THE RULE OF LAW IN MONETARY AFFAIRS

The global financial crisis and the subsequent sovereign debt crisis in Europe demonstrated that the relationship between law and economics in the design of the monetary system must be revisited. International monetary affairs are usually conducted via domestic monetary policies which are formulated by independent central banks and informed mainly by economics, without much room being left to substantive law. Based on the 2012 World Trade Forum, this volume brings together leading scholars, practitioners and policy-makers in international economic law in order to examine the potential of law and legal methodology to contribute to international monetary stability. It explores the links between and lessons to be learnt from existing international investment and trading systems and studies some specific policy issues which have a direct impact on monetary affairs, such as exchange rate policy, sovereign debt, taxation, competitiveness, trade imbalances, austerity programmes and human rights.

THOMAS COTTIER is Managing Director of the World Trade Institute and Professor of European and International Economic Law at the University of Bern, Switzerland.

ROSA M. LASTRA is Professor in International Financial and Monetary Law at the Centre for Commercial Law Studies, Queen Mary University of London.

CHRISTIAN TIETJE is Professor of International Economic Law, Director of the Institute of Economic Law and Director of the Transnational Economic Law Research Center at the Law School, University Halle, Germany.

LUCÍA SATRAGNO is a Doctoral Fellow at the World Trade Institute, University of Bern.

THE RULE OF LAW IN MONETARY AFFAIRS

World Trade Forum

Edited by

THOMAS COTTIER

ROSA M. LASTRA

and

CHRISTIAN TIETJE

Associate Editor

LUCÍA SATRAGNO

CAMBRIDGE
UNIVERSITY PRESS

CAMBRIDGE
UNIVERSITY PRESS

University Printing House, Cambridge CB2 8BS, United Kingdom

Cambridge University Press is part of the University of Cambridge.

It furthers the University's mission by disseminating knowledge in the pursuit of education, learning and research at the highest international levels of excellence.

www.cambridge.org
Information on this title: www.cambridge.org/9781107063631

First published 2014

Printed in the United Kingdom by Clays, St Ives plc

A catalogue record for this publication is available from the British Library

Library of Congress Cataloguing in Publication data
The rule of law in monetary affairs : world trade forum / edited by Thomas Cottier, Rosa M. Lastra and Christian Tietje ; Associate Editor Lucia Satragno.
pages cm
ISBN 978-1-107-06363-1 (Hardback)
1. Finance – Law and legislation. 2. Foreign trade regulation. I. Cottier, Thomas, editor of compilation. II. Lastra, Rosa Maria, editor of compilation. III. Tietje, Christian, editor of compilation. IV. Satragno, Lucia, editor of compilation.
K1066.R85 2014
343′.032–dc23
2014001843

ISBN 978-1-107-06363-1 Hardback

CONTENTS

FIGURES

TABLES

CONTRIBUTORS

KERN ALEXANDER, Professor of Law, Chair for Law and Finance at the Law Faculty, University of Zurich; Senior Research Fellow, Centre for Financial Analysis and Policy, The Judge Business School, University of Cambridge

THOMAS COTTIER, Managing Director, World Trade Institute, Professor of European and International Economic Law, University of Bern

ISABEL FEICHTNER, Assistant Professor, Goethe University Frankfurt

FRANÇOIS GIANVITI, Former General Counsel of the International Monetary Fund, Honorary Dean of the Faculty of Law and Political Science of the University of Paris XII

MARIO GIOVANOLI, Professor (emeritus) of the Law Faculty of the University of Lausanne, former General Counsel of the Bank for International Settlements, Basel

BERNARD HOEKMAN, Professor and Director, Global Economics Robert Schuman Centre for Advanced Studies European University Institute, Florence

ROBERT HOWSE, Lloyd C. Nelson Professor of International Law and Faculty Co-director, Institute for International Law and Justice, NYU Law School

CHRISTINE KAUFMANN, Professor of Law, Chair for International and Constitutional Law and Head of the Centre of Competence for Human Rights, University of Zurich

MATHIAS KENDE, LL.M., London School of Economics, doctoral candidate, World Trade Institute, University of Bern and Geneva-based diplomat of the Belgian Foreign Ministry

MARKUS KRAJEWSKI, Professor of Public and International Law, University of Erlangen-Nüremberg, Germany

ROSA M. LASTRA, Professor in International Financial and Monetary Law at the Centre for Commercial Law Studies, Queen Mary University of London

JEAN-VICTOR LOUIS, Emeritus Professor, Université libre de Bruxelles (ULB)

FEDERICO LUPO-PASINI, Research Fellow in International Finance, University of New South Wales

IAIN MACNEIL, Professor of Commercial Law, University of Glasgow

GABRIELLE Z. MARCEAU, Counsellor in the Legal Affairs Division of the WTO Secretariat, Associate Professor at the Faculty of Law, University of Geneva, Visiting Professor at the Graduate Institute of International and Development Studies and President of SIEL (Society of International Economic Law)

JUAN MARCHETTI, Counsellor in the Economic Research and Statistics Division of the World Trade Organization

JOHN J. MAUGHAN, former Deputy Director of the Global Challenges Forum Foundation in Geneva, Master of International Affairs at the Graduate Institute of International and Development Studies

ERNST-ULRICH PETERSMANN, Emeritus Professor of International and European Law and former head of the Law Department of the European University Institute (EUI), Florence, Chairman of the International Trade Law Committee of the International Law Association

NADIA RENDAK, Senior Counsel at the Legal Department of the International Monetary Fund

MICHELE RUTA, Counsellor in the Economic Research and Statistics Division of the World Trade Organization

LUCÍA SATRAGNO, Doctoral Fellow, World Trade Institute, University of Bern, LL.M., Queen Mary University of London

ROBERT TEH, Counsellor in the Economic Research and Statistics Division of the World Trade Organization

CHRISTIAN TIETJE, Professor of International Economic Law, Director of the Institute of Economic Law and Director of the Transnational Economic Law Research Center, Law School University Halle, Germany

ANNAMARIA VITERBO, Assistant Professor of International Law, Faculty of Law, University of Turin

ROLF H. WEBER, Professor of Law, Chair for International Business Law and Director of the Centre for Information and Communication Law, University of Zurich, Visiting Professor, Law Faculty of Hong Kong University, Attorney-at-Law, Zurich

CLAUS D. ZIMMERMANN, Associate, Sidley Austin LLP, Geneva, DPhil in Public International Law from the University of Oxford; PhD in Economics from the University Paris 1 'Panthéon-Sorbonne'

PREFACE

The World Trade Forum series was established in 1997 as a meeting hub for academia, policy-makers, international organisations and civil society representatives, with the aim of addressing some of the most pertinent questions facing the international trading system. The global financial crisis of 2007–9 gravely affected international trade, and although it was able to recover, high levels of protectionism are still being kept at bay. Hence, fundamental questions remain as to the role of law and legal principles in monetary affairs. Much attention has been paid to the law regulating financial services and to the supervision of private banking but much less has been given to monetary issues, albeit the two cannot be separated. The matter is essentially left to economic analysis, models and policy-making and the law plays little or no role in defining the monetary policies of central banks worldwide. It has been limited to allocating regulatory and discretionary powers, essentially safeguarding the independence of central banks. The rule of law in monetary affairs is thus both a provocative and a normative programme that we intend to explore in this volume.

Based upon the experiences in the field of trade regulation and investment, the World Trade Forum 2012 seeks to expound the potential of legal principles and substantive norms, beyond allocation of powers and the establishment of institutions. It explores the legal foundations and evolution of monetary affairs and the main policy and procedural issues by discussing its relationship with the international trading and investment systems, in particular the lessons to be learnt from the institutional architecture of the World Trade Organization (WTO), its global rules on trade and its dispute settlement mechanism.

This book is based upon papers presented at the World Trade Forum held in October 2012 at the World Trade Institute, University of Bern, Switzerland. It brought together leading scholars and practitioners and policy-makers from the monetary and trade fields in an effort to learn more about the role and rule of law in what may be called trade in monies. Particular thanks are owed to the authors of the chapters who agreed to present and debate the preliminary versions of their papers at the Forum and promptly went on to produce revised versions for publication. We should very much like to thank for their participation and most enriching comments during the debates: Marc Auboin, Ernst Baltensperger, Jappe Eckhardt, Manfred Elsig, Matthias Goldmann, Christian Häberli, Peter Kugler, Rafael Leal-Arcas, Georg Rich, Frieder Roessler, Anirudh Shingal and Matthias Oesch.

We extend special thanks to Margrit Vetter and Christian Steiger, World Trade Institute, for support in organising the conference in Bern. We are most grateful to Susan Kaplan, the scientific editor of the World Trade Institute, for reviewing the manuscripts. Finally, our thanks go to Kim Hughes and her excellent team at Cambridge University Press for their support throughout the project and their strong commitment to the World Trade Forum Series.

ABBREVIATIONS

AB	Appellate Body
ABSs	asset-backed securities
ACP	African, Caribbean and Pacific Group of States
AD	anti-dumping
AIG	American International Group Ltd.
AML/CFT	anti-money laundering and countering the financing of terrorism
ASCM	Agreement on Subsidies and Countervailing Measures
ASEAN	Association of Southeast Asian Nations
BBA	British Bankers' Association
BBAIRS	BBA standard for interest rate swaps
BCBS	Basel Committee on Banking Supervision
BCEAO	Central Bank of the West African States
BIS	Bank for International Settlements
BIT	bilateral investment treaty
BOP	balance of payment
BRICS	Brazil, Russia, India, China, South Africa
CACs	collective action clauses
CDOs	collateralised debt obligations
CDS	credit default swap
CEREP	central repository for publishing the rating activity statistics and rating performance statistics of credit rating agencies
CESR	Committee of European Securities Regulators
CFTC	Commodity Futures Trading Commission (US)
CGFS	Committee on the Global Financial System
CLOs	collateralised loan obligations
CPC	Ceylon Petroleum Corporation
CPI	consumer price index
CPSS	Committee on Payment and Settlement Systems
CRAs	credit rating agencies
CRD	Capital Requirements Directive
CSCE	Commission on Security and Cooperation in Europe
CV Agreement	Customs Valuation Agreement
CVDs	countervailing duties

DBB	debt-buy-back scheme
DSB	Dispute Settlement Body
DM	Deutsche Mark
DSM	Dispute Settlement Mechanism
DSU	Dispute Settlement Understanding
EBA	European Banking Authority
ECAI	External Credit Assessment Institution
ECB	European Central Bank
ECCU	East Caribbean Currency Union
ECMH	efficient capital market hypothesis
ECOFIN	Economic and Financial Affairs Council
ECOWAS	Economic Community of West African States
ECRM	European Crisis Resolution Mechanism
EEA	European Economic Area
ECOSOC	Economic and Social Council
ECSR Committee	Committee on Economic, Social and Cultural Rights
ECT	European Community Treaty
ED	Executive Director
EDRC	Economic and Development Review Committee
EEC	European Economic Community
EFAC	Exchange Fund Advisory Committee
EFC	Economic and Financial Committee
EFSF	European Financial Stability Facility
EFSM	European Financial Stabilisation Mechanism
EIB	European Investment Bank
EIOPA	European Insurance and Occupational Pensions Authority
EMIR	European Market Infrastructure Regulation
EMU	European Economic and Monetary Union
ESCB	European System of Central Banks
ESM	European Stability Mechanism
ESMA	European Securities and Markets Authority
ESR	External Sector Report
ESRB	European Systemic Risk Board
ETS	emission trading scheme
EU	European Union
Euribor	Euro Interbank Offered Rate
EWE	Early Warning Exercise
FATF	Financial Action Task Force on Money Laundering
FCA	Financial Conduct Authority
FDI	foreign direct investment
FOGS	Functioning of the GATT System
FOMC	Federal Open Market Committee

FRBNY	Federal Reserve Bank of New York
FSA	Financial Services Authority (UK)
FSAP	Financial Sector Assessment Program
FSAs	Financial Stability Assessments
FSB	Financial Stability Board
FSF	Financial Stability Forum (now Financial Stability Board)
FSSA	Financial System Stability Assessment
FTA	free trade agreement
G-20	Group of Twenty
G-20 MAP	G-20 Mutual Assessment Program
GATS	General Agreement on Trade in Services
GAL	global administrative law
GATT	General Agreement on Tariffs and Trade
GC	General Comment
GDDS	General Data Dissemination System
GDP	gross domestic product
GFSR	Global Financial Stability Report
GFTEI	Global Forum on Transparency and Exchange of Information
HIPC initiative	Heavily Indebted Poor Countries initiative
HKMA	Hong Kong Monetary Authority
HRL	human rights law
IAASB	International Auditing and Assurance Standards Board
IADI	International Association of Deposit Insurers
IAIS	International Association of Insurance Supervisors
IASB	International Accounting Standards Board
IBRD	International Bank for Reconstruction and Development
ICANN	Internet Corporation for Assigned Numbers and Names
ICCPR	International Covenant on Civil and Political Rights
ICESCR	International Covenant on Economic, Social and Cultural Rights
ICSID	International Centre for Settlement of Investment Disputes
IEL	international economic law
IFI	international financial institution
IFSs	international financial standards
IIA	international investment agreement
IIF	Institute of International Finance
ILA	International Law Association
ILC	International Law Commission
ILO	International Labour Organization
IMF	International Monetary Fund
IMFC	International Monetary and Financial Committee
IMS	international monetary system

IOPS	International Organisation of Pension Supervisors
IOSCO	International Organization of Securities Commissions
ISD	Integrated Surveillance Decision
ISIN	International Securities Identification Number
ITO	International Trade Organization
Libor	London Interbank Offered Rate
LTROs	long-term refinancing operations
MAD	Market Abuse Directive
MDRI	Multilateral Debt Relief Initiative
MFN	most-favoured nation
MiFID	Markets in Financial Instruments Directive
MIST	Mexico, Indonesia, South Korea and Turkey
MoU	memorandum of understanding
MPC	Monetary Policy Committee (of the Bank of England)
MROs	mainstream refinancing operations
NAFTA	North American Free Trade Agreement
NCBs	national central banks
NIFA I	New International Financial Architecture I
NRSRO	Nationally Recognised Statistical Rating Organisation
NTB	non-tariff barriers
NYSE	New York Stock Exchange
OECD	Organisation for Economic Co-operation and Development
OECS	Organisation of Eastern Caribbean States
OMT	Outright Monetary Transactions Programme
OSI	Official Sector Involvement
OSCE	Organisation for Security and Cooperation in Europe
OTC	over-the-counter
OTS	Office of Thrift Supervision
PBOC	People's Bank of China
PIN	public information notice
PIOB	Public Interest Oversight Board
PRA	Prudential Regulation Authority
PSI	Private Sector Involvement
PTA	preferential trade agreement
QFII Program	Qualified Foreign Institutional Investor Program
REO	Regional Economic Outlook
ROSCs	Reports on Observance of Standards and Codes
RTGS	real-time gross settlement
SCIMF	Subcommittee of the Economic and Financial Committee
SCM Agreement	Agreement on Subsidies and Countervailing Measures
SDDS	Special Data Dissemination Standard
SDRs	special drawing rights

SDRM	Sovereign Debt Restructuring Mechanism
SEC	US Securities and Exchange Commission
SEZs	special economic zones
SGP	Stability and Growth Pact
SOBs	state-owned commercial banks
Sibor	Singapore Interbank Offered Rate
SIFI	systemically important financial institutions
SMP	Securities Markets Programme
SNB	Swiss National Bank
SPS Agreement	Agreement on the Application of Sanitary and Phytosanitary Measures
SSBs	standard-setting bodies
SSM	Single Supervisory Mechanism
TBT	technical barriers to trade
TEU	Treaty on the European Union
TFEU	Treaty on the Functioning of the European Union
TPRB	Trade Policy Review Body
TPRD	Trade Policies Review Division
TPRM	Trade Policy Review Mechanism
TSC	Treasury Select Committee
TSCG	Treaty on Stability, Coordination and Governance
Tibor	Tokyo Interbank Offered Rate
TSR	Triennial Surveillance Review
UCITS	Undertakings for Collective Investment in Transferable Securities
UDHR	Universal Declaration of Human Rights
UEMOA	West African Economic and Monetary Union
UNCITRAL	United Nations Commission on International Trade Law
UNCTAD	United Nations Conference on Trade and Development
USD	US dollar
VCLT	Vienna Convention on the Law of Treaties
WAEMU	West African Economic and Monetary Union
WB	World Bank
WEO	World Economic Outlook
WGTDF	Working Group on Trade, Debt and Finance
WTO	World Trade Organization

1

Introduction and overview

THOMAS COTTIER, ROSA M. LASTRA, CHRISTIAN TIETJE AND LUCÍA SATRAGNO

> [T]he international community needs to make headway on the issue of reform of the international monetary system. Unilateral attempts to change or to retain the status quo will not work. We need an international monetary system which supports cross-border investment and a better allocation of capital across nations and which 'facilitates international trade' – as laid out in the aims of the International Monetary Fund. What we need is a global monetary system which inspires confidence, offers stability and monitors exchange rates more efficiently. One which provides the means through which global imbalances that may risk endangering stability can be addressed.
>
> Pascal Lamy[1]

Monetary affairs are at the heart of, and continue to play a key role in, the development of economic and social systems worldwide. The 2007–9 global financial crisis demonstrated that the malfunctioning of the monetary system impedes growth, generates recession and increases protectionism in international trade. It amounted to a failure of law and economics alike.[2] The profound and long-lasting effects of the financial crisis triggered changes in the regulatory thinking at all levels of governance. Hence, monetary affairs – one of the last bastions of national sovereignty – are at the centre of the debate worldwide.[3] The moment has come to revisit the relationship between law and economics in the field.

[1] Former Director-General of the WTO, opening speech at the WTO Seminar on Exchange Rates and Trade, held on 27 March 2012, available at www.wto.org/english/news_e/sppl_e/sppl222_e.htm.

[2] T. Cottier, 'Challenges Ahead in International Economic Law', *Journal of International Economic Law*, 12:1 (2009), 3–15.

[3] Rosa M. Lastra, *Legal Foundations of International Monetary Stability* (Oxford University Press, 2006), pp. 4–5; Tullio Treves, 'Monetary Sovereignty Today', in Mario Giovanoli (ed.), *International Monetary Law: Issues for the New Millennium* (Oxford University Press, 2000), pp. 111–18.

In comparison with the proliferation and reinforcement of rules in the other areas of international economic law (trade and investment), the role of law in monetary affairs has been a limited one.[4] The focus is on constitutional issues relating to the establishment and the functioning of monetary institutions, in particular securing independence and separation of powers in monetary policy-making. While the law has been important in framing agreements between the institutions and recipient countries, it has not played a significant role in informing monetary policies. Such policies, based upon economic considerations, are usually designed and implemented by national independent central banks, operating within a given legal framework, yet equally independent from legal principles and norms apart from very broadly defined goals. This constellation raises concerns of accountability and legitimacy. Soft law standards issued by the International Monetary Fund (IMF), the Basel Committee on Banking Supervision (BCBS), and the Financial Stability Board (FSB), among others, all try to address such concerns at the global level. However, the global financial crisis highlighted the need for reflections upon the role of hard law and normative guidance.

The crisis enhanced the role of law and regulation in the financial system, improving the framework and the stability for private operators and commercial banks.[5] Financial stability has become a prime principle informing regulation both in national and European law. It is at the heart of the developments on the global level in the creation of new soft law instruments by international standard setters.[6] However, it would seem that relatively little attention has been paid to potential lessons to be drawn from the financial crisis and the subsequent sovereign debt crisis for the global monetary system. The focus on Europe, with the ongoing sovereign debt crisis, the advent of the banking union and the consolidation of the European Central Bank (ECB), has left global concerns related to monetary affairs – other than financial regulation – less prominent. This is certainly true from the legal

[4] See C. Brummer, 'Why Soft Law Dominates International Finance – and Not Trade', *Journal of International Economic Law*, 13:3 (2010), 631 also in T. Cottier, J. H. Jackson and R. M. Lastra (eds.), *International Law in Financial Regulation and Monetary Affairs* (Oxford University Press, 2012), pp. 95–113.

[5] For an extended debate and analysis on the quest for international law in financial regulation, see Cottier *et al.* (eds.), *International Law in Financial Regulation and Monetary Affairs*.

[6] This volume will address the law and policy of the major actors in the international monetary system (the national central banks, the ECB, the IMF, the Bank for International Settlements (BIS), the G-20 and the FSB, among others).

perspective. The focus has been on governance issues, in particular quotas and decision-making, but not so much on normative principles and rules which may inform monetary policies in the coming decades, contributing to the goal of monetary stability.

This edited volume purports to contribute to filling this vacuum by discussing the potential of law and legal methodology to contribute to international monetary stability. To attain this ambitious objective, the book seeks to explore and identify the underlying principles and norms which could guide and contribute to the formulation of policies, which have almost exclusively pertained to the domain of macroeconomics, with recourse to regulatory theory to address the role of law and legal principles in allocating powers and normative guidance for governmental action affecting individuals and society at large. In doing so, it attempts to draw lessons and insights from regulatory theory.[7] It aims to identify to what extent monetary affairs pertain to the field of international economic law and thus to what extent they may share common principles with trade and investment.[8] Comparison and linkages with the fields of international investment law and trade regulation within the WTO, and with the prominent role which law plays in these areas,

[7] See, generally, R. Baldwin, M. Cave and M. Lodge (eds.), *The Oxford Handbook of Regulation* (Oxford University Press, 2010). One of the editors of this volume has given a particular focus to regulation and the principle of legality in his work both constitutionally and in international law, developing a regulatory theory which may also offer guidance in the field of monetary law, T. Cottier, *Die Verfassung und das Erfordernis der gesetzlichen Grundlage*, 2nd edn (Zurich: Verlag Rüeger, 1993); T. Cottier, 'Constitutional Trade Regulation in National and International Law: Structure-Substance Pairings in the EFTA Experience', in M. Hilf and E.-U. Petersmann (eds.), *National Constitutions and International Economic Law* (The Hague: Kluwer Law International, 1993), pp. 409–42; T. Cottier, 'Towards a Five Storey House', in C. Joerges and E.-U. Petersmann (eds.), *Constitutionalism, Multilevel Governance and International Economic Law* (Oxford: Hart, 2011), pp. 495–532.

[8] Georg Schwarzenberger, known as one of the fathers of international economic law, noted in 1948 that international economic law is a special branch of international public law which involves different subject matters with the economic element as the common denominator. Hence, he remarked that 'an admittedly extraneous criterion is made the test of whether a subject falls within this new branch of international law'. See Georg Schwarzenberger, 'The Province and Standards of International Economic Law', *International Law Quarterly* 2:3 (1948), 405–6. Later on, he pointed out that each branch of international law 'has its own legal principles and standards which distinguish it from the general principles of international law and from each other'. See Georg Schwarzenberger, 'The Frontiers of International Law', *Yearbook of World Affairs* 246:6 (1952), 249. More recently, S. Charnovitz, while trying to address the question of what international economic law is, states that 'a body of law needs to be based on unifying principles (e.g. economic logics) or motivated by underlying theory of law'. See S. Charnovitz, 'What is International Economic Law', *Journal of International Economic Law* 14:1 (2011), 6.

complement and enrich the analysis. The history of international monetary institutions, in particular the Bretton Woods system, shows a very close interaction between trade, investment and monetary affairs. When the IMF was founded, trade imbalances and the balance of payments were the main concerns, and monetary affairs were discussed closely related to trade policy issues. Monetary interests and policies were mainly shaped in line with the trade interests of a country.[9] The institutional divide between trade, investment and monetary affairs considerably loosened the link to the real economy of goods and services, which it primarily ought to serve under stable monetary conditions. An effort thus should be made to revisit this relationship, seeking to bring about greater coherence among these different fields.

This book explores the field on the basis of the doctrine of multilevel or multilayered governance, identifying appropriate layers of vertical governance and the need for greater coherence between domestic and international spheres. Studies on specific policy issues that have direct impact on monetary affairs, such as exchange rate policy, sovereign debt, competitiveness, trade imbalances, austerity programmes and the human rights dimensions, are provided to illustrate the complexity of the issues and the role that the law can play in such realms. We are confronted with the problem that there is no consensus among economists as to what constitutes good monetary policy and what the role of central banks should be. As *The Economist* put it in September 2013:

> Yet for every critic who believes that central banks have done too little, there is one who fears they have done far too much. By propping up asset prices artificially, some complain, central bankers are stoking inequality, rewarding financial firms despite their past misdeeds and sowing the seeds of the next crisis. Many, especially on the right in America, give warning that the massive increase in the money supply QE [quantitative easing] entails can lead only to a debasement of the currency and hyperinflation. Others gripe that low interest rates in the rich world have sent a flood of hot money towards emerging markets, generating financial instability.[10]

Competing interests and conflicts are inherent to the task of law and we are committed to exploring to what extent the law can assist in guiding monetary policies and affairs under the legal principles of both domestic

[9] See B. Steil, *The Battle of Bretton Woods: John Maynard Keynes, Harry Dexter White and the Making of the New World Order* (Princeton University Press, 2013).

[10] 'Monetary Policy after the Crash: Controlling Interest', *The Economist*, 21–27 September 2013, 62–3.

and international law. We are far from finding all the pertinent answers in what amounts to an incipient field of international economic law. Yet, the first step consists in asking the appropriate questions and stimulating and informing further debate among lawyers and economists.

To achieve its objective, the book is divided according to four thematic areas, which aim to provide the reader with a comprehensive understanding of the current problems affecting the field and some of the lessons that can be learnt from other areas of law. These four thematic areas are as follows:

(i) the legal foundations and evolution of the international monetary system;
(ii) the specific policy issues in monetary affairs;
(iii) the interaction between World Trade Organization (WTO) law and monetary affairs; and
(iv) the quest for law in monetary policy.

Part I of the book gives an introductory overview of the international monetary system, its present state and likely future development, and describes the current international architecture and institutional aspects by paying special attention to the unique role of central banks. This part also focuses on the lack of global substantive principles and rules in monetary affairs and introduces the debate about what role the law can or should play in this field. Christian Tietje puts the current challenges into a historical and conceptual perspective and draws a picture of international monetary affairs in relation to the other areas of international economic law. He points out some broad structural principles that are essential for strengthening the rule of law in international monetary affairs. Mario Giovanoli describes the evolution and present situation of the international financial and monetary architecture from an institutional perspective. He states that despite the increasing relevance of the international financial standards (IFSs), a number of issues remain unresolved and open to debate, such as the implementation of the standards, the legitimacy of the standard-setting bodies (SSBs), the transparency of the standard-setting process and the lack of legal remedies. Rosa Lastra discusses the fundamental and evolving role of central banks in monetary affairs with special reference to the US Federal Reserve System and the ECB. She argues that the law must govern the relationship of the central bank upwards with the government and downwards with the banking and financial system. Jean-Victor Louis focuses on the European Economic and Monetary Union (EMU) by analysing the role of national central banks (NCBs) in times of crisis and the difficult insertion of the euro area into the global system. He contends that these two aspects of the EMU, together with the move towards a banking and fiscal union, will enhance the global position of the euro area.

Part II of the book looks at specific policy and procedural issues in the international monetary system. Bernard Hoekman starts by analysing the spillover effects of policies that have an impact on international competiveness from a global governance perspective. With regard to macroeconomic and monetary policies, he argues that a more open discussion and a more specific analysis of the spillover effects of such policies is needed. Claus Zimmermann explores the conflicting objectives in the setting of global benchmark interest rates both by central banks and by the private sector and their impact upon competitiveness. In this context, he reviews the recent London Interbank Offered Rate (Libor) manipulation scandal and suggests that the replacement of private benchmark rates by alternative benchmarks based on central bank key rates should be considered. Iain MacNeil assesses the extent to which credit rating agencies (CRAs), as major players in the international financial and capital markets, should be regulated and what level of reliance on ratings is more appropriate in the pursuit of financial stability. Nadia Rendak gives an overview of the functioning and current challenges of the IMF's function of surveillance. She also looks at the potential lessons that the IMF can learn from other monitoring mechanisms, such as the WTO Trade Policy Review Mechanism (TPRM) and the Organisation for Economic Co-operation and Development (OECD) surveillance tool. Annamaria Viterbo and Isabel Feichtner follow on by taking up some particular topical and controversial issues related to the effects that sovereign debt has on monetary affairs. While Viterbo discusses the impact of sovereign debt restructurings in the context of the ongoing eurozone crisis, Feichtner offers an analysis of the role that taxation plays in the reduction of sovereign debt in times of austerity.

Part III of the book addresses and explores the relationship between specific areas of WTO law and monetary affairs. Robert Howse opens by exploring the underlying principles potentially informing monetary policy and trade, in particular the role of equity. Based on the broad precepts of this overarching principle, hardly ever referred to in this context, he offers reflections on a more coherent integration of finance, trade and sustainable development in international economic law, and the interaction of WTO law and the IMF in particular. Juan Marchetti, Michele Ruta and Robert Teh examine the relationship of trade and monetary policies from the point of view of economics, addressing trade imbalances and exchange rate misalignments. They argue that multilateral trade cooperation is fundamental in correcting persistent global imbalances. However, trade rules alone will not be enough and urgent solutions for the existing 'coherence gap' in global governance are needed. Gabrielle Marceau and John Maughan discuss the complex relationship between exchange rates and trade from a legal perspective. They scrutinise potential issues involving exchange rates which could be brought before the WTO dispute settlement body (DSB). Mathias Kende ends Part III by assessing the extent to which the TPRM takes into account monetary and financial policies in the revision of trade policies and shows the scope for potential refinement.

Part IV of the book deals with the quest for law in monetary affairs from a theoretical perspective while identifying the linkages and lessons from some other areas of international economic law. Thomas Cottier and Lucía Satragno discuss and analyse the potential of law and legal methodology in monetary affairs from the perspective of regulatory theory and on the basis of the doctrine of multilayered governance. They identify important lessons from other areas of law where there is close interaction between law and economics, showing the potential for identifying appropriate economic factors and considerations to be legally taken into account in monetary policy. Ernst-Ulrich Petersmann examines the international monetary system under the framework of multilevel governance and the role of human rights. He states that stronger 'multilevel regulation' of 'governance failures' and judicial protection of cosmopolitan rights is most needed under a transnational rule of law. Christine Kaufmann and Rolf Weber stress the importance of enhanced transparency in monetary affairs from a three-dimensional perspective, institutional and procedural elements, substantive foundation, and accountability. Markus Krajewski follows on by discussing the human rights dimension in monetary affairs with a focus on the austerity measures implemented in the context of the eurozone debt crisis. Human rights have an important role to play when assessing austerity policies and conditionalities of monetary policies applied to countries under duress and need. Kern Alexander links financial regulation and monetary policy. He describes the regulatory shift in international financial regulation to a macro-prudential focus. In this context, he asks whether international trade law commitments undertaken in the WTO General Agreement on Trade in Services (GATS) limit WTO members' policy autonomy to implement macro-prudential regulatory reforms. François Gianviti explores the interaction between monetary and exchange rate policies. He notes that even though such policies are under the realm of the monetary sovereignty of the states, they should be limited by the rules of the international monetary system. Finally, Federico Lupo-Pasini observes the difficulties in balancing monetary stability and investment protection from a theoretical perspective. He argues that the IMF should assume a central role in the definition of monetary and financial stability in investment agreements and in monitoring abuses.

The contributions offer interesting and relevant building blocks for use in the quest for law in monetary affairs. We conclude that the relationship between law and monetary affairs bears the potential for a greater role of law and legal principles, linking this field to other areas of international economic law. Also, we note that the law is not limited to strict rules, which are hardly suitable for monetary policy, but that legal principles and economic factors as defined by law may assist in developing an appropriate framework offering guidance to policy-makers and macroeconomics. Linkages with trade policy can be further refined and work is needed on the interaction between trade and monetary affairs fostering mutual learning and more interaction on the common issues. It is not a matter of attracting monetary affairs to the trading regime, but of empowering the IMF and central banks to deal with potential conflicts more effectively, taking recourse to law and legally defined principles and procedures to link relevant international institutions in a more coherent manner. While the suggestions proposed and answers provided differ, all contributors agree that the relationship between law and monetary affairs should be revisited and reshaped in order to promote a more stable and predictable international monetary system contributing to the financial stability goal embraced in the aftermath of the recent global financial crisis.

PART I

Legal foundations and the evolution of the international monetary system

2

The role of law in monetary affairs: taking stock

CHRISTIAN TIETJE

A. Introduction

The global financial crisis of 2007–9, which is more than symbolically tied to the breakdown of Lehman Brothers on 15 September 2008, and the ongoing sovereign debt crisis in Europe, intrinsically tied to Greece, resulted in challenges for governments and markets alike. Governments – providing the framework for market activities, having the capacity to intervene in a market if necessary and being major creditors in the international financial markets – and the market as a self-regulatory mechanism are trying to cope with the problem of how to prevent a future global economic crisis and how to cope with the current levels of debt. For governments, both at the national level and with regard to efforts at international cooperation and coordination, 'better' regulation and supervision of financial markets and 'better' policy measures for currency systems are called for. Modified and/or new models of regulation, supervision and economic policy coordination are central in providing for stable domestic and international financial and monetary markets in the future. The role law plays and the importance of law in this exercise are obvious.

Yet, strengthening regulation and supervision is in potential conflict with essential freedoms in financial and monetary markets. There is always a necessity to seek an equilibrium between the two components. The tension between regulation or supervision and market freedom is not a new phenomenon in financial and monetary law. What is new, however, is that by strengthening regulation and supervision today one has also to take into account the need for – at least partial – international regulatory and supervisory cooperation and coordination. The same is true with regard to sovereign debt issues and democratic control of regional and/or international efforts to effectively manage sovereign debt crises and currency issues.

This chapter draws extensively on C. Tietje, 'The International Financial Architecture as a Legal Order', *German Yearbook of International Law* 54 (2011), 11–45.

These challenges are essentially linked to the rule of law as an 'indispensable foundation to a more peaceful, prosperous and just world', as emphasised in the Declaration of the High-Level Meeting of the 67th Session of the General Assembly of the United Nations on the rule of law at the national and international levels of 24 September 2012.[1] However, even though the rule of law is crucial in international financial and monetary affairs, the exact role law plays in this system is less clear. This chapter will try to shed some light on this, in line with the general thrust of this volume. This will be done from a historical and conceptual perspective and with regard to current challenges. In doing so, monetary law will not be understood in a (too) narrow sense of only dealing with currency issues. Instead, the term 'monetary law' will be used in a broader sense, drawing upon a constitutional and administrative perspective on currency and financial markets. In this regard, the starting point for the discussion will be currency issues. However, as will become obvious, currency law and currency affairs cannot be separated from other areas of international economic law, i.e. regulatory challenges in the areas of financial markets, sovereign debts, trade and investment.

B. From 1929 to 2009: the development of the international systems of currency, sovereign debt and financial markets

I. *Early roots*

1. Currency system

Currency law and international efforts to coordinate currency systems are a relatively new development in the international system. This is because monopolies of currency within single states were unknown throughout most of history. On the contrary, it was normal to have competing currencies within one territory. This situation slowly began to change after the establishment of the modern state with the Westphalian Peace Treaties of 1648. However, real monopolies on currencies, i.e. an exclusivity of one currency in one territory, were factually only developed in the eighteenth century. It was not until the nineteenth century that the first currency monopoly was legally established. This happened with the Banking Charter Act of 1844 in the United Kingdom. This development continued globally into the second half of the nineteenth

[1] unrol.org/files/Official%20Draft%20Resolution.pdf.

century. It was not until World War II that customary international law began recognising currency monopolies.[2]

2. Sovereign debt

The current international currency system is influenced to a large extent by sovereign debt. The history of sovereign debt problems is long, with numerous cases of default on payments due to foreign creditors. Spain, for example, defaulted thirteen times between the sixteenth and nineteenth century. During that period, France defaulted eight times, while Portugal and the German states defaulted six times each. In addition, the Latin-American states and the Ottoman Empire declared that they were unable to fulfil their obligations towards foreign creditors several times during the nineteenth and twentieth centuries.[3] In fact, the twentieth century was characterised by up to ten cases of state default per decade. The 1930s are an exception in this regard, with more than twenty sovereign defaults due to the world economic crisis after the stock market crash of 1929.

Even though sovereign defaults are a relatively normal phenomenon in history, international rules pertaining to a state insolvency regime have not been developed. Historically, the normal reaction by a creditor to a state's default was the threat of military action, which is of course prohibited today by Article 2(4) of the UN Charter,[4] which requires resolution by the classical means of diplomatic protection.[5]

Although state practice was restricted for a long time to classical public international law instruments in case of sovereign defaults, it is interesting to see that scholars were already developing innovative concepts to increase the legal security of private creditors in dealings with states as debtors in the late nineteenth and early twentieth centuries, namely by granting private individuals an international legal personality.[6] State practice at that time did

[2] B. J. Cohen, 'Monetary Governance and Capital Mobility in Historical Perspective', in R. Grote and T. Marauhn (eds.), *The Regulation of International Financial Markets – Perspective for Reform* (Oxford University Press, 2006), pp. 27, 32 ff.

[3] A. C. Porzecanski, 'Dealing with Sovereign Debt: Trends and Implications' in C. Jochnick and F. A. Preston (eds.), *Sovereign Debt at the Crossroads* (Oxford University Press, 2005), www.law.georgetown.edu/international/documents/Porzecanski_000.pdf.

[4] Charter of the United Nations, 26 June 1945, UNCIO 15, 335.

[5] On diplomatic protection in a situation of sovereign default, see, e.g., PCIJ, *Case Concerning the Payment of Various Serbian Loans Issued in France*, Judgment of 12 July 1929, Series A, No. 20, 17 ff.; on the history of military activities because of sovereign default see, e.g., K. Pflug, *Staatsbankrott und internationales Recht* (Munich: Schweitzer, 1898).

[6] For details and references, see K. Nowrot, *Normative Ordnungsstruktur und private Wirkungsmacht – Konsequenzen der Beteiligung transnationaler Unternehmen an den*

not adopt such proposals. Moreover, it was unclear whether sovereign debts were even legally relevant in domestic law, as famously indicated by Sir George Jessel MR in *Twycross* v. *Dreyfus*: '[t]he result, therefore, is that these so-called bonds amount to nothing more than engagements of honour, binding so far as engagements of honour can bind, the government that issued them, but are not contracts . . .'.[7] The entire legal development was summarised by Georg Schwarzenberger in 1988 as follows: '[a]nalyses of State bankruptcy . . . in international law may lead to the perhaps over-simplified conclusion that, at least for the purpose of international law, the problem does not exist. More searching minds may conclude that . . . the problem exists, but is insoluble'.[8]

3. (Private) financial markets

For a long time public international law paid no attention to private financial markets, which are different from currency markets and sovereign debt markets. This is surprising as the internationalisation of financial markets is entrenched in history.[9] More than sovereign defaults, private financial crises and banking crises have been a regular feature throughout history in both developed and developing countries.[10] However, it is important to note that international financial markets have not been developed as primarily private financial markets. Instead, cross-border financial transactions in history largely fulfilled the purpose of financing state budgets.[11] In addition, for a long time private banking crises only affected the domestic economy, thus they did not have a systemic global impact. For all these reasons, there was no need to develop specific international rules for private financial markets.

Rechtssetzungsprozessen im internationalen Wirtschaftssystem (Berlin: Berliner-Wissenschafts-Verlag, 2006), pp. 347 ff.

[7] *Twycross* v. *Dreyfus* (1877) 5 Ch D 605.

[8] G. Schwarzenberger, 'State Bankruptcy and International Law', in W.P. Heere (ed.), *International Law and Its Source – Liber Amicorum Maarten Bos* (Heidelberg: Springer, 1988), pp. 137, 144; on development in general, see A. Szodruch, *Staateninsolvenz und private Gläubiger – Rechtsprobleme des Private Sector Involvement bei staatlichen Finanzkrisen im 21. Jahrhundert* (Berlin: Berliner-Wissenschafts-Verlag, 2008), pp. 72 ff.

[9] For details, see D. Held, A. McGrew, D. Goldblatt and J. Perraton, *Global Transformations: Politics, Economics and Culture* (Stanford University Press, 1999), pp. 190 ff.

[10] C.M. Reinhart and K. Rogoff, *This Time is Different: Eight Centuries of Financial Folly* (Princeton University Press, 2009); C.P. Kindleberger and R. Aliber, *Manias, Panics, and Crashes: A History of Financial Crises*, 5th edn (Hoboken, NJ: John Wiley & Sons Inc, 2005).

[11] D. Held *et al*., *Global Transformations*, pp. 191 ff.

However, for quite some time there have been factual interrelationships between international capital movement and private financial markets. The main cause was the lack of restrictions on capital movement at the end of the nineteenth century. Thus, substantial international capital flows to emerging markets took place in the form of bonds. Because of this, the time before World War I has been termed the 'golden age for emerging market bonds and international capital flows to emerging markets'.[12]

The difference between before World War I and today is the number of creditors involved in international capital transactions. Before World War I there was no real globalised financial market. After World War I the international financial centre moved from London to New York. Furthermore, at the end of the 1920s, about 800,000 US citizens held foreign bonds. At that time, bonds were the most important international financial market instrument. States were almost exclusively the recipients of international financial transactions, thus an international financial market with private parties on both sides of the transaction, i.e. a real international private financial market, did not exist.[13] However the interdependence of bonds, sovereign debts and private capital markets was already becoming apparent.

II. Bretton Woods: Keynes and White

The establishment of the Bretton Woods system in 1944 was the first truly multilateral attempt to establish an international monetary system. The Bretton Woods system was created on the basis of the prevailing factual setting of the international financial markets. The most important influencers were the head of the US delegation, Harry Dexter White, and British economist John Maynard Keynes. Although White and Keynes sometimes disagreed,[14] the traumatic experience of the world economic crisis of 1929 and what is known today as 'Keynesianism' united them. Moreover, both agreed that fixed but adjustable exchange rates are necessary in order to enable free international trade in goods and services. This must be supplemented by general (Keynes) or at least possible (White) capital controls,

[12] P. Mauro, N. Sussmann and Y. Yafeh, *Emerging Market Spreads: Then Versus Now*, IMF Working Paper WT/00/190, www.imf.org/external/pubs/ft/wp/2000/wp00190.pdf (accessed on 19 November 2011), 3; Szodruch, *Staateninsolvenz und private Gläubiger*, p. 73.

[13] For details, see *ibid.* pp. 73 ff.

[14] See J. M. Boughton, 'Why White, not Keynes? Inventing the Postwar International Monetary System', IMF Working Paper, WP/02/52; R. M. Lastra, *Legal Foundations of International Monetary Stability* (Oxford University Press, 2006), pp. 345, 351 ff.

they argued.[15] Indeed, the discussion about financial markets at Bretton Woods involved only capital controls. With regard to further aspects of financial markets, everybody at that time accepted what Keynes wrote in 1933: '. . . above all, let finance be . . . national'.[16]

In spite of some common beliefs, some fundamental differences concerning the appropriate approach towards the international monetary systems remained, and in the end White's position prevailed. This is true not only regarding the regulation of bilateral monetary relations between the US and the UK (Keynes), but also in establishing a multinational and integrated system for monetary, investment and trade issues.[17] However, the IMF was kept small and was prevented from being a lender of last resort as a consequence of this approach.[18]

III. *Bretton Woods and the international economic system*

As a result of the Bretton Woods conference in July 1944, the International Bank for Reconstruction and Development (IBRD) (part of the World Bank) and the International Monetary Fund (IMF) were established. The original idea of the World Bank was just to function as a bank and to give money via credits or guarantees to those regions of the world severely affected by World War II.[19] In this regard, the World Bank was originally seen as representing the investment pillar of the international economic system of which trade and finance were the other two pillars.[20] However, since the US started its own financial support programme in 1948, the European Recovery Program,[21] the World Bank actually never got a chance to fulfil its original mandate.

[15] *Ibid.*, p. 11; for details on the opinion of John Maynard Keynes concerning capital controls see, e.g., Cohen, '*Monetary Governance and Capital Mobility*', pp. 45 ff.; comprehensively also M. Moschella, *Governing Risk – The IMF and Global Financial Crises* (Basingstoke: Palgrave Macmillan, 2010), p. 5.

[16] John Maynard Keynes, 'National Self-Sufficiency', *Yale Review* 22 (1933), 755, 769.

[17] Boughton, 'Why White, Not Keynes?', 13 ff. [18] *Ibid.*, 16 ff.

[19] For details see, e.g., S. Schlemmer-Schulte, 'Internationales Währungs- und Finanzrecht', in C. Tietje (ed.), *Internationales Wirtschaftsrecht* (Berlin: De Gruyter, 2009), § 9, paras. 77 ff.; A. F. Lowenfeld, *International Economic Law*, 2nd edn (Oxford University Press, 2008), pp. 93 ff.

[20] D. Arner and R. P. Buckley, 'Redesigning the Architecture of the Global Financial System', *Melbourne Journal of International Law* 11:2 (2010), 1, 6; Lastra, *Legal Foundations*, pp. 345, 354 ff.

[21] For details, see A. de Zayas, 'Marshall Plan (European Recovery Program)', *Max Planck Encyclopaedia of Public International Law*, www.mpepil.com.

Thus, the Bank quickly changed its focus and became a development institution.[22]

The original mandate of the IMF, as the second Bretton Woods institution, was restricted to stable currency systems in direct connection with liberalised trade in goods and services.[23] Of course, this mandate was dependent on the establishment of a third Bretton Woods institution responsible for liberalised international trade in goods and services. The establishment of an International Trade Organization (ITO), as designed by the Havana Charter of 1948, would have completed the architecture of the international economic system. Since the Havana Charter never entered into force and the ITO was never established,[24] the IMF was thus never able to fulfil its original mandate in a comprehensive way, even though it worked quite successfully after its establishment. This was largely due to the rather simple structure and thus also limited rule of law in the original Bretton Woods system of fixed exchange rates. The IMF essentially had the task of negotiating the initial exchange rates of a country and had the power to grant permission to countries to devalue their currencies in specific situations. This was supplemented with the possibility for the IMF to lend money to countries that face balance of payment problems. In turn, Member States of the IMF were obliged to maintain the value of their currency and to purchase or sell the currency by use of reserve in case of a deviation from the fixed value.[25] Regarding international financial markets, it is however important to note that the legal order of the IMF only provided for the possibility of control of capital transfers. Based on Article VI (Section 3) IMF Agreement,[26] the entire issue of financial markets was therefore left to the sovereign discretion of States, which is in alignment with the

[22] Schlemmer-Schulte, 'Internationales Währungs- und Finanzrecht', § 9, para. 81.

[23] See Article 1 Articles of Agreement of the International Monetary Fund, 27 December 1945, UNTS 2, 40 (IMF Agreement):

> 'The purposes of the International Monetary Fund are: . . . (ii) To facilitate the expansion and balanced growth of international trade, and to contribute thereby to the promotion and maintenance of high levels of employment and real income and to the development of the productive resources of all members as primary objectives of economic policy. (iii) To promote exchange stability, to maintain orderly exchange arrangements among members, and to avoid competitive exchange depreciation'.

[24] See, e.g., Lowenfeld, *International Economic Law*, pp. 23 ff.

[25] See, e.g., A. F. Lowenfeld, 'Monetary Law International' *Max Planck Encyclopedia of Public International Law*, www.mpepil.com.

[26] 'Members may exercise such controls as are necessary to regulate international capital movements . . .'.

above-mentioned quote by Keynes to 'let finance be . . . national'.[27] The idea of nationalising finance was based on the firm belief that the international financial and economic crisis of 1929 was due to speculative financial transactions, and that capital controls could therefore have prevented it.[28] As a logical consequence of this prevailing opinion at the time, states envisaged the dissolution of the Bank for International Settlements (BIS) while establishing the Bretton Woods System.[29] As this never happened, the deficiencies of the system become obvious.[30] Moreover, this historical conception and development makes it clear why international law did not play much of a role in international monetary affairs after World War II.

Furthermore, the original plan was to integrate the Bretton Woods institutions completely into the UN System. In accordance with Articles 57 and 63 UN Charter, the intent was to divide labour between the UN, namely the Economic and Social Council (ECOSOC), which would be responsible for the overall international economic and financial system, and the Bretton Woods institutions, which would concentrate on more technical issues.[31] It is well known that the East–West conflict prevented any effective political work by ECOSOC. Moreover, the World Bank and the IMF, which were joined by the World Trade Organization (WTO), quickly established a rather reluctant position towards the UN.[32] As a consequence of these developments, the UN system has never played much of a legal and political role in international monetary affairs.

In sum, it is important to emphasise that the design of Bretton Woods was not intended to establish a comprehensive international economic or financial order in terms of an integration of trade, finance, investment and currency based on the rule of law. Furthermore, a genuine lender of last resort was not established. With the exception of capital control, financial market stability was not addressed, and with the exception of balance of payment questions, the entire issue of sovereign debt was left open. Finally,

[27] Keynes, 'National Self-Sufficiency'.

[28] For details on this opinion namely of Keynes, see Moschella, *Governing Risk*, p. 5; Boughton, 'Why White, not Keynes?', 10.

[29] Lastra, *Legal Foundations*, pp. 345, 354 ff.

[30] Arner and Buckley, 'Redesigning the Architecture of the Global Financial System', 5 ff.

[31] *Ibid.*, 4 ff.

[32] On the 'special' relationship of the IMF with the UN, see D. D. Bradlow, '*The Governance of the IMF: The Need for Comprehensive Reform*' (2006), 20, www.g24.org/brad0906.pdf (accessed on 19 November 2011); see also the Special High-level Meeting of ECOSOC with the Bretton Woods Institutions, the World Trade Organization and the United Nations Conference on Trade and Development, 10–11 March 2011, www.un.org/esa/ffd/ecosoc/springmeetings/2011/index.htm.

the envisaged integration of the Bretton Woods institutions into the legal and political system of the UN failed.

IV. The (re-)invention of the system: 1970 to 2007

1. First steps

Even though the Bretton Woods system was far from complete, the institutions themselves quickly found their respective roles in the international economic system. The World Bank became an important player in the area of development policy. The IMF worked successfully in a system of fixed exchange rates in the 1950s and the 1960s, and the framework of the General Agreement on Tariffs and Trade (GATT), which came into force on 1 January 1948, liberalised world trade.[33] However, (private) international financial markets did not play a significant role in the international economic system after 1945. Most states had restrictions on capital movement in force at that time, which limited opportunities for international financial transactions. Fred Hirsch and Peter Oppenheimer described the situation of the international financial system at the end of the 1960s as 'like a mini-golf course, with some hole or other always accessible, but others shut off and a variety of shifting obstacles to be negotiated'.[34]

The situation changed at the end of the 1960s. At this time, private international financial markets became more visible and began to play a significant role in the international economic system. This also had an important impact on the international monetary system. The somewhat radical change in the international financial and monetary system at that time was due to the introduction of 'eurobonds' in 1963. Eurobonds are bonds issued in a currency other than that of the country of issuance, which are usually placed on different domestic financial markets simultaneously by big banks or banking consortiums. Some consider eurobonds to be a 'genuinely de-territorialised form of finance'.[35] Eurobonds had the effect that the international financial market, until the 1960s almost totally

[33] General Agreement on Tariffs and Trade, 30 October 1947, UNTS 55, 187.

[34] F. Hirsch and P. Oppenheimer, 'The Trial of Managed Money: Currency, Credit, and Prices, 1920–70', in C. M. Cipolla (ed.), *The Fontana Economic History of Europe: The Twentieth Century, Part Two* (Glasgow: Collins, 1976), p. 661, cited by E. Helleiner, *States and the Reemergence of Global Finance – From Bretton Woods to the 1990s* (Ithaca, New York: Cornell University Press, 1994), pp. 81 ff.

[35] Szodruch, *Staateninsolvenz und private Gläubiger*, 52, with further references on eurobonds in general; Lastra, *Legal Foundations*, pp. 371, 396 ff.

controlled and restricted by states, was opened up to the private sector. However at that time the important private actors in the financial market were exclusively large banks and banking consortiums.

In addition to the factual changes in the international financial market, important structural developments occurred in the 1970s. First there was the well-known shift from fixed to flexible exchange rates after the US removed the link between the US dollar and the gold standard on 15 August 1971. This development, which was at least partly due to the problems of the US state deficit at that time, put pressure on the IMF to redefine its task. After the first modification of the IMF Agreement concerning special drawing rights (SDRs) in 1968, the member states of the IMF reacted to the change with a substantial revision of Article VI IMF Agreement and thus an extension of the IMF mandate in 1976. This revision gave the IMF a new mandate to supervise the international currency system with regard to macroeconomic considerations.[36] This development goes hand in hand with the introduction of conditionality as an essential policy tool of the IMF even today. The reason for this was that around the beginning of the 1970s, the IMF had almost exclusively developing countries as 'clients'. This marked the beginning of the IMF's slow transformation into a development institution.[37] Even though the Washington Consensus defines the conditionality policy of the IMF with regard to trade, foreign investment and financial markets, those issues were never included in the IMF mandate.

The shift in the mandate of the IMF at the beginning of the 1970s goes hand in hand with a fundamental change in the global structure of sovereign debts. Most developing countries financed their state budgets after World War II with the help of credits they received from developed countries and the Bretton Woods institutions. As already indicated, private capital played hardly any role and only became relevant with the introduction of eurobonds. However, the energy crisis at the beginning of the 1970s led to massive profits being made by the oil-exporting countries. These countries placed their currency reserves – known as petro dollars – on the euro-dollar markets, i.e. in accounts held with branches of US banks in the UK, namely London. The banks themselves used these savings to invest in Latin American states. This was done with hardly any risk insurance. In 1982, oil-importing countries owed debts of about US$ 300.8 billion to foreign private creditors. At the same time,

[36] See, e.g., Arner and Buckley, 'Redesigning the Architecture of the Global Financial System', 10.

[37] Schlemmer-Schulte, 'Internationales Währungs und Finanzrecht', § 9, paras. 50 ff.

US banks invested about 211 per cent of their capital in credits to emerging economies.[38]

The Bretton Woods system was more or less unaffected by these developments. Instead, a structure parallel to Bretton Woods, and largely based on soft law dealing with the emerging challenges described above, developed, under the auspices of the BIS in Basel, Switzerland. As a result of the insolvency of the German Herstatt Bank, the US Franklin National Bank and the Israel–British Bank in London, the governors of the central bank of the G-10 countries founded the Standing Committee on Banking Regulations and Supervisory Practices, which was renamed the Basel Committee on Banking Supervision in 1990.[39] The insolvencies of these banks, however, were only the immediate cause of the establishment of the Basel Committee. The real genesis lies in the introduction of new actors and an increase in the volume of international financial markets, i.e., in the emerging globalisation of financial markets in the 1970s. Essentially, the establishment of the Basel Committee was a reaction to the lack of international standards for the globalised financial market at that time.[40] However, it is obvious that the task of the Basel Committee was and is limited to rather microeconomic issues. Exchange rate stability, sovereign debts and other challenges to the international economic system are not of primary interest for the Basel system.

Along with the founding of the Basel Committee, soft law international regulatory structures also emerged in the area of securities. In 1974, the World Bank and the Organization of American States jointly established the regional Inter-American Association of Securities Commissions and Similar Organizations as an informal discussion group.[41] This group became the basis for establishing the International Association of Securities Commissions in 1983–4, which today is the most important

[38] Szodruch, *Staateninsolvenz und private Gläubiger*, pp. 89 ff.

[39] For details, see B. Rost, 'Basel Committee on Banking Supervision', in C. Tietje and A. Brouder (eds.), *Handbook of Transnational Economic Governance Regimes* (Leiden: Martinus Nijhoff, 2009), p. 319.

[40] J. J. Norton, 'NIFA-II or "Bretton-Woods-II"? The G-20 (Leaders) Summit Process on Managing Global Financial Markets and the World Economy – Quo Vadis?' *Journal of Banking Regulation* 11 (2010), 261, 266.

[41] C. Möllers, 'Transnationale Behördenkooperation: Verfassungs- und völkerrechtliche Probleme transnationaler administrativer Standardsetzung', *Zeitschrift für ausländisches öffentliches Recht und Völkerrecht* 65 (2005), 351, 360; D. Zaring, 'Informal Procedure, Hard and Soft, in International Administration', *New York University Public Law and Legal Theory Working Papers* 3:12 (2006), 11 ff.

regime for international security regulation.[42] Furthermore, attempts to harmonise accounting standards also started in the mid-1970s. This process began with attempts by the Organisation for Economic Co-operation and Development (OECD) and the UN and led to the establishment of the International Accounting Standards Committee on 29 June 1973, which was replaced by the International Accounting Standards Board (IASB) in April 2001.[43]

With the establishment of the aforementioned organisations and standard-setters, an overall movement towards the creation of several intermediate and private international and regional standard-setting bodies and other forms of cooperation and coordination concerning global financial markets started. Without going into detail, it is clear that with an increase in the intensity of globalisation of financial markets in the 1970s, the complexity of the web of informal, intermediate and non-governmental regimes of cooperation and coordination on and for financial markets increased too.[44] Thus, an important part of what is today called global administrative law (GAL) emerged.[45] Soft law elements are a typical characteristic of this system. It is thus not surprising that soft law still dominates the international regulatory structure of international financial law.[46]

The emerging global (soft) regime on financial markets of the 1970s was, however, not restricted to typical forms of administrative coordination and cooperation concerning microeconomic issues. Instead, a similar development occurred with regard to macroeconomic questions and political structures relevant to the international financial and monetary system. The first important event in this regard was on 25 March 1973 as the finance ministers of Germany, France, the UK and the US

[42] For details, see Rost, 'Basel Committee on Banking Supervision'; D. Alexander, 'International Organization of Securities Commissions', in C. Tietje and A. Brouder (eds.), *Handbook of Transnational Economic Governance Regimes* (Leiden: Brill, 2009), p. 439.

[43] For details see Rost, 'Basel Committee on Banking Supervision', 169 ff.; B. Rost, 'International Accounting Standards Board', in C. Tietje and A. Brouder (eds.), *Handbook of Transnational Economic Governance Regimes* (Leiden: Brill, 2009), pp. 367 ff.

[44] For details see comprehensively Norton, 'Nifa-II or "Bretton-Woods-II"?', 266 ff.

[45] On global administrative law, see, e.g., B. Kingsbury, N. Krisch and R. B. Stewart, 'The Emergence of Global Administrative Law', *Law & Contemporary Problems* 68 (2005), 15; S. Cassese, B. Carotti, L. Casini, M. Macchia, E. MacDonald and M. Savino (eds.), *Global Administrative Law – Cases, Materials, Issues*, 2nd edn. (Institute for International Law and Justice, 2008), www.iilj.org/GAL/documents/GALCasebook2008.pdf; for a comprehensive overview on Global Administrative Law see Bibliographical Resources, www.iilj.org/GAL/documents/GALBibliographyMDeBellisJune2006.pdf.

[46] C. Brummer, *Soft Law and the Global Financial System* (Cambridge University Press, 2012); Lastra, *Legal Foundations*, pp. 447, 453 ff.

met in the White House library to discuss the challenges of the international economic and financial systems after the shift from fixed to flexible exchange rates. After this meeting, the group met on a regular basis and, after Japan joined the talks, it became known as the G-5. Over the years the group expanded the scope of the issues it discussed to encompass general political topics relevant to the international system. It was the basic conviction of the G-5 that the then existing international forum, namely the UN, was neither effective nor capable of coping with the challenges to the international economic system, i.e., that there was no existing effective global economic governance structure. It was on this basis that the G-7 and G-8 emerged. However, throughout the history of the 'Gs', its focus on international governance shifted further and further away from questions of the international financial and monetary system.[47]

2. New International Financial Architecture I (NIFA I)

The developments in the 1970s concerning administrative and political (gubernative[48]) cooperation and coordination finally led, in the 1990s, to the establishment of what has been called the New International Financial Architecture I (NIFA I).[49] The immediate background for the NIFA I was the financial crisis in Mexico in 1994 ('Tequila crisis'), the Asian crisis in 1997 and the Brazilian and Russian crises in 1998–9. The G-7 finance ministers reacted to these crises in May 1998 with the report entitled 'Strengthening the Architecture of the Global Financial System'. With this report, a new dimension of international cooperation based on the rule of law concerning the global financial markets began. The NIFA I worked quite successfully until about 2000, specifically with regard to surveillance, standard-setting, better transparency and exchange of information. Important successes include the establishment

[47] P. I. Hajnal, *The G8 System and the G20 – Evolution, Role and Documentation* (Farnham: Ashgate, 2007), 11 ff; A. Brouder, 'G8', in C. Tietje and A. Brouder (eds.), *Handbook of Transnational Economic Governance Regimes* (Leiden: Brill, 2009), pp. 95, 96 ff, with further references.

[48] 'Gubernative' refers to the part of government being responsible for political decisions and leadership. On the notion of gubernative and the necessity to differentiate between administrative and gubernative structures, see A. von Bogdandy, *Gubernative Rechtssetzung*, (Tübingen: Mohr-Siebeck, 2000), pp. 107 ff; C. Tietje, *Internationalisiertes Verwaltungshandeln* (Berlin: Duncker & Humblot, 2001), pp. 188 ff, with further references.

[49] Very comprehensively on this Norton, 'NiFA-II or "Bretton Woods-II"?', 272 ff.

of the Financial Stability Forum (FSF)[50] (now: Financial Stability Board), the Financial Sector Assessment Program (FSAP),[51] and the Reports of the Observance of Standards and Codes (ROSCs), also as a joint initiative with the IMF and the World Bank. Moreover, NIFA I is characterised by the enlargement of G-7 to the G-20 finance ministers[52] and certain reforms of the IMF. The reforms of the IMF made the organisation more of a standard-setter in itself.[53]

The ambitious structure of NIFA I was successful for some time, namely in its combination of political leadership by G-8/G-20 countries and technical cooperation within institutions such as the FSF and the IMF. This is true with regard to both the international financial and the international monetary system. In this regard, the development in the 1990s clearly strengthened the rule of law in the international economic system, even though soft law dominated.

However, around 2000, and at the latest from 11 September 2001 onwards, the focus of the G-8/G-20 shifted from financial and monetary market stability to more general political topics, namely the fight against international terrorism. As we know today this was a fatal development, because some of the real causes of the financial crisis of 2007–9 emerged during that time. Even though it is hard to single out any one cause of the financial crisis of 2007–9, the low interest rates policy of the Federal Reserve played a role. This policy was only possible because of the surplus of financial resources in the US market due to China's policy of investing its foreign currency reserves, which is currently about US$ 3 trillion[54] in the US.[55] The foreign currency reserves of

[50] On the FSF, see T. Porter, 'Financial Stability Board', in C. Tietje and A. Brouder (eds.), *Handbook of Transnational Economic Governance Regimes* (Leiden: Brill, 2009), p. 345.

[51] Founded in 1999. For details, see www.imf.org/external/np/fsap/fsap.asp.

[52] Norton, 'Nifa-II or "Bretton-Woods-II"?', 275 ff. [53] *Ibid.*, 280.

[54] 'China Foreign Currency Reserves Surged Past US$3 Trillion in March': China's Central Bank, *The China Post*, 15 April 2011, www.chinapost.com.tw/business/asia-china/2011/04/15/298686/China-foreign.htm.

[55] On the causes of the crisis see, e.g., M. Hellwig, *Finanzmarktregulierung – Welche Regelungen empfehlen sich für den deutschen und europäischen Finanzsektor? – Finanzkrise und Reformbedarf –, Gutachten E zum 68. Deutschen Juristentag* (Munich: C. H. Beck, 2010), pp. 365 ff; C. Ohler, 'International Regulation and Supervision of Financial Markets After the Crisis', *European Yearbook of International Economic Law* 1 (2010), 3, 6 ff; comprehensively M. Obstfeld and K. Rogoff, 'Global Imbalances and the Financial Crisis: Products of Common Causes', (2009), www.frbsf.org/economics/conferences/aepc/2009/09_Obstfeld.pdf; R. M. Lastra and G. Wood, 'The Crisis of 2007–09: Nature, Causes, and Reactions', *Journal of International Economic Law* 13 (2010), 531.

China are, to some extent, a result of the export performance of the country after its accession to the WTO on 11 December 2001.

Therefore the interdependence of trade, currency and financial markets becomes obvious, even though this phenomenon did not receive any attention in NIFA I. Only after 2002, and only on a domestic level, namely in the US, did the issue of China's foreign currency reserve and a possible 'currency manipulation' become an issue.[56] The ignorance about the interdependence of trade, currency and financial markets is demonstrated by the fact that even though Article III:5 of the Agreement Establishing the WTO[57] provides for cooperation of the WTO, 'as appropriate, with the International Monetary Fund and with the International Bank for Reconstruction and Development and its affiliated agencies' with a view 'to achieving greater coherence in global economic policy-making', WTO members in fact constantly restricted the mandate of the organisation with regard to cooperation with other international agencies.[58] Even though the topic is not at all new,[59] no real attempt to achieve greater coherence in global economic policy-making was made.[60] This is also true with regard to the role of the IMF concerning currency imbalances or even currency manipulation. Even though the IMF is active within its surveillance measures in advising states about exchange rate policies and is sometimes criticised for its mission creep, i.e., extensive use of originally rather restrictive competences,[61] it has never made an official declaration that a state is in violation of Article IV section 1 IMF Agreement, i.e., is guilty of 'currency manipulation' or

[56] For a detailed discussion, see M. Franke, *Chinas Währungspolitik in der Kritik des US-amerikanischen und des internationalen Wirtschaftsrechts* (Halle: Universitäts-Verlag Halle-Wittenberg, 2008), pp. 13 ff; see also the contributions in S. J. Evenett (ed.), 'The US-Sino Currency Dispute: New Insights from Economics, Politics and Law' (April 2010), www.voxeu.org/reports/currency_dispute.pdf.

[57] Marrakesh Agreement establishing the World Trade Organization, 15 April 1994, UNTS 1867, 3 (WTO Agreement).

[58] For details, see C. Tietje, 'Global Governance and Inter-Agency Co-operation in International Economic Law', *Journal of World Trade* 36:3 (2002), 501 ff.

[59] See, e.g., Declaration adopted by the Trade Negotiations Committee on 15 December 1993, Contribution of the WTO to Achieving Greater Coherence in Global Economic Policymaking, www.wto.org/english/docs_e/legal_e/32-dcohr.pdf.

[60] See, e.g., M. Auboin, 'Fulfilling the Marrakesh Mandate on Coherence: Ten Years of Cooperation between the WTO, IMF and World Bank', WTO Discussion Paper 13 (2007), www.wto.org/english/res_e/booksp_e/discussion_papers13_e.pdf.

[61] See, e.g., D. D. Bradlow, 'International Law and the Operation of the International Financial Institutions', in D. D. Bradlow and D. B. Hunter (eds.), *International Financial Institutions and International Law* (Alphen aan den Rijn: Kluwer Law International, 2010), pp. 1, 15 ff.

some other form of currency policy that has negative effects on the world economy.[62] Because of the very limited role the IMF plays in currency policy, the US has been trying for some time to make a WTO case out of the problem. However, Article XV GATT and the WTO Agreement on Subsidies and Countervailing Measures (ASCM) are hardly suitable for dealing with currency manipulation because it is essentially impossible to distinguish legitimate currency policies of a country from any kind of currency manipulation.[63] This clearly indicates that the role law plays or ought to play in monetary affairs has inherent limits.

In contrast to the issue of interdependence of trade, currency and financial markets, the IMF intensively discussed the problem of state insolvency as an important cause of currency instabilities. In the aftermath of the insolvencies in the 1990s in Mexico, Russia and Brazil as well as that of Argentina in 2001, the IMF realised the connection between sovereign debt and stability of the international financial and monetary markets. Anne Krueger, the First Deputy Managing Director of the IMF, proposed at that time the establishment of a 'Sovereign Debt Restructuring Mechanism'.[64] This proposal never gained any political support and the IMF officially rejected it at the spring meeting in 2003.[65] Therefore even today there is no international legal regime dealing comprehensively with the complexity of international and domestic law affected by a sovereign default. Moreover, the topic overall is not integrated in any way into the international financial and monetary architecture, even though current events, e.g., the financial situation in Greece, demonstrate how important the interrelationship between a budgetary crisis of a state and the stability of the international financial and monetary markets is.

The real problem of leaving out the topic of state insolvency from any legal regulation in the international monetary system is not that the world has seen some spectacular bankruptcies of states in the last few years, but the phenomenon of 'private sector involvement', i.e. the historically unprecedented interdependence of private international

[62] E. A. Posner and A. O. Sykes, 'International Law and the Limits of Macroeconomic Cooperation', Institute for Law and Economics Working Paper No. 609, July 2012, 36, ssrn.com/abstract=2120890.

[63] *Ibid.*, 39.

[64] 'International Financial Architecture for 2002: A New Approach to Sovereign Debt Restructuring', Address by Anne Krueger, First Deputy Managing Director, International Monetary Fund, Given at the National Economists' Club Annual Members' Dinner American Enterprise Institute, Washington, DC, 26 November 2001, www.imf.org/external/np/speeches/2001/112601.htm.

[65] C. Ohler, 'Der Staatsbankrott', *Juristenzeitung* 60 (2005), 590, 598.

financial markets, currency stability and sovereign debts.[66] Private sector involvement has its roots in developments that occurred at the end of the 1980s. It became obvious around 1989 that something had to be done to break the everlasting cycle of financing state budgets by credits provided by a limited number of international banks, leading to sovereign default of that state some years later, necessitating financial aid from international organisations such as the IMF and debt restructuring based on new international credits by large banks, further sovereign default a number of years later and so on. To get out of this never-ending cycle, a radical restructuring of sovereign debt was necessary. Such a new system was proposed by the Brady Plan. According to the principles developed by US Treasury Secretary Nicholas F. Brady in March 1989, large credits to emerging economies are restructured to bonds which are put on the international financial markets in order to finance the original credit. With this, the structure and indeed the number of creditors dramatically changes. In the past, only a limited number of international banks had served as creditors; now, theoretically, an unlimited number of bondholders in different jurisdictions have this ability. Due to private sector involvement in state budget finance, today sovereign defaults necessarily entail crises in the financial and also the currency markets. However, with the exception of certain attempts to harmonise the law of collective action clauses,[67] the international political and legal community hardly reacted to this radical new structure of state debts or its inherent interdependence with private international financial and public currency markets.

Therefore, it is evident that the fragmentation of NIFA I had several causes. First, the possibility of creating a comprehensive lender of last resort was never in question. On the contrary, the IMF lost almost all significance after the Asian crisis as its tasks were taken over, at least to some extent, by the FSF and the G-20. Moreover, the IMF reached the limits of its financial resources, which became more and more marginal in relation to the total volume of international financial markets. In this regard, the IMF got into a liquidity crisis with itself.[68] In addition, as

[66] Comprehensively Szodruch, *passim*.

[67] For details, see E. B. Koch, 'Collective Action Clauses – The Way Forward', *Georgetown Journal of International Law* 35 (2004), 665; S. Schill, 'Der völkerrechtliche Staatsnotstand in der Entscheidung des BVerfG zu Argentinischen Staatsanleihen – Anachronismus oder Avantgarde?', *Zeitschrift für ausländisches öffentliches Recht und Völkerrecht* 68 (2008), 45, 65.

[68] Moschella, *Governing Risk*, p. 125.

indicated above, NIFA I did not make any serious political or legislative attempt to integrate trade, finance, currency issue and state debt problems. Further, the political leadership by the G-8 and G-20, at least after 11 September 2001, shifted its focus away from international financial and currency stability. This resulted in NIFA I more or less becoming an exercise of standardisation and technical and administrative cooperation concerning certain actors and instruments on private financial markets in emerging economies.[69] Once NIFA I had become focused on technical and administrative issues, the international financial system became a prominent field of research for those scholars following the approach of GAL.[70] However, apart from soft law structures in terms of GAL, no 'hard' legal principles or rules governing international financial and monetary affairs emerged.

C. Today's international financial architecture (New International Financial Architecture II?)

The rather fragmented, incomplete and soft-law oriented structure of NIFA I became obvious with the outbreak of the financial crisis in 2007. The logical consequence was that international regulatory efforts to abate the crisis became quickly focused on reforming NIFA I, in this sense creating a 'new new' international financial architecture: a NIFA II. This was done by using the unique governance structure that had been developed in NIFA I, which consisted of a patchwork of several international regimes for technical and administrative standardisation, coordination and cooperation under the auspices of the G-20 finance ministers.[71]

The substantial debate concerning NIFA II circled around attempts to overcome the structural deficits of NIFA I. The first 'real' G-20 summit on 15 November 2008, immediately after the breakdown of Lehman Brothers, made it clear at that time that 'market principles, open trade and investment regimes, and effectively regulated financial markets' were at stake, as they are 'essential for economic growth, employment, and poverty reduction'.[72] The G-20 directed this statement at the

[69] Norton, 'NiFA-II or "Bretton Woods II"?', 281.

[70] E. J. Pan, 'Challenge of International Cooperation and Institutional Design in Financial Supervision: Beyond Transgovernmental Networks', *Chicago Journal of International Law* 11 (2010), 243.

[71] Moschella, *Governing Risk*, p. 127.

[72] Declaration – Summit on Financial Markets and the World Economy, 15 November 2008, para. 2, www.g20.org/Documents/g20_summit_declaration.pdf.

above-mentioned interface problem of integrating trade, finance, currency and investment.[73] Moreover, the G-20 made it clear that they claimed political leadership for the entire international economic system. This was successful, at least for some time during the crisis, as evidenced by the modest use of protectionist measures at that time.[74] However, at that time hardly any attention at all was paid to currency issues.

Next to the re-establishment of political leadership for the international economic system, the G-20 concentrated on modification and reorganisation of the international financial architecture to make it more efficient.[75] This strategy was in line with an insight elucidated some time later in the De Larosière Report: 'the key failure in the past was not so much a lack of surveillance, although the message emerging from the surveillance could have been sharpened, but a lack of policy action'.[76]

The G-20 summits and meetings of G-20 finance ministers with central bank governors which subsequently took place followed the goals and principles formulated in November 2008. In addition to several regulatory efforts concerning standardisation, cooperation and surveillance, the G-20 initiated important steps towards strengthening the international financial architecture. One important reform project in this regard was the transformation of the FSF into the current FSB together with an enlargement of its mandate.[77] Developing its formerly soft structure into a more concrete and legally definable organisation is comparable with the evolution of the Commission on Security and Cooperation in Europe (CSCE) into the Organization for Security and Cooperation in Europe (OSCE)[78] or the GATT in

[73] Norton, 'NiFA-II or "Bretton Woods-II"?', 284.

[74] For details, see Robert Wolfe, 'Did the Protectionist Dog Bark? Transparency, Accountability, and the WTO During the Global Financial Crisis', Policy Report, March 2011, papers.ssrn.com/sol3/papers.cfm?abstract_id=1802783.

[75] See Declaration – Summit on Financial Markets and the World Economy, paras. 5 ff.; Arner and Buckley, 'Redesigning the Architecture of the Global Financial System', 25 ff.

[76] The High-Level Group on Financial Supervision in the EU (De Larosière Report), 2009, ec.europa.eu/internal_market/finances/docs/de_larosiere_report_en.pdf, 63.

[77] See Financial Stability Board Charter, June 2012 (FSB Charter), www.financialstabilityboard.org/publications/r_120809.pdf. For details, see E. R. Carrasco, 'Global Financial and Economic Crisis Symposium: The Global Financial Crisis and the Financial Stability Forum: The Awakening and Transformation of an International Body', *Transnational Law & Contemporary Problems* 19 (2010), 203.

[78] U. Fastenrath and K. Weigelt, 'Organization for Security and Cooperation in Europe (OSCE)', *Max Planck Encyclopaedia of Public International Law*, www.mpepil.com.

1947.[79] In line with the institutional evolution of the FSB, the division of labour between the IMF and the FSB was clarified. The idea in this regard is that the IMF would be responsible for macroeconomic surveillance, whereas the FSB would concentrate on microeconomic issues, namely standardisation.[80] In this regard, the G-20 highlighted that the IMF has the 'leading role in drawing lessons from the current crisis, consistent with its mandate' and needs to be equipped with better funding.[81] Finally, an important reform concerned the enlargement of membership in all relevant international financial institutions in parallel to the structure of the G-20.[82] This is in line with the modification of quotas and voting rights in the IMF that was decided upon during the spring meeting in 2008.[83]

In sum, the actions taken principally by the G-20 during the crisis of 2007–9 were modest. They are in line with the structure of the international financial architecture developed in the 1990s. However, two developments are new and systemically important: the already mentioned enlargement of membership in relevant financial institutions and the role of the G-20.[84]

D. Legal elements of an international financial and monetary order

Based on the foregoing considerations, it is possible to identify some basic elements of an international financial and monetary order, i.e., a legal order that goes beyond the rather descriptive characterisation of an international financial architecture or an international system for monetary affairs. This does not mean, however, that such a coherent and comprehensive

[79] C. Tietje and M. Lehmann, 'The Role and Prospects of International Law in Financial Regulation and Supervision', *Journal of International Economic Law* 13 (2010), 663, 676 ff.

[80] IMF, *The Fund's Mandate – An Overview*, 22 January 2010, www.imf.org/external/np/pp/eng/2010/012210a.pdf, para. 11.

[81] G-20 Summit on Financial Markets and the World Economy, Washington, DC, 15 November 2008, Action Plan to Implement Principles for Reform, Reforming International Financial Institutions, www.pittsburghsummit.gov/resources/125137.htm; see also R. M. Lastra, 'The Role of the IMF as a Global Financial Authority', in Christoph Herrmann and Jörg Philipp Terhechte (eds.), *European Yearbook of International Economic Law* (Berlin: Springer, 2011), pp. 121–36.

[82] This concerns, e.g., the Basel Banking Committee and IOSCO; see Arner and Buckley, 'Redesigning the Architecture of the Global Financial System', 25 ff.

[83] The G-20 Seoul Summit Leaders' Declaration, 11–12 November 2010, The Seoul Summit Document, www.g20.org/Documents2010/11/seoulsummit_declaration.pdf, para. 16.

[84] For more details, see C. Tietje, 'The International Financial Architecture as a Legal Order', *German Yearbook of International Law* 54 (2011), 11, 30 ff.

international financial and monetary order already exists. The current international financial and monetary system is fragmented and incomplete. Moreover, it is obvious that, as the basic structure of the current system dates back to the 1990s, it was not capable of preventing the global financial crisis of 2007–9[85] and the European sovereign debt crisis of 2010–11. This is a clear indication that the reform efforts made after September 2008 did not go far enough. One critical aspect in this regard is the missing regulatory link between trade, finance, sovereign debt and currency issues, even though some rather limited attempts to address the interface problem were made, for example at the G-20 meeting of finance ministers and central bank governors in Paris in February 2011[86] and the spring meeting of the IMF and the World Bank in April 2011.[87] A further aspect one always has to keep in mind while looking at the rule of law in the current monetary system is that this system is dominated by soft institutions and soft law. The significance of soft law in the global financial and monetary system is not necessarily a negative phenomenon. Brummer has discussed this, and further aspects, in his recent book on *Soft Law and the Global Financial System*.[88] However, a stable international monetary system cannot rely exclusively on soft law. In fact, one may argue that the entire phenomenon of soft law essentially rests on the existence of 'hard' law. Soft law fills gaps and in this it depends on gaps, gaps in a legal system.

Based on these considerations, some broader structural principles essential for strengthening the rule of law in international monetary affairs shall be discussed.

I. International financial and monetary stability and domestic embeddedness of financial market instruments and currency policy

First, it is important to be clear as to what the normative basis of the regulatory structure of the international financial monetary order is.

[85] Arner and Buckley, 'Redesigning the Architecture of the Global Financial System', 37.

[86] Meeting of Finance Ministers and Central Bank Governors, Paris, 18–19 February 2011, Communiqué, www.g20.org/Documents2011/02/COMMUNIQUE-G20_MGM%20_18-19_February_2011.pdf, para. 3.

[87] IMF, 'G-20 Moves Forward to Tackle Global Imbalances, IMF Survey online', 16 April 2011, http://www.imf.org/external/pubs/ft/survey/so/2011/NEW041611A.html; G-20 Communiqué, Meeting of Finance Ministers and Central Bank Governors, Washington, DC, 14–15 April 2011, www.g20.org/Documents2011/04/G20%20Washington%2014-15%20April%202011%20-%20final%20communique.pdf.

[88] C. Brummer, *Soft Law and the Global Financial System – Rule Making in the 21st Century* (Cambridge University Press, 2012).

Three aspects are crucial in this regard: first, financial and currency stability, as essential elements of any international financial and monetary order, are global public goods.[89] Second, the domestic embeddedness of financial market products is today essential also for monetary issues in general. Financial market products are inherently linked to a specific domestic legal order; they are indeed the progeny of domestic jurisdiction. For instance an investor buying shares in a Luxembourg investment fund is trusting not only the issuer, but also Luxembourg's well-known quality of legislation and administrative practices in the area of finance. This is a unique feature of financial market products. Unlike physical products and most services, financial market products always feature a particular jurisdiction. Thus they are products that are deeply rooted in one specific domestic legal order, on the one hand, and increasingly traded on global markets on the other. They are offered not only on their domestic market, but also worldwide, and in this sense they are 'international' or better – 'transnational'. Therefore, one may speak of transnational financial products and markets by highlighting the above-described double character of products and markets as being both domestic and international.[90]

This unique feature of financial market products has consequences for any attempt at international regulation because there are inherent limitations due to the domestic embeddedness, which may also be characterised in terms of regulatory competition.[91] Because of the domestic embeddedness of financial market products, in most instances regulation and supervision in this area are aimed not only at financial market stability, but are also

[89] H. Dieter, 'The Stability of International Financial Markets: A Global Public Good?', in S. A. Schirm (ed.), *New Rules for Global Markets – Public and Private Governance in the World Economy* (Basingstoke: Palgrave Macmillan, 2004), p. 23; M. Camdessus, 'International Financial and Monetary Stability: A Global Public Good', in P. B. Kenen and A. K. Swoboda (eds.), *Reforming the International Monetary and Financial System* (Washington, DC: International Monetary Fund, 2000), p. 9; G. R. D. Underhill, 'The Public Good versus Private Interests and the Global Financial and Monetary System', in D. Drache (ed.), *The Market or the Public Domain? Global Governance and the Asymmetry of Power* (London: Routledge, 2001), p. 274.

[90] Tietje and Lehmann, 'The Role and Prospects of International Law', 668 ff.; see also R. H. Weber, 'Multilayered Governance in International Financial Regulation and Supervision', *Journal of International Economic Law* 13 (2010), 683.

[91] Tietje and Lehmann, 'The Role and Prospects of International Law', 663 ff.; similar Weber, 'Multilayered Governance', 684: 'International regulation and supervision is not "naturally superior" to regional or national rules and supervisory practices or vice versa'; for details see also J. P. Trachtman, 'The International Law of Financial Crisis: Spillovers, Subsidiarity, Fragmentation and Cooperation', *Journal of International Economic Law* 13 (2010), 719.

influenced by many other considerations, including consumer protection, protection of creditors and the fiscal interests of the government.[92] These regulatory aims are not necessarily connected to the character of financial market products as (global) public goods, but also based on purely political considerations.

Third, one must realise that there is no one-size-fits-all optimal monetary policy for all countries worldwide. Already the theoretical concept of optimal monetary policy is unclear and in dispute. Moreover, the effects of monetary policy of central banks leading to inflation or deflation depend to a certain, maybe even to a large extent, on specific micro and macroeconomic circumstances in a given country or economic region.[93] Moreover, there is increasing demand for a more integrated and comprehensive policy by central banks concerning monetary issues. The Committee on International Economic Policy and Reform made this point convincingly in its September 2011 report 'Rethinking Central Banking':[94]

> Central banks should make clear that monetary policy is only one part of the policy response and cannot be effective unless other policies – fiscal and structural policies, financial sector regulation – work in tandem.[95]

The inherent complexity and the lack of a single globally applicable optimal monetary policy create serious obstacles for international coordination and cooperation in monetary affairs. As Eric A. Posner and Alan O. Sykes recently wrote, '[a]bout the most one can expect is occasional ad hoc cooperation among the subset of central banks confronting an immediate short-term problem'.[96]

In sum, there are limitations on comprehensive international harmonisation, coordination and cooperation concerning financial market regulation and supervision and monetary affairs. Thus, the international financial and monetary order will always be characterised by a certain element of decentralisation. The rule of law in international financial and monetary affairs thus also has inherent limits.

[92] L. Garicano and R. M. Lastra, 'Towards a New Architecture for Financial Stability: Seven Principles', *Journal of International Economic Law* 13 (2010), 597, 599.

[93] For a comprehensive discussion on this, see Posner and Sykes, 'International Law and the Limits of Macroeconomic Cooperation', 41 ff.

[94] See also R. M. Lastra, 'The Role of Central Banks in Monetary Affairs: A Comparative Perspective', Chapter 4, this volume.

[95] Committee on International Economic Policy and Reform, Rethinking Central Banking, September 2011, p. iii.

[96] Posner and Sykes, 'International Law and the Limits of Macroeconomic Cooperation', 44.

II. *Integrating macro- and micro-prudential regulation and supervision*

The structure of the international financial monetary order also reflects an increasing necessity to integrate approaches of macro- and micro-prudential regulation and supervision.[97] Practical evidence for this increasingly accepted perspective is demonstrated in the 2011 restructuring of regulation and supervision of financial markets in the EU. The new EU system is based on three institutions focusing on microeconomic risks and the European Systemic Risk Board (ESRB), which is responsible for the macro perspective.[98]

The international integration of macro- and micro-prudential regulation and supervision is not without legal problems. This derives from the notion that the mandate of the IMF is, in its original sense, limited to those issues of international finance that have an impact on the international currency system, namely with regard to balance of payments. Financial market stability in a broader sense is not part of the mandate of the IMF.[99] Thus, even today the IMF is influenced by its historical construction.[100]

[97] For a definition see, House of Lords' European Union Committee, The Future of EU Financial Regulation and Supervision, 14th Report of Session 2008–09, 17 June 2009, www.publications.parliament.uk/pa/ld200809/ldselect/ldeucom/106/106i.pdf, paras. 27 ff.

> Macro-prudential supervision is the analysis of trends and imbalances in the financial system and the detection of systemic risks that these trends may pose to financial institutions and the economy. The focus of macroprudential supervision is the safety of the financial and economic system as a whole, the prevention of systemic risk. Micro-prudential supervision is the day-to-day supervision of individual financial institutions. The focus of micro-prudential supervision is the safety and soundness of individual institutions as well as consumer protection. The same or a separate supervisor can carry out these two functions. If different supervisors carry out these functions they must work together to provide mechanisms to counteract macro-prudential risks at a micro-prudential level.

See K. Alexander, 'International Economic Law and Macro-Prudential Regulation', Chapter 20, this volume.

[98] For details, see M. Lehmann and C. Manger-Nestler, 'Die Vorschläge zur neuen Architektur der europäischen Finanzaufsicht', *Europäische Zeitschrift für Wirtschaftsrecht* 21 (2010), 87; M. Lehmann and C. Manger-Nestler, 'Das neue Europäische Finanzaufsichtssystem', *Zeitschrift für Bankrecht und Bankwirtschaft* 13 (2011), 2.

[99] IMF, *The Fund's Mandate – The Legal Framework*, 22 February 2010, www.imf.org/external/np/pp/eng/2010/022210.pdf.

[100] See notes 14 ff.

However, the IMF has gradually moved its activities towards macro and microeconomic surveillance of member states' financial markets, particularly after the Asian crisis in the 1990s. Most important in this regard were the introduction of the Financial Sector Assessment Program (FSAP), together with the World Bank, and the Reports on the Observance of Standards and Codes (ROSCs) in 1999.[101] However, these programmes and activities of the IMF have limits, such as voluntary participation for member states, discretionary obligations to submit individual bank data (see Article VIII(5)(b) IMF Agreement) and restrictions on countries that allow the FSAP and ROSCs. As a result, the IMF currently does not have the formal capability to make an assessment of global financial stability; any such attempt would be outside its mandate,[102] even though the Fund itself seems to adopt a less strict perspective on this matter. Indeed, FSAP is now part of formal surveillance according to the revised IMF decision on surveillance of 2007 and 2012, even though the legal background remains unclear.

As there seems to be no political willingness to amend the IMF Agreement in order to allow for a broader mandate of the Fund, the only alternative is to set up an informal structure outside the IMF. The FSB mandate accomplishes this (Article 2(1)(a) FSB Charter[103]). As a result, the FSB may very well be defined as the fourth pillar of global economic governance – alongside the WTO, the IMF and the World Bank.[104] However, it remains doubtful whether the FSB will actually be able to fulfil its mandate effectively, as any report or other result of the work of the FSB has to be accepted by the FSB Plenary by consensus (Article 9(2) FSB Charter). As practice within the IMF demonstrates, states tend to be hesitant about adopting and publishing reports criticising their financial or economic system, especially in the lead-up to domestic elections.[105]

[101] K. Alexander, R. Dhumale and J. Eatwell, *Global Governance of Financial Systems – The International Regulation of Systemic Risk* (Oxford University Press, 2006), p. 259: '. . . marks a turning point in the Fund's surveillance activities . . .'.

[102] For details on the mandate, see IMF, *The Fund's Mandate.* [103] See note 77.

[104] See the contributions in S. Griffith-Jones, E. Heilleiner and N. Woods (eds.), *The Financial Stability Board: An Effective Fourth Pillar of Global Economic Governance?* The Centre for International Governance Innovation, June 2008, arts.uwaterloo.ca/~bmomani/documents/FSBeditedspecialreport.pdf.

[105] On this problem with regard to the IMF, see H. Siebert, 'Zur Reform des Internationalen Währungsfonds', *Kieler Diskussionsbeiträge* 438 (2007), 7.

III. *Constitutional perspective: Articles 1(3), 55 and 56 UN Charter*

A constitutional roof that emanates from Articles 1(3), 55 and 56 UN Charter tightly holds the aforementioned rather technical, institutional pillars of the international financial order together. According to these provisions, the UN itself and its member states are obligated '[t]o achieve international co-operation in solving international problems of an economic, social, cultural, or humanitarian character' and to promote 'solutions of international economic, social, health, and related problems; and international cultural and educational cooperation'. These fundamental principles that shape the constitutional framework of the international economic order are rooted in those parts of the Atlantic Charter dealing with international economic cooperation.[106] They are an important part of the overall concept of the international system as a value-oriented international legal order based on human rights and social justice – the 'supreme paradigm of peace as a legal order'.[107]

Referring to Articles 1(3), 55 and 56 UN Charter does not necessarily give any answer on the specific role of the UN itself in the international financial and monetary order. Rather, the provisions are important for member states because they indicate the legal responsibility of a state while engaging in efforts to build and maintain the international financial architecture. As in any other area of international relations, states and other international actors are not free to take whatever action they choose; international politics are determined by international law, at least in the sense of some broad legal principles. The states adhere to such principles, as indicated in the 'Outcome of the Conference on the World Financial and Economic Crisis and Its Impact on Development', adopted by consensus by General Assembly Resolution 63/303 of 9 July 2009. In this document, states declared as follows:

> We reaffirm the purposes of the United Nations, as set forth in its Charter, including 'to achieve international cooperation in solving international problems of an economic, social, cultural, or humanitarian character' and 'to be a centre for harmonising the actions of nations in the attainment of these common ends'. The principles of the Charter are particularly relevant in addressing the current challenges. The United

[106] R. Wolfrum, 'Article 55', in B. Simma (ed.), *The Charter of the United Nations*, vol. II, 2nd edn (Oxford University Press, 2002), para. 3.

[107] J. Delbrück, 'Peaceful Change' in R. Wolfrum (ed.), *United Nations: Law, Policies and Practice*, vol. II (Munich: C. H. Beck, Leiden: Martinus Nijhoff, 1995), pp. 970, 977.

> Nations, on the basis of its universal membership and legitimacy, is well positioned to participate in various reform processes aimed at improving and strengthening the effective functioning of the international financial system and architecture.[108]

It is important to keep in mind the constitutional or principle-oriented perspective on international cooperation, also with regard to the international financial and monetary order. Moreover, this perspective indicates that it is not sufficient, and it may even be wrong, to analyse the international financial and monetary system as a network or network of networks exclusively from the perspective of GAL.[109] GAL might be interesting in order to understand the functioning of certain international financial institutions and organisations. However, as GAL essentially ignores public international law, it is not in a position to actually contribute to the debate on a comprehensive international financial order. Moreover, as the role of the G-20 as a gubernative institution during the crisis of 2007–9 demonstrated, global economic governance is more than just technical or administrative networks.[110]

IV. *Further elements of the rule of law in international monetary affairs*

The design and operation of the international monetary order has to adhere to the constitutional values of the UN Charter. Thus, it has to be based on the general obligation of international cooperation aiming at the achievement of economic and social welfare. This obligation is supported by the insight that international financial and monetary stability are global public goods and that financial market products and monetary policy objectives are always domestically embedded. Hence, it is obvious that the legal structure of the international financial and monetary order has to be decentralised and cannot achieve full harmonisation. Regulation and supervision of financial markets and monetary policy will thus always be characterised by the coexistence of

[108] GA Res. 63/303 of 13 July 2009, Annex, para. 2; on the vote see UN Doc. A/63/PV.95 (2009), 3.

[109] For such an approach see, e.g., M. De Bellis, 'Global Standards for Domestic Financial Regulations: Concourse, Competition and Mutual Reinforcement between Different Types of Global Administration', *Global Jurist Advances* 6 (2006), www.bepress.com/gj/advances/vol6/iss3/art6.

[110] Zaring, 'Informal Procedure', 500.

international, regional and domestic regulatory efforts.[111] This feature of any international financial and monetary system is one of the reasons why trying to create a more centralised system of financial regulation and supervision in the EU has been so difficult.

1. Integration of real economy, financial markets, foreign investment and sovereign debts

As mentioned above, the multilayered system of an international financial and monetary order not only has a vertical but also a horizontal dimension. This horizontal dimension is concerned with the integration of the real economy (trade in goods and services), financial markets, currency policy and sovereign debts as an important, if not the most important, challenge facing the international economic order. Even though the crisis of 2007–9 and the European sovereign debt crisis of 2011 are prime examples of the factual interdependence of the international economy, hardly any efforts are being made to modify the international financial and monetary architecture accordingly. A first and necessary step in this direction would be to intensify the cooperation of the IMF, World Bank, WTO and FSB as the four pillars of global economic governance. This, however, requires the members of the respective organisations to grant sufficient autonomy to the executive organs of the institutions. This is problematic, particularly with regard to the WTO as a 'member-driven' organisation[112] and because the WTO Secretariat is not even an organ of the institution. As long as the members are unwilling to change their attitude towards giving more autonomy to the executive organs of international economic organisations, closer cooperation between these organisations, which is needed to achieve greater coherence in international economic governance, is impossible.

Moreover it must be emphasised that the problem of sovereign debts has to be integrated into the broader framework of the international financial and monetary order. If no adequate regulatory answers are found to deal with the increasing interdependence of sovereign debt on the one side and international financial and currency markets on the other, the lack of coherence in the system will be perpetuated.[113] This is

[111] Weber, 'Multilayered Governance', 683 ff.; Tietje and Lehmann, 'The Role and Prospects of International Law', 663 ff.

[112] J. H. Jackson, 'The WTO "Constitution" and Proposed Reforms: Seven "Mantras" Revisited', *Journal of International Economic Law* 4 (2001), 67.

[113] See, e.g., R. P. Buckley, 'The Bankruptcy of Nations: An Idea Whose Time Has Come', *International Lawyer* 43 (2009), 1189.

evident from the Greek sovereign debt crisis of 2011 and its repercussions on the international financial markets.

In this regard, it is also necessary to discuss possible regime conflicts in the international economic system concerning monetary, financial, investment and trade issues. A prime example in this regard is capital control. In certain situations, restrictions on capital movement may be an appropriate regulatory response to instabilities of the financial and monetary market. However, even though the IMF Agreement basically leaves decisions on capital control within the sovereign domain of states, bilateral investment treaties, investment chapters in preferential trade agreements, and – to a certain extent – WTO law impose restrictions on unilateral capital control measures by states.[114]

A further area of increasing concern with regard to overlapping regulatory issues is financial and monetary measures and international investment law.[115] Explicit reference to financial services and monetary measures is made – in accordance with a long-standing practice – in the BITs of Canada and the US. The more or less similar provisions on financial services in the BITs of Canada[116] and the US[117] with third countries have the same structure: first, they provide for a general exception for 'measures relating to financial services for prudential reasons, including for the protection of investors, depositors, policy holders, or persons to whom a fiduciary duty is owed by a financial services supplier, or to ensure the integrity and stability of the financial system'.[118] Second, a similar non-application of the treaty is provided for with regard to 'monetary and related credit policies or exchange rate policies'; this, however, does not affect the freedom of capital and related transfer, and the general prohibition of so-called performance

114 See, e.g., E. L. Broomfield, 'Reconciling IMF Rules and International Investment Agreements: An Innovative Derogation for Capital Controls', *Columbia FDI Perspectives* No. 78, 10 September 2012.

115 This chapter on investment law and financial/monetary issues is taken from: C. Tietje, J. Finke and D. Dietrich, *Liberalisation and Rules on Regulation in the Field of Financial Services in Bilateral Trade and Regional Integration Agreements* (Eschborn: GIS, 2010), www2.gtz.de/wbf/4tDx9kw63gma/gtz2010-en-Financial-Services-FTAs.pdf.

116 See, e.g., Article XI Agreement between the Government of Canada and the Government of the Republic of Ecuador for the Promotion and Reciprocal Protection of Investments, 29 April 1996.

117 See Article 20 US Model Treaty (2012) Concerning the Encouragement and Reciprocal Protection of Investment.

118 Article 20(1) US Model BIT. The US Model BIT defines 'that the term, prudential reasons includes the maintenance of the safety, soundness, integrity, or financial responsibility of individual financial institutions'. See footnote 14 to Article 20 US Model BIT (2004).

requirements.[119] Third, with regard to disputes which might occur concerning the above-mentioned provisions on financial services, a special dispute settlement procedure is provided for in the BIT. This special procedure essentially provides for a 'financial services veto' of the competent financial authorities of both state parties to the BIT. Such 'financial services veto' – a mechanism that is also applied with regard to tax matters (tax veto)[120] – allows the competent authorities to exclude the application of the BIT based on a mutual decision that the subject matter of the dispute is a prudential, monetary or exchange rate measure.

Even though it seems that the US and Canadian BIT practice provides for quite far-reaching exceptions for prudential and monetary or exchange rate measures, it is important to note that the US Model BIT stipulates, in addition to the sentence already quoted on the possibility for prudential measures, that '[w]here such measures do not conform with the provision of this Treaty, they shall not be used as a means of avoiding the Party's commitments or obligations under this Treaty'.[121] This restriction on the possibility for a contracting state to enact and apply prudential measures is highly controversial; some lawyers argue that it actually is 'self-cancelling', or at least 'creates a burden of proof in favour of the investor and against the government'.[122] This opinion, however, disregards the above-mentioned 'financial services veto' which allows the competent authorities to issue a decision on the disputed prudential measure that is binding for an arbitral tribunal.

Explicit provisions on prudential and similar measures are only seen in the model BITs that have followed a North American style. The European BIT approach is different. Just as with regard to tax measures, European BITs do not contain any specific provisions on prudential or related measures. Regulatory measures affecting the financial market are thus subject to the protection against expropriation and the so-called treatment standards of the more than 1,000 BITs that have been

[119] Articles 7 and 8 US Model BIT.

[120] For details, see extensively K. Kampermann, *Steuersouveränität und internationales Investitionsschutzrecht* (Halle: Universitäts-Verlag Halle-Wittenberg, 2009), pp. 92 ff. and *passim*.

[121] Article 20(1), second sentence US Model BIT (2012).

[122] R. K. Stumberg, at the Hearing before the Committee of Ways and Means, US House of Representatives on Investment Protection in US Trade and Investment Agreements, One Hundred Eleventh Congress, First Session, May 14, 2009, Serial 111–200; see also Kevin P. Gallagher, 'US BITs and Financial Stability', *Columbia FDI Perspectives, Perspectives on Topical Foreign Direct Investment Issues by the Vale Columbia Center on Sustainable International Investment*, No. 19, 23 February 2010.

concluded by EU Member States with third countries. Most important in this regard is the standard of 'fair and equitable treatment'.[123] The notion of 'fair and equitable treatment' is obviously broad. It is thus not surprising that the financial and monetary regulatory measures taken by governments are challenged as being in violation of the guarantee of fair and equitable treatment. Next to the numerous cases following the financial crises and the monetary measures adopted by Argentina in 2001–2 and the cases likely to emerge in the near future out of the sovereign debts crises of Greece, Spain and other countries, one may refer, e.g., to a case that was decided in March 2006. In this case Saluka, a Dutch subsidiary of the Japanese bank Nomura, was awarded US$ 181 million plus US$ 55 million interest in a claim against the Czech Republic. The tribunal in this case followed the investor in its claim that the Czech Republic acted in violation of the fair and equitable treatment standard while – in the grip of a country-wide banking crisis – it bailed out some Czech banks, but not the one in which Saluka held a stake.[124] In another investment arbitration currently still pending, certain issues of the global financial crisis of 2007–8 are at stake. In the International Centre for Settlement of Investment Disputes (ICSID) case of *Deutsche Bank AG* v. *Democratic Socialist Republic of Sri Lanka*[125] the claimant argues that the suspension of payments under a derivatives deal between Deutsche Bank and the state-owned Ceylon Petroleum Corporation (CPC) is in violation of the Germany–Sri Lanka BIT. The above-mentioned derivatives deal had been concluded by CPC in an effort to hedge against rising oil prices. The deal started to cause political problems in Sri Lanka when oil prices dropped sharply during the global financial crisis.[126]

2. Coordination and cooperation

As well as the necessity for a more integrated approach, coordination and cooperation in a multilayered system presents a major challenge for

[123] See, e.g., Article 2(2) German Model BIT (2008): 'Each Contracting State shall in its territory in every case accord investments by investors of the other Contracting State fair and equitable treatment as well as full protection under this Treaty'.

[124] *Saluka Investments BV (The Netherlands)* v. *The Czech Republic*, UNCITRAL Arbitration, Partial Award of 17 March 2006.

[125] ICSID Case No.ARB/09/2; for background information see Peterson, IAReporter, 2 April 2009.

[126] It is important to note that disputes of this kind are usually settled by commercial arbitration based on provisions of the International Swaps and Derivatives Association (ISDA) Master Agreements.

the international economic and financial order. The international financial and monetary system is represented by a multitude of different domestic, regional and international actors, as well as steering instruments. This causes distinct challenges for coordination and cooperation based on the well-established basic obligation for inter-institutional cooperation of Article 56 UN Charter.[127] Legally, however, this duty to cooperate only addresses the subject of public international law, i.e. in this context, states and international organisations. It is more complicated to establish a legal obligation to coordinate and cooperate with regard to the numerous private and intermediate actors evident in the international financial and monetary system, as they do not have (international) legal personality. The system has adopted a pragmatic approach to solve this problem. The FSB has been entrusted with a comprehensive mandate 'to promote coordination and information exchange among authorities responsible for financial stability'.[128] However, it is questionable whether the FSB is able to effectively fulfil this mandate because it lacks political authority and, in analogy with the British Crown, has the simple function 'to advise, encourage and to warn'.[129] It has been known for quite some time that the Executive Committee of the IMF experiences a similar problem.[130]

3. Political leadership ('gubernative')

Based on the above, it is clear that the essential challenges presenting themselves to an international financial and monetary order call for more than merely technical administrative structures. In addition to what has already been outlined, an effective and efficient gubernative structure, i.e. a structure of political leadership, is necessary within the international financial architecture. As indicated, the G-20 seems to represent this function, at least from its own perspective. However, it is questionable whether the G-20 is well suited to ensure the stability and

[127] For details, see Tietje, 'Global Governance and Inter-Agency Co-operation', 501 ff.; C. Tietje, 'The Duty to Cooperate in International Economic Law and Related Areas', in J. Delbrück (ed.), *International Law of Cooperation and State Sovereignty* (Berlin: Duncker & Humblot, 2002), 45.

[128] Article 2 (1)(b) FSB Charter.

[129] D. W. Arner and M. Taylor, 'The Global Financial Crisis and the Financial Stability Board: Hardening the Soft Law of International Financial Regulation?' *AIIFL Working Paper* 6 (2009), p. 11, www.law.hku.hk/aiifl/documents/AIIFLWorkingPaper6June2009_000.pdf.

[130] W. Bergthaler and W. Bossu, 'Recent Legal Developments in the International Monetary Fund', *European Yearbook of International Economic Law* 1 (2010), 391, 402 ff.

effective decision-making essential for an institution responsible for political leadership. This is less a problem of legitimacy of the G-20 itself, as the G-20 'represent[s] around 90 per cent of global gross national product, 80 per cent of world trade (including EU intra-trade) as well as two-thirds of the world's population'.[131] Rather, the lack of institutional structure, a probable cause of the rather negative compliance record of the G-20, is problematic. Even the G-7 and G-8 had had severe compliance problems.[132] It is not surprising that some G-20 member states have called for more institutional structure with the establishment of a secretariat.[133]

In addition to the internal structure of the G-20, a further major problem is caused by the exclusion of the United Nations from international financial and monetary governance structures. As already mentioned, the original initiative was to establish the ECOSOC as 'the' political leadership institution in international economic and financial governance. This concept was aligned with the overall notion of the role of the United Nations in the international system generally and with a structure of international economic governance more specifically, as already developed in the famous Bruce Report of 22 August 1939.[134] It is important to note that from this historical perspective no strict separation of 'political' (gubernative) and technical administrative issues was planned; a rather more integrated approach based on differentiation according to concrete task was foreseen. This approach flows through to the UN and the specific function(s) of ECOSOC in global economic governance.

Today there is little evidence of the original concepts of a global economic governance structure, particularly regarding horizontal and vertical integration of trade, finance, monetary issues, investment and sovereign debt. Even though the G-20 has a certain, to some degree successful, role in political leadership and developed its concrete ideas on 'Reinforcing International Cooperation and Promoting Integrity in Financial Markets' in March 2009,[135] it lacks the necessary infrastructure. Such an institutional

[131] See G-20, About G-20, www.g20.org/about_what_is_g20.aspx.

[132] For a discussion of the compliance issue, see A. Brouder, 'G8', 113.

[133] The Chosunilbo, Who Would Host a G20 Secretariat?, 15 November 2010, english.chosun.com/site/data/html_dir/2010/11/15/2010111500563.html.

[134] For details, see K. Dicke, *Effizienz und Effektivität internationaler Organisationen*, (Berlin: Duncker & Humblot, 1994), pp. 71 ff.

[135] G-20 Working Group on Reinforcing International Cooperation and Promoting Integrity in Financial Markets, Final Report, 27 March 2009, www.minefe.gouv.fr/directions_services/dgtpe/international/g20/090403gr2_en.pdf.

infrastructure is essential to the effective coordination and guidance of the activities of numerous governmental and non-governmental organisations. Unlike the G-20, organisations such as the IMF and the FSB certainly have the resources and the infrastructure to fulfil such a task; however, they lack the political authority necessary in a complex multilayered international financial and monetary system.

The problem of having insufficient political leadership in the structure of global economic governance, if it even exists, was recognised and addressed in the Stiglitz Commission's report to the President of the UN General Assembly of 21 September 2009: '[o]n Reforms of the International Monetary and Financial System'. The Commission proposed the establishment of a Global Economic Coordination Council supplemented by a panel of experts.[136] According to the Commission, the main function of the new Coordination Council would be to take up the role of real political leadership over the Bretton Woods organisations – including the WTO, which is not part of the UN system. This proposal aims at replacing or at least reactivating the originally proposed functions of ECOSOC. This may indicate that the Stiglitz Commission has circumvented the decades-long impossible task of reforming ECOSOC.[137]

The main problem with the proposal of the Stiglitz Commission is that it has little chance of gaining global political support. Thus, for the time being, it has to be accepted that the only political leadership structure within the current system of global economic governance is the G-20.[138] This clearly indicates, however, that public international law and international legal scholarship need to take an interest in the G-20.

[136] Report of the Commission of Experts of the President of the United Nations General Assembly on Reforms of the International Monetary and Financial System, 21 September 2009, www.un.org/ga/econcrisissummit/docs/FinalReport_CoE.pdf; for a discussion, see, e.g., F. Schröder and J. Stetten, 'Mythos Weltwirtschaftsrat', *Vereinte Nationen* 58 (2010), 104 ff.

[137] T. G. Weiss, *ECOSOC is Dead – Long Live ECOSOC*, Perspective – Friedrich Ebert Stiftung New York, December 2010, library.fes.de/pdf-files/bueros/usa/07709.pdf; G. Rosenthal, 'The Economic and Social Council of the United Nations – An Issue Paper', *Dialogue on Globalization Occasional Papers* 15 February 2005, library.fes.de/pdf-files/iez/global/50091.pdf.

[138] See also Report of the Secretary-General, Global Economic Governance and Development, UN Doc. A/66/506 (2011).

3

The international monetary and financial architecture – some institutional aspects

MARIO GIOVANOLI

A. Introduction

This chapter discusses a limited number of issues of current interest relating to institutional aspects of the global monetary and financial architecture, in particular with regard to setting international financial standards (IFSs), which plays an important role in promoting international financial stability – and hence in preventing or mitigating as far as possible international financial crises.[1] The chapter is divided into four sections.

B. The current international monetary and financial architecture and its main characteristics

I. *From the Bretton Woods system to a decentralised global financial architecture*

In order to fully understand the present situation, it may help to recall the fundamental evolution that has occurred over the last forty years. Under the Bretton Woods system of fixed exchange rates, which prevailed between 1944 and 1973, national economies were far less interdependent than at present and the essential function of the International Monetary Fund (IMF) was to oversee the international monetary system based on fixed exchange rates.[2] This situation changed radically as a consequence of globalisation and deregulation, leading not

The views expressed in this chapter are those of the author.

[1] The equally important issues relating to crisis resolution, sovereign debt and default, including the Paris Club and the London Club, are not addressed in this chapter, nor are the issues concerning the reform and increase of resources of the International Monetary Fund (IMF); on the latter, see the G-20 Leaders Declaration, published at the end of the Los Cabos Summit of June 2012, www.g20.org.

[2] For a description of the evolution of the Bretton Woods system, see C. Tietje, 'The Role of Law in Monetary Affairs: Taking Stock', Chapter 2, this volume.

only to the end of the Bretton Woods system following the adoption of floating exchange rates, but unfortunately also to recurrent financial crises.[3] As a result, a global market-led financial system emerged, with no central institution having the overall responsibility for regulating or overseeing it.

The vacuum left by the retreat of the IMF from its primary function was progressively filled by a number of mushrooming bodies, which came into existence without any precise plan or design. The creation of these bodies was more often than not prompted by a financial crisis. Symptomatically, the first and most prominent of the standard-setting bodies (SSBs), the BCBS,[4] was set up at the Bank for International Settlements (BIS) by the G-10 central bank governors in 1974 under the pressure of the Herstatt Bank crisis. Initially, the main concern was that the international financial markets (then called 'euromarkets'), particularly the large banking institutions with global banking activity, largely escaped oversight and regulation by domestic supervisors. The BCBS was to become a permanent institution and one of the major SSBs in the financial world. Many other SSBs were created in the following decades, some 'top down', by an initiative of the G-10 (CPSS, CGFS) or the G-7 (FATF), others organised themselves 'bottom up' as associations between the regulatory or supervisory authorities concerned (IOSCO, IAIS, IADI). This decentralised process can be described as a sort of legal existentialism, as it occurred outside any clear legal framework or institutional coherence.[5]

The call for integration of the various initiatives in this field into a rational and coherent framework, a so-called 'international financial architecture', became insistent after the 1997 Asian crisis. Various international efforts in the aftermath of this crisis led to the creation of two new bodies in 1999 with a view to strengthening the architecture of the international financial system, namely the G-20 and the Financial Stability Forum, renamed Financial Stability Board (FSB) ten years later.

[3] M. Goldstein, 'The International Financial Architecture', in F. Bergsten (ed.), *The United States and the World Economy: Foreign Economic Policy for the Next Decade* (Washington, DC: Institute for International Economics, 2005), pp. 373–406 (Chapter 12). Since then, two further crises have occurred, the subprime bank crisis of 2008–9 and the eurozone sovereign debt crisis of 2010–12.

[4] A full list of acronyms of the SSBs with their websites is provided at the end of Appendix 1.

[5] The first attempt to introduce a degree of consistency between the work of the various SSBs was the establishment of the Joint Forum between the BCBS, the IOSCO and the IAIS to deal with issues of common interest.

Both these bodies – although very different in nature – are meant to have overarching functions in order to coordinate and where necessary initiate the work of the various existing SSBs.

At the highest policy level, the major industrialised countries have regularly gathered since 1975 at the level of heads of state or heads of government to discuss economic and financial issues, first as the G-5 (US, UK, France, Germany and Japan)[6] and soon afterwards as the G-7[7] (with Canada and Italy). In 1999, the need for a larger group, including major emerging economies and additional systemically important markets[8] was felt and this led to the creation of the G-20 as a wider forum of consultation and cooperation on matters pertaining to the international financial system. For nearly a decade, the G-20 remained largely dormant and no summits at the highest level took place.[9] It was only at the height of the 2008–9 international financial crisis that the first of a series of 'Leaders' Summits' took place (the November 2008 Washington Summit) and the G-20 agreed on a substantial reform of the international financial architecture (London Summit of April 2009) and designated itself as 'the premier forum for our international economic cooperation' (Pittsburgh Summit of September 2009). At the same time, reporting lines to the G-20 were established or redefined from the FSB (and similarly from the FATF and the Global Forum on Transparency and Exchange of Information (GFTEI) to the G-20), while the sectoral SSBs are expected to report on their work to the FSB (or sometimes directly to the G-20). Hence, the G-20 now appears, with respect to the international financial architecture, to have superseded both the G-7[10] and the G-10,[11] which had initially created the FATF, the FSF and many SSBs including the BCBS.

[6] The first meeting took place in Rambouillet (France) in 1975.

[7] For a clear and thorough presentation of all the various 'Gs', see the IMF factsheet at www.imf.org/external/np/exr/facts/groups.htm.

[8] Twelve countries (plus the European Union (EU)) were added to the original G-7, i.e. the so-called 'BRICS' (Brazil, Russia, India, China, South Africa), the four 'MIST' countries (Mexico, Indonesia, South Korea and Turkey) as well as Argentina, Australia and Saudi Arabia.

[9] However, during that period, the G-20 central bank governors and finance ministers met annually.

[10] It is unclear what the respective roles of the G-7 and the G-20 should be in the future with respect to the international financial architecture. The G-7 did meet in anticipation of the Los Cabos G-20 Summit of June 2012. The G-8 (G-7 plus Russia) will continue to meet mainly to discuss security issues.

[11] For all practical purposes, it seems that the G-10 (which never met at the level of heads of state and governments) has ceased any activity since 2005 (the year of the last paper

At the more practical level of coordinating the work of the various SSBs, the Financial Stability Forum was initially a relatively light structure created specifically to improve coordination between the various bodies responsible for financial stability, in addition to assessing vulnerabilities affecting the international financial system. In order to strengthen the surveillance of financial markets and the process of international financial standard-setting, the G-20 leaders decided to expand the membership of the Financial Stability Forum, and to rename it Financial Stability Board, with a stronger institutional basis including the publication of an FSB Charter (London Summit April 2009). At the Los Cabos Summit (June 2012), the G-20 again decided to improve the institutional and operational basis of the FSB, by revising its Charter.

Eventually, as a result of these efforts, a fairly structured – although far from perfect – international financial architecture emerged, which is summarised graphically in Figure 3.1. It comprises three levels: at the top, the G-20 as an informal steering group; one level below is the FSB with the primary mission[12] of coordinating the activity of the sectoral SSBs in the field of financial regulation and supervision, and finally come the sectoral SSBs themselves. As will be discussed later,[13] the incorporation of these standards, generally deemed to be mere recommendations ('soft law'), into national legislation ('hard law') or administrative practice is left to the national jurisdictions, although the implementation of the IFSs is strongly encouraged by the various international bodies at all three levels. It should be noted that in the case of standard setting both in the fields of money laundering/terrorist finance and transparency/exchange of information in tax matters, there are only two levels, as the FATF and the GFTEI directly establish the relevant standards and report to the G-20.

This decentralised 'architecture' was progressively put in place over nearly four decades in parallel with the four pre-existing international financial institutions (IFIs), which are classic intergovernmental organisations, three of them being international deposit and/or credit institutions (BIS, IMF, World Bank). Although the IFIs are involved to various degrees in international standard setting (in particular with regard to the implementation of IFSs), the new architecture is based on a very

published at www.bis.org/list/g10publications). It also appears that the account for the domain g10.org has been suspended.

[12] It should be noted that the FSB also acts directly as an SSB, in particular with regard to intersectoral issues.

[13] In Part D.

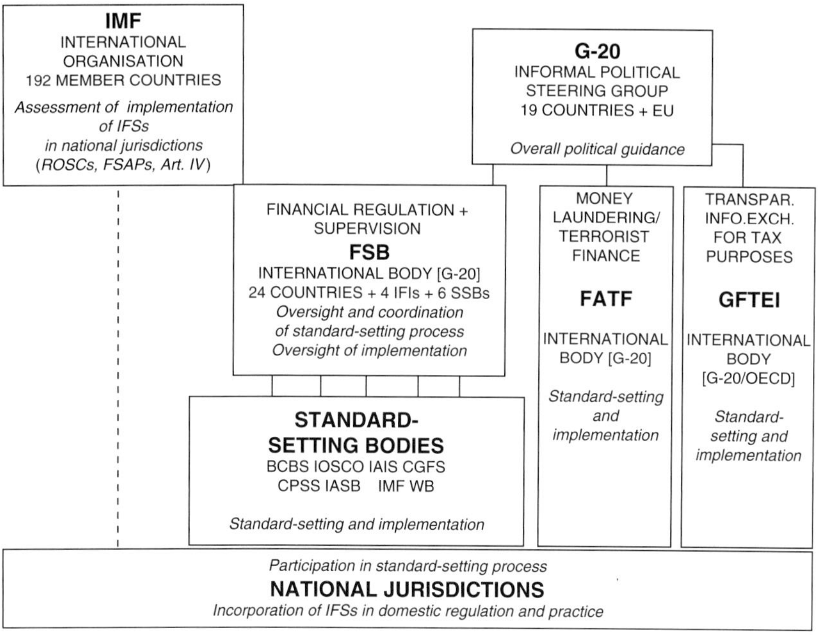

Figure 3.1. International financial architecture – general structure

different process, the 'horizontal' cooperation of national regulators under the aegis of the G-20, as opposed to the institutional 'vertical' process within fully-fledged treaty-based international organisations. Thus the current international financial architecture is based on two pillars: the IMF and the other three IFIs on the one hand, and the pyramid G-20, FSB (plus FATF and GFTEI in their respective spheres) and the various SSBs, on the other hand. Conceivably this process could also have taken place within the ambit of the IMF, which lost the predominant if not nearly exclusive position it occupied at the time of the Bretton Woods system.

II. *The main players and their legal status*

Unsurprisingly, the legal status of the various bodies involved in international standard setting is very diverse.[14] There are several descriptions of

[14] On the legal issues relating to IFSs setting, see the seminal and comprehensive study by R. Bismuth, *La coopération internationale des autorités de régulation du secteur financier*

these bodies, which can be easily consulted.[15] For this reason, it was considered sufficient for this chapter to provide in Table 3.1 in Appendix 1 an overview of the main bodies involved, with a list of their acronyms and websites. Let us now review them by category.

Four pre-existing international organisations (IMF, World Bank, BIS and OECD) have been involved to various degrees in this activity. Their legal status is not discussed here as it is clearly defined in intergovernmental treaties.[16] It is interesting to note that in most if not all cases, the involvement in standard setting represents an extension of the original sphere of activity of these organisations.[17]

The G-20 is a self-appointed political steering group, which is not based on any specific international instrument. It is essentially a *de facto* group lacking legal personality. A nomadic body, it has neither a permanent organisation and seat nor a permanent secretariat and staff. The proposal made in 2010–11 to establish a permanent secretariat was not pursued. The chair rotates annually among the members and is selected from a different regional grouping of countries each time. The

et le droit international public (Brussels: Bruylant, 2011). In English, see the shorter but very comprehensive study by C. Brummer, *Soft Law and the Global Financial System – Rule Making in the 21st Century* (Cambridge University Press, 2012). See also S. Battini (ed.), *La regolazione globale dei mercati finanziari*, Special issue of *Rivista trimestrale di diritto pubblico*, vol. 3 (Milan, 2007), with contributions by G. Bertezzolo (on the BCBS), A. Cassatella (on IOSCO), S. Pellizari (on IAIS), E. Rotolo (on IASB and IAASB) and S. Morettini (on the IMF and global networks of regulators); V. Schreiber, *International Standards – Neues Recht für die Weltmärkte?* (Berne: Haupt, 2005).

15 In particular in the two earlier articles published on this subject by the author, which also provide a general account of the evolution of the SSBs since the inception of the process in 1974: M. Giovanoli, 'The International Financial Architecture and its Reform after the Global Crisis', in M. Giovanoli and D. Devos (eds.), *International Monetary and Financial Law – The Global Crisis* (Oxford University Press, 2010), pp. 3–39; M. Giovanoli, 'A New Architecture for the Global Financial Market: Legal Aspects of International Financial Standard Setting', in M. Giovanoli, *International Monetary Law – Issues for the New Millennium* (Oxford University Press, 2000), pp. 3–59. See also R.M. Lastra, *Legal Foundations of International Monetary Stability* (Oxford University Press, 2006), in particular Chapter 14 on International Financial Architecture; P. Nobel, *Swiss Finance Law and International Standards* (Berne/The Hague: Stämpfli, 2002), in particular Chapter 7.

16 For details, see Appendix 1 and the websites of these organisations, which contain or refer to their respective fundamental legal documents.

17 For the IMF, the involvement in monitoring the implementation of IFSs is an extension of its surveillance and technical assistance functions; in the case of the BIS, dedicated to central bank cooperation, the creation of the Basel Committee in 1974, followed by other BIS-based SSBs, and the hosting of the FSB and other non-BIS SSBs broke new ground in the field of international financial stability, as was the case in governance matters with the OECD hosting FATF, GFTEI and IOPS.

past, present and future chairs form a revolving three-member management group referred to as the Troika.[18] The incumbent chair establishes a temporary secretariat for the duration of its term, which coordinates the group's work and organises its meetings. The role of the Troika is to ensure continuity in the G-20's work and management across host years. Preparations for the summits are made by the so-called 'Sherpas' track (formed by the personal representatives of the heads of state and government) with regard to non-financial issues and by the financial track (the ministers of finance and central bank governors) with regard to financial issues, as well as by working groups.

The mostly annual G-20 Leaders' Summits (since 2008, with two meetings in 2009 and 2010 owing to the financial crisis) have been compared[19] with the Congress System (Concert of Europe), which prevailed in Europe between 1815 (the Vienna Congress) and 1848, when the 'G-5' of the time (Austria, France, Great Britain, Prussia and Russia) regularly convened[20] to discuss international issues in order to seek consensus-based arrangements. However, at the time, these congresses, if at all, were only marginally concerned with monetary, economic and financial issues.

To conclude these remarks on the G-20, it should be recalled that this group emerged as a major actor at the height of the 2008–9 international crisis and took the lead in reshaping the international financial architecture. Since then, the G-20 has also been concerned with a wider range of topics, some of which are not or are only loosely related to international financial issues.[21] One wonders whether the G-20's reform of the global financial architecture has not lost momentum and focus, following the shift from a global banking crisis to sovereign debt concerns in the eurozone.

Since its inception, the FSB[22] has been (and for the moment still is) a *de facto* group and has no legal personality either under international law or under domestic public or private law. In particular, it cannot be

[18] Not to be confused with the 'Troika' formed by the European Commission, the ECB and the IMF for monitoring the conditions of financial assistance to overindebted countries of the eurozone.

[19] The comparison also applies to the G-5 and the G-7, predecessors of the G-20.

[20] In particular the congresses in Aachen 1818, Carlsbad 1819, Troppau 1820, Laibach (Ljubljana) 1821, Verona 1822 and London 1832.

[21] Such as commodities markets, energy and growth, disaster risk management, development, anti-corruption, climate and food security.

[22] On the FSB (but before the planned transformation into an Association under Swiss law), see E. Hüpkes, 'The Financial Stability Board and its Role in the International

considered as a form of association or partnership (*société simple*),[23] as the participants have never expressed the legally relevant will to join such an association or partnership.

At the G-20 Cannes Summit (November 2011), the G-20 leaders agreed to strengthen the FSB's capacity, resources and governance, including its establishment on an enduring organisation footing. Consequently, a high-level working group made proposals, which were approved by the FSB Plenary and submitted with an amended Charter[24] to the G-20, who endorsed the proposals.[25] Interestingly, the Report states that the FSB considers a treaty-based intergovernmental organisation not to be an appropriate legal form at this juncture, but that creating an association under Swiss law would be an appropriate option for vesting the FSB with legal personality. One can only guess at the reasons behind this course of action: avoiding the need for parliamentary approval required in many countries for the creation of an international organisation; following the precedents of the International Association of Insurance (IAIS) and International Association of Deposit Insurers (IADI);[26] preserving the informal character of IFSs setting; reluctance to create a too powerful international organisation.

As regards its resources, the FSB continues for the moment to rely on the BIS for its entire funding as well as for other support-service needs and remains under the BIS umbrella in order to enjoy immunities in Switzerland.[27] An appropriate service agreement is to be concluded with the BIS at the expiry of which the FSB could consider introducing a membership fee.

The publication of the FSB Charter (approved in its revised form at the June 2012 Los Cabos G-20 Summit) is a significant step towards increased transparency and accountability of the institution. However,

Financial Architecture', in A. Heinemann, R. M. Hilty, P. Nobel and R. Sethe (eds.), *Festschrift für Rolf H. Weber* (Zurich: Schulthess, 2011), pp. 855–72.

[23] The latter analysis would involve joint and several liability of the participants, a consequence that is obviously against their will.

[24] Report to the G-20 Los Cabos Summit on Strengthening FSB Capacity, Resources and Governance, dated 12 June 2012, with the text of the revised Charter.

[25] G-20 Leaders Declaration, Los Cabos 18–19 June 2012, section 46.

[26] However, the situation of the FSB differs from that of 'bottom up' SSBs (like IAIS and IADI) where the initiative to create the SSB as an association came from the (future) members themselves.

[27] Under the 1987 Headquarters Agreement between the BIS and the Swiss Confederation.

it contains a provision denying any legal effect to the Charter,[28] which appears strange in this context, particularly in light of the establishment of the FSB as an association under Swiss law with legal personality: indeed the Articles of Association expressly refer to the Charter[29] and it would be ludicrous to continue to deny it any legal effect.

With regard to their legal status, the sectoral SSBs can be divided into three groups. The first comprises the bodies that were created 'top down' (often by the G-10) like the BCBS,[30] the Committee on Payment and Settlement Systems (CPSS) and the Committee on the Global Financial System (CGFS). These SSBs can in principle be considered as *de facto* groups without legal personality, as 'soft institutions' of the same type as the FSB (before its planned transformation into an association): hence what has been said above with respect to the FSB also applies to this group of SSBs. Presumably the FATF and the GFTEI also belong to this group (subject to special arrangements with the OECD). It should be noted that legal personality is not indispensable whenever an SSB is fully sponsored by an international organisation with regard to its infrastructure and funding.[31] The second group, the 'bottom up' sectoral SSBs, are typically associations with legal personality, created spontaneously among national regulators, supervisors or other agencies. This is the case of IAIS[32] and IADI, hosted by the BIS in Basel, and presumably of the International Organisation of Securities Commissions (IOSCO)[33] (although its articles of association have not been published), which

[28] Article 23 of the FSB Charter: 'The Charter is not intended to create any legal rights or obligations.'

[29] See Article 10 of the FSB Articles of Association adopted on 28 January 2013: 'The policy making and related activities of the Association shall be governed by the FSB charter.'

[30] On the legal status of the BCBS, see C. Goodhart, *The Basel Committee on Banking Supervision* (Cambridge University Press, 2011). Although this comprehensive book deals only with the early years of the BCBS, it contains a valuable contribution (Chapter 14) on the legal position of the BCBS and on 'soft law', pp. 542–59. See also Bismuth, *La coopération internationale*, pp. 269–87, however with some doubts on his analysis of the BCBS as an 'independent agency' of the BIS.

[31] However, an SSB without legal personality cannot conclude contracts in its own name and its situation with regard to potential liability for torts is unclear.

[32] On the legal status of IAIS, see Bismuth, *La coopération internationale*, pp. 334–40.

[33] On the legal status of IOSCO, see *ibid.* pp. 324–34.

benefits from a special status in Spain with particular immunities. Finally, there is the special case of private bodies as SSBs. At first sight, it seems problematic for a private body like the IASB (accounting standards) and the IAASB (auditing standards) to set international financial standards, as they depend on private professional associations. To overcome this problem and to ensure that public interest will prevail in an IFS setting, these bodies have been submitted to the scrutiny and monitoring of either a special foundation (Public Interest Oversight Board (PIOB)) in the case of IASB or a monitoring board in the case of the IAASB.

In general, the academic literature tends to categorise the whole process of international standard setting and the various bodies involved (with the possible exception of those that have taken a specific legal form, such as an association or a foundation, and of course excluding the IFIs) as a phenomenon of 'transnational governmental networking',[34] a 'transnational or transgovernmental regulatory network', 'soft law institutions' or the emergence of 'global administrative law'.[35] As intellectually stimulating as they may be, these descriptive concepts do not contribute much towards assessing the legal nature and effects of the phenomenon.

[34] J. Norton, 'Comment on the Developing Transnational Networks in the Area of International Financial Regulation: the Underpinnings of a New Bretton Woods II Global Financial System Framework', *International Lawyer* 43 (2009), 175; K. Raustiala, 'The Architecture of International Cooperation: Transgovernmental Networks and the Future of International Law', *Virginia Journal of International Law* 43 (2002), 1, ssrn.com/abstract_id=333381; A. M. Slaughter, 'Global Government Networks, Global Information Agencies, and Disaggregated Democracy', papers.ssrn.com/abstract=283976; A. M. Slaughter and D. Zaring, 'Networking Goes International: An Update' in *Annual Review of Law and Social Science* (2006), ssrn.com/abstract=960484; D. Zaring, 'International Law by Other Means: The Twilight Existence of International Financial Regulatory Organizations', *Texas International Law Journal* (April 1998), 282.

[35] In particular B. Kingsbury, N. Krisch and R. B. Stewart, 'The Emergence of a Global Administrative Law', IILJ Working Paper 2004/1 (Global Administrative Law Series 2004), ssrn.com/abstract=6926208, see also 68 *Law & Contemp. Probs.* (Summer/Autumn 2005); B. Kingsbury, 'The Concept of "Law" in Global Administrative Law', IILJ Working Paper 2009/1 (Global Administrative Law Series), NYU School of Law, Public Law Research Paper No. 09–29, ssrn.com/abstract=1397308; B. Kingsbury, 'The Administrative Law Frontier in Global Governance', ASIL Proceedings 2005; B. Kingsbury, 'Symposium on Global Governance and Global Administrative Law in the International Legal Order' (ed. with Nico Krisch), *European Journal of International Law* 17 (2006), 1–278.

III. *Some major challenges*

No doubt, the process of IFSs setting should be considered a major achievement in the interest of international financial stability, indispensable as a reaction to the globalisation of financial markets. The 'corpus' of IFSs produced over some forty years is impressive, and there is hardly an issue of international financial law which has not been addressed over time. And yet, it must be admitted that the IFSs, more often than not produced as reactions to financial crises, did not succeed in preventing several major international financial crises.

This does not mean that the effort should not be made in the future. However, a number of challenges need to be addressed in order to foster acceptance, efficiency and implementation of IFSs in a changing world. Among the major legal issues, let us mention:

- the legitimacy of the process and the institutions involved;
- the status of 'soft law' rules in international and municipal law; and
- the implementation of the standards and legal remedies in case of disputes.

C. International financial standards: representativity, decision making, reporting

I. *Representativity and legitimacy*

As regards the question of legitimacy, in other words how representative they are, the IMF and the World Bank are nearly universal organisations, of which almost all jurisdictions are members. From time to time, reservations have been expressed about the principle of weighted voting power (based on quotas taking into account *inter alia* the economic weight of each market), viewed by some as being undemocratic (as opposed to the principle of one country, one vote).[36] However, in a financial institution like the IMF or the World Bank, it seems perfectly appropriate to take into account the economic and financial weight of member countries in defining their voting rights. Of course, the respective weight of each country must be assessed on the basis of fair and objective criteria. Hence the revision of IMF quotas currently under

[36] This seems to be the main reason why Bismuth, *La coopération internationale*, p. 691 believes that the IMF, while at first sight the most appropriate institution to take over the leading role in IFS setting, should nevertheless be disregarded.

way, in order to provide more voting power to emerging markets. At the same time, efforts are being made to rearrange the voting constituencies to this effect.[37]

Universality of membership is not the case for the BIS, the members of which are the sixty most important central banks of the world; however, this does not appear to raise any problem of legitimacy, as the BIS's role in the standard-setting process is confined to initiating, hosting and/or financing a number of SSBs,[38] without being directly involved in the process itself. The situation is less clear with respect to the OECD, with only thirty-four members, and which is directly involved in drafting IFSs,[39] in addition to its role of hosting the FATF, the GFTEI and the International Organisation of Pension Supervisors (IOPS).

The G-20 claims its legitimacy from the fact that its members produce some 85 per cent of the global gross domestic product (GDP) and comprise more than two thirds of the world's total population. No doubt, these figures underpin the huge factual influence of the group, but do they really carry the day from the legal viewpoint of legitimacy and fair representation of all countries? In the absence of any treaty providing a mandate to the G-20 for its activities and criteria or a process for the selection of its members,[40] it is difficult to argue from the legal perspective that this self-appointed group 'represents' anybody but itself. Hence the G-20 has no power to impose any decision on non-member countries; however, the factual weight of the group is such that it is difficult for a non-member country not to take its recommendations into account. In other words, from the viewpoint of political science, this informal steering group appears as a sort of lobby for a sound international financial architecture in line with the major interests of its member countries.

It has been suggested that a sort of United Nations (UN) World Economic Council or a Global Economic Coordination Council under the aegis of the UN at a level equivalent to the UN Security Council could

[37] It would be more rational if all EU countries were consolidated in a given number of constituencies, rather than for many of them to be included in 'mixed' constituencies comprising both EU and non-EU countries.

[38] In particular the BCBS, the CGFS, the CPSS, the IADI, the IAIS and the FSB.

[39] The FASB Compendium of Standards lists sixteen standards in which the OECD was involved.

[40] The current membership of the G-20 leaves out Norway and Switzerland. Although both are among the twenty non-EU countries with the highest GDP, they are not even indirectly represented by the EU in the G-20.

provide a democratically representative alternative to the G-20.[41] Another possibility would be to entrust the functions of the G-20 to a body (within or outside the IMF) based on the constituency system, which applies to the Executive Board of the IMF (although the constituency system reflecting the position of each country in the global economy has also been criticised as being non-democratic).[42] However, it is doubtful whether any such proposal is realistic given the current geopolitical situation. One also wonders whether a larger and more formal body would be as efficient in consensus finding as an informal political steering group such as the G-20.

Before its enlargement in 2009, the restricted membership of the FSF/FSB and of the BCBS was widely criticised.[43] At the Washington Summit of November 2008, the G-20 had called for an expansion of the membership of the FSF (now the FSB) to include more emerging economies and the expansion was effected in March 2009. In parallel, the BCBS expanded its membership in March and June 2009. As a result, twenty-four jurisdictions are now represented in the FSB[44] (the former FSF) and twenty-seven in the BCBS.[45] This is still a relatively small number, but it is questionable whether larger bodies could work as efficiently to elaborate consensus-based recommendations and standards. Furthermore, both bodies have put in place a network for worldwide consultations before finalising IFSs. Finally, in the case of the FSB, the Charter explicitly provides for periodic membership reviews,[46] without however specifying either the timing or the criteria of this review. No similar provision or declaration of intent has been published to date by the BCBS.

41 See the proposal of the UN Commission of Experts on Reforms of the International Monetary and Financial System (chaired by Prof. Stiglitz) published on 19 March 2009, as well as F. Stewart and S. Daws, 'An Economic and Social Security Council at the United Nations', Working Paper 68, Queen Elizabeth House, University of Oxford, March 2001; J. Eatwell and L. Taylor, *Global Finance at Risk – The Case for International Regulation* (New York: New Press, 2000), proposing the creation of a World Financial Authority.

42 For instance by Bismuth, *La coopération internationale*, p. 6.

43 For a comprehensive analysis of this type of criticism (democracy deficit due to restricted membership) see *ibid.*, pp. 478–82.

44 All nineteen jurisdictions represented in the G-20, plus Hong Kong Special Administrative Region, the Netherlands, Singapore, Spain and Switzerland. In addition, the FSB includes four IFIs, six SSBs, the EC and the ECB.

45 All twenty-four jurisdictions represented in the FSB, plus Belgium, Luxembourg and Sweden, plus the EU.

46 Article 5(2) of the FSB Charter: 'The eligibility of Members will be reviewed periodically by the Plenary in the light of the FSB objectives.'

To conclude on this point, it seems that the issue of restricted and selective membership (and hence of an impaired representativity) remains for all 'top down' SSBs such as BCBS, CPSS and CGFS as well as for the 'private law' bodies such as IASB and IAASB. By contrast, the 'bottom up' SSBs are usually open associations, with a much wider membership[47] and which accept new members meeting predefined criteria.[48]

II. *Decision making*

At all levels, decisions in the standard-setting process appear to be based on consensus, although there seem to be very few explicit provisions to this effect. In the case of the FSB, the Charter specifies that decisions are taken by consensus by the Plenary, which is the sole decision-making body, and the Report to the G-20 states that decision making continues to be based on consensus.[49] In fact decision making by consensus appears to be the general practice, even when in isolated cases, there are provisions for a majority vote.[50] The consensus approach based on a wide consultation process ensures the credibility of international standard setting and facilitates the acceptance and subsequent implementation of the standards. The point has been nicely made in a statement by a former BCBS chairman:

> The policy guidance developed and promoted by the Basel Committee is based on consensus rather than on formal international legal agreements. An important objective of the Committee therefore is to promote credible, practical and flexible mechanisms to achieve effective policy implementation in a wide range of countries.[51]

What exactly is meant by consensus? According to the general view, consensus means a procedure for the adoption of a text within a given

[47] However, the degree of effective participation in setting up IFSs may vary considerably among the members, with the important financial centres presumably dominating the discussions.

[48] This seems to be the case for instance for the IOSCO.

[49] Article 9(1) and (2) of the FSB Charter; Section 1 of the Report on the FSB to the G-20 Los Cabos Summit.

[50] For instance, Article 12(1)(c) of the IAIS by-laws provides that the General Meeting may adopt principles and standards by a two-thirds majority, when the decision has been deferred to it from the Executive Committee. In practice, however, it seems that the consensus-principle prevails.

[51] N. Wellink, 'Goals and Strategies of the Basel Committee' *BIS Review* 122 (2006), 1.

body without voting provided that no participant has expressed a formal objection.[52] The consensus method is not limited to the final adoption of standards; it extends to the process of developing the standards, in particular to the preparatory documents published for consultation among the members of the relevant SSB and even beyond the circle of members. The method can also have a negative effect, in so far as it excludes the adoption of a text whenever a participant raises a formal objection.[53]

As successful as the consensus approach has been in the standard-setting process, it is not fully exempt from drawbacks. Consensus finding involves a degree of confidentiality and does not generally foster open debate (which may make consensus finding more difficult). Hence there is definitely an issue of transparency in developing and adopting IFSs. However, the wide consultation process, which has been vastly improved over time and now usually extends far beyond the circle of participants in the various SSBs, significantly mitigates the problem.

Another issue that is not absolutely clear concerns the body which is supposed to be competent for the final adoption of a given standard. Who has the final word in the 'authentication' of a standard developed in one of the SSBs? Is it the governing body of each sectoral SSB? This seems to be mostly the case. However, the situation is less clear when standards are discussed within the FSB, or when a report is made to the G-20. How significant is the approval by the G-20? Is it a sort of rubber stamp needed for the final 'authentication' of the standard or merely a welcoming gesture of the policy guidance group?

III. Reporting

The IFIs of course do not formally report to the G-20, as they act on the basis of their own fundamental documents. However, the G-20 hold a majority in the IMF and the other IFIs, so that productive cooperation

[52] In this context the following definition given in a draft resolution of The Institute of International Law may be helpful: '[a] decision is adopted by consensus when the officer presiding over a meeting declares that, as no Member State present at that meeting formally objects to the proposed decision or has asked for a vote, the decision should be considered as having been approved by consensus.' IIL Yearbook, 67 (1) (1997), 114, Article 2.

[53] See also the detailed presentation of the consensus approach under international law in Bismuth, *La coopération internationale*, pp. 452–69.

between them and the bodies involved in IFSs setting can be taken for granted. Furthermore, all four IFIs are members of the FSB.[54]

Within the pyramid G-20–FSB–SSBs, the situation is slightly more complex. Specific reporting lines exist between the FSB and the G-20[55] and similarly between the FATF and the G-20 (as successor to the G-7 in this context). The sectoral SSBs are nearly all members of the FSB and are committed to report to it under the FSB Charter for their work; however, this is without prejudice to their existing reporting lines or their independence.[56] This means that all these bodies maintain their administrative independence and are not subject to instructions or supervision from the body or bodies to which they report for their work. This applies both to the bodies initially created by the (now defunct) G-10 or the G-7 and to the spontaneously created associations of regulators (such as IOSCO and IAIS) whose independence has been reaffirmed. Finally, it should be noted that from time to time the major SSBs, such as the BCBS and the IOSCO, also submit reports directly to the financial track of the G-20[57].

D. International financial standards: soft law and consultation process

I. *Predominance of soft law*

According to the documents published after the G-20 Summits, the essential principles inspiring the reformed IFA, and consequently the contents of the IFSs, may be summarised as follows:

[54] Article 6(4) of the FSB Charter: 'The international financial institutions participate as Members in the FSB in accordance with their respective legal framework and policies.'

[55] Article 4 of the FSB Charter: 'The FSB will discharge its accountability, beyond its members, through publication of reports and, in particular, through periodical reporting of progress in its work to the Finance Ministers and Central Bank Governors of the Group of Twenty, and to Heads of State and Governments of the Group of Twenty.'

[56] Article 6(3) of the FSB Charter: 'In support of the mandate and tasks laid down in Article 2(1)(e), the standard setting bodies will report to the FSB on their work without prejudice to their existing reporting arrangements or their independence. This process should not undermine the independence of the standard setting process but strengthen support for strong standard setting by providing a broader accountability framework.'

[57] For instance at the Los Cabos Summit of June 2012, the BCBS submitted a Report to G-20 Leaders on the Implementation of Basel III and the IOSCO an Update to G-20 on IOSCO's work on Market Integrity and Efficiency.

> All systemically important financial (1) intermediaries, (2) markets and (3) products irrespective of type must be subject to appropriate regulation and supervision (4) in all jurisdictions.[58]

Both in quantitative[59] and qualitative terms, international financial standards are predominantly, if not exclusively, in the form of non-binding recommendations, i.e. so-called soft law. All of the twelve key standards listed by the FSB (see Table 3.2 in Appendix 2)[60] belong to this category, and so do all of the seventy-seven standards issued over the last five years (2008–12) listed in the Compendium of standards published on the FSB's website.[61] The same would apply to the standards endorsed by the FATF and by the GFTEI. As regards the contents of IFSs and the ongoing workflow, reference is made to the FSB website and to the regular progress reports published.[62]

What is the basis for the generally accepted characterisation of international financial standards as 'soft law'?[63] First, the various international standard-setting bodies have no legislative or treaty-making power; their recommendations do not have any legal force on their own. Second, in order to become legally binding rules (the non-observance of which typically involves a sanction), IFSs need to be incorporated into domestic legislation, regulation and administrative

[58] G-20 London Summit, Leaders' Statement of 2 April 2009, section 15, fourth bullet point; Declaration on Strengthening the Financial System, 2 April 2009, section 'The scope of regulation', introductory paragraph. About the claim to apply these principles worldwide, see the Statement of the Chairman of the FSB to the IMFC of 25 April 2009, available at www.financialstabilityboard.org.

[59] Over the years, the 'corpus' of IFSs with the accompanying commentaries and methodologies has reached a volume equivalent to the legislation of a midsize developed jurisdiction.

[60] For more details, consult the FSB's website.

[61] See www.financialstabilityboard.org, *Compendium of Standards*. The list comprises only standards issued over the last five years and is therefore subject to changes. As at 15 August 2012, seventy-seven standards had been compiled.

[62] See in particular 'Overview of Progress in the Implementation of the G-20 Recommendations for Strengthening Financial Stability, Report of the Financial Stability Board to G-20 Leaders 19 June 2012', as well as the so-called 'scoreboard report' of 19 June 2012 published under the title 'Progress in implementing the G-20 Recommendations on Financial Regulatory Reform – Status report by the FSB Secretariat', both available on the FSB's website. On the concept and the various types of IFSs, see Bismuth, *La coopération internationale*, pp. 369–401.

[63] For a discussion of this issue, see Giovanoli 'A New Architecture', pp. 33–44; Bismuth, *La coopération internationale*, pp. 46–51 and 521–7.

practice by the relevant national legislators of each jurisdiction.[64] Third, the financial intermediaries are not directly the addressees of the 'recommendations' contained in IFSs, which are aimed more at national legislators, regulators and supervisors who are 'encouraged' to implement them in their respective jurisdictions. Fourth, IFSs are not based on an international treaty and thus, at least in theory, their implementation by national authorities is 'voluntary'.[65] Finally, according to the prevailing view, the IFSs are not part of international customary law,[66] as there is no general consensus on their compulsory nature (*opinio juris*).[67]

There is however little doubt about the IFSs' bearing on regulations, codes of conduct and administrative practice or their relevance to the interpretation of, and closing of gaps in, legislation. Indeed, the IFSs are based on a consensus (and perhaps even a commitment) of supervisors or experts from the jurisdictions of the major financial centres.[68] The implementation of IFSs[69] is actively promoted by a number of incentives, both official incentives (e.g. FSAPs, ROSCs, peer pressure) and market incentives. Furthermore, the members of the FSB have committed to pursue the maintenance of financial stability, to implement IFSs (including the twelve key standards), and to undergo periodic peer reviews and FSAPs.[70] There is also a growing recognition of the

[64] It should be noted that unlike in the case of domestic soft law (codes of conduct, etc.), there is no threat of legislative intervention in the case of non-compliance with IFSs.

[65] However, within the EU the contents of the major IFSs have been integrated into European directives, the implementation of which is compulsory for the twenty-seven member countries. On this aspect, see G. Bertezzolo, 'The European Union Facing the Global Arena: Standard-setting Bodies and Financial Regulation', *European Law Review* (2009), 257–80.

[66] Symptomatically, the SSBs themselves (as well as the G-20 and the FSB) carefully avoid any language which might be interpreted as suggesting a legally binding character of their activities, and many of them leave their legal status more or less undefined. SSBs typically use expressions like 'standards' and 'codes of conduct' (rather than rules or regulations), 'ownership' (rather than legitimacy), 'implementation' (rather than enforcement), 'concordat' or 'accord' (rather than agreement or treaty).

[67] Same view in Bismuth, *La coopération internationale*, pp. 522–6.

[68] According to A. Lowenfeld, *International Economic Law*, 2nd edn (Oxford University Press, 2008), p. 845 (see also p. 813), while the Basel Accords on capital requirements for international banks are not treaties within the meaning of international law, they 'are more than "soft law"; they reflect mutual commitments made after intense negotiations, and taken together, they contain both incentives for compliance and at least the suggestion of meaningful sanctions for non-compliance'. These remarks obviously apply to most if not all IFSs.

[69] On implementation of IFSs, see Section E.I.

[70] Article 6 FSB Charter. See also the G-20 document published at the 2009 London Summit: 'Declaration on Strengthening the Financial System', 2 April 2009, p. 1.

relevance of IFSs under international law, particularly in the ambit of the UN[71] and the WTO.[72]

II. *Soft law – or not so soft?*

The developments which have occurred since 2009 with respect to countermeasures to be taken against non-cooperative jurisdictions[73] (or at least the generalisation of such measures hitherto only applied in particular areas) no doubt shed a new light on the concept of soft law. At first sight it seems difficult to reconcile the concept of 'soft law', i.e. rules without the option of legal sanction in case of non-compliance, with the idea of countermeasures in case of non-observance. Beyond the general question of the legal nature of IFSs under international law (are they still 'soft law' or are they quasi-mandatory rules?), there are a number of issues of practical relevance to be considered in connection with potential countermeasures, such as the legal basis of standards,[74] the degree of discretion and flexibility for single countries implementing IFSs and the general principles of public law (e.g. non-discrimination, proportionality or subsidiarity). In addition, several issues need to be clarified with regard to procedural guarantees (such as the possibility of review, the right to be heard, legal remedies and guarantees of due process) and to methods of conflict resolution available to jurisdictions that did not consent to certain standards, facing countermeasures.

III. *Democratic control and consultation process*

One of the classic criticisms of IFSs setting is the alleged lack or at least deficit of democratic control over this process. According to this view, international technocratic bodies establish rules in a relatively closed

[71] Thus, the principles developed by the OECD/GFTEI on information exchange for tax purposes have been reflected in the UN Model Tax Convention, as mentioned in the 'Declaration on Strengthening the Financial System', 2 April 2009, section 'Tax Havens and Non-cooperative Jurisdictions'.

[72] On this aspect, see R. Bismuth, 'Financial Sector Regulation and Financial Services Liberalization at the Crossroads: The Relevance of International Financial Standards in WTO Law', *Journal of World Trade* 44:2 (April 2010).

[73] On these developments, see Section E. II.

[74] Including a clear legal basis for the standards, legitimacy of SSB, compliance with procedural rules for standard-setting consultation process where applicable, transparency of standard setting process, final endorsement of a given international standard making it 'quasi-compulsory'.

environment, largely outside democratic control and accountability, thus resulting in an erosion of the authority of domestic parliaments.[75] Perhaps it is useful to recall that a similar issue arises when formal international treaties are negotiated, often through confidential contacts, until such time as the results of the negotiation are made public and the treaty is eventually submitted to parliament when necessary. Democratic control at the level of national implementation is also possible in the case of IFSs established by consensus among IFS setters.[76] This said, there is indeed a need to give all stakeholders a fair chance to express their views and thus to participate at least indirectly in the decision making.

To overcome this problem, the various bodies involved in IFS setting have vastly improved their consultation procedure over the years. At the top level, the G-20[77] is very conscious of the issue, as made apparent in the Report on the FSB endorsed at the June 2012 Los Cabos Summit. In this connection, the G-20 approved the following course of action:

> 7. The FSB should adopt a structured mechanism for public consultation on FSB policy proposals; it should also engage in dialogue with market participants and other stakeholders, including through round-tables, hearings and other appropriate events.
> 8. The FSB's Regional Consultative Groups and their role in providing a structured consultative mechanism that enables non-FSB members to provide input into the policy formulation process should be appropriately reflected within the FSB Charter as a component of the FSB structure.

These principles have expressly been embodied in the revised FSB Charter, which provides that the FSB 'should consult widely amongst its Members and with other stakeholders including private sector and non-member authorities'.[78] The Chair may invite non-FSB members to the Plenary. Finally, a detailed mechanism for including non-members via Regional Consultative Groups has been established.[79] As regards

[75] See Giovanoli, 'A New Architecture', p. 43. An extensive discussion of these aspects is provided by Bismuth, *La coopération internationale*, pp. 159–67 (at the domestic level) and particularly pp. 469–81 (at the international level).

[76] At least to the extent that the standards imply changes in the legislation, the involvement of parliament is required in principle.

[77] The G-20 itself regularly invites a few non-member countries to its summits.

[78] Article 3 FSB Charter. In particular, the FSB should have a structured process for public consultation on policy proposals.

[79] Article 20 FSB Charter. There currently are six Regional Groups (Americas, Asia, Commonwealth of Independent States, Europe, Middle East and North Africa, sub-Saharan Africa).

accountability and transparency, the FSB will discharge its duty of accountability, beyond its members, through publication of substantive and progress reports to the G-20 financial track and to the G-20 leaders.[80]

The consultation process and information policy followed by the various sectoral SSBs has also been vastly improved over the years, in particular by the BCBS, the IOSCO and the IAIS,[81] so that a genuine and efficient global outreach has now been established. However, this is not a full substitute for participation in decision making.[82]

E. 'Procedural aspects': implementation of IFSs and dispute settlement

I. *Implementation*

As a consequence of their characterisation as 'soft law', IFSs are not, in principle, compulsory under international law,[83] despite the persuasive pressure emanating from an influential group of countries (the G-20 standing behind the larger groups of countries participating in the FSB, FATF and GFTEI) that are now sponsoring the standard-setting process. Hence the reliance on a number of 'incentives' to encourage their implementation, including both market incentives and 'official' incentives.

Market incentives (the expectation that market participants will take into account in their credit and pricing decisions the degree and quality of implementation of IFSs in a given country),[84] appear to some extent to have receded. There may be doubts about their effectiveness: indeed, the global financial crisis has been widely perceived as a failure of market mechanisms to maintain financial stability.

Unsurprisingly, the G-20 emphasised the so-called 'official incentives', especially the assessments by the IMF and the World Bank,

[80] Article 4 FSB Charter.

[81] Detailed information on the evolution of the consultation process towards a greater degree of democracy and inclusiveness is provided by Bismuth, *La coopération internationale*, pp. 487 ff (on the BCBS), 494 ff (on IOSCO) and 499 ff (on the IAIS).

[82] This said, for the sake of efficiency, it is easier to reach consensus in a relatively small and homogeneous group of major regulators than in a wide international gathering. In fact, in the SSBs with a wide circle of members, it seems that the discussions are largely dominated by the major players.

[83] See Sections D.I and D.II.

[84] On market incentives, see Giovanoli, 'A New Architecture' p. 14.

and the peer reviews conducted by the various SSBs. Since the 2009 London Leaders' Summit, the G-20 has invited on various occasions the FSB and the IMF, along with the FATF (for money laundering and terrorist finance issues) and the GFTEI (for tax havens and non-cooperative jurisdiction issues), to monitor progress.[85] At the Pittsburgh Summit, the G-20 reaffirmed their commitment

> to take action at the national and international level to raise standards together so that our national authorities implement global standards consistently in a way that ensures a level playing field and avoids fragmentation of markets, protectionism, and regulatory arbitrage.[86]

The Reports on Observance of Standards and Codes (ROSCs), produced jointly by the IMF and the World Bank,[87] provide summary assessments of an economy's progress in observing standards on data dissemination, fiscal transparency, auditing and accounting, insolvency and creditor rights systems, corporate governance and the financial sector. The more specialised Financial Sector Assessment Programs (FSAPs) provide for a joint evaluation of financial sector standards by the IMF and the World Bank. The FSAPs cover, in particular, those standards established by the BCBS, IOSCO, the IAIS and the CPSS. This surveillance function has been 'officialised' by the G-20 and now appears as one of the major missions of the IMF in connection with the global financial system. Unlike the Article IV surveillance of the IMF,[88] participation and publication of ROSCs and FSAPs is voluntary, but most countries have made the assessments publicly available.[89] Other 'official incentives' include peer pressure and peer reviews in the ambit of the various SSBs

[85] 'Declaration on Strengthening the Financial System', 2 April 2009, last section ('Next Steps'). See also the Leaders' Statement, The Pittsburgh Summit, 24–25 September 2009, Section 12, and subsequent declarations of G-20 Leaders.

[86] Leaders' Statement, Pittsburgh Summit, 24–25 September 2009, para 12.

[87] On the IMF and World Bank monitoring of the implementation of IFSs, see in particular Bismuth, *La coopération internationale*, pp. 598–604.

[88] On Article IV Surveillance by the IMF, see 'IMF Surveillance, A Factsheet', June 2009, www.imf.org/external/np/exr/facts/surv.htm and the contribution of N. Rendak, 'Monitoring and Surveillance of the International Monetary System – What Can Be Learnt from the Trade Field?', Chapter 9 this volume.

[89] ROSCs are available at www.imf.org or www.worldbank.org. See also (on ROSCs and FSAPs) F. Gianviti, 'Legal Aspects of the Financial Sector Assessment Program', in *Current Developments in Monetary and Financial Law*, Vol. 3 (Washington DC: IMF, 2005), pp. 219–28. The issue is whether in the longer run FSAPs and ROSCs should be made compulsory under the Article IV surveillance through a revision of the Articles of Agreement. See Bismuth, *La coopération internationale*, pp. 648–54.

and the FSB,[90] as well as in the FATF and the GFTEI. As already noted, FSB members are committed to implement the IFSs and to undergo FSAPs and peer reviews with respect to the IFSs.[91]

II. Countermeasures against non-cooperative jurisdictions

A more radical change might well affect the legal character of IFSs. At the 2009 London Summit, the G-20 agreed that 'the relevant international bodies identify non-cooperative jurisdictions and develop a tool box of effective counter-measures',[92] such as increased disclosure requirements, withholding taxes, denying deductions, reviewing tax treaties and investment policies and alike.

Although these countermeasures are aimed particularly at inducing non-cooperative jurisdictions to adhere to principles endorsed by the G-20 in the field of information exchange in tax matters, it seems that similar or other countermeasures would be applied more generally in the future with regard to the implementation of many, if not all, international financial standards.[93] Once again, in the conclusions of the Pittsburgh Summit, the implementation of prudential standards and IFSs on tax havens, money laundering, proceeds of corruption or terrorist financing appears to be placed on the same footing with respect to the fight against non-cooperative jurisdictions:[94]

> Our commitment to fight non-cooperative jurisdictions (NCJs) has produced impressive results. We are committed to maintain the momentum

[90] On monitoring of the implementation of IFSs by the FSB, see Bismuth, *La coopération internationale*, pp. 591–8. The FSB has established a Standing Committee on Standards Implementation, Article 16 of the FSB Charter.

[91] Article 6 FSB Charter. See also the G-20 document published at the 2009 London Summit: 'Declaration on Strengthening the Financial System', 2 April 2009, p. 1.

[92] G-20 Communiqué, Meeting of Finance Ministers and Central Bank Governors, United Kingdom, 14 March 2009, www.g20.org and especially the 'Declaration on Strengthening the Financial System', 2 April 2009, section 'Tax Havens and Non-cooperative Jurisdictions'.

[93] The introductory paragraph to the section on countermeasures is quite general: 'It is essential to protect public finances and international standards against the risks posed by non-cooperative jurisdictions. We call on all jurisdictions to adhere to the international standards in the prudential, tax and AML/CFT areas. To this end, we call on the appropriate bodies to conduct and strengthen objective peer reviews, based on existing processes, including through the FSAP process.' See 'Declaration on Strengthening the Financial System', 2 April 2009, section 'Tax Havens and Non-cooperative Jurisdictions'.

[94] Leaders' Statement, The Pittsburgh Summit, 24–25 September 2009, Section 15.

in dealing with tax havens, money laundering, proceeds of corruption, terrorist financing, and prudential standards.

This approach looks very much like a potential extension of the practice of blacklisting non-cooperative countries and territories, which apparently originated within the ambit of the FATF, but is also a technique used by the OECD, the GFTEI and the UN. This does not mean that the timing for applying appropriate countermeasures in fighting NCJs will be the same with respect to prudential rules or standards against money laundering, terrorist finance, tax havens and corruption, nor that the measures would necessarily be the same in all these cases. However, the trend is clear: NCJs are going to face not only increased pressure to adopt global financial standards, but also sets of countermeasures.

It should be noted that countermeasures or sanctions can be based on multilateral (e.g. G-20, FATF) or unilateral decisions (a blacklist established by a given country). The countermeasures themselves may emanate from international bodies (for instance with regard to financial or technical assistance, or membership in international bodies or working groups), or (more often) may be taken by national jurisdictions (e.g. additional conditions imposed upon foreign financial entities for accessing the domestic market,[95] or on domestic entities for transactions with certain jurisdictions,[96] or reporting requirements and systematic monitoring of business relations and transactions with countries and territories considered as NCJs).

III. Dispute settlement

To the extent that IFSs are made quasi-mandatory, what are the legal remedies for countries that have not been consulted or have made reservations with respect to certain rules? The issue arises in particular when a given country or a financial institution of that country has been put on a grey or blacklist and/or faces disadvantages in its financial relations with other countries. This issue seems to be largely unexplored. Presumably, the question would be dealt with more at a political level

[95] For instance, foreign banking subsidiaries that are not included in the consolidated supervision in their country of origin may be subjected to consolidated supervision by the supervisory authorities of the host country.

[96] Thus, the European Directive on Alternative Investment Fund Managers provides that shares or units of a foreign alternative investment fund may only be marketed in an EU country if the country of origin implements the GFTEI principles on information exchange for tax purposes.

than by legal means, but the possibility cannot be excluded that some countries will attempt to use long-arm jurisdiction or extraterritorial application of their legislation or regulations against countries (or their financial institutions) that fail to implement internationally recognised standards.[97]

From a more technical viewpoint, there is a growing recognition of the relevance of the IFSs under international law particularly within the ambit of the UN and the WTO. Thus, the principles developed by the OECD/GFTEI on information exchange for tax purposes have been reflected in the UN Model Tax Convention. The relations between WTO law aiming at liberalisation of financial services within the ambit of the GATS, on the one hand, and international financial standards directed at improving financial stability through better regulation and supervision, on the other hand, no doubt need to be more deeply investigated.[98] The relevance of the IFSs[99] in WTO law is gaining momentum and developments regarding dispute settlement need to be carefully followed.

F. Concluding observations

Recent developments have no doubt further enhanced the international financial architecture since the reform prompted by the global financial crisis of 2008–10.[100] In particular, the institutional underpinning has again been improved, especially as regards the FSB. However, a number of issues remain unresolved, or at least open to debate, some of which deserve special attention.

[97] This may be particularly sensitive in the field of the FATF standards or GFTEI principles, but similar developments cannot be excluded within the ambit of prudential regulation.

[98] On this topic, see the well documented article by R. Bismuth, 'Financial Sector Regulation and Financial Services Liberalization at the Crossroads: The Relevance of International Financial Standards in WTO Law', *WTO Law, Journal of World Trade* 44:2 (2010), 489–514; and also the detailed developments in Bismuth, *La coopération internationale*, pp. 624–45.

[99] This relevance may be recognised for instance on the basis of the trend towards including IFSs in the IMF's surveillance mechanism through FSAPs (Bismuth, *La coopération international*, pp. 648 ff), on the basis of IMF conditionality for financial assistance (pp. 654 ff), or on the basis of the UN Charter (pp. 658 ff).

[100] For a broad presentation of this reform, see the article by M. Giovanoli, 'The International Financial Architecture'.

First, there seems to be some reluctance of various financial centres to implement international financial standards, which are still growing fast in terms of quantity and complexity. This is particularly apparent with regard to the Basel III standards of the BCBS. Competing national interests, the fear of overregulation and of substantial additional cost for the industry, as well as a degree of fatigue with respect to further and increasingly complex international rules, may play a role in this regard.

Second, the shift of focus from the global financial crisis mainly affecting financial markets and internationally active banks towards issues of state indebtedness (especially, but not exclusively, with respect to 'peripheral' European economies) may well have taken some of the steam out of the international efforts to enhance financial regulation and supervision at the global level.

Third, it seems that after the striking success of IFSs over the last thirty years, the limits of international financial 'soft law' have become more apparent.

Despite significant progress in extending the circle of participating jurisdictions, there still are shortcomings as regards legitimacy of SSBs and transparency of the standard-setting process, not to speak of the lack of legal remedies in case of possible disputes. It is also questionable whether IFSs are always the most appropriate means of fostering international financial stability.[102]

To sum up, without minimising the contribution of IFSs to international financial stability, it is important to recognise their limits: they are not a talisman warding off international financial crises and are certainly not a substitute for the prudent behaviour of all stakeholders, including not only financial institutions and their regulators, but also monetary authorities and politicians, acting with a view to preventing excessive credits or over-indebtedness leading to dangerous bubbles.

[101] The IFSs were unable to avert the financial crisis of 2008–10 and some standards may even have contained negative incentives. Formal compliance with abstract IFSs could arguably create a false sense of security and push risky transactions into less supervised segments. Finally, certain issues (such as putting in place an international resolution process (bankruptcy) for defaulting banks) seem at first sight to be beyond the reach of soft law.

Appendix 1

Table 3.1. *International financial architecture: overview of main bodies involved in setting international financial standards (IFSs)*

1. *Intergovernmental organisations*

Name	Year created	Members[a]/seat	Status	Staff	Finance	Governing body	Reporting/ FSB memb.	Sphere of activity	Involvement in IFSs
IMF	1946 [reformed in 1973]	188 Washington, DC	Intergov.org.	2400	Capital subscription from member countries	Board of Governors (24)	– FSB: yes G-20	International monetary cooperation; surveillance	Standard-setting and implementation FSAPs, ROSCs, Art. IV
World Bank (IBRD)	1944	188 Washington, DC	Intergov.org.	9000	Return on equity + margin on lending operations	Board of Directors (25)	– FSB: yes G-20	Financial + technical assistance to developing countries	Standard-setting and implementation FSAPs, ROSCs
BIS	1930	60 Basel	Intergov.org.	590	Return on equity + margin on banking operations	Board of Directors (19)	– FSB: yes	Central bank cooperation; bank for central banks	Hosting FSB, BCBS, IAIS, IADI
OECD	1961 [OECE: 1948]	34 Paris	Intergov.org.	2500	Members' contributions	OECD Council (35)	– FSB: yes	Economic cooperation and governance	Hosting FATF, GFTEI, IOPS

[a] Members = number of jurisdictions represented.

2. *Political steering group*

Name	Year created	Members[a]/ seat	Status	Staff	Finance	Governing body	Reporting/ FSB memb.	Sphere of activity	Involvement in IFSs
G-20	1999 (2008) [successor to G-7/8 (1975) and G-10 (1962)]	20 No permanent seat	*De facto* group	No permanent staff; rotating presidency; 'Troika', ministerial meetings + working groups (financial + Sherpas' track)	Each participant bears own costs	G-20 Leaders' summit (heads of state or government)	– FSB reports to G-20	Informal forum for discussion + cooperation between advanced + emerging countries on economic, monetary and financial stability issues	General incentives for standard-setting process and implementation

[a] Members = number of jurisdictions represented.

3. *Coordinating and standard-setting bodies*

Name	Year created	Members[a]/ seat	Status	Staff	Finance	Governing body	Reporting/ FSB memb.	Sphere of activity	Involvement in IFSs
FSB	2009 [1999 as FSF]	24 (+ 12 org.) Basel (at BIS)	*De facto* group [established as Association under Swiss law in January 2013]	35	Funded by BIS	FSB Plenary	To G-20	Coordination of standard-setting process (sectoral SSBs)	Coordination, standard-setting and implementation

FATF	1989	34 Paris (at OECD)	*De facto* group	21	Members' contributions	FATF Plenary	To G-20 (formerly to G-7)	Combating money laundering and terrorist finance	Standard-setting and implementation
GFTEI	2000	108 Paris (at OECD)	Subgroup within OECD [OECD Council decision of 17 September 2009]		Members' contributions	GFTEI Plenary	To G-20 (formerly to G-7)	Promoting transparency and exchange of information (tax standards)	Standard-setting and implementation

[a] Members = number of jurisdictions represented.

4. *Sectoral standard setting bodies (SSBs)*[a]

Name	Year created	Members[b]/ seat	Status	Staff	Finance	Governing body	Reporting/ FSB memb.	Sphere of activity	Involvement in IFSs
BCBS	1974	27 Basel (at BIS)	*De facto* group	17	Funded by BIS	GHOS[c] [at BIS]	To FSB (on its work)	Banking supervisory matters	Standard-setting and implementation
IOSCO	1983 [1974]	70 Madrid	Association Spanish law	18	Members' contributions	Presidents Committee	To FSB (on its work)	Financial markets' oversight	Standard-setting and implementation
IAIS	1994	190 Basel (at BIS)	Association Swiss law	30	Members' contributions	General meeting	To FSB (on its work)	Supervision of insurance industry	Standard-setting and implementation
IADI	2002	63 Basel (at BIS)	Association Swiss law	7	Members' contributions		To FSB (on its work)	Deposit insurance	Standard-setting

4. (*cont.*)

Name	Year created	Members[b]/ seat	Status	Staff	Finance	Governing body	Reporting/ FSB memb.	Sphere of activity	Involvement in IFSs
CPSS	1990 [1980]	24 Basel (at BIS)	*De facto* group	5	Funded by BIS	Global Economic meeting (31 central bank governors at BIS)	To FSB (on its work)	Payment, settlement and clearing systems	Standard-setting
IASB	2001	15 London	Independent body sponsored by IFRS, a Delaware foundation	100 +	Fundraising	IASB Board (15) Monitoring Board	To Trustees of IFRS Foundation; To FSB (on its work)	International accounting standards	Standard-setting
IAASB	1977	17	Independent body sponsored by IFAC (New York)		IFAC	Oversight by PIOB, a Spanish foundation	To IFAC	International auditing standards	Standard-setting

[a] Further SSBs (not included in this table) are the Committee on the Global Financial System (CGFS) (a *de facto* group hosted by the BIS with members from twenty-three jurisdictions) and the International Organisation of Pension Supervisors (IOPS) (an independent body hosted by the OECD with seventy members representing approximately sixty jurisdictions).

[b] Members = number of jurisdictions represented.

[c] GHOS = Group of Governors and Heads of Supervision.

5. *List of abbreviations and websites*

BCBS	Basel Committee on Banking Supervision	www.bis.org/bcbs
CGFS	Committee on the Global Financial System	www.bis.org/cgfs
CPSS	Committee on Payment and Settlement Systems	www.bis.org/cpss
FATF	Financial Action Task Force	www.fatf-gafi.org
FSB	Financial Stability Board	www.financialstabilityboard.org
G-20	Group of Twenty	www.g20.org
GFTEI	Global Forum on Transparency and Exchange of Information	www.oecd.org/tax/transparency ; www.eoi-tax.org
IAASB	International Auditing and Assurance Standards Board	www.iaasb.org
IADI	International Association of Deposit Insurers	www.iadi.org
IAIS	International Association of Insurance Supervisors	www.iaisweb.org
IASB	International Accounting Standards Board	www.ifrs.org
IBRD	International Bank for Reconstruction and Development (= WB)	www.worldbank.org
IFAC	International Federation of Accountants	www.ifac.org
IFRS	International Financial Reporting Standards Foundation	www.ifrs.org
IMF	International Monetary Fund	www.imf.org
IOPS	International Organisation of Pension Supervisors	www.iopsweb.org
IOSCO	International Organization of Securities Commissions	www.iosco.org
OECD	Organisation for Economic Co-operation and Development	www.oecd.org
PIOB	Public Interest Oversight Board	www.ipiob.org
WB	World Bank (= IBRD)	www.worldbank.org

Appendix 2

Table 3.2. *FSB list of key standards for sound financial systems*

Area	Standard	Issuing body
Macroeconomic policy and data transparency		
Monetary and financial policy transparency	Code of Good Practices on Transparency in Monetary and Financial Policies	IMF
Fiscal policy transparency	Code of Good Practices on Fiscal Transparency	IMF
Data dissemination	Special Data Dissemination Standard / General Data Dissemination System[a]	IMF
Financial regulation and supervision		
Banking supervision	Core Principles for Effective Banking Supervision	BCBS
Securities regulation	Objectives and Principles of Securities Regulation	IOSCO
Insurance supervision	Insurance Core Principles	IAIS
Institutional and market infrastructure		
Crisis resolution and deposit insurance[b]	Core Principles for Effective Deposit Insurance Systems	BCBS/IADI
Insolvency	Insolvency and Creditor Rights[c]	World Bank
Corporate governance	Principles of Corporate Governance	OECD
Accounting and auditing	International Financial Reporting Standards (IFRS)	IASB
	International Standards on Auditing (ISA)	IAASB
Payment, clearing and settlement	Principles for Financial Market Infrastructures	CPSS/IOSCO
Market integrity	FATF Recommendations on Combating Money Laundering and the Financing of Terrorism & Proliferation	FATF

[a] Economies that have, or seek access to, international capital markets are encouraged to subscribe to the more stringent Special Data Dissemination Standard (SDDS) and all other economies are encouraged to adopt the General Data Dissemination System (GDDS).

Table 3.2. (*cont.*)

[b] The FSB supports the inclusion of one or more standards on resolution regimes under this policy area, and intends to make a selection once relevant policy development work is completed.
[c] The World Bank, working with UNCITRAL and internationally recognised experts, has completed and implemented the ICR ROSC Assessment Methodology. The ICR ROSC Methodology is based on the current Creditor Rights and Insolvency Standard (ICR Standard), derived from the World Bank's Principles and Guidelines for Effective Insolvency and Creditor Rights Systems, and the recommendations included in the UNCITRAL's Legislative Guide on Insolvency Law.

4

The role of central banks in monetary affairs: a comparative perspective

ROSA M. LASTRA

A. Introduction

This chapter presents a comparative approach to the study of central banks, with emphasis on the evolving role of the US Federal Reserve System and the ECB. A central bank is the key monetary authority in a given jurisdiction, which is typically the jurisdiction of the nation state, though in the case of a monetary union, the area of jurisdiction is supranational. A central bank is both a regulatory agency and a bank. An underlying theme of this chapter, in line with the general thrust of this volume – namely the limited role that law has played in monetary affairs – is that central banks inhabit a 'world of policy' and that we need to further develop central banking law. This chapter looks first at the changing nature of monetary policy and the goal of monetary stability and considers the rebalancing of central bank objectives – the increasing focus on financial stability matters – in the aftermath of the global financial crisis. The federalisation of supervision and crisis management that is taking place in the European Union (EU) replicates the experience of the Federal Reserve System and the Federal Deposit Insurance Corporation in the US one century ago. The chapter then discusses the special relationship between the central bank and the government – bearing in mind that central banks hold a unique position

This chapter, an earlier version of which was prepared for the conference on 'The Rule of Law in Monetary Affairs: Lessons from the Trade Field', WTI, Bern, 12 October 2012, draws on earlier writings by the author, including *Central Banking and Banking Regulation* (London: LSE, 1996) and *Legal Foundations of International Monetary Stability* (Oxford University Press, 2006). I thank George Rich for insightful and detailed comments and Thomas Cottier and other participants at the conference for their feedback. My thanks also go to Jean-Victor Louis, with whom I have co-authored a commentary on EMU Law entitled 'European Economic and Monetary Union: History, Trends and Prospects', *Yearbook of European Law* (2013), 1–150.

because they are both banker to the government and banker to the banks – and considers briefly the issue of monetary sovereignty.

B. The changing nature of monetary policy and other central banking functions

When central banks were first established (e.g., Bank of England in 1694, Banque de France in 1800 and the Banco de España in 1782) their main rationale was to print money (that is to issue notes) and to finance the government's needs. But from the outset, they have also fulfilled additional functions which were often added in the wake of difficulties and crises or for reasons of convenience. In many countries these essentially include monetary policy, banking supervision and regulation, banker's bank and lender of last resort (LOLR), smooth operation of the payment systems, management of gold and foreign reserves, conduct of foreign exchange operations, debt management, exchange controls and development and promotional tasks.[1] The evolution in the US offers a prime example. The creation in the US of the Federal Reserve System in 1913 was motivated by the need to counteract (via LOLR – discount window lending – and supervision) the damaging banking crises that in 1907 had ravaged the then still emerging US banking system.[2] But the establishment of the Federal Reserve System did not prevent the next big financial crisis in the US (1929–33). Following the failure of the Federal Reserve System to act decisively after the stock market crash of 1929 and the

[1] The list of central bank functions is open-ended and dynamic and may comprise additional tasks. For an analysis see Lastra, *Central Banking and Banking Regulation*, pp. 249–86 and chapter 2 ('Central Banking') in the forthcoming second edition of *Legal Foundations of International Monetary Stability* (entitled *International Monetary Law*, to be published by Oxford University Press in 2014). See also P. Pollard, 'A Look Inside Two Central Banks: The ECB and the Federal Reserve', *Federal Reserve Bank of St Louis* (2003), 18.

[2] The Panic of 1907, also known as the 1907 Bankers' Panic commenced in New York and spread throughout the nation. The panic might have deepened if not for the intervention of financier J. P. Morgan who pledged large sums of his own money, and convinced other New York bankers to do the same, to shore up the banking system. At the time, the US did not have a central bank to inject liquidity back into the market. In 1908 Senator Nelson W. Aldrich, father-in-law of John D. Rockefeller, Jr., established and chaired a commission to investigate the crisis and propose future solutions, leading to the creation of the Federal Reserve System. See minneapolisfed.org/publications_papers/pub_display.cfm?id=3816.

ensuing Great Depression,[3] the Federal Deposit Insurance Corporation was established in 1933. The federalisation of crisis management, first with regard to LOLR (1913) and then with regard to deposit insurance and bank insolvency (1933) took place following major financial crises. The New Deal legislation (Banking Act 1933) also led to the creation of the Federal Open Market Committee. The latter is relevant in that it signals the advent of monetary policy as the 'queen function' of central banks in the twentieth century. This development was reinforced with the establishment of the independent Bundesbank in 1957 with a clear mandate to conduct monetary policy to achieve price stability. This was the model that inspired the ECB (the Maastricht Treaty was heir to the economic theories and consensus reigning at the time of its creation) and that provided the template for nearly all central banking law reforms in the last two decades of the twentieth century. These lessons learned in the process of federalisation are instructive for the resolution of the current problems in the eurozone,[4] in particular with regard to the proposals to grant supervisory and crisis management powers (early intervention) to the ECB first published by the European Commission on 12 September 2012.[5] The Regulation on the Single Supervisory

[3] Milton Friedman and Anna Schwartz in their celebrated *Monetary History of the United States 1867–1960* (first published by Princeton University Press in 1963) and in *The Great Contraction, 1929–1933* (Princeton University Press, NBER Book Series Studies in Business Cycles, 1965) provide the definitive analysis of how the Fed's inaction contributed to the Great Depression. They were the first to argue that the excessively tight monetary policy of the Federal Reserve turned an otherwise normal recession into the Great Depression of the 1930s. Previously, the consensus of economists was that loss of investor and consumer confidence following the Wall Street Crash of 1929 was the primary cause of the Great Depression. The Fed's Chairman Bernanke is an expert on the study of the Great Depression and his stewardship of the Federal Reserve System in the aftermath of the financial crisis has undoubtedly been motivated by this intellectual legacy.

[4] See, generally, Takis Tridimas, 'EU Financial Regulation: Federalization, Crisis Management and Lender of Law Reform', in Paul Craig and Gráinne de Búrca (eds.), *The Evolution of EU Law*, 2nd edn (Oxford University Press, 2011), pp. 783–804.

[5] See ec.europa.eu/internal_market/finances/committees/index_en.htm#maincontentSec1. See European Commission, Proposal for a Council Regulation conferring specific tasks on the European Central Bank concerning policies relating to the prudential supervision of credit institutions, COM (2012) 511 Final, (Sept. 2012) available at ec.europa.eu/internal_market/finances/docs/committees/reform/20120912-com-2012-511_en.pdf and European Commission, Proposal for a Regulation of the European Parliament and of the Council amending Regulation (EU) No 1093/2010 establishing a European Supervisory Authority (European Banking Authority), COM (2012) 512 Final (Sept. 2012), available at ec.europa.eu/internal_market/finances/docs/committees/reform/20120912-com-2012-512_en.pdf.

Mechanism (SSM) was approved in October 2013,[6] while the package pertaining to single resolution and deposit insurance was approved by the European Parliament on 15 April 2014.[7]

In 1996 I wrote: 'nowadays the main rationale for central banking is no longer note-issue and finance of government, but monetary policy and banking supervision'.[8] Eighteen years later, monetary policy and banking supervision remain fundamental central banking functions, but their contours continue to change.[9] The link between supervision and crisis management, as well as the advent of macro-prudential supervision continue to expand the realm of supervision.[10] Monetary policy – the actions taken by the central bank to influence the availability and cost of money and credit in the pursuit of one or more goals – comprises today an ever-growing number of non-standard and non-conventional instruments, in addition to the traditional instruments of monetary control (open market operations, discount policies, reserve requirements). The non-standard measures are meant to be exceptional and transitory, extraordinary measures for extraordinary circumstances. The list though has become longer and longer. Non-conventional measures of monetary policy raise questions about the domains of monetary policy and fiscal policy and remain controversial. Through their programmes of quantitative easing (QE), the Bank of England, the Bank of Japan and the Federal Reserve System have entered uncharted territory.[11] Quantitative easing (QE) raises a number of economic issues, such as the potential for so-called 'currency wars',[12] the interaction between monetary policy and

[6] See Council Regulation (EU) No 1024/2013 of 15 October 2013 conferring specific tasks on the European Central Bank concerning policies relating to the prudential supervision of credit institution, eur-lex.europa.eu/LexU riSe rv/LexU riServ .do?u ri=OJ: L:2013 :287:0063:0089:EN:PDF.

[7] EU Parliament approves Recovery and Resolution Directive, Single Resolution Mechanism and revised Deposit Guarantee Schemes Directive, www.consilium.europa.eu/uedocs/cms_data/docs/pressdata/en/ecofin/137627.pdf.

[8] Lastra, *Central Banking and Banking Regulation*, p. 286.

[9] See, generally, Luis Garicano and Rosa Lastra, 'Towards a new Architecture for Financial Stability: Seven Principles', *Journal of International Economic Law*, 13:3 (2010), 597–621.

[10] In his contribution to this volume Kern Alexander explains the redesign of the international financial regulation with a macro-prudential focus. See K. Alexander, 'International economic Law and Macro-Prudential Regulation', Chapter 20, this volume.

[11] See www.bankofengland.co.uk/monetarypolicy/Pages/qe/default.aspx. See also speech by Chairman Bernanke on QE at www.federalreserve.gov/newsevents/speech/bernanke20121001a.htm. For the latest round of QE in the US, see www.federalreserve.gov/newsevents/press/monetary/20120913a.htm.

[12] The phrase 'currency war' was coined by Brazilian Minister of Finance Guido Mantega in 2010. The issue however is not new. Competitive currency devaluations have

fiscal policy, and the relationship between the central bank and the financial system (dependency on a quasi life-support mechanism) and indeed the difficulties of ending QE.[13] The issues surrounding forward guidance and macro-prudential supervision have also raised much controversy.

pernicious effects upon the economic relations between states, in particular upon their trading relations. As explained in Chapter 13, what the IMF lost through the abandonment of the par value regime (original Article IV) was the jurisdictional power over exchange rates. Since the entry into force of the Second Amendment, the Fund has no substantive legal rights with respect to the choice of exchange rate arrangements of its members. But exchange rates were and are a key focus of Article IV consultations and Article IV prohibits currency manipulation. Article XV of GATT provides the legal link between the IMF and WTO (and it was not amended following the collapse of the par value regime). Article XV establishes that 'the contracting parties shall not, by exchange actions, frustrate the intent of the provisions of this agreement, nor by trade action, the intent of the provisions of the Articles of Agreement of the IMF'. In a working paper 2013 entitled 'The (Mis)Alignment of the Trade and Monetary Legal Orders', Gregory Shaffer and Michael Waibel claim that 'While trade in goods, and to a lesser extent trade in services, are highly regulated by legal rules backed by an enforcement mechanism, currency valuation is now determined by the discretionary activities of central banks and treasury departments run largely by economists with little to no guidance from law'. Also, see F. Gianviti, 'Relationship between Monetary Policy and Exchange Rate Policy', Chapter 21, this volume.

13 I discuss these issues in Chapter 2 of the second edition of *Legal Foundations of International Monetary Stability* entitled *International Monetary Law* (to be published by Oxford University Press in 2014). The mere hint by former Fed Chairman Bernanke of a possible 'tapering' of quantitative easing in a Congressional testimony in May 2013 sent shockwaves throughout global stock markets and government bond markets (bond yields around the world rose sharply as investors anticipated an end to QE, thus triggering a sell-off in bond markets), with the US dollar rising and with the uncertainty also undermining the so-called 'carry trades' (borrowing in a low interest rate currency to invest in higher yielding assets). See James Politi, 'Fed Chief Hints on Money Flow' *Financial Times* (22 May 2013). It is remarkable that major market movements can be triggered by comments shrouded in a degree of uncertainty, if not 'mystery'. (A mystery is defined in the Oxford English dictionary as 'something that is difficult to understand or explain'.) Small wonder then that investors scrutinise every word uttered by the chairman of the Fed. This signalling of the unwinding of QE on 22 May 2013 was followed by a more precise statement on 19 June 2013, in which Chairman Bernanke set out the case for slowing the pace of QE as the US economy picks up momentum. The transcript of Bernanke's press conference is available at www.federalreserve.gov/media-center/files/FOMCpresconf20130619.pdf:

'First, today the Committee reaffirmed its expectation that the current exceptionally low range for the funds rate will be appropriate at least as long as the unemployment rate remains above 6½ percent so long as inflation and inflation expectations remain well behaved in the senses described in the FOMC statement …. The second policy tool being employed by the Committee is asset purchases …. Although the Committee left the pace of purchases unchanged at today's meeting, it has stated that it may vary the pace of purchases as economic conditions evolve. … If the incoming data are broadly consistent with this forecast, the Committee currently anticipates that it would be appropriate to moderate the monthly pace of purchases later this year. And if the

The ECB has used standard and non-standard measures of monetary policy in response to the crisis to ensure the proper working of monetary transmission and the provision of liquidity to the euro area banking system.[14]

Standard measures are open market and credit operations (Article 18 European System of Central Banks (ESCB) Statute), and minimum reserves (Article 19 ESCB Statute).[15] Article 20 of the ESCB Statute allows for other instruments of monetary control. Following standard measures (in accordance with Article 18 of the ESCB Statute) the ECB lowered interest rates in November and December 2011. Recent history shows a frequent recourse to non-standard measures by the ECB. From September 2007, the ECB started providing extra liquidity to address the paralysis in the interbank market as well as liquidity in dollars, following a swap agreement with the Federal Reserve System. In October 2008, the ECB decided on further extraordinary liquidity measures, carrying out weekly refinancing operations with a fixed rate tender procedure with full allotment, i.e., with the interest rate set in advance and the ECB providing as much liquidity as the banks requested, provided they offered collateral of sufficient quality. In July 2009 the ECB Governing Council decided to start a purchase programme

subsequent data remain broadly aligned with our current expectations for the economy, we would continue to reduce the pace of purchases in measured steps through the first half of next year, ending purchases around midyear. In this scenario, when asset purchases ultimately come to an end, the unemployment rate would likely be in the vicinity of 7 percent, with solid economic growth supporting further job gains, a substantial improvement from the 8.1 percent unemployment rate that prevailed when the Committee announced this program.'

As reported by Atkins, Jaime Caruana (BIS General Manager) highlighted that central banks not only have to manage expectations about short term interest rates but also face the 'unfamiliar' challenge of managing long-term interest rates. See Ralph Atkins, 'Bond Markets Jitters Support Bears' Case for Plunge to Earth', *Financial Times* (5 June 2013). Atkins also points out that 'QE has artificially lifted asset prices globally'.

[14] See ECB Monthly Bulletin, 'The ECB's Non Standard Measures – Impact and Phasing Out', July 2011. See also www.ecb.europa.eu/pub/pdf/scpwps/ecbwp1290.pdf and www.europarl.europa.eu/document/activities/cont/201208/20120820ATT49767/20120820ATT49767EN.pdf and R. Lastra, 'The Evolution of the European Central Bank', *Fordham International Law Journal*, 35, Special Issue, Spring 2012, 'From Maastricht to Lisbon: the Evolution of European Union Institutions and Law', 1260–81.

[15] Following 'standard measures', the ECB lowered interest rates by twenty-five basis points in November 2011, and by another twenty-five basis points in December 2011. See Lecture by Peter Praet, Member of the Executive Board of the ECB, Geneva, 20 February 2012, www.ecb.europa.eu/press/key/date/2012/html/sp120220.en.html.

of covered bonds to help revive this segment of the market which is important for the refinancing of banks.[16]

In 2010 the financial crisis mutated into a sovereign debt crisis, following the debt problems in Greece. In light of the no-bailout clauses of Article 123 (prohibition of monetary financing) and Article 125 (no bailout of governments) of the Treaty for the Functioning of the European Union, and considering the desire of the European and national authorities to bail out Greece rather than inflict losses upon creditors via debt restructuring (as recommended by Buchheit and Gulati[17]), the authorities first established ad hoc and temporary facilities for financial assistance (European Stabilization Mechanism[18] and a European Financial Stability Facility). Eventually, they created a permanent mechanism, via the ESM Treaty (European Stability Mechanism).[19] The ECB continued to work within its mandate, stretching the instruments available to it in order to deal with the crisis. The Securities Markets Programme was established by the ECB in May 2010 as an instrument of monetary policy (non standard measure adopted by the ECB bearing in mind the constraints of the Treaty) following the Greek debt crisis. As stated in the preamble to the Decision establishing the SMP (Decision of the European Central Bank of 14 May 2010 establishing a Securities Markets Programme),[20] the objective of the SMP was to restore the monetary policy transmission mechanism:

[16] Decision (ECB/2009/16) of 2 July 2009. See Varii Autori, 'The Impact of the Eurosystem's Covered Bond Purchase Programme on the Primary and Secondary Markets', ECB Occasional Paper Series, No. 122, January 2011. See also ECB Monthly Bulletin 'The ECB's non-standard measures', 55–69.

[17] Lee Buchheit and Mitu Gulati, 'How to Restructure Greek Debt', 7 May 2010, papers.ssrn.com/sol3/papers.cfm?abstract_id=1603304.

[18] Council Regulation (EU) 407/2010 of 11 May 2010 establishing a European Stabilisation Mechanism, OJ 2010, L 118/1.

[19] A Treaty establishing the European Stability Mechanism (ESM) was signed by the Finance Ministers of the euro area on 11 July 2011. For an explanation of these facilities, see, generally, J.-V. Louis and R. Lastra, 'European Economic and Monetary Union, History, Trends and Prospects', *Yearbook of European Law* (2013), 1–150. On 28 November 2012, the European Court of Justice (ECJ) confirmed the compatibility of the European Stability Mechanism (ESM) with EU law in Case C-370/12 (*Pringle*), judgment of 28 November 2012, www.curia.europa.eu.

[20] See www.ecb.int/ecb/legal/pdf/l_12420100520en00080009.pdf. See generally, Lastra, 'The Evolution of the European Central Bank', 1260–81. Under the SMP, the ECB and the Eurosystem NCBs were entitled to purchase on the secondary market eligible debt instruments issued by central governments or public entities of the eurozone, as well as private debt securities.

(1) Pursuant to Article 18.1 of the Statute of the ESCB, national central banks of Member States whose currency is the euro (hereinafter the 'euro area NCBs') and the ECB (hereinafter collectively referred to as the 'Eurosystem central banks') may operate in the financial markets by, among other things, buying and selling outright marketable instruments.
(2) On 9 May 2010 the Governing Council decided and publicly announced that, in view of the current exceptional circumstances in financial markets, characterised by severe tensions in certain market segments which are hampering the monetary policy transmission mechanism and thereby the effective conduct of monetary policy oriented towards price stability in the medium term, a temporary securities markets programme (hereinafter the 'programme') should be initiated. Under the programme, the euro area NCBs, according to their percentage shares in the key for subscription of the ECB's capital, and the ECB, in direct contact with counterparties, may conduct outright interventions in the euro area public and private debt securities markets.
(3) The programme forms part of the Eurosystem's single monetary policy and will apply temporarily. The programme's objective is to address the malfunctioning of securities markets and restore an appropriate monetary policy transmission mechanism.

In December 2011, at a time when the problems were significant in a number of euro area member states leading the European Council to consider further measures (including the Fiscal Compact), the Governing Council of the ECB announced additional enhanced credit support measures to support bank lending and liquidity in the euro area money market.[21] The ECB Governing Council decided to conduct two long-term refinancing operations (LTROs) at the rate of 1 per cent with a maturity of thirty-six months and the option of early repayment after one year, and to increase collateral availability by: (i) reducing the rating threshold for certain asset-backed securities (ABSs) and (ii) allowing national central banks (NCBs), as a temporary solution, to accept as collateral additional performing credit claims (i.e. bank loans) that

[21] See www.ecb.int/press/pr/date/2011/html/pr111208_1.en.html. The regular short-term mainstream refinancing operations (MROs) serve to steer short-term interest rates, to manage the liquidity situation and to signal the stance of monetary policy in the euro area. The LTROs aim to provide additional, longer-term refinancing to the financial sector.

satisfy specific eligibility criteria.[22] The first LTRO in December 2011 provided €489 billion in liquidity to the banking sector and the second LTRO in February 2012, an amount of €529 billion. This provision of liquidity to financial institutions was useful during a period of paralysis of the interbank financing; however, it further reinforced the vicious link between banks and sovereigns.

In August 2012[23] the ECB Governing Council announced its controversial bond purchasing programme: the so-called 'Outright Monetary Transactions' (OMTs). On 6 September 2012, the President of the ECB announced the adoption by the Governing Council of decisions on a number of technical features of outright monetary transactions (OMTs) in secondary sovereign bond markets and announced, at the same time, that the SMP was terminated following this decision.[24] The legal basis of this OMT programme is Article 18.1 of the ESCB Statute; its objective is to safeguard the monetary policy transmission mechanism in all countries of the euro area, to preserve the singleness of the ECB's monetary policy and to address severe distortions in government bond markets which originate from fears on the part of investors about the reversibility of the euro. The ECB felt that, if not addressed, these conditions would have severe consequences for the maintenance of price stability. The OMT, as opposed to the SMP, is to apply strict conditionality. (The ECB will subordinate the launching of an OMT to the conditionality attached to an appropriate EFSF/ESM programme).

However, Bundesbank President Jens Weidmann stated in 2012 that it (the ECB's bond purchasing programme) was too close to state financing via the money press.[25] Even though the German Constitutional Court (Bundesverfassungsgericht) has no jurisdiction over the ECB, it commenced hearings to consider the legality of the OMT programme on 11 June 2013.[26]

In a crisis it is difficult to separate the monetary policy function from the provision of extraordinary liquidity assistance (LOLR, which often becomes

22 Decision of ECB of 14 December 2011 (OJ L 341) on additional temporary measures relating to the Eurosystem refinancing operations and eligibility of collateral.

23 See www.ecb.int/press/pr/date/2012/html/pr120906_1.en.html.

24 'Technical Features of Outright ECB Press Release, 6 September 2012, *Monetary Transactions*', www.ecb.int/press/pr/date/2012/html/pr120906_1.en.html.

25 Interview with Spiegel (29 August 2012), at www.spiegel.de/international/europe/spiegel-interview-with-bundesbank-president-jens-weidmann-a-852285.html.

26 See, generally, economistsview.typepad.com/economistsview/files/Siekmann.and.Volker.pdf and www.bundesverfassungsgericht.de/pressemitteilungen/bvg13–029. On 7 February 2014, the German Constitutional Court requested the Court of Justice of the European Union to issue a preliminary ruling on the OMT. See www.bverfg.de/en/press/bvg14-009en.html; see more at: europeanlawblog.eu/?p=2219#sthash.

lender of primary resort). The legal situation of the ECB in this regard is complex. The ECB has competence to provide market liquidity according to Article 18 of the ESCB Statute and Article 127(2) TFEU, and the ECB has indeed provided hugely expanded liquidity operations during the twin crises (financial and sovereign debt crises) and has made ample use of the considerable set of operational tools at its disposal to handle a liquidity crisis. However, what constitutes 'ordinary' liquidity assistance as opposed to 'emergency'/LOLR liquidity assistance becomes blurred during a crisis, since the drying up of the interbank market gives the central bank a primary role in the provision of liquidity. Although the ECB is competent to provide liquidity assistance to 'financially sound' banks,[27] the classic LOLR assistance (collateralised loans to troubled illiquid but solvent banks) remains a national competence (unless the problems originate in the payment system[28]). In 1998 the ESCB adopted a restrictive reading of the ECB competences, concluding that the provision of LOLR assistance to specific illiquid individual institutions was a national task of the NCBs in line with Article 14.4 of the ESCB Statute (a provision which allows NCBs to perform non-ESCB tasks on their own responsibility and liability).[29] With the advent of banking union, this restrictive interpretation must be reversed. The ECB should be the lender of last resort for those banks it now supervises.

C. The goal of monetary stability and other central banking objectives

Between 1989 and 2008 a consensus developed around the world (in economic and policy-making circles) that the primary objective of monetary policy as an instrument of economic policy should be price stability. Most modern central bank laws still refer to this goal as their most important objective.[30]

[27] See ECB, 2008, www.ecb.europa.eu/pub/pdf/other/gendoc2008en.pdf, p. 11.

[28] According to Article 127.2 TFEU.

[29] Article 14.4 reads as follows: 'National central banks may perform functions other than those specified in this Statute unless the Governing Council finds, by a majority of two thirds of the votes cast, that these interfere with the objectives and tasks of the ESCB. Such functions shall be performed on the responsibility and liability of national central banks and shall not be regarded as being part of the functions of the ESCB'.

[30] This was based on economic theory (vertical Philips curve in the long-run and time inconsistency) and supported by empirical evidence: ICBs do a better job than politicians at controlling inflation. See Lastra, *Central Banking and Banking Regulation*, pp. 13–24. With regard to the economic literature on this issue, see, *inter alia*, Alex Cukierman, *Central Bank Strategy, Credibility and Independence: Theory and Evidence* (Cambridge MA: MIT Press, 1994).

Monetary stability can be defined in positive terms or in negative terms. In positive terms, monetary stability refers to the maintenance of the internal value of money (i.e., price stability) as well as of the external value of the currency (i.e., the stability of the currency vis-à-vis other currencies, which is, in turn, influenced by the choice of exchange rate regime).[31] In negative terms, monetary stability refers broadly to the absence of instability.

The economic literature in the latter part of the twentieth century – which has influenced legal and political developments – relied on a notion of monetary stability primarily focused on its internal dimension, i.e., keeping inflation under control.[32] Monetary stability is the lack of instability in the movement of prices. Monetary instability can be caused both by rapidly rising prices (inflation) or by rapidly falling prices (deflation), particularly when such phenomena are 'unanticipated' or when they occur on a continuous basis. The phenomenon of deflation, once considered a ghost of the past, has made its reappearance and Japan has experienced falling prices since the mid-1990s.[33] The risks of deflation are real in today's economy.

Monetary stability is a fundamental economic goal. However, there are other important economic goals that the government needs to take into account in the design of its economic policies, such as growth and employment. The following question then arises: what is the best way of achieving several goals? Up until the financial crisis, the solution adopted by the political authorities in many countries was to pursue growth and employment directly through fiscal policy and other instruments of economic policy – typically under political instruction – and to delegate the mandate of price stability and the conduct of monetary policy to an independent central bank. This model relied upon the pursuit of one

[31] The stability of exchange rates (the exchange rate being the price of a currency in another currency) and the issue of the best exchange rate arrangement for a given country (fixed, floating or some version of managed float) remain a matter of great controversy in the economic literature. This means that the law tends to refer to the external dimension of monetary stability (the stability of the currency) in rather ambiguous terms.

[32] The standard definition of inflation is that it is a fall in the value of money, not just a rise in the consumer price index. See definition of 'inflation' in Peter Newman, Murray Milgate and John Eatwell (eds.), *The New Palgrave Dictionary of Money & Finance* (London: Macmillan, 1992). Inflation is a process of continuously rising prices, or equivalently, of a continuously falling value of money.

[33] See, e.g., Tim Callen and Jonathan D. Ostry (eds.) *Japan's Lost Decade. Policies for Economic Revival* (Washington, DC: International Monetary Fund, 2003).

goal, namely monetary stability, using one instrument – monetary policy – conducted by one agency, the central bank.

A crucial aspect of the institutional reform proposals in response to the financial crisis of 2007–9 involves having the monetary authorities more closely involved in financial supervision, a return to the financial stability mandate. This is a reversal of the trend that prevailed in the late 1980s and in the 1990s, where the emphasis on stable money as the primary objective of monetary policy was often accompanied by a move away from the supervisory tasks. It also vindicates longstanding central banking traditions, aptly summarised by Vera Lutz Smith (a student of Hayek), who explained in her excellent book, *The Rationale of Central Banking*, that the twin mandate of central banks was stable money and sound banking. In modern parlance: monetary stability and financial stability.[34]

The US Federal Reserve Act of 1913 is an important example of a central bank whose law includes other objectives such as growth, employment and the stability of the financial system in addition to monetary stability. The introduction to the Federal Reserve Act reads as follows: 'To provide for the establishment of Federal Reserve Banks, *to furnish an elastic currency*, to afford means of rediscounting commercial paper, to establish a more effective supervision of banking in the United States, and for other purposes'.[35] Elastic is not stable; elastic means adaptable, the ability to stretch and then return to its original form. The 'stability culture' is in itself a modern phenomenon, which has influenced legislative developments in recent decades. In the early 1930s – during the Great Depression – the emphasis was on growth and employment, not on controlling inflation. Indeed, until World War II, during the times of peace from 1850 to 1939 inflation was zero in the US. Of course the historical experience in Germany of hyperinflation

[34] See Vera C. Smith, *The Rationale of Central Banking and the Free Banking Alternative* (Indianapolis: Liberty Press, 1990) pp. 189–90. The book was originally published in 1936.

[35] See also Section 2(a) of the Federal Reserve Act (12 USC 225a), which was added by Act of 16 November 1977 (91 Stat 1387) and amended by Acts of 27 October 1978 (92 Stat 1897) and 23 August 1988 (102 Stat 1375) and 27 December 2000 (114 Stat 3028) referring to 'stable prices'. Section 2(a) also refers to other policy objectives: 'The Board of Governors of the Federal Reserve System and the Federal Open Market Committee shall maintain long run growth of the monetary and credit aggregates commensurate with the economy's long run potential to increase production, so as to promote effectively the goals of maximum employment, stable prices, and moderate long-term interest rates'.

during the Weimar Republic in the interwar period still influences German attitudes towards central banking.[36]

However, for much of the post-World War II period, policy-makers in developed and developing countries have been concerned about rising inflation, especially during the late 1970s and early 1980s. The US Federal Reserve Act was modified to give due emphasis to the notion of 'stable prices' as an important goal to be pursued by the Board of Governors and the Federal Open Market Committee.[37] The so-called 'oil shock' of 1973 – i.e., the quadrupling of oil prices which plunged much of the industrialised world into an era of soaring inflation and low and volatile growth, known in economic jargon as stagflation – is a historical development which marked a turning point in the understanding of the need for price stability. The oil shock destroyed the post-war pattern whereby governments had tried to buy a little more growth with a little more inflation (Philips curve), instead of entrenching price stability as their primary concern.

Against this background the case for central bank independence – the need to delegate control over the money supply – was also a recognition of the importance given to monetary policy in the overall design of economic policy. Under the Keynesian policy modalities of the 1950s and 1960s, fiscal policy had primacy and demand management policies (goals of growth and employment) were prevalent. An independent central bank gives priority to a monetary policy aimed at achieving price stability. It should be noted however that although independent central banks became the preferred institutional arrangement to keep inflation under control in the latter part of the twentieth century, there are other arrangements that can promote monetary stability, such as legislated monetary rules (akin to the ones proposed by Milton Friedman[38]) and currency boards. The rules versus discretion

[36] See, generally, Chapter 2 of Lastra, *Legal Foundations* for an extensive analysis of the anti-inflationary tradition in Germany and how this tradition influenced the history of the Bundesbank, which served as a 'functional model' for the ECB.

[37] Section 2a of the Federal Reserve Act (12 USC 225a), which was added by Act of 16 November 1977 (91 Stat 1387) and amended by Acts of 27 October 1978 (92 Stat 1897) and 23 August 1988 (102 Stat 1375), refers to 'stable prices'.

[38] Milton Friedman formally proposed his monetary rule – for a constant growth of the money supply at a rate roughly equal to underlying productivity growth – in Milton Friedman, *Program for Monetary Stability* (New York: Fordham University Press, 1960). Friedman had already advanced some of his ideas in 1948, in Milton Friedman, 'A Monetary and Fiscal Framework for Economic Stability', *American Economic Review* 38 (1948), 245.

literature[39] and the quantity theory of money influenced the economic debate, the teaching of monetary economics and the actual conduct of monetary policy in North America and Europe in the mid 1970s and early 1980s. However, strict monetary targeting (i.e., reliance on rigid monetary rules) had been abandoned or modified by the mid 1980s in the US and the UK.[40] Following the granting of operational independence to the Bank of England in 1998, reliance on inflation targeting[41] (i.e., a numerical target for the rate of inflation, according to Article 12.1 of the Bank of England Act 1998[42]) characterised conventional monetary policy until the financial crisis.

In the context of the rules versus discretion monetary debate, it is interesting that the advent of central bank independence granted a substantial degree of discretion (technical, not political) to central bankers within the realm of their legal mandate to strive for monetary stability.

The emphasis on price stability as the primary goal of monetary policy is therefore a development that needs to be understood within the historical context provided by the country experiences, economic policies and economic thinking which prevailed in the second half of the

[39] The rules versus discretion economic literature – which interestingly resembles the rules versus discretion debate in administrative law – dates back to Henry C. Simons, 'Rules versus Authorities in Monetary Policy', *Journal of Political Economy* 1 (1936), 44. Most of the economic literature on central bank independence has followed the so-called time inconsistency argument, first formulated by Finn E. Kydland and Edward C. Prescott, 'Rules rather than Discretion: The Inconsistency of Optimal Plans', *Journal of Political Economy* 86 (1977), 473, and further developed by Robert J. Barro and David B. Gordon, 'Rules, Discretion, and Reputations in a Model of Monetary Policy', *Journal of Monetary Economics* 12 (1983), 101.

[40] However, from an operational point of view there is a beneficial legacy of monetary targeting, namely the continuing, albeit non-mechanical concern, with the growth of a range of financial assets (included in monetary aggregates) and the understanding of the value of publishing and monitoring detailed information about the authorities' actions and intentions.

[41] New Zealand was the first country to adopt inflation targeting, according to the Reserve Bank of New Zealand Act 1989. The theoretical work on inflation targeting was developed by Lars E. O. Svensson in his seminal articles Lars E. O. Svensson, 'Inflation Forecast Targeting: Implementing and Monitoring Inflation Targets', *European Economic Review* 41 (1997), 1111 and Lars E. O. Svensson, 'Inflation Targeting as a Monetary Policy Rule', paper presented at the Sveriges Riksbank–IIES Conference on Monetary Policy Rules in 1998, later published as Lars E. O. Svensson, 'Inflation Targeting as a Monetary Policy Rule', *Journal of Monetary Economics* 43 (1999), 607.

[42] Section 12.1 of the Bank of England Act, 1998, reads as follows: 'The Treasury may by notice in writing to the Bank specify for the purposes of Section 11 (a) what price stability is to be taken to consist of, or (b) what the economic policy of Her Majesty's Government is to be taken to be.'

twentieth century. This development had important legal implications nationally and internationally, particularly in the 1990s, as a substantial number of domestic laws as well as some international treaties (most notably the Maastricht Treaty on European Union) made this the primary goal of central banks or monetary agencies. The trade-off between objectives is often a political decision.[43] It is subject to economic and political developments. As I wrote in 2006:

> Perhaps in the twenty-first century we will witness the emergence of a rebalanced framework of macro-economic policy (with fiscal policy regaining part of its earlier role) that may lead to a realignment of the goals to be pursued by the monetary authorities, which in turn will lead to a new wave of legal reforms. Though the importance of monetary stability as a foundation of the economic order, nationally and internationally, will remain, it may lose the quasi-sacrosanct nature that it has enjoyed during the last quarter of the twentieth century.[44]

The subsequent crisis has certainly reinforced such findings.

D. The special relationship between the central bank and the government

The relations between the central bank and the government have always been the subject of much controversy, as the nickname given to the Bank of England, the Old Lady of Threadneedle Street, reminds us.[45] These relations involve several aspects: ownership, separate juridical

[43] In Germany, the Bundesbank Law stated that price stability was its primary objective. The secondary objective of the Bundesbank was to support the general economic policies of the Government (including growth and employment). German commentators on the Bundesbank Law referred to this provision of the law (which is also replicated in the EU Treaty with regard to the ESCB: supporting the general economic policies of the Union, without prejudice to price stability) as the 'squaring of the circle', given that such economic policies could sometimes conflict with the sacrosanct goal of price stability.

[44] See Chapter 2 of Lastra, *Legal Foundations*.

[45] The nickname comes from a Thomas Gillray cartoon published in May 1797, following a speech that a Member of Parliament, Richard Brinsley, had made in the House of Commons alluding to the Bank as an 'elderly lady in the City of great credit and long standing, who had unfortunately, fallen into bad company'. The bad company in question was the company of Prime Minister Pitt, who had required the Bank to make large loans to the Government to finance a war against France.

personality, and dependence or independence (which in turn is related to the issue of control).[46]

Most central banks these days enjoy separate juridical personality, which means that they can sue or be sued, and are the subject of rights and obligations. They can also enter into some international treaties, as is the case of the Bank for International Settlements (BIS), whose members are central banks and monetary authorities.[47] This is an important dimension when considering the rule of law in monetary affairs.

The issue of legal personality becomes interesting in complex central banking systems, such as the US Federal Reserve System or the European System of Central Banks. The US Federal Reserve System itself is not an entity; the entities with legal personality are the Board of Governors, which is a federal government agency (i.e., a public body) created by Congress and accountable to Congress, and which performs administrative functions[48] (central banking functions), and the twelve Federal Reserve Banks, which are separate, privately owned,[49] legal entities,[50] organised as corporate entities, each with a different legal personality. The Federal Reserve Banks perform dual functions: central banking functions[51] (e.g., administration of monetary and credit policies) and

[46] The issue of public or private ownership is of marginal importance these days, although the ownership of reserves and the allocation of central bank profits can be a source of contention in privately owned central banks, since the interests of private shareholders may conflict with the central bank's public responsibilities. A great number of central banks were nationalised in the twentieth century (e.g., the Bank of England was nationalised in 1946), while others that were created as public agencies, were typically endowed with public ownership.

[47] The members are the central banks and monetary authorities of Algeria, Argentina, Australia, Austria, Belgium, Bosnia and Herzegovina, Brazil, Bulgaria, Canada, Chile, China, Colombia, Croatia, the Czech Republic, Denmark, Estonia, Finland, France, Germany, Greece, Hong Kong SAR, Hungary, Iceland, India, Indonesia, Ireland, Israel, Italy, Japan, Korea, Latvia, Lithuania, Luxembourg, Macedonia (FYR), Malaysia, Mexico, the Netherlands, New Zealand, Norway, Peru, the Philippines, Poland, Portugal, Romania, Russia, Saudi Arabia, Serbia, Singapore, Slovakia, Slovenia, South Africa, Spain, Sweden, Switzerland, Thailand, Turkey, the United Arab Emirates, the United Kingdom and the United States, plus the European Central Bank.

[48] 12 USC 241. In addition, the Federal Open Market Committee (FOMC) was established in 1933.

[49] 12 USC 282, 323. See also Article 4 of the by-laws of the Federal Reserve Bank of New York (FRBNY).

[50] Section 4 of the Rules of Organization of the Board of Governors, issued pursuant to 5 USC 552.

[51] The central banking functions are conferred by statute or by express delegation of authority pursuant to 12 USC 248 (k).

corporate functions proper of a bank (e.g., managing depository accounts for other banks).[52]

The ESCB is composed of the ECB and the NCBs. The Eurosystem comprises the ECB and the NCBs of the Member States that have adopted the euro.[53] Neither the ESCB nor the Eurosystem have legal personality, and therefore, they are not holders of rights and obligations. The entities that do have a legal personality are the ECB and the NCBs. The legal position of the ECB and its independence have been the subject of much debate in recent years. The European Court of Justice defined the limits of the independence of the ECB in the *OLAF* case,[54] adopting a functional approach anchored in EU law.

The attribution of separate legal personality is different from the granting of independence in the exercise of some delegated government functions. In exercising its responsibilities, the central bank can be dependent on or independent from political instruction. Independence can be restricted to one function, such as monetary policy,[55] or can encompass several or all the functions a central bank performs. There are however degrees of dependence and independence.[56] At one end of the spectrum, a dependent central bank is subordinated to the dictate of the political authorities, as in many European countries before the

[52] See *Bank Markazi Iran* v. *Federal Reserve Bank of New York*, Case No. 823 presented before the Iran–United States Claims Tribunal at the Hague, the Netherlands (1997–99). The Tribunal reached its decision on 16 November 1999, Award No. 595–823–3.

[53] Article 282 of the Treaty on the Functioning of the European Union enshrines in law the term 'Eurosystem', which was already used in the praxis of the ECB.

[54] See Case 11/00 *Commission of the European Communities* v. *European Central Bank* [2003] ECR 00, para. 92. This case is referred to as 'the *OLAF* (*European Anti-Fraud Office)* case'.

[55] The case for central bank independence has generally been advocated in the conduct of monetary policy. In this respect, central bank independence provides an intermediate solution between full depoliticisation, as advocated in the free-banking proposals, and politicisation, in which all economic policy is under governmental control.

[56] Legal guarantees concerning the organisation and functions of central banks, on the one hand, and the integrity and professionalism of central bankers, on the other hand, are an important measurement of legal central bank independence. The incentive structure of independent central bankers is different from that of elected politicians. Political economy and political science have contributed to the understanding of this 'incentive structure'. However, these incentives need to be enshrined in the law in order to be effective and enforceable. The independent central bank can be seen as a form of pre-commitment by the political system to tie its hands, like Ulysses at the mast, to avoid taking destructive actions when the siren of inflationary temptation appears.

advent of central bank independence.[57] At the other end of the spectrum, an independent central bank enjoys freedom from Government interference (greater in the case of 'goal independence' than in the case of 'instrument independence'). The notion of control is not the same as the notion of dependence or independence. Independent central banks are still subject to a degree of control over their activities by the government. They are also accountable to parliament, to the judiciary and to the elected government.

During the 1990s, central bank independence became a kind of 'graduation issue' for countries wishing to exhibit or consolidate their credentials in monetary stability and fiscal restraint. Over the past two decades central bank laws in numerous jurisdictions have granted independence or greater operational autonomy to their central banks, with an explicit price stability mandate. Despite the economic merits of central bank independence, the actual decision to grant independence is a political one.

The link between economics and politics is complex and differs between countries and over time. This is true both for developed and for developing countries. In non-democratic societies, the control of the money supply has traditionally been an important instrument of economic policy that can address various political needs, in particular the financing of government activities. In a democracy, political parties try to appeal to various constituencies and – according to economic and political theories that became widely accepted in the latter part of the twentieth century – in its eagerness to increase economic activity, the incumbent party may engage in inflationary policy in the period immediately before an election in order to raise employment and create a strong, if temporary, sense of euphoria among voters that translates into votes for the politicians then in office. Of course these theories somehow presuppose a certain cynicism about politics and public office, and appear to ignore the existence of individuals who take up public office – shunning the monetary incentives of private business – expressly to serve their country. I have encountered over the last twenty years many of these altruistic individuals who could have become immensely

[57] Before the advent of central bank independence, the relationship between the Treasury or Minister of Finance and the Central Bank was a principal–agent type of relationship in which the Treasury or Minister of Finance instructed the Central Bank what to do, and the latter was subservient to the wishes of the former, whether that meant to finance government deficits, or to use interest rate policy for a variety of government objectives.

wealthy had they dedicated their amazing talent and intelligence to profit-maximising activities. I have also met bankers for whom serving the public interest is irrelevant.

The phenomenon of 'independence' is not unique to central banking. It is a feature inherent in an administrative law tradition in which certain powers are delegated to certain agencies, with regulatory powers. This feature of functional decentralisation, initially favoured in countries which also supported geographical decentralisation (i.e., a federal structure, such as the US, Germany and Switzerland), has become widespread around the world when it comes to monetary affairs. The skills, expertise and superior qualifications of technocrats (e.g., central bankers and energy regulators) compared to politicians with regard to the conduct of their delegated functions, reinforce the case for independence.

There are two principal limits on central bank independence that all democratic societies should maintain. One is 'the goal constraint'. Important as stable prices are in ordinary times, the commitment to preventing inflation should not impair a nation's ability to respond to fundamental threats, exceptional circumstances (like the great financial crisis of 2008 and its aftermath) or basic changes in its identity. Indeed, as discussed below, the US Federal Reserve System has a broader statutory mandate that encompasses employment and growth in addition to stable prices. The other limit concerns the issue of democratic legitimacy and is related to the debate about central bank accountability. A democratic society always retains the discretion to reinvent itself; and should the people of a country make a considered, deliberate choice to seek some other goal or another instrument, the institutions of central bank independence should respect that decision.

Since independent central banks can seldom choose their goals, the discussion about central bank independence mainly focuses on the scope of powers delegated to central banks for the achievement of their statutorily defined objectives.

E. Money and monetary sovereignty

The power to issue currency is a sovereign monopoly power, one of the attributes of the general sovereignty of the state under international law. This sovereign power is exercised by the central bank.[58] Making a central

[58] In its judgment of 12 July 1929, *Serbian and Brazilian Loans Cases*, the Permanent Court of International Justice stated that 'it is indeed a generally accepted principle that a state is

bank independent interferes – to some extent – with the sovereign's right concerning the creation and regulation of money (*lex monetae*). Article I, section 8, clause 5 of the US Constitution gives Congress the power 'to coin money, regulate the value thereof, and of foreign coin'.[59] Congress delegated some powers to the Federal Reserve System when it enacted the Federal Reserve Act in 1913.

The notion of monetary sovereignty is not expressly recognised or defined as such in the Charter of the United Nations, nor in the Articles of Agreement of the International Monetary Fund nor in other key instruments of international law.[60] Some authors argue that the concept of monetary sovereignty predates by thousands of years the concept of political sovereignty that was developed in the Renaissance following feudalism, since the authority to create money had been proclaimed by the rulers or priesthood of ancient civilizations (Sumer, India, Babylon, Persia, Egypt, Rome and others).[61]

We recall that the modern understanding of the attributes of sovereignty is rooted in the political thought that was developed in the Renaissance. The history and evolution of sovereignty is intrinsically linked to the history and evolution of the nation state. Both concepts were developed in Western Europe between the end of the fifteenth century and the sixteenth century.

Monetary sovereignty has a territorial dimension. The law of a currency is always confined to a territory. It can only be enforced in that territory. There are of course significant extraterritorial effects with reserve currencies. As Richard Fisher, President of the Dallas Federal

entitled to regulate its own currency' *Serbian and Brazilian Loan Cases*, Permanent Court of International Justice (PCIJ), Judgment of 12 July 1929, Publications of the Court, Series A, Nos. 20–1, 44 and 122. See also the publications of the judgments (*Payment of various Serbian loans issues in France* and *Payment in gold of Brazilian loans issued in France*) in *World Court Reports* (Manley O. Hudson, ed.), vol. II, (Washington, DC: Carnegie Endowment for International Peace, 1935), pp. 323 and 427.

59 [US] Congress' right to regulate interstate commerce (Article 1, Section 8, Clause 3) encompasses banking and other financial services as the courts have come to define and interpret this clause. Congress also has the right to make any law that is 'necessary and proper' for the execution of its enumerated powers (Article I, Section 8, Clause 18).

60 See also Ernst Baltensperger and Thomas Cottier, 'The Role of International Law in Monetary Affairs', *Journal of International Economic Law* 13 (2010), 911.

61 See Robert A. Mundell, 'Money and the Sovereignty of the State', in Axel Leijonhufvud (ed.), *Monetary Theory and Policy Experience* (Basingstoke: Palgrave 2001 in association with the International Economic Association), pp. 298–302. For a study of monetary sovereignty, see, generally, Chapter 1 of Lastra, *Legal Foundations*. Claus Zimmermann has written an excellent PhD thesis on 'A Contemporary Concept of Monetary Sovereignty' (Oxford University Press, 2013).

Reserve, pointed out, even central banks whose influence extends way beyond their own shores remain accountable to national constituencies. 'It is an oddity in a globalized world', he admitted.[62]

Monetary sovereignty has been eroded (or at times surrendered) as a result of various developments and forces. There are consensual limitations of monetary sovereignty such as a monetary union or the obligations that stem from participation in the International Monetary Fund, and there are *de facto* limitations.[63] Consensual limitations represent a voluntary surrender of monetary sovereignty. *De facto* limitations are the result of globalisation, the information revolution and of economic and financial developments during the last three decades of the twentieth century.

The adoption of a single currency, the euro, and the creation of the European System of Central Banks signified the voluntary surrender of monetary sovereignty by those Member States that agreed to transfer sovereign rights to the European Union. This was a limited surrender, a non-exclusive transfer of sovereign powers. The members of the eurozone retain their national sovereignty in those domains where no other consensual limitation has been agreed.[64]

The holder of monetary sovereignty for those Member States whose currency is the euro is not the ECB, but the Union in the form of the

[62] Interview with the *Financial Times*, 24 June 2013. See also Ralph Atkins, *Financial Times* 26 June 2013, 'ECB Needs a Timely Response to Fed's QE Tapering Move'.

[63] As George Rich stated in his comments on my chapter, when it comes to the determination of the exchange rate, a simple illustration can help us understand some of the limits of monetary sovereignty. He confines himself in his example to a world of two countries, each issuing a national currency, but trading with one another on a foreign exchange market. Although there are two countries there is only one exchange rate to be set in that market. If the two countries regard the exchange rate as an instrument of policy – or at least as a magnitude to be influenced by policy – they face a problem: two countries cannot independently set or manipulate the single exchange rate; they must agree on its appropriate level. He then goes on to summarise the options of fixed and freely floating exchange rates, and he concludes that, unless we live – like Robinson Crusoe – on an island in complete autarky, we always have to accept, *de jure* or *de facto*, some loss of monetary sovereignty.

[64] The European Court of Justice ruled in the *Costa/Enel* case that 'by creating a Community of unlimited duration, having its own institutions, its own personality, its own legal capacity and capacity of representation on the international stage and, more particularly, real powers stemming from a limitation of sovereignty or a transfer of sovereign powers from the States to the Community, the member states have limited their sovereign rights, albeit within limited fields, and have thus created a body of law which binds their nationals and themselves'. See Case 6/64, *Costa/Enel* (1964) ECR 585, para. 9, 593.

seventeen member states (2012) that have pooled monetary sovereignty and form the Eurosystem.[65] The Union's 'exclusive competence' in monetary policy is exercised by the ESCB/ECB, and since the ECB is the institution that has legal personality (the ESCB and the Eurosystem do not), it is the ECB that is the holder of rights and obligations.

However, the partial transfer of 'attributes of monetary sovereignty' led to grave problems during the twin banking and sovereign debt crises in the eurozone. Banking union[66] addresses the flaws of institutional design[67] and transfers further attributes of monetary sovereignty by granting responsibility to supervise eurozone banks (and banks of non-eurozone member states that choose to become part of the Single Supervisory Mechanism or SSM) to the European Central Bank (based upon Article 127.6 of TFEU).

The limitations imposed by the Articles of Agreement of the International Monetary Fund were greater with the par value regime under the original Articles of Agreement than they are nowadays. Since the collapse of the Bretton Woods regime (*de facto*), and the Second Amendment to the Articles of Agreement (*de jure*), IMF member states reaffirmed some of the attributes of their monetary sovereignty with regard to the conduct of exchange rate policy. However, IMF members must still comply with the obligations under Article IV and Article VIII of the IMF Articles of Agreement, where the jurisdiction (regulatory powers) of the Fund applies. Multilevel governance – as discussed elsewhere in this volume by Petersmann – provides a valuable framework for assessing which functions or powers should remain at the national level and which can be better carried out supra-nationally or internationally.[68]

As for the *de facto* limitations, to begin with, the government has the monopoly over the issue of currency only – i.e., notes and coins in

[65] This is in line with the established doctrine of monetary sovereignty, where the state, as representative of the will of the people, is the holder of such sovereignty, even if the exercise or implementation of some of its prerogatives – such as the monopoly of note issue – is the responsibility of the central bank. See generally Lastra, *Legal Foundations*, chapter 1.

[66] See notes 6 and 7.

[67] See, generally, R. Lastra, 'Banking Union and Single Market: Conflict or Companionship?' *Fordham International Law Journal*, 36:5 (2013). An analysis of the weak economic pillar of EMU is provided in Lastra and Louis, 'European Economic and Monetary Union', 1–150.

[68] E. Petersmann, 'Framework of Analysis: Towards Multilayered Governance in Monetary Affairs', Chapter 17, this volume.

circulation – but not over other assets that individuals might hold instead of currency and that are contributing to the blurring of the definition of money and to a *de facto* erosion of monetary sovereignty. Commercial banks have an important role in the process of money creation: checking accounts (demand deposits) are used as means of payment. Demand deposits constitute the major part of the narrow definition of the money supply (M1). This characteristic of bank liabilities provides the rationale for many monetary and banking laws and regulations.

There have also been radical proposals, suggesting the reliance on 'private money'. Hayek (and other economists in the 'free banking school') have advocated the 'denationalization of money', opening up the provision of currency to competition both from the private sector and from foreign issuers of currency.[69]

The degree to which a currency is a good store of value in international monetary relations ('hard currencies' and 'soft currencies') is an economic consideration that can also limit in practice the effectiveness of monetary control. Depreciation (the loss in value of a currency vis-à-vis other currencies under a system of flexible exchange rates) and devaluation (the loss in value of a currency vis-à-vis other currencies by official intervention under a system of managed exchange rates) can lead to a *de facto* erosion of national monetary sovereignty.

The choice of exchange regime adopted by a state clearly affects the external value of the currency. Under a fixed exchange rate system, a national central bank only enjoys control over monetary policy if it is the central bank which sets monetary policy for the whole area. In the case of a currency board arrangement, monetary sovereignty is greatly reduced. In the case of dollarisation, there is a surrender of monetary sovereignty.[70]

The experience of inflation can be viewed as an 'abuse of sovereignty'.[71] Inflation makes people turn to other forms of payment, e.g., foreign currencies. The public authorities have various ways of gaining command

[69] See Friedrich A. von Hayek, *Denationalization of Money* (London: Institute of Economic Affairs, 1976). Hayek's first writing on this subject dates back to 1937, *Monetary Nationalism and International Stability* (reprint, New York: Augustus M. Kelly, 1971). For further references on this issue, see Lastra, *Central Banking and Banking Regulation*, pp. 252–7.

[70] See, generally, Chapter 1 of Lastra, *Legal Foundations*.

[71] See Robert Mundell 'Monetary Unions and the Problem of Sovereignty', *Annals of the American Academy of Political and Social Science* 579 (2002), 127.

over real resources: expropriation, taxes, bond issues and the issue of currency.[72] In a market economy, taxes and bond issues are preferred. However, the temptation to print money to finance government expenses remains a powerful argument for depoliticising the management of money; hence the support for monetary independence.[73]

F. Concluding observations

Monetary law is characterised by the existence of overlapping jurisdictions, with a predominance of national law. Central banks retain a fundamental – albeit changing – role in the conduct of monetary affairs. One of the defining features of the financial crisis has been the extraordinary assistance provided by central banks through liquidity provision and non-conventional instruments of monetary policy in order to stabilise the financial markets and to provide stimulus to the real economy.[74] This extraordinary assistance has been questioned by academics and central bankers.[75]

Central banking law, once relegated to the abstruse universe of a few specialists, is now a growing corpus of scholarship and knowledge. Its proper understanding requires a mix of administrative law, commercial law and international law and a constant dialogue with economists.

This chapter has analysed the monetary powers of central banks in the light of their statutory goal or goals, considering how these goals change over time and how the recent crisis has reignited the need to focus on the financial stability mandate. The chapter has also briefly considered – drawing upon earlier writings – the nature of

[72] See Charles Goodhart, *Money, Information and Uncertainty*, 2nd edn (London and Basingstoke: Macmillan, 1989), p. 44.

[73] A forceful defence of this monetary independence has been made by Bundesbank President Jens Weidmann as noted earlier.

[74] 'The success of institutions is to tread carefully on what is extraordinary and try to channel the instruments at their disposal towards a return to ordinary times. Central banks often act as last resort: purchasers of last resort, lenders of last resort, liquidity of last resort, investors of last resort. These last resort considerations are suited for extraordinary times. It is the immediacy of the availability of central bank liquidity that makes such liquidity essential when other sources either dry out or become prohibitively expensive'. See Lastra, 'The Evolution of the European Central Bank'.

[75] Bundesbank President Jens Weidmann raised concerns about monetary policy taking on fiscal tasks and wants a return to conventional monetary policy. See www.bundesbank.de/Redaktion/EN/Interviews/2012_09_26_weidmann_nzz.html.

delegated powers, the uneasy relationship between the central bank and the government and the tension between independence and accountability.

Central banks are at the centre, equidistant from the government and the financial system (they are both banker to the government and banker to the banks). Central banking is thus defined by the relationships of the central bank upwards with the government and downwards with the banking and financial system. The law must govern both relationships.

5

Monetary union and the law: some comments

JEAN-VICTOR LOUIS

A. Introduction

This chapter addresses two aspects of the European Economic and Monetary Union (EMU) which have great relevance as they reflect some original perspectives and could be useful for the sake of comparison with other monetary experiments around the world. They concern the transformation and the evolution, in times of crisis, of the role of national central banks (NCBs) within the Eurosystem and the difficulty of insertion of the euro area into the global system.

The concept of the 'Eurosystem' was introduced by Article 282, paragraph 1 of the Treaty on the Functioning of the European Union (TFEU),[1] formerly the Treaty on the European Community, as modified by the so-called Lisbon Treaty, which entered into force on 1 December 2009. From the start of the final stage of the EMU, on 1 January 1999, this denomination of Eurosystem has identified, within the European System of Central Banks (ESCB), the group formed by the NCBs that have adopted the euro as a single currency and the European Central Bank (ECB). Only these NCBs of Member States are 'integral parts'[2] of the ESCB, which includes all the NCBs of the European Union (EU), whether or not they have adopted the single currency. We will analyse this situation in the first section and try to focus on the evolution and possible changes in relation to the original conception of the Treaty.

[1] All references to the Treaty on the European Union (TEU) and to the Treaty on the Functioning of the European Union (TFEU) (in the version of the Treaty of Lisbon, entry into force 1 December 2009) are to the consolidated version, OJ, C 326, 26 October 2012, eur-lex.europa.eu/JOHtml.do?uri=OJ%3AC%3A2012%3A326%3ASOM%3AEN%3AHTML.

[2] See Article 14.4 of the Protocol to the Treaties on the EU and on the Functioning of the EU, on the Statute of the European System of Central Banks and the European Central Bank.

The second section will be dedicated to the uneasy insertion of the euro area within the complex of institutions and bodies in charge of international financial cooperation. Here also the Lisbon Treaty has introduced new provisions in the TFEU on the obligation for the euro area to speak with one voice and on the representation in international institutions and conferences. We refer to Article 138 TFEU, which up to now has received very little attention from the Member States and the institutions. The prospects of the creation of a banking union and a fiscal union, as well as meaningful advancement in economic governance, already realised or in progress, should be a stimulus for the necessary evolution in this matter.

B. The national central banks within the Eurosystem

Article 282, paragraph 1 TFEU reads as follows:

> The Europe Central Bank, together with the national central banks, shall constitute the European System of Central Banks (ESCB). The European Central Bank, together with the national central banks of the Member States whose currency is the euro, which constitute the Eurosystem, shall conduct the monetary policy of the Union.

The somewhat curious formulation of this Article means that it is the Eurosystem, i.e., both the ECB and the NCBs, which 'shall conduct the monetary policy of the Union'. This answers an opinion that the ECB addressed on 2 September 2003 to the intergovernmental conference negotiating the adoption at the time of the Treaty Establishing a Constitution for Europe – the predecessor to the Lisbon Treaty – which never entered into force.

The rest of the Article does not explain what 'conduct' really means. It is significant that the text does not use the verb 'adopt'. This would not have been in line with the other provisions of the Treaty and the Statute in general. The same Article, in particular, after having mentioned, in paragraph 2, that the ESCB shall be governed by the decision-making organs of the ECB and having listed the objectives of the system, only mentions the ECB as the decision-making organ. Furthermore, the Treaty of the European Union makes the ECB, and not the Eurosystem, an 'institution' of the EU, according to Article 13, paragraph 1 and the same Article 282 TFEU, paragraph 3, which confirms what was already provided in the Maastricht Treaty[3]: 'The European Central Bank shall

[3] The Treaty on European Union (Maastricht Treaty) of 7 February 1992, which entered into force on 1 November 1993, was published in OJ C 191, 29 July 1992. It modifies the original Treaty of Rome of 25 March 1957. This modified Treaty is referred to as the ECT.

have legal personality'. This reflects the specific nature of the ECB among the other institutions because it is not only the organ adopting the monetary policy for the euro area, but it is also a bank with the capacity to conduct financial operations and to establish relations with other financial authorities and central banks.

The verb 'conduct' in Article 282, paragraph 1, should be understood as including both the adoption of monetary policy by the ECB and its implementation with the participation of NCBs. In this way, it is understandable to speak of the Eurosystem as the 'monetary authority of the euro area', an expression used by the 'Mission Statement of the Eurosystem', a declaration adopted in January 2005 with a 'Declaration of mission of the ECB' and 'Strategic Orientations'.[4] NCBs, as such, do not participate in the adoption of monetary policy decisions. The governors of NCBs of the euro area participating in the decisions on monetary policy adopted by the Council of Governors of the NCBs are acting in conformity with the requirement of institutional independence provided by Article 130 TFEU and Article 7 of the Protocol on the Statute of the ESCB and ECB (the Statute) forbids 'any member of their [of the NCBs' or of the ECB's] decision-making bodies' to 'seek or take instructions from Community institutions or bodies, from any government of a Member State or from any other body', including the NCB chaired by the respective governors.[5] They have a personal responsibility within the Governing Council. This feature is reflected in the fact that, for monetary policy decisions, votes are not weighted in proportion to the key applicable to the subscription in the capital, like for questions related to the finances of the institution. Each Governor has one vote, be it the Governor of the Central Bank of Malta or the President of the Bundesbank, a situation which is increasingly contested in Germany[6] but which reflects the basic philosophy of the ESCB: Central Bank Governors are (independent) experts adopting monetary policy in the general interest of the Union.[7] Furthermore, if sometimes the concept of

[4] Published on the website of the ECB, www.ecb.int/home/html/index.en.html

[5] See on this point the *ECB Convergence Report 2012*, 22, www.ecb.int/pub/conrep/cr2012

[6] The Federal Republic was in favour of introducing a system of weighted votes in the decision-making organs of the ECB in charge of managing the Single Supervisory Mechanism (SSM) with the argument based on the importance of the banking sector in Germany.

[7] On the preparatory works related to this principle, see the PhD thesis of C. C. A. van den Berg, *The Making of the Statute of the European System of Central Banks. An Application of Checks and Balances* (Vrije Universiteit Amsterdam, 2004), pp. 405 ff.

a 'team' is used to qualify the Eurosystem,[8] one should realise that the ECB is not just another central bank with specific powers, it is the 'principal' or the 'captain' of the team, and there are necessarily provisions that establish this primacy. In this respect, we quote Article 14.3 of the Statute, which states that the NCBs shall act in accordance with the guidelines and instructions of the ECB; Article 14.4 which allows the Council of Governors to decide, as we will see, that functions other than ESCB ones interfere with the objectives and tasks of the ESCB; Article 32 which provides for the surveillance by the ECB of exchange operations on non-transferred reserves; and Article 35.6 which permits the ECB to appeal against an NCB before the Court of Justice for infringement of the rules of the Treaties and the Statute. All these provisions are symbolic of the central role the ECB plays.

If the NCBs' Governors are requested to act within the Governing Council as independent experts in the general interest of the Union,[9] this logic has not led the authors of the organic provisions of the NCBs to provide EU rules for the appointment of the Governors, except concerning their term of office: Article 14.2 of the Statute of the ESCB and the ECB requires that the statute of NCBs 'shall ... provide that the term of office of a Governor of a national central bank shall be no less than five years', a prescript easily circumvented by a commitment to resign before the completion of the term or an appointment being made some years before retirement age. No other rules are provided in the Statute for the appointment of Governors (or for other members of the Board of NCBs, in particular those who could deputise for the Governor for participation in the organs of the ECB), which is in strong contrast with the guarantees offered by the Statute for the relief from office of the Governor (security of tenure) including the right of the Governor concerned, and the ECB, to appeal before the Court of Justice if these rules are not respected.[10] This

[8] On the concept of 'team', see ECB, *The Eurosystem, the Union and Beyond: The Single Currency and Implications for Governance* (Frankfurt am Main, 2005) Session I, A single currency and a team of 13 central banks, pp. 9–36.

[9] This is the reason why the ECB rightly objected to a form of oath imposed on the Governor or member of the Board (Monetary Committee) of an NCB, which includes, in particular, a commitment to be faithful to their country and to fulfil their office for the benefit of their people, without taking into account and reflecting the fact that the Governor acts in a dual capacity as a member of the Monetary Council of its NCB and of the ECB's decision-making bodies, see Opinion of the ECB of 5 April 2012 on amendment to the Law on the Magyar Nemzeti Bank (CON/2012/26), point 5.3 and note (10).

[10] See Article 14.2, second sub-paragraph: 'A Governor may be relieved from office only if he no longer fulfils the conditions required for the performance of its duties or if he has been guilty of serious misconduct. A decision to this effect may be referred to the Court

difference in approach was observed, among others, by two authors[11] who underlined that 'Governors now perform a European function'. They suggested that their appointment should be 'subject to approval of the European Parliament and/or of the Council of Ministers, in analogy to the nomination of the Executive Board members'. Under Article 283, paragraph 2, second subparagraph TFEU, the Executive Board members are appointed by the European Council deciding by a qualified majority on a recommendation by the Council and after consultation of the European Parliament and the Governing Council, among persons of whom the authority and professional experience in the monetary and banking field are recognised. A number of formulas are conceivable for taking into account the European feature of NCBs' Governors, as members of the Governing Council, ranging from a veto right attributed to this body (an idea which would be resisted by Member States) to the need to consult an independent committee composed similarly to the Article 255 TFEU consultative committee, which has been acting since the entry into force of the Lisbon Treaty for the appointment of the members of the Court of Justice.[12] This committee should make sure that the candidates meet the conditions for appointment that new provisions in the Statute and the Treaty would require. Experience has shown that it is difficult for the authority in charge of the appointment to designate a person who has not received the 'green light' from such a committee.

The lack of provisions in the Treaty and the Statute regarding the criteria for the appointment of NCB Governors, which could 'Europeanise' the procedure, reflects the hesitation of the Contracting Parties to allow the interference of European rules in a decision that traditionally is seen as an important internal political act[13] and the dominant idea at the time of drafting the statute of the ESBC, that NCBs should preserve, as far as

of Justice by the Governor concerned or the Governing Council on grounds of infringement of this Treaty or of any rule of law relating to its application'.

[11] See L. Bini Smaghi and D. Gros, *Open Issues in European Central Banking* (Basingstoke: MacMillan Press and Brussels: CEPS, 2000), p. 172. See also M. J. Neumann, 'Les problèmes de l'Union monétaire européenne' in Collectif, *Du franc Poincaré à l'Écu*, (Paris: Comité pour l'histoire économique et financière de la France/IGPDE, 1993), p. 772; J.-V. Louis, 'L'Union économique et monétaire' in *Commentaire Mégret. Le droit de la CEE*, Vol. 6, 2nd edn (Éditions de l'Université de Bruxelles, 1995), p. 69. We concluded at the time on the limits of the 'communitisation' of the NCBs' Governors who remain organs of national sovereignty.

[12] See on this committee, Bo Vesterdorf, 'La nomination des juges de la Cour de justice de l'Union européenne', *Cahiers de droit européen* 47 (2011), 601–10.

[13] The idea was strongly opposed by Matthias Goldmann, Senior Research Fellow at the Max Planck Institute for Comparative Public Law and International Law (Heidelberg),

possible, their national statute. We realise the importance of this element but we are of the opinion that the qualifications and experience of future NCB Governors should weigh more heavily than considerations of national politics. The same respect for the specificities of the NCBs explains why the EU institutions did not receive under the Treaty a formal competence to harmonise the statutes of NCBs,[14] which operate under different legal forms, such as public law entities or companies limited by shares, sometimes admitting shareholders other than the state and public authorities, and which may be tasked by the legislator or the government with relatively important responsibilities. Under Article 14.4 of the Statute, NCBs may still perform non-ESCB functions, 'unless the Governing Council finds, by a majority of two thirds of the votes cast, that these interfere with the objectives and tasks of the ESCB'.[15] But, compatibility of national legislation with the Treaties and the Statute is required. Any incompatibility should be removed according to Article 131 TFEU.[16] This compatibility is one of the convergence criteria which are to be observed (legal convergence) for the adoption of the euro under Article 140 TFEU. But central bank independence (under Article 130 TFEU and Article 7 of the Statute) and confidentiality have to have already been realised for admission to the EU, as must the compatibility with a number of Treaty provisions, like, for example, the prohibition of monetary financing under Article 123 TFEU. For the adoption of the euro, NCBs' legislation should permit the 'full legal integration of NCBs into the Eurosystem', in order to allow for 'the effective operation of the Eurosystem once the Member State concerned has adopted the euro'.[17]

The lack of competence for harmonising national legislations in the EU Treaties is somewhat balanced out by the exercise of the consultative power conferred on the ECB under Article 127.4 and 282.5 TFEU.[18] The consultation bears on all proposed Union acts and all proposals for

discussant at the presentation of the paper upon which this chapter is based, whom we thank for his comments.

14 See *ECB Convergence Report 2012.*

15 It is significant that it is to the Governing Council and not to the Executive Board that such a mission is conferred.

16 See, e.g., *ECB, Convergence Report 2012*, p. 23. The obligation also covers incompatibilities with EU secondary legislation.

17 *Ibid.* p. 40.

18 There is an important body of literature on consultation. See, *inter alia*, K. Würtz, 'The Legal Framework Applicable to ECB Consultations on Community Acts', *EUREDIA* (2005), 283–327, (in particular, 290–1); A. Arda, 'Consulting European Central Bank. Legal Aspects of the Community and National Authorities' Obligations to Consult the ECB Pursuant to Article 105(4) EC' *EUREDIA* (2004), 111–52, 142–6.

regulation at national level, in its fields of competence.[19] These fields are understood broadly. One example is a relatively recent Opinion of the ECB of 5 December 2011 on fiscal responsibility (CON/2011/96).[20] The consultation was about a Slovak draft Constitutional Act on Fiscal Responsibility and, in particular, on the debt threshold. This did not prevent the ECB from giving an answer. The consultative competence constitutes an important activity for the ECB and has allowed it, without the intervention of EU legislation, to build a legal environment for NCBs. This environment evolves, in a flexible way, influenced by sometimes unforeseen events. The Opinions have often been quoted to support statements included in the Convergence reports that the ECB publishes every two years in compliance with Article 140, paragraph 1 TFEU on the preparation of the Member States with derogation to the adoption of the euro, or more often at the request of a Member State wishing to adopt the euro. In the 2012 Convergence Report, quoted above, references to views expressed in the Opinions and quotations from these Opinions had become systematic. This demonstrates the richness of the

[19] The versions of the two articles differ: in the English version of the TFEU, one finds in Article 127.4 'any *legislative* provision in its field of *competence*'; in Article 282.5, one can read 'Within the areas falling within its *responsibilities*, the ECB shall be consulted on . . . all proposals for *regulation* at national level'. In French, one reads in Article 127.4: respectively 'dans les domaines relevant de ses *compétences*' and 'tout projet de *réglementation*' and in Article 282.3: 'dans les domaines relevant de ses *attributions*' and 'sur tout projet de *réglementation* au niveau national' (author's italics). We have chosen the interpretation actually retained in practice. A Decision of the Council sets out the framework for consultation (Decision 38/415/EC of 29 June 1998 on the consultation of the European Central Bank by national authorities regarding draft legislative provisions, OJ L 189, 3 July 1998, p. 42). Article 2 of this Decision does not list exhaustively the matters which are within the competence of the ECB. Conflicts of interpretation may occur. There are approximately one hundred Opinions adopted every year. The Legal Department is in charge of the preparation of the Opinion in collaboration with interested departments and the opinion – after being submitted to the LEGCO (Legal Committee composed of legal advisers to the NCBs and chaired by the Director General of the Legal Department) and, on rare occasions, to the Executive Board – is approved by the Governing Council, or, if it concerns the legislation of a State with a derogation, the General Council of which all the ESCB Central Banks Governors are members. Both Councils decide by a written procedure, except when some Governors wish to raise the question for discussion at their meetings. The ECB has published a *Guide to Consultation of the ECB by National Authorities. Regarding Draft Legislative Provisions*, June 2005 (endorsed by the Governing Council on 17 March 2005) and a booklet on *The ECB's Advisory Role. Overview of opinions (1994–2008)*, May 2009.

[20] All the opinions are available in chronological order or in the eight main sections reflecting the fields of competence of the ECB, under the 'legal framework' section of the ECB website at: www.ecb.int/home/html/index.en.html.

corpus of doctrine elaborated by the ECB, especially on the delicate question of NCB independence. This increases the usefulness of the consultation for national legislators and allows this doctrine to be adapted in line with specific new problems. The non-consultation or other violations of the general principles on consultation (for example, the modification without new consultation of a draft submitted to consultation or the request for opinions at too short notice) by a Member State are infringements of the Treaty, which could be the object of the procedure provided by the TFEU, with the possibility for the Commission to appeal to the Court of Justice under Articles 259 and 260 TFEU. Until recently, the Commission, which is informed by an ECB annual report on the problems met in the application of the consultation procedure (like acts repeatedly adopted too quickly after the request for advice), had never started an infringement procedure for violation of the obligation for the Member States to consult the ECB on their draft regulations. The first time that the Commission started such an infringement procedure[21] was, among other grievances, in relation to measures taken by Hungary which were considered incompatible with the independence of the NCB. Either the Hungarian Government did not consult the ECB or it did not act in conformity with the procedure for consultation, for example, by amending, before the end of the consultation process, a draft law which was submitted for consultation.[22]

As we mentioned above, NCBs are the agents of the monetary policy adopted for the Eurosystem by the ECB's Governing Council. There is, under Article 119 TFEU, one single currency and one single monetary policy for the Member States that have adopted the euro. This policy has to be implemented 'in a uniform manner throughout the Member States whose currency is the euro'.[23] This requirement is often characterised under the 'one size fits all' slogan. It includes, in particular, one interest rate for the main refinancing operations and, since 1 January 2007, after

[21] See European Commission, Press Releases, MEMO/12/165, 7 March 2012. 'Hungary is . . . asked to inform the Commission and the ECB on the new procedural steps it intends to take in order to consult the ECB in a systematic and timely way on any draft legislative provision in its field of competence, including the forthcoming draft law', europa.eu/rapid/press-release_MEMO-12-165_en.htm.

[22] See Opinions of 5 December 2011 (CON/2011/96), 14 December 2011 (CON/2011/104), 5 April 2012 (CON/2012/26), 31 May 2012 (2012/43).

[23] See Guideline of the European Central Bank of 20 September 2011 on monetary policy instruments and procedures of the Eurosystem (recast) (ECB/2011/14), OJ L 331/1 14 December 2011, and in Annex I the 'General Documentation on Eurosystem monetary policy instruments and procedures', whereas (2).

a transitional stage during which there was a two-tier system, one single list of collateral.[24] Before the crisis, one noted a strong convergence in financial conditions across euro area countries and a highly integrated euro area money market. More generally there was a low level of heterogeneity in financial conditions across euro area countries. The crisis has dramatically changed this situation.[25] Mechanisms of transmission of monetary policy, i.e., 'the process through which monetary policy decisions affect the economy and the price level in particular'[26] were perturbed by the resuming heterogeneity of the financial conditions, which reflect the way euro area countries have been affected by the crisis. The ECB has adopted a number of measures called non-standard (or non-conventional) measures[27] in order to step up the intermediation between banks in a situation in which the interbank money market has been greatly impaired. On the other hand, a number of Guidelines and Decisions were taken by the ECB in order to temporarily derogate to the General Documentation with the purpose of increasing the discretion of NCBs. Examples of such measures include, in particular, the Decision of the ECB of 14 December 2011 on additional temporary measures relating to the Eurosystem refinancing operations and eligibility of collateral[28] and a Guideline of 2 August 2012[29] which relates to instruments that NCBs are not obliged to use as collateral. This latter text concerns, in particular, bonds issued by Member States under a European

[24] Article 18.1, second indent of the Statute of the ESCB and the ECB, provides that the ECB and the NCBs 'conduct credit operations with credit institutions and other market participants with lending being based on adequate collateral'. Article 18.2 provides that 'the ECB shall establish general principles for open market and credit operations carried out by itself or the national central banks, including for the announcement of conditions under which they stand ready to enter into such transactions'. The principles are part of the General Documentation, mentioned above.

[25] 'Heterogeneity in Euro Area Financial Conditions and Policy Implications', ECB, *Monthly Bulletin*, 8 (2012), 63–75.

[26] See ECB, *The Monetary Policy of the ECB* (Frankfurt am Main, 2011), p. 58.

[27] See 'The ECB's Non Standard Measures – Impact and Phasing Out', ECB, *Monthly Bulletin* 7 (2011), 55–69, www.ecb.int/pub/pdf/mobu/mb201107en.pdf, R. Lastra and J.-V. Louis, 'European Economic and Monetary Union: History, Trends and Prospects', *Yearbook of European Law* (2013), 1–150, yel.oxfordjournals.org/content/early/2013/03/27/yel.yet003.full.pdf and R. Lastra, 'The Role of Central Banks in Monetary Affairs: A comparative Perspective', Chapter 4, this volume.

[28] Decision on additional temporary measures relating to Eurosystem refinancing operations and eligibility of collateral (ECB/2011/25), OJ L 341, 22 December 2011, p. 65.

[29] Guideline of the ECB of 2 August 2012 on additional temporary measures relating to Eurosystem refinancing operations and eligibility of collateral and amending Guideline (ECB/2007/9), OJ L 218, 15 August 2012, 20.

Union/International Monetary Fund (IMF) programme or, more generally, by a Member State whose credit assessment does not meet the Eurosystem benchmark establishing its minimum requirement for high credit standards, as set out by the General Documentation. The Guideline also concerns the increase in the levels of own-use of government-guaranteed bank bonds. The NCBs have the obligation to report on the use of derogations to the General Documentation and, in some cases, to ask for prior approval of the Governing Council. In exceptional cases, the Governing Council may decide on derogation to some rule included in the Guideline. This demonstrates that, due to the crisis and the rupture of the channels of transmission of monetary policy, temporary measures provide for a margin of discretion regarding the eligibility of collateral. The traditional rules established by the General Documentation are that the eligibility of collateral does not include any selectivity element in a list of collateral which is mandatory. Under the measures necessitated by the great heterogeneity of the financial situations, these principles have ceased to be absolute. Some commentators are inclined to conclude that this means a renationalisation of monetary policy in an effort to introduce some discretion and they welcome this move because it breaks with the 'one size fits all' principle, which could be a source of moral hazard. This judgment is perhaps exaggerated because the discretion allowed to NCBs is not an unfettered one. The Governing Council is, as we have mentioned, in charge of scrutinising the measures taken under the temporary guidelines.[30] This kind of discretion and the surveillance it requires call for a Governing Council of which the members are, in the most visible way, independent and of an impeccable standing. Any suspicion that this might not be the case is counterproductive to the reputation and legitimacy of the ECB. This allows us to make the link with what was proposed earlier for improving the procedure for the appointment of NCB Governors. These recent developments give a new relevance to the debate on decentralisation within the Eurosystem which was active in its first ten years.[31] The discretion

[30] This task fully corresponds to the provisions of Article 14.3, second sentence of the Statute: 'The Governing Council shall take the necessary steps to ensure compliance with the guidelines and instructions of the ESCB, and will require that any necessary information be given to it'.

[31] The principle of decentralisation (see, *inter alia*, E. de Lhoneux, 'Decentralisation and Specialisation in the Eurosystem', *Bull. Banque centrale du Luxembourg* (2009), 144–63, www.bcl.lu/fr/publications/bulletins_bcl/Bulletin_BCL_2009_1/Chapitre_4.pdf. It responded to the choice made by the authors of the Treaty in favour of a European System of Central Banks and not for a European Central Banking System, which would

left to NCBs is requiring a strict 'pilotage' by the ECB of the use being made by the NCBs of the derogations to fundamental principles of monetary policy.

This rapid and undoubtedly incomplete inventory of some aspects of the position of the NCBs within the Eurosystem reveals the unavoidable tensions between the centre and the periphery. We have evoked in point 1 the elements that are typical of the primacy of the ECB, but it is difficult for the outsider to judge the way the ECB, and in particular its Governing Council, effectively uses these powers. Under Article 10.4 of the Statute, 'The proceedings of the meetings [of the Governing Council] shall[32] be confidential. The Governing Council may decide to make the outcome of its deliberations public'.[33] Furthermore, the Decision of the ECB of 4 March 2004 on public access to ECB documents[34] denies access to documents which would jeopardise the public interest as

have left a more modest place to the NCBs which would have become sort of branches of the ECB. It is especially applicable in the statistics field (Statute, Article 5). Two other provisions are more enigmatic. Article 9.2 of the Statute only prescribes that the tasks of the ESCB are implemented either by its own activities or through the NCBs pursuant to Articles 12.1 and 14 of the Statute. Article 12.1, 3rd subpara. states that 'To the extent deemed possible and appropriate and without prejudice to the provisions of this Article [which provide for the specific responsibilities of the Governing Council and the Executive Board regarding monetary policy], the ECB shall have recourse to the national central banks to carry out operations which form part of the tasks of the ESCB'. We have already quoted Article 14 above.

32 See Case T-590/10, *Gabi Thesing and Bloomberg Finance LP* v. *ECB*, General Court (7th chamber), Judgment of 29 November 2012.

33 In academic writings and in the European Parliament, requests were made, at the start of monetary union, for the publication of the minutes of the Governing Council and disclosure of the votes. Harsh polemics took place between Otmar Issing, member of the Executive Board of the ECB at the time and Willem Buiter, who was then a Cambridge professor of international macroeconomics but also a member of the Monetary Policy Committee of the Bank of England. See the exchange of letters between the two economists in *The Financial Times*, 21 and 22 September 1998 and the articles published as CEPR Policy Papers and also in the *Journal of Common Market Studies*, 37:2 and 3 (1999) respectively by W. Buiter, 'Alice in Euroland', 181–209 and by O. Issing, 'The Eurosystem: Transparent and Accountable or Willem in Euroland', 503–19. Apart from the question of the publicity given to documents, the article by W. Buiter includes interesting questions that are still pertinent. We should mention in this context the article by P. Magnette, '"Accountable independence"? Parliamentary Control of the ECB and the Rise of a New Democratic Model' *European Law Journal* 6 (2000) 326–40. On 1 August 2013 the President of the ECB, Mario Draghi, has announced a proposal in order to improve the communication of the Bank.

34 OJ L 80, 18 March 2004, 42. See also the Decision of the European ombudsman closing his inquiry into complaint 2016/2011/AN against the European Central Bank, www.ombudsman.europa.eu/fr/cases/decision.faces/en/11770/htlm.bookmark.

regards the monetary and economic policy of the EU or a Member State (Article 4(1) (a)). The monthly press conferences chaired by the President and the Vice President of the ECB, which are organised after each meeting of the Governing Council dedicated to monetary policy, relate only to this topic. There is an important '*face cachée*' in the activities of the Governing Council for what are surely good motives.

It is, for example, possible that the Governing Council prefers to discreetly settle possible subjects of controversy among its members than to engage in a formal procedure. Unsurprisingly, the ECB has never appealed to the Court of Justice against a member central bank under Article 35.6 of the Statute. It was decided by a memorandum of understanding (MoU) to settle disputes, if possible, by an agreement concluded either bilaterally or upon recommendation of an independent panel. This MoU on the procedures for settling disputes within the ESCB was signed on 1 May 2007. It replaces an older one.

The few remarks made above are intended to reflect the evolving integration of NCBs within the Eurosystem and the progressive Europeanisation one can observe in their functioning. They also show the limits of this process. One can observe some reluctance to recognise the qualitative move which has occurred through the building of a monetary union. This is also, and perhaps more so, the case for the external action of the Eurosystem and, more generally, of the EU in financial and monetary affairs.

C. The euro area on the global scene

The question of the expression of a single voice by the EU and later on by the Eurosystem, and its representation in international financial and monetary institutions, is an old one which has generated an abundant literature[35]

[35] Without any pretention to being exhaustive, we will mention R. S. T. Martha, 'The Fund Agreement and the Surrendering of Monetary Sovereignty', *Common Market Law Review*, 30 (1993) 749–86; R. Smits, *The European Central Bank* (The Hague: Kluwer International, 1997), pp. 443 ff.; J. Lebullenger, 'La projection externe de la zone euro' *Review trimestrielle de droit européen*, (1998) 459 ff; R. Torrent, 'Whom is the ECB Central Bank of? Reaction to Zilioli and Selmayr', 35 (1998), *Common Market Law Review*, 459 ff.; M. López Escudero, *El euro en el sistema monetario internacional* (Madrid: Tecnos, 2004); J.-V. Louis, 'L'espace euro, l'Union européenne et le FMI' *Revue d'Économie Financière* 88 (2007), 123–39; J.-V. Louis, 'The International Projection of the Euro and the International Monetary System', in M. Telò (ed.), *The European Union and Global Governance* (London-New York: Routledge, 2007), pp. 64–86; A. Ahearne and B. Eichengreen, 'External Monetary and Financial Policy

especially after the conclusion of the Maastricht Treaty (Treaty on European Union). The Rome Treaty establishing the European Economic Community (EEC Treaty) included some reference to monetary cooperation and instituted a Monetary Committee (Article 105 EEC) for this purpose, but the Bretton Woods agreements creating the IMF and the International Bank for Reconstruction and Development (IBRD) seemed to allow for the benign neglect of monetary questions by the then recently born Community. The situation changed in the early 1970s after the fall of the Bretton Woods system and with the insertion, twenty years later, of the objective of progressive realisation of an EMU in the Maastricht Treaty. An Article (Article 109, renumbered as 111 European Community Treaty (ECT), applicable only to the Member States having adopted the euro, provided for the exercise of exchange rate and external monetary policy by the European Community (para. 1 and 2), and the conclusion of monetary agreements (para. 3) as well as participation in the international scene in para. 4:

> Subject to paragraph 1 [on exchange rates regime], the Council shall, on a proposal from the Commission and after consulting the ECB, acting by a qualified majority decide on the position of the Community at international level as regards issues of particular relevance to economic and monetary union and, acting unanimously, decide its representation in compliance with the allocation of powers laid down in Articles 103 and 105.[36]

This provision presented various limitations and ambiguities. It was only related to the adoption of a position by the Community, but made no provision for a single voice expressing this position. It regarded 'issues of a particular relevance' to EMU, an expression which could give rise to different interpretations. The decision on the representation of the Community was to be submitted to unanimous vote and had to take into account the allocation of powers in the fields of economic and monetary union. This obligation was in line with the respective allocation of competences between the Member States and the institutions. This generated a controversy as to the nature of the competences of the

Review and a Proposal' in A. Sapir (ed.), *Fragmented Power: Europe and the Global Economy* (Brussels: Bruegel Books, 2007), pp. 128–55; R. Smits, 'International Representation of Europe in the area of Economic and Monetary Union' *EUREDIA* (2009), 297–333; S. Hagan '10 Years of the Euro: A Perspective from the IMF', (2009) speech at the ECB in Frankfurt am Main, www.imf.org/external/np/speeches/2009/012909.htm.

[36] Para. 1 referred to the adoption of an exchange rate regime; Article 103 ECT was the key provision on the coordination of economic policies (now, Article 121 TFEU) and Article 105 ECT related to the single monetary policy (now, Article 127 TFEU).

IMF in relation to the possible joint/single participation of the EC/EU: was it a monetary institution or, in order to qualify its nature, was it necessary to take into account the surveillance of the economic policy of its members? Lastly, the expression 'at international level' needed clarification: was the bearing of Article 111.4 limited to the single voice and the representation of the Community as a legal person or was its participation as an observer or as an actor in matters pertaining to soft law also directed by the provision?

In the field of monetary policy, the Maastricht Treaty provides for the attribution of legal personality, both internal and external, to the ECB (Article 107.2, now Article 282.3 TFEU) and Article 6 of the Statute of the ESCB and the ECB reads as follows:

> 6.1. In the field of international cooperation involving the tasks entrusted to the ESCB, the ECB shall decide how the ESCB shall be represented.
>
> 6.2. The ECB and, subject to its approval, the national central banks may participate in international monetary institutions.
>
> 6.3. Articles 6.1 and 6.2 shall be without prejudice to Article 138 of the Treaty on the Functioning of the European Union.[37]

Member States were reluctant to apply Article 111, para. 4 ECT. Despite the presentation of a proposal on this matter by the Commission, the European Council meeting at Vienna in December 1998 decided for the adoption of pragmatic procedures that were partly rejected by G-7 partners because they increased the representation of the EU by adding new participants to its delegation. The regime of representation still varies from one international institution or body to another. Weak coordination processes at the level of the EU were organised for IMF-related questions both in Brussels and in Washington. The status accorded to the EU varies from the role of observer, for the Commission or the ECB, *de facto* or under a specific regime in international institutions, to full membership in some standard-setting bodies (SSBs) and in groups like the G-20 before the crisis, where the representation was shared, depending on the body concerned, between the Council of the EU, the Commission or the ECB.

Article 6.2 of the Statute was drafted with the idea of allowing the continuation of the participation of NCBs in the Bank for International

[37] The text of Article 6.3 of the Statute before the Lisbon Treaty ended as follows: 'without prejudice to Article 111(4) of this Treaty'. The implicit limitations included in the mention of Articles 103 and 105 ECT have disappeared with the reference to Article 138 TFEU which did not provide for these limitations.

Settlements (BIS). The ECB became a shareholder of the BIS and this institution modified its Statute in order to admit what was termed in Article 56 of its Statute as an element of a 'cross-border central banking system',[38] an expression which is not uncontroversial. The ECB used its international legal personality in order to conclude technical cooperation agreements, for example, with Interpol for the fight against counterfeiting and to enter into swap agreements with other central banks, like the Federal Reserve Bank of New York. The clause 'without prejudice' in para. 3 of Article 6 of the ESCB Statute was a caveat guarding against the expansion of ECB external policy outside monetary policy, in the spirit of Article 111.4 at the time of the Maastricht Treaty. In any case, exchange rate policy clearly came under Article 111.1 ECT (now Article 219.1 TFEU), a field in which the Council was and still is preponderant under the Treaty. The ECB had no vocation to replace the EU Member States in international organisations. It received, from the beginning of the final stage of monetary union on 1 January 1999, the right to appoint an observer to the Executive Board of the IMF for a list of subjects more or less precisely defined. It plays the same role at the bi-annual meetings of the International Financial and Monetary Committee. The experience demonstrates that this role is not fully satisfactory for the expression of the ECB's views.

With the Treaty of Lisbon, Article 138 TFEU has replaced Article 111.4 ECT. It is part of a group of provisions specific to the Member States having adopted the euro. The innovations introduced by Article 138 are important. This Article fixes an objective of creating common positions: they are provided in order 'to secure the euro's place in the international monetary system', an expression that should not receive a limited interpretation. The matters addressed by the new provision are those 'of particular interest' (the expression is still there) 'for economic and monetary union' (which could be seen as an enlargement of the scope of the definition of common attitudes) and the text replaces the rather vague mention of the 'international level' in Article 111.4 ECT with the phrase 'within the competent international financial institutions and conferences'. The adoption of common positions is an obligation for the

[38] Statutes of the Bank for International Settlements (of 20 January 1930, text as amended on 27 June 2005), Article 56 (a): 'central bank means the bank or banking system in a country to which has been entrusted the duty of regulating the volume of currency and credit in that country; *or, in a cross-border central banking system, the national central banks and the common central banking institution which are entrusted with such duty.*' (author's italics) available at www.bis.org/about/statutes-en.pdf.

Council (with the vote of euro area member states) acting on a proposal by the Commission and after consulting the ECB.

Article 138.2 TFEU provides for the same procedure in order to adopt 'appropriate measures to ensure unified representation within the international financial institutions and conferences'. The main difference from para. 1 of this Article is that para. 2 is not a '*shall*' but a '*may*' provision. It is first of all an enabling clause for the EU because the realisation of the objective of 'unified representation' needs to gain the agreement of the institution concerned and be possible under its constitutional rules. These rules matter as much as the political will of its members and only these members can remove this obstacle.

The use of 'may' in lieu of 'shall' does not mean that the question is left to the political discretion of the EU institutions. The action has to be in conformity with the allocation of competences between the Member States and the EU and the new perspectives that open up with the evolution of the EMU. It does not necessarily result in a substitution of the EU for its member states but a single delegation helps when presenting common views.

The case of the IMF has to be looked at separately from the specific problems that arise with the participation of the EU in the Groups or SSBs, because of the different nature of these entities.

The situation in the organs of the IMF is characterised by an over-representation of industrialised and, more especially, European countries[39] and a fragmented representation of the EU and in particular of the euro area. Of twenty-four Executive Board members, there are eight or nine, who are 'European', whether euro area members, or EU or non-EU Executive Directors (EDs). Other euro area countries are located in constituencies led by non-euro area members, a dispersion which does not help the coordination of their positions. The relations of the EU/euro area with the IMF at present include the following:

The presence of an ECB observer in the Executive Board and in the International Monetary and Financial Committee (IMFC), the stable (2 years) chair for the group of euro area EDs, the presence of a Commission observer at the IMFC and of one of its officials in the office

[39] A. Ahearne and B. Eichengreen, 'External Monetary and Financial Policy Review and a Proposal', in *Fragmented Power: Europe and the Global Economy* (Brussels: Bruegel Books 2007), pp. 128–55; Report of High-Level Commission on Modernisation of the World Bank Group Governance, the so-called Zedillo Commission Report, October 2009, siteresources.worldbank.org/NEWS/Resources/WBGovernanceCOMMISSIONREPORT.pdf.

of an ED of a euro area country and the coordination assured within the *Eurimf* (grouping the EU Member States' EDs) in Washington, with the help of the Commission representation, as well as in Brussels through a subcommittee of the Economic and Financial Committee (SCIMF). These various links and committees do not succeed in providing euro area standpoints on each important subject. And the move towards a single chair for the euro area seems far away.

It is well known that under Article II of its Articles of Agreement,[40] the IMF is an organisation of 'countries' and does not admit international organisations as members. Furthermore, the euro area has no legal personality of its own. Among the many proposals contemplated in order to assure the representation of the euro area in the Bretton Woods institutions, the constitution of one single constituency for euro area countries was the one which appeared the least problematic, at least in principle and with regard to the rules of the IMF. One obstacle – but one which did not seem to be insuperable – is that according to Schedule E, point 4 of the Articles of Agreement, voting power of a constituency is limited to 9 per cent of the votes for the appointment of an ED. It would be a transition towards a single seat.[41] As is well known, the Fund is still in a process of reform re-launched by the G-20 Summit held in London in April 2009 under the pressure of emerging market and developing countries, which require representation that better reflects their (increasing) role in the global context. The first result of this process was achieved through the so-called Gyeongju compromise endorsed by the G-20 Summit in Seoul on 11–12 November 2010.[42]

One point of the agreement includes 'Greater representation for emerging market and developing countries at the Executive Board through two fewer advanced European chairs, and the possibility of a second alternate for all multi-country constituencies'. It was also, among other items, decided to move to an all-elected Board (no more EDs designated by single – big – countries) and to review the composition of the Board every eight years.

The entry into force of the Seoul reform is still blocked by the lack of ratification by the US. The new deadline fixed for the entry into force is

[40] Articles of Agreement of the IMF, www.imf.org/external/pubs/ft/aa/index.htm.

[41] See European Commission, Communication, *A Blueprint for a Deep and Genuine Economic and Monetary Union. Launching a European Debate*, 28 November 2012, COM(2012)777 final/2, ec.europa.eu/commission_2010-2014/president/news/archives/2012/11/pdf/blueprint_en.pdf.

[42] www.mofa.go.jp/policy/economy/g20_summit/2010-2/document.pdf.

now 1 January 2015, with the hope that for this date, the necessary ratifications would be attained. In the context of this reform, Belgium and the Netherlands decided after a long negotiation to merge the Constituencies they traditionally led.[43] For its part, Austria, which had appointed until then the alternate to the Belgian IMF ED, decided to establish a constituency of its own led in rotation by Austria, Turkey and emerging Central and Eastern European countries.[44] Each of the two new constituencies include countries which are not European or, if they are, are neither in the EU nor, of course, in the euro area. This development appears as a kind of protection against possible initiatives of bigger European countries for the implementation of the Gyeongju compromise. Whatever the short-term economic and political merits of what appears to have been a diplomatic success for those who clinched the deal, it is a step backwards for improved representation of the euro area within the IMF. It does not contribute to the definition and defence of a single attitude in external fora and seems to be in contradiction with Article 138 TFEU.

The development of groups of countries, like the G-7/G-8, G-10 and G-20 and of a number of SSBs,[45] is an important feature of the international financial system. All those groupings have in common the fact that they are not created by international treaties and they do not adopt binding decisions. There are sources of the so-called soft law, i.e. rules that are not compulsory by themselves but are not without, sometimes important, indirect legal effect.

For their part, acting as screening entities, the groups partially remedy the lack of coordination within the international system between a growing number of international institutions and specialised agencies. The SSBs are building corpuses of mostly technical 'rules' that are conceived as guidelines for national or regional legislation over which

[43] 'Réforme du FMI: la Belgique et les Pays-Bas ont conclu un accord sur la création d'une nouvelle constituante'. See www.stevenvanackere.be/fr/actua/reforme-du-fmi-la-belgique-et-les-pays-bas-ont-conclu-un-accord-sur-la-creation-d%E2%80%99une-nouvelle, 6 July 2012.

[44] 'IMF: New Central and Eastern European Constituency, www.oenb.at/en/presse_pub/aussendungen/2012/2012_q3/pa_20120711_iwf__neue_zentral-_und_osteuropaeische_stimmre_249027_page.jsp, 11 July 2012.

[45] 'Standards set out what are widely accepted as good principles, practices, or guidelines in a given area' on the website of the FSB, www.financialstabilityboard.org/cos/standards.htm. On SSBs, see in particular the works of Mario Giovanoli mentioned in 'The International Monetary and Financial Architecture – Some Institutional Aspects', Chapter 3, this volume.

they exercise a noteworthy influence. The standards adopted are becoming the universal references for good practice, for example in financial markets, insurance, and accountancy, among others.

The status of the EU within the groups has evolved over time. The Vienna European Council (1998) decided that it would be for the president of the Council of Economic and Financial Affairs ministers (ECOFIN) if the country having the six-month presidency has adopted the euro and the president of the Eurogroup,[46] if the country has not adopted the euro, who would represent the EC/EU with the president of the ECB at the G-7 at the rank of finance minister and governors of central banks. The president of the Commission regularly attends the G-7/G-8 summits. When the G-20 was created in 1999, it was decided that the ECOFIN President and the ECB President would represent the EC/EU. Since the Ottawa Summit (2010), the President of the European Council and the President of the Commission have represented the EU at the G-20 Summits. These representations are additional to those of the EU Member States who are members of the Group: the so-called G-4 (Germany, France, Italy and the UK) for the G-7/G-8 and G-20 (Spain and the Netherlands were invited to the first summits). EU coordination is organised before G-20 meetings, at the level of the European Council or at both the G-4 and European Council levels. The EU delegation is not the speaker for the G-4 countries and the expression of diverse standpoints or nuances on sensitive subjects does not seem to be excluded.

The Commission and the ECB are members of other bodies like the very influential Financial Stability Board (FSB). The Charter[47] of the FSB proclaims, on the one hand that 'This Charter is not intended to create any legal rights or obligations' (Article 23 on 'legal effect') and, on the

[46] Informally created at the beginning of the final stage of the monetary union, the existence of a Eurogroup where finance ministers of the countries with the euro as their currency is recognised in Article 137 TFEU and a Protocol has also been added to the Treaty regarding this informal organ. At present, the Treaty on Stability, Coordination and Governance in the EMU (signed on 2 March 2012 by twenty-five member states, still in the process of ratification) has established (Article 12) a Summit of the Euro Area composed of the heads of state and government of the contracting parties of which the euro is the currency with the participation of the President of the European Commission, the President of the ECB being invited to take part in the meetings. As for the Eurogroup, the 'institutionalisation' does not make it into an organ with decision-making power. Both will remain 'informal', www.european-council.europa.eu/home-page/highlights/treaty-on-stability,-coordination-and-governance-signed?lang=en.

[47] www.financialstabilityboard.org/publications/r_120619c.pdf.

other hand, it lists the 'commitments of Members', which include the implementation of international financial standards, periodic peer reviews, implementation monitoring of agreed commitments and FSB periodic reports 'on the degree of adherence by the Members to these commitments and the evaluation process' (Article 6). This adherence is part of the scrutiny in the Financial Sector Assessment Programs (FSAP) of the IMF and World Bank, which includes a chapter on the Reports on the Observance of Standards and Codes (ROSC). It may also be a criterion for the IMF's decision on a request for financial assistance. The adherence to standards adopted by the Basel Committee on Banking Supervision, one of the most famous SSBs, is submitted by the Committee to a review process. Recently the EU had a negative review of the way it implements the rules of Basel 3 on capital requirement. As in other committees, a number of EU member states' financial authorities participate with the Commission and the ECB, apparently without, at least systematically, speaking with a single voice on a common position. This is not in conformity with Article 138 TFEU which does not limit the discipline it imposes to institutions with regulatory power or for the negotiation of legally binding agreements. The development of the banking union with all its components[48] as is being undertaken within the euro area, and which will possibly also be extended to some non-euro area member states, underscores the necessity of complying with these requirements. It will first be necessary to find formulas which will reconcile the defence of the general interests of the euro area/EU with the expertise of national specialists. There is a stark contrast between the way the IMF and the G-20 are increasingly considering the euro area as a unit and the attitudes of a number of EU Member States which are not prepared to face all the consequences of their participation in a monetary union.

It is noteworthy that the European Commission has included in its recent blueprint for a deep and genuine economic and monetary union

[48] See Report, 'Towards a Genuine Economic and Monetary Union', 26 June 2012, ec.europa.eu/economy_finance/focuson/crisis/documents/131201_en.pdf, and the Declaration of the Heads of State and Government of the Euro Area of 29 June 2012, www.consilium.europa.eu/uedocs/cms_data/docs/pressdata/en/ec/131359.pdf. The EU has engaged in a process of building a banking union, a fiscal union, increased economic union and elements of political union (greater legitimacy and democracy). The banking union includes a Single Supervisory Mechanism (SSM) with a single rule book for banking, a centralised resolution mechanism and a centralised deposit guarantee. This will necessarily have repercussions for external action.

an Annex related to the 'External representation of the euro area' which includes proposals for the short-term and the long-term vision of a single seat at the IMF for the euro area.[49]

D. Conclusion

If a word of conclusion to the preceding comments is needed, we would point to the fact that EMU has contributed perhaps more than expected to 'Europeanising' NCBs although some further progress is still possible and indeed desirable.[50] A European model of central banks has developed. Originally, there was a natural insistence on the dual nature of NCBs, as part of the system and as national institutions.[51] The evolution of the system has demonstrated how deep the involvement of NCBs was in the tasks of the Eurosystem and the importance of the loyalty of central banks and their Governors to the system. This loyalty is a condition for maintaining credibility.[52]

The Lisbon Treaty has allowed for important provisions which could substantially enhance the role of the EU as an international actor. Much resistance has to be overcome, but it is to be hoped that the move towards a banking union, a fiscal union and new and important progress in the field of economic union will contribute to a better international projection for the euro area.

[49] See European Commission Communication. A Blueprint for a Deep and Genuine Economic and Monetary Union. Launching a European Debate, 28 November 2012, Annex 2.

[50] P. Athanassiou, 'Reflections on the Modalities for the Appointment of NCB Governors', *European Law Review*, 39:1 (2014), 27–46.

[51] See R. Lastra, 'The Division of Responsibilities between the European Central Bank and the National Central Banks within the European System of Central Banks', *Columbia Journal of European Law*, 6:2 (2000), 167–80.

[52] A message which seems not always to be fully understood. See 'Debt Crisis: Central Bank Action is Work of the Devil, says Germany's Jens Weidmann', www.telegraph.co.uk/finance/financialcrisis/9551348/Debt-crisis-central-bank-action-is-work-of-the-devil-says-Germanys-Jens-Weidmann.html, 18 September 2012; 'Bundesbank wäre für Euro-Crash gut gerüstet', www.welt.de/wall-street-journal/article109292889/Bundesbank-waere-fuer-Euro-Crash-gut-geruestet.html, 18 September 2012.

PART II

Specific policy issues in monetary affairs

6

Global governance of international competitiveness spillovers

BERNARD HOEKMAN

A. Introduction

Competitiveness concerns are front and centre in the economic sections of newspapers around the world. Improving competitiveness is a key objective for policy-makers in Europe but is equally central in policy debates in the US.[1] Many of the concerns are driven by monetary and macroeconomic policies that are pursued by countries. Numerous high-income countries face an urgent need to reduce public sector deficits and pay down high debt burdens that increased rapidly following the 2008 financial crisis. In part this will require an increase in net exports – which is only possible if the countries concerned are able to produce goods and services that are 'competitive' on world markets. The extent to which this can happen will depend primarily on economic policy reforms implemented by the countries concerned. A complicating factor is that such measures will be (or are being) taken by many countries, so that whatever a government seeks to do to improve the competitiveness of firms based in its own territory may be offset to a greater or lesser extent by actions that are taken in other countries. The policies that governments pursue may generate negative international pecuniary spillovers.[2] The

I am grateful to Petros Mavroidis, Jose Guilherme Reis and Anirudh Shingal for helpful comments. This chapter draws in part on presentations made at the Banque de France/ CEPII/PSE conference, 'After the Collapse, the Reshaping of Trade' Paris, 26 May 2011; the APEC SOM2 meeting on Structural Reform, Big Sky, Montana, 16 May 2011; and the VIIIth Symposium on International Trade, American University, Washington, DC, 17 October 2012.

[1] M. Porter and J. Rivkin, 'The Looming Challenge to US Competitiveness,' *Harvard Business Review*, 90:3 (2012), 54–61.

[2] A pecuniary spillover refers to the monetary equivalent value of the effect of an action by one entity on another.

effect of economic policies and regulatory measures implemented by a given jurisdiction on the firms located in other jurisdictions has long been the focus of debate and controversy. Actual or perceived spillover effects may motivate reactive (retaliatory) policies and become the focus of efforts to negotiate agreed rules of the game.

An influential strand of the economic theory of trade agreements is premised on the notion that the motivation for governments to negotiate trade agreements is to internalise the pecuniary externalities that are created by the unilateral use of trade-related policies that affect the terms of trade. The set of such policies is large, and extends well beyond the traditional focus of trade negotiators on tariffs and quotas that are applied at the border. While economists view trade agreements and international cooperation as driven by terms of trade externalities and/or political economy factors (trade agreements as commitment mechanisms), politicians, business people and civil society more generally often tend to frame concerns regarding the effects of policy measures taken by foreign countries in terms of their impact on the competitiveness of national industry. Abstracting from the current economic challenges confronting countries with unsustainable debt burdens and government budget deficits, competitiveness is a key focus of policy debates the world over, reflecting the recognition that in open societies the survival and growth of firms – and thus the creation of employment opportunities for the workforce – depends on their ability to increase their productivity. Many policies may affect the competitiveness of firms, either directly, or more frequently, indirectly.

'Competitiveness concerns' have been a staple feature of efforts to cooperate on economic policies, especially in the context of trade agreements and formal economic integration efforts. Indeed, one driver of such agreements has been the desire to 'level the playing field' for firms located in the participating countries. A recurring conundrum has been what policies to include; what should remain sovereign and what should become subject to common disciplines. During the period leading to the creation of the European Economic Community (EEC), Jelle Zijlstra, the Dutch Minister of Economic Affairs, argued that tariff removal also required 'common policies on taxes, wages, prices and employment policy'[3] in order for firms to have a level playing field. Similarly, the Belgian coal mining industry argued in the late 1940s that a common

[3] A. Milward, *The European Rescue of the Nation State* (Berkeley, CA: University of California Press, 1992), p. 188.

market could only be accepted if German wage and social security costs were raised to Belgian levels. French officials persistently demanded policy harmonisation in the social area – equal pay for both sexes, a uniform working week – as a precondition for trade liberalisation (French standards in this area were higher than in other countries).[4]

The European Union (EU) is the most far-reaching economic integration initiative extant involving sovereign states. Many policy areas that are excluded from shallower trade agreements are covered. Members of the European Monetary Union (the eurozone) have attained the deepest level of integration among EU Member States. Notwithstanding the depth of the European integration effort, however, there are very large differences in the competitiveness of firms and industries between EU member states. Indeed, these differences are a key factor in the unfurling of the ongoing eurozone crisis. The same is true for countries that are not parties to integration agreements – and in practice, notwithstanding the large number of preferential trade agreements (PTAs) that are in force, much global trade takes place between countries that do not have PTAs. Bilateral trade between the EU, the US, Japan and China does not occur under the auspices of PTAs as none of these four entities have a PTA with each other. These stylised facts suggest that there exists substantial scope for countries to pursue greater cooperation ('deep integration'), but the example of the EU and the eurozone illustrates that moving down this path – even if it proves to be feasible – will not necessarily remove or address competitiveness concerns.

Different approaches can be envisaged for dealing with (perceived) cross-border negative pecuniary spillovers created by policies in addition to reactive domestic policies. International law is one option. Others include 'soft law' forms of bilateral or multilateral cooperation and delegation to independent entities that are given a transparency and analysis mandate – e.g., tasked with assessing whether and how large any negative spillovers are. In many cases there will be significant uncertainty as to what the *net* effects of policies are, taking into account the *overall* impact of the relevant policy measures that have a bearing on firm-level competitiveness. A precondition for agreement on binding international rules is a shared recognition that the negative spillovers associated with a policy (or set of policies) are significant and that a specific set of disciplines will result in greater efficiency (lower costs). At present there is no such recognition when it comes to important policy

[4] B. Hoekman and M. Kostecki, *The Political Economy of the World Trading System* (Oxford University Press, 2009)

areas that generate negative competitiveness spillovers. One implication is that countries need to work towards putting in place the preconditions for stronger forms of international cooperation – by improving the transparency of applied policies; supporting independent analysis of the effects of policies; and establishing mechanisms through which governments can consult and exchange information.

B. Competitiveness and its determinants

The term 'competitiveness' is widely used and many definitions have been suggested. Economists tend to take the view that competitiveness is a notion that applies at the level of an enterprise, whereas many commentators and pundits apply the concept to territories – cities, provinces, regions and nations. Krugman has argued forcefully that the concept should not be applied to nations.[5] Countries do not compete, firms do, and a focus on competitiveness at the national level can very easily result in an incorrect and perverse zero-sum view of international exchange.[6] Firms compete in global markets, with some firms winning (expanding their profits and growing) at the expense of other firms that lose market share, are forced to contract and may go bankrupt. At the firm level there are winners and losers, but for countries as a whole the competitive process is welfare-enhancing. That said, it is important for policy-makers to take a nation-level perspective of competitiveness because locational factors help shape firm-level competitiveness (positively or negatively) by determining the availability and cost of production inputs and the operating and transactions costs. Competitiveness is the result of firms exploiting the sources of comparative advantage that prevail in a given location, many of which are endogenous in the sense of being the result of economic policies and institutions that have been put in place over time.

Analysts often equate a country's competitiveness with the real exchange rate (and changes in the real exchange rate over time), usually defined as the relative price of a basket of goods in two countries (consumer price index) or relative unit labour costs.[7] Another frequently used indicator is the

[5] P. Krugman, 'Competitiveness: A Dangerous Obsession,' *Foreign Affairs*, 73:2 (1994), 28–44.

[6] P. De Grauwe, 'Introduction,' in P. De Grauwe (ed.), *Dimensions of Competitiveness* (Cambridge, MA: MIT Press, 2010), pp. ix–xvi.

[7] A. Boltho, 'The Assessment: International Competitiveness', *Oxford Review of Economic Policy*, 12:3 (1996), 1–16.

(trend in) market (export) shares for a country.[8] Neither of these variables is necessarily informative about the determinants of either the level of or the changes in the indicators used, which is of course the key question for policy. Many factors can affect relative unit labour costs and the evolution of market share. The most broadly accepted definition of aggregate national competitiveness is total factor productivity.[9] Delgado *et al.* define what they term foundational competitiveness as the expected level of output per working-age individual (i.e., potential workers as opposed to those actually employed) given the overall quality of a country as a place to do business.[10] The rate of increase in productivity determines the rates of return on investment, which in the aggregate determine economic growth rates in the longer run – the ability to generate greater output from any given supply of inputs. In such a longer-run perspective, competitiveness will be a function of the ability of firms to allocate and deploy resources to the most productive, highest valued activities. This in turn will depend on the feasibility and cost of reallocating and redeploying resources, with more productive firms expanding and others contracting or closing down. There is growing evidence that productivity differences *within* national industries is a major factor in determining cross-country differences in productivity[11] and that the performance of services sectors plays an important role in this respect.[12] One implication is that competitiveness will be a function of the efficiency of product, labour and capital markets, as well as of macroeconomic policies and the availability and quality of public goods provided by governments (e.g., infrastructure, security of property rights).

In an extensive empirical analysis and survey of the literature, Delgado *et al.* highlight three interrelated drivers of national competitiveness: (i) 'social infrastructure' and political institutions, (ii) macroeconomic policy, and (iii) the microeconomic environment (including the business climate broadly defined to encompass factor markets,

[8] E.g., M. Del Gatto, F. di Mauro, J. Grube and B. Mandel, 'The Structural Determinants of the US Competitiveness in the Last Decades: A "Trade-Revealing" Analysis', *ECB Working Paper* 1443 (2012).

[9] M. Porter, *The Competitive Advantage of Nations* (New York: Free Press, 1990).

[10] M. Delgado, C. Ketels, M. Porter and S. Stern, 'The Determinants of National Competitiveness', *NBER Working Paper* No. 18249 (2012).

[11] See C. Syverson, 'What Determines Productivity?' *Journal of Economic Literature*, 49:2 (2011), 326–65 and C. Altomonte, T. Aquilante and G. Ottaviano, *The Triggers of Competitiveness: The EFIGE Cross-country Report* (Brussels: Bruegel, 2012).

[12] J. Francois and B. Hoekman, 'Services Trade and Policy', *Journal of Economic Literature*, 48:3 (2010), 642–92.

product market contestability, trade openness, physical infrastructure and the sophistication of company operations and strategy).[13] All three are found to be significant drivers of competitiveness, but the last is argued to be most important in that it has the greatest impact on firm-level productivity. The other two broad drivers are economy-wide in their impact – affecting all firms or broad groups of firms similarly. The business/microeconomic environment, in contrast, may have very differentiated impacts by influencing the ability of entrepreneurs to start new activities and the ease of expanding and contracting economic operations. Moreover, the relevant variables can be influenced by numerous actors, including municipal or regional governments, as opposed to primarily being determined by the central government as is the case for macroeconomic and monetary policy.

The approach taken by Delgado *et al.* is very broad, spanning a large number of the relevant variables that affect competitiveness. Efforts to determine what matters from a narrower trade perspective tend to take institutional and macroeconomic framework conditions as given and focus on policy areas that can be changed in the short run. The World Bank, for example, has developed a trade competitiveness policy toolkit that centres on three broad areas: economic policies that affect overall incentives; factors affecting operating costs; and policies that may be used to address national market failures (Figure 6.1).

Figure 6.1. Three pillars of trade competitiveness

[13] Delgado *et al.*, 'The Determinants of National Competitiveness'.

In operationalising this framework the focus is on:

(i) *the incentive framework for trade*: anti-export biases created by trade and tax policy; the regulatory environment and investment climate faced by firms; and external market access conditions;
(ii) *factor inputs and trade costs*: labour markets, skills and the sophistication of management, accessibility and cost of production inputs, capital equipment, utilities, finance and business services, as well as trade logistics and transport services; and
(iii) *proactive trade promotion policies*: the capacity, incentives and institutions that impact on innovation processes, standards and certification systems, and export and investment promotion mechanisms, including special customs regimes and economic zones, clusters and sector-specific support (industrial policy).[14]

Note that this narrower focus on the determinants of *trade* competitiveness still spans a large number of policy areas, illustrating the challenge of identifying, let alone agreeing on, an international framework to 'govern' the use of policies that impact on competitiveness.

C. Competitiveness drivers and international spillovers

The empirical literature on competitiveness and its determinants is informative as it helps to identify policies that impact on competitiveness. At the same time a problem from an international law or rule-making perspective is that almost anything can matter for competitiveness. The challenge is to determine what types of policies create the greatest negative pecuniary spillovers and where there is scope for international coordination to improve outcomes for all participating countries. The empirical literature suggests that the microeconomic environment is key,[15] whereas the centre of attention in policy debates on competitiveness spillovers is often on macroeconomic variables such as monetary policy, intervention in the foreign exchange market or allegations that countries target recurring current account surpluses that in turn result in large global imbalances. Macroeconomic policies will shift incentives for the whole distribution of firms located in a country as opposed to targeting or affecting the

[14] See J. G. Reis and T. Farole, *Trade Competitiveness Diagnostic Toolkit* (Washington, DC: World Bank, 2012).

[15] See Altomonte *et al.*, *The Triggers of Competitiveness* and Delgado *et al.*, 'The Determinants of National Competitiveness'.

growth of the most productive and innovative firms. Macroeconomic policy can have major impacts on export performance and economic growth and development in low-income countries with distorted domestic markets, but the literature on competitiveness suggests that good macroeconomic policy is a necessary, but alone not a sufficient, condition for competitiveness. What matters more (most) from an overall productivity growth perspective is the *micro*economic incentive framework.

I. *Macroeconomic policies*

Macroeconomic policies may generate negative spillovers if a country is large enough to affect world prices and/or interest rates. The export-driven growth strategy that has been pursued by China with great success is often claimed to be a case in point, with critics arguing that China has pursued a policy mix that targets an undervalued exchange rate, subsidising its exports to the detriment of employment in other countries.[16] Exchange rates have often been the source of economic tension between trading partners. Countries that are running large current account deficits – that import much more than they export – frequently claim that surplus countries are 'unfairly' manipulating the exchange rate so as to give their exporters a competitive advantage – increasing the domestic prices of imports and reducing the foreign currency denominated export prices. In the 1980s such claims were frequently made against Japan and the Asian 'tigers'; in the 2000s it was the turn of China to bear the brunt of such complaints.

A depreciation of the exchange rate can be equivalent to a combination of raising import tariffs for all traded goods and providing local firms with an across-the-board export subsidy. Governments have long been concerned with the possibility that a trading partner might pursue policies to engineer a depreciation of the exchange rate so as to undo trade liberalisation commitments negotiated in trade agreements. Such concerns have become particularly prominent in recent years as a result of the build-up of large current account surpluses and foreign exchange reserves by a number of countries, especially China. Perceptions that exchange rates are being manipulated can generate pressures for protection by businesses facing competition on both their home and export

[16] F. Bergsten and J. Gagnon, 'Time for a Fightback in the Currency Wars', (2012) www.iie.com/publications/opeds/oped.cfm?ResearchID=2207.

markets. More generally, large swings in exchange rates can also have major impacts on the debt service levels of countries that have borrowed in the affected currencies, giving rise to fiscal pressures. The rise in the US dollar in the 1980s was a factor in the debt crisis of that time and affected both debt restructuring and the required increase in net exports by borrowers.

Maintaining a competitive real exchange rate is important for economic growth, but the national welfare case for targeting the exchange rate is premised on tradable sectors suffering disproportionately from market failures. Whether this is true is an empirical matter. The extent to which undervaluation will 'work' in expanding net exports will depend on many factors, including the behaviour of nominal wages (if these increase, the competitive impact will be undone); the ability of the monetary authorities to control inflationary effects (which can generate macroeconomic instability with associated costs that far outweigh the temporary advantages given to exportables); the extent to which firms rely on imported inputs (in an increasingly supply-chain-driven world, a tax on imports is a direct tax on exports that embody the imports – so that the competiveness effects of a depreciation will be offset the higher the degree of integration into global value chains and/or the import dependence of firms); the degree to which exporters hedge against foreign exchange risk; and the currency in which they invoice their products. All these factors matter for the effectiveness of the policy for the country pursuing it, and thus for any assessment of the extent to which there are negative spillovers for other countries.

II. Assessing spillover effects

Deliberate policy intervention that aims at lowering the exchange rate can generate negative international competitiveness spillovers for competing exporting firms, but this is not the case for policies and institutions that incentivise firms to improve productivity performance. As mentioned above, there is a large set of policies and institutions that have a bearing on productivity growth (competitiveness). Countries that put in place an appropriate enabling microeconomic environment – such as an innovation regime that encourages investment in human capital and R&D; a financial system that provides firms with access to start-up equity capital and funding for expansion; actions to enhance competition on services markets so as to reduce the cost of services inputs and increase quality; corporate governance mechanisms that reward performance; and an open trade and investment regime – will presumably experience higher productivity growth rates and generate more competitive firms that grow market share internationally. However, this does not constitute a negative spillover. The same is true for more fundamental determinants of national competitiveness that will take longer to change such as public health and educational attainment, or for factors that cannot be changed – such as location and natural endowments.

Whether major negative spillover effects are associated with specific policies is an empirical matter. In cases where there are negative pecuniary spillovers, a key issue is to disentangle intent from effects. To revert to the case of deliberate undervaluation of the exchange rate, this can be one element of a policy aimed at stimulating economic growth by increasing the profitability of the tradable sector in contexts where firms face a bad investment climate and high operating costs as a result of domestic distortions.[17] If there are also positive externalities associated with expanding the exports of manufactures, measures such as currency depreciation may be welfare-improving for the country concerned as well as for the world as a whole.[18] Freund and Pierola find that significant increases in manufactured exports that are sustained for at least seven years (what they call export surges) in many developing countries were often preceded by a real devaluation of the exchange rate.[19] This generates not just an expansion in existing exports but also enables entry into new export products and new markets. The latter are important, accounting for 25 per cent of export growth during the surge in developing countries. The authors argue that maintaining a competitive currency leads firms to expand the product and market space for exports, inducing a considerable reorientation of the tradable sector.[20]

The cost and quality of numerous services inputs will affect the competitiveness of firms, as services are important elements of production and transactions costs. The costs of services may be increased as a

[17] D. Rodrik, 'The Real Exchange Rate and Economic Growth', *Brookings Papers on Economic Activities*, No. 2 (2008), 365–412.

[18] M. Eden and H. Nguyen, 'Correcting Real Exchange Rate Misalignment: Conceptual and Practical Issues', *World Bank Policy Research Working Paper* 6045 (2012).

[19] C. Freund and D. Pierola, 'Export Surges: The Power of a Competitive Currency,' *World Bank Policy Research Working Paper* 4750 (2008).

[20] Disentangling the two can be very difficult in practice, in that the objective of a policy may be to offset an externality, but the instrument used goes beyond what is needed to do so.

result of limited competition that allows prices to reflect significant markups over costs. Actions to reduce these excess costs and improve quality will enhance the competitiveness of firms located in the markets concerned, with an aggregate effect that is akin to a depreciation of the real exchange rate. If it is difficult to address the various distortions in an economy that give rise to excess costs for firms, it may be more straightforward to seek to depreciate the exchange rate as a way of offsetting (some of) the excess operating costs. There are many market failures that can have a negative effect on competitiveness of firms. A common example is credit constraints for small and medium-sized firms – e.g., lack of financing for investment in new technology or new business lines – that prevent upgrading and the production of higher value-added products. While policy interventions should be targeted at the source of market failures, in the interim 'compensating measures', such as maintaining an undervalued exchange rate, may help firms to exploit their competitive advantages.

Much can be learned from successful countries concerning what types of policies and institutions matter, but the fact that some countries do better than others is not a justification for the latter to argue that the actions put in place by the former are detrimental. To the contrary – higher productivity performance and growth in successful nations creates greater economic opportunities for all countries, as long as markets are open. Less dynamic countries that are not able to put in place an incentive framework that supports competitiveness may have lower growth and gross domestic product (GDP) per capita, but that is the result of their own implicit or explicit choices. This is not to deny that policies that target specific industries or firms can generate negative international spillovers. However, the policies and institutional factors identified in the literature as drivers of competitiveness are not sector- or product-specific but focus on activities that are 'general inputs' into productivity growth. Common examples would be designing the tax regime so as to generate incentives for investments in R&D and actions to ensure (greater) availability of finance and venture capital, as well as measures to ensure that markets are contestable so as to facilitate expansion by dynamic firms into new activities and to enable them to grow.

D. Some implications for international cooperation

Generally applicable regulation and other government policies that affect relative prices for firms will affect competitiveness. But for there to be a case for seeking to agree on international rules there need to be spillovers – terms of trade externalities – or coordination failures that result in prisoner's dilemma-type inefficient outcomes. There also needs to be clarity on the policies that generate the externalities – it is not enough to point to outcomes such as current account surpluses or large bilateral trade imbalances as these can be the result of many factors of a structural nature as well as policies. As discussed below, this is a major problem when it comes to thinking about what rules might be appropriate and what remedy to apply in cases where such rules are being violated. Thus, international cooperation may be difficult to achieve. Even if specific policies can be identified, coordination or harmonisation may not enhance national economic welfare, especially if specific outcomes (e.g., current account balances) reflect aggregate savings and investment behaviour and/or differences between countries in social preferences, demographics and so forth.

In many of the policy areas that are the focus of attention in 'competitiveness' debates, differences in policies – e.g., with respect to labour standards, social security or similar forms of regulation, including competition policies (antitrust) – may not affect the ability of firms to compete on world markets. If firms in 'high labour standards' countries can ensure that the incidence of the implicit tax is borne by workers – that is, that the workforce pays for the resulting benefits through lower wages – labour costs may be unaffected.[21] Moreover, insofar as the cost-raising effects of workers' rights cannot be fully shifted to workers, the resulting increase in product prices (due to higher costs) will put pressure on the exchange rate (because foreign demand for exports falls as prices increase, all other things being equal). The resulting depreciation will lower the standard of living by raising the cost of imports. While the whole economy thus bears the burden of the higher standards, the exchange rate adjustment allows firms to continue to compete on world markets. As long as the labour standards or other social regulation in force reflect the desires of citizens, the costs of implementation simply reflect the trade-off between monetary and non-monetary wealth that society has made.[22]

[21] R. Ehrenberg, *Labor Markets and Integrating National Economies* (Washington, DC: Brookings Institution, 1994).

[22] These issues were analysed in depth by scholars in the 1990s – see, e.g., J. Bhagwati and R. Hudec (eds.), *Harmonization and Fair Trade: Prerequisite for Free Trade?* (Cambridge, MA: MIT Press, 1996) and R. Lawrence, A. A. Bressand and T. Ito, *A Vision for the World Economy: Openness, Diversity, and Cohesion* (Washington, DC: Brookings Institution, 1996).

What matters for rule-making is not just whether there are clear (agreed) policy-specific externalities and coordination failures but also whether an agreement can be enforced. The dispute settlement system of the General Agreement on Tariffs and Trade (GATT)/World Trade Organization (WTO) has been a major factor motivating suggestions that the WTO should be expanded to include more disciplines on policies that (are claimed to) impact on competitiveness. Thus the ability of dispute settlement to deal effectively with conflicts is another criterion to take into account when considering binding international rules in an area.[23]

The WTO and regional trade agreements tend to focus on discrimination at the level of a product or a sector. Even where there are rules that discipline the use of general policies – such as the ban on export subsidies or quotas – the application of such policies is generally specific to a product or a sector. Much of the debate on competitiveness revolves around policies that are general in the sense that they affect production costs or relative prices – such as the (real) exchange rate – or affect the dynamics and potential growth performance of an economy as a whole. As noted above, the literature suggests that the key driver of competitiveness in the longer term is the microeconomic incentive framework – the investment climate/business environment broadly defined. If this is dealt with ineptly, there is a good case in the short run for targeting the (real) exchange rate to offset the associated disincentives. This is not a longer term solution of course. There is a need to address the various distortions and/or disincentives directly, and this needs to be pursued in parallel (and will of course in turn be reflected in the evolution of the real exchange rate). Whether the concern is a product-specific policy or more general economic policies that impact on the real exchange rate, the key to international cooperation is that there is a terms of trade externality or coordination failure. The solution to the former may be binding international rules, while the latter type of problem may be more effectively addressed through other forms of cooperation.

What follows is a discussion of several policy areas that seem particularly germane from a competitiveness perspective: macroeconomic

[23] There are different dimensions to this but a key one is that trade remedies (import protection) need to be effective in dealing with the effects of the policies that are deemed to violate a WTO commitment. See K. Maskus, 'Regulatory Standards in the WTO: Comparing Intellectual Property Rights with Competition Policy, Environmental Protection, and Core Labor Standards', *World Trade Review* 1:2 (2002), 135–52.

policies that have an impact on trade and microeconomic policies that promote or support the allocation of resources to dynamic and/or innovative firms.

I. *Macroeconomic policies*

Misaligned exchange rates ('currency manipulation') can cause negative spillovers and thus international cooperation could in principle be globally welfare improving. Defining the specific international disciplines that would result in such improvements is extremely difficult, however, in part because it may not be clear whether there is in fact a significant negative spillover, and if so, what the appropriate remedy is. As has been discussed in depth in the literature on this subject there may be very good reasons why exchange rates diverge from 'equilibrium' levels for long periods and which have nothing to do with a desire to circumvent market access commitments. Nor is undervaluation necessarily a reflection of deliberate attempts to engage in beggar-thy-neighbour, mercantilist behaviour aimed at generating large trade surpluses. It is important to recognise that current account balances reflect the difference between aggregate savings and investment in a country, and that these variables are driven by many factors such as demographics, the financial system, social preferences, investment opportunities and the pension regime. Seeking rules on maximum allowable global current account surpluses over a given period of time, or on the extent to which the real exchange rate can deviate from its 'equilibrium rate' over a given period, would constitute significant intrusion into economic policy in that it implies a need to commit to a willingness to intervene to change savings and investment rates and to second guess WTO members' social policies and preferences. It would also imply a major shift away from the approach that has been pursued to date in international trade cooperation by targeting outcomes as opposed to agreeing to disciplines on specific policies that generate spillovers.

Given that the IMF cannot force governments to adjust exchange rates – it can only advise – there have been suggestions that the WTO members should agree to stronger rules in this area that can be enforced through dispute settlement. At the moment, the WTO does not provide this possibility, other than through GATT Article XV. This calls for WTO members to cooperate and consult with the IMF on matters relating to foreign exchange reserves, the balance of payments and exchange rate issues. It states that the Contracting Parties and the IMF 'may pursue a coordinated policy with regard to exchange questions' and that contracting parties 'shall not, by exchange action, frustrate the intent of the provisions of the GATT'. The existence of the IMF helps in understanding why the GATT/WTO disciplines are not very specific: it is left to the IMF to address exchange rate misalignments.

Mattoo and Subramanian argue that if there is a clear finding of undervaluation and if this is clearly due to government action, this should be regarded as fully equivalent to a violation of import tariff bindings and the ban on export subsidies.[24] They recognise that undervaluation can result from a number of factors, including fiscal and monetary policies, policies related to capital flows, taxes and subsidies, and intervention in foreign exchange markets, but argue that there is a clear hierarchy of policy actions in terms of proximate causation. Prolonged one-way intervention in foreign exchange markets by the central bank or by government and quasi-government agencies, redenomination of domestic debt into foreign currency, and extensive forward market operations are policy actions that can clearly be identified as causes of undervaluation. In such cases, they propose that countries bring cases to the WTO, with the IMF – as is already the case when members invoke the GATT balance of payments articles – being tasked to assess whether the member's exchange rate is misaligned and whether this is a consequence of government action. Thorstensen *et al.* and De Lima-Campos and Gaviria have argued that WTO members should launch countervailing duty investigations against currency manipulators, defined as countries with sustained exchange rate levels that are greatly depreciated as compared to the levels that applied when tariff concessions were negotiated.[25] Gagnon argues that WTO rules should be reformed to facilitate the use of import tariffs on the exports of countries found to be currency manipulators.[26]

[24] A. Mattoo and A. Subramanian, 'Currency Undervaluation and Sovereign Wealth Funds: A New Role for the World Trade Organization', *World Economy* 32 (2009), 1135–64.

[25] One problem in pursuing this suggestion is that the WTO requires subsidies to involve a financial contribution by the government and be product-specific in order to be actionable. An undervalued exchange rate will affect all exports and is not specific. See V. Thorstensen, E. Fernandes Marçal and L. Ferraz, 'EU-Mercosur Trade Relations: Implications of Exchange Rate Misalignments on Tariffs', *CEPS Working Paper* No. 372 (2013) and A. De Lima-Campos and J. A. Gaviria, 'A Case for Misaligned Currencies as Countervailable Subsidies', *Journal of World Trade* 46:5 (2012), 1017–44.

[26] J. Gagnon, 'Combating Widespread Currency Manipulation', *Petersen Institute for International Economics Policy Brief* (2012), www.iie.com/publications/pb/pb12-19.pdf.

There are compelling arguments as to why efforts to go down the path of invoking the WTO's contingent protection or dispute settlement mechanisms are likely to do much more harm than good in terms of sustaining multilateral cooperation or addressing the underlying source of the externality. One reason is that it is necessary to consider the overall current account and not bilateral trade balances. One deficit country taking trade action against a surplus country may not have much effect on the balance of overall imports and exports of the two countries concerned. Moreover, as a result of the rapid rise in vertical specialisation and intra-industry trade, much of a surplus country's exports may embody imports sourced from the deficit country – so that an import surcharge by the latter may also negatively affect its exports. The level of the real exchange rate is not a policy instrument on which a government can make specific commitments. It is endogenous, and will reflect a mix of fiscal and monetary policies. Deciding whether a government is engaging in deliberate undervaluation is inherently a subjective exercise, not least because there are different methodologies and approaches to determining the 'equilibrium' real exchange rate, which may generate quite different benchmarks.[27] Even if the assessment is left to the IMF – as required by GATT Article XV – it will be very difficult to assess objectively in a specific disputed case whether there is currency manipulation, and if so, to what extent a country is undercutting its trade policy commitments to liberalise access to its markets and/or is subsidising its exports. There are many other objectives that may underpin an active monetary and exchange rate management policy that have nothing to do with seeking to circumvent trade policy commitments.[28]

Current account surplus countries have historically never been willing to subject themselves to binding international disciplines. Policies that result in large current account surpluses are costly to the countries adopting them as they imply suppression of domestic consumption. Over time there will be endogenous pressures limiting the magnitude of sustained imbalances and pushing towards adjustment of the underlying policies – as has been occurring in the case of China. Equally important is recognising that from a competitiveness perspective, countries running large, sustained current account deficits that reflect an excess of consumption over income need to put their own house in

[27] See Eden and Nguyen, 'Correcting Real Exchange Rate Misalignment'.

[28] R. Staiger and A. Sykes, '"Currency Manipulation" and World Trade', *World Trade Review* 9:4 (2010), 583–627.

order – by focusing on improving both the macro and microeconomic environment that determines productivity performance. This entails, for example, improving product market regulation (reducing barriers to competition in services sectors, including network industries); permitting foreign ownership; lowering trade barriers; labour market reform to enhance labour mobility; eliminating fiscal distortions (e.g., non-renewable energy subsidies); improving educational quality and outcomes, R&D and innovation incentives and the quality of infrastructure; controlling the cost of healthcare.

That said, whatever one's views, doing more to clarify, analyse and discuss the effects of prevailing policies would help to identify the extent of negative spillovers and possible actions that could be taken to enhance competitiveness in deficit and/or low productivity countries. The same is true with respect to the possible spillover effects on capital flows of the monetary policies that are pursued by large countries – e.g., the current debates about the impact on the rest of world of monetary easing by the US and the EU, which some countries argue generates capital inflows and thus puts pressure on their exchange rates and/or their competitiveness. As argued by Irwin, there is a clear case for the IMF and the WTO to work out how they can help defuse current and future disputes over exchange rates and monetary policy and, more specifically, whether agreement can be obtained on specific 'rules of the game'.[29] Gagnon, Irwin, Mattoo and Subramanian[30] and many others involved in the policy-making community in the US and Europe take the view that trade retaliation should be on the table as a remedy if these rules are violated. This is arguably seriously misconceived as it can easily lead to the unravelling of the open multilateral system of trade and impair the predictability of the policy environment in which traders operate. Trade policy should not be seen as an appropriate tool to address monetary policy-related conflicts. If countries can agree to stronger rules, given that much of the concern relates to the effects of the induced capital flows, taking action to tax capital inflows (raising the cost of buying domestic bonds or other financial instruments) is a more appropriate remedy, one that is currently unconstrained under the WTO and that

[29] D. Irwin, 'Esprit de Currency', *Finance and Development* 48:2 (2011), www.imf.org/external/pubs/ft/fandd/2011/06/irwin.htm.

[30] See Gagnon, 'Combating Widespread Currency Manipulation' (2012), above n 26, Irwin, 'Esprit de Currency'; and Mattoo and Subramanian, 'Currency Undervaluation and Sovereign Wealth Funds'.

can be implemented unilaterally by governments as an instrument to manage the impacts of capital flows.[31]

II. Spillovers from microeconomic policies affecting competitiveness

As noted earlier, much of what matters for longer-run competitiveness should not generate negative spillovers and thus does not give rise to a need for international disciplines. Potential exceptions are industrial policy type sector-specific interventions. This is a well-known issue area for international rule-making, as reflected in WTO disciplines on the use of export subsidies and trade policies that can be used to offset tariff reduction commitments, such as local content requirements. The 2008 financial crisis gave rise to a significant increase in the use of subsidies of different types, some of which were aimed at stimulating demand – e.g., 'cash for clunkers' programmes to stimulate demand for cars – while others involved support for specific sectors (e.g., governments taking direct equity stakes in financial services and car companies) (see the Global Trade Alert website).[32] Clearly such policy interventions affected competition on the markets concerned. Looking forward there may be more recourse to subsidy-type policies as traditional border trade policies (tariffs, quotas) have become much less effective in supporting domestic economic activity as a result of global production fragmentation and the organisation of production in international value chains. Rather than restrict access to markets – which raises the costs of imports that increasingly are direct inputs into export production – governments

[31] Restrictions on capital flows can play a useful role in coping with surges of capital inflows and the associated spillovers (asset bubbles, potential financial instability) that are in part the result of monetary policies in large trading partners. See, e.g., N. Magud and C. Reinhardt, 'Capital Controls: An Evaluation', *NBER Working Paper* 11973 (2006); J. D. Ostry, A. R. Ghosh, K. Habermeier, M. Chamon, M. S. Qureshi and D. B. Reinhardt, *Capital Inflows: The Role of Controls* (Washington, DC: IMF, 2010) and O. Canuto and M. Cavallari, 'Monetary Policy and Macroprudential Regulation: Whither Emerging Markets', *World Bank Policy Working Research Paper* 6310 (2013). Of course, this is not a panacea: one country's success in using capital controls will increase the difficulty for other nations doing the same (Committee on International Economic Policy and Reform, *Rethinking Central Banking* (Washington, DC: Brookings Institution, 2011)), pointing to the need for greater communication between authorities and justification of the measures taken (O. Canuto, C. Garcia-Kilroy and A. Silva, 'The New Financial Landscape: What it means for Emerging Market Economies', *Economic Premise* 87 (Washington, DC: World Bank, 2012).

[32] www.globaltradealert.com.

may respond to pressures to create or safeguard jobs at home by providing subsidies to local economic activity, whether *de jure* or *de facto*.

The WTO Agreement on Subsidies and Countervailing Measures (SCM Agreement) prohibits export subsidies and establishes conditions under which domestic subsidies that cause adverse effects on other WTO members can be challenged or countervailed. The WTO does not restrict the ability of governments to use subsidies or to allocate subsidies to domestic producers only – Article III:8 GATT explicitly excludes subsidies from the national treatment rule. To be actionable, subsidies must be *specific*, entail a *cost* to government and create a *benefit* for firms. Adverse effects are defined in trade terms: the subsidies create adverse trade effects for other WTO members. The SCM Agreement does not specify any types of specific subsidies that are permitted and thus are not actionable.[33] The problem that arises is that subsidies may be an appropriate instrument to address market failures – along the lines of the case for an undervalued exchange rate to offset domestic distortions – but may give rise to international competitiveness spillovers. At the moment the focus of WTO rules is only on the latter; it is irrelevant as far as the WTO is concerned what the subsidy aims to achieve. As is well known, a subsidy can be an efficient instrument to offset some types of market failures. If a subsidy offsets or corrects market failures, in principle it cannot be held to create a negative spillover on foreign interests and/or to raise a competitiveness issue. The problem is that the WTO ignores what a subsidy is aimed to achieve – the focus is only on trade effects. If a country has made tariff commitments and subsequently decides to use a policy instrument, such as a specific subsidy, this may have an adverse trade effect on trading partners and thus be actionable even if the sole objective of the measure is to correct a domestic distortion.[34]

The WTO makes allowances for countries to invoke a general exceptions provision (Article XX GATT) to enable them to use otherwise prohibited trade policies as long as these do not discriminate between domestic and foreign goods and are necessary to achieve a regulatory objective (e.g., to protect health and safety or to conserve

[33] A provision that did so for some specific subsidies was time-bound and lapsed in 2001.

[34] One result is that the rules may distort what governments are willing to commit to in the WTO. See K. Bagwell and R. Staiger, 'Will International Rules on Subsidies Disrupt the World Trading System?', *American Economic Review* 96:3 (2006), 877–95 for an analysis of the incentive effects of existing WTO rules on subsidies.

non-renewable natural resources), but this provision does not (cannot) apply to non-prohibited subsidies (as these are not disciplined by the SCM Agreement, which only lays out when domestic subsidies are actionable) and cannot be used to justify specific subsidies because of the non-discrimination requirement.[35] Moreover, an exception will not insulate a country against countervailing actions.[36] As a result, governments may be pressed to take unilateral action against imports produced by firms that are deemed to have benefited from subsidies whatever the rationale or effect of the subsidies beyond trade. Thus, 'competitiveness concerns' may conflict with the objective of addressing market failures and give rise to pressures for countervailing action by other countries.

A key policy issue is whether and what types of specific subsidies, motivated on the basis of market failures, should be permitted. For example, should free allowances made under emission trading schemes (ETSs) be actionable? Feed-in tariff programmes that pay renewable energy producers a premium for green energy generation? Given the rapid increase in green tax and/or subsidy-related trade disputes and countermeasures (anti-dumping and countervail cases for solar panels; feed-in tariffs; the EU decision to extend the ETS to all airlines landing in its territory), international agreement on what constitutes 'acceptable' targeted policies that are beneficial for the environment (address market failures) and should be non-actionable would help reduce the scope for globally welfare-reducing actions taken under the banner of competitiveness.[37] The same is true of other subsidy policies that can be justified as aiming to offset specific market failures. A case in point is the treatment of special economic zones (SEZs) and the scope for SEZs to fall foul of the ban on export subsidisation. Just as deliberate targeting of a competitive exchange rate may be a short-term instrument to offset the effects of a bad investment climate, SEZs can be effective instruments to insulate firms against an unsupportive business environment that impedes investment in tradable industries.

35 P. C. Mavroidis, *Trade in Goods*, 2nd edn (Oxford University Press, 2012).

36 R. Howse, *Climate Mitigation Subsidies and the WTO Legal Framework: A Policy Analysis* (Geneva: International Institute for Sustainable Development, 2010).

37 L. Henschke, 'Going it Alone on Climate Change a New Challenge to WTO Subsidies Disciplines: Are Subsidies in Support of Emissions Reductions Schemes Permissible Under the WTO?', *World Trade Review* 11:1 (2012), 27–52.

E. Improving global governance and policy coordination

A common theme of the literature on competitiveness is to identify a set of policies that can be pursued by governments to enhance the long-term productivity performance of the economy. A feature of virtually all the literature is that the focus is on countries. While there is much cross-country comparison and analysis of policy indicators and outcomes, little attention is generally given to the potential for negative pecuniary spillovers, let alone empirical estimates of how large spillover effects are. One reason for this is that what drives competitiveness is mostly determined by national governments and polities – what other countries do certainly has impacts on competition on global markets but in many, if not most, countries it is the national investment climate broadly defined that is the main determinant of the ability of national firms to compete effectively on world markets. The exceptions are the literatures on 'industrial policy' (targeted intervention that impacts on production incentives for specific industries or economic activities) and on 'global imbalances' (the strand that focuses on 'export mercantilism', i.e., deliberate exchange rate undervaluation aimed at sustaining large current account surpluses).

In neither of these areas are matters clear-cut when it comes to the global welfare effects of specific policies and the magnitude (or even sign) of negative spillovers. As discussed above, there is a serious tension between concerns about the competition effects of industrial policies and the need for intervention to address market failures. One can (and should) question whether policies do in fact address such failures, but this is not to deny that policy intervention can improve allocative (and dynamic) efficiency. As argued above, there is a clear case for revisiting the current WTO rules in the area of subsidies. On the macroeconomic sources of potential spillovers, there are numerous possible rationales for why countries might have current account surpluses – including self-insurance against exogenous shocks and 'sudden credit stops'; financial repression implemented as part of an economic development strategy; regulation of product and factor markets that reduces competition and raises costs of entry and operations, thereby decreasing investment; limited financial market development and weak governance that generates excessive corporate savings; or weak social protection (safety nets, health insurance, pension systems) that induces high precautionary savings by households.

The underlying drivers of large current account imbalances are likely to impede long-run growth and thus are unlikely to be sustained in the long run. Rebalancing must involve changes in economic structure. The associated 'competitiveness agenda' overlaps to a significant extent with the need for 'structural reforms' to increase competition in services sectors (health, financial services (pension systems), professional and business services, transport and logistics), as well as product and labour market regulation. Developing countries face significant difficulties in designing such reforms, in part because of concerns about the realisation of regulatory objectives. There are multiple players with different objectives within governments that have a role in setting regulation. Moreover, efficient provision of services often involves a cluster of activities that cuts across multiple regulatory agencies, making it more difficult to determine what is needed to improve competitiveness.

These are areas where it will be difficult to agree to binding rules on the substance of regulation through negotiations, even in cases where there are negative spillovers or terms of trade effects. A problem for international cooperation is that policies and their effects are frequently not transparent – not enough is known about extant policies and their impacts. More systematic collection of information on relevant policies and objective analysis of their effects on competitiveness and any spillovers is a precondition for any effort to arrive at a common understanding of any specific situation. This is partly being done by organisations like the OECD and the World Bank, but it arguably needs to become much more central to the work of the WTO. Bolstering voluntary mechanisms that are open to all countries, which focus on the identification of beneficial structural reforms, including in services sectors, from a national self-interest perspective, could help prepare the ground for possible enforceable agreements on specific policies once there is a common understanding that this would benefit all participating countries.[38]

Hoekman and Mattoo suggest the formation of 'knowledge platforms' that would act as vehicles through which countries can assess and analyse the impacts of current policy regimes and identify potentially beneficial reforms and the investments needed to implement them. Such platforms would connect stakeholders to different sources of expertise – local, regional and global; facilitate knowledge exchange; build on

[38] Accordingly, Marchetti *et al.* argue that, 'services trade liberalization, supported by WTO negotiations, would enhance competition and efficiency, and raise productivity in all economies, including surplus countries'. See J. Marchetti, M. Ruta and R. Teh, 'Trade Imbalances and Multilateral Trade Cooperation', Chapter 13, this volume.

existing networks of regulators and industry associations; and connect with both the donor community, for support for implementation of reforms in developing countries, and the business community – which has a direct stake in pro-competitive reforms and needs to play an active role in monitoring progress in implementing reforms and holding governments accountable for results.[39] While undoubtedly a complex, resource-intensive and time-consuming exercise, shifting the focus more in this direction is arguably a necessary condition for 'ownership' and political support for putting in place policies that will enhance competitiveness.

Such forms of cooperation are sometimes incorporated into PTAs. Often this takes the form of provisions to provide technical and other forms of assistance, and the establishment of mechanisms for the exchange of information, interactions between business associations, investors and civil society groups, and non-economic forms of cooperation (e.g., student or cultural exchanges). PTAs often also create a variety of official bodies that are tasked with implementation of the agreement in specific areas and that can act as mechanisms through which the regulators and other officials from the participating countries establish working relationships. One lesson from successful North–South PTAs is that the prospects for the agreements to enhance the welfare of developing country signatories are improved if the focus extends beyond market access (i.e., terms-of-trade externalities) and government-to-government interaction. Including complementary measures that aim at improving the domestic regulatory environment; bolstering related institutions; the provision of technical and financial assistance; and active engagement by the private sector in surveillance and enforcement of commitments is equally if not more important.

F. Concluding remarks

Although the rapid increase in global integration and production-sharing (international supply chains) means that trade policy is likely to feature much less prominently in the toolbox of governments in the future than it has in the past, other instruments such as monetary, fiscal or industrial (sector) policies continue to have an important role to play.

[39] B. Hoekman and A. Mattoo, 'Liberalizing Trade in Services: Lessons from Regional and WTO Negotiations', *International Negotiation*, 18:1 (2013), 131–51.

These are appropriate instruments for governments to use in the pursuit of growth and development goals, but they can have beggar-thy-neighbour features and thus generate international tensions. Addressing such conflicts – which in part will be the consequence of successful pursuit of export-led growth and thus be difficult to disentangle from more general competitive pressures – in a cooperative manner is important both to prevent recourse to unilateral trade 'retaliation' by trading partners and to allow those countries that are most in need of effective proactive policies to use them without fear of negative reactions from the rest of the world.

For there to be a rationale for countries to negotiate internationally binding rules on specific policies, they need to generate terms of trade spillovers. This also applies to policies that impact on the competitiveness of firms in a country: the question is to what extent such policies generate negative pecuniary spillovers. The literature on the determinants of competitiveness suggests that policies and institutions that support the emergence of productive firms and boost overall total factor productivity do not generate negative spillovers. What this suggests from a global governance perspective is that mechanisms are needed that generate greater transparency and facilitate learning about what works and what matters for competitiveness. This is the focus of work by many organisations, including the IMF, the OECD and the World Bank. It is not however a focal point for the WTO. Thus, one conclusion suggested by the discussion in this chapter is that the membership of the WTO – the primary international organisation where competitiveness concerns will arise and can be addressed – should consider doing more to promote such exchanges.

Deep integration based on internationally agreed, binding norms that are applied on a non-discriminatory basis to all traders may enhance global welfare. But, the need for deeper integration on most issues that impact on competitiveness is arguably limited. Frequently, shallow integration will be a more powerful instrument – i.e., competition between regulatory regimes that reflect national circumstances. In areas such as social regulation and macroeconomic policies it will be very difficult to achieve deep integration (coordination or harmonisation of policy). A necessary condition is a common understanding of how regulation and/or policy affects competitiveness. This can be pursued via creation of processes through which governments and domestic stakeholders can identify the effects of policies and alternatives that are likely to enhance competitiveness. Entry barriers such as non-recognition of professional certification and qualifications and conformity assessment regimes that imply redundant costs for foreign suppliers are examples of regulatory areas where domestic reform can do much to foster greater competitiveness. Binding international law that spells out the substance of the relevant regulatory requirements is not likely to be feasible or desirable, however. A focus on agreement on good regulatory principles (process- and transparency-related) and creation of mechanisms through which firms can interact with governments to identify market-segmenting impacts of prevailing policies and less trade restrictive alternatives is likely to be a more productive path.

The same applies to macroeconomic and monetary policies, where the first step should also be more open discussion and specific analysis of the spillover effects of policies. Reaching an agreement on binding rules seems very unlikely – it is difficult to imagine large countries ever agreeing to be subject to binding legal disciplines outside the framework of a monetary union, if they imply a diminution of national sovereignty (and even then the eurozone illustrates that the degree of integration that is required is very far-reaching). The most that can realistically be expected to be feasible is pursuit of greater procedural cooperation in the IMF to consult and bolster the ability (mandate) of the organisation to strengthen Article IV surveillance with greater analysis of the spillover effects of national monetary and exchange rate policies.[40] As discussed previously a greater focus on enhancing communication and dialogue on such matters in the WTO, but also in organisations such as the OECD and deep PTAs would also be beneficial.

Deficit nations are ultimately subject to market discipline, while surplus countries face 'only' political market discipline – where large, sustained surpluses are the result of deliberate policies, governments will be subject to political pressure from their citizens if the costs in terms of consumption and investment returns forgone become too high. It is important in this connection to recognise that the recent period that has given rise to macroeconomic policy-induced competitiveness concerns has been unique in that it is associated with China's re-integration into the global economy. This has been very beneficial to China as well as the world as a whole, but the rapidity and magnitude of the resulting shifts in trade shares and relative incomes has been unprecedented,

[40] For an analysis on the IMF surveillance framework, see N. Rendak, 'Monitoring and Surveillance of the International Monetary System – What Can Be Learnt from the Trade Field?', Chapter 9, this volume.

giving rise to major adjustment costs for other countries. However, it has also created great opportunities as the effective size of the world economy has increased substantially. The policy challenges of leveraging this opportunity into sustained higher growth are primarily domestic – putting in place a supportive business environment and investment climate that generates high quality jobs for citizens.

7

Global benchmark interest rates: conflicting objectives and increasing hybridisation

CLAUS D. ZIMMERMANN

A. Introduction

The setting of key interest rates, such as the Federal Funds Target Rate determined by the Federal Open Market Committee (FOMC) in the US, the Bank of England Base Rate, set by the Bank of England's Monetary Policy Committee (MPC), or the key interest rates determined by the Governing Council of the European Central Bank (ECB), is one of the three main tools of monetary policy.[1] The other two are open market operations (by which the quantity of money in circulation is managed through the purchase and sale of financial instruments such as treasury bills and foreign currency) and reserve requirements (by which central banks determine the minimum reserves (in the form of vault cash or deposits with the central bank) that each commercial bank must hold of customer deposits and notes). In addition, the regulation of the banking system (and therewith of the availability and cost of credit) and of the payments system (clearing and settlement) are increasingly important tools for controlling the money supply in a modern economy.[2]

Claus D. Zimmermann is an associate in the international trade and arbitration practice of Sidley Austin LLP in Geneva. This chapter represents his personal views only and not those of Sidley Austin LLP or any of the firm's clients. This chapter benefited greatly from comments by participants in the World Trade Forum 2012, in particular by Professor Peter Kugler from the University of Basel. Parts of Section B and the beginning of Section C.I of this chapter are based on material published previously by this author in C. D. Zimmermann, *A Contemporary Concept of Monetary Sovereignty* (Oxford University Press, 2013), pp. 25–8, 76–81. The final manuscript of this chapter was completed on 1 October 2013; unless stated otherwise, all Internet links referred to in the chapter were last accessed that day. With the exception of an important update included prior to the chapter's conclusion subsequent developments could not be taken in account.

[1] These days, the vast majority of modern economies have delegated the conduct of monetary policy to independent central banks.

[2] A given monetary policy, and, intrinsically related, interest rate policy, is commonly referred to as being contractionary if it reduces the size of the money supply, notably by

Depending on their respective, explicit or implicit, mandate, most central banks aim to achieve either a certain target inflation *rate* or a target inflation *range*. Their common monetary policy objective thus is to achieve monetary stability,[3] which can be regarded as a synonym for price stability.[4] Importantly, although central banks often also seek to achieve not only the stability of domestic prices but also external price stability, i.e., a stable exchange rate, it is economically inconsistent in the medium or long term to pursue both objectives simultaneously.[5] In addition, some central banks, notably the US Federal Reserve System (Fed), also aim to achieve a desired level of growth in real activity as part of their monetary policy. Thus, in early December 2012, the Fed went as far as to explicitly specify that its objective was to push the US unemployment rate below 6.5 per cent and that it would therefore leave interest rates at close to zero provided its inflation expectations did not rise beyond 2.5 per cent.[6]

Interestingly, under the effect of ever-increasing economic integration and financial innovation, it is not the key interest rates set by central banks, but certain reference rates set by the private sector, that have evolved into the key benchmarks for the vast global trade in innovative financial instruments such as interest rate swaps, foreign currency options and forward rate agreements. The best known among these benchmark rates is the London Interbank Offered Rate (Libor), the

raising key interest rates. By contrast, an expansionary policy increases the money supply in the economy, notably by decreasing interest rates. Similarly, a monetary policy referred to as being accommodative is one that is intended to create economic growth, while a tight policy would be one that is intended to reduce inflation.

[3] *Financial* stability, the other key objective pursued by most central banks beside that of *monetary* stability, is not strictly speaking a monetary or interest rate policy objective. This chapter will therefore address it only very briefly in order to point out the limits of achieving both the objective of monetary stability and that of financial stability simultaneously. See Section B below.

[4] The Governing Council of the ECB, e.g., has clarified that, in pursuing price stability as the ECB's primary policy objective, it seeks to keep inflation below, but close to, 2 per cent over the medium term.

[5] F. Gianviti, 'The Objectives of Central Banks', in M. Giovanoli and D. Devos (eds.), *International Monetary and Financial Law: The Global Crisis* (Oxford University Press, 2010), pp. 449–83 and F. Gianviti, 'Relationship between Monetary Policy and Exchange Rate Policy', Chapter 21, this volume. For a detailed definition and nuanced discussion of monetary stability as key central bank objective, see, e.g., R. M. Lastra, *Legal Foundations of International Monetary Stability* (Oxford University Press, 2006), pp. 34–9 and R. M. Lastra, 'The Role of Central Banks in Monetary Affairs', Chapter 4, this volume.

[6] R. Harding and J. Politi, 'Fed Links Interest Rates to US Unemployment Figures', *Financial Times* (13 December 2012), www.ft.com/intl/cms/s/0/3713f096-447e-11e2-8fd7-00144feabdc0.html.

average of hypothetical interest rates that leading banks operating in the City of London estimate they would be charged by their peers if they were borrowing unsecured funds from each other short-term. Most eurodollar contracts and eurobond products are based on US dollar (USD) Libor rates.[7] Similar reference rates set by the private sector are the Euro Interbank Offered Rate (Euribor), the Tokyo Interbank Offered Rate (Tibor) and the Singapore Interbank Offered Rate (Sibor).

Although private benchmark rates such as the Libor are not meant, in principle, to have macroeconomic ramifications, the 2012 Libor scandal, which, as will be explained in detail in this chapter,[8] involved various instances of significant fraud and collusion by member banks connected to rates submissions, revealed that such rate manipulation does indeed have the potential to significantly affect the world economy.

This chapter examines the hybrid reality of global benchmark interest rates. This reality comprises both the key interest rates set by central banks under domestic public law and the transnational,[9] private, benchmark rates set by associations of globally operating banks. It will be argued in this chapter that the common characteristic of the setting of key interest rates, both by central banks and bankers' associations, is one of conflicting objectives at various levels and that these conflicts, as well the overly hybrid nature of monetary affairs when it comes to the setting of benchmark rates, potentially endanger the attainment of the overarching objectives pursued by central banks, i.e., monetary and financial stability.

Distinct from the above-mentioned dual object of analysis of the present chapter, i.e., the key interest rates set by central banks as a matter of monetary policy and the short-term private benchmark rates such as the Libor, are the long-term interest rates prevailing in a given economy. These long-term interest rates, determined by pure market forces, play a decisive role notably as part of one of the four criteria of sustainable convergence for adoption of the euro. Thus, as stipulated by Article 4 of Protocol 13 on the Convergence Criteria attached to the EU treaties:

> The criterion on the convergence of interest rates referred to in the fourth indent of Article 140(1) of [the Treaty on European Union] shall mean that, observed over a period of one year before the examination, a Member State

[7] For a detailed definition of eurodollars and eurobonds, see below, Section C.I.

[8] See Section C.II.

[9] Transnational law is commonly defined as the body of rules – national, international, public or private – that regulates actions across national borders by all types of actors, i.e., not only states and their official organs but also international organisations and businesses, as well as other public or private persons.

> has had an average nominal long-term interest rate that does not exceed by more than two percentage points that of, at most, the three best performing Member States in terms of price stability. Interest rates shall be measured on the basis of long-term government bonds or comparable securities, taking into account differences in national definitions.

In the following, this chapter succinctly examines the lack of harmonised objectives in the pursuit of interest rate policies by central banks (Section B), looks in detail into the elusive role of the law when it comes to reference short-term interest rates determined by the private sector (Section C) and concludes with several thoughts on how to remedy the identified deficits (Section D).

B. The lack of harmonised objectives in the pursuit of interest rate policies by central banks

Achieving monetary stability is usually the central target of monetary and, more specifically, interest rate policies as conducted by central banks. It emerges from a detailed study of central bank objectives undertaken by François Gianviti, a former general counsel of the IMF, that, in most central banking laws worldwide, monetary stability is defined as the stability of domestic prices.[10] As explained in detail by Gianviti, this is due to the economic reality that *external* price stability (in terms of the exchange rate with a given major currency) and *domestic* price stability, are in fact two distinct objectives, incompatible with each other in the long run.[11] For example, a central bank increasing the monetary base in order to prevent its currency from appreciating in line with economic fundamentals, thereby aiming to maintain an unrealistic currency peg, will in the long run fuel inflation, thus endangering domestic price stability.

Gianviti's survey further shows that what precisely is understood by domestic price stability is often not explicitly defined unless the country concerned is one of those with a specific procedure in place for the formulation of an explicit inflation target or some other form of quantified price objective.[12] In countries lacking a formal definition of the objective of domestic price stability, the understanding of that objective is subject to the central bank's case-by-case interpretation and, to the extent that the central bank is not entirely independent,[13] to the approval

[10] Gianviti, 'The Objectives of Central Banks', p. 468. See also Lastra, *Legal Foundations*, p. 35.

[11] Gianviti, 'The Objectives of Central Banks', p. 473. [12] *Ibid.*, p. 468.

[13] For an insightful analysis of the theory and practice of central banks independence, see Lastra, *Legal Foundations*, pp. 41–61. On the economic rationale for central bank

and review by the government.[14] However, Gianviti's survey identifies a global trend towards the adoption of quantified price objectives as opposed to leaving central banks to conduct monetary policy without publicly announcing specific objectives.[15]

Gianviti's study indicates that there now seems to be a common understanding on what is meant by the objective of domestic price stability. Thus, while domestic prices are those of domestic goods and services, asset prices are not usually covered by the term. As regards 'stability', there now appears to be broad consensus that while a total absence of inflation would discourage investment and thus stifle economic growth, an annual price increase of 2 per cent would still be consistent with the objective of price stability.[16]

Thus, some countries have adopted inflation ceilings whereas others consider the setting of inflation targets to be the preferable approach.[17] An inflation target may take the form of a 'point inflation target', i.e., a specific percentage increase in consumer prices, such as the Bank of England's inflation target of 2.0 per cent,[18] or of a 'target inflation range' which seems to be the more common approach and which is adhered to, for example, in Canada and Sweden.[19] An interesting example in that context is the approach taken by the Governing Council of the ECB, which has shifted from an outright inflation ceiling of 2 per cent to a hybrid definition of price stability that might appropriately be qualified as a 'targeted inflation ceiling'.[20]

Despite this significant convergence of the ways in which the objective of price stability is being pursued by central banks, it is important to stress that the remaining differences are not limited to scenarios where a country accords priority to external price stability as opposed to focusing on inflation. Thus, it makes a huge difference whether a central bank adheres to an inflation ceiling of 2 per cent, which will be met even if inflation is zero, or if it aims to achieve a target inflation rate of 2 per cent, which

independence, see S. Fischer, 'Central-Bank Independence Revisited', *The American Economic Review* 85:2 (1995), 201, as well as the various references listed therein.

[14] Gianviti, 'The Objectives of Central Banks', pp. 468–9. [15] *Ibid.*, p. 472.

[16] *Ibid.*, p. 470.

[17] On the reasons that led to the widespread adoption of inflation targeting towards the end of the last century, see F. S. Mishkin, 'Inflation Targeting: True Progress or Repackaging of an Old Idea', in *The Swiss National Bank 1907–2007* (Zurich: Swiss National Bank, 2007), pp. 599–623.

[18] For the Bank of England's recent Inflation Report of August 2013, see www.bankofengland.co.uk/publications/Pages/inflationreport/2013/ir1303.aspx.

[19] Gianviti, 'The Objectives of Central Banks', p. 471.

[20] For the relevant definition, see above, n 4.

means neither more nor less. Inflation targeting may thus be considered as having a built-in bias towards a consistently moderate level of inflation, favourable, at least in the short term, to growth and employment.[21]

This leads us directly to what is arguably the contemporary key difference between the interest rate policies pursued by different central banks. While the formal adoption of an inflation target (or target range) amounts to an implicit acknowledgement that the central bank wishes to contribute, via the way it conducts monetary policy, to economic growth and employment, some central banks, as noted earlier, also aim to achieve a desired level of growth in real activity as part of their monetary policy. These different approaches explain to a large extent existing discrepancies in the interest rate policies conducted on both sides of the Atlantic. They also help to understand the continuous struggle between the EU's two largest economies, Germany and France (whose Banque de France formerly played a major role in stimulating the real economy), regarding the ideal monetary policy to be conducted by the ECB.

Pursuing a dual objective of both price stability and growth in real activity becomes problematic when both objectives enjoy equal priority. Under such a scenario, pursuing an objective of promoting growth in real activity may prove incompatible with the objective of controlling inflation. Whereas price stability, as sole or primary monetary policy objective, makes action by the central bank predictable and reliable, a dual objective undermines the central bank's commitment to price stability. This may happen if the population gains the impression that, faced with the dilemma of choosing between an economic downturn and higher inflation, the central bank will attach higher importance to its objective of full employment.[22]

The Fed's and the ECB's different responses to the onset of the 2007–9 Global Financial Crisis offer significant insight in this context. The Fed reacted with a series of interest rate cuts aimed at saving employment while the ECB kept interest rates unchanged for much longer in order not to endanger price stability. This illustrates that the current lack of harmonisation in the way interest rates policies are being conducted by central banks may lead to major differences in how similar economic problems are tackled by different countries. Analysing precisely the extent to which such different interest rate policy approaches introduce avoidable distortions for conducting business in a globalised world economy lies beyond the scope of this chapter.

[21] Gianviti, 'The Objectives of Central Banks', p. 471. [22] See *ibid.*, p. 473.

Finally, a few words at least need to be said about the other key objective pursued by most central banks besides that of monetary stability: the objective of financial stability. As already noted in the introduction, that objective is strictly speaking not a monetary or interest rate policy objective. Many different definitions have been advanced in the economics literature for financial stability. Usually, the concept is approached indirectly by defining the opposite of financial stability, i.e., financial instability. A broad and systemic approach defines financial instability as the prevalence of a financial system that is unable to ensure, in a lasting way and without major disruptions, the efficient allocation of savings to investment opportunities.[23] Financial regulation on minimum capital ratios for commercial banks is the main, but not the only, tool for avoiding financial instability.

Although a common position on the precise nature of the interdependence of monetary stability and financial stability does not seem to exist in the economics literature, it appears to be broadly accepted that these phenomena are intrinsically linked and reinforce each other, which seems equally true for the two instability scenarios.[24] Thus, as pointed out by Gianviti, while in most cases, securing financial stability will support the achievement of monetary stability, a central bank may face a conflict of objectives in the conduct of its monetary and interest rate policies once it becomes engulfed in a financial crisis.[25] Gianviti cites the example of a major financial crisis in which the central bank, in order to safeguard a financial system on the verge of collapse, decides to bail out numerous systemically important financial institutions, partly without collateral, on top of lowering its interest rates and injecting short-term liquidity into the banking system; in addition, the central bank may even be exposed to significant public pressure to purchase large amounts of government bonds to finance budget deficits arising from countercyclical measures taken to mitigate the crisis.[26] In the long run, these amounts of central bank money, all injected in the name of financial stability, may endanger monetary stability in the sense of domestic price stability.

Based on the above, it would be wrong to conclude that central banks should not aim to safeguard financial stability in addition to pursuing

[23] O. Issing, 'Monetary and Financial Stability: Is there a Trade-off?' (2003) Paper presented at the ECB Conference on 'Monetary Stability, Financial Stability and the Business Cycle' held at the Bank for International Settlements (BIS), Basel (28–29 March 2003), www.ecb.int/press/key/date/2003/html/sp030329.en.html.

[24] See, e.g., *ibid.* [25] Gianviti, 'The Objectives of Central Banks', p. 481. [26] *Ibid.*

their monetary policy objective(s), in particular as both monetary and financial stability will in most cases reinforce each other. However, while a sovereign state is free to determine in the statutes of its central bank that the objective of monetary stability takes priority over that of financial stability, such an order of priority would effectively have to be abandoned in the case of a severe crisis. Although, strictly speaking, financial stability is not an objective of monetary and interest rate policies, the central bank of a modern economy has little choice but to pursue both these objectives simultaneously. This appears to be true despite the above-mentioned potential for conflict between the two objectives. This clearly distinguishes the pair 'financial stability–monetary stability' from the wholly separate choice as to whether or not to pursue an economic growth objective as part of monetary policy on top of the objective of price stability.

Having completed this succinct overview of the lack of harmonised objectives in the pursuance of interest rate policies by central banks, this chapter now turns to examining the elusive role of the law when it comes to reference interest rates set by the private sector.

C. The elusive role of the law with respect to reference interest rates set by the private sector

In order to fully expose the complex economic and legal dimensions of the phenomenon of global benchmark interest rates as set by the private sector, this section takes a close look at the irresistible emergence of what may be called a truly transnational monetary and financial system (Section C.I) prior to focusing on the Libor manipulation scandal and its implications (Section C.II).

I. The irresistible emergence of a truly transnational monetary and financial system

The emergence, and extensive use, of private benchmark interest rates such as the Libor and the Euribor, is intrinsically linked to the huge success of eurocurrencies and of financial innovation, i.e., the creating and marketing of new types of securities.

Eurocurrencies are deposits, denominated in whatever currency, that are made with a financial institution, of whatever nationality, situated outside the territory of the issuing state. The eurocurrency market first emerged in the 1960s when significant amounts of USD accumulated outside the US. Several aspects of domestic US regulation at the time created strong incentives for those holding dollars abroad not to reintroduce them into the US, but to both deposit and reinvest them overseas. Thus, the eurocurrency markets originally developed as eurodollar markets in order to allow USD transactions, mainly between large financial institutions, outside the US.[27] Later, the phenomenon broadened in scope and eurocurrency markets emerged for other global currencies.[28]

Originally, eurocurrency markets were limited to their two fundamental components: eurocurrency deposits and eurocurrency loans, the latter being essentially the use by the recipient financial institution of the eurocurrency deposits as a means of funding for customers not wishing to rely on the capital markets in the issuing state. The multiplier effect arising from the lending activities of financial institutions has traditionally been more pronounced for eurocurrencies than for domestic currency, because domestic reserve requirements usually do not apply to deposits made outside the territory of the issuing state. The operation of the banking system thus created, and continues to create, eurocurrencies at a significantly faster pace than lending operations within the territory of the issuing state with respect to domestic currency, for which states, or, more accurately, their respective central banks, retain at least some control over the evolution of the money supply via reserve requirements and the setting of key interest rates.[29]

Intrinsically related, the large amounts of eurocurrency deposits also triggered the evolution of the market for eurobonds,[30] i.e., bonds issued

[27] See C. Proctor, *Mann on the Legal Aspect of Money* 6th edn (Oxford University Press, 2005), pp. 50–5.

[28] Notably for Deutsche Mark, Japanese yen, pound sterling, Swiss franc, and, more recently, the euro.

[29] The eurocurrency market has reached dimensions that no one would have imagined when that market first emerged. By the end of 2009, loans granted and deposits placed in the five major eurocurrencies amounted to the equivalent of approximately USD 13,500 billion. Deposits received and borrowing in these same five major eurocurrencies amounted to the equivalent of approximately USD 15,500 billion, with USD accounting each time for approximately 60 per cent (source: unpublished BIS international locational banking statistics by residence. Communicated by Mr Swapan-Kumar Pradhan (personal email correspondence 4 June 2010, on file with author)). These numbers appear even more impressive when compared to the world's total foreign exchange holdings, which, according to the IMF, amounted to the equivalent of just over USD 8,000 billion by the end of 2009 (www.imf.org/external/np/sta/cofer/eng/cofer.pdf).

[30] By the end of 2006, the eurobond market had already reached a total volume of more than USD 4,000 billion (D. Carreau and P. Juillard, *Droit international économique* 3rd

in a eurocurrency. The great success of the eurobond market stems from the fact that eurobonds are issued in bearer form, with interest payments being free of withholding taxes. This makes them very attractive to investors wishing to remain anonymous or to avoid taxes. Subject to the agreement between the financial institutions involved, eurobonds may possess varying maturities, at either fixed interest rates, or at floating rates linked to private benchmarks such as the Libor or the Euribor.

What renders the legal regime of eurocurrencies[31] complex and unique is the fact that any financial transaction relying on eurocurrencies will be subject concurrently to two national legal regimes: the law governing the underlying contract, the *lex contractus*, and the law of the state whose currency is relied upon as eurocurrency, the *lex monetae*. Two distinct types of money can thus be identified for every currency that has risen to the status of a eurocurrency on international capital markets. The underlying support currency, whose supply is at least to some extent still subject to the control of the issuing state, would appear as 'public and national money'.[32] By contrast, the related eurocurrency has been convincingly analysed by Carreau as 'derivative', as 'private and transnational money', created by the private sector overseas, but subject, at least in theory, not only to the *lex contractus*, but also to the *lex monetae*.

Triggered by the impressive evolution of eurocurrency and eurobond markets, and fuelled by the spread of derivatives as new financial instruments, a private monetary and financial system has thus emerged alongside the traditional public and intergovernmental monetary system. With both systems having become increasingly intertwined and interdependent, the global monetary system appears to have become an

edn (Paris: Dalloz, 2007), p. 643), which is several times the total lending capacity of the IMF (the amount the IMF has readily available for new (non-concessional) lending is indicated by its one-year forward commitment capacity, which, in April 2013, stood at USD 399.4 billion (www.imf.org/external/np/tre/liquid/2013/0413.htm).

[31] The legal nature of eurocurrencies has been thoroughly analysed in the existing literature, see notably D. Carreau, 'Le système monétaire international privé (UEM et euromarchés)', *Recueil des Cours* 274 (1998), 309, 350–79. Additional, timeless sources of insight are J. Dach, 'Legal Nature of the Euro-Dollar', *American Journal of Comparative Law* 13 (1964), 30; and R. C. Effros, 'The Whys and Wherefores of Eurodollars', *The Business Lawyer* 23 (1968), 629.

[32] Strictly speaking, this analysis appears convincing only if one adheres to the societary theory of money. According to the traditional state theory of money, a huge proportion of this 'public and national money' as described by Carreau – the scriptural money created by domestic lending activities – would not amount to money in the legal sense, but to credit. A detailed analysis of this issue lies beyond the scope of this chapter.

outstanding example of a legal framework that has become truly transnational in nature, going beyond the traditional, and increasingly somewhat artificial, boundaries between public and private law as well as between domestic and international law.

Over the years, the originally separated markets for the lending and borrowing of eurocurrencies short-term (in the form of eurocurrency deposits and loans) and long-term (under the form of eurobonds) have become increasingly intertwined under the impact of financial innovation and the use of derivatives.[33] This led to the creation of a dense network of hardly visible links between these formally distinct components of the global market for capital, resulting in their horizontal integration.[34] In addition, the traditional key role of banks in financial intermediation has been shuffled by the emergence, beginning in the 1980s, of securitisation, as a result of which an increasing proportion of borrowing operations by professional market players has been undertaken via the issuance of securities. Classical bank loans, including eurocurrency loans, have thus been replaced, at least to some extent, by new financial products.

Throughout the early 1980s, the City of London established itself as a centre for loan syndication and an increasing number of banks in London were actively trading the new financial products, such as forward rate agreements and interest rate swaps. While many banks found the new products very attractive, they felt the need for a uniform benchmark as a convenient reference for the new products. This is why they asked the British Bankers' Association (BBA)[35] to devise such a rate, in order to make benchmarking more objective and transparent. Thus, the work of several working groups set up by the BBA together with other parties, such as the Bank of England, led to the development of the

33 There are three main categories of derivatives: swaps, options and futures (also called forwards). Swaps are contracts by which the parties involved exchange some benefits of one party's financial instrument against some benefits of the other party's financial instrument. Options are contracts that give the owner the right, but not the obligation, to buy (in the case of a call option) or sell (in the case of a put option) an asset. Futures, finally, are contracts on buying or selling an asset on or before a future date at a price already specified. By combining selected elements of these three basic types of derivatives, and by additional contractual arrangements, it is possible to create more complex derivatives, which illustrates the potential of financial innovation.

34 Carreau and Juillard, *Droit internationale économique*, p. 644.

35 The BBA is the trade association for the banking and financial services industry of the United Kingdom (UK). Its 250 members, with headquarters in fifty different countries, operate in 180 countries worldwide.

Libor's predecessor, the BBA standard for interest rate swaps, also known as the BBAIRS terms. Libor rates were officially fixed for the first time on 1 January 1986 and the Libor has since established itself as the key reference rate for a large number of key financial instruments relied upon both in financial and commercial markets.[36]

Until July 2013, Libor rates were calculated for ten different currencies with fifteen maturities (also so-called 'tenors') quoted for each (ranging from overnight to a year). Since then, as a result of the 2012 manipulation scandal to be addressed below, the number of Libor rates quoted daily has been reduced from 150 to 35 (five different currencies, seven maturities). For each Libor currency, the BBA, advised by the Foreign Exchange and Money Markets Committee, maintains reference panels composed of between six and eighteen contributor banks. In their daily submissions to Thomson Reuters, the designated calculation agent for the Libor, contributor banks are asked to answer the following question: 'At what rate could you borrow funds, were you to do so by asking for and then accepting inter-bank offers in a reasonable market size just prior to 11 a.m.?'[37] Thus, even though the recent reduction of the number of Libor rates that are calculated daily serves to increase the likelihood that the reported rates are underpinned by real trades, Libor rates are not necessarily based on actual transactions but upon the lowest perceived rate at which a bank could obtain funding, for a given maturity and currency, on the London inter-bank money market. Upon receipt of the submissions, Thomson Reuters ranks them in descending order, excluding the highest and lowest 25 per cent. It then calculates the arithmetical average for the remaining contributions, for every currency and maturity, to produce 35 (150 until July 2013) Libor rates every day. The rates are published through Thomson Reuters at 11:30 a.m.[38]

Distinct from euro Libor rates, which are among the rates calculated by Thomson Reuters under the auspices of the BBA in London, is the Euribor which came into being in 1999, when Frankfurt's Fibor, Paris' Pibor and Helsinki's Helibor merged. Analogous to the Libor, the Euribor is a daily reference rate calculated exclusively for the euro on the basis of averaged interest rates at which eurozone banks offer to lend

[36] This paragraph summarises the information on the Libor's origins provided on the official website of the BBA Libor, www.bbalibor.com/bbalibor-explained/historical-perspective.

[37] This question has been in place in this form since its latest revision in 1998.

[38] This paragraph summarises the technical information provided on the official website of the BBA Libor at www.bbalibor.com/bbalibor-explained/the-basics.

unsecured funds to other banks. The Libor manipulation scandal also triggered a reform of the Euribor. Thus, while the Euribor used to be calculated for fifteen different maturities ranging from one week to twelve months, it has been decided to reduce the number of different maturities to no more than seven (1 and 2 weeks, 1, 3, 6, 9 and 12 months) as of 1 November 2013.[39] Having comprised well over forty banks until 2012, the panel of eurozone banks contributing to the Euribor consisted of thirty-two banks as of 1 October 2013.[40]

Other private benchmark rates such as the earlier mentioned Sibor, the Tibor and other smaller ones have also been designed in analogy to the Libor.

The reliability of the Libor and other private benchmark rates, and their reputation as objective and transparent reference rates for both financial and commercial markets, has recently come under fire as a result of a manipulation scandal that gradually emerged over recent years and which, by 1 October 2013, had triggered major legal and regulatory consequences which raise serious questions about the future of private benchmark interest rates in what has become a truly transnational monetary and financial system as explained above.

II. The Libor manipulation scandal and its implications

After presenting the key features of the Libor manipulation scandal and its main regulatory consequences (Section C.II.1), this section looks briefly at the Libor scandal from the angle of competition law (Section C.II.2).

1. The key features of the scandal and the main regulatory consequences

Attention to potential irregularities in the way Libor rates are determined was raised for the first time by a controversial study released by the *Wall Street Journal* on 29 May 2008,[41] which suggested that literally all banks participating in the setting of Libor rates, notably CitiGroup, WestLB

[39] See European Banking Federation, 'Reduction in the Number of Euribor Tenors as of 1 November 2013' (23 September 2013), press release D2832–2013, www.euribor-ebf.eu/assets/files/D2832A-2013-Euribor%20tenors%20to%20be%20reduced%20as%20of%201%20November%202013.pdf. For detailed information on the Euribor's recent reform, see the Euribor website of the European Banking Association, www.euribor-ebf.eu/euribor-org/euribor-reform.html.

[40] For a regularly adjusted list of the panel of contributing banks, see www.euribor-ebf.eu/euribor-org/panel-banks.html.

[41] C. Mollenkamp and M. Whitehouse, 'Study Casts Doubt on Key Rate', *Wall Street Journal* (29 May 2008), online.wsj.com/article/SB121200703762027135.html.

and HBOS, may have consistently understated their borrowing costs. The suspected reason for this was that the banks may have wished to appear healthier than they actually were during the 2007–8 credit crunch. In the same vein, in September 2008, Willem Buiter, a former member of the Bank of England's MPC, called for the replacement of the Libor which he was quoted as having characterised as 'the rate at which banks don't lend to each other',[42] a description which, in November 2008, was also used by Mervyn King, the Governor of the Bank of England, before the UK Parliament House of Commons Treasury Select Committee.[43] However, not only the BBA but also the Bank for International Settlements (BIS), in its March 2008 Quarterly Review,[44] and the International Monetary Fund (IMF), in its October 2008 *Global Financial Stability Review*,[45] rejected these early allegations of manipulation and insisted that the Libor remained a sound benchmark.

Over the course of 2011 and 2012, regulators in various countries, notably the US and the UK, initiated probes regarding instances of Libor manipulation by several participating banks, notably Bank of America, Citigroup and UBS. On 28 February 2012, it was revealed that the US Department of Justice was even conducting a criminal investigation into potential Libor abuse, notably into the submission of rates requested by the bank's own traders in order to procure the latter an unfair advantage in predicting that day's benchmark.[46] That the UK Serious Fraud Office had also opened a criminal investigation into the same matter was announced on 6 July 2012.[47]

The full scale of the manipulation scandal became apparent in June 2012 when it was revealed that at least twelve banks around the world

[42] A. Osborne, 'Former MPC Man Calls for Libor to be Replaced', *The Telegraph* (11 September 2008), www.telegraph.co.uk/finance/economics/2795962/Former-MPC-man-calls-for-Libor-to-be-replaced.html.

[43] For the related Committee records, see UK Parliament, Examination of Witnesses (25 November 2008), www.publications.parliament.uk/pa/cm200708/cmselect/cmtreasy/1210/8112503.htm.

[44] See 'International Banking and Financial Markets Developments', *BIS Quarterly Review*, March 2008, p. 70, www.bis.org/publ/qtrpdf/r_qt0803.pdf.

[45] IMF, Global Financial Stability Report – Financial Stress and Deleveraging (October 2008) p. 76, www.imf.org/external/pubs/ft/gfsr/2008/02/pdf/text.pdf.

[46] C. Mollenkamp, 'Exclusive: U.S. Conducting Criminal Libor Probe', *Reuters* (28 February 2012), www.reuters.com/article/2012/02/28/us-libor-probe-idUSTRE81R1ZG20120228.

[47] See C. Main and E. Rosen, 'Libor Criminal Probe, CFTC Exemptions, Canada: Compliance', *Bloomberg Businessweek* (9 July 2012), www.businessweek.com/news/2012-07-09/libor-criminal-probe-cftc-bank-exemptions-canada-compliance.

were involved in Libor investigations.[48] On 27 June 2012, Barclays Bank became the first bank to face severe consequences, when it was fined GBP 59.5 million by the UK Financial Services Authority (FSA),[49] USD 200 million by the US Commodity Futures Trading Commission (CFTC),[50] and USD 160 million by the US Department of Justice for attempted manipulation of Libor and Euribor rates. It should be stressed that several other banks have been fined, accepted a settlement with the investigating agencies, or are still being investigated. Most notably, on 19 December 2012, UBS agreed to pay the UK, US and Swiss regulators a combined USD 1.5 billion for its share of responsibility in the Libor manipulation scandal.[51]

For the sake of brevity, the following paragraphs will focus on Barclays Bank only, since the condemned conduct of its staff appears to be a particularly powerful illustration of the type of conduct and criminal energy that caused the scandal.

The probes undertaken by the US and UK agencies had revealed that, on a significant number of occasions, Barclays' staff in charge of the daily rate submissions to Thomson Reuters had submitted rates requested by Barclays' traders placing bets on interest rates derivatives. Considering the huge size of the relevant market, USD 554 trillion in 2011, even tiny shifts of the interest rate could have a significant impact on the profits achieved by those traders.[52] As a consequence of the scandal, Bob Diamond, Chief Executive Officer (CEO) of Barclays, Marcus Agius, the bank's Chairman, and Jerry del Missier, Chief Operating Officer of the bank, who admitted having instructed employees in charge of Libor submissions to submit falsified rates to the BBA, all had to resign.

The US Department of Justice found that Barclays manipulated its Libor and Euribor submissions in order to meet at least two distinct objectives:[53] first, from at least as early as 2005, in order to benefit the

48 See 'Libor – Eagle Fried', *The Economist* (30 June 2012), www.economist.com/node/21557772.

49 For the final notice issued by the FSA to Barclays, see www.fsa.gov.uk/static/pubs/final/barclays-jun12.pdf.

50 US CFTC, 'CFTC Orders Barclays to pay $200 Million Penalty for Attempted Manipulation of and False Reporting concerning LIBOR and Euribor Benchmark Interest Rates', Press Release (27 June 2012), www.cftc.gov/PressRoom/PressReleases/pr6289-12.

51 See 'UBS Fined $1.5 bn for Libor Rigging', *BBC* (19 December 2012), www.bbc.co.uk/news/business-20767984.

52 See 'Libor – Eagle Fried'.

53 US Department of Justice, 'Barclays Bank PLC Admits Misconduct Related to Submissions for the London Interbank Offered Rate and the Euro Interbank Offered

financial positions of its traders, thus unfairly raising the bank's profits; and second, during the 2007–8 credit crunch and the ensuing Global Financial Crisis, to make the bank look healthier than it actually was, which in retrospect confirmed the suspicion that the *Wall Street Journal* had raised back in 2008. It goes without saying that both these objectives are diametrically opposed to the ideal of a transparent and objective rate-setting mechanism through which the banks participating in the Libor and similar private benchmarks are supposed to provide a public service for a well-functioning financial system.

Whereas for the first objective, the seeking of unfair trading profits, the criminal nature is obvious, the picture seems less clear for the second one, i.e., safeguarding one's own bank from an overly nervous reaction of financial markets at a time of global financial distress. However, it would be erroneous to conclude that, by understating their borrowing costs in its Libor submission, Barclays, and any other bank engaging in similar conduct, may in fact have contributed to systemic stability. By misleading market participants, and financial supervisors, about its actual borrowing costs, an ailing financial institution merely postpones the moment at which it will be driven out of the market or when it will have to be rescued by its peers or the central bank as the lender of last resort. In the long run, this will likely create greater harm and costs to the financial system than would have been the case under accurately reported rates.

Yet, it may well have been out of fear of a nervous reaction of financial markets that neither the Fed nor the Bank of England took any noteworthy action against the serious allegations of fraud, which, as documents released by the New York Fed in July 2012 clearly show, they had been aware of since at least 2007.[54] Hence, it seems appropriate for central banks and regulators to take part of the blame for the scale of the Libor manipulation scandal. Although regulators and central banks may thus have been mistaken when judged from a long-term perspective, it is important to realise that requiring the banks participating in setting the Libor to report their actual borrowing costs and nothing else, appears to have conflicted with the short-term objectives of central bankers and financial regulators during the credit crunch. This may well explain why

Rate and Agrees to Pay $160 Million Penalty', *Justice News* (27 June 2012), www.justice.gov/opa/pr/2012/June/12-crm-815.html.

[54] M. Gongloff, 'New York Fed's Libor Documents Reveal Cozy Relationship Between Regulators, Banks', *HuffPost* (13 July 2012), www.huffingtonpost.com/2012/07/13/new-york-fed-libor-documents_n_1671524.html.

they preferred to turn a blind eye to what was going on with the setting of Libor rates.

In light of the above, it is not surprising that the report[55] prepared by the Treasury Select Committee (TSC) of the UK Parliament's House of Commons severely criticises the FSA for failing to ensure adequate supervision and for its inability to take action upon specific information from various sources that Libor rates were being manipulated.[56] According to Andrew Tyrie, the TSC's chairman, manipulation of Libor rates was 'made possible by a prolonged period of extremely weak internal compliance and board governance at Barclays, as well as a failure of regulatory supervision'.[57] In its report, the TSC recommended, *inter alia*, that the FSA and, upon entry into force of what was then still the Financial Services Bill, its successors,[58] impose a wider range of fines, levying much higher penalties on firms that fail to cooperate.[59] It also required that the FSA report to the FSC on how it will improve its supervisory efforts to counter weak compliance in the future,[60] and recommended that the Government, following the presentation of the review conducted by Martin Wheatley (the so-called 'Wheatley Review'), then still managing director of the FSA and now CEO of the new Financial Conduct Authority (FCA), into the origins of the Libor scandal,

[55] House of Commons Treasury Committee, *Fixing LIBOR: Some Preliminary Findings* (18 August 2012), www.parliament.uk/documents/commons-committees/treasury/Fixing%20LIBOR_%20some%20preliminary%20findings%20-%20VOL%20I.pdf.

[56] S. Dale, 'TSC slams FSA Over Role in Libor Scandal', *MoneyMarketing* (18 August 2012), www.moneymarketing.co.uk/politics/tsc-slams-fsa-over-role-in-libor-scandal/1056501.article.

[57] UK Parliament, Commons Select Committee, 'Treasury Committee Publishes LIBOR Report', Press Release (18 August 2012), www.parliament.uk/business/committees/committees-a-z/commons-select/treasury-committee/news/treasury-committee-publishes-libor-report/.

[58] Upon entry into force of the Financial Services Act 2012 on 1 April 2013, the FSA was indeed abolished and its responsibilities were shared between two new agencies and the Bank of England. Thus, the Financial Conduct Authority (FCA) has since been in charge of supervising both retail and wholesale financial services firms in the UK. The prudential regulation of financial firms, including banks, investment banks, building societies and insurance companies, is being carried out by the Prudential Regulation Authority (PRA), which forms part of the Bank of England. For detailed information and links to background material on the Financial Services Act, see www.gov.uk/government/policies/improving-regulation-of-the-financial-sector-to-protect-customers-and-the-economy.

[59] House of Commons Treasury Committee, *Fixing LIBOR: Some Preliminary Findings*, para. 16.

[60] *Ibid.*, para. 36.

consider clarifying the FSA's (and its successors') power to initiate criminal proceedings where there is serious fraudulent conduct in financial markets.[61] As will be explained towards the end of this Section, the UK Government has already created a related criminal offence in the meantime.

Providing for such criminal sanctions to cover the manipulation of benchmark rates would be perfectly in line with the European Commission's legislative reaction to the Libor manipulation scandal. On 25 July 2012, the Commission adopted amendments to the proposals for a Regulation and a Directive on insider dealing and market manipulation, including criminal sanctions, which it had originally tabled on 20 October 2011, in order to explicitly prohibit the manipulation of benchmark rates such as the Libor and Euribor and to make such manipulation a criminal offence.[62] As of 1 October 2013, the legislative process on both complementary instruments, most importantly on the Directive providing for the potential imposition of criminal sanctions, was still underway; it was hoped that the necessary political agreement could be reached by the end of 2013.[63]

The above-mentioned Wheatley Review into various aspects of the setting and usage of Libor was presented on 28 September 2012.[64] It made a number of nuanced recommendations to the Government, submitting notably a ten-point plan for the comprehensive reform of the Libor. Its key conclusions/recommendations, which have largely been followed in the subsequent reform of the Libor and the related regulatory framework, can be summarised as follows.

First, the Review concluded that a transition to a new benchmark or set of benchmarks would pose an unacceptably high risk of significant financial instability, and risk large-scale litigation between parties holding contracts that reference the Libor and that there was therefore a clear case in favour of comprehensively reforming the Libor, rather than

[61] House of Commons Treasury Committee, *Fixing LIBOR: Some Preliminary Findings*, para. 202.

[62] For the Commission's amended proposals for a Regulation and a Directive as well as related press releases and other background documents, see the website of Internal Market and Services Commissioner Michel Barnier, ec.europa.eu/commission_2010-2014/barnier/headlines/news/2012/07/20120725_en.htm.

[63] See European Commission, 'European Parliament's Endorsement of the Political Agreement on Market Abuse Regulation', MEMO/13/774 (10 September 2013) europa.eu/rapid/press-release_MEMO-13-774_en.htm.

[64] The Wheatley Review and related materials can be downloaded from the Government's website, www.hm-treasury.gov.uk/wheatley_review.htm.

replacing the benchmark.[65] This approach has clearly been followed in reaction to the recent manipulation scandal. Instead of replacing the main private-sector benchmark rates with something completely new, the main rates such as the Libor and the Euribor have merely been redesigned (fewer maturities (seven) for fewer currencies (five), as explained earlier[66]). In addition, they have been placed in a revised legal framework. Thus, as already mentioned,[67] the FSA was abolished and its responsibilities were shared between two new agencies (the FCA and PRA) and the Bank of England. In addition, in early 2014 the BBA is due to be replaced by NYSE Euronext Rate Administration Limited, a subsidiary of NYSE Euronext, as the new administrator of the Libor.[68] With the new administrator being a London-based, UK-registered company, the administration of the Libor has become a regulated activity overseen by the FCA.

Second, the Wheatley Review concluded that actual transaction data, and not hypothetical data, should be used to support Libor submissions under strict and detailed processes for verifying submissions against transaction data and with the number of different Libor rates being limited to those currencies and maturities ('tenors') that are supported by sufficient transaction data. As noted earlier, the recent reduction of the number of currencies and maturities for which Libor rates are calculated (bringing the total number of rates that are calculated daily from 150 down to 35) clearly serves to increase the likelihood that the reported rates are underpinned by real trades. It still remains, of course, that by definition, Libor rates are not based on actual transactions.

Third, the Review concluded that while Libor needed to be reformed to remedy its weaknesses, it would not be appropriate for the authorities to completely take over the process of producing a benchmark that exists primarily for the benefit of market participants. According to the Wheatley Review, market participants are in the best position to identify the most reliable and verifiable benchmark for any given transaction. The role of the authorities is primarily to ensure the integrity of the process by which benchmarks are determined rather than to direct users

[65] It should be added, however, that the Wheatley Review acknowledges that given the difficulties identified with attempting to replace the Libor quickly, it has not attempted to conduct a detailed evaluation of alternatives that might, over time, come to be used by market participants.

[66] See the final paragraphs of Section C.I above.

[67] See above, n 58.

[68] NYSE Euronext, 'NYSE Euronext Subsidiary to Become New Administrator of Libor', Press Release (9 July 2013), www.nyse.com/press/1373365567815.html.

to adopt a particular benchmark.[69] In reaction to these recommendations, the BBA adopted a new code of conduct for the banks participating in the Libor. Knowingly or deliberately making false or misleading statements in relation to the setting of benchmarks was made a criminal offence under the Financial Services Act 2012.[70] Maybe most importantly, it was decided that individual rate submissions by the participating banks would only be published after an embargo of three months. Without affecting the daily calculation of the various Libor rates, this change will likely diminish the incentive for participating banks to make inaccurate statements serving to appear overly healthy.[71]

2. The Libor manipulation scandal and competition law

The analysis provided by this chapter would not be complete without also taking a look at the Libor scandal from the angle of competition law. The fact that the manipulation of private benchmark interest rates may well trigger legal consequences under domestic and European competition rules is yet another powerful expression of the increasingly hybrid nature of contemporary monetary law as a body of truly transnational law combining both public and private law aspects and emerging from formerly separate legal disciplines.

On 13 July 2012, EU Competition Commissioner Joaquín Almunia was quoted as having said:

> The alleged rate-rigging is a major competition concern .... This is why the Commission started investigating a number of banks last year for their possible concerted manipulation of [interest rate] benchmarks such as Libor, Euribor and Tibor, the Tokyo rate, for several currencies. ... The investigations have top priority because this sort of collusion can seriously harm competition worldwide and on our continent in particular.[72]

[69] The information provided in this paragraph is a summary of the information provided on pages 6–8 of the Wheatley Review, see *ibid.*

[70] See HM Treasury, 'Financial Services Bill receives Royal Assent', Press Release (19 December 2012), www.gov.uk/government/news/financial-services-bill-receives-royal-assent.

[71] BBA Libor, 'Announcement of Libor Changes' (12 June 2013), www.bbalibor.com/news/announcement-of-libor-changes.

[72] 'Libor scandal: EU Probe into "Shocking" Rate-rigging Includes Japan, says Joaquín Almunia', *The Telegraph* (13 July 2012), www.telegraph.co.uk/finance/newsbysector/banksandfinance/9397354/Libor-scandal-EU-probe-into-shocking-rate-rigging-includes-Japan-says-Joaquin-Almunia.html.

Shortly thereafter, on 24 July 2012, Almunia gave an optimistic outlook on the progress of the investigations, noting that: 'The evidence we have collected is quite telling, so I am pretty sure this investigation will not be closed without results.'[73] Two months later, on 24 September 2012, Almunia indicated that in these investigations, which the Commission was reported to have placed on its top-priority list,[74] high fines might be imposed: 'According to [competition] rules we need to enforce and implement, based on the sales, turnover figures affected by the cartel. We also need to account for gravity of infractions. I think [in this case] [the] level of gravity is above average.'[75]

So far at least, the Commission's current probe under EU competition rules appears to focus exclusively on collusion between rival undertakings under Article 101 of the Treaty on the Functioning of the European Union (TFEU), as opposed to investigating the unilateral or joint abuse of a dominant position under Article 102 TFEU. The reasons for this choice are not obvious. Article 102(a) TFEU explicitly states that the direct or indirect imposition of unfair purchase or selling prices or other unfair trading conditions is one type of abuse covered by Article 102. This seems to be sufficiently broad to cover the manipulation of benchmark interest rates. Hence, it seems more likely that the Commission's decision not to investigate under Article 102 TFEU was made for different reasons. Perhaps the Commission reached the preliminary conclusion that the market shares of the banks involved were not big enough to put them into a dominant position, particularly in light of the fact that the highest and lowest 25 per cent of reported rates are entirely disregarded when calculating Libor rates. Verifying this assumption would require a more detailed factual analysis than can be undertaken as part of this chapter. It seems equally plausible that the Commission adheres to the view that the manipulation of benchmark interest rates as a unilateral act should not be addressed under Article 102 TFEU. Rather it should come under the two pieces of new EU legislation which, as noted in the preceding subsection, it has deliberately amended in reaction to the Libor scandal in order for the manipulation of benchmark interest rates to be explicitly prohibited and become subject to criminal sanctions in all EU Member States.

[73] A. R. Rego and R. McLeod, 'EU Probes into Interest-rate Benchmarks Yields "Telling" Evidence, Almunia Says', *MLex market intelligence* (24 July 2012).

[74] A. R. Rego, '"Gravity" of Conduct over Interbank Rates "Above Average", Almunia says', *MLex market intelligence* (24 September 2012).

[75] *Ibid.*

Returning to the Commission's investigations on potential collusion, Article 101.1 TFEU prohibits, as incompatible with the internal market, agreements between undertakings, decisions by associations of undertakings and concerted practices which may affect trade between Member States and which have as their object or effect the prevention, restriction or distortion of competition within the internal market. Article 101.1 (a)–(e) TFEU adds a non-exhaustive list of agreements, decisions or concerted actions that are thus prohibited. It seems likely that the Commission is focusing its current investigations on subparagraph (a) of Article 101.1 TFEU which outlaws agreements, decisions or concerted actions, 'which directly or indirectly fix purchase or selling prices or any other trading conditions'.

This calls for four succinct comments. First, the crucial issue in the Commission's investigations will be whether it can establish the existence of an actual agreement, decision or concerted practice among various banks to report understated borrowing costs. While numerous exchanges between the traders and rate submitters within the *same* banks, such as those discovered in Barclays' case, prove the attempt to manipulate Libor rates, they do not show anything that would amount to a relevant agreement, decision, or concerted practice under Article 101 TFEU which would have to be identified as among *different* banks. Second, even if it were to take the view that banks submitting understated borrowing costs did so primarily in order to avoid a nervous reaction by the markets at a time of crisis, and not to distort competition, the Commission may still find a violation of Article 101.1 TFEU as that provision outlaws agreements, decisions or concerted practices with the object *or effect* of preventing, restricting or distorting competition. Third, even if collusion to manipulate Libor rates can be shown, the banks involved might argue that their doing so stabilised the financial markets at a time of crisis, and that their agreement, decision or concerted practice promoted economic progress and should thus benefit from an exemption under Article 101.3 TFEU. However, as explained earlier, in the long run the reporting of understated borrowing costs may well be more harmful than the early market exit of an ailing institution, which is why such an excuse would probably fail to gain acceptance. Fourth, if the Commission were to find that Article 101 TFEU has been infringed, those who consider that they have been harmed by the rigged interest rates could sue the banks involved for damages in their domestic courts without having to establish liability. Domestic courts would be bound by the Commission's findings and would turn directly to assessing what damages were caused, which may itself be a tricky issue.[76]

As regards the probable outcome of the Commission's investigations, which were still ongoing when this book went to press, it was reported that the Commission would seek to reach a settlement with the investigated banks by the end of 2013.[77] Under the applicable EU provisions, such settlement, a rather frequent phenomenon in the realm of competition law, could lead to lower fines for the banks concerned in return for an outright admission of wrongdoing.

3. Update on the outcome of the Commission's investigations

On 4 December 2013, the Commission announced that it had fined eight financial institutions a total of EUR1.71 billion for participating in illegal cartels in markets for interest rate derivatives dominated in both euro and yen, such collusion being prohibited by Article 101 TFEU and Article 53 of the European Economic Area Agreement.[78] As expected, the related decisions were adopted under the Commission's cartel settlement procedure, with the companies' fines being reduced by 10 per cent for their willingness to settle.[79] Both Barclays and UBS received full immunity for revealing the existence of the respective cartels and thereby avoided fines of EUR690 million and EUR2.5 billion respectively.[80] EU Competition Commissioner Joaquín Almunia commented as follows on the conclusion of the investigations:

> What is shocking about the LIBOR and EURIBOR scandals is not only the manipulation of benchmarks, which is being tackled by financial regulators worldwide, but also the collusion between banks who are supposed to be competing with each other. Today's decision sends a

[76] See C. Bristow, 'Libor Manipulation: Breach of Competition Law?' (20 July 2012), www.collyerbristow.com/fileserver.aspx?oID=1929&IID-0.

[77] L. Brinded, 'Libor Fixing Scandal: EU Eyes Bank Case Settlements By 2014', *International Business Times* (1 July 2013), www.ibtimes.co.uk/articles/485104/20130701/libor-fixing-scandal-euribor-almunia-eu-ec.htm.

[78] See European Commission, 'Antitrust: Commission Fines Banks € 1.71 billion for Participating in Cartels in the Interest Rate Derivative Industry', Press release, IP/13/1208 (4 December 2013), europa.eu/rapid/press-release_IP-13-1208_en.html (accessed 9 December 2013).

[79] *Ibid.*

[80] *Ibid.* For the precise amounts of the fines imposed on the various financial institutions involved in the two cartels, see *ibid.*

> clear message that the Commission is determined to fight and sanction these cartels in the financial sector. Healthy competition and transparency are crucial for financial markets to work properly, at the service of the real economy rather than the interests of a few.[81]

D. Conclusion

It is economic reality that certain short-term interest reference rates set by the private sector, such as the Libor, have evolved into the key benchmark rates for the vast global trade in innovative financial instruments. The hybrid reality of global benchmark interest rates thus consists of both classical central bank interest rates, set under domestic public law, and of transnational, private, benchmark rates set by associations of globally operating banks.

This chapter has attempted to show that the setting of global benchmark interest rates, both by central banks and bankers' associations, is characterised by conflicting objectives at various levels: between different central banks, between central banks, the government and regulators, between the private sector and regulators, between the primary interest of private banks in raising their profits and their obligation to provide a public service by contributing to the setting of private benchmark interest rates, among others. It has been argued herein that these conflicts, as well the overly hybrid nature of monetary affairs when it comes to the setting of benchmark rates, potentially endanger the attainment of the overarching objectives pursued by central banks, i.e., monetary and financial stability.

In this conclusion, it seems worth recalling that the potential conflict between the central bank objectives of monetary and financial stability and the conflict that may arise within the dual objective of price stability and economic growth are distinctly different in nature. Although, strictly speaking, financial stability is not an objective of monetary and interest rate policies, the central bank of a modern economy has little choice but to pursue both monetary and financial stability in parallel. By contrast, it would make sense in light of the arguments presented herein that those central banks that formally pursue an economic growth objective switch to a single objective of domestic price stability. As explained above, even without an explicit growth objective, the inherent inflation bias of an inflation target still ensures a constant economic stimulus, yet without

[81] *Ibid.*

raising doubts about the central bank's commitment to the objective of price stability at a time of crisis.

As regards the lessons to be drawn from the Libor manipulation scandal, this chapter largely agrees with the sensible recommendations made by the UK Parliament's House of Commons TSC and those submitted by the Wheatley Review for the UK Government's further consideration. As explained, the reforms undertaken in the wake of the Libor manipulations scandal are broadly in line with these recommendations. However, this chapter recommends that the feasibility of the radical option of replacing private benchmark rates such as Libor and Euribor by alternative benchmarks based on central bank key rates be nevertheless examined in more detail. As a potential long-term alternative to the existing scheme this option should not be too readily dismissed.

There is indeed little doubt that a radical transition to a new benchmark or to a set of benchmarks, if undertaken hastily, would pose a significant risk of financial instability, and might lead to large-scale litigation between parties holding contracts that rely on the Libor as a reference. However, one cannot stress enough that even a comprehensive reform of the way Libor rates are calculated, such as the one undertaken in the aftermath of the recent Libor scandal, essentially falls short of resolving the fundamental conflict of interests that arises from a situation in which staff members, who are all on the payroll of the same institution, and who see each other over lunch and who play golf with each other, are in charge both of contributing to the setting of a transparent and objective benchmark, thus providing a public service to the financial system, and of making money by betting on the evolution of the very same interest rates. In hindsight, the only thing that really is surprising in the entire Libor scandal is that anybody ever believed that the existing system would not be rigged.

8

Credit rating agencies: regulation and financial stability

IAIN MACNEIL

A. Introduction

Credit rating agencies (CRAs) were largely excluded from regulation until 2006 in the US and until 2010 in the European Union (EU). That approach was predicated on the view that reputational concerns provided adequate incentives to CRAs to produce accurate ratings.[1] The financial crisis changed that perception as it became apparent that CRAs were prone to serious errors. Those responsible for regulating CRAs responded by moving the focus on to the role of CRAs as market actors who should fall within the scope of the regulatory perimeter. The main objective of regulating CRAs is to improve the accuracy of ratings, thereby assisting investors in debt instruments to estimate more accurately the degree of (credit) risk to which they are exposed.

More recent regulatory developments have moved beyond that agenda to focus on over-reliance by regulators and investors on ratings. Although not generally framed in such terms, this process should be seen as correcting an error on the part of policy-makers, regulators and investors that is on a par with the errors of the CRAs. In retrospect, it now seems clear that the widespread adoption of ratings as a risk-control mechanism in financial regulations was misguided. The primary purpose of recent moves to limit reliance on credit ratings in regulatory rules is to mitigate mechanistic reliance on credit ratings by investors as well as the pro-cyclical effect of rating downgrades which have the capacity to cause 'cliff effects' when regulatory capital and investment portfolios are adjusted in response to rating downgrades. Reducing reliance on ratings is predicted to promote financial stability and resilience by reducing the

[1] See, generally, R. Levich, G. Majnoni and C. Reinhart (eds.), *Ratings, Rating Agencies and the Global Financial System* (Boston, MA: Springer, 2002).

tendency for investors to act in a co-ordinated manner in response to rating downgrades.

Since there has been more analysis and progress with regard to the regulation of CRAs, this chapter focuses in particular on over-reliance on ratings in financial regulation and financial contracting. It begins with an overview of those characteristics of CRAs and ratings which are relevant for the discussion which follows. It then outlines the main features of the EU and US regulatory regimes for CRAs. The nature and extent of regulatory reliance on ratings as well as the role of ratings in the private law domain of financial contracting is then examined. Section E explores the links between ratings and financial stability while Section F considers potential solutions. Section G concludes.

B. Ratings and the credit rating industry

A credit rating measures the relative risk that an entity or transaction will fail to meet its financial commitments, such as interest payments and repayment of principal, on a timely basis.[2] While there are differences in the rating methodologies employed by the leading CRAs, there are three characteristics that they share. First, ratings are characterised by CRAs as an ordinal measure[3] of credit risk rather than specific estimates of credit risk metrics such as default probability or expected loss. Second, they distinguish so-called investment grade from non-investment grade or speculative debt securities.[4] Third, rating stability is a key objective of the CRAs. This means that a rating should be capable of surviving an economic trough and that a recession or tightening in liquidity should not in itself trigger a downgrade. All three characteristics have implications for the regulatory use of ratings which are considered in more detail below. At this point, it may simply be observed that these characteristics inherently limit the role that may be performed by ratings, especially when they are relied on to operate in a manner or a context for which they were not designed.

Ratings can be either solicited (by the issuer) or unsolicited. In the case of sovereign debt, ratings are normally unsolicited but in the case of corporate debt most ratings are solicited (and paid for by the issuer).

[2] IMF, *Global Financial Stability Report* (2011), p. 88.

[3] An ordinal measure is a simple ranking system which does not seek to measure the distance between variables. The medals awarded in the Olympic Games are a classic example.

[4] IMF, *Global Financial Stability Report*, p. 90. These scales refer to long-term debt. There are separate scales for short-term debt.

This has implications for the sources of information on which ratings are based. Unsolicited ratings rely on public information whereas solicited ratings are generally based on private information made available to CRAs by the issuer. Changes to ratings are generally signalled in advance by negative 'review' or 'watch' notifications to indicate that a downgrade is likely within the next ninety days. Negative 'outlook' provides a longer-term form of warning of the potential for a downgrade.

Ratings are said to perform three main roles. First, they reduce information asymmetry between issuers and investors.[5] Their success in that role varies between different debt instruments, with a relatively good record in corporate debt being overshadowed by more recent failures in structured finance.[6] A related function of ratings is their role in reducing the cost to investors of engaging in their own individual assessments of credit quality.

Second, ratings play a key role in financial regulation. Their most significant role lies in determining the application of regulatory rules related to capital (such as the Basel framework for banking regulation). Expansion in that role since the 1970s has led to the claim that the primary role of CRAs is to grant a 'regulatory licence' to issuers and investors in rated debt instruments rather than solving information asymmetry.[7] The concept of a regulatory licence is that the function of a rating is primarily to facilitate compliance by the issuer and/or investors with relevant financial regulations, thereby lowering funding costs and complying with relevant portfolio regulations. Ratings also have a regulatory role with regard to asset identification, such as the definition of permissible investments and concentration limits. Both of these roles have been linked to official recognition of CRAs by regulatory authorities, although it is only relatively recently that the approval process has become more formal and rigorous.

[5] BIS, *Credit Ratings and Complementary Sources of Credit Quality Information* (2000). The informational content of ratings has, however, been disputed in the academic literature: for a review of the literature and finding that rating changes have a meaningful role with regard to the interpretation of previously disclosed information see M. Clement, B. Jung and S. Yang, 'The Interpretive Information Content of Credit Ratings Changes for Stock Investors', www.uic.edu/cba/accounting/Documents/Young-paper-Sp12.pdf.

[6] See UK Tripartite Authorities, *The United Kingdom Authorities Response to the European Commission Internal Market and Services Consultation Document on Credit Rating Agencies* (2010), p. 5.

[7] A. Partnoy, 'The Siskel and Ebert of Financial Markets? Two Thumbs Down for the Credit Ratings Agencies', *Washington University Law Quarterly* 77:3 (1999) 619–714, proposing removal of references to ratings and their replacement by CDS spreads.

Third, ratings perform an important role in the private law framework governing financial contracting and institutional investment. In that sphere they operate, *inter alia*, as contractual limitations on the investment powers of fund managers as well as a potential guide for courts to the fiduciary duties owed by fund managers to their clients.[8]

Two aspects of the CRA industry have attracted attention from regulators. The first is the concentrated nature of the industry and the dominance of the 'big three'. Although there are about 130 CRAs operating around the world, the industry is dominated by the 'big three': Moody's, Standard & Poor's and Fitch who have a combined global market share of 95 per cent.[9] The dominance of the big three, combined with the increasing reliance of regulators and investors on ratings, raises questions about whether there is effective competition in the CRA industry.[10] That issue has implications for the 'reputational capital' rationalisation for reliance on the accuracy of ratings, which claims that CRAs can be relied on to produce accurate ratings because their reputation and ability to generate future revenue depends on it.[11] The market dominance of the big three suggests that lack of competition may lead to less accurate ratings across the industry (as well as rent-extraction by the big three in setting fees) and therefore increased competition has been on the agenda as part of the regulatory debate.

The second issue which has attracted attention is the 'issuer pays' model according to which the issuer pays for a rating. While in the early stage of development of the ratings industry the 'investor pays' model had been the most common form of payment, the 'issuer pays' model is now the most widespread method of payment for ratings.[12] That model

8 *Ibid.*, 641.

9 EU Commission Staff Working Paper, *Impact Assessment Accompanying the Document Proposal for a Regulation amending Regulation (EC) No 1060/2009 on Credit Rating Agencies etc.*, SEC (2011) 1354, p. 7.

10 The preference for the big three may be partly explained by investors' preferences for a broad, cross-sectional, cross-border rating coverage from the same agency. This may create an entry barrier for new agencies and incentives to exaggerate their coverage: see, e.g., www.sec.gov/news/press/2012/2012-75.htm.

11 See, generally, S. Schwarcz, 'Private Ordering of Public Markets: The Rating Agency Paradox', *University of Illinois Law Review* (2002), 1. For the contrary view, arguing that CRAs are not reputationally constrained, see A. Johnston, 'Corporate Governance is the Problem, Not the Solution: A Critical Appraisal of the European Regulation on Credit Rating Agencies', *Journal of Corporate Law Studies* 11:2 (2011), 395.

12 The 'issuer pays' model accounts for more than two thirds of CRA revenues: see EU Commission, *Public Consultation on Credit Rating Agencies* (5 November 2010), p. 144.

raises an obvious concern with regard to conflicts of interest since a CRA which is paid by an issuer may become more concerned with short-term revenue generation than with its long-term reputation for accurate ratings. That concern is exacerbated when CRAs provide advisory and consulting services to issuers in connection with a rating because in that situation the aggregate remuneration of the CRA is clearly linked to generating the 'right' rating outcome to enable the issuer to meet its funding objectives.

C. CRA regulation: 'be right or be good'

Historically, CRAs were unregulated private sector organisations that did not attract the attention of regulators as a subject of regulation. However, two developments in particular led to the conclusion that there was a market failure in the production of accurate ratings for debt securities. The first was the failure of Enron in 2001 which prompted a review of the role of CRAs and eventually led to the passing of the Credit Rating Agency Reform Act of 2006 in the US. At this stage, the official view in the EU was that self-regulation, in the form of compliance with the International Organization of Securities Commissions (IOSCO) Code of Conduct Fundamentals,[13] provided an adequate response.[14] However, the onset of the financial crisis boosted support for a more formal and rigorous approach to regulation with the result that a regulation on CRAs was adopted by the EU in September 2009.[15] In terms of regulatory intensity this represented a third stage of development through the creation of a regime that built on but went beyond both the IOSCO Code and the US Act of 2006.

The rationale underlying both the US and EU initiatives was that regulation could improve the quality of ratings by making them reflect credit risk more accurately. Thus the primary regulatory response was a

Note that the unsolicited nature of ratings for sovereign debt means that there is normally no payment for a rating in this large segment of the debt market.

[13] IOSCO, *Code of Conduct Fundamentals for Credit Rating Agencies* (December 2004). While IOSCO reported in 2007 that the big three complied with its Code, subsequent investigations by the US Congress and US Senate suggested otherwise: see P. Yeoh, 'External Credit Assessment Institutions: Clash of Expectations and Accountability Issues', *Journal of Corporate Law Studies* 12:2 (2012), 393, 403.

[14] See Communication from the Commission on Credit Rating Agencies, OJ 2006 C 59/02, 59/5.

[15] Regulation (EC) No 1060/2009 on Credit Rating Agencies, OJ 2009 L 302/1 (as amended).

prescription that ratings should 'be right'. That objective was pursued indirectly through regulation of the organisation and governance of CRAs rather than by direct regulation of their rating methodology. While no explicit consideration was given to the inevitable outcome that not all ratings can be right at all points in time, the implicit regulatory prescription is that if CRAs cannot be right they should at least 'be good', meaning that they operate in a manner which promotes accountability and transparency.[16] This approach is now considered in more detail by reference to the primary regulatory techniques that are employed in the US and EU systems: registration and supervision; control of conflicts of interest; and the imposition on CRAs of disclosure and transparency requirements.

Registration of CRAs acts as a form of control of entry by linking registration to the use of ratings by financial institutions in connection with regulatory rules.[17] It does not in itself require that financial instruments must be rated nor that investors must invest only in rated securities.[18] The registration process requires a CRA to submit information regarding its rating methodology. While the prescribed information is more extensive in the EU than the US, the US Securities and Exchange Commission (SEC) has a residual power to require information that may be necessary in the public interest.[19] Both systems require submission of rating methodology and the organisational structure of the CRA. Registration and supervision in the US remains in the hands of the SEC, but the EU has adopted a novel approach whereby the European Securities and Markets Authority (ESMA) rather than the national regulatory authorities is responsible for registration and supervision of CRAs.

[16] See Annex 1A of the CRA Regulation and Johnston ('Corporate Governance is the Problem', 439) noting that many of the governance requirements set by the CRA Regulation were already in place for the big three CRAs prior to the financial crisis under the listing rules of the New York Stock Exchange (NYSE) and therefore reliance on that approach may be misguided.

[17] Article 4(1)(98) of the CRD IV Regulation (575/2013, OJ 2013 L 176/1) removed the anomaly whereby approval as an ECAI (External Credit Assessment Institution) was required in addition to registration under the CRA Regulation in order for EU financial institutions to rely on ratings: any CRA registered under the CRA Regulation is now deemed to be an ECAI. See further EU Commission, *Impact Assessment*, p. 18.

[18] Incentives to have a rating or to invest in rated securities are created indirectly by the reliance of regulations on ratings.

[19] Compare Article 15(1) of and Annex II to the EU CRA Regulation with Section 15E of the Securities Exchange Act 1934 (15 USC 78o-7) as amended by Dodd-Frank.

Regulatory rules on conflicts of interest address the inherent conflict that is present in the 'issuer pays' model. The primary focus is on ensuring that a credit rating is an independent[20] and objective assessment of credit quality that is free from all political and economic influences or constraints. Both the US and EU systems implement this objective through rules relating to organisation (governance of a CRA), operational requirements and rules relating to rating analysts.[21] An important feature is the prohibition in both systems on the provision of consultancy or advisory services to rated entities, which was an important feature of the ratings inflation in structured finance which preceded the financial crisis.[22] The conclusion implicit in that solution is that the conflict of interest posed by advisory services is of a different order to the other conflicts faced by CRAs and not capable of resolution by disclosure, internal management or regulatory rules. Under both the EU Regulation and Dodd-Frank, remuneration of CRA staff is left to the independent directors to determine.[23]

Disclosure and transparency requirements focus on providing investors and the public with a better understanding of the rating process and ensuring better accountability on the part of CRAs for their actions. Both the US and EU regimes require public disclosure (and updating) of rating procedures and methodologies as well as historical performance data on the accuracy of ratings. Reflecting the particular problems in that sector, the EU requires ratings for structured finance to carry a symbol to distinguish it from other ratings.[24] The EU system in effect treats a rating as a public good by requiring that all ratings are made public, even those that are distributed by subscription.[25]

[20] See, generally, P. Leyens, 'Intermediary Independence: Auditors, Financial Analysts and Rating Agencies', *Journal of Corporate Law Studies* 11 (2011) 33–66 proposing a public law model of independence as a correlative to market access.

[21] The greater intensity of EU regulation is evident in the requirement of Article 7(4) of the CRA Regulation for analyst rotation. There is no equivalent requirement in the US.

[22] See Article 6(2) CRA Regulation and Annex B para. 4; and for the US, 17 CFR 240.17(g)–5(c) and SEC *Federal Register* 73(123) (25 June 2008).

[23] See Johnston, 'Corporate Governance is the Problem', 430, noting that Moody's and S&P already followed this practice in conformity with the NYSE Listing Rules.

[24] Article 10(3) of the CRA Regulation. That approach has not been followed in the US although it may be introduced in due course to implement §938 of Dodd-Frank: see Johnston, 'Corporate Governance is the Problem', 431; and SEC *Federal Register* 74(25) (9 February 2009) n 1.

[25] Article 10(1) CRA Regulation.

It remains to be seen how far these measures will improve the accuracy of ratings. In the meantime the more pressing problem is the risk to financial stability posed by reliance on ratings.

D. Reliance on ratings

The use of ratings in regulatory rules first emerged in the US in banking regulation in the 1930s.[26] However, the two crucial developments for the integration of ratings into the regulatory framework did not occur until much later. First, the creation and deployment of the concept of a Nationally Recognised Statistical Rating Organisation (NRSRO) by the SEC in the 1970s led to much greater reliance on ratings within the rules of the agency.[27] Second, at the international level, the use of ratings in the 1996 market amendment to the Basel I framework and their subsequent adoption in the credit and market risk framework of Basel II was a key development. It resulted in ratings becoming a key determinant of regulatory capital and prompted the use of a range of strategies which attempted to expand banks' balance sheets either with no additional capital or using forms of capital which provided less protection against losses. The regulatory regime for investment firms that fall within the market regime of the Basel framework has a similar reliance on credit ratings but (at least outside the US) regulation of the insurance sector has been less reliant on credit ratings because it is focused on matching regulatory capital with the risks arising from insurance policies, which are associated more with accidents and mortality than with credit risk. In general it has been noted that the US is more reliant than the EU on credit ratings across the entire system of financial regulation.[28]

Regulatory systems rely on ratings for three main purposes: first, as a measure of risk for the purposes of determining regulatory capital; second, as a method to identify permissible assets; and third, to determine disclosure requirements and prospectus eligibility in the context of securities offerings.[29] Each is now considered in more detail.

[26] See, generally, Partnoy, 'The Siskel and Ebert of Financial Markets', 636.

[27] See, generally, J. Hunt, 'Credit Rating Agencies and the "Worldwide Credit Crisis": The Limits of Reputation, the Insufficiency of Reform, and a Proposal for Improvement', *Columbia Business Law Review* (2009) 109.

[28] Basel Committee on Banking Supervision (BCBS), The Joint Forum, *Stocktaking on the Use of Credit Ratings* (2009), p. 14.

[29] *Ibid.* at 3.

The determination of regulatory capital under the Basel regime requires the aggregation of capital requirements attributable to various forms of risk. For commercial banks, credit risk is the major component, whereas for investment banks and securities firms market risk is the more important factor. Credit risk is determined by a process of weighting assets (such as bonds, collateralised debt obligations (CDOs) and loans) according to their quality and a primary determinant of quality is ratings allocated by recognised rating agencies. A similar process occurs in the calculation of market risk for debt securities. In both instances sovereign debt classified as 'step 1' under Basel (equivalent to AAA in CRA terms) is zero-weighted, meaning that there is no capital requirement.[30] For lower rated corporate debt, however, the risk weighting can exceed 100 per cent of the exposure at default.[31] Thus, ratings directly influence the regulatory capital requirement of banks and securities firms. Moreover, the greater the leverage within those firms, the greater will be the effect of changes to ratings on capital requirements.

In some jurisdictions (excluding the UK) ratings are commonly used to determine permissible assets and/or required investments and concentration limits. The most extensive use occurs in the US, where (SEC) regulation of money market funds[32] and (state) insurance regulation control permissible assets by reference to ratings. In the EU, the Undertakings for Collective Investment in Transferable Securities (UCITS) framework[33] for investment fund regulation does not refer expressly to ratings but recent changes in the regulation of money market funds do refer to ratings in their definition of permissible assets.[34]

The use of ratings in disclosure rules and prospectus rules serves a different purpose. While it is common to require rated entities to disclose their ratings and any changes to them, that simply has the effect of ensuring that a rating has a 'public good' character through being available to all investors at no cost. On the other hand, prospectus

[30] See, generally, S. Gleeson, *International Regulation of Banking* (Oxford University Press, 2010), Chapters 5 and 6.

[31] For a term loan, the exposure at default is normally the amount of the loan plus unpaid interest. See further Gleeson, *International Regulation of Banking*, Chapter 6.

[32] See 17 CFR § 270.2a-7, setting out the risk-limiting provisions applicable to money-market funds.

[33] The UCITS IV framework is contained in Directive 2009/65, OJ 2009, L 302/32.

[34] See Committee of European Securities Regulators (CESR/10–049), *CESR's Guidelines on a Common Definition of European Money Market Funds*. The role of CESR has since been taken over by ESMA.

eligibility rules, especially those in the US and Canada, which provide access to short-form prospectuses for securities with certain credit ratings, rely on credit ratings as a substitute for full disclosure. The underlying assumption is that a credit rating may justify less due diligence on the part of investors and can partly perform the role of disclosure in price formation and the efficient operation of markets. It can be argued that substitution is valid to the extent that CRA scrutiny (with access to private information from the issuer) may be more effective for determining credit quality than investor scrutiny of a prospectus. That approach, however, is not followed in the EU.

The implications of these forms of reliance on ratings in regulatory regimes can be considered at two levels. The first is the capacity of those links to cause mechanistic reactions to downgrades, resulting in herding in investor behaviour and 'cliff effects' which amplify procyclicality in the financial system. That issue is considered in more detail in Section E below. The second is the potential for those links to create the impression that regulators endorse ratings, thereby limiting the incentives for investors to undertake their own due diligence as to credit quality.[35] Moreover, regulatory endorsement encourages reliance by investors on ratings in private contracts, thereby exacerbating the risks to financial stability. This form of reliance is seen particularly in the investment mandates[36] of asset managers where ratings determine permissible investments and in the counterparty collateral requirements of trading markets where ratings are used to determine the amount of collateral that must be posted against trading positions. The latter form of reliance featured prominently in the collapse of Enron and AIG, both of which were triggered by spiralling collateral requirements linked to rating downgrades.[37]

E. Financial stability and the role of ratings

Financial stability has become the main focus of financial regulation at the international, regional and national levels since the onset of the

[35] In BCBs Joint Forum *Stocktaking* p. 14, more than half of the national regulator respondents viewed regulatory references to ratings as implying an official endorsement of such ratings and/or agencies.

[36] See R. Cantor, O. Gwilym and S. Thomas, 'The Use of Credit Ratings in Investment Management in the U.S. and Europe', *The Journal of Fixed Income* 17:2 (2007).

[37] IMF, *Global Financial Stability Report*, p. 92.

financial crisis. The change in focus reflects a failure in the past to pay sufficient attention to systemic risk by comparison with the risk of failure of individual financial institutions. While the concept of financial stability is still in the process of development, it implies at least that the financial system should be sufficiently robust to withstand shocks and thereby to mitigate the effects of financial sector distress for the remainder of the economy.[38]

The presence of systemic risk in the financial system is linked with the interconnected nature of the system. The financial system has been compared with networks that operate in other spheres and like them its robustness is related to the number of nodes within the network and the degree to which the nodes are connected.[39] On a variety of different measures the global financial system became more interconnected in the pre-crisis era, implying that its robustness had declined and the potential threat posed by systemic risk had increased.[40] A related development was greater homogeneity among banks as they shed idiosyncratic risk through risk transfer techniques such as securitisation and credit default swaps (CDSs).[41] Moreover, that process occurred at a time when two other developments might well have led to the impression that systemic risk was in decline or at least under control: one was the introduction of the more risk-sensitive system for the setting of regulatory capital under Basel II, and the other was the development of risk transfer techniques such as CDOs/CLOs (collateralised loan obligations) and CDSs which increased the complexity risk across the entire financial system but at the same time gave the impression that risk was being diversified across the system. In retrospect that impression was something of an illusion made possible by the lack of clear focus in pre-crisis regulatory regimes on defining or measuring systemic risk. That failure facilitated a process whereby banks were able to become less risky individually (for the

[38] W. Allen and G. Wood, 'Defining and Achieving Financial Stability', *Journal of Financial Stability* 2:2 (2006) 152–72; C. Borio and M. Drehmann, '*Towards an Operational Framework for Financial Stability: "Fuzzy" Measurement and its Consequences*', BIS Working Papers, No. 284 (2009).

[39] A. Haldane, '*Rethinking the Financial Network*' (2009), www.bankofengland.co.uk/publications/Pages/speeches/2009/386.aspx.

[40] *Ibid.*, p. 12. Also, see K. Alexander, 'International Economic Law and Macro-prudential Regulation', Chapter 20, this volume, for a more general study of the new macro-prudential approach in international financial regulation.

[41] See R. Nijskens and W. Wagner, 'Credit Risk Transfer Activities and Systemic Risk: How Banks Became Less Risky Individually but Posed Greater Risks to the Financial System at the Same Time', dx.doi.org/10.2139/ssrn.1319689.

purposes of regulatory capital) but posed greater risks to the financial system at the same time.[42]

As ratings are integrally linked with the process of funding financial institutions, setting regulatory capital and distributing risk across the financial system, they are a central part of the structure of the financial system and therefore linked closely with financial stability. The influence of ratings extends throughout their lifespan. An initial rating controls access to funding as a result of the link between ratings and regulatory capital (especially but not solely for banks) and the role of ratings in the investment mandates of institutional investors. Subsequent changes to ratings (or stages in that process such as review and rating watch) are linked to financial stability as a result of their capacity to cause herding among investors and 'cliff effects' in the markets for rated instruments as a result of simultaneous sales. That process is exacerbated by increased structural reliance on short-term wholesale market funding, collateral and securitisation, which has increased the sensitivity of banks' balance sheets to fluctuations in credit ratings.[43] In the case of sovereign debt, ratings have broader implications as a determinant of a country's borrowing costs in international capital markets and as a *de facto* ceiling for the rating of domestic financial institutions.[44] Thus, ratings have a distributional effect among and within countries because they have direct implications for the capacity of a country to finance public expenditure.

In an idealised world in which all ratings were correct at all points in time, ratings would perform a function similar to disclosure as a technique to mitigate systemic risk, especially when disclosure is used to inform investors about the nature and location of risk within the financial system. However, a crucial difference between ratings and disclosure in the conventional sense is that ratings represent an opinion which may turn out to be wrong whereas disclosure generally relates to facts that can be objectively verified. Thus, the role of ratings with respect to financial stability has to take account of the possibility that they may be inaccurate.[45] Moreover, the alternative regulatory prescription for

[42] *Ibid.* Interestingly, the market seemed to appreciate the risk associated with those techniques because the share price *beta* of such banks rose considerably as they employed those techniques.

[43] See IMF Staff Position Note SPN 09/09 'Policies to Mitigate Procyclicality' (2009), p. 5.

[44] EU Commission *Impact Assessment*, p. 136.

[45] An analogy might be made here with the role of markets in the efficient capital market hypothesis (ECMH). According to the strong version of ECMH prices reflect all

CRAs ('be good') is focused on public accountability and while that is a worthy objective in its own right, it may not contribute much to financial stability directly.

Errors in ratings can cause too much risk to build up within the financial system by causing investors to underestimate the risks to which they are exposed. As shown by the recent crisis, that risk is particularly prominent in the case of innovative financial instruments for which the CRAs and investors lack a relevant history upon which they can assess risk. Moreover, even without errors, changes in ratings have the capacity to cause a 'cliff effect' whereby holders of the relevant instrument simultaneously face the prospect of having to sell just at the time when liquidity is likely to dry up because the downgrade limits the number of buyers in the market.[46] As demonstrated by the recent crisis, the systemic effects of such downgrades are likely to be particularly severe when there are widespread and severe downgrades within a particular asset class (such as structured finance) where transmission and amplification mechanisms may aggravate financial distress.[47] The effects may extend beyond banks to assets managers, money market funds and insurers, for whom ratings may control permissible assets and concentration limits. Moreover, the impact on funding liquidity for banks may be particularly severe in view of the reliance of banks on funding from these sources.

The primary transmission mechanisms of systemic risk are contracts and markets.[48] Contracts represent a direct form of transmission since they give rise to direct obligations between counterparties. The failure of one party to meet contractual obligations has implications for the counterparty and for other market participants who may be exposed to that counterparty. The effect of contracts is most evident in bilateral

information (whether public or not) and therefore investors cannot 'beat the market'. A CRA whose ratings were always right would be performing a role similar to a market under the strong form of ECMH but that possibility seems as unlikely for a CRA as it does for a market. Weaker forms of efficiency seem inevitable in both instances. For a general introduction to ECMH, see K. Pilbeam, *Finance and Financial Markets* 3rd edn (Basingstoke: Palgrave, 2010), Chapter 10.

[46] See M. Pagano and P. Volpin, 'Credit Ratings Failures: Causes and Policy Options', in M. Dewatripont, X. Freixas and R. Portes (eds.), *Macroeconomic Stability and Financial Regulation: Key Issues for the G20* (London: Centre for Economic Policy Research, 2009), pp. 129–48, www.voxeu.org/reports/G20_Ebook.pdf.

[47] See E. Benmelech and J. Dlugosz, 'The Credit Rating Crisis', *NBER Working Paper* 15045, June 2009.

[48] See, generally, I. Anabtwai and S. Schwarz, 'Regulating Systemic Risk: Towards an Analytical Framework', *Notre Dame Law Review* 86:4 (2011), 1349.

over-the-counter (OTC) derivatives markets where counterparty credit risk can be difficult to gauge as a result of a lack of transparency as to the nature or scale of the commitments that have been entered into by market participants.[49] This lack of transparency can cause a 'similarity effect' to lead to contagion extending to anyone suspected of being exposed to the relevant entities or instruments. Markets represent a more indirect form of transmission mechanism since they transmit market risk (the risk of a fall in the value of a traded financial instrument) to all holders of that instrument. The transmission operates in tandem with 'mark to market' accounting rules and has the effect that the value of the instrument must be written down to its market value.[50] Markets also transmit liquidity risk in the sense that there may no longer be a market or the same depth of market for a particular instrument as a result of financial distress.

The payments system and psychology are additional transmission mechanisms of systemic risk. The payments system has implications for the liquidity requirements of the financial system in aggregate: for example, real-time gross settlement (RTGS) systems have higher liquidity requirements than systems that settle on a net basis at the end of each day and thus the demand for central bank money will vary as between the two systems and that in turn has implications for the policy rate at which the central bank can supply liquidity.[51] Similarly, shocks within the payment system (such as default by a commercial bank) may disrupt the normal pattern of demand for short-term central bank liquidity and cause volatility in short-term interest rates. Psychology introduces another complication in the sense that official announcements or guidance with respect to monetary policy may have effects that extend far beyond the immediate action that is envisaged as investors interpret the implied future path of monetary policy. This

[49] Recent regulatory reform requiring increased disclosure and transparency in the derivatives market has addressed this problem. It is implemented through the European Market Infrastructure Regulation (EMIR) in the EU and Dodd-Frank in the US.

[50] In a simple 'domino model' of financial contagion, asset prices are fixed at book value and balance sheets are affected only by default (see M. Brunnermeir, A. Crockett, C. Goodhart, A. D. Persaud and H. Shin, *Fundamental Principles of Financial Regulation* (Centre for Economic Policy Research, 2009). Nowadays, however, market price adjustments are a more powerful transmission mechanism than defaults.

[51] S. Schmitz, 'How Payment Systems Affect Monetary Policy', www.centralbanking.com/central-banking-journal/feature/2069864/payment-systems-affect-monetary-policy.

aspect has been particularly noticeable in 2013 as investors anticipated the effects on asset prices of the withdrawal of the US Federal Reserve from its programme of quantitative easing.[52]

Ratings are directly implicated in these transmission mechanisms. They are often used to determine contractual obligations (such as collateral requirements in OTC derivative contracts) or portfolio restrictions for investors as well as the eligibility of assets for use as collateral in the money market. Thus, ratings downgrades are closely linked to the transmission of systemic risk through contracts and the payments system. Similarly, ratings downgrades are linked with market transfer of risk since a downgrade may itself be the cause of a fall in market value. In the context of sovereign debt in particular, CDS contracts play an important role as a channel through which downgrades in one country may cause a 'spillover' effect in other countries, especially when downgrades are close to speculative grade.[53]

Moreover, ratings have a pro-cyclical effect in the transmission of systemic risk. In the Kindleberger-Minsky model of booms and busts[54] the role played by rating agencies in the expansion of credit and inflation in asset values is comparable to the herding instinct of investors. Thus CRAs contribute to the boom by systematically underestimating credit risk and supporting the development of new credit instruments. Rather than providing a prognosis of the evolving boom that might help to contain it, credit ratings provide an ostensibly rational basis for participation in the boom and an equally rational basis for exit when downgrades follow, although by that time it is quite likely that the market will have already collapsed.

Another consideration is that shocks may become amplified as they are transmitted across the system, with the result that a relatively small shock has the capacity to destabilise the system.[55] Two forms of

[52] See, e.g., G. Davies, 'No Tapering Yet for Global Central Banks', blogs.ft.com/gavyndavies/2013/07/16/no-tapering-yet-for-global-central-banks/, observing that guidance issued by the US Federal Reserve with regard to the withdrawal of its quantitative easing programme caused global bond yields to rise by 70 basis points in two months.

[53] See R. Arzeki, B. Candelon and N. Amandou, 'Sovereign Rating News and Financial Markets Spillovers: Evidence from the European Debt Crisis', *IMF Working Paper* 11/68 (March 2011).

[54] See C. Kindleberger, *Manias, Panics, and Crashes* (New York: Basic Books, 1978).

[55] M. Brunnermeir, 'Deciphering the Liquidity and Credit Crunch 2007–2008', *Journal of Economic Perspectives* 23:1 (2009), 77–100.

amplification are a loss spiral and a margin spiral. A loss spiral forces investors in a particular financial instrument (especially leveraged investors such as banks) to sell as the price declines so as to preserve their own capital at the initial level. These forced sales depress the price even further because other similar investors are also forced to sell and potential buyers prefer to wait until there is some sign of the market stabilising. A margin/haircut spiral reinforces the loss spiral because a fall in the value of underlying financial instruments will cause a rise in the margin/haircut requirements for associated derivative contracts, thereby triggering further sales of the underlying instruments to fund the higher requirements and preserve the original financial position.[56] Rating downgrades exacerbate these amplification mechanisms because they are likely to cause forced sales that might not otherwise occur. Thus, absent a requirement to meet regulatory capital or portfolio requirements that are linked to ratings some investors might well choose to hold on to instruments through a period of turbulence rather than sell.

It is clear therefore that rating downgrades (and associated stages in the process) play a destabilising role as a result of their linkage to financial regulation and financial contracting. The potential solutions to this problem are considered in the following section.

F. Potential solutions

Two regulatory strategies are available to address the problems associated with credit ratings. The first is to adjust the existing regulatory regimes so as to promote more accurate ratings. The second is to reduce the reliance on ratings in financial regulation through a process of 'unravelling'. The main options available to implement each strategy are now considered.[57]

I. Regulate to make ratings more accurate

In view of the considerable effort already devoted to this objective in the regulatory systems in the US and EU, the incremental benefits from this approach may be limited, at least so long as the radical solution of removing the 'issuer pays' model remains off-limits. Alternative

[56] *Ibid.*

[57] For a more extensive discussion of all options, see the EU Commission, *Impact Assessment*, p. 1354.

solutions focusing on more competition, the civil liability of CRAs and the regulatory characterisation of ratings would not fundamentally alter the ratings process and are probably best viewed as fine-tuning of the regulatory frameworks for CRAs that are already in place in the EU and US.

1. Remove or adjust the 'issuer pays' model

A radical solution to the conflict of interest faced by CRAs would be to prohibit the 'issuer pays' model and require that investors obtain and pay for their own rating before they purchase a particular financial instrument.[58] That option has not attracted widespread support because it is open to the risk that 'free-riding' might occur when ratings paid for by a single investor are leaked to the market as well as the risk that reluctance on the part of investors to pay might marginalise ratings for smaller issuers and less liquid instruments.

Proposed adjustments to the 'issuer pays' model have taken three main forms. The first is the prohibition on the provision by CRAs of ancillary services, which has already been introduced in the EU and US.[59] The rationale for the prohibition is to remove the risk that reliance on fees from ancillary services provided to an issuer may compromise the integrity of a rating assigned to an issuer or its securities. A second proposal has been that independent directors of the issuer should play a leading role in selecting a CRA, thereby limiting the possibility of collusion between the executive directors of an issuer and a CRA.[60] A third option is a variant of the so-called 'Cuomo plan' according to which CRAs should be paid an upfront fee irrespective of whether or not a rating is issued and 'credit shopping' (as well as ancillary services) should be prohibited. It is not certain, however, that this proposal would eliminate implicit collusion between issuers and CRAs, especially when they have a long-term relationship.

2. Promote more competition among CRAs

The oligopolistic structure of the CRA industry and its high barriers to entry prompted policy-makers and regulators to conclude that more

[58] See Pagano and Volpin, 'Credit Ratings Failures', p. 17; EU Commission Public Consultation on Credit Ratings Agencies, p. 27. Responses to the Commission Consultation generally favoured retention of the issuer pays model.

[59] See n 22 above and accompanying text.

[60] See European Commission, 'Roundtable on Credit Rating Agencies' (6 July 2011), p. 4.

competition may improve the quality of credit ratings. In Europe the focus has been on the potential role of the ECB and national central banks in providing ratings.[61] While this approach builds on the existing role of some central banks in credit assessment, there are inherent limitations to this solution arising from the independence of the ECB and national central banks (ruling out a compulsory system) and the existing prohibition on national central banks rating the sovereign debt of their own country.[62] In the US, the main focus has been on promoting competition through greater formality in the Nationally Recognised Statistical Rating Organisation (NRSRO) designation and more disclosure so as to foster comparability and monitoring of the performance of ratings.[63]

It remains to be seen, however, whether those measures actually do reduce the market power of the big three by encouraging new entrants into the market. And even if that does occur, it is not entirely clear that increased competition will result in the sort of material improvement in the quality of ratings that is predicted at a theoretical level.[64]

3. Extend the civil law liability of CRAs to promote accountability and accuracy

According to the EU Commission, a specific civil liability regime for CRAs would 'improve legal certainty for investors, prevent forum shopping and have a preventive disciplining effect on credit rating agencies'.[65] That approach has been followed in the US, where Dodd-Frank removed the protection from 'expert liability' previously enjoyed by NRSROs.[66] Elimination of the exemption makes all CRAs potentially liable as experts for misrepresentations or omissions of

[61] There has been less focus on whether CRAs may have acted in breach of competition law: for an analysis of this issue see Yeoh, 'External Credit Assessment Institutions', 423.

[62] See EU Commission, Public Consultation on Credit Ratings Agencies, p. 19, and Article 2(2)d(3) CRA Regulation.

[63] See SEC, Annual Report on NRSROs (March 2012) pp. 23–4, www.sec.gov/divisions/marketreg/ratingagency/nrsroannrep0312.pdf.

[64] See B. Becker and T. Milbourn, 'How did Increased Competition Affect Credit Ratings?', *Harvard Business School Working Paper* 09–051, 15 September 2010, www.hbs.edu/research/pdf/09-051.pdf, finding that ratings quality at Moody's and Standard & Poor's deteriorated as a result of increased competition from Fitch.

[65] EU Commission, Public Consultation on Credit Rating Agencies, p. 24.

[66] Securities Act 1933 Rule 436(g) was repealed by the SEC in July 2010. That development led NRSROs to withhold permission for inclusion of ratings in documentation that would lead to expert liability: see 'Raters go on strike', *Financial Times*, 23 July 2010.

material facts in SEC registration statements. A related provision of Dodd-Frank provides for a private right of action against CRAs for securities law violations based on the NRSRO's failure either to conduct a reasonable investigation of the rated security with respect to the factual elements it relied upon in its methodology for evaluating credit risk or to obtain reasonable verification of such factual elements from other sources.[67]

However, even if it is accepted that extending legal liability may promote greater accuracy, there remain difficulties in formulating a liability regime and beyond that in framing a harmonised liability regime.[68] The CRA Regulation in the EU initially avoided this issue although it did provide for fines and periodic penalty payments to be imposed by ESMA on CRAs and recognised that civil law claims could be pursued under domestic law. However, the CRA 3 reforms to the CRA Regulation make provision for civil liability where a CRA has committed intentionally or with gross negligence a number of specific infringements of the regulation and thereby caused loss to an investor.[69] This expands the options available to investors[70] but it remains to be seen how effective it will prove to be. Three factors suggest a limited impact. One is the role of factors other than ratings (e.g., economic downturn or poor liquidity) in causing losses to investors albeit that there is no requirement for investors to prove causation under the liability provisions of the CRA Regulation (it is only necessary to show reasonable reliance on a credit rating for a decision to invest into, hold or divest from a financial instrument covered by that rating). A second factor is that while the CRA Regulation does not preclude further liability claims being made under national law, such claims may be limited by appropriate contractual exclusions subject to the 'reasonable and proportionate' test in Article 35a(3). It is not yet clear how that test will affect the standard 'no third party beneficiary' provisions typically

[67] Dodd-Frank §933, amending §15E(m) of the Securities Exchange Act of 1934. See, generally, Yeoh, 'External Credit Assessment Institutions', 416.

[68] See UK Tripartite, Authorities *Response*, part IV. The same issue has already arisen in the context of liability for prospectuses but the EU Prospectus Directive does not attempt to harmonise liability regimes in the EU. The roles of intent, reliance and causation are all problematic, albeit not insurmountable issues (which are addressed in national liability regimes for prospectuses but not harmonised).

[69] See (new) Article 35a CRA Regulation as amended by Article 22 CRA 3 (Regulation No 462/2013 amending Regulation No 1060/2009), OJ 2013 L 146/1.

[70] See the EU Commission, *Impact Assessment* for civil liability regimes in different member states of the EU.

found in agreements between CRAs and issuers which aim to exclude liability to investors.[71] The third factor is the limited success of parallel civil liability provisions in other areas of financial regulation (at least in the EU context which generally lacks the incentives for private litigation that are present in the US).[72]

4. Characterise ratings as investment recommendations

Ratings are generally characterised as opinions with the result that they are differentiated from investment research undertaken by financial analysts (often working for 'sell-side' investment banks).[73] The rationale for that approach is that ratings do not express any view as to whether investors should buy, sell or hold a particular financial instrument. According to that view, ratings are more similar in character to the audit opinion provided by an auditor, albeit there are important differences in the timeframe and perspective of each opinion (e.g., ratings are inherently more forward-looking than audit opinions).

The case for characterising ratings as recommendations is that *de facto* they may perform a similar function to recommendations by influencing (through regulatory and contractual linkages) the financial instruments that are held by financial institutions. On that basis, the issue of ratings should be subject to an equivalent regulatory regime to investment recommendations to ensure that they are objective and free from conflicts of interest. Taking the EU as an example, the result of treating ratings as a form of investment recommendation[74] would be to bring CRAs and ratings within the scope of the Markets in Financial Instruments Directive (MiFID) regulatory regime and to subject CRAs, their analysts and the ratings process to a more intense system of

[71] See, further, Yeoh, 'External Credit Assessment Institutions', 420–1.

[72] In the UK, e.g., the civil liability provisions in the Financial Services and Markets Act 2000 have not been used frequently. That may of course be interpreted differently as the operation of an effective deterrent.

[73] See Recital 10 of Commission Directive 2003/125/EC OJ L 339/73 (implementing the Market Abuse Directive with regard to investment recommendations).

[74] It would require very little adjustment to the MiFID definition of 'investment recommendation' in the EU to encompass ratings: see Article 1(4) of Commission Directive 2003/125 (implementing MiFID). Note that investment recommendations differ from 'investment advice', which is a *personal* recommendation to a client (see Article 4(1)(4) MiFID).

regulation.[75] To date, the development of regulatory regimes for CRAs has been premised on the basis that they are inherently different from investment research. However, that premise has not been adequately articulated and some jurisdictions (such as Australia[76]) have chosen to treat ratings as investment recommendations (equivalent to investment research in the EU). Such an approach has the merit of applying a consistent regulatory regime to activities that perform a similar function (the provision of investment research to investors) and where regulation pursues a similar objective (independence of the provider and elimination of conflicts of interest). Moreover, since the regulatory obligations applicable to CRAs have come to resemble those applicable to investment research in many respects, a unified regime would represent a more coherent structure.

II. Reduce reliance on ratings in regulation

Even if regulation succeeds in improving the quality of ratings, there remains the separate issue of over-reliance on ratings in financial regulation. This has now become a matter of considerable concern for international agencies, the EU and national authorities. The objectives are succinctly expressed by the Financial Stability Board (FSB) Principles for Reducing Reliance on CRA Ratings which are focused on removing or replacing references to ratings in regulatory rules and reducing market participants' reliance on ratings.[77] However, it has proven much easier to set an objective of reducing reliance than to implement it. The problem is not just one of finding alternative metrics to ratings but to some extent it is also one of stopping and reversing a path-dependent process that was set in motion by the regulatory reliance on ratings. This remains so even in those cases (such as the US) where the process of reducing reliance has been mandated by statute since the

[75] Characterisation as an investment recommendation would also effectively remove the exemption enjoyed by CRAs from the Market Abuse Directive (see n 81 below), but that would only bring the EU into line with the US.

[76] For a summary of the position in Australia, see www.esma.europa.eu/system/files/2012_-259_0.pdf. In Australia, ratings fall within the definition of 'financial product advice' which is defined as 'a recommendation or statement of opinion, or a report of either of those things, that: (i) is intended to influence a person or persons in making a decision in relation to a financial product or class of financial products, or an interest in a particular financial product or class of financial products; or (ii) could reasonably be regarded as being intended to have such an influence' (para. 214).

[77] See Financial Stability Board, *Principles for Reducing Reliance on CRA Ratings* (2010).

legislative process focused more on the objective than on solutions.[78] The options available and the progress that has so far been made are now examined.

1. Alternatives to ratings

As recognised by the FSB, 'references to CRA ratings should be removed or replaced only once alternative provisions in laws and regulations have been identified and can safely be implemented'.[79] In some cases it has been possible simply to remove references to ratings in regulatory rules without specifying an alternative metric. This has occurred in the US, e.g., with respect to eligible securities for money market funds and issuer disclosure in securities offerings.[80] The EU has followed suit, with a target date of 2020 set for the removal of references to credit ratings in Union law for regulatory purposes 'provided that appropriate alternatives to credit risk assessment have been identified and implemented'.[81] However, that approach could not be applied more widely and certainly not with regard to the (standardised) regulatory capital regime in the Basel Accords, which relies heavily on ratings for the purposes of risk weighting. In that context some alternative metric for risk would be required if the principle of risk-weighting is to retain its dominant role. One possibility is to look to some form of market measure of credit risk on the basis that markets may be better able to estimate credit risk than CRAs. While Partnoy proposed in 2006 that credit default spreads might perform this role,[82] widespread evidence from the financial crisis that markets are just as prone to mispricing as CRAs are to rating errors resulted in little or no official endorsement for that proposal.[83] Some market-based solutions[84] have emerged but do not appear to have

[78] The provisions of the Dodd-Frank Act § 939 largely delegate responsibility for removing references to ratings to the SEC. For a general overview on progress in the US, see SEC, *Annual Report on NRSROs* (2012), www.sec.gov/divisions/marketreg/ratingagency/nrsroannrep0312.pdf.

[79] Financial Stability Board, *Principles for Reducing Reliance on CRA Ratings*.

[80] While the EU has focused on banks, the US has adopted a broader approach, reflecting its greater reliance on ratings across the entire system of financial regulation.

[81] See Article 5c CRA Regulation as amended by CRA 3.

[82] Partnoy, 'The Siskel and Ebert of Financial Markets?', 704.

[83] See the UK Tripartite Authorties, *Response*, para 1.25, noting that movements in market prices are driven by factors other than credit risk, such as depth and liquidity of the market.

[84] See The Covered Bond Label, www.coveredbondlabel.com/; and Prime Collateralised Securities, pcsmarket.org/.

attracted widespread support. The loan level data initiatives of the European Central Bank and the Bank of England adopt a different approach by providing data to support investors' own assessment of creditworthiness.[85]

A simpler approach to bank regulation which focused more on a simple leverage ratio (assets relative to capital) rather than risk weighting of assets would provide much greater scope for reducing reliance on ratings, but that would represent a reversal of the trend towards sophistication and complexity in the Basel framework over time.[86] Absent that shift in focus, it seems unlikely that there can be a substantial reduction in the use of ratings in regulations and contracts in the medium term. The Capital Requirements Directive (CRD) IV reforms to banking regulation include a leverage ratio as a Pillar 2 measure available to supervisors as an option to be applied to individual institutions, but no binding measure is envisaged before 2018 at the earliest although it may well be that the market will demand disclosure of a leverage ratio in some form.[87] While disclosure of a leverage ratio would provide another useful perspective on risk, it would not in itself reduce reliance on ratings and so it follows that other options for reducing reliance must play a greater role.

2. Enhance transparency and comparability of rating information

Enhancing the transparency of rating information would permit investors to look more closely into the 'black box' of the rating process, thereby assisting them in understanding the ratings and facilitating due diligence on their own part. This objective has been implemented in both the US and EU regulatory regimes through requirements to disclose rating methodology and the results of back-testing of ratings as well as a requirement to distinguish ratings for structured financial products from other financial instruments. Another option that has been proposed but not implemented is that CRAs provide a longer period to countries for which they are issuing a rating to review the rating and correct factual information.[88] In the EU, measures put in place by the

[85] See www.ecb.int/paym/coll/loanlevel/html/index.en.html and www.bankofengland.co.uk/markets/Documents/marketnotice100719.pdf, respectively.

[86] See A. Haldane and V. Madouros, 'The Dog and the Frisbee', www.bankofengland.co.uk/publications/Pages/speeches/default.aspx.

[87] See europa.eu/rapid/press-release_MEMO-13-690_en.htm?locale=en.

[88] EU Commission, Public Consultation on Credit Rating Agencies, para 2.1.

CRA Regulation for a credit rating repository (CEREP)[89] aim to improve transparency and comparability between the ratings of different agencies.

However, these changes to transparency do not put investors in an equivalent position to CRAs with regard to information made available by issuers. CRAs in the EU have access to 'inside information' that is not available to investors as a result of information privileges which facilitate access to and use of inside information by CRAs in their ratings.[90] While that access can be viewed as supporting the accuracy of ratings and the role of CRAs as an information conduit to the market, an alternative view is that these privileges encourage over-reliance on ratings and that a level playing field as between investors and CRAs with regard to information disclosure would result in less reliance on ratings.[91] The alternative view has been partially implemented in the US by withdrawing the CRA exemption from Regulation Fair Disclosure.[92] The result is that CRAs no longer have a special exemption from the prohibition against selective disclosure but they can still be given access to inside information if they are bound by an obligation of confidentiality.[93] It has been noted that in practice little has changed in the US since CRAs may still have access to inside information subject to appropriate confidentiality agreements.

3. More due diligence

Requiring investors to carry out more own due diligence rather than relying on ratings has been the option for reducing reliance on which most progress has been made to date. The Basel II framework was an early mover on that front through its requirement that securitisations be deducted from regulatory capital if banks do not collect data on the

[89] See Article 11 CRA Regulation and ESMA, CESR's Guidelines for the Implementation of the Central Repository (CEREP), www.esma.europa.eu/system/files/10_331.pdf.

[90] That access is made possible as a result of Article 6.3 Market Abuse Directive (MAD) which allows an issuer to disclose information privately to a third party which is under a duty of confidentiality; and the characterisation of ratings as opinions rather than investment recommendations under Directive 2003/125 (see Recital 10), which permits CRAs to use that information in their ratings without breaching Article 3(b) MAD.

[91] N. Veron, 'Rating Agencies: An Information Privilege Whose Time Has Passed', Breugel Briefing Paper available at www.bruegel.org/publications/publication-detail/publication/235-rating-agencies-an-information-privilege-whose-time-has-passed/.

[92] Regulation Fair Disclosure, adopted by the SEC in 2000: see www.sec.gov/rules/final/33-7881.htm.

[93] See Amendment to 17 CFR Part 243, implementing § 939B of Dodd-Frank.

underlying assets so as to be able to make their own assessment of credit and other risk.[94] In the EU, further measures have been adopted for banks and investment firms in the form of obligations to form their own internal credit opinion on material exposures; to develop internal ratings-based approaches where there are a material number of exposures in a given asset class; and to verify external ratings internally when they are used.[95] A parallel obligation is imposed on the EU level regulatory bodies (European Systemic Risk Board (ESRB), European Banking Authority (EBA), ESMA and European Insurance and Occupational Pensions Authority (EIOPA)) to avoid references to ratings in their guidelines in future and to review and remove where appropriate all such reference in existing versions.[96] The US is further ahead in terms of implementation of the principle, with the SEC having been particularly active with regard to investment funds and disclosure in public offers.[97] Moreover, these regulatory initiatives have been accompanied by guidelines adopted by private sector bodies encouraging greater due diligence on the part of institutional investors so as to discharge their legal and professional obligations to clients.[98]

While this approach may well reduce the impact of over-reliance on ratings produced by CRAs, it will give rise to considerable costs for financial institutions and may not necessarily result in aggregate in more accurate credit assessment across the financial system as a whole if individual institutions cannot match the resources and expertise of the CRAs. While there can be little doubt that more due diligence is required for some asset classes, there is some irony in resolving the problem of over-reliance by requiring market participants to rely less on a better informed agent, which has specialised expertise, and more on their own judgment. Moreover, the failure of regulatory oversight of internal

[94] See Article 122a of the Capital Requirements Directive (CRD) 2006/48, OJ (2006) L 177/1 for implementation in the EU.

[95] See Recitals 70–3 and Articles 76, 77(2), 79 and 161(3) CRD 4, Directive 2013/36/EU, OJ (2013) L 176/338; Article 5a CRA Regulation (as amended by CRA 3); and Directive 2013/14/EU OJ (2013) L 145/1 (applicable also to pension funds and UCITS).

[96] See Article 5b CRA Regulation as amended by CRA 3; and Directive 2013/14/EU, OJ (2013) L 145/1.

[97] See SEC, Annual Report on NRSROs (March 2012), p. 4, www.sec.gov/divisions/marketreg/ratingagency/nrsroannrep0312.pdf.

[98] See, e.g., the Asset Management Industry Guidelines to Address Over-Reliance Upon Ratings, www.investmentfunds.org.uk/press-centre/2008/20081211/.

models employed for regulatory capital under the Basel IRB approach[99] suggests that the capacity of supervisors to monitor and control effectively a new set of internal credit models may well be limited.

G. Conclusions

The immediate response to the failings of CRAs demonstrated by the financial crisis was to regulate according to the prescription 'be right or be good'. A new regulatory regime in the EU and refinements to the pre-crisis regime in the US introduced measures that may well improve the accuracy of ratings over time. Importantly, they also address the public accountability of CRAs as organisations which wield substantial power in global financial markets. However, those regulatory reforms did not directly address the issue of over-reliance on ratings by regulators and investors. Over-reliance represents a threat to financial stability because it induces herding among investors and cliff effects as a result of rating downgrades. However, solutions to the problem of over-reliance have proven difficult to identify. The best option appears to be increased due diligence by investors albeit this will result in additional costs for investors and extended monitoring duties for supervisors. It may also be that as leverage reduces in the banking system with the implementation of Basel III over time, the risks posed to financial stability by reliance on ratings will decline as there will be greater capacity to absorb downgrades within the system.

[99] This approach permits banks, subject to supervisory approval, to calculate their own regulatory capital requirements using internal models of risk (normally based on 'value at risk' models).

9

Monitoring and surveillance of the international monetary system: what can be learnt from the trade field?

NADIA RENDAK

A. Introduction

The recent international financial crisis has intensified discussions among policy-makers and experts on the international financial architecture and how it can be strengthened to better anticipate and resolve economic and financial crises. Particular emphasis in this debate has been placed on enhancing mechanisms for monitoring economic and financial developments and on early detection of vulnerabilities that, if left unnoticed and unaddressed, can undermine economic and financial stability at the national and global levels.

As an international financial institution with an almost universal membership and a key mandate in economic surveillance, the International Monetary Fund (IMF) has been at the forefront of this debate.[1] This chapter provides a brief overview of IMF surveillance and explores potential lessons from other monitoring mechanisms, such as the WTO Trade Policy Review Mechanism (TPRM) and the Organisation for Economic Co-operation and Development (OECD)

This chapter was prepared for and presented at the World Trade Forum 'The Rule of Law in Monetary Affairs: Lessons from the Trade Field' organised by the World Trade Institute (WTI) at the University of Bern, 12–13 October 2012 (www.wti.org/world-trade-forum). The views expressed herein are those of the author and should not be attributed to the International Monetary Fund, its Executive Board or its management. The author would like to thank François Gianviti and Rosa Lastra for their comments on this chapter, and also Francis Chukwu and Natalia Stetsenko of the IMF Legal Department for their assistance with research.

[1] The other two key functions of the IMF under its charter, the Articles of Agreement, are the provision of financial assistance to help its members resolve their balance of payment problems (often referred to as 'IMF lending') and the provision of technical and financial services.

surveillance in bringing about early warning systems and debate on monetary affairs.[2]

The chapter is organised as follows: Section B provides an overview of the legal and operational framework for IMF surveillance and discusses some of the recent developments in this area. Section C discusses the economic monitoring under the WTO's TPRM and that done by the OECD and what can be learnt from those other mechanisms. Section D concludes.

B. Surveillance at the IMF

Surveillance is a key function of the IMF and is mandatory for the Fund and its members.[3] Surveillance generally refers to regular monitoring and assessment by the Fund of the exchange rate and the economic and financial policies of the member countries and of the global economy. In the conduct of surveillance, the Fund identifies vulnerabilities and advises countries on the necessary policy adjustments. The main objective of surveillance is crisis prevention. In particular, effective surveillance would minimise the likelihood of an economic crisis and consequently the need for the IMF to provide financial assistance to a country facing balance of payment problems.

The legal basis for IMF surveillance is set forth in Article IV of the IMF Articles of Agreement (the 'Articles'), as revised at the time of the Second Amendment in 1978. Under Article IV, the IMF is authorised to conduct two types of surveillance: *bilateral surveillance* refers to the monitoring by the Fund of the economic and financial policies of each of its member countries; *multilateral surveillance* refers to the Fund's authority to oversee the international monetary system, in order to ensure its effective operation. While legally distinct, bilateral and multilateral surveillance are closely interrelated in practice. The remainder of this section

[2] While this chapter discusses only surveillance at the IMF, the OECD and the WTO, a review of other surveillance frameworks, such as the Bank for International Settlements (BIS) and the European Union (EU), could provide additional insight. For a broader perspective, see, e.g., K. Shigehara and P. Atkinson, *Surveillance by International Institutions: Lessons from the Global Financial and Economic Crisis*, www.oecd-ilibrary.org/docserver/download/5kgchzchkvd2.pdf?expires=1355442305&id=id&accname=guest&checksum=3D96133F2168EBABF688805213481CE7.

[3] The term 'surveillance' originates from Article IV, Section 3(b): 'In order to fulfill its functions under (a) above, the Fund shall exercise *firm surveillance* over the exchange rate policies of members' (emphasis added).

highlights the key elements of the legal framework for the Fund surveillance and describes its modalities.

I. IMF surveillance – legal framework

1. Bilateral surveillance

Bilateral surveillance is conducted by the Fund *vis-à-vis* each member country. From the legal perspective, it constitutes *an assessment by the Fund of members' compliance with their obligations set forth in Article IV, Section 1.*[4] This provision reads as follows:

> **Section 1. General obligations of members**
>
> Recognizing that the essential purpose of the international monetary system is to provide a framework that facilitates the exchange of goods, services, and capital among countries, and that sustains sound economic growth, and that a principal objective is the continuing development of the orderly underlying conditions that are necessary for financial and economic stability, each member undertakes to collaborate with the Fund and other members to assure orderly exchange arrangements and to promote a stable system of exchange rates. In particular, each member shall:
>
> (i) endeavor to direct its economic and financial policies toward the objective of fostering orderly economic growth with reasonable price stability, with due regard to its circumstances;
> (ii) seek to promote stability by fostering orderly underlying economic and financial conditions and a monetary system that does not tend to produce erratic disruptions;
> (iii) avoid manipulating exchange rates or the international monetary system in order to prevent effective balance of payments adjustment or to gain an unfair competitive advantage over other members; and
> (iv) follow exchange policies compatible with the undertakings under this Section.

(i) Coverage: exchange rate vs. domestic policies, spillovers It is evident that under Article IV, Section 1 members have (i) a general obligation to collaborate with the Fund and other members to assure orderly exchange

[4] IMF Articles of Agreement, Article IV, Section 3(a).

arrangements and to promote a stable system of exchange rates, and (ii) specific obligations on the conduct of exchange rate and domestic economic and financial policies set forth in clauses (i)–(iv). In addition, members have a procedural obligation to engage in discussions of their economic policies with the Fund and to provide the Fund with the necessary information.

While members' obligations cover all types of policies, exchange rate and other ('domestic' economic and financial) policies are treated differently, with the emphasis on exchange rate policies. In particular, obligations on exchange rate policies are established as 'firm' obligations, while the latter are 'soft', i.e., formulated on a best-effort basis, and do not require members to achieve the specified objective. The soft nature of the obligations on domestic policies reflects the post-war focus on exchange rates and the reluctance of countries at the time to grant more control over domestic policy-making to an international institution like the IMF. As discussed below, the asymmetry in the treatment of exchange rate and domestic policies complicates the Fund's assessment of members' compliance with their obligations and creates a challenge for the effectiveness of the Fund.[5]

This asymmetry is also reflected in the provisions authorising the Fund to conduct surveillance: in addition to the general oversight over members' compliance with their obligations under Article IV, Section 1, the Fund is also required to pay special attention to members' exchange rate policies. In particular, Article IV, Section 3(b) provides: 'In order to fulfill its functions under (a) above, the Fund shall exercise firm surveillance over the exchange rate policies of members, and shall adopt specific principles for the guidance of members with respect to those policies.' The specific requirement that the Fund should focus on exchange rate policies reflects the historical importance of exchange rate policies and the necessity to concentrate on this issue at the time when the Fund was established in the 1940s. However, over the years, the Fund has recognised that national and global stability is affected not only by exchange rate policies but also by domestic policies and resulting spillovers.

Effective surveillance in a globalised world is not possible without considering the impact of individual countries' policies on other

[5] On the analysis of Article IV, Section 1, see Joseph Gold, *Exchange Rates in International Law and Organization* (Washington, DC: American Bar Association, 1989), p. 89. Also, for a broader overview of the legal issues of Fund surveillance, see '2011 Triennial Surveillance Review – Review of the 2007 Surveillance Decision and the Broader Legal Framework for Surveillance', www.imf.org/external/np/pp/eng/2011/082611.pdf.

countries and the global economy as a whole. In this respect bilateral surveillance has limitations which are rooted in the design of Article IV. More specifically, bilateral surveillance focuses on the stability of the exchange rate system and thus covers spillovers from countries' exchange policies. However, bilateral surveillance is not so well-suited to address spillovers from domestic policies because it assesses members' compliance with their obligations, which are limited with respect to domestic policies to the promotion of a country's own stability. To address this issue, the recently adopted Integrated Surveillance Decision (ISD)[6] uses the Fund's multilateral surveillance mandate to enhance the analysis of spillovers from countries' domestic policies. (See Section B.III below.)

(ii) Principles for the guidance of members' policies and indicators As required by the Articles, the Fund has adopted, through an Executive Board decision, principles to guide members on their policies. These principles[7] are as follows:

A. A member shall avoid manipulating exchange rates or the international monetary system in order to prevent effective balance of payments adjustment or to gain an unfair competitive advantage over other members.
B. A member should intervene in the exchange market if necessary to counter disorderly conditions, which may be characterized inter alia by disruptive short-term movements in the exchange rate of its currency.
C. Members should take into account in their intervention policies the interests of other members, including those of the countries in whose currencies they intervene.
D. A member should avoid exchange rate policies that result in balance of payments instability.
E. A member should seek to avoid domestic economic and financial policies that give rise to domestic instability.

From a legal perspective, these principles, with the exception of Principle A, constitute recommendations to members. Therefore, while observance of the Principles creates a presumption of a member's compliance

[6] Decision No. 15203-(12/72) on Bilateral and Multilateral Surveillance ('Integrated Surveillance Decision'), adopted 18 July 2012.

[7] While the Articles do not require the Fund to adopt principles for guidance of members on domestic policies, the Fund is not precluded from doing so. Originally, the guiding principles, only on exchange rate policies, were adopted in the 1977 and 2007 Surveillance Decisions. A new principle on domestic policies was added in 2012 in the ISD.

with its obligations under Article IV, Section 1, a failure to observe Principles B–E would not *per se* constitute a breach of obligation,[8] and such a finding would require the Fund to take additional steps.

In addition to the Principles, the Fund has also adopted a list of indicators as signposts for assessing compliance with the Principles. Indicators are policy developments that may trigger the need for additional discussion with a country on whether the Principles are being observed.

(iii) Data provision To conduct effective surveillance, the Fund needs reliable information. Accordingly, the Articles require members to provide information needed for the Fund's activities.[9] The list of data that constitutes the necessary minimum is set forth in Article VIII, Section 5.[10] The members' obligation to provide data to the Fund is limited in several important respects. One limitation concerns a country's capacity, as the data only has to be provided if the country has the ability to do so.[11] Another limitation is that members are under no obligation to provide data 'in such detail that the affairs of individuals or corporations are disclosed'.[12]

In practice most countries provide much more information to the Fund than is legally required under the Articles. In some cases the Fund also obtains institution-specific data on a voluntary basis from the authorities, subject to assurances on confidentiality.[13] However, the legal limitation on requiring institution-specific data has an impact on the Fund's ability to conduct effective surveillance.

8 As Principle A reiterates the obligation set forth in Article IV, Section 1(iii), a finding of non-observance of this Principle would also constitute a breach of obligation.

9 The requirement to provide the Fund with the information for surveillance is set forth in Article IV, Section 3(b), with respect to exchange rate surveillance, and more generally in Article VIII, Section 5.

10 The original list was expanded in 2004 to include additional data. Decision No. 13181-(04/10), adopted on 30 January 2004, as subsequently amended.

11 Article VIII, Section 2(b): 'In requesting information the Fund shall take into consideration the varying ability of members to furnish the data requested'. A country with no capacity to provide the required data cannot be found in breach of its obligation; however, the country would then be required to work to improve its data provision framework.

12 IMF Articles of Agreement, Article VIII, Section 5(b).

13 Article VIII, Section 5(b) also allows the Fund to obtain additional information by agreement with members. It also authorises the Fund to act as a 'centre for the collection and exchange of information on monetary and financial problems, thus facilitating the preparation of studies designed to assist members in developing policies which further the purposes of the Fund'.

(iv) Consequences of non-compliance with obligations The formulation of members' policy obligations in Article IV makes it difficult to find a member in breach of these obligations.[14] If, however, a member is found to be in breach, the Fund may impose sanctions specified in Article XXVI, which include: declaration of ineligibility to use the general resources of the Fund; suspension of the voting rights; and compulsory withdrawal from the Fund. Given the severity of the sanctions and the generally cooperative nature of the Fund, sanctions are rarely applied. In case of surveillance, reliance on sanctions may be especially problematic. Thus, while there has been considerable debate lately on strengthening 'enforcement' of the Fund's surveillance, the Fund has so far continued to rely on a cooperative approach, and there is also currently no interest among the membership to change this approach.[15]

2. Multilateral surveillance

The activity known as the Fund's multilateral surveillance is described in just two lines in the Articles: Article VI, Section 3(a) provides that 'the Fund shall oversee the international monetary system, to ensure its effective operation'. Until recently there has been no additional guidance in the form of decisions of the Executive Board on multilateral surveillance. However, the recently adopted ISD has for the first time defined the meaning of international monetary system (IMS) and has provided guidance to the Fund and its members on multilateral surveillance.

There are important differences between bilateral and multilateral surveillance. First, they have a different subject matter. Bilateral surveillance focuses on the policies of individual countries, while the objective of multilateral surveillance is the effective operation of the IMS. Second, while bilateral surveillance must assess members' compliance with the substantive policy obligations specified in the Articles, the Articles establish no substantive policy obligations for multilateral surveillance. In other words, members have no obligation under the Articles to

[14] This difficulty is due, in particular, to the vagueness of the language on the obligations on domestic policies and the intent element in the obligation not to manipulate the exchange rate. Since the second amendment, no member has been found in breach of its obligations under Article IV.

[15] Several reports have recently discussed these issues. See, e.g., Edwin M. Truman, 'Strengthening IMF Surveillance: A Comprehensive Proposal', www.iie.com/publications/pb/pb10-29.pdf; 'Reform of the International Monetary System: A Cooperative Approach for the Twenty First Century (Palais-Royal Initiative)', global-currencies.org/smi/gb/telechar/news/Rapport_Camdessus-integral.pdf.

conduct their economic and financial policies in a manner that would promote the effective operation of the IMS.[16] Third, in terms of the process, bilateral surveillance is conducted *vis-à-vis* each country member of the Fund and involves discussions with the country authorities. Multilateral surveillance, on the other hand, has so far been conducted by the Fund mainly through the preparation of analytical reports, such as World Economic Outlook (WEO), Global Financial Stability Report (GFSR) and Fiscal Monitor.[17] These reports deal mainly with global developments and are not designed to provide country-specific policy recommendations, and therefore their preparation normally does not involve in-depth discussions with individual countries' authorities. Finally, as multilateral surveillance focuses on the effective operation of the IMS, in conducting it the Fund can examine developments and spillovers from any of the members' policies that may have an impact on the IMS, including through the impact on global economic and financial stability,[18] and regardless of the channel through which such spillovers may be transmitted.

Despite these differences and the fact that bilateral and multilateral surveillance are legally two separate activities, from the economic point of view the need for closer integration is obvious. After all, national economies form the global economy, and the conditions in the global economy depend on the economic, financial, exchange rate and other policies implemented at the national (and sometimes regional) level. Recognising the importance of such integration, all the IMF's Executive Board decisions on surveillance to date have required that the analysis of individual economies be conducted in the context of global developments. However, integrating bilateral and multilateral surveillance continues to be a challenge.

II. The conduct of surveillance

Procedures for conducting surveillance are established in the decisions of the Executive Board.[19] While the 1977 and 2007 decisions covered

[16] However, as stated in the ISD (para. 15), members do have a procedural obligation to consult with the Fund, if required to do so, to enable the Fund to conduct multilateral surveillance.

[17] In 2006–7 the Fund conducted a multilateral consultation. See Section B.II.2.

[18] See IMF Policy Paper 'The Integrated Surveillance Decision', www.imf.org/external/np/pp/eng/2012/062612.pdf and 'Modernizing the Legal Framework for Surveillance – Building Blocks Toward an Integrated Surveillance Decision', www.imf.org/external/np/pp/eng/2012/031612a.pdf.

[19] The first surveillance decision was adopted in 1977, with the introduction of new Article IV. The 1977 Decision was replaced with a new decision in 2007, and the most recent

only bilateral surveillance, the recently adopted ISD for the first time covers both bilateral and multilateral surveillance. (The ISD is discussed in more detail in Section B.III below.)

1. Bilateral surveillance

As discussed above, from the legal standpoint the Fund, in its bilateral surveillance, must assess members' compliance with their policy obligations set forth in Article IV. In practice, however, surveillance has evolved more as a cooperative exercise and a continuing dialogue between the Fund and the countries on their economic policies. This has been recognised in all Fund decisions on surveillance.[20]

Regular Article IV consultations between the Fund and each member country have traditionally been the key instrument for the conduct of bilateral surveillance.[21] These consultations are held on a regular schedule that varies between twelve and twenty-four months.[22] For the majority of Fund members Article IV consultations are completed on schedule, although consultations with a few countries have recently been substantially delayed. As Article IV consultations are important for the Fund's ability to conduct effective surveillance, the Fund recently adopted a framework to address such delays.[23]

one, the ISD, was adopted in July 2012. The ISD provided for a six-month transition period and will apply to Article IV consultations concluded after 18 January 2013.

[20] For example, the ISD provides:

> 'Dialogue and persuasion are key pillars of effective surveillance. The Fund, in its bilateral surveillance, will clearly and candidly assess relevant economic developments, prospects, and policies of the member in question, and advise on these. Such assessments and advice are intended to assist that member in making policy choices, and to enable other members to discuss these policy choices with that member. In the context of bilateral surveillance, the Fund will foster an environment of frank and open dialogue and mutual trust with each member and will be evenhanded across members, affording similar treatment to members in similar relevant circumstances.'

[21] Under the ISD, Article IV consultations have become a vehicle of both bilateral and multilateral surveillance. See Section B.III.

[22] A country can be put on a longer consultation cycle (18–24 months) if, for example, it receives financial assistance from the Fund (as programme reviews provide another opportunity for regular monitoring) or if it is not of systemic or regional importance and is not perceived to be at risk.

[23] See IMF policy paper 'Proposed Steps to Address Excessive Delays in the Completion of Article IV Consultations', www.imf.org/external/np/pp/eng/2012/020212.pdf. The framework provides for a range of escalating measures, starting from a written notification of the member whose Article IV consultation is significantly delayed to the imposition of sanctions.

Article IV consultation discussions include discussions between the staff and the authorities, and other stakeholders. They are normally conducted during the IMF staff's visit ('mission') to the country and address such issues as exchange rate and monetary, fiscal, financial and structural policies that may impact the country's domestic and balance of payment stability, and the relevant spillovers from the country's policies.

Upon return from the visit, staff prepare a report on members' policies that is submitted to the Executive Board.[24] To ensure that the information and analysis submitted to the Board remains relevant, the Fund limits the expected lag between the completion of the discussions with country authorities and the Executive Board's consideration of the Article IV consultation report.[25] The Executive Board usually discusses the Article IV consultation report in a meeting, and thereby concludes the consultation.[26] The consideration of the Article IV consultation report by the Executive Board serves as a peer review mechanism, through which other members of the Fund can discuss and express views on the country's policies. These views are conveyed to the authorities by the Executive Director for that country.

Most Article IV consultation reports are published shortly after the Board meeting. While publication requires consent of the member concerned, the Fund has a policy under which publication of surveillance reports is voluntary but presumed. In the past decade, the publication rate for Article IV consultation reports has increased dramatically, with few reports currently not published. Apart from the staff report, the Fund normally also publishes a public information notice (PIN), which draws on the Chairman's summing up[27] and thus conveys to the general public the views expressed by other members of the Fund during the Board meeting.

In addition to the regular surveillance procedure, the Fund has developed a special framework for countries that are members of a currency

[24] An Article IV report may include papers analysing a specific policy area in greater depth, which may be prepared at the initiative of staff or at the request of the authorities.

[25] The expected lag is sixty-five days for most countries and ninety days for low-income countries.

[26] There is also a procedure for concluding Article IV consultation without a Board meeting.

[27] For each meeting, the Chairman of the Executive Board meeting prepares a summing up, which is a document that summarises the views of the Executive Board expressed at the Board meeting.

union. Since members of a currency union delegate certain policies to the union-level institutions, the regular Article IV discussions for such countries are supplemented by discussions with the institutions of the relevant currency union on policies implemented at the union level. These not only form an integral part of the Article IV process for each country, but the report on the union level discussions is also incorporated by reference into the individual Article IV consultation reports of member countries of the currency union.

Also, in 2010, the regular Article IV process was complemented by less frequent mandatory Financial Stability Assessments ('FSAs') for twenty-five countries with systemically important financial sectors.[28] The key objective of the FSAs is to identify the main vulnerabilities that could trigger a crisis. Teams conducting FSAs discuss with the authorities the soundness of the banking and other financial sectors; conduct stress tests; review the quality of bank, insurance and financial market supervision against accepted international standards; and evaluate the ability of supervisors, policy-makers and financial safety nets to respond effectively in case of systemic stress. The FSA's analysis and conclusions are presented in a Financial System Stability Assessment (FSSA) report, which is usually discussed by the Executive Board together with the Article IV consultation report for the country.

2. Multilateral surveillance

Unlike bilateral surveillance, which is conducted through a continuous dialogue with the countries' authorities, multilateral surveillance is conducted mainly through the preparation of analytical reports on global economic developments. In addition to WEO and GFSR reports, the Fund also organises regular briefings on capital and financial market developments.

In 2006–7, the Fund experimented with a new modality – a multilateral consultation. The objective of the first (and so far the only) multilateral consultation on global imbalances was to bring together the authorities of several major countries to facilitate the discussion on global economic imbalances and a coordinated policy response. Consultation participants included China, Japan, Member States of the European Union, and the United States. The 2006–7 multilateral

[28] See 'Integrating Stability Assessments Under the Financial Sector Assessment Program into Article IV Surveillance', www.imf.org/external/np/pp/eng/2010/082710.pdf.

consultation was initiated by the Managing Director of the IMF and was conducted on a voluntary basis. It included several rounds of discussions between staff and the participating authorities, on the basis of which staff prepared a report that included, *inter alia*, policy commitments by each participating country to help address global imbalances. The report was discussed at the Executive Board and presented by the IMF Managing Director to the International Monetary and Financial Committee (IMFC).[29] Because the follow-up from the participants of the first multilateral consultation on the agreed commitments was weak, it was generally not considered a success, and no attempts were made to hold another multilateral consultation.

3. Other inputs into surveillance

The exercise by the Fund of its surveillance mandate through Article IV consultations and other modalities discussed above is informed and supported by many complementary activities. These activities include staff visits; informal Board meetings on country matters; assessments under the Financial Sector Assessment Program (FSAP); implementation of the standards and codes initiative, which results in Reports on Observance of Standards and Codes (ROSCs); World Economic and Market Developments sessions; spillover reports; Early Warning Exercise (EWE) conducted by the Fund jointly with the Financial Stability Board (FSB); the new pilot External Sector Report (ESR);[30] the Fund's contribution to the G-20 Mutual Assessment Program (G-20 MAP) process; and outreach activities.[31] While participation in some of these activities is voluntary, many of the issues discussed (for example, financial sector issues) do fall within the scope of surveillance. Some of these tools are briefly described below.

[29] See the IMFC Communiqué of 14 April 2007, www.imf.org/external/np/sec/pr/2007/pr0771.htm and Press Release No. 07/72 of 14 April 2007, www.imf.org/external/np/sec/pr/2007/pr0772.htm.

[30] For a description of other tools that support IMF surveillance see, e.g., Box 2 of the paper 'Biennial Review of the Implementation of the Fund's Surveillance and of the 1977 Surveillance Decision – Overview' prepared for the 2002 biennial surveillance review, www.imf.org/external/np/pdr/surv/2002/031302.pdf.

[31] Some of these activities are part of surveillance, while others are voluntary both for the Fund and for the members. For a detailed explanation of the role of the FSB and the G-20 in the international financial architecture, see the contribution of M. Giovanoli, 'The International Monetary and Financial Architecture – Some Institutional Aspects', Chapter 3, this volume.

The FSAP is a joint programme of the IMF and the World Bank established in 1999 in the aftermath of the Asian financial crisis. Under the FSAP, staff conduct a comprehensive and in-depth assessment of a country's financial sector that provides key input in financial sector analysis in Fund surveillance. The IMF is primarily responsible for the financial stability component of the FSAP (FSAs, discussed above), while the World Bank is responsible for the financial development component (the 'development module'). Participation in the FSAP is voluntary for the countries, except for the twenty-five countries for which FSAs are part of bilateral surveillance and thus mandatory.[32]

Reports on Standards and Codes (ROSCs) are also used to inform surveillance. A ROSC summarises the extent of a country's compliance with certain internationally recognised standards and codes, which are benchmarks of good practices in different areas. The IMF has recognised twelve areas and associated standards as useful for the operational work of the Fund and the World Bank. These include accounting; auditing; anti-money laundering and countering the financing of terrorism (AML/CFT); banking supervision; corporate governance; data dissemination; fiscal transparency; insolvency and creditor rights; insurance supervision; monetary and financial policy transparency; payments systems; and securities regulation.[33] Reports summarising countries' observance of these standards are prepared in the context of an FSAP assessment or on a stand-alone basis and can be published at the request of the member country.[34]

Since 2010, Fund surveillance has been supplemented by enhanced analysis of spillovers from policies of five major economies (US, UK, the euro area, Japan and China). This analysis, conducted with the consent of relevant members, is presented in individual spillover reports and a consolidated spillover report prepared once a year. The reports focus on the impact individual country policies may have on other countries and the global economy as a whole. These reports cover all major spillovers originating from *any* policy transmitted through *any* channel, and thus go beyond a more limited spillover analysis conducted in the context of Article IV consultations. The consolidated surveillance report draws together the analysis and conclusions from individual

[32] More information on the FSAP is available at www.imf.org/external/np/exr/facts/fsap.htm.

[33] The Fund will shortly consider a standard on cross-border bank resolution and the related methodology.

[34] More information on ROSCs is available at www.imf.org/external/np/exr/facts/sc.htm.

reports and summarises them in a concise document designed for top policy-makers.[35]

Introduced in late 2008, following the request from the G-20, the Early Warning Exercise (EWE) assesses low probability but high impact risks to the global economy and identifies policies to mitigate them. The EWE, which initially covered only emerging economies but was later extended to advanced economies as well, is conducted jointly by the IMF and FSB and aims to provide an integrated perspective on risks and vulnerabilities. The Fund tends to take a leading role on economic, macro-financial and sovereign risk concerns, with FSB leading on financial system regulatory and supervisory issues. The key output of the EWE is a confidential presentation of risks and vulnerabilities to the IMFC. Following discussions at the IMF Executive Board and at the FSB, the findings from the EWE are presented to senior officials during the Spring and Annual Meetings. The findings also contribute to the Fund surveillance more generally.[36]

Regional Economic Outlook (REO) reports discuss recent economic developments and prospects for countries in various regions. They also address economic policy developments that have affected economic performance in the regions and discuss key challenges faced by policy-makers.

In July 2012, the Executive Board considered for the first time an External Sector Report (ESR). The ESR provides a snapshot of multilaterally consistent analysis of the external positions of major world economies at a point in time. The first report, prepared on a pilot basis, combines the insights from analysis by the Fund's staff working on individual economies with results from multilateral analysis, including models, and provides an important input into Fund surveillance.[37]

III. Selected recent developments in surveillance

The IMF surveillance is constantly evolving, and this evolution reflects the efforts to adapt surveillance to a changing global economic environment.[38] Over the years the coverage of surveillance has been expanded beyond the original focus on exchange rate, monetary and fiscal policies

[35] The 2012 Consolidated Spillover Report is available at www.imf.org/external/np/pp/eng/2012/070912.pdf.

[36] More information on the EWE is available at www.imf.org/external/np/exr/facts/ewe.htm.

[37] The pilot ESR is available at www.imf.org/external/np/pp/eng/2012/070212.pdf.

[38] Box 1 of the paper 'Biennial Review of the Implementation of the Fund's Surveillance and of the 1977 Surveillance Decision – Overview' prepared for the 2002 biennial surveillance,

and relevant trade issues, to better cover structural and institutional issues, to extend the analysis of financial sector issues and matters related to international capital flows, and to include more explicit and comprehensive analysis of crisis vulnerabilities and spillover effects from members' policies.

This section provides an overview of selected recent developments in surveillance, namely: (i) the 2011 Triennial Surveillance Review (TSR) and the new ISD, (ii) work on international capital flows, and (iii) the Fund's work on the G-20 MAP.

1. The 2011 TSR and the Integrated Surveillance Decision

An important feature of the IMF surveillance is a built-in review mechanism. Recognising that surveillance would evolve in light of the changing global environment and experience gained with the exercise, the first (1977) surveillance decision established biennial reviews of the decision itself and the implementation of surveillance. At each review up until 2004[39] the Executive Board would analyse the conduct of surveillance during the relevant period, draw lessons and establish priorities for the upcoming period.[40]

The most recent review of surveillance was completed in October 2011. It assessed the implementation of surveillance since 2008 and identified the remaining gaps, drawing in large part on lessons from the global financial crisis. Unlike previous reviews that focused on bilateral surveillance, the 2011 review took a comprehensive approach, covering both bilateral and multilateral surveillance. It also drew extensively on feedback from all major stakeholders, analysis by IMF staff and commentaries and studies by external experts. For the first time, the review was assessed and endorsed by an independent External Advisory Group.[41]

The key conclusion of the TSR was that, although the Fund has made important progress in strengthening its surveillance, more should be done to strengthen assessments of risks and prospects for economies

www.imf.org/external/np/pdr/surv/2002/031302.pdf provides a good illustration of the impact of the international financial crisis of the 1980s and 1990s on Fund surveillance.

[39] The last biennial review of surveillance under the 1977 Decision took place in 2004. In 2007, the 1977 Surveillance Decision was replaced by a new decision and the expected frequency of surveillance reviews was changed to every three years.

[40] See, e.g., documents for the 2002 and 2004 biennial reviews of surveillance, available, respectively, at www.imf.org/external/np/pdr/surv/2002/ and http://www.imf.org/external/np/pdr/surv/2004/082404.htm.

[41] The 2011 TSR materials are available at www.imf.org/external/np/spr/triennial/.

around the world, delivery of policy advice and to achieve better traction of the Fund's advice. As required under the current legal framework, the TSR incorporated the review of the then effective (2007) surveillance decision and broader legal framework for surveillance. The review identified significant shortcomings in that framework, the most important of which are (i) exchange rate bias, (ii) insufficient integration of bilateral and multilateral surveillance, and (iii) legitimacy deficit among membership.

On the first point, the review emphasised the existence of the exchange rate bias of the economic framework underlying the legal construct of Article IV. As a result, the legal framework: (i) defines too narrowly the scope of the collaboration obligation of members; (ii) makes an artificial distinction between domestic and external policies and fails to acknowledge that all policies contribute to a country's and to global stability; and (iii) establishes asymmetrical obligations by requiring members to take into account the external effects of their exchange rate policies but not their domestic policies. It was found that the framework did not foster sufficient integration of bilateral and multilateral surveillance (in particular, by hampering the analysis of spillovers from members' policies) and the integration of financial sector analysis into surveillance. The review also observed that the exchange rate bias rooted in Article IV undermines the legitimacy of the Fund, as some members regard the focus on exchange rate policies – and surveillance itself – to be discriminatory against members with fixed exchange rate regimes.

The review identified options to address the limitations of the current framework. Key among those were: to establish an integrated framework for promoting global and country-level stability, while rebalancing the focus of surveillance away from exchange rates, and (ii) developing an Integrated Surveillance Decision within the confines of the existing Articles. In the absence of broad support among the membership for amending the Articles, it was decided to proceed with the new decision, which was approved on 18 July 2012.

The ISD builds on the earlier surveillance decisions and maintains important features of the existing legal framework including no change in the scope of members' obligations under the Articles and preserving the emphasis of bilateral surveillance on members' exchange rate policies. At the same time, it allows the Fund to engage more effectively with member countries on their domestic economic and financial policies, and continues to emphasise the collaborative nature of surveillance, the importance of dialogue and persuasion, the need for candour and evenhandedness, and the importance of paying due regard to country circumstances.

At the same time, the ISD enhances the existing framework in several important ways. First, it provides a conceptual link between bilateral and multilateral surveillance by clarifying that surveillance should focus on economic and financial stability both at an individual country level and at the global level. Second, it recognises that it is the overall mix of policies that contributes to a country's stability. Third, it clarifies that the IMF can discuss with member countries the full range of spillovers from their policies when they may have a significant impact on global stability. The ISD has made Article IV consultations a vehicle not only for bilateral but also for multilateral surveillance, thus promoting a more comprehensive and integrated economic analysis at the national and global level. For the first time, the ISD explicitly encourages countries to be mindful of the impact of their policies on global stability, even though countries have no obligation to change their policies as long as they promote their own stability. Finally, the decision defines, for the first time, the scope and modalities of multilateral surveillance, and establishes a framework for potential multilateral consultations.[42]

2. Stepping up work on international capital flows

The Fund has long recognised the importance of international capital flows, and of the policies to manage them, in maintaining stability both in individual countries and globally.[43] However, developing a comprehensive view on these issues has been challenging, not least because of the limited jurisdiction that the Fund has over international capital movements. Indeed, while the Fund has extensive jurisdiction over payments and transfers for current international transactions,[44] the Articles

[42] More information on the ISD is available at www.imf.org/external/pp/longres.aspx?id=4673.

[43] All surveillance decisions to date have required the Fund to include capital flows in its analysis while evaluating members' economic policies. Also the introduction or substantial modification by a member for balance of payments purposes of restrictions on, or incentives for, the inflow or outflow of capital is included in the list of indicators that could trigger the need for discussion with a member about the observance of the guiding principles for economic, financial and exchange rate policies.

[44] Article VIII, Section 2(a) prohibits members from imposing restrictions on the making of payments and transfers for current international transactions unless they are authorised by the Fund. This provision is in turn grounded in the purposes of the Fund, one of which is 'to assist in the establishment of a multilateral system of payments in respect of

give members the right to 'exercise such controls as are necessary to regulate international capital movements'.[45]

At the same time, member countries have increasingly turned to the IMF for advice on policies related to capital flows. In response to these requests and the 2011 request from the IMFC, work to come up with a 'comprehensive, flexible, and balanced' Fund institutional view on capital flows and policies affecting them has intensified. This work, which has built on countries' experiences and the earlier work on capital flows, has culminated in the adoption by the Executive Board in November 2012 of an institutional view on the liberalisation and management of international capital flows. The institutional view emphasises that capital flows can have substantial benefits for countries but can also carry significant risks, which should be carefully managed. It describes the conditions under which countries can benefit most from liberalising capital flows, provides a framework for managing inflows and outflows, and encourages greater cooperation between countries that generate and receive capital flows.[46] The 'institutional view' – which does not change members' obligations under the Articles or other international agreements – would provide a consistent basis for Fund advice to all members on issues related to international capital flows.

3. Fund's input in G-20 MAP

The MAP is a new approach to policy collaboration, conceived and owned by the G-20 member countries, whose leaders pledged at the 2009 Pittsburgh Summit to work together to ensure a lasting recovery and strong and sustainable growth over the medium term. To meet this goal, they launched the Framework for Strong, Sustainable and Balanced Growth. The backbone of this framework is a multilateral process through which G-20 countries identify objectives for the global economy, the policies needed to reach them, and the progress towards meeting these shared objectives – the so-called MAP.

The MAP is an evolving process. Its first stage involved aggregating the G-20 members' policy and macroeconomic frameworks, assessing

current transactions between members and in the elimination of foreign exchange restrictions which hamper the growth of world trade'.

45 Article VI, Section 3. There was an attempt to expand the Fund's jurisdiction to include international capital flows in the mid-1990s but it failed in the aftermath of the Asian crisis.

46 More information on the IMF institutional view on capital flows and related documents are available at www.imf.org/external/np/sec/pn/2012/pn12137.htm.

whether members' policies would help achieve the G-20's objectives and evaluating alternative policy scenarios. It then moved to identifying and assessing imbalances through the use of indicative guidelines and indicators, and identifying policy actions by each participant to help achieve the set growth objectives.[47] Reports for countries with large imbalances were prepared and progress towards external sustainability by G-20 members was assessed. In November 2011, the G-20 leaders adopted the Cannes Action Plan for Growth and Jobs and announced other steps, reinforcing commitment to the spirit of multilateral cooperation that lies at the heart of the MAP.[48]

At the request of the G-20, the IMF has supported and continues to support the MAP by providing the technical analysis needed to evaluate how members' policies fit together and whether, collectively, they can achieve the G-20's goals. This work, but not the surveillance from the legal perspective, draws on the analysis conducted by the Fund in bilateral and multilateral surveillance and, in turn, informs and deepens surveillance at all levels.

IV. *Is the Fund surveillance effective?*

While the IMF has made considerable effort over the years to enhance its surveillance, much remains to be done. Several recent studies of the IMF surveillance conducted inside and outside the Fund[49] stressed that the

[47] In February 2011, the G-20 authorities reached agreement on the key indicators (public debt, fiscal deficits, private saving rate, private debt, etc.) and in April 2011 an agreement was reached on indicative guidelines (developed with technical input from IMF staff), i.e., qualitative or quantitative benchmarks against which the indicators would be assessed to identify the presence of large imbalances.

[48] In particular, G-20 leaders reiterated the importance of expeditiously implementing measures to address the eurozone crisis, committed to take significant strides towards a more stable and resilient international monetary system, which was reflected in the agreement on *Coherent Conclusions for the Management of Capital Flows*, and agreed to continue strengthening financial regulation. They also endorsed policy actions by members that aim to correct imbalances over the medium term and ensure progress towards strong, sustainable and balanced growth, and committed to working with greater resolve on pressing social issues, including high unemployment and inadequate social safety nets.

[49] See, e.g., Report of the Independent Evaluation Office of the IMF 'Performance in the Run-Up to the Financial and Economic Crisis: IMF Surveillance in 2004–07', www.ieo-imf.org/ieo/files/completedevaluations/Crisis-%20Main%20Report%20(without%20Moises%20Signature).pdf, Reform of the International Monetary System: A Cooperative Approach for the Twenty First Century (Palais-Royal Initiative), global-currencies.org/smi/gb/telechar/news/Rapport_Camdessus-integral.pdf, IMF, the 2011 Triennial Review of Surveillance, www.imf.org/external/np/spr/triennial/.

Fund should become more effective in providing early warnings to countries about potential risks and vulnerabilities, delivering solid policy advice and achieving better traction with policy-makers.[50]

In particular, the recent IEO report recommended that, in order to address its shortcomings, the Fund surveillance should be strengthened by: (i) creating an environment that encourages candour and considers dissenting views; (ii) modifying incentives to 'speak truth to power'; (iii) better integrating macroeconomic and financial sector issues; (iv) overcoming the silo mentality and insular culture; and (v) delivering a clear, consistent message on the global outlook and risks. Improvements to the Fund surveillance have also been recommended by outside experts. For example, the Palais de Royal Report[51] noted that strengthened IMF surveillance

> should contain, in particular, the following key elements: (a) stronger multilateral obligations, backed by clear, objective norms or quantitative benchmarks on economic and financial policies and performance to function as alarm signals with appropriate thresholds; (b) assessment procedures that permit judgment about the causes and implications of any deviation from those policy norms; and (c) consequences, including the possibility of both incentives and sanctions. While all countries should be subject to the same obligations and assessment procedures, particular attention should be directed to countries whose policies have a larger potential impact on the stability of the international monetary system. This new surveillance process should also aim at eliciting a supportive response from financial markets, helping to orient market

[50] E.g., a recent report by the IMF Independent Evaluation office (IEO), www.ieo-imf.org/ieo/files/completedevaluations/01102011Crisis_III._IMF_Messages_in_the_run_Up_to the_Crisis.pdf found that the Fund provided few clear warnings about the risks and vulnerabilities associated with the impending crisis before its outbreak and that surveillance paid insufficient attention to risks of contagion or spillovers from a crisis in advanced economies. The Palais de Royal Report, discussing the structural weaknesses of the existing international monetary arrangements, observes that:

> 'The [international monetary] system lacks effective discipline and countries can accumulate large current account imbalances – whether surpluses or deficits – for extended periods without facing effective pressures for adjustment. The peer review over the policies of member countries to be exercised by the IMF ("surveillance") has often been ineffective in bringing about policy adjustment on the part of countries with internal and external imbalances, especially when they have no need to borrow from the Fund. This reflects, among other issues, the lack of teeth of IMF procedures.'

[51] Available at www.global-currencies.org/smi/gb/telechar/news/Rapport_Camdessus-integral.pdf.

sentiment towards stability objectives that have been agreed at a multilateral level.

These challenges are not unique to the Fund and are present in other monitoring mechanisms, e.g., the WTO's TPRM and the OECD's surveillance, which are discussed below.

C. Surveillance at the WTO and the OECD – what can be learnt?

I. *The WTO's TPRM*

The Trade Policy Review Mechanism (TPRM), established on a provisional basis in 1989 and made permanent in 1995, is the WTO's principal surveillance tool. The TPRM's key objectives are to increase the transparency and understanding of countries' trade policies and practices through regular monitoring, to improve the quality of public and intergovernmental debate on the issues and to enable a multilateral assessment of the effects of policies on the world trading system.[52]

While all countries are reviewed on a regular basis, the frequency of the review depends on the size of the country, with larger countries coming under review more often.[53] The reviews focus on members' own

[52] The TPRM is based on the provisions of Annex 3 of the Agreement Establishing the WTO (The Marrakesh Agreement), which established the Trade Policy Review Body (TPRB) responsible for carrying out the trade policy reviews. For more information, see www.wto.org/english/tratop_e/annex3_e.htm. See also P. C. Mavroidis 'Surveillance Schemes: The GATT's New Trade Policy Review Mechanism', *Michigan Journal of International Law* (1992), 374, and M. Kende, 'Monetary Affairs in the WTO Trade Policy Review', Chapter 15, this volume. Besides the TPRM, other types of surveillance in the GATT/WTO system include special meetings of the GATT Council to review compliance of the contracting parties with the GATT requirements and general developments in the trading system, regular reviews by the Committee on Trade and Development of the operation of Part IV of the General Agreement and the implementation of the enabling clause, regular reporting to the Committee on Balance of Payment Restrictions, Surveillance under the MTN Codes and some others. See, generally, R. Blackhurst, 'Strengthening the GATT Surveillance of Trade-Related Policies, The New GATT Round of Multilateral Trade Negotiations', *Studies in Transnational Economic Law*, 5 (1988), 123, 131–5. More information on the TPRM is available at www.wto.org/english/tratop_e/annex3_e.htm. See also Mavroidis, 'Surveillance Schemes'.

[53] The four biggest traders (the European Union, the US, Japan and China) are examined approximately once every two years, the next sixteen countries every four years, and the remaining countries are reviewed every six years.

trade policies and practices, although they also take into account the countries' wider economic and developmental needs, their policies and objectives, and the external economic environment.

For each review, two documents are prepared: a policy statement by the government under review and a detailed report written independently by the WTO Secretariat. These documents, together with the proceedings of the Trade Policy Review Body's meetings, are published shortly after the meeting.

Unlike the IMF surveillance, TPRM was not designed as an enforcement instrument for members' compliance with their trade policy obligations.[54] Rather, these 'peer reviews' by other WTO Members were designed to enhance transparency of Member's practices and indirectly encourage governments to follow more closely the WTO rules and commitments. The reviews also enable outsiders to understand a country's policies and circumstances, and provide feedback to the country being reviewed on its performance in the system.[55]

While TPRM has generally been considered a success, particularly for increasing transparency and its capacity to promote inter-agency cooperation,[56] it has also been criticised for, *inter alia*, falling short on specifics, being unduly accommodating to misreporting by members, and paying inadequate attention to developing countries.[57]

[54] However, the TPRM also plays an important role in the general system of ensuring compliance with the WTO obligations. See, e.g., S. Laird, 'The WTO's Trade Policy Review Mechanism – From Through the Looking Glass', *World Economy* 9 (2002), 741–64; Marc D. Froese, 'Between Surveillance and Transparency: Trade Policy Review and North American Dispute Settlement at the WTO' (1 April 2012), gsrn.com/abstract=2038036.

[55] For a more detailed discussion of the TPRM, see, e.g., A. H. Qureshi, 'The New GATT Trade Policy Review Mechanism: An Exercise in Transparency or "Enforcement"?', *Journal of World Trade* (1990), 147, 152–4.

[56] See, e.g., S. Grammling, 'WTO Trade Policies Review Mechanism: Explanations and Reflections', www.library.fes.de/pdf-files/bueros/genf/06316.pdf.

[57] See, e.g., A. Ghosh, 'Developing Countries in the WTO Trade Policy Review Mechanism', journals.cambridge.org/action/displayFulltext?type=1&fid=7809815&jid=WTR&volumeId=9&issueId=03&aid=7809812; R. Abbott, 'GATT and the Trade Policy Review Mechanism: Further Reflections on Earlier Reflections', *Journal of World Trade* 27 (1993), 117–18 (who, while acknowledging the economic benefits of the TPRM, argues that its efficacy is not to be founded on its 'so-called' prescriptive or normative attributes, and that the reviews do not attempt to evaluate specific measures or aspects of policy for their conformity with GATT rules; nor do they reach any decisions as such, which the country concerned has to follow).

II. Surveillance at the OECD

The OECD surveillance is an important tool in achieving the OECD's mandate of promoting sound economic policies of its member states.[58] The two principal tools for the OECD surveillance are peer reviews (e.g., Economic Survey) and *Economic Outlook*.

The OECD peer review is an examination of one country's performance or practices in a particular area (e.g., macroeconomics, financial or fiscal matters, labour, education, the environment) by other countries.[59] While the reviews may take various forms, the best known and the most long-standing are regular Economic Surveys. The Economic Surveys are carried out on a regular basis for every OECD member (and some non-members) by the OECD's Economic and Development Review Committee (EDRC), cover the overall economic performance and prospects of a country and are published every two years for each OECD member country.[60]

The Economic Surveys have evolved over the years. While in the past they were mostly focused on short-term macroeconomic developments and policies, now more emphasis is put on policies viewed as beneficial to the economy's long-run performance,[61] with particular attention to structural policies and their interaction with macroeconomic policies.[62]

[58] Article 1 of the OECD Convention provides:

> 'The aims of the OECD shall be to promote policies designed: (a) to achieve the highest sustainable economic growth and employment and a rising standard of living in Member countries, while maintaining financial stability, and thus to contribute to the development of the world economy; (b) to contribute to sound economic *expansion in Member as well as non-member countries in the process of economic development; and (c) to contribute to the expansion of world trade on a multilateral, non-discriminatory basis in accordance with international obligations*' (emphasis added).

This objective is achieved through the undertakings of the member states stipulated in Article 2 and 3 of the Convention. Article 2 provides for the general undertaking of the states to pursue certain economic and social goals and Article 3 provides for the cooperation, coordinated actions and information exchange between the OECD member states aimed at achieving the aims of Article 1.

[59] See, e.g., F. Pagani, 'Peer Review: A Tool for Co-Operation and Change: An Analysis of an OECD Working Method' *OECD Working Paper*, September 2002. www.oecd.org/dataoecd/33/16/1955285.pdf.

[60] The periodicity of the reviews for non-members depends on the terms of the agreement with such non-members, and a separate survey is prepared on the euro area.

[61] www.oecd.org/eco/economicsurveysandcountrysurveillance/abouteconomicsurveysandtheedrc.htm.

[62] F. Pagani, 'Peer Review'.

Each country's survey builds upon the following general structure of: (i) assessment and recommendations, including recent trends, prospects and macroeconomic policy requirements; (ii) an overview of structural policy developments, key challenges and implementation of structural reforms; and (iii) a country-specific special chapter (e.g., on taxation, public sector expenditure, population ageing, environmental sustainability).[63]

The country reviews are carried out by the EDRC[64] in close cooperation with the authorities of the member country under review. After discussion by the members (with designated members acting as reviewers leading the examination), the report is revised by the OECD Secretariat in consultation with the member country under review to take account of the EDRC's recommendations and comments and finally published.

The OECD also publishes on a semi-annual basis its analysis on the major economic trends and prospects for the next two years in the *OECD Economic Outlook*.[65] The *Outlook*, which includes policy assessment and numerical forecasts, is prepared by the OECD Economics Department and includes the set of macroeconomic data for thirty-four OECD member states and six non-members (Russia, Brazil, China, India, Indonesia and South Africa).

Peer review has been practised by the OECD since its inception in 1961 and has shaped the work of the organisation in most policy areas. The success and relative effectiveness (although disputed) of the OECD peer review has been attributed, *inter alia*, to its limited and largely homogeneous membership.[66] The fact that most members share a similar level of development and similar political and economic concerns is considered as an advantage in establishing a closer dialogue and reaching

[63] A. Schafer, 'A New Form of Governance? Comparing the Open Method of Co-ordination to Multilateral Surveillance by the IMF and the OECD', *Journal of European Public Policy* 13:1 (2006), 70–88.

[64] The Economic and Development Review Committee (EDRC) has one member from each OECD country plus the European Commission, and the final survey reflects the joint views of the OECD countries.

[65] OECD Economic Outlook compares to the IMF's WEO.

[66] See, e.g., K. Shigehara, 'Multilateral Surveillance: What the OECD can Offer', Global Finance Lecture University of Birmingham, October 1996. The OECD currently has thirty-four member countries which include many of the world's most advanced countries and emerging countries like Mexico, Chile and Turkey. At first the OECD's membership was limited to eighteen European countries plus the US and Canada. Russia is negotiating to become a member of the OECD, while close relations of the OECD with Brazil, China, India, Indonesia and South Africa are maintained through the 'enhanced engagement' programme.

understandings on complex policy issues.[67] Indeed, effective peer review involves value-sharing within the member countries for purposes of evaluation, mutual trust regarding the dissemination of accurate data, confirmation of a standard level of commitment from the member states and credibility of the OECD.[68] All these considerations contribute to the 'peer pressure', which is a driving force behind the reviews and is exercised through (i) a mix of formal recommendations and informal dialogue by the peer countries; (ii) public scrutiny, comparisons and, in some cases, even ranking among countries; and (iii) the impact of all the above on domestic public opinion, national administrations and policy-makers. It is made more effective by the influence of public opinion on domestic policy-makers: publicising the outcome of the OECD reviews and their scrutiny by public media plays an important role in creating an incentive for policy change and provides support to domestic policy-makers for sometimes unpopular reforms.[69]

In evaluating the OECD surveillance, the following benefits are commonly noted: increased policy dialogue, enhanced transparency of members' policies and the ability to draw on others' experience, capacity building through identifying and sharing 'best practices', and increased compliance through peer pressure and soft enforcement.[70] Criticisms of the OECD surveillance include: limited membership (especially in the face of the increasing importance of the OECD's non-members as agenda-setters), 'vetting' of the final surveillance reports and a lack of clarity and consistency of warnings and policy recommendation,[71] 'soft law' shortcomings and the lack of a stronger enforcement

[67] K. Shigehara and P. Atkinson, 'Surveillance by International Institutions: Lessons from the Global Financial and Economic Crisis', *OECD Economics Department Working Papers* No. 860 (2011).

[68] Reference from 'Evaluating the Effectiveness of the OECD Surveillance', John C. Whitehead School of Diplomacy and International Relations, Seton Hall University, May 2012.

[69] F. Pagani, 'Peer Review'.

[70] One recent study focused on evaluating OECD surveillance in twenty-four randomly selected member countries. It concluded that 52 per cent of the OECD's economic recommendations are adopted by its members. 'Adoption' was understood as any official policy change, regardless of magnitude, that is in the spirit of the prior OECD recommendations. This level of adoption was estimated consistent over time and across different types of issues.

[71] The published versions of the OECD surveillance reports are often considered 'sanitised' because of the need for political agreement between the OECD member states before these reports are published. Warnings and policy recommendations could be more clear, succinct and consistent. See Shigehara and Atkinson, 'Surveillance by International Institutions'.

mechanism (a 'peer review' can function properly only if there is an adequate level of commitment by the participating countries), lack of coordination between multilateral and bilateral surveillance activities, and a lack of explicitly agreed policy requirements or guidelines that constitute the basis for judgment of the macroeconomic performance in the OECD surveillance process.

III. What can be learnt from the TPRM and the OECD surveillance?

The recent international financial crisis has revealed gaps in the existing international surveillance mechanisms and has demonstrated the need to strengthen the ability of these mechanisms to provide early warnings about risks and vulnerabilities and to facilitate the appropriate policy responses. So what can surveillance in the international monetary field learn from the trade field? The experience with the surveillance mechanisms described in this chapter reveals that different institutions conducting surveillance in the monetary and trade fields face many of the same challenges, and that successfully addressing these challenges is the key to improving the effectiveness of surveillance. Some of the common issues and challenges are discussed below.

First, an effective surveillance mechanism should involve a continuous dialogue between the institution conducting the monitoring and countries' authorities and other stakeholders. It should also establish modalities for other members of the institution to discuss and express views on a country's policies (such as consideration of Article IV consultation reports by the IMF Executive Board and discussions at the OECD's EDRC). This continuing dialogue and regular reviews or assessments are crucial for early detection of potential risks and vulnerabilities and for promoting the policy debate.

Second, more work needs to be done to develop a better understanding of the origin and mechanisms of transmission of potential vulnerabilities that could trigger a crisis. While trade-related risks and vulnerabilities are relatively well understood, financial globalisation, with its growing interconnectedness between countries and individual financial institutions, has posed particular challenges, as demonstrated by the recent financial crisis. To address these challenges, the IMF has developed and has been implementing an ambitious agenda on financial sector surveillance, in close cooperation with its member countries and other international institutions and organisations.

Third, transparency is essential to effective surveillance and to promoting public debate about national policies and their impact on other countries and on global stability. The past decade has witnessed a dramatic shift towards more publicity in many institutions, including the WTO, the OECD and the IMF. However, communication of early findings of risks and vulnerabilities poses difficult challenges. For example, if the IMF makes public its views on a risk that has not yet materialised, this may trigger a market reaction that may cause or exacerbate a crisis. Thus, risks associated with premature disclosure of such information should be carefully considered. More generally, the trend towards greater transparency has to be balanced with the need for candour, and it may pose special challenges if an institution, such as the IMF, fulfils a dual role of a 'truth teller and enforcer' and a 'confidential advisor'.

Fourth, effective surveillance in general, and early identification of risks and vulnerabilities in particular, are difficult without the necessary data. While each institution engaged in surveillance has its own legal framework for data provision, such a framework may not always be consistent with the evolving data needs. For example, the IMF Articles do not obligate members to provide certain types of data, such as institution-specific data, which the IMF considers important to enable it to conduct effective surveillance of the financial sector. It is thus important that frameworks be developed, where necessary, based on voluntary cooperation, to bridge such gaps.

Finally, no international surveillance mechanism on its own has proven to be effective in predicting, preventing or resolving crises. Therefore, cooperation between the institutions engaged in economic monitoring is important, in order to make surveillance more effective at the national and global level.

D. Conclusion

A number of international organisations and institutions, including the IMF, the OECD and the WTO, are involved in the conduct of economic surveillance at the national and global levels. While the scope and modalities of these surveillance activities are rooted in institution-specific legal frameworks, they share many of the same challenges, including how to engage most effectively with members and other stakeholders, how to detect risks and vulnerabilities before they develop into a crisis, and how to increase traction of their advice with policy-makers in individual countries.

As each institution strives to make its surveillance more effective, these efforts should be informed by the experience of others. There are also benefits in strengthening cross-institutional cooperation that could exploit synergies and complementarities of each framework with the objective of promoting national and global economic and financial stability.

10

The impact of sovereign debt on EU monetary affairs

ANNAMARIA VITERBO

A. Introduction

Sovereign insolvencies have always existed but, following the recent wave of crises, sovereign debt restructuring has gained centre stage in academic debate.[1] Economists, policy-makers and lawyers are discussing causes, common traits and consequences of sovereign debt crises, as well

[1] 'While there is no universally accepted definition, a sovereign debt restructuring can be defined as an exchange of outstanding sovereign debt instruments, such as loans or bonds, for new debt instruments or cash through a formal process. Sovereign debt here refers to debt issued or guaranteed by the government of a sovereign state. One can generally distinguish two main elements in a debt restructuring: debt rescheduling, defined as a lengthening of maturities of the old debt, possibly involving lower interest rates; and debt reduction, defined as a reduction in the face (nominal) value of the old instruments' (IMF, 'A Survey of Experiences with Emerging Market Sovereign Debt Restructurings', 5 June 2012, p. 3).

On sovereign debt see, among others: M. Audit (ed.), *Insolvabilité des États et dettes souveraines* (Paris: LGDJ, 2011); C. A. Primo Braga and G. A. Vincelette (eds.), *Sovereign Debt and the Financial Crisis* (Washington, DC: World Bank, 2011); R. Kolb (ed.), *Sovereign Debt: From Safety to Default* (Hoboken, NJ: John Wiley & Sons, 2011); R. Olivares-Caminal, 'Sovereign Debt Restructuring', in N. Segal and L. Chan Ho (eds.), *Debt Restructuring* (Oxford University Press, 2011), pp. 379–459; E. C. Schlemmer, 'The Enforcement of Sovereign Debt', in M. Giovanoli and D. Devos (eds.), *International Monetary and Financial Law: The Global Crisis* (Oxford University Press, 2011), pp. 418–48; F. Sturzenegger and J. Zettelmeyer, *Debt Defaults and Lessons from a Decade of Crises* (Cambridge, MA: MIT Press, 2007); M. Waibel, *Sovereign Defaults before International Courts and Tribunals* (Cambridge University Press, 2011); K. Rogoff and J. Zettelmeyer, 'Bankruptcy Procedures for Sovereigns: A History of Ideas, 1976–2001', *IMF Staff Papers*, 2002; D. Carreau and M. Shaw (eds.), *La dette extérieure/The External Debt*, The Hague Academy of International Law, Recueil des Cours – Colloques, Vol. 17 (The Hague: Martinus Nijhoff, 1995). See also L. Buchheit and R. M. Lastra, 'Sovereign Debt', in ILA, *Committee on International Monetary Law*, Sofia Conference Report, 2012, www.mocomila.org; ILA, Sovereign Insolvency Study Group, State Insolvency: Options for the Way Forward, presented at the ILA The Hague Conference, 2010, www.mocomila.org.

as preventive policy measures and legal instruments to proceed with orderly restructurings.

Currently, however, the legal framework on sovereign debt remains rather fragmented, its major flaw being the absence of either a single forum or a single procedure for the adjudication of disputes concerning restructurings or defaults.

Applicable rules and procedures are envisaged by many bodies of law, both at domestic level (for instance, national laws governing bond contracts, usually the laws of England or the State of New York) and at international level, with a major role played by the Paris and London Clubs, as well as the International Monetary Fund (IMF).

This fragmentation among different institutions, procedures and sources of law reflects the historical evolution of sovereign debt crises and the heterogeneity of creditors.[2]

As a result of this evolution, four restructuring tools are now in place: (i) the Paris Club, the leading institutional framework for restructuring external bilateral sovereign debt (in other words public or publicly-guaranteed debt owed to foreign governments);[3] (ii) the London Club, a less institutionalised process for the renegotiation of debt between a government and commercial banks;[4] (iii) the IMF, which, together with

[2] Das, Papaioannou and Trebesch provide a detailed classification of all sovereign debt restructurings since 1950 (U. S. Das, M. G. Papaioannou and C. Trebesch, 'Sovereign Debt Restructurings 1950–2010: Literature Survey, Data, and Stylized Facts', *IMF Working Paper*, August 2012, WP/12/203).

[3] After World War II, governments largely relied on borrowing from other states through bilateral agreements rather than resorting to the private market. Negotiations over the public debt of a country began to be managed by the Paris Club in 1956, when it met for the first time upon request of Argentina. Since then this informal group of official creditors seeking coordinated and sustainable solutions for nations facing payment difficulties has negotiated more than 400 agreements for eighty-nine debtor countries. The scope of Paris Club negotiations covers the medium and long-term external public debt of a country, issued before an agreed cut-off date. Its work is based on a number of principles (such as the principle of comparability of treatment) agreed by creditor countries to facilitate decision-making processes and the adoption of rescheduling or cancellation agreements. Once consensus is reached at Paris Club level, the rescheduling terms and conditions are included in binding bilateral agreements.

[4] In the aftermath of the oil shock of the 1970s, commercial bank lending to developing countries boomed. Following the successful negotiations with Peru and Zaire of 1976, the London Club developed as an informal group of international commercial banks that gather to protect their claims against a sovereign debtor in distress: the debtor voluntarily initiates a process in which a Bank Advisory Committee or Steering Committee is appointed to conduct the negotiations. Chaired by a leading financial firm, the Committee includes representatives from other banks with large exposure to the debtor state. Once the restructuring agreement is signed, the Committee is dissolved.

the World Bank and other multilateral institutions, provides debt relief to highly indebted poor countries;[5] and (iv) exchange offers typically aimed at restructuring the debt held by bondholders.[6]

Soft-law instruments also play an important role. The Institute of International Finance (IIF) and the United Nations Conference on Trade and Development (UNCTAD) have established principles to guide states and private creditors in debt management, under both normal conditions and severe financial distress.[7] They promote a restructuring process centred on the principles of good faith and fair treatment, and have been praised for their contribution to the overall transparency in sovereign finance, as well as to risk management and accountability.

Only a few of the instruments described above, however, proved useful in the context of the sovereign debt crisis affecting the European Monetary Union (EMU).

B. Sovereign debt restructuring in the EMU

I. The EMU's 'original sin'

The eurozone sovereign debt crisis is the most severe faced by Europe since World War II and the challenges it poses are enormous. According to many commentators, the crisis stems from the EMU's 'original sin': the introduction of a common currency in the absence of a common state.[8]

[5] The IMF and the World Bank launched the Heavily Indebted Poor Countries initiative (HIPC initiative) in 1996 and the Multilateral Debt Relief Initiative (MDRI) in 2005. As of late the IMF has been providing debt relief to wealthier countries too.

[6] In the 1990s the composition of sovereign debt changed again, shifting towards tradable debt securities held by international bondholders. It is worth noting that reliance on the issuance of sovereign bonds as a new source of finance brought new challenges. Sovereign debt restructuring involves institutional investors and thousands of individual creditors and retail bondholders. Such a dispersed creditor structure is prone to holdouts and vulture creditors risks and makes it extremely difficult to achieve high participation in exchange offers.

[7] On the IIF Principles for Stable Capital Flows and Fair Debt Restructuring, see R. Ritter, 'Transnational Governance in Global Finance: The Principles for Stable Capital Flows and Fair Debt Restructuring in Emerging Markets', *ECB Occasional Paper Series*, No. 103, April 2009.

On the UNCTAD Principles on Promoting Responsible Sovereign Lending and Borrowing, see C. Espósito, Y. Li and J. P. Bohoslavsky (eds.), *Sovereign Financing and International Law: The UNCTAD Principles on Responsible Sovereign Lending and Borrowing* (Oxford University Press, 2013).

[8] Tommaso Padoa-Schioppa was among the first to warn of the dangers of a currency without a state: T. Padoa-Schioppa, *The Euro and Its Central Bank: Getting United after the Union* (Cambridge, MA: MIT Press, 2004), p. 36.

This is the peculiar feature that distinguishes the eurozone from federal countries like the US (which have a single currency area, a federal budget and taxation powers).

The founding fathers of the EMU were aware of the intrinsic risks brought about by the introduction of a single monetary and exchange rate policy, while at the same time leaving full powers to each member over its national fiscal policies.[9]

As financial markets were unlikely to drive governments towards sustainable levels of public deficit and debt, the Maastricht Treaty was drafted so as to include a number of institutional arrangements for sound public finances. The following measures were introduced: the prohibition of monetary financing (now Article 123 Treaty on the Functioning of the European Union (TFEU)), the prohibition of privileged access to financial institutions (now Article 124 TFEU), the no-bailout clause (now Article 125 TFEU), fiscal provisions to avoid excessive government deficits and the excessive deficit procedure (now Article 126 TFEU).

In the late 1990s, countries were incentivised towards sound fiscal policies in order to qualify for the third stage of the EMU in compliance with the Maastricht convergence criteria; fiscal laxity led to exclusion from the single currency. Once participation in the eurozone had been decided on, the focus on fiscal discipline faded substantially, since a relaxation of budgetary efforts was perceived as having only negligible consequences on budget financing. In fact, in the eurozone integrated bond market, risk premiums no longer provided a true representation of the quality of national debts, giving rise to free-riding and opportunistic behaviours.

In 1997, the Stability and Growth Pact (SGP) was introduced through two Council Regulations.[10] The SGP rules were intended to counterbalance the waning attention to rigour, but did not have the desired

[9] Report on Economic and Monetary Union in the European Community (so-called 'Delors Report'), 12 April 1989: 'an economic and monetary union could only operate on the basis of mutually consistent and sound behaviour by governments and other economic agents in all member countries. In particular, uncoordinated and divergent national budgetary policies would undermine monetary stability and generate imbalances in the real and financial sectors of the Community' (para. 30). Also, see F. Gianviti, 'Relationship between Monetary and Exchange Rate Policy', Chapter 21, this volume.

[10] Resolution of the European Council on the Stability and Growth Pact, 17 June 1997, eur-lex.europa.eu/LexUriServ/LexUriServ.do?uri=CELEX:31997Y0802(01):EN:HTML; Council Regulation (EC) 1466/97 of 7 July 1997 on the strengthening of the surveillance of budgetary positions and the surveillance and coordination of economic policies (OJ L 209, 2 August 1997, p. 1); Council Regulation (EC) 1467/97 of 7 July 1997 on speeding up and clarifying the implementation of the excessive deficit procedure (OJ L 209, 2 August 1997, p. 6).

effect. The fiscal rules contained in the SGP were only loosely enforced and were even relaxed in 2005 to introduce more flexibility and discretion in the corrective arm.[11] Germany and France – the two most fervent advocates for the adoption of the SGP – became the promoters of these changes after both countries proved unable to stay below the 3 per cent public-deficit-to-GDP threshold.

The SGP reform eroded the moral authority of Germany and France, which were no longer in a position to take firm action within the Council of Economy and Finance ministers (ECOFIN Council) against states pursuing unsound fiscal policies. Other EMU members felt justified in neglecting the fiscal parameters enshrined in the SGP. The rules were not the real problem: the problem was their lax implementation.[12]

II. *Sovereign debt in a monetary union*

In their study, Das, Papaioannou and Trebesch affirm that only a few instances of sovereign debt restructuring occurred within monetary unions.[13]

[11] See European Council, Brussels 22–23 March 2005, Presidency Conclusions, Annex II – Improving the Implementation of the Stability and Growth Pact, ue.eu.int/ueDocs/cms_Data/docs/pressData/en/ec/84335.pdf; Council Regulation (EC) No 1055/2005 of 27 June 2005 amending Regulation (EC) No 1466/97 on the strengthening of the surveillance of budgetary positions and the surveillance and coordination of economic policies (OJ L 174, 7 July 2005, p. 1); Council Regulation (EC) No 1056/2005 of 27 June 2005 amending Regulation (EC) No 1467/97 on speeding up and clarifying the implementation of the excessive deficit procedure (OJ L 174, 7 July 2005, p. 5). In 2005, the ECB recommended a rigorous application of the excessive deficit procedure (EDP) in the interests of fiscal prudence: ECB, 'The Reform of the Stability and Growth Pact', *ECB Monthly Bulletin* (August 2005), 59–74, at 70. See also J.-V. Louis, 'The Review of the Stability and Growth Pact', *Common Market Law Review* 43 (2006), 85–106 and J.-V. Louis, 'The Legal Foundations of the SGP in Primary and Secondary EC Law', in F. Breuss (ed.), *The Stability and Growth Pact: Experiences and Future Aspects* (Vienna: Springer, 2007), p. 3.

[12] See European Commission, 'A Blueprint for a Deep and Genuine Economic and Monetary Union: Launching a European Debate', COM(2012) 777 final/2, Brussels, 30 November 2012, p. 2. It should be noted, however, that the SGP was amended and complemented by the new set of rules on enhanced EU economic governance – the so-called Six Pack (five Regulations and one Directive) – which entered into force on 13 December 2011 (OJ L 306, 23 November 2011). In addition, on 23 November 2011, the Commission proposed two draft Regulations to strengthen the budgetary surveillance framework for all euro-area member states, in particular for those countries that have excessive deficits, that are experiencing or are at serious risk of financial instability, or that are under a financial assistance programme. Fiscal discipline was also reinforced by the adoption of the Treaty on Stability, Coordination and Governance (TSCG).

[13] Das *et al.*, 'Sovereign Debt Restructurings 1950–2010', pp. 55–6.

The West African Economic and Monetary Union (WAEMU)'s largest member, Côte d'Ivoire, restructured its debt twice: in 1998 and in 2009. As regards the East Caribbean Currency Union (ECCU), three members defaulted and requested debt renegotiation: Dominica in 2004, Grenada in 2005 and Antigua and Barbuda in 2010.[14] Since the WAEMU was founded in 1994 and the ECCU in 1983,[15] the frequency of restructuring events so far appears to be rather high. However, the authors claim that those crises had no negative consequences for the stability of the respective monetary union. The same cannot be argued for the EMU. As demonstrated by the case of Greece, a debt crisis in any country of the eurozone undermines the financial and political stability of the area as a whole.

Members of a monetary union lose their capacity to issue debt in a currency over which they have full control.[16] De Grauwe illustrates the possible consequences of this loss of sovereignty when a member of a monetary union is hit by solvency problems. In this scenario, investors' loss of confidence or 'changing market sentiments can lead to "sudden stops" in the funding of the government debt, setting in motion a devilish interaction between liquidity and solvency crises'.[17] Liquidity is withdrawn from the national market, interest rates on sovereign borrowings are pushed up as are the spreads of state bonds and – in a self-fulfilling prophecy – the liquidity crisis turns into a solvency crisis. The state in distress is hampered in its capacity to decide on effective counter-cyclical budgetary measures. The loss of confidence in the capacity of the state to service its debt leads to an increase in interest rates, which in turn translates into a harsher recession

[14] Côte d'Ivoire, Grenada and Antigua and Barbuda agreed on a restructuring of their public external debt with the Paris Club.

[15] The WAEMU was established in the framework of the Economic Community of West African States (ECOWAS) with the Treaty of Dakar, Senegal, signed on 10 January 1994 by the heads of state and governments of Benin, Burkina Faso, Côte d'Ivoire, Mali, Niger, Senegal, and Togo.

The ECCU was established in 1983 among the members of the Organization of Eastern Caribbean States (OECS): Antigua and Barbuda, Dominica, Grenada, St. Kitts and Nevis, St. Lucia, and St. Vincent and the Grenadines.

[16] See also X. Debrun, 'Sovereign Debt Crises in Monetary Unions: Prevention, Prevention and Prevention', *Reflets et perspectives de la vie économique* 49:4 (2010), 59–69; K. Featherstone, 'The JCMS Annual Lecture: The Greek Sovereign Debt Crisis and EMU: A Failing State in a Skewed Regime', *Journal of Common Market Studies* 49:2 (2011), 193–217.

[17] P. De Grauwe, 'The Governance of a Fragile Eurozone' (2011), www.econ.kuleuven.be/ew/academic/intecon/Degrauwe/PDG-papers/Discussion_papers/Governance-fragile-eurozone_s.pdf, p. 7.

and even greater budget deficit, leading to deflation and a crisis of the banking system.

Conversely, in countries retaining full powers over their own currency, the central bank can always provide liquidity that, although it causes inflation, greatly reduces the risk of a default.[18]

According to Gianviti *et al.*:

> The greater possibility of sovereign default in a monetary union is just the dark side of the well-known argument that highly indebted countries benefit from euro-area membership in terms of lower interest rates paid on their public debt because the monetary union makes the commitment to low inflation more credible. By closing the inflation channel, monetary union leaves a country with only three ways out of a situation of excessive debt: severe and harmful fiscal retrenchment, default, and being bailed out by the other members of the monetary union.[19]

III. The actions taken so far: the Greek sovereign debt restructuring

In late 2009, fears of a default by Greece, which was no longer in a position of being able to service its huge public debt, marked the beginning of the eurozone sovereign debt crisis. Despite the adoption of an initial rescue package by the IMF and eurozone countries (the so-called Greek Loan Facility) coupled with drastic austerity measures,[20] in February 2012 Greece was forced to partially restructure its debt under the Private Sector Involvement voluntary deal (PSI deal).[21]

The PSI deal was 'voluntary' in the sense that its terms and conditions were negotiated *ex ante* between the Greek government, the representatives of the private creditors (see below on the IIF involvement) and in

[18] In this sense, see *ibid.*, p. 27. However, it is also possible that the central bank will generate hyperinflation, triggering a complete loss of confidence in the government and the monetary authority. In these circumstances, the public will refuse to hold any money and bonds issued by the authorities. A default by the government in that case will thus be inevitable (in this sense G. Rich, 'Comment on "The Impact of Sovereign Debt Monetary Affairs" by Annamaria Viterbo', WTI, World Trade Forum 2012, Bern, 12–13 October 2012).

[19] See F. Gianviti, A. O. Krueger, J. Pisani-Ferry, A. Sapir, and J. von Hagen, 'A European Mechanism for Sovereign Debt Crisis Resolution: A Proposal', *Bruegel Blueprint Series* (2010), 6, www.bruegel.org/publications/publication-detail/publication/446-a-european-mechanism-for-sovereign-debt-crisis-resolution-a-proposal.

[20] In the period 2009–11, Greece's fiscal adjustment amounted to almost 12.6 per cent of its GDP, an unprecedented level in economic history.

[21] Euro Summit Statement, Brussels, 26 October 2011.

consultation with the official sector (eurozone authorities, EU institutions and the IMF).

The heads of state or government of the eurozone had already agreed upon the PSI deal on 26 October 2011: while deeming the PSI deal necessary, they affirmed it was being adopted because Greece's situation was exceptional and unique.[22]

Only a minority of the outstanding bonds had been issued under English law, while approximately 90 per cent of them were governed by Greek law, which did not include collective action clauses (CACs).[23]

CACs became common after the IMF's proposal to create a Sovereign Debt Restructuring Mechanism (SDRM) was rejected in 2003.[24] Governments preferred to rely on a contractual approach, which bases sovereign debt restructuring on privately negotiated agreements between a sovereign and its creditors, rather than on an institutional approach. CACs are designed to streamline the restructuring process and limit the possibility for individual bondholders to initiate disruptive litigation. These clauses make the amended terms of a renegotiated debt agreement binding upon all creditors if approved by a qualified majority of bondholders, thus not leaving minorities with the power to obstruct the process.[25]

On 23 February 2012, the Greek Parliament introduced Law 4050/2012 on 'Rules on the Modification of Titles Issued or Guaranteed by the Greek State with the Bondholders' Agreement' (the so-called Bondholder Act),[26] by which CACs were to be retroactively introduced

[22] On the Greek debt restructuring debate, see M. G. Gulati and J. Zettelmeyer, 'Making a Voluntary Greek Debt Exchange Work', *Capital Markets Law Journal* 7:2 (2012), 169–83; L. C. Buchheit and M.G. Gulati, 'Greek Debt – The Endgame Scenarios', (2011), ssrn.com/abstract=180701; L.C. Buchheit and M.G. Gulati, 'How to Restructure Greek Debt', (2010), ssrn.com/abstract=1603304.

[23] Nor did they include *pari passu* or cross-default clauses.

[24] In 2001, following the outbreak of the Argentinian crisis, Anne Krueger, at the time First Deputy Managing Director of the IMF, proposed the creation of a Sovereign Debt Restructuring Mechanism (SDRM), which was rejected in 2003 (see the IMFC Communiqué of 12 April 2003). For a description of the SDRM, see, in particular, IMF, 'Proposed Features of a Sovereign Debt Restructuring Mechanism', 12 February 2003. See also S. Hagan, 'Designing a Legal Framework to Restructure Sovereign Debt,' *Georgetown Journal of International Law* 36:2 (2005), 299.

[25] See J. Dey, 'Collective Action Clauses: Sovereign Bondholders Cornered?', *Law and Business Review of the Americas* 15 (2009), 485–529.

[26] Law 4050/2012 'Rules of Amendment of Titles Issued or Guaranteed by the Hellenic Republic with the Bondholders' Agreement,' published in Government Gazette A 36/23.02.2012 of the Hellenic Republic. See also ECB Opinion of 17 February 2012 on the Terms of Securities Issued or Guaranteed by the Greek State (CON/2012/12), www.ecb.int/ecb/legal/pdf/en_con_2012_12_f_sign.pdf.

on all Greek bonds issued before 31 December 2011. The aim was to force bondholders to accept the exchange offer, which was to be launched by the Hellenic Republic.

On 24 February 2012, Greece announced a debt exchange operation for bonds with an aggregate outstanding face value of approximately € 200 billion, which would have substantially reduced its debt level and interest expenditure, thus contributing to the sustainability of government debt and a return to financial stability.

Pursuant to the Bondholder Act, the high level of participation – 83.5 per cent of private creditors accepted the debt swap offer – was sufficient to allow the activation of the CACs.[27] On 9 March 2012, the Greek Council of Ministers acknowledged that the decision by a large majority to accept the swap had become binding upon all holders of Greek bonds, thus forcing also creditors who had refused the deal to suffer a nominal haircut of 53.5 per cent on their principal. As a result, Greece received a seemingly unprecedented large reduction of its debt (amounting to € 106 billion, almost 50 per cent of its GDP), which was, however, counterbalanced by a corresponding increase in its indebtedness associated with the second support programme.

The debt exchange operation covered € 177 billion of bonds regulated by Greek law, € 8 billion of foreign law bonds and € 9.5 billion of debt issued by state-controlled enterprises guaranteed by the Greek government. The terms of the PSI deal included:

(i) a 53.5 per cent reduction in the nominal value of eligible Greek government bonds, for which bondholders received in exchange:
  (a) new bonds with a face value amounting to 31.5 per cent of the face value of the debt exchanged,[28] and
  (b) European Financial Stability Facility (EFSF) short-term notes maturing within twenty-four months amounting to 15 per cent of the face value of the debt exchanged;

(ii) a 2 per cent fixed-rate annual coupon to be paid on the new bonds in 2013–15, increasing to 3 per cent in 2016–20, 3.65 per cent in 2021 and reaching 4.3 per cent from 2022 onwards; and

(iii) GDP-linked securities of a nominal amount equal to the face value of the new bonds, capped at 1 per cent of the notional amount of new bonds.[29]

[27] With the activation of the CACs, private creditors' participation reached almost 97 per cent.

[28] The new bonds issued by Greece contain a CAC in line with the new EU standards, and are made subject to English law and UK jurisdiction.

[29] Source: IMF, 'Country Report on Greece,' No. 12/57, March 2012, p. 88.

As part of a package of measures approved by the Eurogroup on 27 November 2012,[30] Greece offered to buy back various categories of its sovereign obligations with a view to lowering its debt from a projected 190 per cent in 2014 to 124 per cent of GDP by 2020. Through the debt-buy-back scheme (DBB), the Greek government purchased back about € 30 billion in debt owed to private creditors – about half of the outstanding bonds – at a third of their face value. The operation was a precondition for unlocking the release of the next disbursement of loans from the eurozone and the IMF.

It is worth noting that the IIF took part in the negotiation process of the PSI deal, first through the Task Force on Greece and later through the Private Creditor–Investor Committee (composed of representatives of about thirty of the largest private investors in Greek sovereign bonds).[31] The IIF Principles for Stable Capital Flows and Fair Debt Restructuring served as a framework for the negotiations and demonstrated the validity of the voluntary, cooperative and market-based approach (as opposed to a unilateral, top-down approach). However, some features of the Greek restructuring raised concerns and made it more difficult to fully adhere to the IIF core Principles (open dialogue, transparency, good faith and the fair and comparable treatment of all creditors). The issues of major concern included: the complexities deriving from Greece being a member of a currency union; the exemption from the debt exchange of bonds held by EU official entities and the subordination of private investors' claims (considered not fully consistent with the equal treatment of creditors); and the retroactive introduction of a collective action mechanism in bonds issued under domestic law (which threatened the sanctity of financial contracts).[32]

[30] Eurogroup Statement on Greece, www.consilium.europa.eu/uedocs/cms_data/docs/pressdata/en/ecofin/133857.pdf. See also Hellenic Republic, Ministry of Finance, Press Releases, 3 December 2012 and 10 December 2012.

[31] IIF, 'Report on Implementation by the Principles Consultative Group', October 2012, pp. 12–13.

[32] IIF, 'Report of the Joint Committee on Strengthening the Framework for Sovereign Debt Crisis Prevention and Restructuring', October 2012. The Greek experience was carefully assessed in order to revise the existing framework for sovereign debt crisis prevention and resolution (see in particular the Addendum to the IIF Principles endorsed by the Group of Trustees of the Principles at its Annual Meeting in Tokyo, 14 October 2012 and published in the above-mentioned IIF Report).

First, membership in the EMU and its institutional features were considered to impose policy constraints and add a layer of complexity that resulted in longer discussions and less effective decision making.

Second, the ECB and the national central banks (NCBs) of the Eurosystem were *de facto* awarded senior creditor status and their holdings of Greek bonds – mainly acquired under the Securities Markets Programme (on which see Section V) – were shielded from bearing any losses.[33] In fact, before the exchange offer was launched, the ECB and the NCBs swapped their Greek bonds for new bonds of identical structure and nominal value, but with different International Securities Identification Number (ISIN) numbers that, at a later stage, would not be involved in the application of retroactive CACs. Also the holdings of the European Investment Bank (EIB) were carved out of the restructuring. These decisions raised the spectre of discriminatory treatment to the detriment of private creditors.[34] On 8 March 2012, the President of the ECB, Mario Draghi, explained that:

> the SMP was a monetary policy instrument. So the purchases of Greek bonds done under that program responded to public interest policy – general policy considerations. And as such, they deserve protection. This is one reason. The other reason is that I think the balance sheet of the ECB should be protected, because only through the integrity of the balance sheet of the ECB you can have the ECB independence in pursuing price stability in the whole of the euro area, and price stability is in the interest of all the members. So I think that's one other reason why this exchange of bonds was quite right to do. But there is a third reason, I think, that people rarely think about this. I mean, we forget that this money is taxpayers' money. And so the ECB has, in a sense, the duty to do everything to protect the taxpayers' money that was entrusted with it. So this exchange of bonds was actually the right thing to do from this point of view as well.[35]

[33] IMF, 'Euro Area Policies: 2012 Article IV Consultation – Selected Issues Paper', IMF Country Report No. 12/182, July 2012, 47. For a brief study of the role of the NCBs within the Eurosystem in time of crises, see also, J-V. Louis, 'Monetary Union and the Law: Some Comments', Chapter 5, this volume.

[34] The ECB, NCBs and EIB holdings amounted to more than 20 per cent of the total outstanding bonds. According to the IIF Joint Committee on Strengthening the Framework for Sovereign Debt Crisis Prevention and Resolution, 'the exclusion of the ECB holdings from the debt exchange could be rationalized . . ., but the exclusion of the official body holdings [NCBs and EIB] deviated from the normal principle of non-discrimination' (IIF, Report of the Joint Committee on Strengthening the Framework for Sovereign Debt Crisis Prevention and Restructuring', October 2012, p. 52).

[35] Mario Draghi, President of the ECB, 'Transcript of the Press Conference', 8 March 2012, www.ecb.int/press/pressconf/2012/html/is120308.en.html.

Another argument in favour would have been based on Article 123 TFEU (on which see Section V): this provision can be interpreted as preventing the ECB from accepting losses deriving from the restructuring of Member States' sovereign bonds. It follows that any voluntary restructuring or rescheduling of the ECB's holdings could amount to monetary financing if a dogmatic interpretation of Article 123 TFEU were to be favoured over one that is more in tune with the prevailing exceptional circumstances. In fact, Article 123 TFEU (as well as Article 125 TFEU) has essentially a preventive nature, its objective being to reduce as far as possible the risk of public debt crises.[36] This provision, however, was drafted with normal rather than turbulent times in mind, and at a time when a sovereign debt crisis in the eurozone was unforeseeable. If the fiscal discipline objectives of Article 123 have not been attained in normal times (which is clearly the case with Greece), to insist on strict compliance with the monetary financing prohibition at a time of acute, almost existential, crisis is to actively counteract the efforts of indebted Member States to return to fiscal discipline. If the participation of the ECB and NCBs in an Official Sector Involvement (OSI)[37] or a debt-buy-back scheme can help Greece (or, in the future, other troubled sovereign states) to return to fiscal discipline (rather than to default), the main goal of Article 123 will be not only preserved, but also well served.

Third, the retroactive insertion of CACs in the outstanding domestic bonds changed the original terms of their issuance contract. This might be deemed inconsistent with the obligations taken on in the investment treaties ratified by Greece (more than forty bilateral investment treaties (BITs), with both EU and non-EU countries). Most Greek BITs contain a broad definition of investment, which does not explicitly exclude sovereign debt instruments from the scope of their application. Moreover, to protect domestic creditors from the risk of a so-called double adjustment (i.e., the losses due to the haircut on their claims and the costs associated with austerity measures, unemployment and high interest rates), they were offered preferential conditions as compared with foreign bondholders. This, however, could be construed as a breach of the standard of

36 See ECJ Judgment (Full Court), *Thomas Pringle* v. *Ireland*, Case C-370/12, 27 November 2012, para. 59.

37 According to many observers and analysts, Greece may face a further restructuring, possibly involving the official sector creditors, which now hold around four-fifths of Greece's debt.

national treatment contained in investment treaties.[38] Also at stake is the standard of fair and equitable treatment, due to the 'take it or leave it' nature of the debt exchange offer. The Bondholders Act might also be challenged on the grounds of the umbrella clause: in fact, Greece unilaterally amended the terms of a contractual obligation by a sovereign act. Last but not least, a breach of the free transfer of funds clause and a form of indirect expropriation are to be considered.

The possibility of opting for investor–state arbitration to challenge debt restructuring was further grounded by the decision of the International Centre for Settlement of Investment Disputes (ICSID) Tribunal in the *Abaclat et al.* v. *Argentina* case, which opened a Pandora's box[39] by upholding jurisdiction to hear the claims of more than 60,000 bondholders on the alleged breach of the Italy–Argentina BIT.[40] It is, therefore, likely that German bondholders will bring a claim before an ICSID tribunal on the basis of the 1961 Germany–Greece BIT.[41] This also raises the question of discrimination among EU investors, as not all of them have the possibility of resorting to arbitration under a BIT.

[38] See E. Norton, 'International Investment Arbitration and the European Debt Crisis', *Chicago Journal of International Law* 13 (2012), 291–315; D. Strik, 'Investment Protection of Sovereign Debt and Its Implications on the Future of Investment Law in the EU', *Journal of International Arbitration* 29:2 (2012), 183–204. See also M. Waibel, *Sovereign Defaults before International Courts and Tribunals* (Cambridge University Press, 2011), pp. 273 ff.; A. Caliari, 'Risk Associated with Trends in the Treatment of Sovereign Debt in Bilateral Trade and Investment Treaties', in UNCTAD, *Compendium on Debt Sustainability and Development* (New York and Geneva: UN Publications, 2009), p. 211; K. Cross, 'Arbitration as a Means of Resolving Sovereign Debt Disputes,' *American Review of International Arbitration* 17:3 (2006), 335–82.

[39] Waibel anticipated this development in M. Waibel, 'Opening Pandora's Box: Sovereign Bonds in International Arbitration', *American Journal of International Law* 101 (2007), 711–59.

[40] *Abaclat and others* v. *Argentina* (case formerly known as *Giovanna A. Beccara and others* v. *Argentina*), ICSID Case No. ARB/07/5, Decision on Jurisdiction and Admissibility, 4 August 2011 and Dissenting Opinion of the arbitrator Georges Abi-Saab, 28 October 2011. The decision on the merits is still pending. See also *Giovanni Alemanni and others* v. *Argentina*, ICSID Case No. ARB/07/8 and *Giordano Alpi and others* v. *Argentina*, ICSID Case No. ARB/08/9.

The *Abaclat* decision was fiercely criticised: see, among others, S. Manciaux, 'Decisions et sentences commentées: Abaclat et a. c. Argentine', *Journal du droit international* 139: 1 (2012), 286–316; A. De Luca, 'Collective Actions in ICSID Arbitration: The Argentine Bonds Case', *Italian Yearbook of International Law* 21(2011) (published 2013), 211–39; J. Beess und Chrostin, 'Sovereign Debt Restructuring and Mass Claims Arbitration before the ICSID: The Abaclat Case', *Harvard International Law Journal* 53 (2012), 505–17.

[41] See J. Wilson and G. Wiesmann, 'Germans Seek Lawsuits over Greek Debt Swap', *Financial Times*, 12 March 2012.

Moreover, a mass claim is going to be brought before the ECHR by a group of Italian holders of Greek bonds claiming a violation of the right to property (Article 1 Protocol 1).[42]

IV. The actions taken so far: the inclusion of CACs in European bonds

As noted above, the majority of Greek sovereign bonds were issued under domestic law and did not contain CACs. This is not uncommon in Europe, where – before the crisis – government bonds were predominantly issued under domestic laws and the inclusion of CACs remained an exception. The Greek debt restructuring, though, showed how critical CACs were.

As early as 2003, to promote orderly restructurings in the event of sovereign debt crises, EU Member States had agreed to include CACs in government bonds issued under a foreign jurisdiction and/or governed by a foreign law.[43] European CACs would have been consistent with the recommendations adopted by the G-10 Working Group on Contractual Clauses in its report of September 2002.[44] However, this development concerned only international sovereign bonds and – as we have seen – the majority of European bonds continued to be regulated by domestic law.

In 2010, the worsening Greek crisis drove the Eurogroup to take a more decisive step towards the adoption of CACs. The issue was included in the discussions on the European Stability Mechanism (ESM).[45]

[42] See www.bondgreci-azionilegali.it.

[43] See the speech by the ECOFIN President to the IMFC in April 2003.

[44] G-10, 'Report of the Working Group on Contractual Clauses' (the so-called 'Quarles Group'), 26 September 2002.

[45] Eurogroup Statement of 28 November 2010, 'General Features of the Future Mechanism', annexed to the Conclusions of the European Council of 16–17 December 2010, EUCO 30/1/10 REV 1, p. 9, www.consilium.europa.eu/uedocs/cms_data/docs/pressdata/en/ec/118578.pdf.

The decision of the Eurogroup was later confirmed by the Eurosummit and the European Council: Conclusions of the Heads of State of Government of the Euro Area of 11 March 2011, www.consilium.europa.eu/uedocs/cms_data/docs/pressdata/en/ec/119809.pdf; and Conclusions of the European Council, Annex II 'Term Sheet on the ESM', para. 2, 24/25 March 2011, EUCO 10/1/11, www.consilium.europa.eu/uedocs/cms_data/docs/pressdata/en/ec/120296.pdf.

The seventeen eurozone countries signed the first version of the ESM Treaty on 11 July 2011, and the second version (now in force) on 2 February 2012.[46] Both versions included a recital whereby identical and standardised CACs would be mandatorily included in all new eurozone government securities (bills, bonds, debentures, notes and other debt securities) with maturity beyond one year.[47]

The Sub-Committee on EU Sovereign Debt Markets of the Economic and Financial Committee (EFC) was entrusted with the task of drafting standardised and identical CACs consistent with those contained in New York and English Law bonds. On 18 November 2011, the EFC agreed on a draft text and a final version of the model clause was published in February 2012 after having taken into account comments received as part of a public consultation process.[48]

The eurozone CACs draw a distinction between modification of reserved and non-reserved matters, the latter concerning the less important terms and conditions and requiring a lower majority of bondholders' affirmative votes.[49] Moreover, the modification could be proposed in relation to either a single series of bonds or different series (cross-series modification), with different approval thresholds applicable.

[46] The European Stability Mechanism (ESM) is an international organisation that provides financial assistance to members of the eurozone in financial difficulty. The ESM is intended to replace the European Financial Stability Facility (EFSF) and the European Financial Stabilisation Mechanism (EFSM). The ESM Treaty entered into force on 27 September 2012, following the deposit by Germany of its instrument of ratification. The text of the ESM Treaty is available at www.european-council.europa.eu/media/582311/05-tesm2.en12.pdf. On the ESM, see ECB, 'The European Stability Mechanism', *ECB Monthly Bulletin*, July 2011, 71–84; A. Viterbo and R. Cisotta, 'La crisi del debito sovrano e gli interventi dell'UE: dai primi strumenti finanziari al Fiscal Compact', *Diritto dell'Unione europea* 2 (2012), 325–68.

[47] See Recital 11 and Article 12.3 of the ESM Treaty. On European CACs, see L. C. Buchheit and M. G. Gulati, 'Drafting a Model Collective Action Clause for Eurozone Sovereign Bonds', *Capital Markets Law Journal* 6:3 (2011), 317–25; J. B. Gott, 'Addressing the Debt Crisis in the European Union: The Validity of Mandatory Collective Action Clauses and Extended Maturities', *Chicago Journal of International Law* 12 (2011), 201–28; J.-V. Louis, 'The Unexpected Revision of the Lisbon Treaty and the Establishment of a European Stability Mechanism', in D. Ashiagbor, N. Countouris and I. Lianos (eds.), *The European Union After the Treaty of Lisbon* (Cambridge University Press, 2012), pp. 284–320, at 314–19.

[48] EFC, 'CACs Common Terms of Reference', 17 February 2012, europa.eu/efc/sub_committee/pdf/cac_-_text_model_cac.pdf. See also EFC, Supplemental Provisions, 17 February 2012, europa.eu/efc/sub_committee/pdf/cac_-_supplemental_provisions.pdf.

[49] The modification of a reserved matter requires an affirmative vote of not less than 75 per cent of the aggregate principal amount of the outstanding bonds represented at a duly called meeting.

Disenfranchisement became a very hot topic in the context of the EU after the ECB started buying sovereign bonds on the secondary market within the framework of the Securities Markets Programme (SMP) (see below).[50] A disenfranchisement clause bars certain bondholders from voting on restructuring plans, excluding them from quorums and majorities needed for amendments. Therefore, the disenfranchisement of bonds directly or indirectly owned or controlled by a sovereign issuer and its public entities is a way to protect ordinary creditors from manipulation of votes.

Some suggested including a disenfranchisement clause in European CACs for investors with interests similar to those of the issuer, who predictably would vote in favour of modifications or who are likely to be motivated by circumstances other than the direct effect of a modification on the value of their holdings.[51] The latter is the position in which the ECB – or a national central bank – would find itself when holding foreign state bonds in its portfolio.

According to the EFC Sub-Committee on EU Sovereign Debt Markets, since the ECB and the Eurosystem NCBs are independent from governments' interference, their holdings of eurozone public securities do not have to be disenfranchised under the model CACs. This is because:

> Article 130 TFEU and Article 7 of the ECB Statute expressly prohibit euro area national central banks and members of their decision-making bodies from seeking or taking instruction from European Union institutions or bodies, from any government of a Member State of the European Union or from any other body. As a result, a euro area national central bank's decision to vote for or against the proposed modification of securities acquired in connection with, for instance, its Eurosystem operations must, as a matter of law, be made by the bank acting in its own interest.[52]

The Sub-Committee focuses therefore on one of the key principles of the EMU: the independence of the ECB and of NCBs. This same principle, though, could be interpreted in the opposite way, as to motivate their disenfranchisement. In fact, due to its independence, the ECB should not be forced to accept the outcome of a majority vote that might result in the central bank bearing losses.[53] Moreover, the ECB could find itself in the

[50] See K. Drake, 'Disenfranchisement in Sovereign Bonds', *Duke Law Working Paper* (2012), papers.ssrn.com/sol3/papers.cfm?abstract_id=2007294.

[51] EFC Sub-Committee on EU Sovereign Debt Markets, 'Model Collective Action Clause Supplemental Explanatory Note', 26 March 2012, europa.eu/efc/sub_committee/pdf/supplemental_explanatory_note_on_the_model_cac_-_26_march_2012.pdf.

[52] *Ibid.* [53] Said losses might result in a breach of Article 123 TFEU.

awkward position of having to increase its bond holdings in order to influence majority decisions in which it is enfranchised.

All the issues related to disenfranchisement highlight the challenges posed by the new role that quasi-sovereigns are acquiring as active participants in the sovereign debt market.[54]

V. The actions taken so far: the ECB's intervention in the public debt securities market

Together with other non-standard monetary policy measures, in May 2010 the ECB began to purchase outright, through the SMP, European sovereign bonds in the secondary market.[55] In adopting this purchasing programme, the ECB reversed its long-held policy of avoiding intervention in sovereign bond markets, which it deemed compromising for its independence.

Under the SMP, the ECB and the Eurosystem NCBs were to purchase, on the secondary market, eligible debt instruments issued by central governments or public entities of the eurozone, as well as private debt securities.

The ECB Governing Council adopted the SMP decision due to 'the exceptional circumstances in financial markets, characterized by severe tensions in certain market segments, which were hampering the monetary policy transmission mechanism and thereby the effective conduct of monetary policy oriented towards price stability'.[56]

The SMP was to be applied temporarily and, *de facto*, it was discontinued in September 2012,[57] when the ECB announced the introduction of the new Outright Monetary Transactions programme (OMT programme).

[54] A. Gelpern, 'Bankruptcy, Backwards: The Problem of Quasi-Sovereign Debt', *Yale Law Journal* 121 (2012), 888–942: the author investigates recent proposals to adapt bankruptcy institutions for US states and members of the European Union, that to different degrees have ceded important aspects of their sovereignty to a central government or supranational institution in the name of economic and political integration.

[55] See ECB, 'The ECB's Non-Standard Measures – Impact and Phasing Out', *Monthly Bulletin* (July 2011), 66; D. Zandstra, 'The European Sovereign Debt Crisis and Its Evolving Resolution', *Capital Markets Law Journal* 6:3 (2011), 285–316, 291.

[56] Recital 2 of the ECB Decision of 14 May 2010 establishing a securities markets programme (ECB/2010/5), OJ L 124/8, 20 May 2012.

[57] According to the Eurogroup Statement on Greece of 27 November 2012, starting from 2013 member states would pass on to Greece (in a segregated account) an amount equivalent to the profits on the SMP holdings of Greek bonds held by their national central bank. States receiving financial assistance are not required to participate in the scheme.

Under the OMT programme, the ECB and the NCBs will conduct outright transactions in secondary sovereign bond markets with the aim of safeguarding an appropriate monetary policy transmission and the singleness of the monetary policy. Interventions by the ECB on the secondary market will be carried out only for countries that have requested EFSF/ESM support,[58] and provided that the request is approved by the Eurogroup. The ECB would purchase bonds on the secondary market, while the EFSF/ESM would conduct primary market purchases. No *ex ante* quantitative limits are set on the size of OMTs, and both the amount of holdings and their market values will be disclosed.[59]

The argument put forward by the ECB is that the divergence in government bond yields is hampering monetary transmission in the whole eurozone and therefore also its efforts at maintaining price stability, which is the ECB's primary objective. Therefore, even though the purchase of bonds will concern only countries receiving EFSF/ESM support, the singleness of the monetary policy will be safeguarded.

The main qualitative difference between the SMP and the OMT is that countries whose bonds are being purchased by the ECB through the OMT will be subject to stricter conditionality.[60] Conditionality will be defined in the context of an EFSF/ESM macroeconomic adjustment programme or of a precautionary programme.

It should be noted that both the EFSF and the ESM envisage a role for the European Commission and the IMF in designing conditionality. In particular, the conditionality attached to ESM financial assistance

[58] The European Financial Stability Facility (EFSF) is a special purpose vehicle established on 9 May 2010 by the eurozone countries to safeguard financial stability in Europe by providing financial assistance to member states in economic difficulty. The EFSF is also authorised to intervene both in the primary and secondary markets, usually upon request from the member state concerned to the President of the Eurogroup. In particular, intervention on the secondary market serves to support the functioning of the debt markets and appropriate price formation in government bonds in exceptional circumstances where the limited liquidity of markets threatens financial stability and pushes sovereign interest rates towards unsustainable levels. See EFSF, 'Guideline on Interventions in the Secondary Market', 29 November 2011, www.efsf.europa.eu. Once the European Stability Mechanism (ESM) is fully operational, the EFSF will only remain active in financing previously started programmes.

[59] See ECB Press Release, 'Technical Features of Outright Monetary Transactions', 6 September 2012, www.ecb.int. The ECB Governing Council has not yet adopted a decision detailing the legal framework for the OMT programme.

[60] An element of conditionality was also present in the context of the SMP (see Recital 4 of Decision ECB/2010/5).

instruments will be detailed in a Memorandum of Understanding (MoU) adopted pursuant to the procedure set out by Article 13(3) of the ESM Treaty: the European Commission, in connection with the ECB, and 'wherever possible' together with the IMF (the so-called 'Troika') will be entrusted by the ESM Board of Governors[61] with the task of negotiating the MoU with the ESM member concerned.[62] Furthermore, the Troika will also be responsible for monitoring compliance with the conditionality attached to the financial assistance facility. The European Commission and the IMF would therefore become relevant players in the design and monitoring of conditionality, putting the ECB's independence at stake. This is especially so because the ECB will terminate its OMTs when the member country fails to comply with the macroeconomic adjustment or precautionary programme.

According to the ECB, however, its independence will be safeguarded since the Governing Council has full discretion to decide on the start, continuation and suspension of the OMTs in accordance with its monetary policy mandate (OMTs will only be used to achieve the objective of maintaining price stability).[63]

Doubts may also be raised on the consistency of both the SMP and the OMT programmes with the prohibition of monetary financing enshrined in Article 123 TFEU (on which see also Section III). This provision explicitly forbids the ECB and the NCBs to purchase debt instruments from central governments and other public authorities, but it only applies if these instruments are purchased 'directly'. Under the prevailing interpretation of Article 123 TFEU, although it is prohibited from purchasing in the primary market, the ECB would still be allowed

[61] The ESM Board of Governors is composed of the Ministers of Finance of the euro area member states as voting members, with the European Commissioner for Economic and Monetary Affairs and the ECB President as observers (its composition is therefore similar to that of the Eurogroup). The Board of Governors is chaired by the President of the Eurogroup, Jean-Claude Juncker, while Klaus Regling is the ESM Managing Director.

[62] Pursuant to Article 5 of the ESM Treaty, the Board of Governors adopts, among others, the following decisions by mutual agreement (unanimity): the decision to provide stability support by the ESM, including the economic policy conditionality as stated in the MoU, and to establish the choice of instruments and the financial terms and conditions; the decision to give a mandate to the European Commission to negotiate, in liaison with the ECB, the economic policy conditionality attached to each programme of financial assistance.

[63] ECB, 'Compliance of Outright Monetary Transactions with the Prohibition on Monetary Financing', *Monthly Bulletin* (October 2012), 7–9.

by the adverb 'directly' to operate in the secondary market in the fine-tuning of its monetary policy (Article 18 ECB Statute).[64]

The recent German Federal Constitutional Court (FCC) decision on the ESM, however, while it has shed new light upon the issue, has also given rise to new concerns.[65] The FCC explains – in an *obiter dictum* – that Article 123 TFEU prevents the ECB from '[using] the funds at its disposal for *direct* financial stabilization of its members', adding that 'an acquisition of government bonds on the secondary market by the ECB aiming at financing the Members' budgets independently of the capital markets is prohibited as well, as it would circumvent the prohibition of monetary financing' (para. 246).[66] This leaves open the question of what conclusions the FCC will draw in its final judgment, since if the ECB ever took part 'voluntarily' in a debt restructuring, this would be construed as monetary financing, as the OMT is also a monetary instrument.

To determine whether the OMT purchases might indirectly infringe the monetary financing prohibition, it has been suggested that it would be necessary to look at its rationale and objectives,[67] namely to safeguard: (i) the ECB's ability to maintain price stability, (ii) fiscal discipline, and

[64] M. Ruffert, 'The European Debt Crisis and European Union Law', *Common Market Law Review* 48:6 (2011), 1777–805, at 1787–8.

[65] Decision on the application for a temporary injunction of the German Federal Constitutional Court (Bundesverfassungsgericht) of 12 September 2012, 2 BvR 1390/12, 2 BvR 1421/12, 2 BvR 1438/12, 2 BvR 1439/12, 2 BvR 1440/12, 2 BvE 6/12, paras. 246–7. At the time of writing, the Court has not yet ruled on the merits. On 14 January 2014, the German FCC separated from the proceedings related to the ESM and the Treaty on Stability, Coordination and Governance in the Economic and Monetary Union (the so-called 'Fiscal Compact') the matters related to the SMP and OMT programme. Furthermore, the proceedings related to the SMP/OMT were stayed and a referral for a preliminary ruling was submitted by the German FCC (for the first time in its history) to the Court of Justice of the European Union on the OMT consistency with EU law: according to the GFCC, the OMT programme falls outside the Monetary policy mandate of the ECB and is incompatible with the monetary financing prohibition set forth by Article 123 TFEU (BVerfG 2 BvR 2728/13 14 January 2014 Absatz-Nr. (1–105), www.bverfg.de/entscheidungen/rs20140114_2bvr272813en.html).

[66] Reference should also be made to the 7th Recital of Council Regulation (EC) No. 3603/93 of 13 December 1993 specifying definitions for the application of the prohibitions referred to in Articles 104 and 104b(1) of the Maastricht Treaty (renumbered after the Lisbon Treaty as Article 123 and 125 TFEU), OJ L 332/1 31 December 1993. According to said recital 'purchases made on the secondary market must not be used to circumvent the objective of Article 104 of the Treaty [now Article 123 TFEU]'.

[67] See ECB, 'Compliance of Outright Monetary Transactions with the Prohibition on Monetary Financing', *ECB Monthly Bulletin* (October 2012), 7–9 and P. Athanassiou, 'Of Past Measures and Future Plans for Europe's Exit from the Sovereign Debt Crisis: What is Legally Possible (and What is Not)', *European Law Review* 4 (2011), 566–7.

(iii) central bank independence. If caution is needed in assessing the OMT impact on the ECB's independence for the reasons stated above, certainly the other objectives of the monetary financing prohibition are not impaired by the OMT programme, which on the contrary is conducive to their achievement.[68]

It is worth noting that, when it is purchasing bonds issued by eurozone countries through the OMT programme, the ECB will accept being *pari passu* with ordinary creditors,[69] in accordance with the terms of the bonds (the same does not apply to SMP bond holdings).[70] On this issue, it was observed that 'the ECB can promise to be *pari passu*, until

[68] According to Georg Rich, monetary financing may be conducted in two different ways. The first method entails the central bank purchasing sovereign debt in order to lower the costs to the government of financing. If the government's financing needs are large, the central bank may be prompted to expand the money supply excessively, fuelling inflation. Inflation will reduce the real value of currency and sovereign debt held by the public, which will thus be forced to accept capital losses and to bear the costs of the central bank absorbing such debt. However, monetary financing may also involve purchases of sovereign debt without the central bank engendering inflation. The central bank may be able to neutralise the effects of the debt purchases on the money supply by selling other assets or by issuing its own interest-bearing securities. If ailing governments default on their debts, the central bank will see its profits shrink or it may even incur losses. Therefore, resources will be shifted from the central bank to the ailing government, without any necessity for inflation to rise. Once again, taxpayers ultimately have to pick up the bill by incurring capital losses on their own holdings of sovereign debt and by an increase in taxes required to offset the fall in central bank profits that would otherwise accrue to the government. The ECB seems to be mainly concerned about the second variant of monetary financing as the prospect of a significant rise in inflation is small – at least at present. Nevertheless, worried observers ask themselves whether the ECB is not taking an overly big gamble. When in the more or less distant future the eurozone economy starts to recover and the need for tightening monetary policy arises, will the ECB be able to quickly reduce the money supply? Will the ailing countries have gained sufficient health to allow the ECB to sell their sovereign debt? If that debt cannot be sold without rekindling the fiscal crisis, does the ECB possess a sufficiently wide range of other instruments for reducing the money supply? At the moment, there are no clear-cut answers to these questions. But one thing is certain: the risk that the ECB's current purchases of ailing government debt will ultimately evolve into monetary financing of the first or second kind or both is substantial (G. Rich, 'Comment on "The Impact of Sovereign Debt Monetary Affairs" by Annamaria Viterbo', WTI, World Trade Forum 2012, Bern, 12–13 October 2012).

[69] The ECB will not claim preferred creditor status as compared to private investors. See ECB Press Release: 'Technical features of Outright Monetary Transactions', 6 September 2012, www.ecb.int. The ECB Governing Council has not yet adopted a decision detailing the legal framework for the OMT programme.

[70] See M. Draghi, President of the ECB, and V. Constâncio, Vice-President of the ECB, 'Introductory Statement to the Press Conference (with Q&A) of 6 September 2012', Frankfurt am Main, www.ecb.int.

a default threatens and it can then pressure "Euritania" to let it swap into local or international bonds without CACs that receive special treatment, exactly as it did with Greece'.[71] In this case, if a proper *pari passu* clause was contained in the bond contract, the other creditors could claim breach of contract.[72]

Last but not least, it is interesting to note that, in the 2012 Article IV Report on the eurozone, the IMF seems to imply that the ECB exemption from the Greek PSI deal (even if unique and exceptional) might have made the SMP (and now the OMT) less effective due to subordination risk.[73]

VI. What could have been done: a European Crisis Resolution Mechanism (ECRM)

Since a debt crisis within a eurozone country can undermine financial stability and the common currency, it has been argued that a permanent European mechanism for sovereign debt crisis resolution should be put in place.[74]

In November 2010, François Gianviti and other distinguished scholars put forward the proposal to create a European Crisis Resolution Mechanism (ECRM).[75] The ECRM would have been activated upon request of a government whose debt had reached unsustainable levels. The country in question would immediately stop servicing its debt to national and international creditors and there would be a stay on litigation for individual creditors seeking repayment. The mechanism would provide a framework for negotiations only between the debtor and its private creditors, while bilateral creditors would continue to refer

[71] D. Nowakowski, 'How Can the ECB Address Concerns on Seniority?', *Roubini Global Economics*, 5 September 2012.

[72] The sovereign bonds issued under Greek law before the restructuring did not contain a *pari passu* clause. On the *pari passu* clause, see L. Buchheit and J. Pam, 'The Pari Passu Clause in Sovereign Debt Instruments', *Emory Law Journal* 53:3 (2004), 869; R. Olivares-Caminal, 'To Rank Pari Passu or Not to Rank Pari Passu: That Is the Question in Sovereign Bonds' (2008), ssrn.com/abstract=1291751. See, in particular, United States Court of Appeals, Second Circuit, *NML Capital LTD* v. *Argentina*, 26 October 2012, 2012 WL 5275014 (CA2 (NY).

[73] IMF, 'Euro Area Policies: 2012 Article IV Consultation – Selected Issues Paper', IMF Country Report No. 12/182, July 2012, pp. 47 ff. It is noteworthy that the ESM will have a preferred creditor status second only to that of the IMF: this, however, might have an adverse effect on the perceived credit risk of new issues of euro area sovereign bonds.

[74] For an overview of proposals for a sovereign insolvency framework, see Das *et al.*, 'Sovereign Debt Restructurings', p. 88.

[75] Gianviti, *et al.*, 'A European Mechanism for Sovereign Debt Crisis Resolution', p. 21.

to the Paris Club. Binding decisions on behalf of all creditors were to be taken by a supermajority, thus locking in potential holdouts. The proposed ECRM would have been made up of three organs: (i) a legal body responsible for the settlement of disputes; (ii) an economic body to guide negotiations and assess debt sustainability; and (iii) a financial body entrusted with the task of providing interim financial assistance on behalf of the EU.

The foregoing proposal attracted criticism from other economic scholars, who argued that it would raise a moral hazard issue and that it would attract speculative pressure, to the point of precipitating a crisis, with contagion spreading to solvent countries as well.[76]

C. Conclusions

Only some of the tools available under international law for sovereign debt restructuring have been applied in the context of the European crisis.

To tackle the eurozone debt crisis, the leaders of EU countries relied on a variety of measures: the Greek sovereign debt restructuring, the introduction of CACs in European government bonds, the ECB's non-standard measures and the adoption of financial assistance mechanisms (like the EFSF and the ESM), as well as the reform of the European economic governance and of the SGP, the Fiscal Compact, and the project for a banking union.

Similar to what happened at the beginning of the 2000s for the SDRM proposal,[77] the creation of the ECRM drew attention, but not enough consensus to move beyond political discussions.

The contractual approach therefore remains the preferred one, even if, within the EU legal framework, the introduction of a mechanism with a stronger element of public authority could have been expected.[78] This leaves the ECB in the difficult position of safeguarding monetary stability in the whole eurozone with few policy tools at its disposal, and which are often stretched to their limits.

[76] See Louis, 'The Unexpected Revision of the Lisbon Treaty', p. 37.

[77] See above footnote 24.

[78] See A. von Bogdandy and M. Goldmann, 'Sovereign Debt Restructurings as Exercises of International Public Authority: Towards a Decentralized Sovereign Insolvency Law', paper presented at the ESIL-IEL-IG Workshop of Valencia, 13 September 2012 (on file with author).

The European sovereign debt crisis demonstrates therefore that the EMU project – a common currency without a state – did not take into account all of the possible implications. As a matter of fact, 'the European Union is [still] only a polity in the making, lacking important functions and constitutional characteristics of a political union and retaining some features of an old model of strategic contest between independent states'.[79] The EMU and the EU are at a crossroads: the choice is between leaving out non-compliant states, putting both the EMU and the EU at risk of disintegrating, or decisively moving towards further integration, in particular through the establishment of a fiscal union and greater tax cooperation. Are we ready for a federal European government?

[79] T. Padoa-Schioppa, *The Euro and Its Central Bank: Getting United after the Union* (Cambridge, MA: MIT Press, 2004), p. 50.

11

Taxation in times of austerity: a question of political economy

ISABEL FEICHTNER

A. Introduction: taxation in times of austerity

Taxation – as the main source of public revenue in market economies – plays (next to expenditure cuts) a crucial role in the reduction of sovereign debt.[1] The revenue raising function of taxation is, however, only the most obvious link between taxation and sovereign debt. The two other functions of taxation – namely redistribution and regulation[2] – are also affected by rising amounts of sovereign debt and, more specifically, the accompanying austerity programmes and economic reforms. In the modern welfare state, taxation has long served as an instrument of redistribution to address different degrees of societal inequality arising in capitalist economies. With the progression of global economic integration after 'embedded liberalism',[3] we have come to believe that this redistributive function had lost its centrality. Yet, recently, redistribution has resurfaced as a central focus in taxation debates due to new and persistent concerns over social inequality[4] and its destabilising effects. Such concerns are often voiced today in the context of debates on (global) justice and ethics, at the centre of which

[1] See, e.g., Memorandum of Economic and Financial Policies, attached to Greece's Letter of Intent to the IMF of 21 December 2012, www.imf.org/external/country/grc/index.htm?type=9998#23, p. 17; Memorandum of Economic and Financial Policies, attached to Ireland's Letter of Intent to the IMF of 29 November 2012, www.imf.org/external/country/irl/index.htm?type=9998#23, p. 6.

[2] See R. S. Avi-Yonah, 'The Three Goals of Taxation', *New York University Tax Law Review* 60:2 (2006), 1.

[3] J. G. Ruggie, 'International Regimes, Transactions, and Change', *International Organization* 36:2 (1982), 379.

[4] P. Olinto and J. Saavedra, 'The World Bank', *Inequality in Focus* 1:1 (2012) (explaining how despite falling international income inequality, global income inequality has remained relatively stable since the 1980s).

we find widespread discontent given that the main burden of fiscal consolidation and public crisis management appears to be falling on middle- and low-income groups.[5]

The regulatory objective of taxation also figures prominently in current discourses on fiscal consolidation and taxation. The reason for this is that regulatory taxation can be presented as a win–win option from an economic point of view: the right type of regulatory taxation, it is argued, can stimulate economic growth while raising public revenue and steering behaviour in desirable directions.[6] Yet, the use of taxation to set incentives for businesses also raises concerns, namely when it affects the competition between jurisdictions to attract economic activities. This phenomenon is usually denoted as 'harmful tax competition'.[7]

Whereas most tax systems attempt to integrate all three objectives – revenue generation, redistribution and regulation – these objectives frequently conflict. Taxes aimed at increasing competitiveness and productivity, for example, may clash with the redistributive aim of taxation. To calibrate the objectives of taxation is a function of governments which still regard taxation as one of the last vestiges of national sovereignty.[8] Yet, governments are cognisant of the limitations concerning their tax policy choices and tax collection capacity that result from regional and global economic integration. In particular, with the liberalisation of capital flows, the promise of embedded liberalism, as formulated by John Ruggie,[9] has come under pressure. Ruggie interpreted the international economic system that had emerged from the Bretton Woods Conference as aiming for global economic integration while maintaining the freedom and capacity of states to intervene domestically in the distribution of the costs and benefits of the capitalist economy.[10] In recent decades this freedom has been shrinking, the area of taxation

[5] On the economic effects of inequality in the US and calling for increased progressivity in taxation, U. Dadush, K. Derviş, S. Puritz Milsom and B. Stancil, *Inequality in America* (Washington, DC: Brookings Institution Press, 2012); J. Stiglitz, *The Price of Inequality* (New York: Norton, 2012); on inequality in the G-20 and recommending progressive taxation, R. Gower, C. Pearce and K. Raworth, 'Left Behind the G20?', 157 *Oxfam Briefing Paper*, 19 January 2012, www.oxfam.org.

[6] See Section C.I.2. On regulatory taxes, see R. S. Avi-Yonah, 'Carbon Tax, Health Care Tax, Bank Tax and other Regulatory Taxes', *Public Law and Legal Theory Research Paper Series*, Paper No. 281 (Ann Arbor, MI: University of Michigan Law School, July 2012).

[7] OECD, *Harmful Tax Competition* (Paris: OECD, 1998); see Section C.II.2.

[8] See Section B.IV.

[9] See Ruggie, 'International Regimes, Transactions and Change'. [10] *Ibid.*

being one where governments' power to intervene in order to address the social costs of economic globalisation and to realise a society's own vision of social justice appears restricted by the threat of loss of competitiveness in the global economy.[11] One reaction to the diminishing 'policy space' of governments takes the form of restrictions on transnational economic activity to restore domestic policy space, another is the turn to international institutions and intergovernmental cooperation in order to integrate or balance economic integration with other societal concerns at the international level.[12]

In the realm of taxation the Organisation for Economic Co-operation and Development (OECD) appears to be the most important international institution to tackle the effects of globalisation: first through the generation of policy advice and, second, through intergovernmental cooperation on tax matters. Yet, in neither of these two fields of activity has the organisation served to save the idea of embedded liberalism. From the policy advice given by the OECD Secretariat on tax matters, it is clear that the organisation has fully embraced the rationality of global economic integration. In the OECD debates among government representatives on international cooperation in the face of increasing competition between different tax systems, concerns about policy space for the pursuit of societal ideas of (redistributive) justice figure more prominently than in the policy papers of the OECD Secretariat. Here too, however, the dominant language is economic: cooperation aims to ensure 'good competition' and combat 'bad (or harmful) competition'. These debates largely sideline the question of how ideas of social justice may be realised through political action at the national level – in this case taxation. Moreover, they hardly address questions of global justice that are equally implicated in the developments that the OECD denotes as harmful tax competition, including the question of how to react to the observation that tax evasion and avoidance hit developing countries much harder than developed countries.[13]

[11] R. S. Avi-Yonah, 'Globalization, Tax Competition, and the Fiscal Crisis of the Welfare State', *Harvard Law Review* 113 (2000), 1573.

[12] *Cf.* D. Rodrik, *Has Globalization Gone Too Far?* (Washington, DC: Institute for International Economics, 1997).

[13] A. Rosenzweig, 'Why Are There Tax Havens', *Legal Studies Research Paper Series*, No. 10-11-03 (St Louis, MI: Washington University Law School, 2010); R. S. Avi-Yonah, 'The OECD Harmful Tax Competition Report', *Public Law and Legal Theory Working Paper Series*, Paper No. 115 (Ann Arbor, MI: University of Michigan Law School, August 2008).

This chapter puts forward the argument that questions of social and global justice are being excluded from the policy advice given by the OECD on taxation as well as from the international cooperation against harmful tax competition as conducted within the framework of the OECD. It calls for acknowledging that decisions about tax policy are expressive of ideas about justice and – more specifically – the distribution of the costs and benefits of economic activity within society and across societies. Consequently, debates and policy advice on taxation cannot or should not attempt to separate neatly questions of economic efficiency and competitiveness from social concerns (as the OECD proposes they should). Only if questions of taxation are perceived as questions of social justice and thus as questions of politics, and not merely of economics, can we hope to maintain a 'political economy'.[14] Motivated by the conviction that debates about global market governance are (and should be) increasingly overlapping with debates on global justice, constitutionalism and global ethics, this chapter takes a step back from the questions addressed in most of the other chapters in this volume. Instead of addressing specific procedural or substantive norms and their effect on the relationship between sovereign debt and taxation it attempts to problematise the role that international economic institutions, in particular the OECD, are playing in keeping these two interconnected debates artificially apart.

Before I turn to the OECD, Section B addresses in more detail how the three objectives of taxation – revenue generation, redistribution and regulation – are affected as governments aim for fiscal consolidation and how government's power to freely pursue and calibrate these objectives has come to appear rather as a myth than the core of sovereignty. Section C demonstrates how the OECD's tax policy advice and cooperation in tax matters react to the constraints on governmental taxation powers; how they aim at economic growth and competitiveness to the detriment of (other) ideas of social justice. The chapter concludes in Section D with a call for (re)integrating social and global justice concerns into debates on taxation.

[14] *Cf.* A. O. Hirschman, 'Exit and Voice' in A. O. Hirschman (ed.), *Essays in Trespassing* (Cambridge University Press, 1981), pp. 236, 239 ('political action or action in the public interest, is liable to escape the fetters of the benefit-cost calculus . . . [and is] fundamental for a genuine "political economy"').

B. Government objectives of taxation and the myth of fiscal sovereignty

Taxation not only serves to generate revenue, it is also an instrument used in the welfare state to redistribute and to steer the behaviour of economic actors. In times of austerity, the focus is on taxation as much as a means to reduce government debt as it is on taxation as a way to distribute the burdens of fiscal consolidation, and as a potentially cost-efficient way to regulate. Yet, while governments cling to the power of taxation as a core power of government, fiscal sovereignty in times of regional and global economic integration appears increasingly to be a myth.

I. Revenue generation

In market economies, governments rely on three main sources for government revenue: charges, taxes and debt instruments, such as government bonds.[15] When governments aim at fiscal consolidation, tax revenue is essential to reduce budget deficits and public debt. Consolidation may follow the recognition that further borrowing to finance the deficit destabilises the economy.[16] It, may, however, also be required by law. Budget rules, such as the so-called debt brake included in the German Constitution (the Basic Law) in 2011[17] and now mandated by the Treaty on Stability, Coordination and Governance in the Economic and Monetary Union,[18] place legal limits on public debt and thus force governments to turn to other sources of revenue. Governments that receive financial assistance from the International Monetary Fund (IMF) may need to increase revenue generation from taxation as part of the conditionality attached to such assistance.[19] Charges, as an alternative source of revenue are, by contrast, of limited value. Whereas they may pay for the provision of public services, for

[15] R. A. Musgrave and P. B. Musgrave, *Public Finance in Theory and Practice*, 4th edn (New York: McGraw-Hill, 1984), pp. 219, 220.

[16] On the relationship between sovereign debt and financial crisis, see C. M. Reinhart and K. S. Rogoff, *This Time is Different* (Princeton University Press, 2009), pp. 49 ff.

[17] The German Federation's budget rule is included in Article 115 of the Basic Law.

[18] Article 3:2 Treaty on Stability, Coordination and Governance in the Economic and Monetary Union (the respective norms shall be 'preferably constitutional, or otherwise guaranteed to be fully respected and adhered to throughout the national budgetary processes').

[19] See note 1.

example public education, they cannot serve directly to reduce the debt burden and, moreover, cannot finance social transfers, such as housing or health benefits.[20] Thus, governments rely on revenue from taxation for reducing their debt burden and – unless the concept of the welfare state is abandoned – for offering social services to those in need.

Some of the causes of sovereign debt, however, limit the potential of taxation to reduce public deficits and debt. An aging population leads to increased public expenditure on pensions and health services while reducing revenue from income taxes; economic recessions may necessitate greater public expenditures in order to sustain social safety nets and at the same time negatively affect tax revenue. Consequently, debates on fiscal consolidation focus as much on the reduction of expenditures as on the increase of government revenue through taxation.[21] Economic recessions raise a further dilemma as tax cuts are among the measures governments should consider to stimulate demand in times of economic downturn. Stimuli other than tax cuts include increases in government spending (another fiscal measure straining the public budget), and the lowering of interest rates as a monetary measure.[22] For governments concerned with fiscal consolidation the choice might well fall on monetary policy to stimulate the economy. Yet, this option can be limited by independent central banks' mandates to control inflation. Moreover, loose monetary policy may increase private indebtedness (shifting the debt burden from the government to the population) and social inequality.[23] Finally, the observation that protracted periods of fiscal austerity decrease the social acceptance of taxation calls into question whether debt can successfully be paid off with tax revenue.[24]

[20] On governments' obligations under international human rights law to provide such benefits, see Markus Krajewski, 'Human Rights and Austerity Programmes', Chapter 19, this volume.

[21] One way suggested to increase revenue without increasing taxes is the reduction of tax expenditures; see Memorandum of Economic and Financial Policies, attached to Ireland's Letter of Intent to the IMF of 29 November 2012, www.imf.org/external/country/irl/index.htm?type=9998#23, p. 6 (announcing the tightening of income tax allowances).

[22] M. Horton and A. El-Ganainy, *Fiscal Policy, Finance and Development* (Washington, DC: IMF), www.imf.org/external/pubs/ft/fandd/basics/fiscpol.htm (last visited 2 November 2013).

[23] J.-P. Fitoussi and F. Saraceno, 'How Deep Is a Crisis?' *OFCE Document de Travail*, No. 2009-31 (Paris: Center for Economic Research, November 2009).

[24] W. Streeck and D. Mertens, 'Politik im Defizit', *Der moderne Staat* 3:1 (2010), 7.

II. Redistribution

In the modern welfare states, taxes have always been aimed at redistribution. Apart from revenue generation for the provision of public goods and to cover the costs of war, governments collected taxes to address the increasing inequalities emerging from industrialisation. When income taxes were introduced on a comprehensive basis the redistributive objective was maintained and realised mainly through progressivity.[25] The guiding principle for taxation has long been the 'ability to pay principle' which aims at horizontal equity (persons with equal incomes should pay equal taxes) and vertical equity (persons with higher incomes should pay higher taxes).[26]

While, until the 1970s, assessment of tax policy was predominantly conducted on the basis of equity considerations a shift occurred in the 1970s and 1980s when tax policy was increasingly tested for its efficiency. Efficiency analysis led both to a questioning of the effectiveness of income taxes as means for distribution (as income tax progressivity may pose a disincentive to work) and of the desirability of redistribution.[27] This change in assessment of tax policy went hand in hand with the increasing mobility of capital. As a result investors can easily move capital to other jurisdictions in order to minimise the tax incurred on capital income.

Many tax systems were changed by cutting income tax rates whilst broadening the tax base, by reducing the progressivity of income taxation and through the adoption of general consumption taxes,[28] which tend to be regressive as the poorer segments of the population spend a higher proportion of their income on consumption than the

[25] For a history of ideas and political economy perspective on the development of European and the US tax systems, see S. Steinmo, 'The Evolution of Policy Ideas', *British Journal of Politics and International Relations* 5:2 (2003), 206.

[26] *Ibid.*, 209 ff. On the two main approaches to tax equity, the 'benefit principle' and the 'ability to pay principle', see Musgrave and Musgrave, *Public Finance in Theory and Practice*, pp. 227 ff.

[27] Steinmo, 'The Evolution of Policy Ideas', 217–20; on the shift from equity to efficiency analysis by tax theorists, see also B. I. Bittker, 'Equity, Efficiency and Income Tax Theory', *San Diego Law Review* 16:4 (1979), 735; generally on the disappearance of redistribution as a concern from economic theory with the emergence of the method of marginalism: H. Hovenkamp, 'Coase, Institutionalism, and the Origins of Law and Economics', *Indiana Law Journal* 86 (2011), 499.

[28] On these convergences in tax systems, see Avi-Yonah, 'Globalization, Tax Competition and the Fiscal Crisis'; OECD, *Tax Policy Reform and Economic Growth* (Paris: OECD, 2010), pp. 25 ff.

wealthier ones do.[29] While the shares of corporate and personal income taxes of the overall tax revenue appear to have remained relatively stable, tax scholars have shown that the tax burden has shifted away from capital to (less mobile) labour.[30]

That tax progressivity has waned and the tax burden been shifted onto labour is partly responsible for the growing inequality in many societies. While poverty has been decreasing overall, the income gap (after tax and benefits) between the small segments of society that are extremely rich and the rest of the population has been expanding in many countries.[31] The gap between the extremely wealthy and the rest of society is not only criticised from the standpoint of social justice; increasingly researchers are pointing out the detrimental effects of inequality on well-being.[32] Economists have come to the conclusion that inequality may in fact be destabilising and endanger economic growth.[33] This research is of particular relevance in a context of austerity, as the financial and debt crises pose the danger of increasing inequality even further. Poor countries at the periphery of the global economy have suffered disproportionately more than wealthy countries, and within the wealthier societies it is the poor and middle-income segments that bear the brunt of the burden of government bail-outs and austerity programmes.[34]

As a consequence, the theme of inequality forcefully reemerges in debates on tax policy[35] and has prompted the following proposals by

[29] OECD, *Tax Policy Reform and Economic Growth*, at 51; F. Bastagli, D. Coady and S. Gupta, 'Income Inequality and Fiscal Policy', *IMF Staff Discussion Note*, 27 September 2012, SDN/12/08 (revised), 12.

[30] Avi-Yonah, 'Globalization, Tax Competition and the Fiscal Crisis', 1618–22 (with further references).

[31] Bastagli *et al.*, 'Income Inequality and Fiscal Policy'; Gower *et al.*, 'Left Behind the G-20?'.

[32] See, e.g., R. Wilkinson and K. Picket, *The Spirit Level* (London: Allen Lane, 2009).

[33] Dadush *et al.*, *Inequality in America*; Stiglitz, *The Price of Inequality*; Bastagli *et al.*, 'Income Inequality and Fiscal Policy'.

[34] J. Stiglitz *et al.*, *Report of the Commission of Experts of the President of the United Nations General Assembly on Reforms of the International Monetary and Financial System* (New York: United Nations, 21 September 2009), pp. 12, 13; K. Pistor, 'Towards a Legal Theory of Law and Finance', *Columbia Law and Economics Working Paper* No. 434 (New York: Columbia University School of Law, 18 November 2012) (arguing that finance is a hierarchical system implying that actors at the periphery will be hit harder by financial crisis than those at the core).

[35] See, e.g., the French government's introduction of a marginal income tax rate of 75 per cent on personal income over € 1 million ('France Unveils Tough Budget Measures', *Financial Times* (21 September 2009)) or the debates in Germany on the introduction of a wealth tax ('A German Wealth Tax', *The Economist* (8 September 2012)).

intellectuals, politicians and civil society organisations: first costs to public finances associated with the financial industry shall be internalised, e.g. through financial transaction taxes.[36] Second, inequality shall be addressed through redistributive taxes on wealth and high incomes.[37] Third, tax evasion and tax avoidance shall be tackled more forcefully. The latter is also considered an equality issue since the opportunities for tax evasion and avoidance grow with income.[38]

III. Regulation

Taxes – if assessed in terms of economic efficiency – constitute costs that influence economic behaviour. Due to their steering effect taxes are frequently used to regulate by deterring or incentivising certain behaviour. In the course of the financial crisis a number of tax policy proposals have aimed at incentivising behaviour that stabilises the economy and at dis-incentivising potentially destabilising economic activities. Thus, for example, it has been suggested to remedy the preferential tax treatment of debt as compared to equity financing, to tax bonuses and to introduce financial transaction taxes.[39]

IV. The myth of fiscal sovereignty

Who decides about the structure of taxation (the proportion of income taxes, property taxes and consumption taxes, the degree of progressivity) or the level of taxation (the tax rates)? The formal legal answer is: the government, subject to domestic constitutional law, EU law (if the state is an EU member) and international law. Taxation is usually seen as one of the last vestiges of national sovereignty. For example, the German

[36] See European Commission, Proposal for a Council Directive on a common system of financial transaction tax and amending Directive 2008/7/EC, COM(2011) 594 final (Brussels, 28 September 2011); United Nations, Department of Economic and Social Affairs, *World Economic and Social Survey 2012. In Search of New Development Finance*, E/2012/50/Rev. 1 (New York: United Nations, 2012), pp. 45 ff.; IMF, *A Fair and Substantial Contribution by the Financial Sector* (Washington, DC: IMF, June 2010), pp. 16 ff. (assessing proposals for the introduction of a financial transaction tax).

[37] V. Tanzi, 'Equity, Transparency, Cooperation and the Taxation of High Net Worth Individuals', *Asia-Pacific Tax Bulletin* (July/August 2012), 299 and the references note 5.

[38] Bastagli *et al.*, 'Income Inequality and Fiscal Policy', p. 19; Tanzi, 'Equity, Transparency, Cooperation and the Taxation of High Net Worth Individuals', 306.

[39] For these proposals, see IMF, *A Fair and Substantial Contribution*. On the financial transaction tax, see also Section C.I.2.

Federal Constitutional Court, in its 2009 Lisbon judgment on European integration, stated that the power to tax was – as a core government function – part of Germany's constitutional identity and could not be transferred to the European Union.[40] According to this understanding, the power to tax is an essential characteristic of statehood which cannot be relinquished.

In the course of global and regional economic integration the ability of governments to tax has, however, been severely limited. Limitations are due to international and regional law that directly or indirectly restrict the power to tax as well as the liberalisation of capital which is as much a consequence of political choices as it is an (unintended) consequence of trade liberalisation and technological change.[41] Examples of legal limitations on governments' powers are found in the WTO Agreements,[42] international investment treaties or double taxation treaties.[43] The power to tax is also limited when tax reform becomes part of conditionality attached to financial assistance granted by the World Bank or the IMF.[44] In addition to these direct limitations, indirect limitations, while formally leaving fiscal sovereignty intact, arguably have had a much further reaching effect on domestic tax systems. Most prominently, the liberalisation of capital flows has allowed capital to move between jurisdictions so as to (legally) avoid or (illegally) evade taxation.[45]

Capital controls had been an important element of the International Monetary System negotiated in 1944 at Bretton Woods.[46] Keynes, in particular, regarded them as essential to allow governments to pursue policies which might otherwise result in capital flight, such as expansive monetary policy to promote full employment.[47] However, capital

40 *Lisbon Case*, BVerfG, 2 BvE/08 of 30 June 2009, para. 252, www.bverfg.de/entscheidungen/es200906302bve000208.html.

41 On the liberalisation of transboundary capital flows, see B. Eichengreen, *The Globalization of Capital*, 2nd edn (Princeton University Press, 2008), pp. 92, 118 ff.

42 E.g., Article III General Agreement on Tariffs and Trade (GATT).

43 On double taxation treaties, see Section C.II.1.

44 M. Stewart and S. Jogarajan, 'The International Monetary Fund and Tax Reform,' *British Tax Review* (2004), 146.

45 In the European Union the free movement of workers, services, capital and freedom of establishment have had a significant impact on member states' tax systems. See D. Birk, *Steuerrecht*, 15th edn (Heidelberg: C. F. Müller, 2012), pp. 67 ff.

46 R. N. Gardner, *Sterling Dollar Diplomacy* (Oxford: Clarendon Press, 1956); Eichengreen, *The Globalization of Capital*, pp. 91 ff.

47 Gardner, *Sterling Dollar Diplomacy*, pp. 77 ff.

controls were not maintained for long. At first the liberalisation of trade in goods made it increasingly difficult to enforce capital controls,[48] and later liberalisation of capital was being promoted, *inter alia*, by the International Financial Institutions, as a policy to further economic growth.[49] Today capital can flow largely unimpeded, and small changes in government policies, including tax policies, can induce capital flight.[50]

Yet, governments still insist on the 'myth of fiscal sovereignty'. This may be explained by the fact that in liberal constitutional democracies taxation is not understood as a technical question of 'optimal tax design', but as a function of conceptions of individual autonomy, collective responsibility and distributive justice[51] – conceptions that are partly laid down in the constitution and in part are the subject of recurring deliberations within the public sphere and the political process.[52] Nonetheless, given the impact on taxation of international law and the globalised economy, issues of taxation are bound to become a matter of transnational and international cooperation. The predominant venue for such cooperation currently is the OECD. Yet, questions of justice and distribution – crucial to taxation as a governmental power – are largely lost in translation when dealt with at the OECD. While the OECD formally acknowledges national fiscal sovereignty, through its policy advice it provides its members with guidelines for the establishment of tax systems that centre around economic growth and efficiency. Instead of aiming at regaining policy space for redistributive tax policies through international cooperation, the OECD seems to fully embrace the integration of the global economy that has led to the erosion of embedded liberalism.

48 Eichengreen, *The Globalization of Captial*, p. 92.

49 For a critical account of this policy and its economic justification, see D. Rodrik, *The Globalization Paradox* (New York: Norton, 2011), pp. 90 ff.; see also J. Stiglitz, *Globalization and its Discontents* (New York: Norton, 2011), Chapter 4; recently the IMF has changed its policy on capital controls, now considering them as 'part of the policy toolkit' of governments, see www.imf.org/external/pubs/ft/survey/so/2011/NEW040511B.htm.

50 See Avi-Yonah, 'Globalization, Tax Competition, and the Fiscal Crisis', 1579 ff, 1631.

51 T. Nagel and L. Murphy, *The Myth of Ownership* (New York: Oxford University Press, 2002).

52 J. Habermas, *Faktizität und Geltung [Between Facts and Norms]* (Frankfurt a.M.: Suhrkamp, 1992), in particular Chapter 3. At the international level responsibility of government to provide a minimum of social welfare is reflected in human rights instruments, in particular the International Covenant on Social, Economic and Cultural Rights.

C. OECD tax policy advice and cooperation

The OECD is the most active international institution in the field of taxation. While membership in the OECD is limited and excludes most developing countries, many OECD activities have effects beyond its membership; the OECD considers itself to be the 'market leader in developing standards and guidelines in the core of International Taxation'.[53] In tax matters, the OECD operates mainly through its Center for Tax Policy and Administration, which forms part of the OECD bureaucracy, and the Committee on Fiscal Affairs[54] which consists of government officials from the OECD member states and can be considered a transnational government network.[55]

In the following I will concentrate first on the OECD's work on tax policy and, second, on the organisation's efforts to mitigate harmful tax competition. With reference to the language employed in the OECD texts, I intend to show how the OECD treats questions of taxation primarily as questions of economic efficiency and competitiveness. Contrary to the logic of embedded liberalism, the OECD in its tax policy advice does not adopt a political economy perspective that ties the freedom of governments in setting tax policies to questions of how to pursue their constituencies' ideas of social justice. Nor does the OECD in its work on harmful tax competition address questions of global justice that result from governments' attempts to tailor their tax systems to attract globally operating businesses.

I. *The eclipse of social justice in tax design for economic growth*

The main objectives of the OECD's work on tax policy are clarified in a recent description of the Committee on Fiscal Affairs' mandate. According to the OECD's Current Tax Agenda 2012 it is

> [t]he overarching objective of the Committee on Fiscal Affairs ... to contribute to the shaping of globalization for the benefit of all through the promotion and development of effective and sound tax policies and guidance that will *foster growth* and allow governments to provide better services to their citizens. Its work is intended to enable OECD and non-

[53] OECD, Focus on Africa, www.oecd.org/tax/40999877.pdf.

[54] For an overview of OECD activities related to taxation, see OECD, *Current Tax Agenda 2012* (Paris: OECD 2012).

[55] A.-M. Slaughter, 'Global Government Networks', *Michigan Journal of International Law* 24 (2003), 1041.

> OECD governments to improve the design and operation of their national tax systems, to promote co-operation and co-ordination among them in the area of taxation and to *reduce tax barriers to international trade and investment.*[56]

While the reduction of tax barriers to trade and investment is primarily pursued by the OECD's work on double taxation,[57] the OECD promotes its growth objective, *inter alia*, with the publication of tax policy studies including recommendations to policy-makers.

1. Revenue generation through taxation that is 'least negative to economic growth'

The emphasis on economic growth coupled with the ideal of global economic integration through liberalised trade and investment has consequences for the policy advice given by the OECD. While the OECD recognises that taxation may serve as an instrument not only to generate revenue but also to address inequality through redistribution, and that decisions on tax policy ultimately have to be made within a democratic political process, its focus lies squarely on the question of how taxation for revenue generation can be reconciled with the promotion of economic growth. The OECD Tax Policy Study 'Tax Policy Reform and Economic Growth'[58] demonstrates how questions of social justice (even though recognised in frequent references to potential equity concerns)[59] are thus being sidelined and how economic growth comes to represent the predominant yardstick by which tax policy should be measured.

The study was prepared by members of the OECD Secretariat. As it dates from 2010 it takes account of the strained budgets of the OECD member states in the wake of the 2008 financial crisis and their need for fiscal consolidation. It states: 'Debt-to-GDP levels can be reduced either by reducing spending or increasing taxes but also by increasing the GDP growth rate. Such considerations point to designing the tax system in such a way that is the *least negative for economic growth.*'[60]

[56] OECD, *Current Tax Agenda 2012*, p. 14 (emphasis added). [57] See Section C.II.1.

[58] OECD, *Tax Policy Reform and Economic Growth.*

[59] Social justice concerns are mainly dealt with under the heading 'Obstacles to Fundamental Tax Reforms', in OECD, *Tax Policy Reform and Economic Growth*, pp. 47 ff.; see also OECD, 'Income Inequality and Growth', *OECD Economics Department Policy Notes*, No. 9 (Paris: OECD, January 2012).

[60] OECD, 'Income Equality and Growth', pp. 9–10 (emphasis added).

Proceeding from the assumption that all taxation impedes growth and distorts competition,[61] the study establishes a ranking of taxes according to the relative weight of their negative effects on economic growth 'in terms of reducing long-run GDP per capita'.[62] The smaller the negative impact on economic decisions of individuals and firms the less negative for economic growth the taxes are judged to be. According to this measurement the study considers corporate taxes to have the most detrimental effects on growth. Income taxes are held to be the second-most detrimental and consumption taxes and regulatory environmental taxes take third place. Finally, taxes on immovable property are found to be least harmful.[63]

On the basis of this ranking the study makes the following recommendations: tax reform should 'shift the burden of taxation from income to consumption and/or residence property' and 'improve the design of a tax regime by broadening the tax base and lowering the rate and/or improve its externality-correcting properties'.[64] The study sees its recommendations partly reflected in recent trends in OECD members' tax structures. Many have already cut personal and corporate income taxes, broadened the tax base and increased the use of the Value Added Tax as a general consumption tax.[65] The study recognises that these changes are partly induced by the mobility of capital.[66] This mobility affords corporations (and individuals) more freedom in their location decisions which, in turn, are becoming more sensitive to tax policies.[67] As a consequence, 'countries increasingly use their tax systems to improve their ability to compete in global markets'.[68]

The study stresses that tax reforms need to be based on solid policy analysis. To assess the revenue and welfare impact of taxation, its authors express a preference for behavioural tax policy models.[69] The study supports its own findings with the potential behavioural consequences of certain tax structures. With respect to top marginal statutory rates on personal income, for example, it argues that their reduction would encourage individual risk-taking and entrepreneurship.[70] By contrast, high progressivity of income taxation will,

[61] Corrective taxes constitute an exception as the report states that environmental taxes may promote 'Green Growth' (*ibid.*, p. 104); on the OECD's view of corrective taxes, see Section C.I.3.

[62] *Ibid.*, p. 20. [63] *Ibid.*, pp. 20, 21. [64] *Ibid.*, p. 21. [65] *Ibid.*, pp. 26 ff.

[66] *Ibid.*, p. 140 (referring to empirical literature for this finding). [67] *Ibid.*, pp. 19, 20.

[68] *Ibid.*, p. 19. [69] *Ibid.*, p. 65. [70] *Ibid.*, pp. 24 and 114, 115.

according to the study, negatively affect the hours worked and productivity (output per hour worked).[71]

The study acknowledges that – if implemented – the proposed reforms would lead to less progressivity (and even regressivity) within tax systems and thus may raise distributional concerns.[72] It presents the potential impact of the proposed reforms on the redistributive function of taxation as a trade-off between GDP growth and equity, which is up to the individual OECD countries to evaluate.[73] It leaves no doubt, however, about the authors' preference for the first and attempts to address equity concerns by making the argument that eventually the proposed reforms will increase societal welfare. In a number of places, moreover, the study points out that the trade-off between equity and efficiency might appear to be non-existent.[74] Where equity concerns persist, policy-makers could respond with the compensation of 'reform losers', preferably, however, through direct transfers rather than through changes to the proposed tax structure.[75]

The interpretation according to which the study does not take equity or social justice seriously as a challenge to the desirability of the implementation of its policy recommendation is further illustrated by the fact that it treats equity concerns in a chapter on 'Strategies for Successfully Implementing Growth-oriented Tax Reforms' as potential obstacles to the implementation of the proposed tax reforms.[76] Generally, the authors of the study regard growth-oriented tax reforms as a necessity in times of increasing sovereign debt to which they see no alternative.[77]

2. Cost-efficient regulation through taxation

The same OECD study includes a recommendation for governments to use taxation in a regulatory mode. More specifically, governments shall 'improve the extent to which taxes correct for externalities'. Where taxes are used as corrective taxes they justify, according to the OECD, a departure from the general guiding principle of a broad tax base and low tax rates.[78]

The rationale for the endorsement of corrective taxes is similar to the justification of the other tax recommendations listed above. Corrective taxation is held not only to be less distortive of economic behaviour than

[71] *Ibid.*, p. 23. [72] *Ibid.*, pp. 13, 22 and 49. [73] *Ibid.*, p. 22.

[74] Residence property taxes, for example, which are frequently regarded as inequitable, according to the OECD, can be justified on the basis of the benefit principle (*ibid.*, p. 52).

[75] *Ibid.*, p. 79. [76] *Ibid.*, pp. 47 ff. [77] *Ibid.*, p. 102. [78] *Ibid.*, p. 10.

other types of taxation, such as income taxes, and less distortive than command-and-control regulation, but it is also said to be able to promote growth by offering incentives for economic activity. Moreover, corrective taxation is held to be preferable to regulation due to its cost-effectiveness: it steers behaviour and raises revenue at the same time.[79] Consequently, the OECD endorses the taxation of environmental pollution. Taxing pollution or abolishing tax benefits for certain industries, such as the fossil fuel industry, is expected to create incentives to reduce pollution and generate government revenue. In the OECD's own words: 'Shifting part of the tax burden onto pollution aligns with the logic of business – it creates market demand for entrepreneurs to develop and sell new smarter and cleaner technologies, thereby promoting *green growth*.'[80]

While the OECD Secretariat endorses environmental taxes as a win–win–win situation in terms of innovation, regulation and revenue generation[81] it is equally clear in its opinion about taxes on financial transactions. In contrast to the EU Commission, which supports the financial transaction tax, *inter alia*, for its potential corrective function by discouraging risky trading activities,[82] the OECD does not share this view. Instead it considers financial transaction taxes to be highly distortive and thus does not advocate them.[83] The OECD's view is shared by the IMF which argues that a financial transaction tax is undesirable, *inter alia*, because its 'corrective function' to reduce 'socially unproductive financial activity' was unclear.[84]

3. The eclipse of social justice, or: economic growth as (the new) social justice

The above interpretation of the OECD's policy advice on tax reform does illustrate the degree to which considerations of social justice risk being eclipsed in the OECD's analysis of taxation. To be sure the emphasis by the OECD on economic growth is in line with its mandate

[79] In its Tax Agenda for 2012, the OECD Secretariat stresses the cost-effectiveness of taxation vis-à-vis regulation, see OECD, *Current Tax Agenda 2012*, p. 50.

[80] *Ibid.*, p. 51 (emphasis added).

[81] See, also, OECD, *Taxation, Innovation and the Environment* (Paris: OECD, 2010).

[82] European Commission, Common Rules for a Financial Transaction Tax. Frequently Asked Questions, MEMO/11/640 (Brussels, 28 September 2011), europa.eu/rapid/press-release_MEMO-11-640_en.htm.

[83] OECD, *Tax Policy Reform and Economic Growth*, p. 21.

[84] IMF, *A Fair and Substantial Contribution*, p. 20, Box 5.

in the Convention on the Organisation for Economic Co-operation and Development of 1960. According to its Article 1(a) '[t]he aims of the Organisation for Economic Co-operation and Development . . . shall be to promote policies designed . . . to achieve the highest sustainable economic growth and employment and a rising standard of living in Member countries, while maintaining financial stability, and thus to contribute to the development of the world economy.'

However, while the Convention explicitly mandates the OECD to promote policies designed to achieve economic growth, it qualifies this aim with the adjective 'sustainable' and complements the objective of growth with further aims – including raising standards of living. Thus, the Convention opens the door for the OECD to integrate into its work the long-standing and increasing criticism of taking GDP as a measure of social progress and well-being.[85] And indeed the OECD acknowledges that 'there is not necessarily a direct link between economic growth and overall wellbeing'. Nonetheless it posits that 'there are good reasons for OECD countries to try to increase the rate of economic growth'.[86]

While it may be worthwhile to analyse the effect of tax policies on economic growth, what is being criticised here is, first, that the analysis and recommendations as put forward by the OECD leave very little room for the integration of social justice concerns (apart from economic growth) into the process of tax policy-making; and, second, that the OECD's own analysis, by tying any justification of taxation to the concept of economic growth, which is in itself ambivalent, renders the evaluation of taxation a quasi-scientific and neutral-objective exercise even where it is based on value or moral judgments. In its presentation as a trade-off between two apparently irreconcilable policy goals, the OECD juxtaposes taxation that furthers (or at least does not impede) economic growth with taxation that aims at redistribution. Coupled with the presentation of economic growth as an inevitable necessity and the arguments that present efficiency and competitiveness as equitable, the

[85] For recent initiatives to consider indicators other than GDP to measure societal progress and well-being, see A. Sen, J.-P. Fitoussi and J. Stiglitz, *Report of the Commission on the Measurement of Economic and Social Progress* (2009); UN General Assembly Res/65/309, 'Happiness. Towards a Holistic Approach to Development' (25 August 2011); J. Helliwell, R. Layard and J. Sachs (eds.), *World Happiness Report* (2012); for the OECD's own Measuring Well-being Agenda, see www.oecd.org/statistics/measuring well-beingandprogressresearchanddevelopmentprojects.htm.

[86] OECD, *Tax Policy Reform and Economic Growth*, pp. 28, at 9.

OECD clearly does not see room for redistributive aims in tax-policy making.[87]

Effectively, the OECD appears to pit economics against politics. In that vein, economic analysis is referred to to tell us how tax policy should be designed. Yet, what the OECD reveals only implicitly is that of course any assessment of what is economically efficient already relies on value or moral judgments about what is considered good (or bad) as well as certain predictions about human behaviour.[88] This becomes particularly apparent in the discussion of corrective taxes where the OECD hails the taxation of 'bads' for its economic efficiency and consequently recommends environmental taxes as promoting 'green growth'. What the OECD does not say is that this policy advice is based on a presupposition as to which effects of economic activities are to be considered as 'bads' – for example, what constitutes 'pollution' – as well as a certain understanding as to the behavioural effects of taxation. Even more crucially the OECD's assumption that taxation generally impedes growth ignores the fact that most economic activity relies on tax-funded infrastructure and thus ultimately on government.[89]

The OECD's policy advice thus stands in stark contrast to the concept of embedded liberalism. Instead of testing and delineating the policy space for governments to pursue redistributive policies domestically (or by means of transnational collaboration), it embraces the desirability of policy convergence directed towards the overarching aims of growth, efficiency and competitiveness, which are portrayed as self-explanatory.

II. *The eclipse of global justice in international cooperation to avoid harmful tax competition*

Whereas the OECD Secretariat's advice on tax policy reform rather unquestioningly embraces the pressures that economic globalisation

[87] See *ibid.*, p. 49: 'Distributional Considerations might become an obstacle to implementation [of the proposed reforms].' The study goes on to suggest other measures to address inequality: 'The question, of course, arises as to which degree governments would want to use the tax system to redistribute income. Non-tax policy measures that stimulate education, for instance, increase individuals' earning capacity and may therefore contribute to a more equal income distribution' (*ibid.*).

[88] *Cf.* G. Myrdal, 'Institutional Economics', excerpt reprinted in Ö. Appelqvist and S. Andersson (eds), *The Essential Gunnar Myrdal* (New York: New Press, 2004), pp. 236 ff.

[89] This point is stressed by Nagel and Murphy, *The Myth of Ownership*.

puts on taxation, the concern of governments about their shrinking policy space has figured prominently in the work of the OECD's Committee on Fiscal Affairs (a body of government representatives). Here too, however, in the respective OECD documents, concerns about diminishing fiscal sovereignty are clothed in the economic language of competitiveness. Private economic competition, considered to be welfare enhancing, is to be facilitated through the elimination of barriers to transboundary economic activities including double taxation. By contrast, governmental competition for capital through the use of tax incentives is judged as potentially harmful for global welfare as it distorts private competition. Through this focus on competition, questions of justice again are sidelined, this time questions of *global* justice that can be seen to lie at the heart of the OECD debates on harmful tax competition.

1. International tax law to further economic integration and private competition

Under the OECD Convention members agree to 'pursue their efforts to reduce or abolish obstacles to the exchange of goods and services and current payments and maintain and extend the liberalisation of capital movements' (Article 2(d)). The OECD complies with this mandate, *inter alia*, by the maintenance of the OECD Model Tax Convention on Income and on Capital.

The OECD Model Tax Convention provides a blueprint for the (mainly bilateral) double taxation treaties concluded between states.[90] These aim, first, at preventing double taxation of transboundary economic activities and, second, at delineating the allocation of tax revenue between the different jurisdictions that lay a claim to taxes, mainly the state of the source of the income and the state of residence. The OECD postulates that the international tax law based on its Model Tax Convention serves to remove obstacles to the international exchange of goods and services and the cross-border movement of capital, technology and persons as well as to offer security and predictability for tax payers.[91]

Arguably, however, the second aim – the allocation of tax revenue between the source and the residence state – constitutes the more

[90] Y. Margalioth, 'Double Taxation' in R. Wolfrum (ed.), *Encyclopedia of Public International Law* (Oxford University Press, 2008), online edition, www.mpepil.com.

[91] OECD, *Model Tax Convention on Income and on Capital 2010 (updated 2010)* (Paris: OECD, 2012), p. I-1.

important rationale for double taxation treaties.[92] The fact that the OECD Model Tax Convention gives preference to the residence state has prompted the United Nations to set up and administer its own Model Tax Convention – the United Nations Model Double Taxation Convention Between Developed and Developing Countries. In comparison with the OECD Model Convention it favours the source country`s taxation rights over those of the investor's residence country and thus aims at greater tax revenue for developing countries (which are frequently host countries to foreign investors rather than capital exporters).[93]

2. International tax law and cooperation to counter 'harmful tax competition'

While both the OECD and the UN Model Tax Conventions aspire to avoid double taxation as an impediment to transboundary trade and investment, they are only partially successful in containing what has come to be known as 'harmful tax competition'.[94] With the liberalisation of capital flows, governments have attempted to attract capital through their tax laws. As a result the tax burden was shifted from labour to capital, and progressivity in taxation decreased. Apart from the convergence of tax systems, countries have adopted preferential tax schemes which grant benefits to multinational enterprises – either to keep them from shifting residence to another jurisdiction or to induce them to locate production facilities in their jurisdiction.[95] These developments, coupled with the existence of so-called offshore tax havens with no or nominal tax rates and strict bank secrecy laws, have facilitated and increased opportunities for tax avoidance and tax evasion.[96] The

[92] R. S. Avi-Yonah, 'Double Taxation Treaties. An Introduction' in K. P. Sauvant and L. E. Sachs (eds.), *The Effect of Treaties on Foreign Direct Investment. Bilateral Investment Treaties, Double Taxation Treaties, and Investment Flows* (Oxford University Press, 2009), p. 99.

[93] United Nations, *Model Double Taxation Convention Between Developed and Developing Countries* (New York: United Nations, 2011), p. vi.

[94] For an argument that international tax law promotes tax competition, see Rosenzweig, 'Why Are There Tax Havens?'.

[95] Avi-Yonah distinguishes between production tax havens and headquarters tax havens: Avi-Yonah, 'Globalization, Tax Competition, and the Fiscal Crisis', 1588 ff.

[96] *Ibid.*; see also N. Shaxson, *Treasure Islands* (London: Vintage, 2012 (first published 2011)); R. Murphy, 'Closing the European Tax Gap', www.socialistsanddemocrats.eu/gpes/media3/documents/3842_EN_richard_murphy_eu_tax_gap_en_120229.pdf (estimating that 'tax evasion in the European Union is approximately € 860 billion a year' (at p. 2)).

beneficiaries have been multinational enterprises and high-income individuals, including dictators and criminals, who are frequently able to channel their income so as to escape taxation almost entirely.[97]

The losers are the populations of developed countries who incur higher taxes on labour and higher consumption taxes and who are living in increasingly unequal societies. Even worse off, however, are the populations of developing countries. While the OECD member states through tax reforms as well as the international cooperation described below have been able to safeguard their tax revenues, developing countries are losing revenue.[98] Such observations constitute important elements in an emerging perspective on 'tax competition' as an issue of global distributive justice.

However, this is not how the OECD governments, conscious of the threat to their national budgets, have been addressing this issue. Rather, the official stance has maintained that the problem remains one of *fair* versus *unfair competition*. In the 1998 OECD Report on Harmful Tax Competition, redistribution is mentioned only in passing, when the report's authors state that competition in taxation 'hampers the application of progressive tax rates and the achievement of redistributive goals'.[99] Overall the OECD's message is that global economic integration and, in particular, the mobility of capital across borders is welfare enhancing; the resulting tax reforms are denoted as 'modernisations' of tax systems that improve capital neutrality.[100] The problem that is identified instead is the distortion of global competition through preferential tax regimes and tax havens. According to the OECD 'location decisions should be driven by economic considerations and not primarily by tax factors';[101] levelling the playing field is considered 'essential to the continued expansion of global economic growth'.[102] Governments are reprimanded if they engage either in 'harmful tax competition' by exploiting the interaction of tax systems or they free-ride on public goods financed by other jurisdictions' tax revenues. As a consequence, the OECD attempted in its report to single out factors that can help in identifying tax havens and preferential tax regimes[103] based on which the OECD issued recommendations to governments.[104]

[97] Shaxson, *Treasure Islands*, Chapter 1.
[98] Avi-Yonah, 'The OECD Harmful Tax Competition Report'.
[99] OECD, *Harmful Tax Competition*, p. 14.
[100] *Ibid.*, pp. 13, 14: 'Globalisation . . . has encouraged countries to reduce tax barriers to capital flows and to modernise their tax systems to reflect these developments.'
[101] *Ibid.*, p. 9. [102] *Ibid.* [103] *Ibid.*, pp. 21 ff. [104] *Ibid.*, pp. 65 ff.

The core OECD activities against harmful tax competition so far have been the promotion of information exchange based on the OECD standard on transparency and information exchange and the establishment of the Global Forum on Transparency and Information Exchange that monitors the implementation of this standard.[105] In order to enforce information exchange, the OECD lists uncooperative tax havens on so-called blacklists.[106] When the G-20, motivated by the urgency of fiscal consolidation, threatened to take countermeasures against tax havens,[107] the OECD initiative received a renewed impetus leading to the conclusion of a large number of information exchange agreements.[108]

The evaluation of the success of these activities differs. While some consider them a charade[109] others believe they have helped OECD governments to prevent the erosion of their tax bases.[110] Empirical evidence shows, however, that they have had no positive effect on developing countries which, unlike developed countries, have been suffering from an erosion of their tax bases. This erosion is mainly due to tax evasion and avoidance, which is facilitated by the tax laws of developed countries.[111] By way of illustration, developing countries have an incentive to grant preferential tax treatment to multinational enterprises as long as these enterprises can avoid paying taxes in their country of residence. As a consequence, stopping tax competition among developing countries would require a concerted effort by developed countries to end tax avoidance by their multinationals.[112]

105 The Global Forum, in its Terms of Reference of 2009, refers to the transparency and information exchange standards in the OECD Model Agreement on Exchange of Information and Article 26 of the OECD Model Tax Convention and breaks them down to ten essential elements against which tax jurisdictions that participate in the Global Forum are reviewed; see Global Forum on Transparency and Exchange of Information for Tax Purposes, Terms of Reference (2010), www.oecd.org/tax/transparency/keydocuments.htm.

106 Currently no country is listed on the OECD's List of Uncooperative Tax Havens, www.oecd.org/ctp/harmfultaxpractices/listofunco-operativetaxhavens.htm.

107 G-20, Leaders' Statement, London Summit 2 April 2009, para. 15; G-20, Leaders' Statement, Pittsburgh Summit, 24 September 2008, para. 16.

108 Information on these agreements can be found on the OECD's website, www.oecd.org/tax/transparency/exchangeoftaxinformationagreements.htm.

109 Shaxson, *Treasure Islands*, Chapter 10; M. J. McIntyre, 'How to End the Charade of Information Exchange', *Tax Notes International* 56:4 (26 October 2009), 255.

110 Avi-Yonah, 'The OECD Harmful Tax Competition Report'.

111 *Ibid.*; see also Shaxson, *Treasure Islands*, Chapter 8.

112 Avi-Yonah, 'The OECD Harmful Tax Competition Report'; for a recent initiative in this respect, see the EU Commission's Action Plan to strengthen the fight against tax fraud and tax evasion, COM(2012) 722 final (6 December 2012).

3. The eclipse of global justice, or: 'fair competition' as global justice

As the integration of the global economy continues to diminish the capacity of individual governments to autonomously set their tax policies, international cooperation appears to be one way to reconcile economic integration with the pursuit of redistributive policies by governments. International cooperation on redistribution seems all the more important as it becomes apparent that the promise that economic globalisation will benefit all countries and eventually also all human beings remains unfulfilled. International cooperation in the field of taxation could mean that the redistributive role of taxation is debated at the global level and that governments agree on measures such as global taxes that are aimed at redistribution across societies.[113]

Such cooperation has, however, not been the route taken by the OECD. Instead of initiating a global debate on tax justice, it seeks to expand the logic of economic competition among private actors to cover governmental policy. With respect to taxation this means that international cooperation should aim at levelling the playing field and reducing harmful tax competition. And once again the seemingly technical language hides the underlying, highly contested, value judgments and conceptions of justice.

D. Conclusion: taking the justice dimension of taxation seriously

I. *Competing ideas of social justice*

Critiques abound with regard to the mantra of economic growth in terms of GDP as the all-purpose measure of social progress and well-being.[114] So far, however, *alternative* visions of a successful society have not really entered into the mainstream analysis of economic policy as conducted at the OECD. Instead economic growth, to be pursued through economic competition, remains the yardstick against which economic policy is measured. Despite the many disappointments of economic globalisation,

[113] For a recent proposal on global taxes to finance development, see United Nations, Department of Economic and Social Affairs, *World Economic and Social Survey 2012*, pp. 36 ff; for historical overviews, see P. Wahl, *International Taxation* (Berlin: WEED, 2005); M. J. Frankman, 'International Taxation', *World Development* 24:5 (1996), 807.

[114] See note 85; see also A. Sen, *Development as Freedom* (Oxford University Press, 1999).

including increasing inequality and environmental degradation, the hopes for social progress remain confined, it seems, to the realm of private economic freedom.

The role of government is not diminished within this conception of social progress, but it is different from the role of governments within embedded liberalism. As government provides the infrastructure for economic activities and ensures 'fair competition' through regulation, it becomes a facilitator of the economy. Taxation is still necessary to provide revenue to pay for regulatory capitalism.[115] It ceases, however, to be considered as an important instrument for redistribution for fear of the distortive effects such market governance would have on competition and economic output.

To perceive economic liberty and free competition as the main (and only) aims of societal ordering represents one vision of a 'good or just society', which may have its advantages and which finds support in political and economic theory.[116] It is important, however, to recognise it as such – as only a contingent concept of social order and the role of government that is not without alternative. Whether to choose this concept or another cannot be a question of economic analysis, but falls within the ambit of political processes, be they domestic, regional or global.

II. Politics and uncertainty

To recognise that decisions about taxation imply political choices among competing visions of social justice also entails embracing the fact of indeterminacy and uncertainty. Economists may, using certain models, predict the effect of certain tax measures on certain economic variables on the basis of certain assumptions. How tax policies work in reality, however, is a different matter[117] and it would be fallacious to assume that the answer could be predicted with certainty. The adoption of one economic policy or another ultimately is a political decision between two options both of which hold uncertain futures.[118]

115 J. Braithwaite, *Regulatory Capitalism* (Cheltenham: Edward Elgar, 2008), pp. 23, 24.

116 See only F. A. Hayek, *The Constitution of Liberty* (University of Chicago Press, 1960).

117 Critical with respect to the transposition of economic findings based on specific economic models into economic policy advice is Rodrik, *The Globalization Paradox*, Chapter 6.

118 N. Luhmann, 'Die Paradoxie des Entscheidens', *Verwaltungsarchiv* 84 (1995), 289.

Nonetheless international economic institutions, such as the OECD and the IMF, regularly base policy recommendations on the results of economic analysis thus ignoring the role of political choice in light of uncertainty.

This attitude towards political decision-making can be illustrated by reference to the diverging treatment by the IMF and the United Nations of the question as to whether to introduce a financial transaction tax. The IMF simply recommended against its adoption because it would not have a corrective effect on financial volatility and would impede growth.[119] By contrast, debates within the framework of the United Nations on the introduction of a financial transaction tax to finance development openly embraced uncertainty.[120]

In 2000 the UN General Assembly adopted a resolution in which it called for 'a rigorous analysis of the advantages, disadvantages and other implications of proposals for developing new and innovative sources of funding, both public and private, for dedication to social development and poverty eradication programmes'.[121] In reaction to this call the UN Department of Economic and Social Affairs asked the World Institute for Development Economics Research (UNU-WIDER) to study 'innovative sources for development finance'. The assessment of UNU-WIDER of a financial transaction tax differs markedly from that of the IMF. Like the IMF, UNU-WIDER addresses the economic implications of a financial transaction tax. Unlike the IMF it is, however, much more cautious in its conclusions. While the IMF is quite unequivocal in its finding of distortive effects, and, as a result, does not recommend the adoption of a financial transaction tax,[122] UNU-WIDER concludes that the final distributional effects of a financial transaction tax are hard to predict. More importantly, it clarifies that the decision on whether or not to introduce such a tax implies a political choice. A political decision that balances the potential benefits – finances for development and stabilisation of financial markets – against the potential drawbacks – including increases in the prices of commodities, which might disproportionately affect the poor.[123]

[119] See IMF, *A Fair and Substantial Contribution*.

[120] A. B. Atkinson, 'New Sources of Development Finance. Funding the Millennium Development Goals,' *Policy Brief* No. 10 (Helsinki: UNU-WIDER, 2004).

[121] UN General Assembly Res/S-24/2 (15 December 2000), para. 142 (g).

[122] IMF, *A Fair and Substantial Contribution*, p. 21.

[123] Atkinson, 'New Sources of Development Finance'.

III. *Experimental taxation*

Given the uncertainty attached to any predictions on the effects of taxation, governments would be ill-advised to base their tax policy decisions exclusively on such forecasts. *Experimentation* with tax policy may ultimately be more fruitful than relying solely on the advice of economic experts. While economists come to diverging conclusions, e.g., about the behavioural effects of progressive income taxes,[124] only the imposition of such taxes can reveal their true effects. Detrimental or unforeseen consequences may be limited by evaluating the effects of such taxes after a certain period or by including sunset clauses in the tax legislation.

Finally, experimental tax policy-making and legislation may play an important role in establishing a counter-narrative to that of economic growth and competitiveness. In such a narrative citizens may be perceived as stakeholders of the global economy who call for multinational enterprises and individual profiteers of capitalism to bear a fair share of the cost of government and contribute towards a just distribution of economic benefits through paying taxes. Thus, taxation might not be perceived merely as a necessary evil in times of austerity but restored to its place as an essential element of a just society.

[124] For references, see Bastagli *et al.*, 'Income Inequality and Fiscal Policy', pp. 13, 14.

PART III

The interaction between WTO law and monetary affairs

12

Towards an equitable integration of monetary and financial matters, trade and sustainable development

ROBERT HOWSE

A. Recourse to equity

In Section III of the Millennium Declaration entitled 'Development and Poverty Reduction' United Nations (UN) member states committed themselves 'to create an environment – at the national and global levels alike – which is conducive to development and to the elimination of poverty'.[1] This depends on 'good governance within each country' and on 'good governance at the international level, and on transparency in the financial, monetary and trading systems'. Hence, they 'are committed to an open, equitable, rule-based, predictable and non-discriminatory multilateral trading and financial system'. In 2002 the Monterrey Consensus also reaffirmed the UN members' commitment to trade liberalisation, but noted that developing countries need 'appropriate institutions and policies' to benefit fully from trade.

The concept of equity in international trade and financial rules and institutions has not been explicitly defined and is the subject of debate and speculation among philosophers and political theorists.[2] At the same time a notion of equity has played an important role in the settlement of disputes in public international law, especially with regard to allocation

I thank Ernst Baltensperger and Thomas Cottier for helpful and detailed comments.

[1] 55/2 United Nations Millennium Declaration. Resolution 55/2 adopted by the General Assembly, 8 September 2000, Chapter II para. 12.

[2] For a critical discussion, focusing on the approach of Thomas Pogge to these matters, see Robert Howse and Ruti Teitel, 'Global Justice, Poverty, and the International Economic Order' in Samantha Besson and John Tasioulas, *The Philosophy of International Law* (Oxford University Press, 2010).

of natural resources.[3] Thomas Cottier suggests, 'Achieving broad goals of global welfare and equity is not a matter of international charity, but of common and shared interests in the light of the "ticking time bombs" of excessive population, mass migration, poverty and destitution facing many parts of the globe.'[4] Economists are often sceptical as to whether the trade and financial systems should be understood at all in terms of justice rather than as instruments of economic policy coordination. Nevertheless, it will be observed that the actual rules often do depend, explicitly or implicitly, on a concept of fairness. For instance, one of the rules that will be discussed in this chapter, contained in Article IV of the International Monetary Fund (IMF) Articles of Agreement, required that IMF Members do not 'manipulate exchange rates or the international monetary system in order to prevent effective balance of payments (BOP) adjustment or to gain an *unfair* competitive advantage over other members' (emphasis added).[5] In the trading system, the WTO rules on subsidies, including fiscal measures such as tax incentives, suppose a conception of fair competition; as the WTO Appellate Body (AB) noted in one case, there are situations where market-based benchmarks for fairness will be inapplicable given the pervasive interconnection of public policies and market structures. The concept of equity is then inescapable in the interpretation and application of the law of international trade and financial systems. The question is whether there are legal and policy sources that allow us to give a definite meaning to this concept as we apply it to particular rules and disputes in the trade and financial systems. Such sources are more various and more instructive than one might have originally imagined. This approach, pursued in this chapter, can usefully be compared to that of Thomas Pogge, who seeks to judge (and condemn) the existing system of rules in international economic law against an abstract conception of global justice, emphasising the priority of eliminating poverty and, therefore, a counterfactual of an ideal system of international economic law that would adequately reflect

[3] See Thomas Cottier, 'Equity Revisited: An Introduction' in '*Equitable Principles of Maritime Boundary Delimitation in International Law: Legal Foundations and Methodology*' (forthcoming). This chapter contains a very helpful review of the concept of equity both in domestic legal systems and international law, as well as the secondary literature.

[4] *Ibid.*, p. 20.

[5] Articles of Agreement of the International Monetary Fund, adopted at the United Nations Monetary and Financial Conference Bretton Woods, New Hampshire, 22 July 1944, entered into force on 27 December 1945, as subsequently amended, www.imf.org/external/pubs/ft/aa.index.htm.

that principle.[6] Rather, this chapter begins without assuming the manifest injustice of the existing norms of international economic law, and assumes instead that we can help achieve more equitable outcomes through appreciating better the elements of equity implicit or sometimes explicit in those rules, and interpreting and applying them together with or in light of other norms of international law, such as those entrenched in the UN human rights covenants, for example. The approach of beginning with the possible concrete applications of concepts of equity to specific disputes or challenges and problems in international economic law, and with the jurisprudential *acquis*, rather than with philosophical dogma and abstraction, is in many ways akin to that of Cottier.[7] The aim is not radical critique with a view to comprehensive reconstruction, but a careful consideration of how relevant conceptions of equity have been sidelined or distorted in the way the existing rules have been applied and interpreted within and across international economic and other regimes under conditions of fragmentation. The end point might well be characterised as realistic utopia or more perfect expression or elaboration of the ideals of equity already reflected in a range of positive international legal norms, through the interpretative transcendence of 'self-contained regimes'.

This last point requires some elaboration. The international monetary and financial system does not have its own 'court'. As will be discussed, its rules and practices may take effect as legal norms through their interpretation within the trade regime, which does have a highly developed dispute settlement arrangement, including an appellate tribunal.[8] Given that the trade regime is not integrated into the UN system, there is a risk that the WTO dispute settlement organs will view the rules of global finance from a rather narrow perspective on growth, development and equity, without consideration of the norms that have emerged from the UN institutions concerned with human rights and development.

One aspect of equity that is widely reflected in international instruments concerning trade, finance and development (for example, the Doha Declaration and its references to special and differential treatment) is the notion that rules should be adjusted to the different

[6] For an elaboration of this approach and a critique of its abstract utopianism, see Howse and Teitel, 'Global Justice, Poverty, and the International Economic Order'.

[7] Cottier, 'Equity Revisited'.

[8] On the way in which the legal norms in one regime may have effects through their interpretation and application by another, see Howse and Teitel, 'Beyond Compliance: Rethinking Why International Law Really Makes', *Global Policy* 1:2 2009, 127–36, 130–33.

situations of different states, in terms of their development needs. Thus, there is widespread agreement that formal legal equality, treating everyone the same regardless of their particular situation, is *not* equitable.[9] At the same time, there is disagreement among states on how much differential treatment is justified in a given situation. The WTO rules on the BOP, designed to work in close relation to IMF principles, allow, e.g., additional policy space to developing countries to use trade restrictions for purposes of monetary stability, in recognition that the alternative of tight monetary and fiscal policies to achieve stability might be at odds with development goals (as we shall see below, unfortunately these flexibilities have not been interpreted broadly enough in dispute settlement).

There is an interesting parallelism between the conception of equity as treating 'unlikes' *differently* and the recognition, in recent economic literature, that – contrary to what was implied in the Washington Consensus orthodoxy of the international financial institutions – there is no single formula or pathway to development that will work for all countries.[10] Another dimension of equity that is reflected in international human rights instruments is that of voice and participation. These instruments suggest that people should not have a vision of development forced on them or decided by others. The Declaration on the Right to Development stipulates that the right to development includes 'free and meaningful participation in development'.[11] This has become an issue, with, for example, Aid for Trade, where critics have pointed to inadequate ownership of these initiatives in the communities towards which they are directed.

Further, there is a concept of equity implicit in the 2015 Millennium poverty reduction goals.[12] Acceptance of these goals implies that existing inequalities of wealth, to the extent that they leave billions in dire poverty, are

[9] A very clear statement of this principle is given by the AB in its first ruling in the *Shrimp – Turtle* case; interpreting the chapeau of Article XX of the GATT, the AB held that non-discrimination between countries where similar conditions prevail implies the duty to treat countries differently where different conditions prevail. Along similar lines, in the *EC – Tariff Preferences* (GSP) case, the AB held that treating different developing countries differently based on their particular development needs was consistent with, and might even be required by, the non-discrimination norm in the Enabling Clause.

[10] See, for instance, Dani Rodrik, *The Globalization Paradox* (New York: Norton, 2011); cf. also Thomas Cottier, 'Sovereign Equality and Graduation in International Economic Law', in *Festschrift Ernst Ulrich Petersmann*, booksandjournals.brillonline.com/content/books/b9789004228832s015.

[11] UN General Assembly, Declaration on the Right to Development: resolution adopted by the General Assembly, 4 December 1986, A/RES/41/128, www.refworld.org/docid/3b00f22544.html (accessed 30 July 2013).

[12] www.un.org/millenniumgoals/poverty.shtml (accessed 30 July 2013).

unacceptable. The focus on reducing *poverty* not just increasing *growth*, implies that increased wealth does not necessarily lead to an acceptably just or equitable distribution of wealth without positive redistributive measures. This is reflected by a recent statement by the WTO Director-General candidate from Indonesia, Mari Pangestu, that opening up a country's markets to trade should be done in a manner that does not disadvantage lower-income households.[13] Closely related to this notion of equity is the concept of social and economic justice or equity expressed in the UN Covenant on Social and Economic and Cultural Rights. Article 11 of the Covenant provides:

> 1. The States Parties to the present Covenant recognize the right of everyone to an adequate standard of living for himself and his family, including adequate food, clothing and housing, and to the continuous improvement of living conditions. The States Parties will take appropriate steps to ensure the realization of this right, recognizing to this effect the essential importance of international co-operation based on free consent.[14]

While not all states – most notably the US – have embraced the rights in the Covenant as treaty or customary international law, even the US has participated in the Declaration on the Right to Development, which to a large extent affirms these rights.

It is important to note that the Covenant does require a specific notion of redistribution between countries as a means of realisation of the rights in question. The primary obligation is of states to their own peoples. However, a concrete implication of this notion of equity is that the rules of the international trade and financial system at a minimum should not *undermine* and ideally should *facilitate* the ability of states to discharge their obligations under the Covenant to implement social and economic rights. In this respect, the UN Human Rights organs have correctly grasped that they have a mandate to evaluate the rules of the trade and financial system against their impact on the ability of states, individually and collectively, to fulfil their obligations under the Covenant.[15]

[13] 'Indonesia's Pangestu Offers an Incremental Approach to Reviving WTO', *Institutional Investor*, 21 April 2013, www.institutionalinvestor.com/Article/3194496/Banking-and-Capital-Markets/Indonesias-Pangestu-Offers-an-Incremental-Approach-to-Reviving-WTO.htm.

[14] United Nations, Treaty S United Nations, Treaty Series, vol. 993, p. 3; see Robert Howse and Ruti Teitel, 'Beyond the Divide: The Covenant on Economic, Social and Cultural Rights and The World Trade Organization', Occasional Paper No. 30, Friedrich Ebert Stiftung, Geneva, April 2007.

[15] See, e.g., Liberalization of Trade in Services and Human Rights, Report of the High Commissioner for Human Rights (E/CN.4/Sub.2/2002/9). Globalisation and its Impact

Finally, equity has been considered by UN members to imply a fair global distribution of burdens and benefits from the operations of the international economic system. This goes beyond a notion that the system(s) should enable states to achieve social and economic justice within their borders to a conception of global solidarity. Thus, according to the Millennium Declaration, solidarity requires that 'global challenges must be managed in a way that distributes the costs and burdens fairly in accordance with basic principles of equity and social justice. Those who suffer most, or who benefit least, deserve help from those who benefit most.'[16]

B. Calling for coherence

The normatively justified bridging of specialised regimes seems a logical implication of the recognition of equity as a fundamental ingredient of the international trade and financial systems; while, as noted, there are rules and policies in the system that are *expressions* of equity those rules and policies mostly leave unarticulated – and in some sense presuppose – relevant conceptions or articulations of equity. These are found, as we have seen, in the instruments and institutions primarily of the UN that address human rights and development. Coherence, then, means in the first instance coherence between the rules and policies of the institutions where equity is articulated and defined normatively and the rules and policies of the international trading system. But there is a further aspect to the relationship between equity and coherence: inequity may result from *uncoordinated rules as between* the trading system and the financial system.[17]

For example, the IMF may ask a country to improve its BOP and the trading system may prevent the use of certain instruments for doing so, such as import surcharges or concessional export financing. Furthermore, there may be strong reasons why these policy options have been constrained by the international trading system. However, without greater sensitivity by the IMF to the constraints imposed by that

on the Full Enjoyment of Human Rights; Report of the High Commissioner for Human Rights (E/CN.4/2002/54). The report considers the WTO's Agreement on Agriculture; The Human Rights, Trade and Investment, Report of the High Commissioner for Human Rights (E/CN.4/Sub.2/2003/9); Impact of the TRIPS Agreement on the Enjoyment of all Human Rights, Report of the High Commissioner for Human Rights (E/CN.4/Sub.2/2001/13).

16 See, for an elaboration of these notions, Ruti Teitel, *Humanity's Law* (Oxford University Press, 2011), Chapter 6.

17 'Economic Policy Challenges in an Open Economy: Coherence Between Trade and Finance', Communication of UNCTAD to the WTO Working Group on Trade, Debt and Finance, WT/WGTDF/W/27, 24 November 2004.

system *and their underlying policy reasons* and a broader and more palatable range of policy options, developed to accommodate the trading system while achieving the IMF's goals for a given client state, such states may well feel those policy options are their only viable choices. If these options remain foreclosed without the provision of other viable trading system friendly options, states may be forced to have recourse to policy instruments that threaten social equity, and result in poverty and unemployment, if they are to obey the prescriptions of the financial system as well as respect the rules of the trading system.

An early explicit attempt to address coherence at the WTO[18] is the Uruguay Round Declaration on the Contribution of the World Trade Organization to Greater Coherence in Global Economic Policymaking.[19] Paragraph 2 of the Declaration reads, in relevant part,

> Trade liberalization forms an increasingly important component in the success of the adjustment programmes that many countries are undertaking, often involving significant transitional social costs. In this connection, Ministers note the role of the World Bank and the IMF in supporting adjustment to trade liberalization, including support to net food-importing developing countries facing short-term costs arising from agricultural trade reforms.

The most important text in the Declaration is arguably to be found in Paragraph 5:

> The interlinkages between the different aspects of economic policy require that the international institutions with responsibilities in each of these areas follow consistent and mutually supportive policies. The World Trade Organization should therefore pursue and develop cooperation with the international organizations responsible for monetary and financial matters, while respecting the mandate, the confidentiality requirements and the necessary autonomy in decision-making procedures of each institution, and avoiding the imposition on governments of cross-conditionality or additional conditions. Ministers further invite the Director-General of the WTO to review with the Managing Director of the International Monetary Fund and the President of the World Bank, the implications of the WTO's responsibilities for its cooperation with the Bretton Woods institutions, as well as the forms such cooperation might take, with a view to achieving greater coherence in global economic policymaking.

[18] There were earlier efforts, during the pre-WTO GATT era. See the excellent account by Chien-Heui Wu, 'Greater Coherence in Global Economic Policymaking: Progress and Prospect', in C. Herrmann, M. Krajewski and J. P. Terhechte (eds.), *European Yearbook of International Economic Law* 5 (2013), pp. 67–92.

[19] WTO, *The Legal Texts* (Cambridge University Press, 1999), p. 386.

It is to be noted that, while Paragraph 2, for example, mentions the important social costs of trade liberalisation and economic reform and singles out the situations of developing countries, the Declaration does not extend the idea of coherence to cooperation with those international institutions whose mandate is development policy, such as UNCTAD and UNDP, nor those concerned with social equity and justice in particular, such as the UN Human Rights institutions. Instead, the need for coherence is limited to those international institutions 'responsible for monetary and financial matters'. Nevertheless, Paragraph 5 does state the imperative of avoiding 'cross-conditionality', a situation where a government is forced to pursue a harmful policy or set of policies, or even inconsistent policies, because otherwise it will fall foul of uncoordinated conditions or strictures imposed by different international economic institutions.

In 1996, the WTO entered into a cooperation agreement with the IMF providing for consultations between the WTO and the IMF and for the exchange of information. Paragraph 10 of that agreement provides:

> The Fund's staff shall consult with the WTO Secretariat on issues of possible inconsistency between measures under discussion with a common member and that member's obligations under the WTO Agreement. The WTO Secretariat shall consult with the Fund's staff on issues of possible inconsistency between measures under discussion with a common member and that member's obligations under the Fund's Articles of Agreement.

This provision would appear to be crucial to coherence; it appears both to strengthen and implement Paragraph 5 of the Uruguay Round Declaration on Coherence by requiring (the obligatory 'shall', is used here) discussions about possible inconsistency, while measures are 'under discussion', i.e. to avoid a conflict in the first place. As we shall see, however, in at least one prominent WTO dispute, it became clear that this consultation requirement had not been followed and unfortunately the AB of the WTO did not attach much importance to it.

Keeping this in mind, we turn to specific interlinkages of trade, finance and monetary affairs.

C. Exchange controls and convertibility measures: GATT Article XV and the SCM Agreement

I Introductory remarks

The GATT rules on exchange controls and convertibility reflect the international financial and monetary system designed at Bretton Woods at the end of World War II.[20] The post-war arrangements contemplated a system of fixed exchange rates tied to the gold standard. Under this system, a country would, in theory,[21] be required to hold sufficient reserves of gold to back the quantity of its currency in circulation. Where a temporary imbalance of payments occurred (i.e., where a country could not meet payments for imports with its receipts of foreign currency from export sales without selling gold for foreign currency), this would be financed by a country borrowing from the IMF.

In the case of a structural or persistent imbalance, a country would devalue its currency under the supervision of the IMF, which might recommend domestic policy adjustments to ensure that further devaluations were not required in order to maintain the BOP. While it had already been under tension for some time, and arguably suffered from the inherent contradiction that it could not guarantee that actual gold reserves matched currency in circulation, the Bretton Woods system broke down in the 1970s when the US unilaterally opted out of the system by explicitly refusing to back the dollar with gold reserves.

In the case of developing countries, rapid progress towards convertibility and the removal of exchange controls became the economic orthodoxy in the 1980s and 1990s. Such reforms were thought to have the effect of encouraging foreign investment and creating domestic financial systems as well as access to global financial networks that would underwrite growth and development. The Asian and Latin American financial crises of the 1990s led to considerable rethinking of this story. Some economists, such as Bhagwati, believe that too rapid financial liberalisation contributed to the crises, which led to widespread human misery in a number of countries.[22] Nobel Prize-winning economist Stiglitz takes a similar view, and when he was at the World Bank he resisted the IMF-led orthodoxy of rapid financial liberalisation, largely predicting the kind of consequences discussed by Bhagwati.[23] Both Stiglitz and Bhagwati, economists of the first rank who disagree on

[20] The following sections draw from Michael J. Trebilcock, Robert Howse and Antonia Eliason, *The Regulation of International Trade*, 4th edn (London and New York: Routledge, 2012), Chapter 5 'Trade, Exchange Rates and the Balance of Payments'.

[21] But in theory only (hence one might say that the system contained the seeds of its own destruction). See the excellent account in Benn Steil, *The Battle of Bretton Woods: John Maynard Keynes, Harry Dexter White, and the Making of a New World Order* (Princeton University Press, 2013).

[22] J. Bhagwhati, *In Defense of Globalization* (Oxford University Press, 2004), pp. 199–200.

[23] J. Stiglitz, *Globalization and Its Discontents* (New York: W.W. Norton, 2002).

many issues, nevertheless see capital controls as a valuable instrument in stemming a panic flight of short-term capital and thereby preventing the kind of financial collapse that sent millions back into poverty in the late 1990s. The Report of the UN Commission, chaired by Stiglitz in the wake of the recent global financial crisis, has re-emphasised these considerations.[24]

With respect to exchange rates, the IMF Articles of Agreement provide that an IMF Member shall not 'manipulate exchange rates or the international monetary system in order to prevent effective balance of payments adjustment or to gain an unfair competitive advantage over other members'.[25] Currency manipulation as such is defined in the surveillance provisions of the IMF Articles as 'protracted large-scale intervention in one direction in the exchange market'.

However, the concept of an '*unfair*' competitive advantage is not defined. Thus, the international community is required to supply a relevant conception of 'equity'. Arguably, under an approach to fairness influenced by conceptions of sustainable development and the right to development, one essential aspect of the question when considered in relation to China's exchange rate policy by way of example would be whether such policy represents a legitimate exercise of its right to development, and thus the way in which the policy figures in its development needs and strategies. As Erik Denters argues, pegging the renminbi to the dollar may well have encouraged foreign investment, a crucial part of China's development strategy.[26] At the same time, as already noted in relation to Brazil, one would have to ask if China's exchange rate actions undermine the development policies of *other* WTO members. The question is whether the WTO offers a viable normative benchmark to address such competing equities, or if it could.

II. WTO and the IMF

The GATT rules concerning exchange measures and convertibility are contained in Article XV GATT. Article XV:4 states that 'Contracting parties shall not, by exchange action, frustrate the intent of the provisions of this Agreement, nor by trade action, the intent of the provisions

[24] United Nations, Report of the Commission of Experts of the President of the United Nations General Assembly on Reforms of the International Financial System, New York, 21 September 2009.

[25] IMF Agreement Article IV, Section 1(iii).

[26] E. Denters, 'Manipulation of Exchange Rates in International Law: The Chinese Yuan', *ASIL Insights*, November 2003.

of the Articles of Agreement of the International Monetary Fund'. According to the Interpretative Note Ad Article XV, the word 'frustrate' is intended to indicate, for example, that infringements of the letter of any Article of this Agreement by exchange action shall not be regarded as a violation of that Article if, in practice, there is no appreciable departure from the intent of the Article.[27] Thus, a contracting party which, as part of its exchange control operated in accordance with the Articles of Agreement of the IMF, required payment to be received for its exports in its own currency or in the currency of one or more members of the IMF will not thereby be deemed to contravene Article XI or Article XIII of the GATT on quantitative restrictions. Article XV:9 GATT further provides that nothing in the GATT precludes a Member from adopting measures in accordance with the Articles of Agreement of the IMF or under special exchange agreements. According to Article XV:2 GATT, there shall be deference to 'the determination of the Fund as to whether action by a contracting party in exchange matters is in accordance with the Articles of Agreement of the International Monetary Fund'.

These provisions suggest that, where measures have been taken with respect to exchange controls or restrictions, even if such measures would otherwise be considered trade restrictions because of their effect on import and export transactions, *the intent of the GATT is not to impose disciplines beyond those required by the IMF*. Nevertheless, it is inaccurate to view these provisions, as some commentators have, as essentially *ceding jurisdiction* to the IMF. Thus, where an exchange measure is not consistent with the IMF Articles then the 'safe haven' of Article XV GATT disappears, and it becomes the task of the *WTO* dispute settlement organs to determine, as a matter of *WTO* law, whether the measure falls foul of a provision of the GATT, such as Article XI. Thus, where a country disagrees with the Fund on the best course for solving a financial crisis, including in a manner that does not worsen the plight of the least advantaged, the GATT allows for that country to be 'punished' through being found in violation of GATT rules; that is, added to the punishment that the IMF can dish out, is the punishment that can be dished out

[27] Marchetti *et al.* argue that 'Although there is some attempt at clarification with respect to what "frustrate" means, as yet, there has been no jurisprudence or decision of a competent WTO body regarding either the interpretation or application of paragraph 4 of GATT Article XV'. See J. Marchetti, M. Ruta and R. Teh, 'Trade Imbalances and Multilateral Trade Cooperation', Chapter 13, this volume.

through possible retaliatory sanctions for a violation of the GATT. In other words, the GATT/WTO sets itself up as a residual enforcer for the IMF.[28] The original IMF Articles were premised on a world of largely fixed exchange rates adjusted through IMF supervision and, at least in theory, against an objective standard (gold reserves). The world today is a very different one, where because of speculation-driven currency markets and the widespread liberalisation of capital controls, which IMF economists have generally wholeheartedly endorsed, there is no agreed international standard against which a currency can be viewed as over- or under-valued, thus triggering a reasonable obligation to adjust economic fundamentals through means that do not impose unreasonable costs on other countries.

In GATT/WTO practice and jurisprudence, the justifiability of measures under Article XV GATT has been considered on a number of occasions. In the *Argentina – Textiles and Apparel* case, Argentina argued that a 3 per cent ad valorem tax that it collected was for purposes of funding the collection of accurate statistical data on import and export transactions as part of its overall understanding with the IMF on stabilisation and adjustment. The panel held that there was no exception under the GATT that would, for these reasons, limit Argentina's obligations under Article VIII with regard to customs fees. The panel did not consider whether, given that Argentina was maintaining the tax in the context of its arrangements with the IMF, the tax could be deemed to be an exchange measure within the meaning of Article XV:9 of the GATT. The fact that the tax applied to all imports indicates that it was not intended as a protectionist measure to shelter Argentinian industries from competition while lending plausibility to its connection to Argentina's exchange arrangements. The AB upheld the panel's approach.[29]

Argentina had argued that the Declaration on Coherence and the subsequent Agreement between the IMF and the WTO, discussed above, were 'legislative developments' in the WTO which had the effect of creating a meta-norm of avoidance of 'cross-conditionalities', such that its relations with the IMF would require a state to engage in conduct that would violate WTO law. The AB observed that Argentina had not

[28] This kind of double jeopardy or cross-regime magnifying effect is what Teitel and I have labelled 'ultra-compliance'. See Howse and Teitel, 'Beyond Compliance'. In their work in progress, K. Davis and B. Kingsbury deploy the concept of 'obligation overload'.

[29] *Argentina – Measures Affecting Imports of Footwear, Textiles, Apparel and Other Items*, Report of the Appellate Body, WT/DS56/AB/R (adopted 22 April 1998), paras. 69–74.

shown to the panel's satisfaction that the tax had been requested of it by the IMF or there was a conflict of *legal obligation*, i.e., that Argentina had a legally binding agreement with the IMF that would be violated if it did not impose the tax. As interpreted in the WTO dispute settlement system, the WTO rules on exchange actions are likely to be permissive on any macroeconomic policy intervention that has the explicit blessing of, or is specifically required by the IMF; however, where a WTO member takes an action that the Fund is not prepared to endorse, or that it has not required, and such an action falls generally within the kind of exchange measures covered by Article XV there is something close to a presumption that the WTO rules have been violated.

These findings of the AB suggest a far too narrow and formalistic view of the problem of coherence and conflicting conditionalities. In many cases, the IMF's requirements are of a general nature, and linked to the achievement of certain results. The IMF leaves the specific instrumentalities up to the state in question. The fact that the IMF has not requested 'x' policy does *not mean* that 'x' policy does not result from requirements imposed by the IMF – the policy in question may be one of the only feasible ways of satisfying the IMF's demands at reasonable social cost, for example. The notion of legal conflict suggested by the AB is equally problematic. It narrows the meaning of coherence to the notion of avoiding conflicting treaty requirements. However, international law is not the only or even the primary lever that the IMF uses to 'enforce' conditionality; rather, the IMF will simply not disburse further funds to a state that does not meet its conditions, regardless of whether those conditions are formalised as legal requirements or expressed, as is typically the case, in 'memoranda' or 'letters of intent' from the state in question.[30]

The AB placed considerable emphasis on the notion that neither the Declaration on Coherence nor the subsequent Cooperation Agreement between the WTO and the IMF added to or diminished the rights and

[30] See O. Eldar, 'Reform of IMF Conditionality; a Proposal for Self-Imposed Conditionality', *IILJ Working paper* 2005/10, New York University Law School; D. Siegel, 'Legal Aspects of the IMF/WTO Relationship: The Fund's Articles of Agreement and the WTO Agreements,' *American Journal of International Law* 96 (2002), 561, 581: 'even those measures that constitute Fund conditionality do not entail legal obligations to implement the policies in the program. As a legal matter, failure to complete those measures results solely in the non-fulfillment of a condition for the use of Fund resources. Political ramifications may stem from this failure, but the legal consequences are limited to the suspension of financing absent further action by the Executive Board; they do not give rise to a breach of obligation or the possibility of sanctions.'

obligations contained in the WTO Agreements. The AB noted that the effect of cross-conditionalities or possible conflicts between measures that might result from IMF programmes and WTO obligations was specified as 'consultation' between the Fund and the WTO. Yet when it considered whether the panel's failure to consult with the Fund constituted a violation of its obligation to make an objective assessment of the matter, the AB *ignored* the consultation requirement as set out in Paragraph 10 of the Agreement between the IMF and the WTO.

The consultation requirement in Paragraph 10 applies, as a *sui generis* obligation, to discussions between IMF staff and the WTO Secretariat in cases of a possible situation of cross-conditionalities and does not as such demand consultations between a dispute settlement panel and the IMF staff. Nevertheless, the AB failed to consider that this requirement might have relevance for the *interpretation* of Article XV of the GATT and also for the meaning of the obligation 'to make an objective assessment of the facts' under Article 11 of the WTO DSU. Briefly put, the thrust of the Declaration on Coherence and the subsequent Agreement between the IMF and the WTO is that issues that arise from possible inconsistencies between measures taken in relation to Fund programmes on the one hand and WTO obligations on the other ought, at least in the first instance, to be addressed through consultations and cooperation between the WTO Secretariat and the Fund. Arguably, in light of the Agreement between the IMF and the WTO, Article XV:9 could be *interpreted* so as to encompass any measure related to the fulfilment of an IMF programme to restore payments and exchange rate stability that would otherwise be WTO-inconsistent; the Agreement gives meaning to the exception in Article XV by specifying *ex ante* consultations between the WTO Secretariat and the IMF rather than *ex post* dispute settlement, as the means by which possible inconsistencies between IMF measures and WTO measures are resolved. This would explain why, as the AB observed, the Agreement between the IMF and WTO does not contain any 'rules' for resolving conflicts; the Agreement specifies policy coordination, not rule-application through dispute settlement, as the manner in which such measures are to be addressed.

In the *Dominican Republic – Cigarettes* case, the Dominican Republic argued that a foreign exchange fee charged on certain import transactions was an exchange measure within Article XV:9(a) of the GATT and thus justified even if otherwise inconsistent with GATT Article II, because 'it is prescribed by monetary authorities, not by trade or customs authorities; it applies to exchange actions, not to import transactions as such; and it is a charge on foreign exchange transactions imposed through the banking system, not a charge on import transactions levied by customs authorities' (para. 7.124). The panel rejected the Dominican Republic's defence under Article XV:9 on the grounds that 'since Article XV:9 GATT exempts exchange restrictions measures that are applied in accordance with the Fund Articles, from obligations under other Articles of the GATT, the guiding principle that the IMF prescribed as the criterion for the determination of what constitutes an "exchange restriction" should be respected by this Panel' (para. 7.132). This is the same *non sequitur* evident in the panel ruling on the Greek import charge in the 1950s – the leap from the textual requirement of the GATT that a measure justified under Article XV:9 be consistent with the IMF Articles, the constitutional treaty of the IMF, to the conclusion that the IMF and its policies should be determinative *in other respects* of whether the measure falls under Article XV. In jumping to various IMF documents to assess whether the Dominican Republic's measure was an 'exchange restriction' within the meaning of those documents, the panel failed to consider the meaning of the text of Article XV, especially the term, 'exchange restrictions' in light of the purpose and object of the WTO Agreements. It looked at Article XV:9 as if it simply ceded jurisdiction or deferred to the IMF, rather than being intended to fulfil goals of the WTO itself, such as the achievement of full employment and improving standards of living, through allowing a country to safeguard the stability of its currency and payments as a sovereign matter, and not on account of the authority of the IMF. Thus, the panel asked the IMF for a legal opinion as to whether the Dominican Republic measure was an 'exchange restriction' and the Fund replied that in its current form, as a fee charged on importation rather than all foreign currency transactions, the measure was not an 'exchange restriction'. The panel simply deferred to this judgment of the Fund even though, as already noted, the legal meaning of an 'exchange restriction' is not mentioned in the exhaustive list in Article XV:2 of matters on which the panel must defer to the Fund. The rejection of the Dominican Republic's Article XV:9(a) defence was all the more egregious, given that the Fund, having given an opinion on a matter where according to GATT Article XV:2 it has no particular mandate, the interpretation of language in the GATT treaty (in this case the expression 'exchange restriction') *then* stated that it would not go on to give an opinion on the matter where it *is* given a mandate, namely the consistency of the Dominican Republic's measures with the IMF Articles (para. 7.150).

Through a logic so twisted that it is almost impossible to fathom, in light of the IMF's failure to indicate whether the measure was consistent with the IMF Articles, the panel held that the Dominican Republic had not discharged its burden of proof to show that the measure was consistent with the IMF Articles. But how *could* such a burden of proof be reasonably imposed on the Dominican Republic? Article XV:2 states that whether action in exchange matters by a Contracting Party is in accord with the IMF Articles is a matter for determination by the Fund. Thus if, as here, the Fund refuses to make that determination, by the very language of Article XV:2 there is no alternative route open to the Dominican Republic to *prove* consistency with the IMF Articles.

III. The issue of exchange rate manipulation

It is sometimes suggested that exchange rate policies such as China's might be examples of exchange actions that 'frustrate the intent of the provisions of the GATT', by undermining the ability of members to use their comparative advantage to benefit from the market access provided by GATT rules. However, the reference to 'exchange controls and restrictions' in Article XV:9, which qualifies Article XV:4, suggests that what might be intended by the expression 'exchange action' is measures that directly impede market access by limiting the availability of currency that can be exchanged to pay for imported goods (as opposed to intervention in currency markets that affects exchange *rates*). Indeed, this is highly likely since Article XV:9 GATT was drafted in light of the original Bretton Woods assumption of exchange rates tied to the gold standard. While one might adopt an evolutionary interpretation of Article XV:4, taking into account the shift to floating market-based rates, the text seems normatively too thin to assess legitimately whether any given 'exchange action' undermines the intent of any particular provision of the GATT. Hence, even Brazil observes that:

> Article XV was not designed to equip Contracting Parties with the means to deal with new challenges created by the weakness of the international monetary system following the collapse of the gold standard, nor to settle any trade related disputes. It is not a mere coincidence that the dispute settlement mechanisms of the GATT/WTO have never been used to address complaints under Article XV.[31]

[31] 'The Relationship Between Exchange Rates and International Trade: Exchange Rate Misalignment and Trade Remedies: A Conceptual Note by Brazil', WT/WGTDF/W/68, 5 November 2012.

Thus, Brazil takes the view that new WTO norms may be required to provide a remedy for currency manipulation. Along similar lines, a number of commentators have suggested that the WTO dispute settlement system should be used to address currency undervaluation, even if amending Article XV of the GATT is needed to provide more precise rules that refine the notion that 'exchange action' must not frustrate the intent of provisions of the GATT. For example, Mattoo and Subramanian argue: 'There are compelling reasons for the WTO to address exchange rate undervaluation. . . . An undervalued exchange rate is *both* an import tax and an export subsidy and is hence the most mercantilist policy imaginable.'[32] Mattoo and Subramanian admit that it may be difficult to determine the extent to which a given exchange rate is the effect of intentional government action to undermine WTO rules.[33] From Keynes[34] to Stiglitz, leading economic minds have been sceptical about the relationship between exchange rates and trade effects that the arguments of commentators like Mattoo and Subramanian suppose. Gagnon attempts to address the difficulty by undertaking an analysis that claims to isolate export-boosting from other policy influences on exchange rate intervention.[35] But his approach ultimately depends on the notion that the currency interventions of the Asian governments he accuses of manipulation cannot be explained by the concern to have a cushion of foreign exchange reserves as insurance against a crisis. This depends ultimately on the normative judgment that these reserves are in excess of what would be needed for that purpose. Thus, there is no smoking gun here, only a particular point of view on what is an 'excessive' build up of reserves and thus should be regarded with suspicion.

A basic conceptual difficulty with the manipulation hypothesis has been clearly and succinctly stated by Staiger and Sykes:

> Prices in a country that devalues its currency will adjust so that the real effects of the devaluation and implied price changes cancel out and leave

[32] Aaditya Mattoo and Arvind Subramanian, 'Currency Undervaluation and Sovereign Wealth Funds: A New Role for the World Trade Organization', Working Paper WP 08–2, January 2008, Peterson Institute for International Economics, Washington, DC. On this issue, also see the contribution by G. Z. Marceau and J. J. Maughan, 'The WTO Dispute Settlement Mechanism in Matters Involving Exchange Rates and Trade', Chapter 14, this volume.

[33] *Ibid.*

[34] As presented by Irwin, 'Esprit de Currency', *Finance & Development*, February 2011, p. 31.

[35] Joseph E. Gagnon, 'Combating Widespread Currency Manipulation', Policy Brief PB12–19, Peterson Institute for International Economics, Washington, DC, July 2012.

> import and export volumes unchanged ... Two specific points follow. First exchange rate intervention need not imply real trade effects. Indeed, because China's currency policies are longstanding and the yuan has, as noted, appreciated against the dollar in recent years, it is at least possible that any trade effects of Chinese policy have largely washed out in accordance with this long-run scenario.[36]

Staiger and Sykes note that currency undervaluation can have short-term trade effects depending on the currency practices in the invoicing of trade transactions and the stickiness of prices, but I share their scepticism that such effects warrant WTO action. Stiglitz has made the further point that even in the short term if there are low demand elasticities for Chinese goods, revaluation might result not so much in quantity going down but in prices going up, such that the impact of the re-evaluation would be largely to improve the terms of trade for Chinese producers.[37]

The notion that Chinese exchange rate policies, for example, may constitute a countervailable subsidy under existing WTO rules is, however, gaining some traction in the US.[38] Part of presidential candidate Mitt Romney's platform was to declare China a currency manipulator on his first day in office and order the imposition of retaliatory duties.[39] In March 2013 a bill was introduced in the US House of Representatives that, like an earlier initiative in 2010, would direct the relevant US authorities to consider applying countervailing duties where a US industry is injured by a fundamentally undervalued currency.[40] A currency would be considered fundamentally undervalued if during the most recent eighteen-month period for which information was available, the following was established: the government engaged in protracted, large-scale intervention in one or more foreign exchange markets; the real effective exchange rate of the currency is undervalued by at least 5 per cent (based on IMF guidelines); the country has experienced significant and persistent global current account surpluses; and the foreign asset reserves held by the government

[36] Robert W. Staiger and Alan O. Sykes, 'Currency "Manipulation" and World Trade: A Caution', in Simon Evenett (ed.), *The US–Sino Currency Dispute: New Insights from Economics, Politics and Law* (London: Centre for Economic Policy Research, 2010), p. 110.

[37] Stiglitz video interview, *Wall Street Journal* website, 9 October 2010. I am grateful to Joe Stiglitz for conversations on this and other issues discussed in this chapter.

[38] Mattoo and Subramanian, 'Currency Undervaluation'.

[39] For a critique of Romney's position, see R. Howse, 'Obama's Trade Policy Plays by the Rules: Romney's Would Not', *Financial Times*, 9 February 2012, www.ft.com/cms/s/0/baed2df0-51be-11e1-a99d-00144feabdc0.html#axzz28Y1a2I6d.

[40] The Currency Reform for Fair Trade Act, HR 1276.

of the country exceed (i) the amount necessary to repay all debt obligations of the government falling due within the coming twelve months; (ii) 20 per cent of the country's money supply using standard measures of M2; and (iii) the value of the country's imports during the previous four months. The Hong Kong Trade Development Council notes, based on these selective criteria, that while formally the law 'would apply to goods from all countries, it is clear that this measure is targeted specifically at imports from mainland China'.[41] The definition of 'subsidy' in the WTO Subsidies and Countervailing Measures Agreement (SCM Agreement) includes a requirement that there be a 'financial contribution' by government to an industry or firm, not only the conferral of a competitive 'benefit'; exchange rate policies do not appear to conform to any of the meanings of financial contribution stipulated in the SCM Agreement. Nevertheless, Jung has observed:

> Some have argued that 'financial contribution' exists, at least in the case of China's currency exchange regime, because a 'direct transfer of funds' is involved when a Chinese bank exchanges the USD for the RMB for their exporters at the Chinese government's administered exchange rate. This is a noteworthy argument in the case of China's currency regime, because China had once implemented its currency exchange regime by requiring foreign exchange transactions to occur at a government-determined rate rather than a market-determined rate, in addition to implementing other conventional methods of currency intervention. Ordinarily, however, exchange of currencies by banks does not directly cause undervaluation of currency.[42]

Moreover, China's exchange rate policy applies to the entire Chinese economy and therefore would be unlikely to be considered 'specific' and, under both existing US and WTO law, only 'specific' subsidies may be countervailed. In fact the US Department of Commerce has consistently found that the specificity requirement has not been met in the case of petitions complaining that currency manipulation constitutes a countervailable subsidy.[43] Nevertheless the SCM Agreement deems export subsidies to be specific, as these fall under the 'prohibited' category in Article 3 (see Article 2.3 SCM Agreement).

[41] 'Legislation to Address Currency Manipulation Introduced in House', HKTCD Research, 5 April 2013, p. 2.

[42] Haneul Jung, 'Tacking Currency Manipulation with International Law: Why and How Currency Manipulation should be Adjudicated', *Manchester Journal of International Economic Law* 9:2 (2012), 184–200, 199, footnotes omitted.

[43] Above n. 31.

While a principled legal test for currency manipulation is elusive in today's monetary system, the concern is real that states will resort to beggar-thy-neighbour macroeconomic policy responses to financial and economic crises, undermining confidence in the rules that sustain an open trading system. In the wake of the 2007–10 financial and economic crisis, the G-20 grouping of states took the lead in attempting to forestall, through various policy commitments, competitive beggar-thy-neighbour national responses to the crisis. This effort culminated in a more formal agreement, the 'Framework for Strong, Sustainable and Balanced Growth', which was launched at the Pittsburgh Summit in September 2009. Among the commitments in the framework are to 'promote more balanced current accounts' and 'to undertake monetary policies consistent with price stability in the context of . . . exchange rates that reflect underlying economic fundamentals'. Schwanen, however, notes that there is no real surveillance or implementation mechanism attached to the framework, but rather that it is intended to rely on existing IMF monitoring exercises.[44] He argues that the G-20 needs to develop a framework agreement on a set of actions by member states that undermine it in such a way as to justify a complaint, which could be brought to a complaint mechanism. At the meeting of G-20 Finance Ministers and Central Bank Governors held on 15 April 2011, there was a move in the direction of more specific normative benchmarks for implementing the Framework, at least with respect to determining whether imbalances are of such a nature as to justify collective demands for adjustment. Thus, agreement was reached on the 'G20 Indicative Guidelines for Assessing Persistently Large Imbalances'.[45] Essentially, the Guidelines adopt various statistical approaches for determining whether a member state's imbalance requires 'policy action'.

It remains to be seen if these Guidelines will translate into concrete collective policy discipline. One positive feature of the G-20 approach, however, is it puts concern with trade deficits and surpluses and currency misalignment into a broader policy context, avoiding the obsession with simplistic judgments about currency manipulation that have to some extent, as discussed above, fuelled the Chinese exchange rate controversy and the recent arguments by Brazil. At a G-20 meeting in February 2013 there was an effort to censure Japan's move to devalue the yen, and Brazil

[44] Daniel Schwanen, 'The G20 Framework for Strong, Sustainable and Balanced Growth: A Study in Credible Cooperation', CIGI G20 Paper No. 4, 22 June 2010.

[45] G-20, 'Communiqué Meeting of Finance Ministers and Central Bank Governors', Washington DC, 14–15 April 2011, www.g20.org/documents/#p2.

also raised issues concerning the euro; however, the G-20 notably failed to make any judgments about supposed currency manipulation or competitive devaluation. More recently, at the April 2013 G-20 meeting, while the G-20 reiterated their opposition to currency manipulation as a general matter, there was no implication that at present any particular state was engaged in the practice.

D. Trade restrictions for balance-of-payments purposes: GATT Articles XII–XIV

Articles XII to XIV of the GATT elaborate a complex code designed to govern and discipline the use of trade restrictions for BOP purposes. Article XII:1 states the basic right of any Contracting Party to impose quantitative restrictions in derogation from Article XI 'in order to safeguard its external financial position and its balance of payments'. Article XII:2 establishes that such restrictions shall be limited to what is 'necessary: (i) to forestall the imminent threat of, or to stop, a serious decline in monetary reserves, or (ii) in the case of a Contracting Party with very low monetary reserves to achieve a reasonable rate of increase in its reserves'. Such restrictions must be progressively relaxed as the BOP improves.

Furthermore, Contracting Parties 'undertake, in carrying out their domestic policies, to pay due regard to the need for maintaining or restoring equilibrium in their balance of payments on a sound and lasting basis' (Article XII:3). At the same time, no Contracting Party is obligated to take domestic BOP measures that would threaten the objective of full employment (i.e., contracting the domestic money supply to dampen demand for imports, Article XII:3(d)). A process of consultations is envisaged with the GATT Council concerning any new restrictions or increase in restrictions, with periodic review of the necessity of the trade measures and their consistency with Articles XII–XIV. In addition, Article XII contains provisions on dispute settlement, including the authorisation of retaliation where a Party persists in trade restrictions that have been found by the Contracting Parties to violate the GATT. Articles XIII and XIV contain, respectively, the requirement that measures taken pursuant to Article XII:1 be implemented on a non-discriminatory basis and certain narrow exceptions to this non-discrimination requirement, e.g., where discriminatory exchange controls have been authorised by the IMF (see the discussion of substitutability below). In the case of developing countries, there is a much broader exemption for BOP-based trade restrictions. Hence, Article XVIII:2(b) states the principle that developing countries should have additional flexibility 'to apply quantitative restrictions for balance of payments purposes in a manner which takes full account of the continued high level of demand for imports likely to be generated by their programmes of economic development'.

What this suggests is that even though a developing country could address its BOP difficulties through exchange rate adjustments or tighter macroeconomic policies, it should not be expected to do so, given the harm to development that may come from the resultant decline in needed imports. It is recognised that quantitative restrictions will allow a developing country to conserve its limited foreign currency resources for purchases of imports necessary for development – whereas devaluation would result in *all* imports becoming more expensive. In this connection, it bears emphasis that BOP restrictions in general may be discriminatory with respect to products although not with respect to countries. Indeed, it is explicitly stated that 'the contracting party may determine (the) incidence (of restrictions) on imports of different products or classes of products in such a way as to give priority to the importation of those products which are more essential in the light of its policy of economic development' (Article XVIII:B(10)).

The Understanding on the Balance of Payments Provisions of the General Agreement on Tariffs and Trade 1994, incorporated in the Uruguay Round Final Act, is aimed at improving GATT/WTO discipline of trade measures taken for BOP purposes. The Understanding further sets out an elaborate set of procedures for review by the Committee for Balance-of-Payments Restrictions of both the timetables for elimination of existing restrictions and notifications of any new restrictions.

Dissatisfied with the lack of consensus in the Committee on India's use of BOP-based trade restrictions, the US challenged India's continued use of such restrictions in dispute settlement, claiming violations of the GATT and the BOP Understanding. A key threshold issue was the relationship between the mandate of the BOP Committee and the jurisdiction of the WTO dispute settlement organs; India argued that, given the explicit role of the Committee in the surveillance of the challenged measures, the dispute panel should defer to that process. The panel found that its own competence and that of the BOP Committee were not mutually exclusive in these matters. India appealed this finding.

The AB first observed, in disposing of this appeal that, according to Article 1.1 of the Dispute Settlement Understanding (DSU), the dispute settlement procedures apply generally to disputes brought under the dispute settlement provisions of the covered agreements (in this case Article XXIII of the 1994 GATT), and that furthermore the DSU rules and procedures are subject only to special or additional rules identified in agreements as listed in Appendix 2 of the DSU. The AB noted that 'Appendix 2 does not identify any special or additional rules or procedures relating to balance of payments restrictions' (para. 86). In particular, it did not mention Article XVIII:B of the GATT, which calls for review by the Contracting Parties of BOP restrictions maintained on the basis of developmental considerations set out in Article XVIII:B. Thus, one could not infer any limitation on the rights of access to dispute settlement under the DSU, or on the competence of panels to interpret and apply the BOP provisions of the GATT, from the grant of competence to review Article XVIII:B justifications for such restrictions to the Contracting Parties. India, however, also argued that GATT practice with respect to Article XXIII precluded access to dispute settlement for BOP purposes. Since Article XXIII is the very basis on which DSU procedures may be invoked in the case of the GATT, practice with respect to Article XXIII of the GATT *is* relevant to the ultimate scope and limits of authority of panels and the AB when they are applying the GATT. Here, however, any pre-existing GATT practice in this matter was codified and perhaps also modified by the BOP Understanding negotiated in the Uruguay Round. The second sentence of footnote 1 to the BOP Understanding reads: '[t]he provisions of Articles XXII and XXIII of GATT 1994 as elaborated and applied by the DSU may be invoked with respect to any matters arising from the application of restrictive import measures taken for balance-of-payments purposes'. Here, India argued that the expression 'application' somehow limited the competence of the dispute settlement organs in BOP disputes in favour of the BOP Committee. The distinction that India drew was between disputes about the 'application' of BOP measures and those that concerned the substantive justification of the measures.

The AB nevertheless held that the use of the word 'application' merely reflected 'traditional GATT doctrine that, with the exception of mandatory rules, only measures that are effectively applied can be the subject of dispute settlement proceedings' (para. 93). But, at first glance, this very interpretation would seem to risk reducing the word to complete inutility – as that much, the AB is saying, has already been established by GATT practice. However, the BOP Understanding is intended to 'clarify' Articles XII and XVIII:B of the GATT. Such clarifications provide greater legal certainty and security, but will amount in large measure to restatements of what a sound treaty interpreter would already find to exist in the *status quo*. The assumption in treaty interpretation developed in *Reformulated Gasoline* and subsequent cases, that each treaty provision should be assumed to have a discrete, non-redundant legal meaning, may have to be modified in cases where the text being interpreted is an understanding that clarifies and largely affirms other existing legal provisions.

The problem with the AB's reading is in the semantic structure of the footnote. The footnote first asserts that '[n]othing in this Understanding is intended to modify the rights and obligations of Members under Articles XII or XVIII:B of GATT 1994'. The footnote then goes on to express the situation with respect to Articles XXII and XXIII of the GATT in terms of the right to invoke these procedures in matters arising from the application of BOP measures. Now if, as the AB suggests, the effect is simply to confirm existing rights under Article XXIII, then why was Article XXIII not added to the list of GATT provisions containing rights and obligations that the BOP Understanding is not intended to modify?

The AB's interpretation of the word 'application' is also undermined by the structure of Article XVIII:B of the GATT itself. Article XVIII:B(9) contains the criteria for justification of BOP measures under Article XVIII:B, while Article XVIII:B(10) states certain conditions that a member must adhere to in the application of its BOP measures, even if they are justified under Article XVIII:B(9). Thus, the relationship between Article XVIII:B(9) and Article XVIII:B(10) is not dissimilar to the relationship between the various lettered paragraphs of Article XX and the *chapeau*. The most obvious interpretation of 'application' in the footnote is that the BOP Understanding modifies rights and obligations under Article XXIII of the GATT to the extent that it limits dispute settlement action under Article XXIII to claims that the *application* of BOP measures is inconsistent with the criteria for such application contained in Article XVIII:B(10), which would be consistent with exclusive competence for the BOP Committee with respect to review of justification of such measures under Article XVIII:B(9).

Despite all this, there may be good legal reasons why the AB came to the conclusion that footnote 1, second sentence, of the BOP Understanding does not oust the jurisdiction of the dispute settlement organs to consider complaints related to the justification of BOP measures under Article XVIII:B(9). As the AB noted, the DSU itself purports to provide transparency with respect to any special procedures that might apply so as to modify or supplement DSU procedures in the case of particular covered agreements, and the BOP Understanding is not on the list.

In the *India – Balance of Payments* case, the exception relied on by India required that BOP restrictions be removed as soon as the crisis conditions to which they were addressed had passed, unless the removal was likely to provoke the return of those conditions. However, a further proviso was that, in any case, a developing country should not be required to remove BOP import restrictions if doing so could require a change in that country's development policies. India's reliance on this provision required the AB to determine what a development policy is and whether, if India were to remove its BOP restrictions, it would be required to change its policies.

What the AB did was to rely entirely on a judgment of the IMF that India did not need to change its development policies because it could address the consequences of removing its BOP-based import restrictions through 'macroeconomic' policies. Had the AB considered development policy informed by a conception of equity that includes the notion that development policy is a matter in the first instance for participation of those who are affected, it would have analysed the legal issue quite differently.

First, the AB would not have accepted that one institution, and particularly, the technocrats in that institution have 'ownership' of the meaning of a 'development' policy. Second, the AB would not have embraced the stark contrast between 'development policy' and macroeconomic policy. This implies that development policy is restricted to a series of techniques that 'experts' view as formulae for 'development', rather than including all those policies that people – in this case, at a minimum, India and Indians – see as affecting the fulfilment of their approach to development. From the perspective of equity, as informed by the social and economic rights recognised in the UN Covenant on Social, Economic and Cultural Rights, it would be obvious that macroeconomic policies, which affect revenues available for government programmes to fulfil social and economic rights, as well as the cost of imported goods and services needed to fulfil such rights and the reserves of currency with which to pay for them, are 'development policies'.

Third, on the question of whether India would be required to change its development policy in order to be able to remove the BOP restrictions without a return to the crisis conditions that led to their imposition, the

AB and the panel ought to have, for purposes of equity and coherence, considered and indeed solicited the views of a broader range of institutions and social actors – at a minimum the international organisations with express mandates on development, such as UNCTAD and the UNDP. Finally, the AB might have considered that the provision in question is largely a matter of self-declaration – that it empowers India and, above all, Indians to chart their own course in development policy, and therefore that the provision is not intended to invite the dispute settlement organs to examine *de novo* India's judgment that if it removed the restrictions, it would have to change its development policy. In sum, even *if* the overall orthodox economic preference for macroeconomic measures over trade restrictions is correct, in the realm of the second best, trade restrictions, at least of a temporary nature, may be a desirable alternative to a macroeconomic policy move that has very severe social and economic consequences.

E. Trade finance and equitable access to global markets

Increasing exports is a means of addressing indebtedness and BOP difficulties that, instead of reducing employment with the corresponding effect of increasing poverty in many cases, could actually bring more people out of poverty. Yet trade financing – at least short-term financing – is crucial to many export transactions and the very economic conditions that export receipts are needed to address may make access to such financing on the market, particularly in developing countries that have suffered financial crises, very difficult.

In a study of the WTO Secretariat in the late 1990s, Finger and Schulknecht explain the importance of government export credit agencies in trade financing:

> the commercial and political risk of international trade transactions is often much larger than for domestic transactions, because companies lack information about their foreign trading partners, the legal framework may not be well-developed and war, crisis and the sudden implementation of payment restrictions can undermine the proper completion of trade transactions . . . well-functioning ECAs [Export Credit Agencies] are probably even more important for developing country exporters [than for industrial country exporters in developed countries]. [Developing country exporters] (and their banks) are often relatively small and, therefore, less able to generate their own information on commercial and political risk abroad. They are also often likely to obtain less favourable financing terms because of mistrust by importers from

> other countries. This implies that developing country traders have to pay earlier for imports (possibly even cash on order) but they receive payment later (possibly only after delivery), and hence their trade financing needs are greater than for similar exporters from industrialized countries.[46]

A WTO Working Group on Trade, Debt and Finance was established at the fourth Ministerial Conference in Doha in November 2001, with the mandate to examine the relationship between trade, debt and finance, and to make recommendations on the problem of external indebtedness of developing and least-developed countries, and on strengthening the coherence of international trade and financial policies. The General Council was required to report to the fifth Session of the Ministerial Conference on progress in the examination.

This report, formally tabled at the Cancun Ministerial Conference in September 2003, had as its basis the Working Group's own report to the General Council of 11 July 2003, which merely identified a number of 'themes' for ongoing study and examination, namely the effect of the deterioration of the terms of trade on the ability of debtor countries to service their debt, and the need for greater access to facilities for export financing, as well as the issue of coordination and coherence between the WTO and other relevant international institutions including the international financial institutions.

The matter of adequate export financing raised in the report has direct implications for WTO rules. Here the concern, discussed at length in a later discussion paper of the Secretariat,[47] is that, as a consequence of financial crises and indebtedness, many countries have been left with a shortage of private funding for export financing, which is necessary for most export transactions, since there is usually a time gap between the buyer ordering the goods and paying for them; this in turn limits the ability of those countries to use exports as a means of restarting or increasing growth and a source of revenue for debt financing.

In the wake of the 2007–9 financial and economic crisis, concerns that the decline in trade would be exacerbated or compounded by a

[46] K.M. Finger and L. Schulknecht, *Trade, Finance and Financial Crises*, World Trade Organization Special Studies (Geneva: WTO, 1999), pp. 9–10.

[47] Marc Auboin and Moritz Meier-Ewert, 'Improving the Availability of Trade Finance during Financial Crises', Discussion Paper No. 2, WTO Secretariat, November 2003 (footnotes omitted).

reduction in trade finance due to liquidity problems of banks and a reduced appetite for risk led to a number of multilateral and other responses. The first set of responses, in 2008, is summarised by Auboin:

- All regional development banks and the IFC have doubled on average capacity undertrade facilitation programmes between Mid-2008 and the G-20 Meeting. In response to requests by commercial banks of direct co-lending with IFIs, nearly all of them have opened a 'liquidity window', in addition to their traditional risk mitigation activities (trade insurance). As such, such region-specific liquidity windows will usefully complement the IFC's new liquidity pool by way of private to public sector partnership in the industry.
- Export credit agencies have also stepped in essentially with programmes for short-term lending of working capital and credit guarantees aimed at SMEs. For certain countries, the commitment is very large or unlimited in amount (Germany, Japan). In other cases, very large lines of credit have been granted to secure supplies with key trading partners (the USA with Korea and China). In other cases, cooperation is developing to support regional trade, in particular chain-supply operations (establishment of an Asia-Pacific Trade Insurance Network to facilitate intra- and extra-regional flows).[48]

However, despite these measures, there was not a rapid recovery in the trade finance market. Thus, in 2009 at the London Summit, the G-20 made a collective commitment to further boosting trade finance, to 'ensure availability of at least $250 billion over the next two years to support trade finance through our export credit and investment agencies and through the [multilateral development banks]'.

The 2011 G-20 Summit in Seoul asked that:

> the G-20 Trade Finance Expert Group, together with the WTO Expert Group on Trade Finance and the OECD Expert Credit Group [sic] to further assess the current need for trade finance in LICs, and if a gap is identified, will develop and support measures to increase the availability of trade finance in LICs. We call on the WTO to review the effectiveness of existing trade finance programs for LICs and to report on actions and recommendations as for the consideration by the Sherpas through the G20 Development Working Group in February 2011.[49]

[48] Marc Auboin, 'Restoring Trade Finance during a Period of Financial Crisis: A Stocktaking of Recent Initiatives', Staff Working Paper ERSD-2009-16 December 2009 World Trade Organization, Geneva, pp. 14–15.

[49] See WTO ELearning, 'Trade Finance and the WTO', Geneva, March 2013.

A WTO trade finance manual summarises the findings reported to the Sherpas as follows:

> only a third of the 60 poorest countries in the world benefited regularly from the services offered under these trade finance programs. The lack of risk mitigation programs in these countries partly explained the very high fees and collateral requirements paid by local importers. Such high fees were out of line with risk statistics revealed by the International Chamber of Commerce's loss default register on trade finance. . . . too many small businesses in small countries having limited financial sector capacity to oil trade were increasingly requesting support from multilateral development banks.[50]

There has been some concern that the Basel II rules on capital adequacy for banks unduly constrained the availability of trade finance during the crisis; these rules may not fully take into account that trade finance products are relatively low-risk assets for banks. Ravi suggests that the new Basel III rules, designed in the wake of the 2007–9 financial crisis, will significantly increase the costs of trade finance, thus in fact operating at loggerheads with the G-20 and WTO goals of ensuring adequate availability of such goals.[51]

According to a WTO trade finance manual,

> these issues have been discussed by the Basel Committee on Banking Supervision's Policy Development Group and the institutions concerned with trade finance, notably the WTO, the World Bank and the ICC. The Basel Committee on Banking Supervision discussed which measures of the prudential regulation affecting trade finance was most detrimental to trade and trade finance availability, with a particular focus on low income countries. Based on proposals made by the WTO and the World Bank, it decided on October 25, 2011 to waive the obligation to capitalize short-term letters of credit for one full year, as average maturity was established to be between 90 and 115 days. This measure has the potential to unblock hundreds of millions of $ to finance more trade transactions . . . The Director-General of the WTO continued to conduct discussions with the President of the Financial Stability Board (FSB) in 2012, with a view to clarifying the conditions of the waiver on the one-year maturity floor for self-liquidating trade finance instruments, the provisions regarding liquidity rules applying to short-term trade finance (less than 30 days), and the application of the leverage ratio to trade instruments.[52]

50 *Ibid.*, p. 10.

51 Jamuna Ravi, 'Impact of Basel III on International Trade Finance', blog, 30 March 2011, www.finextra.com/community/fullblog.aspx?blogid=5151.

52 Above n. 49, p. 14.

But it is not just the Basel rules that are a problem, it is the WTO's own rules. The public provision of export financing, even short-term instruments, may easily run foul of WTO prohibitions on export subsidies. The relevant provisions are paragraphs (j) and (k) of Annex I to the SCM Agreement, which is entitled 'Illustrative List of Export Subsidies'. Paragraph (j) states that the following would be examples of prohibited export subsidies: 'The provision by governments (or special institutions controlled by governments) of export credit guarantee or insurance programmes, of insurance or guarantee programmes against increases in the cost of exported products or of exchange risk programmes, at premium rates which are inadequate to cover the long-term operating costs and losses of the programmes'. Further examples are to be found in paragraph (k):

> The grant by governments (or special institutions controlled by and/or acting under the authority of governments) of export credits at rates below those which they actually have to pay for the funds so employed (or would have to pay if they borrowed on international capital markets in order to obtain funds of the same maturity and other credit terms and denominated in the same currency as the export credit), or the payment by them of all or part of the costs incurred by exporters or financial institutions in obtaining credits, in so far as they are used to secure a material advantage in the field of export credit terms.
>
> Provided, however, that if a Member is a party to an international undertaking on official export credits to which at least twelve original Members to this Agreement are parties as of 1 January 1979 (or a successor undertaking which has been adopted by those original Members), or if in practice a Member applies the interest rates provisions of the relevant undertaking, an export credit practice which is in conformity with those provision shall not be considered an export subsidy prohibited by this Agreement.

The international undertaking referred to in paragraph (k) is the OECD Export Credit Arrangement. By incorporating this Arrangement into paragraph (k), the WTO SCM Agreement essentially draws a line between prohibited and permissible forms of export financing based on an Agreement negotiated by and for developed countries in a developed country forum, the OECD. The assumed benchmarks are based on mature capital markets and sophisticated risk-spreading and allocation vehicles typical of fully developed economies. Are these fair or reasonable benchmarks for developing countries, especially ones that have had access to private capital severely limited due to debt and/or other financial crises? The Center for International Environmental Law (CIEL) notes concerning the OECD Arrangement:

> The Arrangement can be understood as a cartel-like, price-fixing mechanism, where the largest lenders of export credits establish limits on competition, in terms of the interest and premia fees, to prevent running substantial losses, and thus to avoid risking intensified scrutiny by their own national parliaments or governments. It is an agreement by the richest countries in the world, and therefore its provisions are tailored for their needs.[53]

In the *Brazil – Aircraft* case, where the context was the sale for export of commuter jets that was supported by export credits by both Brazil and Brazil's competitor Canada, Brazil argued that:

> due to the high level of risk perceived by international markets with respect to Brazilian borrowers, the cost to EMBRAER and to Brazilian financial institutions of raising funds to finance exports of Brazilian regional aircraft is higher than the cost to Bombardier and Canadian financial institutions of raising funds to finance exports of Canadian regional aircraft. Because PROEX payments merely offset in part that higher cost of funds, allowing export credit financing for Brazilian regional aircraft on terms that are closer to, but still less favourable than, those available for competing Canadian regional aircraft, those payments are not in Brazil's view used to secure a material advantage in the field of export credit terms.[54]

In other words, Brazil was arguing that the particular financing barriers faced in developing countries should be used in determining the baseline against which an export credit is assessed to determine if it is an unfair export subsidy (para. 7.21). The panel curtly and almost scornfully rejected Brazil's approach. Most disturbingly, the panel suggested that Brazil's claim that the baseline of the 'marketplace' in paragraph (k) be adjusted to the circumstances and needs of developing countries had to be rejected because the paragraph was not on its face a provision concerning special and differential treatment (para. 7.32). It should be noted that Article 27 of the SCM Agreement does provide some time- (and otherwise) limited relaxation of export subsidies disciplines for developing countries.

The interpretative approach of the panel suggests that where special and differential treatment is mentioned explicitly in some provisions in a WTO Agreement the other provisions should be interpreted in a manner

[53] CIEL, 'Export Credit Agencies and the World Trade Organization,' *Draft Issue Brief*, 2003, pp. 4–5.

[54] WTO Panel Report, *Brazil – Export Financing Programme for Aircraft (Brazil – Aircraft)* case WT/DS46/R, adopted 14 April 1999, para. 7.21.

that is blind as to the equities as between developed and developing country members. However, Article 27.1 states a general principle that is much broader than the specific exceptions and limitations in Article 27.2 ff.: 'Members recognize that subsidies may play an important role in economic development programmes of developing country Members.' This principle should inform the interpretation of the entire SCM Agreement – there is certainly no textual indication that it is exhausted by Article 27.2 ff. (Compare the analysis of the AB in *EC – Hormones*, where it found that Article 5.7 of the Sanitary and Phytosanitary Measures Agreement (SPS Agreement) on provisional measures did not exhaust the precautionary principle as an interpretative principle for SPS.) The panel in *Brazil – Aircraft* tendentiously characterised Brazil's approach to the meaning of 'used to secure a material advantage' in paragraph (k) as a 'general lowering' of SCM disciplines, which might be harmful to developing countries as a whole; but, of course, Brazil's notion was not an across-the-board lowering of disciplines, but rather to take into account the difference in financial market conditions of a particular developing country credit-provider in relation to those conditions of its actual developed country competitors to determine whether the developing country producer is really being given a leg up or compensated for structural disadvantage and inequity. It is hard to see how such an approach could be harmful to other developing countries, many of which face much more serious structural disadvantages in terms of access to capital than Brazil.

The AB compounded the indifference to developing country concerns and challenges that was shown by the panel. Although paragraph (k) refers only to the OECD Arrangement as a 'safe haven' in terms of the disciplines of that paragraph, the AB used the benchmarks of the Arrangement – as noted above, negotiated by and for developed country governments in a process where developing countries lack virtually all voice – as the appropriate methodology for determining, in Brazil's case, whether the rates of interest attached to its export credits were such as to conclude that they 'are used to secure a material advantage'.[55]

One solution, debated in the WTO Secretariat discussion paper,[56] is that export financing be provided by multilateral development banks and institutions, since these entities (as opposed to WTO Members) are

[55] *Brazil – Export Financing Programme for Aircraft*, Report of the Appellete Body, WT/DS46/AB/R (adopted 2 August 1999).

[56] Above n. 47.

not, apparently, bound by the WTO subsidies rules (p. 12). However, the paper acknowledges that this view of the SCM Agreement is held only by 'some Members' of the WTO. It also seems rather perverse to use multilateral institutions as a means of, effectively, circumventing WTO rules, rather than making changes to the rules themselves, which would permit governments to provide short-term export financing on a non-discriminatory basis, even in situations where profit-maximising private actors would not do so, given the risks associated with financial crisis conditions.

F. The General Agreement on Trade in Services (GATS), balance of payments and debt sustainability

The regulation of banks and other financial institutions is critical to management of debt and financial crises, especially from an equity perspective. The collapse of financial intermediaries can destroy the savings, as well as the jobs, of ordinary citizens. Thus, the WTO has a special set of rules that apply to liberalisation of financial services within the general context of the GATS. These rules limit and shape in various ways the capacity of governments to regulate the financial sector with a view to stability and equity in the management of debt and financial crises.

Before considering these special rules, it is important to understand the implications of the general framework for services liberalisation, the GATS, for the management of debt and financial crises, in particular through the control of capital flows. The GATS applies to trade in services in four modes: (1) cross-border delivery; (2) presence of the consumer in the territory of the vendor; (3) commercial presence of the vendor in the consumer state; (4) transboundary movement of workers engaged in providing services. Certain obligations in the GATS apply to all services trade in these four modes. For example, limited reservations may be taken in relation to the MFN obligations, by individual WTO Members, and there are certain general exceptions, including in relation to BOP measures, which we shall examine shortly. At the same time, many of the most important obligations in the GATS, such as the national treatment obligation as well the 'market access' rules (prohibiting quantitative restrictions) apply *only* where the particular service sector in question is listed in a particular WTO member's schedule of specific commitments.

Article XI:1 GATS creates a general rule, only, however, applicable to sectors where a member has made specific commitments. Article XI:2 states:

> Nothing in this Agreement shall affect the rights and obligations of the Members of the International Monetary Fund under the Articles of Agreement of the Fund, including the use of exchange actions which are in conformity with the Articles of Agreement, provided that a Member shall not impose restrictions on any capital transactions inconsistently with its specific commitments regarding such transactions, except under Article XII [of GATS] or at the request of the Fund.

The language of Article XI:2 indicates a crucial difference between the GATT and the GATS. However narrowly or restrictively interpreted, the relevant provisions of the GATT, as we have seen, contain only disciplines on *current account* measures. Under the GATS, a Member's specific commitments may prevent it from instituting *capital account* controls, which, as noted above, economists such as Stiglitz, Bhagwati and Rodrik have argued may be desirable or necessary to either forestall or address a financial crisis in a manner consistent with the development and general social needs of the country concerned. An IMF Reference Note suggests: 'While capital controls may be considered a legitimate part of the toolkit to manage capital inflows in certain circumstances, they may, in some cases, be inconsistent with GATS obligations.'[57]

To understand the flexibility that may exist under the GATS to enact such capital controls, it is therefore necessary to look carefully at Article XII, the BOP exception. This exception can only be utilised after satisfying a very complex and long series of conditions.

A number of important features of Article XII are worth noting. First of all, Article XII:1 gives WTO members with developing or transitional economies a clear right to take measures that provide a level of financial reserves 'adequate' for that particular member's programme of economic transition or development. Thus, Article XII:1 GATS affirms that development goals are the legitimate basis for a WTO member determining the kinds of BOP measures it needs. Whereas the measures must 'not exceed those necessary' to deal with 'serious balance-of-payments and external financial difficulties or threat thereof', Article XII:3 affirms that a member 'may give priority to the supply of services which are more essential to their economic or development programmes'. More

[57] International Monetary Fund, Reference Note on Trade in Financial Services, Washington, DC, 3 September 2010, para. 16. Emphasis in original, footnotes omitted.

generally, the concept of 'necessity' ought to be interpreted in the context of Article XII as a whole, which gives considerable emphasis to an individual member's approach to development. There is ample room to read Article XII so as not to require a member to use alternative policy measures, even if less restrictive of services trade, where those measures undermine the concept of equity implicit or explicit in that member's development programme. Here, Article XII should be interpreted in light of the Right to Development, and in relation to the UN Covenant on Economic, Social and Cultural Rights.[58]

Unlike the case with the GATT, deference to the IMF under Article XII extends *only* to statistics and facts and conclusions drawn from such statistics and facts; therefore, a judgment about the consistency of the measures with the IMF Articles may be made independently at the WTO.

Article XII envisages consultations on BOP measures in the Committee on Balance of Payments Restrictions. However, following the logic of the *India – Balance of Payments* case, discussed above, since the GATS provides no exception from dispute settlement for Articles XI and XII of the GATS, the existence of the Committee on Balance of Payments Restrictions forum would not lead to a removal or restriction of panel and AB jurisdiction.

Finally, it is important to appreciate the extent to which GATS-specific commitments may imply limits to the ability to impose capital account controls. Footnote 8 of Article XVI:1 reads:

> If a Member undertakes a market-access commitment in relation to the supply of a service through [mode 1] and if the cross-border movement of capital is an essential part of the service itself, that Member is thereby committed to allow such movement of capital. If a Member undertakes a market-access commitment in relation to the supply of a service through [mode 3], it is thereby committed to allow related transfers of capital into its territory.

Situations where 'movement of capital is an essential part of the service itself' would apply most obviously to certain kinds of financial services (for example, mutual funds), but the other kind of situation mentioned in Footnote 8 is much broader, applying to *all* cases where the service is being supplied through a commercial presence in the other WTO member. Nevertheless, in such circumstances, the requirement of liberalisation seems limited to *inward* movement of capital.

[58] See, generally, Howse and Teitel, 'Beyond the Divide'.

At the same time, some kinds of (outbound) capital controls might be viewed as *conditions* on who can supply services (number of service suppliers) in violation of Article XVI:2(a), or as 'limitations on the total value of service transactions or assets' in violation of Article XVI:2(b) or 'total number of service operations or the total quantity of service output' in violation of Article XVI:2(c). This possibility arises from the extremely broad interpretation of Article XVI:2(a) and (c) by the AB in the *US – Gambling* case. Essentially, the AB suggested that to violate either provision, measures need not take the explicit *forms* described in those provisions provided they have comparable *effects* on restricting market access and are quantitative in nature.[59] Since capital account controls are clearly quantitative measures they may well have effects on the number of service suppliers, the total value of services transactions or assets under Article XVI.

G. 'Prudential' regulation under the GATS

With respect to financial services, commitments in this sector are governed by the Annex on Financial Services. The first sentence of this provision appears to allow any measure 'to ensure the integrity and stability of the financial system' without the need to show that the measure is necessary or least restrictive of trade in services. The second sentence, however, seems drafted in a manner to undermine the regulatory flexibility granted in the first sentence, in that it qualifies the use of the provision as an *exception* to GATS commitments and obligations. Thus, where a measure is not in conformity with the GATS, it 'shall not be used as a means of avoiding the Member's commitments or obligations under the Agreement'. It is difficult to discern the exact implication of this qualifying or conditional language. One reading would be that it imports an intent requirement into 2(a) of the Annex on Financial Services, namely the notion that the measures must be genuinely intended to 'ensure the integrity and stability of the financial system' rather than to protect domestic financial industries. Such an intent requirement might be difficult to apply in the case of a financial crisis, where ensuring the survival of domestic financial institutions may well be part and parcel of ensuring the 'integrity and stability of the financial system' itself.

[59] Report of the AB, paras. 232, 247.

The GATS financial services arrangements do not contain any specific standards defining appropriate prudential regulation and efforts in the WTO Committee on Financial Services to define further the meaning of prudential regulation have gone nowhere. Juan Marchetti has attempted to elaborate on the meaning of the GATS exception for prudential regulation. Marchetti suggests:

> the main function of the GATS prudential carve-out. . .[is] to give enough comfort to financial regulators to adopt measures not only in exceptional circumstances (e.g., a systemic financial crisis) but also on a day-to-day basis, as part of preventive policies aimed at ensuring the stability of the financial system, without being constrained in principle by trade disciplines. . . .[E]nsuring financial system stability involves a continuous examination of potential risks and vulnerabilities that may threaten the functioning of the system and economic activity. . . whether a measure falls under the prudential exception would not depend only on the type of measure (in other words, whether for some it is 'prudential' or not), but on the reasons behind it. And those reasons go beyond a mere focus on microeconomic conditions and the likelihood of failure of individual institutions, and allow for a broader – systemic – perspective that also considers other elements of the financial system, and the system's significance for the whole economy.[60]

There is significant debate among academic commentators as to whether and to what extent the meaning of prudential regulation for purposes of the GATS carve-out should be determined by the standards of the Basel Committee on Banking Supervision.[61] The Basel Committee has promulgated a set of non-binding capital adequacy standards for banks engaged in international transactions. In addition, the Basel Committee has developed 'Core Principles for Effective Banking Supervision'.[62]

Commentators have raised legitimacy concerns about the G-20-dominated Basel process, and questioned whether, in a multilateral regime such as the WTO with a large developing country membership, it is appropriate for the WTO adjudicator to use the Basel standards as a

[60] Juan Marchetti, 'The GATS Prudential Carve-Out', in Pangiotis Delimatsis and Nils Herger, (eds.), *Financial Regulation at the Crossroads: Implications for Supervision, Institutional Design and Trade* (Alphen aan den Rijn: Kluwer Law International, 2011), pp. 290–1.

[61] Lazaros E. Panourgias, *Banking Regulation and World Trade Law: GATS, EU and 'Prudential' Institution Building* (Oxford, Hart: 2006), pp. 106–7.

[62] The following draws from Robert Howse, 'Importing Regulatory Standards and Principles into WTO Dispute Settlement: the Challenge of Interpreting the GATS Regulations on Financial Services and Telecommunications', paper presented at the NYU-CPR Conference on Global Administrative Law, New Delhi, 5 January 2008.

benchmark or baseline against which to assess the regulatory measures a WTO member is seeking to justify under the prudential carve-out.[63] Panourgias suggests that incorporation of the Basel standards into the WTO framework, especially through dispute settlement but even through amendment to the GATS, would raise the 'democracy-related problem of legalization at the multilateral level of international norms, which have been developed by an international forum without the safeguards and transparency of treaty making'. Grynberg and Silva complain of 'lack of representation [for small states]'as well as 'non-transparency'.[64]

Barr and Miller, on the other hand, conclude in their study of the Basel Committee in light of the Global Administrative Law approach: 'The Basel Committee has increased the transparency of its processes and broadened the circle of the Basel Club. It has improved opportunities for public participation. These measures serve to increase the accountability and legitimacy of the Basel Committee's global rule-making.' Still they 'would like to see greater transparency and wider participation.'[65] Trachtman's concern, on the other hand, is not that the Basel standards inadequately reflect the social and development concerns of small and developing countries, i.e., no economic values, but rather that they are indifferent, hostile, or insufficiently oriented to trade liberalisation as a value.[66]

A number of issues arise as to the way in which the Basel standards could properly be used to interpret the prudential exception in the GATS. One view would be that where domestic regulation is more trade-restrictive than that endorsed or required by the Basel standards, it should be presumed to be unjustifiable under the prudential exception. This presumption would be reversible, but the onus can in effect be put on the WTO member seeking to justify its prudential measures to explain *why* it needs to go beyond the international norm, i.e. the *legitimate* rationale for this, given the prudential objective.

However, from the Basel perspective, the standards have been self-consciously understood as minimum *standards*, and this community

[63] See K. Alexander, R. Dhumale and J. Eatwell, *Global Governance of Financial Systems: The International Regulation of Systemic Risk* (Oxford University Press, 2006).

[64] R. Grynberg and S. Silva, 'Harmonization without Representation: Small States, the Basel Committee, and the WTO,' *World Development* 34:7 (2006), 1224.

[65] Michael Barr and Geoffrey Miller, 'Global Administrative Law: the View from Basel,'17 *European Journal of International Law* 1 (2006), 45.

[66] Joel Trachtman, 'Addressing Regulatory Divergence through International Standards: Financial Services,' in A. Mattoo and P. Sauvé (eds.) *Domestic Regulation & Services Trade Liberalization* (Washington, DC: World Bank, 2005), pp. 34–5.

certainly would not discourage stricter or greater regulation, depending on the particular strengths and weaknesses of a country's financial system and financial services markets and institutions. Thus, arguably for the purpose of identifying a baseline against which one can subject to special scrutiny non-conforming regulations, one would need to look at the practice of states in implementing the Basel standards in their domestic regulations, and not to take the standards themselves as evidence of some kind of common or widespread understanding of the maximum necessary level of prudential regulation.

Further, there may be some areas of prudential regulation where Basel does not engage the relevant values, interests or constituencies in the GATS. As Barr and Miller explain, the rationale for Basel is very much connected to the collective action problems and externalities involved in the globalisation of financial markets, where financial instability or the collapse of major financial institutions in one jurisdiction can impose significant negative externalities on others for example, or where capital can easily escape stricter regulations in one jurisdiction by moving to another with laxer standards ('race to the bottom' effects). But there are also other important values and interests at stake in prudential regulation (and the Basel epistemic community would not be likely to deny this). Such regulation for instance is closely related to deposit insurance, which may play important redistributive functions, protecting vulnerable groups that face considerable inequalities of bargaining power and information asymmetries in dealing with financial institutions, as well as systemic stability functions.

The financial and economic crisis has further called into question the wisdom of the GATS approach to financial services liberalisation. Up to the crisis there had been more movement in Doha Round negotiations in the financial services area than in most other sectors. The WTO discussions on financial services appear to have been operating in relative isolation from major efforts to reform and restructure global financial regulation and global standards for domestic regulation in the wake of the crisis (e.g., Basel III), a UN Commission on reform of the international monetary and financial system headed by Joseph Stiglitz recommended in 2009 to review the agreements (including GATS) which limit the revision of the regulatory regimes by the countries, especially capital accounts regulations.[67]

[67] United Nations, 'Report of the Commission of Experts of the President of the United Nations General Assembly on Reforms of the International Financial system', New York, 21 September 2009, p. 104, para. 94.

In June 2012, Ecuador tabled a proposal in the WTO Committee on Trade in Financial Services, seeking 'clear and agreed understanding of existing WTO regulations, in particular in the context of the discussion on new forms of macro-prudential regulation, which has been taking place in a number of relevant international and regional bodies and national institutions'.[68] In its proposal, Ecuador referred to concerns raised in the UNCTAD 2011 *Trade and Development Report*[69] concerning policy space under the GATS for post-crisis financial re-regulation.

H. Conclusions

The WTO rules on exchange actions and BOP justifications for trade restrictions clearly reflect a conception of equity that takes into account the particular needs and situations of developing countries. In certain, very precisely defined matters, the WTO rules entail deference to judgments of the IMF. In dispute settlement, however, those elements in the rules that reflect equity in particular as concerns developing countries have been minimised or ignored; moreover, the dispute settlement organs have gone well beyond the explicit limits of deference to the IMF such that they have deferred to the IMF even in such a matter as the meaning of a country's 'development policy' (the *India – Balance of Payments* case). From the perspective of equity as participation in decision-making concerning development, these tendencies of the dispute settlement organs are of considerable concern, since developing countries have limited and unequal representation and voice in the IMF. Generally, the concept of coherence reflected in the relevant WTO instruments and activities as concerns BOP and exchange matters is too narrowly focused on relations between the IMF and the WTO and does not include cooperation with those international institutions concerned with equity in development. The concept of coherence should be revised to reflect the relationship between equity and coherence as implied in the Millennium Declaration and related instruments.

At the same time, it appears that even within the narrow conception of coherence embraced in the WTO, the agreed mechanism for avoiding cross-conditionalities, namely obligatory consultations between the

[68] Communication From Ecuador: Proposal for discussing progress in respect of macro-prudential regulation and its relationship with GATS rules, S/FIN/W/84, 26 June 2012, para. 5.

[69] For details, see unctad.org/en/docs/tdr2011_en.pdf.

WTO Secretariat and the IMF prior to either taking decisions that could result in cross-conditionalities, has not been closely followed. A comprehensive review should be done of the situations where these consultations have or have not occurred and whether they have been effective in the avoidance of cross-conditionalities.

In the case of the GATS, there is a real possibility that a WTO member's specific commitments combined with general obligations in the GATS could result in a GATS violation if the member adopts capital controls, which may be necessary to address a financial crisis in a manner consistent with social and economic justice. However, there are a number of exceptions and limitations provisions in the GATS that could conceivably justify such measures. International institutions with a mandate related to equity in development should endeavour to produce guidelines for the taking into account of equity in the trade and financial system in the interpretation of such limits and exceptions.

Especially as interpreted in dispute settlement (the *Brazil – Aircraft* case), the rules on export subsidies in the SCM Agreement appear to limit the capacity of developing countries (subject to certain temporal exceptions) to provide trade financing for export transactions, based on market benchmarks devised for and by developed countries in the OECD Arrangement. Consideration should be given to an alternative approach, which would take into account, in an equitable manner, the structural differences of financial markets in developing countries as well as the special challenges of countries that have faced financial and/or debt crises in depending on private capital markets for the financing of export transactions.

13

Trade imbalances and multilateral trade cooperation

JUAN MARCHETTI, MICHELE RUTA AND ROBERT TEH

A. Introduction

The years prior to the global financial and economic crisis were marked by rising current account and merchandise trade imbalances. According to some authors, these imbalances either contributed to or precipitated the crisis.[1] And many agree that, to the extent that these large imbalances create systemic risks, it is desirable that they be reduced.[2] One frequently mentioned factor contributing to the build-up of imbalances is persistent exchange rate misalignments, i.e., an exchange rate that is above or below its equilibrium level. But this is not the only one; other factors related to macroeconomic, structural and financial policies, are also relevant in that regard.

This chapter seeks to examine the contribution that the World Trade Organization (WTO) can make in its three areas of activities – negotiations, rule-making and dispute settlement – to deal with trade imbalances and with the main factors leading to them, including exchange rate misalignments. Beyond that, this chapter also touches on the need to correct failures in international cooperation, which have allowed such imbalances to pose such a threat to the global economy.

The structure of the chapter is as follows. Section B describes the pattern of current account and trade imbalances both before and after the crisis and

An earlier version of this chapter appeared on the WTO website. The authors wish to thank Frieder Roessler and Hector Torres for their many helpful comments. The opinions expressed herein are the sole responsibility of the authors and do not necessarily reflect the views of the members of the WTO or of the WTO Secretariat.

[1] E.g. M. Obstfeld and K. Rogoff, 'Global Imbalances and the Financial Crisis: Products of Common Causes', *Centre for Economic Policy Research* Discussion Paper No. 7606 (2009).

[2] E.g. O. Blanchard and G. M. Milesi-Ferretti, 'Global Imbalances: In Midstream?', *IMF Staff Position Note* SPN/09/29(2009); O. Blanchard and G. M. Milesi-Ferretti, 'Why Should Current Account Imbalances be Reduced', *IMF Staff Discussion Note* SDN/11/03 (2011).

identifies the main explanations for them. Section C considers what we know about the effect of exchange rate changes on the trade balance both in the short-run and the long-run. Section D describes General Agreement on Tariffs and Trade (GATT) and General Agreement on Trade in Services (GATS) rules and disciplines on exchange rate policy, the balance of payments and trade measures. In addition, it discusses the role that trade-contingent measures (anti-dumping, countervailing duties and safeguards) play in responding to the adverse trade consequences of misaligned exchange rates. Section E examines the possible role of the WTO in addressing imbalances. In particular, that section discusses the role that financial reform and liberalisation of trade in financial services, litigation and rule-making can play in correcting imbalances and preventing persistent exchange rate misalignment. Section F offers some final remarks.

B. Current account and trade imbalances: facts and causes

I. *Stylised facts*

We begin by highlighting important trends and patterns in the current and merchandise trade accounts of countries.[3] The world witnessed a large build-up of current account and merchandise trade imbalances, both in absolute and relative terms, prior to the global financial and economic crisis (see Table 13.1 and Figure 13.1). In 2000, China had a current account surplus of only US$ 20.5 billion while Germany was actually in deficit. Seven years later, China's surplus had grown to nearly US$ 354 billion while Germany's shot up to US$ 248 billion. By the same year, Saudi Arabia was generating a surplus equal to a quarter of its gross domestic product (GDP) while Greece and Spain had deficits exceeding a tenth of their GDP.

Current account/merchandise trade surpluses were most pronounced among the East Asian economies, oil exporters and the 'core' eurozone

[3] Although the current account differs from the merchandise trade account by the amount of services trade and international factor payments, the two are highly correlated for most countries. The current account is defined as X − M + R, where X and M are exports and imports of goods and services, and R equals international factor payments. Macroeconomic balance requires that Y = C + I + G + X − M where Y stands for GDP, C for consumption, I for investment, and G for government spending. If we let T equal taxes, we can re-arrange the equation to get: X − M + R = [(Y + R − T) − C] + (T − G) − I. This says that the current account is equal to the difference between domestic saving (made up of private and government saving) and domestic investment. A current account surplus is created if domestic savings exceeds domestic investment: a current account deficit ensues if domestic savings is less than domestic investment.

Table 13.1. *Current account balance, selected countries: 2000–11*

Item	2000		2007		2011	
	US$ (billions)	Percentage of GDP	US$ (billions)	Percentage of GDP	US$ (billions)	Percentage of GDP
Surplus countries						
Oil exporters						
Saudi Arabia	14.3	7.6	93.4	24.3	158.5	26.5
Russia	46.8	18.0	77.0	5.9	98.8	5.3
Norway	25.3	15.0	49.0	12.5	70.3	14.5
East Asian exporters						
China	20.5	1.7	353.9	10.1	201.7	2.8
Japan	119.6	2.5	212.1	4.9	119.3	2.0
euro area ('core')						
Germany	−32.8	−1.7	248.0	7.5	203.9	5.7
Netherlands	7.9	2.0	52.7	6.7	70.9	8.5
Deficit countries						
US	−416.3	−4.2	−710.3	−5.1	−465.9	−3.1
euro area ('periphery')						
Spain	−23.1	−4.0	−144.3	−10.0	−52.2	−3.5
Greece	−9.9	−7.8	−44.7	−14.6	−29.4	−9.8

Source: World Economic Outlook Database (October 2012).

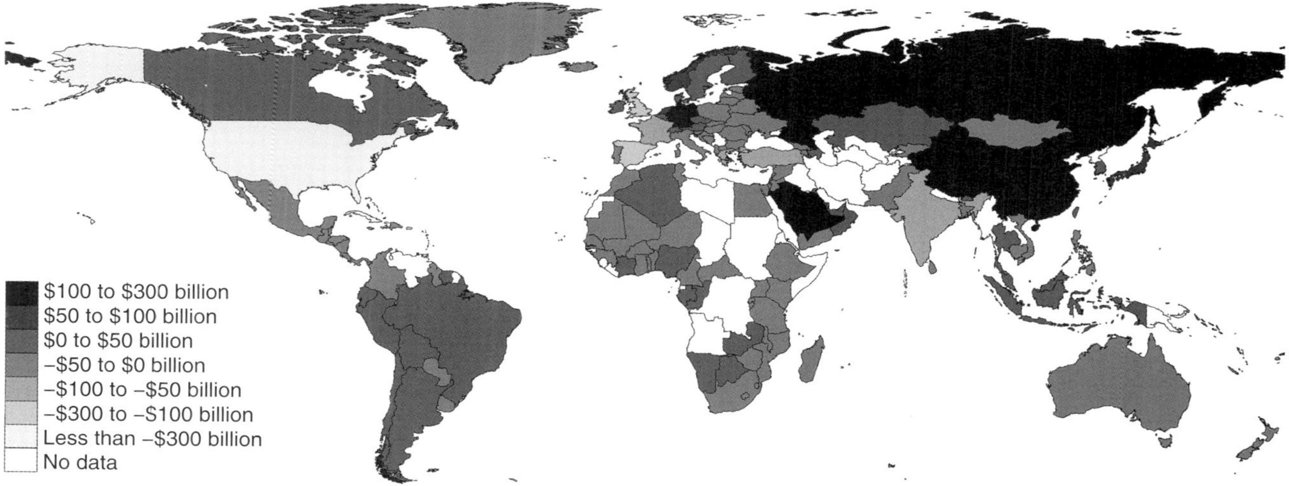

Figure 13.1. Global merchandise trade balances 2007
Note: Figure created using data from UN Comtrade.

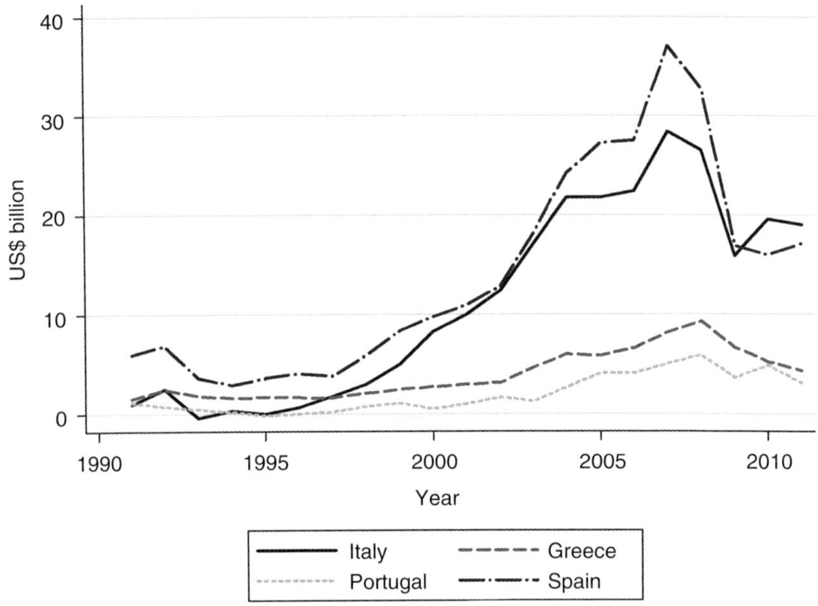

Figure 13.2. German merchandise trade surplus with selected euro area partners
Note: Figure created using data from UN Comtrade.

countries (Germany and the Netherlands). The US and the eurozone periphery countries (Greece, Ireland, Italy, Portugal and Spain) had large and persistent deficits. Beyond simply their size, the fact that a country's surplus or deficit tended to be concentrated on a handful of trade partners was bound to heighten their political sensitivity (see Figures 13.2 and 13.3). For instance, the US trade deficit with China in 2007 (US$ 275 billion) was more than three times larger than its deficit with Japan (US$ 87 billion), the next biggest source of its merchandise trade imbalance.

While imbalances contracted after the crisis (see the narrowing of the distribution of imbalances shown in Figure 13.4), they remain large in absolute terms and relative to GDP. Even after falling from its peak in 2007, the US merchandise trade deficit amounted to US$ 783 billion in 2011 which is about 5 per cent of its GDP. Further, without changes in economic policies, large imbalances are liable to return once the global economy emerges from the crisis.[4]

[4] J. Knight and W. Wang, 'China's Macroeconomic Imbalances: Causes and Consequences', *World Economy* 34 (2011), 1476–506.

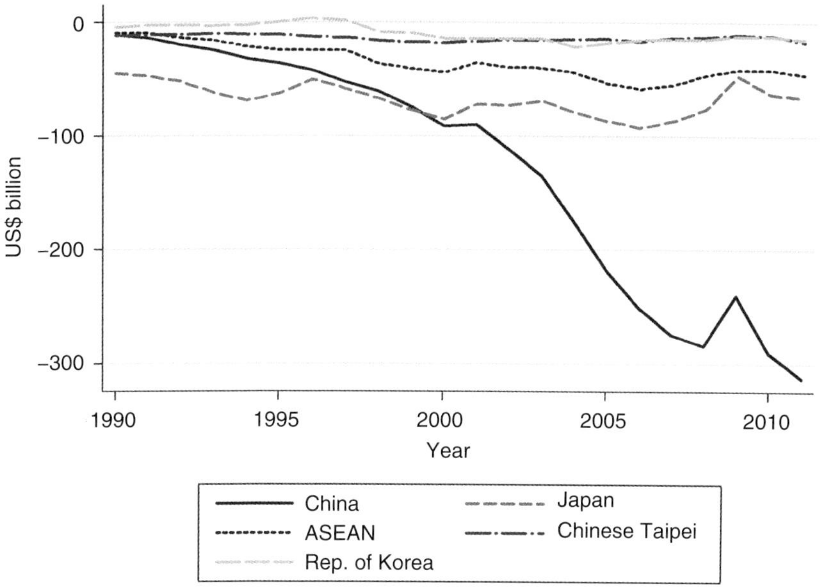

Figure 13.3. US merchandise trade deficit with selected East Asian countries 1990–2011
Note: Figure created using data from UN Comtrade.

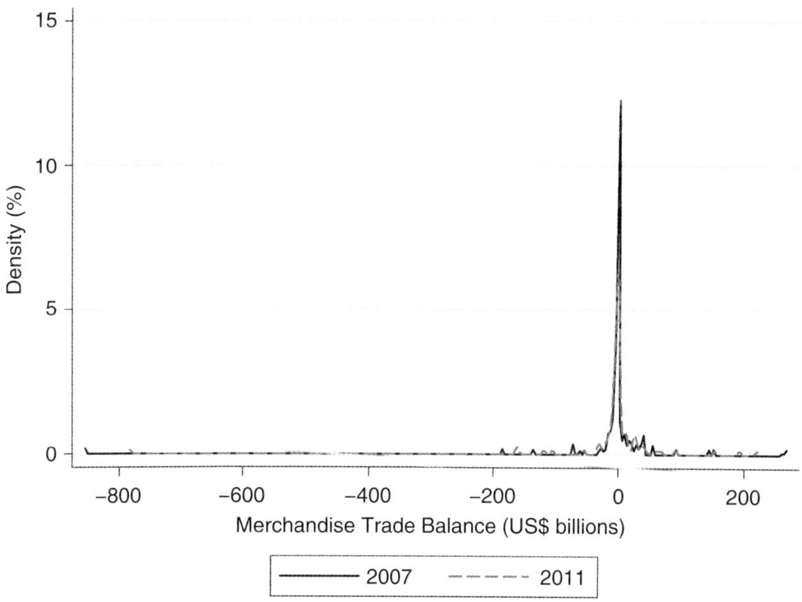

Figure 13.4. Kernel density of merchandise trade balance 2007 and 2011
Note: Figure created using data from UN Comtrade.

II. *Explaining current account and trade imbalances*

International trade theory, being concerned with explaining the pattern of trade, assumes that trade is balanced between any pair of countries. This is equivalent to the requirement that the value of production equals the value of consumption in every period. To explain imbalances, one must relax this assumption and allow countries to consume more (or less) than they produce during any given period of time although they still face a long-term budget constraint (the present value of consumption cannot exceed the present value of output). Imbalances reflect inter-temporal trade, i.e., a situation in which a country exchanges present for future consumption with its trading partner. An excess of savings over investment allows countries with a surplus to acquire claims on assets owned by countries in deficit, which in turn provide the latter with the wherewithal to consume more than they produce. Imbalances therefore reflect international differences in aggregate savings and investment behaviour.

However, the economic identity that links savings/investment behaviour to the current account makes it clear that variables on both sides of the equation are endogenous. Shocks to the trade account can affect the savings–investment gap. A positive shock to the export sector – e.g., an increase in oil production as a result of new finds – increases output and, assuming investment opportunities at home remain unchanged, can lead to greater savings (trade surplus).

Current account imbalances are the outcome of differences between countries in saving patterns, investment patterns and the degree of risk or liquidity of different assets. These differences are sometimes 'good' (leading to 'good' imbalances) and sometimes 'bad' (leading to 'bad' imbalances), to borrow the distinction from Blanchard and Milesi-Ferretti.[5] Those differences in saving patterns, investment patterns and assets are 'good' when they are a natural reflection of differences in levels of development, demographic trends and other underlying economic fundamentals. But they may be 'bad' if they reflect distortions, externalities and risks, at the national and international level.

Familiar examples of 'good imbalances' include the following: the running of current account surpluses (as a result of saving) by countries whose population is ageing faster than their trading partners'; the running of a current account deficit in a country presenting attractive investment opportunities (and therefore relying on foreign savings);

[5] Blanchard and Milesi-Ferretti, 'Global Imbalances'.

and the running of a current account deficit by a country that has deeper and more liquid financial markets that attract foreign capital and therefore leads to currency appreciation. In these cases, it would probably be unwise to take specific measures to reduce imbalances, since they reflect an optimal allocation of capital across time and space.

'Bad' examples may be symptoms, *inter alia*, of underlying domestic distortions. For example, high levels of private savings may reflect a lack of social insurance, which forces people to engage in high precautionary saving. Or it may reflect poor firm governance, which allows firms to retain and reinvest most of their earnings. Conversely, low levels of private savings can be motivated by bubble-driven asset booms, or excessively optimistic expectations about future growth. Poor protection of property rights or lack of competition in the financial sector can lead to excessively low investment. In all these cases, the purpose of policies should not be to reduce the resulting current account imbalances *per se*, but to tackle the underlying distortions. Doing so might ultimately reduce imbalances but this is not the main goal.

Turning now to the pattern of current account and trade balances in recent years, one explanation for the rise of surpluses is the 'savings glut' in emerging east Asia, which can be explained by its demographic structure,[6] a still fledgling social welfare system,[7] the lack of financial and capital market development,[8] and the build-up of foreign exchange reserves to guard against a repeat of the financial crisis of 1997–8.[9] On the other side of the ledger, deficits in the US have arisen mainly because of the low personal savings rate, which averaged just 2.8 per cent of income in the years preceding the crisis, and federal government deficits.[10] The US has also proven to be a magnet for global savings because of its attractiveness as an investment destination, the depth and sophistication of its financial markets

[6] S. J. Wei and X. Zhang, 'The Competitive Saving Motive: Evidence from Rising Sex Ratios and Savings Rates in China', *Journal of Political Economy* 119 (2011), 511–64.

[7] O. Blanchard and F. Giavazzi, 'Rebalancing Growth in China: A Three-Handed Approach', *China and World Economy* 14 (2006), 1–20; M. Chamon and E. Prasad, 'Why Are Saving Rates of Urban Households in China Rising?', *American Economic Journal – Macroeconomics* 2 (2010), 93–130.

[8] K. J. Forbes, 'Why Do Foreigners Invest in the United States?', *Journal of International Economics* 80 (2010), 3–21.

[9] J. W. Gruber and S. B. Kamin, 'Explaining the Global Pattern of Current Account Imbalances', *Journal of International Money and Finance* 26 (2007), 500–22.

[10] M. D. Chinn and H. Ito, 'Global Economic Imbalances: Prospects and Remedies: Global Current Account Imbalances: American Fiscal Policy versus East Asian Savings', *Review of International Economics* 16 (2008), 479–98.

and the role of the dollar as leading international reserve currency.[11] The role of an undervalued renminbi in the US–China trade imbalance has also figured prominently in the literature. We discuss the impact of exchange rate misalignment on trade imbalances in greater detail in the next section.

There are a number of ways to explain the pattern of imbalances in the euro area. For instance, one can ascribe them to differences in fiscal policy and economic performance.[12] However, following Mundell's classic analysis,[13] the most compelling explanation for the imbalances is that they reflect a failure by countries in a single currency area to achieve the required degree of flexibility and openness in product, services and labour markets. This has led real wages to grow out of line with productivity improvements in many euro-area members. Financial markets may have misjudged the extent to which these divergences were occurring given the smooth introduction of the euro and the discipline imposed by the Growth and Stability Pact. Thus, the markets continued to facilitate the flow of capital from core to periphery euro-area members even though the misalignment of wages and productivity eventually required a violent reversal. This point is further elaborated in Section E.I.

Prior to the global crisis, there were those who viewed current account and trade imbalances benignly as a reflection of global capital market integration which allowed a more efficient allocation of savings from surplus countries to deficit countries, where they earned a higher return.[14] This benign perspective applied equally well to the US and China trade balance. Dooley *et al.* in particular, argued that the cross-border transfer of goods and services to the US in exchange for China's financing of US deficits resulted in the successful employment and integration of tens of millions of workers into the global economy.[15] This view implies that the imbalances are sustainable and not subject to sudden reversals.

[11] B. S. Bernanke, 'The Global Saving Glut and the US Current Account Deficit', The Sandridge Lecture, Virginia Association of Economics, Richmond, Virginia, 10 March 2005.

[12] A. Fatás and I. Mihov, 'The Euro and Fiscal Policy', in A. Alesina, and F. Giavazzi (eds.), *Europe and the Euro* (University of Chicago Press, 2010), pp. 287–326.

[13] R. Mundell, 'A Theory of Optimum Currency Areas', *American Economic Review* 51 (1961), 657–65.

[14] R. Cooper, 'Living With Global Imbalances: A Contrarian View', *Institute for International Economics* (2005), www.ile.com/publications/pb/pb05-3.pdf.

[15] M. P. Dooley, D. Folkerts-Landau and P. Garber, 'Direct Investment, Rising Real Wages and the Absorption of Excess Labor in the Periphery' in R. Clarida (ed.), *G7 Current Account Imbalances: Sustainability and Adjustment* (University of Chicago Press, 2006), pp. 103–32.

However, since the advent of the global crisis many more observers have seen an intimate connection between the imbalances and the crisis. A nuanced view is that while the imbalances may not have caused the crisis, they reflected and magnified the ultimate causal factors behind it.[16] The large pool of savings from surplus countries, lax oversight in capital markets and poorly understood financial innovations created a toxic cocktail that led to the crisis. A harsher assessment is that a substantial part of the imbalances reflected economic distortions. Large and unsustainable public sector deficits, restrictions on competition in financial and other services markets, and rigid or undervalued exchange rates contributed to the misallocation of savings. Even the accumulation of reserves as a form of self-insurance is costly, since it is globally inefficient relative to alternative forms of insurance, such as the establishment of credit lines, reserve-pooling arrangements and swap lines.[17] Beyond these costs, the large imbalances played a significant role in the build-up of systemic risk. They contributed to low interest rates and to large capital inflows into US and European banks, which in turn contributed to a search for yield, higher leverage and the creation of riskier assets.[18] The main risk nowadays is that the adjustment will be disorderly and detrimental to global macroeconomic and financial stability. Should the financial flows complementing current account deficits suddenly reverse their course, economies with large deficits will suffer disorderly currency depreciations, and domestic financial sectors might also struggle to absorb efficiently the financial inflows that are the counterpart to the current account deficit. Moreover, the large balance sheet positions that emerge as a consequence of gross financial flows can entail risks because the assets (accumulated outflows) and the liabilities (accumulated inflows) are not interchangeable.[19]

[16] Obstfeld and Rogoff, 'Global Imbalances and the Financial Crisis'.

[17] Blanchard and Milesi-Ferretti, 'Global Imbalances'.

[18] IMF, 'Initial Lessons of the Crisis', prepared by the IMF Research, Monetary and Capital Markets, and Strategy, Policy, and Review Departments, 6 February 2009. Reinhart and Rogoff find that between 2003 and 2007, the trajectory of the US current account deficit was far larger and more persistent than was typical in other crises. See Figure 13.5 and the explanation in Chapter 13 of C. M. Reinhart and K. S. Rogoff, *This Time is Different: Eight Centuries of Financial Folly* (Princeton University Press, 2009).

[19] The Bank for International Settlements explains, e.g., that foreign assets held by some residents, for instance pension funds, cannot generally be used to repay the cross-border debts owed by some other residents, such as real estate developers. And the currency, liquidity and credit risks of assets and liabilities are also likely to vary considerably: the risk characteristics of the pension fund's equity portfolio are very different from those of the real estate developer's loans. Bank for International Settlements, 'The Risks of

This implies that the economic conditions that bred global imbalances need to be untangled with both surplus and deficit countries contributing to the rebalancing. Deficit countries need to shift from domestic to external sources of demand and surplus countries need to shift in the opposite direction. A comprehensive solution requires that the policies, regulatory weaknesses and structural features that created the imbalances all be addressed. Focusing on just one problem will be unlikely to do the trick. Furthermore, the existence of systemic risks means that individual countries may not be fully taking into account the cost of the distortions nor the benefits from rebalancing. This suggests that any solution will require international cooperation. We shall examine the issue of what international cooperation, and specifically, the WTO could contribute to reducing these distortions and systemic risk in greater detail in Section E.

C. What do we know about the impact of exchange rates on imbalances?

Exchange rates affect trade flows through two main channels: currency volatility and misalignments. The first is the extent to which exchange rates move up or down over time. On average, currency volatility is perceived to have a negative impact on trade. This effect, however, is generally found to be small, even though it can be relevant for certain producers or countries that have difficulties with hedging against volatility.[20] More importantly, the theory does not predict that exchange rate volatility will affect the trade balance, but rather that it will lower both imports and exports. Hence the focus of this section is on currency misalignments, that is, on the effects on the trade balance of an exchange rate that is above or below its equilibrium level following the devaluation or revaluation of the currency. It is important to draw a distinction between the immediate and the permanent effects of currency misalignments. This key distinction is reflected in the organisation of the two subsections below.

I. Exchange rates and the trade balance: the short-run

In the short-run, prices and wages may be fixed or slow to adjust. This price 'stickiness' implies that movements in the level of the nominal

International Imbalances: Beyond Current Accounts', *BIS Annual Report 2010/2011*, Basel: Bank for International Settlements 2011, Chapter III.

20 M. Auboin and M. Ruta, 'The Relationship between Exchange Rates and International Trade: A Literature Review', *World Trade Review* 12 (2013), 577–605.

exchange rate can alter relative prices in the economy. These changes, in turn, affect economic decisions and thereby influence international trade flows. Consider, for instance, the short-run impact of currency devaluation. How will the trade balance of a country respond? In textbook models with fixed prices, the nominal devaluation corresponds to a real fall in the value of the domestic currency. Foreign goods become more expensive relative to domestic goods and consumers (both at home and abroad) switch to buying more of the latter and less of the former. As a result, imports fall, exports rise and the trade balance of the domestic economy improves.[21]

Is there empirical evidence of the short-run responsiveness of the trade balance to nominal exchange rate changes? Any study that addresses this question using aggregate trade data suffers from a basic problem: the trade balance itself affects the value of the exchange rate.[22] One way to address this econometric problem is to focus on firms rather than on aggregate trade flows. This is because individual firms' decisions to export respond to the level of the currency but each firm individually is unlikely to have an impact on the exchange rate. Using a dataset of French exporters,[23] Berman *et al.* show that aggregate trade is not very responsive to exchange rate movements. On average, a 10 per cent devaluation of the currency *vis-à-vis* a trading partner leads to an overall increase in the volume of trade of 10 per cent in the short-run (i.e. unit elasticity). Other studies apply the same methodology to a detailed dataset of exporters from China and Brazil.[24]

There are several factors that limit the responsiveness of the trade balance to exchange rate changes. First, if the devaluation is unexpected and, therefore, is not embedded into pre-signed trade orders, the value of

[21] Any international economics textbook contains a detailed description of this basic mechanism. See, e.g., R. C. Feenstra and A. M. Taylor, *International Economics* (New York: Worth, 2008).

[22] In the jargon of economists, exchange rates are not exogenous to trade balances. Rather, exchange rates are endogenous variables that result from a complex interaction of macroeconomic, financial and trade factors.

[23] N. Berman, P. Martin and T. Mayer, 'How Do Different Exporters React to Exchange Rate Changes? Theory, Empirics and Aggregate Implications', *Quarterly Journal of Economics* 127 (2012), 437–92.

[24] Chatterjee *et al.* and Tang and Zhang respectively, find similar results. A. Chatterjee, R. Dix-Carneiro and J. Vichyanond, 'Multi-Product Firms and Exchange Rate Fluctuations', *American Economic Journal: Economic Policy* 5 (2013), 77–110; H. Tang and Y. Zhang, 'Exchange Rates and the Margins of Trade: Evidence from Chinese Exporters', *CESifo Economic Studies* 58:4 (2012) 671–702.

imports increases and that of exports decreases on impact. This suggests that the short-run impact of currency devaluation on the trade balance, rather than being linear, should look more like a J-curve with an initial worsening and then a subsequent improvement. The short-run impact of exchange rates on trade flows also depends on the currency in which domestic producers invoice their products. The case where a nominal devaluation leads to a one-to-one real devaluation assumes that producers set prices in their home currency. However, a large empirical literature shows that the use of the local, a foreign or a third-country currency such as the US dollar by producers depends on a plethora of variables that vary by country.[25] Finally, a third factor affecting this relationship is the trade structure itself. For instance, a high import content of exports (as in the case of economies that are part of global value chains) reduces the impact of a devaluation on the trade balance as exporters pay a higher price to source their inputs.

Besides these limiting factors, it is generally understood that currency misalignments can have short-run effects on the trade balance. A more controversial issue is whether these effects persist in the longer term or disappear as prices adjust. We turn to this question below.

II. Exchange rates and the trade balance: the long-run

Under perfect markets, economic theory suggests that changes in the level of the exchange rate have no long-run impact on the trade balance. The intuition for this result dates back to the essays of David Hume in the eighteenth century.[26] In the long-term, money is like a veil on the real economy. As nominal prices adjust, relative prices go back to where they were before the policy shock created by the movement in the value of the currency. In this environment, real economic variables, including exports and imports, are ultimately not affected.

Essential in the above logic is the initial premise that markets are perfect. What is the trade effect of a currency misalignment in an economy characterised by market failures? Consider, as an example, an economy that has a potentially profitable export sector. And assume that the growth of exporters is limited by market imperfections such as

[25] L. Goldberg and C. Tille, 'Vehicle Currency Use in International Trade', *Journal of International Economics* 76 (2008), 177–92.

[26] David Hume, *Essays, Noval, Political, and Literary*, Eugene F. Miller ed. (Indianapolis, IN: Liberty Fund Inc., 1987), www.econlib.org/library/LfBooks/Hume/hmMPL26.html.

information asymmetries (e.g., the quality of domestic products is unknown to foreign consumers). As a result of these failures, domestic firms face prohibitively high costs of entering foreign markets and the level of exports is inefficiently low. In this context, an undervalued currency may have a long-run impact on the balance of trade, as it allows exporters to overcome high entry costs in foreign markets. For instance, once they enter, foreign consumers can discover the quality of domestic products, eliminating the original problem of asymmetric information. Whatever the details of the mechanism at play, an exchange rate movement is expected to have a permanent effect on the trade balance when market failures are relevant.[27]

Empirical studies on the long-run impact of currency misalignments on trade do not provide definitive and unanimous evidence. However, some common patterns consistent with the theory have emerged. Freund and Pierola and Di Nino *et al.* find that the positive relationship between currency undervaluation and persistent export growth is strong for developing countries, where market failures of the type discussed above are likely to be pervasive.[28] In contrast, regressions including a broader sample of developing and developed countries tend to show that the trade effect of exchange rate misalignments is not statistically significant in the long-term.[29] This indicates that currency misalignments are unlikely to have permanent effects on the trade balance of advanced economies.

III. Conclusions

This section reviewed the effect of a currency misalignment on the balance of trade. In the short-run, when prices are either fixed or slow

[27] This should not be taken as an indication that a competitive devaluation is an efficient export development strategy. First, an exchange rate devaluation is a second-best instrument to address market failures. Second, trading partners generally react to currency undervaluation by using diverse forms of contingent protection (e.g., M. Knetter and T. J. Prusa, 'Macroeconomic Factors and Antidumping Filings: Evidence from Four Countries,' *Journal of International Economics* 61 (2003), 1–17; C.P. Bown and M.A. Crowley, 'Import Protection, Business Cycles, and Exchange Rates: Evidence from the Great Recession', *Journal of International Economics* 90 (2013), 50–64.

[28] C. Freund and M. D. Pierola, 'Export Surges', *Journal of Development Economics* 97 (2012), 387–95, and V. Di Nino, B. Eichengreen and M. Sbracia, 'Real Exchange Rates, Trade and Growth: Italy 1861–2011', *Bank of Italy Economic History Working Papers*, No. 10 (2011).

[29] M. Haddad and C. Pancaro, 'Can Real Exchange Rate Undervaluation Boost Exports and Growth in Developing Countries? Yes, But Not for Long', *Economic Premise* No. 20 (2010) World Bank.

to adjust, exchange rate devaluations (revaluations) are predicted to improve (worsen) the trade balance. While the theory also adds a series of caveats to this basic notion, the evidence is for the most part supportive. The long-run trade impact of currency misalignments is more controversial. Under perfect markets, exchange rates are predicted to have no impact on the trade balance as prices adjust. But long-run effects emerge in models with market failures. The available evidence supports the view that a positive relationship between a currency undervaluation and an improvement in the trade balance exists only for developing countries, where market failures are more pervasive.

D. Multilateral trade rules related to exchange rates and balance of payments

We distinguish between two types of multilateral trade rules relating to exchange rates and the balance of payments. First, there are *de jure* trade rules that discipline WTO members' exchange rate actions and allow them to take trade restrictive measures in the face of a worsening balance of payments. Second, there are other WTO provisions which allow members to limit imports on grounds not explicitly linked to the exchange rate or the balance of payments but which in reality are used by governments in response to an unfavourable movement in those variables. We call the latter *de facto* rules.

I. De jure *rules*

De jure multilateral trade rules are GATT Articles XII, XV and XVIII and GATS Articles XI, XII and XVI.

GATT Article XII allows a member to restrict the quantity or value of merchandise permitted to be imported in order to safeguard its balance of payments. There are conditions attached to the application of these trade restrictions: they should have the least disruptive effect on trade; there should be no more than one type of trade measure for this purpose; and whenever practicable, there should be a time schedule for the removal of the measures.

GATT Article XVIII allows a developing country member to impose quantitative restrictions in order to safeguard its balance of payments, but also requires the member to eliminate those restrictions when conditions no longer justify the measure. There is only one dispute settlement case that has been litigated and resolved involving Article XVIII which is *India – Quantitative Restrictions*.[30]

In contrast, GATT Article XV is about WTO members' exchange rate actions. The main obligation of GATT Article XV is contained in paragraph 4, namely, 'Contracting parties shall not, by exchange action, frustrate the intent of the provisions of this Agreement'. It has been recently argued that the expression 'exchange action' is very broad and would include exchange-rate policy or exchange-rate management.[31] Although there is some attempt at clarification with respect to what 'frustrate' means, as yet, there has been no jurisprudence or decision of a competent WTO body regarding either the interpretation or application of paragraph 4 of GATT Article XV.[32] One possible explanation for this non-use of Article XV is its legal 'vagueness', which makes it difficult to invoke in dispute settlement.[33] The availability of *de facto* rules, which shall be discussed in greater detail below, may have also dampened the need to use the *de jure* rules.

The GATS deals with payments, transfers and capital movements in Articles XI (Payments and Transfers) and XII (Restrictions to Safeguard the Balance of Payments), and in Footnote 8 to Article XVI (Market Access).

GATS obligations on payments and transfers in Article XI are based on a distinction between current transactions and capital transactions.

30 The dispute concerns import restrictions that India claimed were maintained to protect its balance-of-payments situation. The quantitative restrictions covered 2,714 tariff lines within the eight-digit level of the Harmonized System. The WTO dispute settlement panel found that as India's monetary reserves were adequate, the measures were not necessary to forestall the threat of, or to stop, a serious decline in its monetary reserves.

31 Miranda argues that 'the context of Article XV(4) makes it clear that the drafters intended the term "exchange action" in this provision to be very broad, so as to include a multiplicity of modalities of exchange-rate based-measures. Further, the structure of Article XV(2), taken as relevant context, combined with the preparatory work of Article XV lend further support to the proposition that the term "exchange action" in Article XV(4) includes exchange-rate policy or exchange-rate management.' J. Miranda, 'Currency Undervaluation as a Violation of GATT Article XV:4', in S. Evenett (ed.), *The US-Sino Currency Dispute: New Insights from Economics, Politics and Law* (CEPR, Policy Report No. 2, VoxEu Publication, 2010).

32 However, there have been a number of disputes involving the justifiability of measures under other provisions of GATT Article XV. They include the *Argentina – Textiles and Apparel* case and the *Dominican Republic – Import and Sale of Cigarettes* case. These two cases are discussed in greater detail in R. Howse, 'Towards an Equitable Integration of Monetary and Financial Matters, Trade and Sustainable Development', Chapter 12, this volume.

33 G. C. Hufbauer, Y. Wong and K. Ketki Sheth, 'US-China Trade Disputes: Rising Tide, Rising Stakes. Policy Analyses', in *International Economics* 78 (Washington: Peterson Institute for International Economics, 2006).

Under Article XI, a WTO member having undertaken specific commitments on financial services (or in any other services) is under the obligation not to impose 'restrictions on international transfers and payments for current transactions relating to its specific commitments'. The GATS does not define terms such as 'payments and transfers for current transactions', 'current transactions', 'capital transactions', 'movement of capital' or indeed 'restrictions', although some of these terms have been defined in the IMF Articles of Agreement.

The obligation in paragraph 1 of Article XI to allow for unrestricted international payments and transfers for current transactions is qualified by the general proviso contained in paragraph 2 of the same Article to preserve the rights and obligations of Fund members under the Fund's Articles of Agreement, including the use of exchange actions which are in conformity with the Articles of Agreement.

The second part of GATS Article XI:2 deals with capital transactions. In this case, WTO members are obliged not to impose restrictions on any capital transactions inconsistently with their specific commitments regarding those transactions, except under GATS Article XII (i.e., in the event of serious balance-of-payments and external financial difficulties or threat thereof) or at the request of the IMF.

In addition, the extent of capital movements required by specific commitments is defined in Footnote 8 to paragraph 1 of GATS Article XVI. First, if the member undertook a commitment on the cross-border supply of a service (mode 1), 'and if the cross-border movement of capital is an essential part of the service itself, that Member is thereby committed to allow such movement of capital'. Second, if the WTO member undertook a commitment on the supply of a service through commercial presence, 'it is thereby committed to allow related transfers of capital into its territory'. It can be said therefore that Article XI:2 establishes the nature or the obligation with regard to capital transactions, and that Footnote 8 delimits the extent of the obligation with regard to the capital movements involved. In any case, if a country makes a commitment to liberalise trade with respect to a particular financial service in the GATS, it is not, however, making an across-the-board commitment to freedom of capital movements.

GATS Article XII allows WTO members to impose restrictions on trade in services covered by specific commitments (including on payments or transfers for transactions related to such commitments) 'in the event of serious balance-of-payments and external financial difficulties or threat thereof', but also recognises that 'particular pressures on the balance of payments of a [WTO] Member in the process of economic development or economic transition may necessitate the use of restrictions to ensure, inter alia, the maintenance of a level of financial reserves adequate for the implementation of its programme of economic development or economic transition'.

II. De facto *rules*

Beyond these rules, there is a range of measures – primarily anti-dumping, countervailing and safeguard measures – that the available economic literature suggests are often used by governments to respond to business cycle movements and real exchange rate changes.

Knetter and Prusa found that real exchange rate appreciation in the currencies of the traditional users of anti-dumping – Australia, the EU, Canada and the US – against their trade partners usually led to more initiations of anti-dumping proceedings.[34] In particular, a one-standard deviation real appreciation of the domestic against the foreign currency increases anti-dumping filings against the foreign country by one third. A subsequent paper by Niels and Francois that examined Mexico's experience with anti-dumping protection between 1987 and 2000 found a similar pattern[35] – that the number of anti-dumping complaints against a partner increases when the peso appreciates relative to the partner's currency. Finally, a more recent paper by Bown and Crowley extends the analysis beyond anti-dumping to include safeguards and countervailing duties as well.[36] They discover that for a set of industrialised countries and group of countries – the US, EU, South Korea, Australia and Canada – episodes of real exchange rate appreciation against partner currencies from 1998–2008 led to substantial increases in these forms of contingent protection.

In contrast to the non-use of the *de jure* exchange rate and BOP-related rules, these *de facto* trade instruments are frequently invoked. Since the WTO was established in 1995, each year has seen an average of 236 anti-dumping initiations, fifteen countervailing initiations and thirteen safeguard initiations. These measures are also the subject of a

[34] Knetter and Prusa, 'Macroeconomic Factors and Antidumping Filings'.

[35] G. Niels and J.F. Francois, 'Business Cycles, the Exchange Rate, and Demand for Antidumping Protection in Mexico', *Review of Development Economics* 10 (2006), 388–99.

[36] Bown and Crowley, 'Import Protection, Business Cycles, and Exchange Rates'.

large number of WTO disputes.[37] Although not explicitly designed to deal with the trade repercussions of a real exchange rate appreciation, the evidence is strong that many countries employ these measures to respond to real exchange rate appreciations. Nevertheless, they are imperfect substitutes for a remedy that is directly targeted against exchange rate undervaluation. These trade contingent measures require additional conditions to be met before they can be triggered, e.g. dumping behaviour or government subsidies. Furthermore, they are only useful if exchange rate undervaluation results in intensified import competition at home, but are useless if the affected country is concerned about the erosion of its hold in export markets as a result of undervaluation by its competitor.

E. The role of multilateral trade cooperation in addressing imbalances

The policy changes needed to effect global rebalancing will require international cooperation. As stated earlier, imbalances may create systemic risks that individual countries do not fully take into account when they consider the benefits and costs of rebalancing. Furthermore, it will not be enough if only deficit or surplus countries adjust as the conditions that give rise to imbalances have roots in both. In this Section, we will discuss the potential contribution of multilateral trade cooperation in redressing imbalances, focusing on the three traditional areas of WTO work: market access negotiations, rule-making and dispute settlement. We begin with the area of market access negotiations, focusing on the potential contribution of services sector opening, particularly in the financial sector, to the reduction of imbalances. Then, we turn to dispute settlement and the challenges involved in litigating disputes about exchange rates. Finally, we discuss rule-making and examine the arguments for negotiating new rules on exchange rates or strengthening the existing Article XV to limit exchange rate manipulation.

I. Liberalisation of trade in (financial) services

The level of financial sector development is an important determinant of savings rates and, through this channel, also a driver of global imbalances.

[37] As of end of June 2012, the Anti-dumping Agreement had been referred to in ninety-three requests for consultations and the Safeguards Agreement in forty cases.

There are many reasons why an underdeveloped financial sector could in fact lead to a high savings rate.[38] First, in a fast-growing economy where the desired consumption bundle shifts towards durable goods such as cars and houses, the inability to borrow against future income streams could lead to households saving more in order to self-finance their purchases. Second, lack of diversification opportunities for financial assets, as well as lack of social insurance, could lead households to save more for precautionary purposes. Finally, 'financial repression',[39] which results in low or negative real interest rates, could lead to higher savings – the real interest rate elasticity of savings could be negative if the income effect dominates the substitution effect – something referred to in the literature as the 'target savings hypothesis'.[40]

China is a case in point. Although quantitative measures of financial depth (e.g., bank credit to the private sector and banks' assets representing more than 100 per cent and 240 per cent of GDP, respectively) seem to indicate that for the most part China's financial system is on a par with or even ahead of its economic development, the financial system is unbalanced and incomplete.[41] The securities markets and the insurance sector are underdeveloped compared with the banking system. The banking system itself is unbalanced, with the large state-owned commercial banks (SOBs) holding more than half of banking sector assets. There is also imbalance in the capital markets, where stocks dominate and the corporate bond market remains underdeveloped (stock market

[38] E. Prasad, 'Rebalancing Growth in Asia', *NBER Working Paper* 15169 (Cambridge, MA: National Bureau of Economic Research, 2009).

[39] 'Financial repression' occurs when governments implement policies to channel to themselves funds that in a deregulated market environment would go elsewhere. Policies include directed lending to the government by captive domestic audiences (such as pension funds or domestic banks), explicit or implicit caps on interest rates, regulation of cross-border capital movements and (generally) a tighter connection between government and banks, either explicitly through public ownership of some of the banks or through heavy 'moral suasion' (C. M. Reinhart, J. F. Kirkegaard, and M. B. Sbrancia, 'Financial Repression Redux', *Finance and Development*, June 2011).

[40] The basic idea of the 'target savings hypothesis' is that households have a target level of savings that they want to achieve by the end of their working life, which means that savings rates will tend to be negatively correlated with the real returns on savings. This, of course, is just a way of restating the relative importance of substitution and income effects of changes in interest rates on inter-temporal consumption decisions. The usual presumption is that the substitution effect dominates, so that a lower real rate of return on savings leads to a lower savings rate (Chamon and Prasad, 'Why Are Savings Rates of Urban Households in China Rising?').

[41] World Bank and the Development Research Center of China's State Council 'China 2030: Building a Modern, Harmonious, and Creative High-Income Society' (2012).

capitalisation represents 67 per cent of GDP, roughly seven times the size of corporate bonds outstanding).

The Chinese domestic imbalances (both in the financial sector and between industry and services) as well as the external imbalances are largely due to financial repression.[42] Financial repression in China has taken the form of interest rate controls, directed lending (including through SOBs), barriers to entry, state ownership in the banking sector, and capital account restrictions. In addition, social security underdevelopment has been a significant determinant of the extraordinarily high savings rate in China.

If the negative effects of financial repression and underdevelopment are to be redressed, the Chinese financial system must undergo a series of reforms, including the elimination of market access barriers, opening up of the capital account (both to allow further access to foreign investors and further investment abroad by domestic companies and investors), interest rate deregulation, and even greater privatisation.[43] Through

[42] Recent research suggests that there is a non-linear relationship between financial repression and growth. Governments can use financial repression to allocate limited financial resources, skew relative prices and provide capital to preferred sectors. Huang and Wang have shown that financial repression has helped economic growth in China, and have linked this positive relationship to a prudent and gradual approach to liberalisation. Y. Huang and X. Wang, 'Does Financial Repression Inhibit or Facilitate Economic Growth? A Case Study of Chinese Reform Experience', *Oxford Bulletin of Economics and Statistics* 73 (2011), 833–55. However, as highlighted by Johansson (A. C. Johansson, 'Financial Repression and China's Economic Imbalances', in H. McKay and L. Song (eds.), *Rebalancing and Sustaining Growth in China* (Canberra: ANU E Press, 2012)) their findings also show that the impact of financial repression turned from being positive during the first two decades of reform to being negative in the 2000s. It is not so difficult to understand that at the early stages of development, infrastructure projects (e.g., roads, bridges, ports, airports and power plants) have high returns, and the banking system, even if repressed, may easily focus on these, often urged on by political authorities who are rewarded for generating growth. But once infrastructure has been built up, further financing has to become more capable of discriminating between good and bad projects, and this is when the inadequacies of a highly repressed financial sector become more apparent, and why a repressed financial sector may not contribute to economic growth. A similar point is made by Raghuram G. Rajan, 'Has Finance Made the World Riskier?', *European Financial Management* 12:4 (2006), 499–533.

[43] The current context is however particularly challenging for implementing some of these reforms. As explained by the Bank for International Settlements, the extraordinarily accommodative monetary policies implemented in major advanced economies (e.g., the eurozone, Japan, the UK and the US) 'are being transmitted to emerging economies in the form of undesirable exchange rate and capital flow volatility'. Bank for International Settlements, 'The Limits of Monetary Policy', *BIS Annual Report 2011/2012* (Basel; Bank for International Settlements 2012), Chapter IV.

their impact on savings and investment rates, and on domestic consumption, these policies may in turn help reduce China's large current account surplus. Specifically, a more developed social welfare system (which would reduce the need for precautionary saving by households) as well as financial sector reform with a view to deepening the sector and improving its allocation function would contribute to a fall in the savings rate and an increase in investment.[44]

China has already embarked on a series of significant reforms, doing away with decades of financially repressive policies. For example, it has allowed foreign investors to hold up to 100 per cent ownership of non-bank financial institutions (e.g., personal consumption finance companies), and 49 per cent ownership of securities joint ventures (including joint ventures trading commodity and financial futures). China also agreed to shorten the waiting period ('seasoning period') for securities joint ventures to expand its business scope into brokerage, fund management and other trading activities. Subsidiaries of foreign banks are now allowed to underwrite corporate bonds in the interbank bond market, and foreign and domestic automobile-financing companies, currently dependent on China's state-owned banks for funding, have been authorised to issue bonds regularly, including securitised bonds. In addition, in April 2012 China increased the total dollar amount that foreigners can invest in China's stock and bond markets under its Qualified Foreign Institutional Investor (QFII) Program from US$ 30 billion to US$ 80 billion.[45] All these measures will reduce restrictions on the free flow of capital and contribute to capital market development. However, in spite of these reforms, financial repression still remains in the form of state-ownership of banks, foreign ownership restrictions in various financial services, limitations on business scope and, most importantly, interest rate controls. Indeed, although lending and deposit-taking by banks have been deregulated since 2004, they are still subject to benchmarks set by the People's Bank of China (PBOC). Commercial banks may charge lending

While the WTO can help in supporting domestic financial reforms in a country like China, the growing relevance of monetary policy spillovers suggests that central banks, both in surplus and deficit countries, need to take better account of the global implications of their actions. In our view, this reinforces our plea for a first-best solution based on global coordination of macroeconomic policies to redress the adverse effects of large and persistent global imbalances (see Sections E.II and E.III).

44 OECD 'The Impact of Structural Reforms on Current Account Imbalances', *OECD Economics Department Policy Notes*, No. 3 (2011).

45 For an exhaustive description of recent regulatory developments in the Chinese financial sector, see WTO document WT/TPR/S/264 (Trade Policy Review – China – Report by the Secretariat), 8 May 2012; and WTO document WT/TPR/OV/W/6 (Report to the TPRB from the Director-General on Trade-related Developments), 28 June 2012.

rates above the benchmark (but not lower than 90 per cent of the benchmark) and offer deposit rates below – but not above – the benchmark. Market-based interest rates are allowed in the short-term interbank money markets and bond markets.[46] Further deregulation of interest rates would allow Chinese households to earn a higher return on their savings, supporting greater household consumption, and would make exchange rate intervention and the build-up of foreign reserves more costly.

The WTO can provide a suitable forum for negotiating and implementing many of these reforms, in particular those dealing with the elimination of market access barriers (e.g., foreign ownership restrictions, limitations on business scope) and the creation of a level playing field between Chinese and foreign financial service suppliers. Apart from the credibility combined with predictability gains that may ensue from improved GATS/WTO commitments, negotiations can provide for the staging of commitments over time, ensuring an appropriate sequencing of reforms. Appropriate sequencing of policies will be crucial for the success of financial sector reforms in China.[47]

Together with China, Germany and the oil-exporting countries make up the bulk of global current account surpluses. The underlying drivers of these other countries' surpluses are different from China's. Except for the period of re-unification in the 1990s, Germany has been running current account surpluses for decades. However, the current account of the euro bloc, on average, has been balanced. Moreover, a striking feature of the eurozone's experience over its first ten years is that some countries have systematically exhibited current account surpluses while others have had continuous deficits.[48] As long as the eurozone's current

[46] See WT/TPR/S/264.

[47] Johansson ('Financial Repression and China's Economic Imbalances') argues in that regard that although capital account liberalisation is important, a complete opening up of the capital account should come only after other financial reforms. Interest rate restrictions play an important role in fuelling the banking system with cheap capital, so a sudden and comprehensive liberalisation of the capital account could generate a massive outflow of capital. Before a complete reform of the capital account can take place, three preliminary reforms need to be implemented. These are interest rate liberalisation, exchange rate flexibility and strengthening of supervision and regulatory practice in the banking system. There is also a need for sufficiently developed domestic capital markets, because they provide incentives for further commercialisation of domestic banks, enable absorption of large capital inflows and reduce the risk of currency mismatches.

[48] F. P. Mongelli and C. Wyplosz, 'The Euro at Ten: Unfulfilled Threats and Unexpected Challenges', in B. Mackowiak, F. P. Mongelli, G. Noblet and F. Smets (eds.), *The Euro at Ten – Lessons and Challenges* (European Central Bank, 2009).

account is close to balanced, Germany's current account surplus is basically a European – not global – issue.[49]

The factors behind Germany's external surpluses do not primarily reflect market failures or policy-induced distortions.[50] Much of Germany's high level of savings is a rational response to the ageing of its population.[51] Similarly, Germany's strong export performance is a reflection of just how globally competitive its companies are. As said above, generally speaking, large current account balances (either positive or negative) are only undesirable insofar as they reflect distortions in the economy. That said, in mature economies such as Germany's, a current account surplus may arise from investing too little, rather than saving too much. Over the period 1995–2009, Germany had the lowest net investment share in net domestic product among all OECD countries.[52] The decline in domestic investment by the corporate sector in the first half of the 2000s seems to have contributed significantly to the increase in the current account surplus.[53] This decline in domestic business investment was reflected in net capital outflows, which took the form of foreign direct investment in Eastern Europe and foreign net lending by banks.

The reasons for investment being relatively low in Germany are not entirely clear. Several explanations have been suggested, including the uncertainty about the durability of the upswing in external demand; low productivity growth, particularly in the non-tradable sector; and gaps and distorted incentives in the financial sector. In the case of the financial sector, a relatively underdeveloped framework for venture capital and private equity, as well as an inefficient insolvency process, may explain the low investment in high-risk, high-growth sectors. At the same time, large Landesbanken (regional state-owned banks) have been more inclined to invest overseas than domestically. Germany's labour and total factor productivity growth has been lower than the OECD average for the last decade at least, dragged down by a poor performance of its

49 J. Aizenman and R. Sengupta, 'Global Imbalances: Is Germany the New China? A Skeptical View', *Open Economy Review* 22 (2011), 387–400.

50 IMF, 'Germany: Sustainability Report', prepared by the staff of the International Monetary Fund for the G-20 (2011).

51 Aizenman and Sengupta, 'Global Imbalances'; IMF, 'Germany: Sustainability Report'; C. Wyplosz, 'Germany, Current Accounts and Competitiveness', *VoxEu*, 31 March 2010.

52 H.-W. Sinn, T. Buchen and T. Wollmershauser, 'Trade Imbalances: Causes, Consequences, and Policy Measures', in J. T. Boorman and A. Icard (eds.), *Reform of the International Monetary System: The Palais Royal Initiative, Emerging Markets Forum* (Thousand Oaks, CA: Sage, 2011).

53 OECD, *OECD Economic Surveys: Germany* (Paris: OECD, 2010).

services sector. In business services, for example, productivity grew by 0.9 per cent a year in Germany in the period 2000–8, against an average of 1.7 per cent in the OECD.[54] It has been argued that one factor holding back productivity is the burdensome regulation in some services sectors, in particular professional services.[55] Germany ranks twenty-second out of twenty-seven OECD countries in terms of strictness and this is mostly due to domestic regulations, such as restrictions on advertising and fees, compulsory chamber membership, and licence and permit systems more burdensome than those of other countries.[56]

To some extent, these factors affecting Germany's current account surplus are mutually reinforcing.[57] Weak productivity growth, particularly in the services sector, reduces incentives to invest, holding back potential output and income, and thus consumption. In turn, lower domestic demand reduces the incentive to invest, notably in the services sector, thus dampening demand for labour and keeping wages and consumption depressed. A broad reform agenda, for services and for the financial sector in particular, could unleash Germany's domestic growth potential. A larger, more productive services sector would increase the relative importance of the domestic economy. New businesses in the services sector are also likely to trigger higher investment, at least initially, and the creation of new jobs would support consumption. Both higher consumption and investment would tend to increase imports, potentially reducing the current account surplus while strengthening growth. Since the domestic regulations identified as hampering productivity growth in Germany are not amenable to market access negotiations in the GATS, the role of multilateral cooperation in this case seems to be, *prima facie*, relatively limited. That said, future disciplines on domestic regulation under the GATS, with their emphasis on transparency, objectivity and impartiality, simplification of procedures and recognition of equivalence of qualifications, might create over time a dynamic conducive to less trade-restrictive regulation of services, and thus support and consolidate individual countries' efforts in that regard.[58]

[54] OECD, *OECD Economic Surveys: Germany* (Paris: OECD, 2012).
[55] OECD, *Economic Surveys: Germany* 2010. [56] *Ibid.*
[57] IMF, 'Germany: Sustainability Report'.
[58] For a discussion on the development of disciplines on domestic regulation under the GATS, see WTO *World Trade Report 2012 - Trade and Public Policies: A Closer Look at Non-tariff Measures in the 21st Century* (Geneva: World Trade Organization, 2012); in particular pp. 184–6.

Oil exporting countries are nowadays the main counterpart to the US current account deficit.[59] Still, these large surpluses may be considered as structural, reflecting oil price developments. Normally, a large current account surplus would be eroded over time by stronger domestic spending and a higher exchange rate. But these countries' currencies are pegged, or closely linked, to the dollar. While a more flexible exchange rate might assist global rebalancing, floating exchange rates might also lead to excessive volatility and discourage diversification of these economies (by making other sectors uncompetitive as the currency appreciates). At this juncture, the most effective policy tool to reduce oil exporters' current account surpluses seems to be public spending and investment, in particular because of its high import content.[60] Increased public spending on infrastructure as well as on services such as education, health care and housing, as well as the elimination of the remaining market access barriers in various services sectors, could also help these economies diversify away from oil. And here there may be a role for the WTO to play as well. Take the example of Saudi Arabia, the major oil-exporting country, and one which is running a very significant current account surplus on its own. Saudi Arabia made extensive commitments, not least on services, when acceding to the WTO. While access to the Saudi services market should be enhanced, and the remaining barriers eliminated, ideally through multilateral services negotiations, there is an additional WTO area of work that may contribute to improving Saudi Arabia's domestic investment and consumption: the negotiations on government procurement. Opening its domestic procurement market, combined with increased public spending, could increase imports (while ensuring at the same time an efficient allocation of the public sector's resources), thus helping reduce the current account surplus.

We turn now to the 'deficit country' *par excellence*, namely the US. The dominant factor behind the US current account deficits over the past decade has been the decline in domestic savings, both by households (who borrowed against increasing house prices and rising asset prices more generally) and the public sector, which led to significant fiscal deficits.[61] Any reduction of the US current account deficit should

[59] This year the IMF expects oil-exporting countries to run a collective record surplus of US$ 740 billion, three-fifths of which will come from the Middle East. That will dwarf China's expected surplus of US$ 180 billion. Since 2000 the cumulative surpluses of oil exporters have amounted to more than US$ 4 trillion, twice as much as that of China. See 'Petrodollar profusion – Oil exporters are the main drivers of global imbalances', *The Economist*, 28 April 2012.

[60] *Ibid.* [61] Blanchard and Milesi-Ferretti, 'Global Imbalances'.

imply therefore an increase in savings rates by households and reductions of the fiscal deficit through fiscal policy. In that context, there seems to be little the WTO can contribute. However, this first reading may be misleading.

A closer look at the US figures shows that the bulk of the US current account deficit is accounted for by merchandise trade deficit. In the case of services trade however, the US has been constantly running a very significant surplus, while China, Germany and Saudi Arabia in particular have been running trade deficits (see Table 13.2). In other words, when we look at trade in services, the imbalances are reversed. This is a reflection of the overwhelming comparative advantage that the US has in services. It

Table 13.2. *Services trade balance, selected countries: 2007–11*

Item	2007 US$ (billions)	2007 Percentage of GDP	2011 US$ (billions)	2011 Percentage of GDP
Surplus countries				
US	135.7	1.0	185.6	1.2
UK	89.8	3.2	103.3	4.2
euro area ('periphery')				
Greece	23.1	7.6	19.3	6.4
Spain	31.1	2.2	47.1	3.2
financial centres				
Hong Kong, China	42.2	20.4	65.7	27.0
Switzerland	32.7	7.3	47.4	7.2
Deficit countries				
euro area ('core')				
Germany	−41.2	−1.2	−35.7	−1.0
oil exporters				
Saudi Arabia	−30.2	−7.8	−43.8	−7.3
Russia	−17.8	−1.4	−34.5	−1.9
East Asia				
China	−7.6	−0.2	−54.1	−0.7
Japan	−21.6	−0.5	−23.3	−0.4

Source: WTO Secretariat and World Economic Outlook Database (October 2012).
Note: Based on balance of payments data.

becomes clear then that the WTO services negotiations could contribute to a reduction of global imbalances by improving US exporters' access to foreign markets. In addition, services trade liberalisation, supported by WTO negotiations, would enhance competition and efficiency, and raise productivity in all economies, including surplus countries.

II. Litigation in the WTO

A number of scholars have proposed bringing exchange rate controversies within the scope of the WTO.[62] The essential argument is that, since exchange rate misalignments may have trade effects that are comparable to other border measures such as import tariffs and export subsidies, WTO members should be allowed to litigate exchange rate practices in the context of the WTO dispute resolution system. These proposals have created a large academic and policy debate, a significant part of which is collected by Evenett.[63] Since a full review of this literature is beyond the scope of the present chapter, we only attempt to place this issue in the broader context of the debate on trade imbalances and multilateral trade rules.

When thinking of the possibility of litigating exchange rate policy in the WTO, there are essentially two separate (albeit overlapping) issues to consider. A first question concerns the practical implementation of WTO adjudication in this area; the second relates to the efficient design of rules to address the trade effects of exchange rate policy. Let us briefly look at these two issues.

Can exchange rate practices be efficiently adjudicated in the WTO system? There are several concerns that have emerged in the literature. Most of these concerns focus on the legal difficulties of bringing an

[62] C. F. Bergsten, 'The Global Imbalances and the US Economy, Testimony before the Subcommittees on Trade, Ways and Means Committee: Commerce, Trade and Consumer Protection, Energy and Commerce Committee; and Domestic and International Monetary Policy, Trade and Technology', Financial Services Committee of the House of Representatives, 9 May 2007; M. Goldstein, 'Confronting Asset Bubbles, Too Big to Fail, and Beggar-thy-Neighbor Exchange Rate Policies', Peterson Institute for International Economics, Paper based on remarks delivered on 15 December 2009 at the workshop 'The International Monetary System: Looking to the Future, Lessons from the Past', February 2010, www.iie.com/publications/papers/goldstein0210.pdf; Hufbauer *et al.*, 'US-China Trade Disputes'; A. Mattoo and A. Subramanian, 'Currency Undervaluation and Sovereign Wealth Funds: A New Role for the World Trade Organization', *The World Economy* 32 (2009), 1135–64.

[63] S. Evenett, *The US-Sino Currency Dispute: New Insight from Economics, Politics and Law* (London: Centre for European Policy Research, 2010).

exchange rate case to the WTO under current rules. Can Article XV of the GATT form the basis of such a dispute? Or should WTO rules on subsidies be invoked? Here we set aside these considerations altogether and limit ourselves to what appear to us to be the two most pressing concerns from an economic perspective. First, currency manipulation is difficult to identify. An important reason for this is that there are several causes, beyond direct policy actions, that can lead to a currency misalignment. Essentially, this is because exchange rates are endogenous variables that result from the complex interaction of macroeconomic, structural, financial and trade determinants. A second concern is that trade effects of exchange rates may be difficult to establish.[64] For example, even in the short-run when prices are slow to adjust and currency misalignments have an impact on trade, the equivalence between exchange rate policy and trade policy instruments, such as import tariffs and export subsidies, hinges on the invoicing decisions of firms. These observations imply that the application of current WTO rules to exchange rate policy is, at best, a highly complex matter in practice.[65] Needless to say, authors disagree on the extent to which these practical problems can be overcome.

The second element of the debate on the role of WTO dispute resolution in exchange rate matters concerns the design of multilateral trade rules and the broader issue of the place of the trading system in global economic governance. The rules of the WTO are clearly not written in stone and can and should be adjusted as underlying economic problems evolve. But the current debate seems to miss an important point on the nature of exchange rates. As we argued above, currency misalignments are caused by a multiplicity of factors. For example, while both high foreign reserve accumulation and aggregate savings may lead to currency undervaluation, there is an essential difference between the two causes of the misalignment. The first is a policy action under the direct control of the monetary authority, while excess savings are influenced by structural conditions (such as the lack of an adequate social insurance mechanism) that a policy-maker can only change in the medium term. More importantly, correcting these macroeconomic and structural distortions solely

[64] R. W. Staiger and A. O. Sykes, '"Currency Manipulation" and World Trade', *World Trade Review* 9 (2010), 583–627.

[65] For a study on the potential exchange rate disputes that may be brought before the DSB, see G. Z. Marceau and J. J. Maughan, 'The WTO Dispute Settlement Mechanism in Matters Involving Exchange Rates and Trade', Chapter 14, this volume.

through the multilateral trade system does not seem efficient from a global governance perspective. As the cause of such distortions is not trade itself, but rather trade is the channel through which distortions spill over into other countries, a simple first-best argument would suggest that it is international cooperation in macroeconomic and structural policies that needs to be reinforced. In brief, any talk of reform of WTO rules in this domain cannot be dissociated from the nature of exchange rates and the role that the trading system should play in the broader global governance framework.

III. WTO rulemaking

The many proposals we have referred to see WTO rules (whether these rules are embodied in GATT Article XV, the Agreement on Subsidies and Countervailing Measures (SCM Agreement), or a new exchange rule to be negotiated by WTO members), in very narrow terms as instruments to deliver sanctions. This is not to argue that the use of trade sanctions cannot be part of the broader international solution to global imbalances. But the nature of these proposals is a symptom of a 'coherence gap' in global governance that has prompted some to conceive WTO rules as devices to make up for the weakness in international cooperation in macroeconomic, exchange rate and structural policies. The IMF has rules on exchange rates and exchange rate manipulation (Article IV) but these rules have seldom been effectively used.[66] The G-20 has established a working group to deal with the issues of economic growth and global imbalances, the Framework Working Group for Strong, Sustainable and Balanced Growth. While this group has made substantial progress in identifying and monitoring the broad set of policies that are the root causes of imbalances, the idea of introducing simple and enforceable rules has met resistance from several members.

As stated above, the first-best solution is international cooperation in macroeconomic, exchange rate and structural policies to deal with the roots of imbalances. With that in place, a general argument can be made for sanctions to deter countries from either free-riding or defecting from the cooperative outcome. Such arguments have been made to address other problem areas, most notably in the case of international environmental

[66] M. Mussa, 'IMF Surveillance over China's Exchange Rate Policy', Paper presented at the Conference on China's Exchange Rate Policy, Peterson Institute, Washington, DC, 19 October 2007.

externalities.[67] If there is international agreement that sanctions are to form part of the solution to imbalances, they should apply to both surplus and deficit countries. Furthermore, given the manifold roots of the imbalances, policies beyond exchange rates, such as those contributing to fiscal deficits, will need to be subjected to the same or to an even greater degree of international scrutiny. Otherwise, there will be serious gaps in how the global community deals with rebalancing. Sanctions that target only exchange rates would mean that imbalances in currency unions would not be dealt with as part of a broader solution. Also, a trade sanction that targets only surplus countries and focuses on the exchange rate would be politically problematic. There is a danger that the initiative might be seen as targeting specific countries, e.g., China, which would therefore have no incentive to support the idea. Finally, the set of penalties would need to go further than trade sanctions. The idea of a Tobin tax on cross-border capital flows to reduce the incentive for surplus countries to continue accumulating savings and to make importing capital less attractive for deficit countries has been resurrected by some commentators.[68] Krueger has suggested (i) taxes on the new debt or on all new financial instruments issued by deficit countries which fail to take steps to rebalance or (ii) financial penalties along the lines of those envisaged in the EU for surplus and deficit countries.[69]

With this understanding, it will be possible to support efforts to negotiate a new rule on exchange rates as suggested by Mattoo and Subramanian, or to amend existing rules such as GATT Article XV or even the SCM Agreement, so that they can be effectively used by members. As noted above, there are a number of still formidable questions that will need to be resolved – determining whether an exchange rate is undervalued and whether undervaluation is due to government action – but they do not appear to be insurmountable hurdles.

[67] S. Barrett, 'The Strategy of Trade Sanctions in International Environmental Agreements', *Resource and Energy Economics* 19 (1997), 345–61; M. Botteon and C. Carraro, 'Strategies for Environmental Negotiations: Issue Linkage with Heterogeneous Countries', in N. Hanley and H. Folmer (eds.), *Game Theory and Climate Change* (Cheltenham: Edward Elgar, 1998).

[68] H. Dieter and R. Higgott, 'Managing Global Imbalances: Is it Time to Consider Some Form of Sanctions?', in S. Claessens, S. Evenett and B. Hoekman *et al.* (eds.), *Rebalancing the Global Economy: A Primer for Policymaking* (London: Centre for Economic Policy Research, 2010), pp. 197–204.

[69] A. O. Krueger, 'Persistent Global Imbalances', in S. Claessens, S. Evenett and B. Hoekman (eds.), *Rebalancing the Global Economy: A Primer for Policymaking* (London: Centre for Economic Policy Research, 2010), pp. 185–190.

F. Conclusions

The risks presented by large and persistent trade and current account imbalances justify concerted international action towards rebalancing. Multilateral trade cooperation can contribute to this process in two important ways. First, market opening efforts in services, including in the area of financial services, can reduce policy-related distortions and market imperfections in surplus countries that lead to the build-up of unsustainable imbalances. Services liberalisation can also contribute to economic diversification in oil-exporting economies, to a more domestic-demand-driven growth model in other surplus countries, such as China and Germany, and to the expansion of external sources of demand in the US.

Second, we have argued that the first-best solution to correct large and persistent global imbalances is international cooperation in macroeconomic, exchange rate and structural policies with a view to dealing with the roots of the imbalances. In that context, if such a framework could be put in place, there is a general efficiency argument that could be made for the use of sanctions to enforce cooperative behaviour towards rebalancing. However, this requires that both surplus and deficit countries be subject to sanctions, that all important roots of the imbalances be subject to international scrutiny and that sanctions beyond trade be included as well. WTO-triggered trade actions could form part of a broader solution to prevent the build-up of unsustainable imbalances in the future. But this requires addressing a 'coherence gap' in global governance, because trade rules alone would not provide an efficient instrument to compensate for the weaknesses in international co-operation in macroeconomic, exchange rate and structural policies.

14

The WTO dispute settlement mechanism in matters involving exchange rates and trade

GABRIELLE Z. MARCEAU AND JOHN J. MAUGHAN

A. Introduction – the relationship of exchange rates and international trade

Since the advent of the global financial crisis in 2008, the issue of how exchange rates relate to international trade has been a frequent subject of debate. In particular, there has been widespread speculation that the World Trade Organization (WTO) Dispute Settlement Body (DSB) could be called upon to adjudicate a dispute surrounding Members' exchange rate policies. This chapter offers a modest description of the various types of challenges that could arguably be brought before the DSB in potential exchange rate disputes. It does not address the validity or WTO-consistency of potential claims and defences.

The relationship between exchange rates and trade is an old concern addressed in the provisions of the original General Agreement on Tariffs and Trade (GATT), drafted in 1947. The relationship has since been well-established, but remains extremely complex. In the context of the Working Group on Trade, Debt and Finance, the WTO Secretariat prepared a review of economic literature on the relationship between exchange rates and international trade and, in particular, to what extent an exchange rate or currency 'misalignment' could impact on Members' economies.[1] The study offered no firm conclusions on the exact interaction between exchange rates and trade, but rather highlighted the

The views expressed in this article do not bind WTO Members or the WTO Secretariat. Thank you to Christian Häberli for his valuable comments on the chapter, to Melanie Wahl and Susanna Waltman.

[1] See Note by the Secretariat, The Relationship Between Exchange Rates and International Trade: A Review of Economic Literature, WT/WGTDF/W/57, 27 September 2011; Note by the Secretariat, The Relationship Between Exchange Rates and International Trade: A Short Update of Recent Economic Literature, WT/WGTDF/W/65, 18 July 2012. Also see J. Marchetti, M. Ruta and R. Teh, 'Trade Imbalances and Multilateral Trade Cooperation', Chapter 13, this volume.

complexity of the issue, the number of variables at work and the avenues for current economic research in this area.

Although some argue that the WTO is not the proper forum to address exchange-related disputes, others point out the possibility that the trade-related effects of exchange policies could lead to a dispute among WTO Members. For example, some economists have noted that an allegedly undervalued currency could affect trade partners on both the export and import sides, acting in the first case as an export subsidy and, in the second case, as a higher import duty. In that context, it has been suggested that Members could seek to use the WTO dispute settlement mechanism (DSM) to address the alleged currency situation by claiming that a member's exchange measures violate a WTO provision or nullify or impair benefits under the WTO Agreement. Alternatively, some suggest that a member could impose countervailing duties (CVDs), anti-dumping (AD) duties or increased import tariffs to counter the supposed trade effects of an allegedly misaligned currency. The member targeted by these trade remedies could then seek to have them reviewed at the WTO. In either case, the DSB could be obligated to resolve the dispute under the Dispute Settlement Understanding (DSU).

Adding to the complexity of this issue in the realm of international law is the fact that exchange rates and trade are governed by two different international organisations with overlapping and sometimes uncertain jurisdictions. Indeed, Article XV:9 of the General Agreement on Tariffs and Trade (GATT) makes clear that an exchange rate measure consistent with International Monetary Fund (IMF) rules could not be considered inconsistent with GATT Article XV, which prohibits exchange rate measures that frustrate the intent of other GATT provisions. It is probably for this reason that Article XV obliges the WTO under certain circumstances to consult with the IMF. But to what extent must the WTO consult the IMF? If such consultations were to take place, who would consult and how? To what extent would a panel be bound by the determinations of the IMF or technical experts, especially in a matter as complex as the relationship between exchange rates and trade? The DSB has never been asked to adjudicate any exchange-related trade dispute and members have not adopted any formal interpretations or other legal instrument concerned with this topic.

Based on publicly available information, this chapter introduces the various angles through which an exchange-related trade dispute could be submitted to the WTO DSM. It also reviews related procedural issues that could become relevant in the event of such a dispute. As such, this chapter serves as a modest starting point for understanding the procedural elements of using the WTO dispute settlement system in the context of an exchange-related trade dispute.

B. WTO jurisdiction in exchange-related trade disputes

Under the DSU, WTO Members can initiate disputes by making three broad types of claims: a claim of 'violation' of one or more WTO provisions, a claim of 'non-violation' or a 'situation' claim. The most common type, violation claims, may be either *de jure* or *de facto*. This Section introduces these aspects of WTO dispute settlement in the context of exchange-related disputes.

I. Automaticity of the WTO dispute settlement mechanism

The DSB is required to address any dispute initiated by Members under the terms of the DSU and the WTO Agreements it covers. Under the DSU, Members initiate a dispute by filing a request for consultations. After this initial period of consultations, if the Members have not come to an agreement, the complainant may request the DSB to establish a panel.

The WTO adjudication process would begin automatically. DSU Article 6:1 states that, 'If the complaining party so requests, a panel *shall* be established. . .' (emphasis added). Under DSU Article 23:1, the panel's jurisdiction is exclusive and compulsory.[2] The parties' legal and economic interests in the dispute are presumed and the procedural stages remain quasi-automatic throughout the dispute. Any overlapping jurisdiction between the WTO and other international organisations such as the IMF could not prevent a WTO member from initiating dispute settlement proceedings or establishing a panel.

Unless the complainant agrees otherwise, panels and the Appellate Body (AB) have the obligation to adjudicate all disputes brought by WTO Members. So far no panel or AB report has reached a conclusion of *non liquet*.[3]

[2] DSU Article 23:1 states:

> When Members seek the redress of a violation of obligations or other nullification or impairment of benefits under the covered agreements or an impediment to the attainment of any objective of the covered agreements, they shall have recourse to, and abide by, the rules and procedures of this Understanding.

[3] The expression *non liquet* is a legal term derived from Latin, meaning 'it is not clear'. It is used by judges to indicate that there is no law presented to the court to allow it to

If the case proceeds, both parties have the opportunity to submit two sets of written and oral submissions asserting their claims and rebuttals. The burden of proof, according to the AB in *US – Wool Shirts and Blouses*, 'rests upon the party, whether complaining or defending, who asserts the affirmative of a particular claim or defence'.[4] In general, it is for the complainant to establish a *prima facie* case of violation of one or more WTO provisions. The burden then shifts to the responding party to rebut the complainant's *prima facie* case. The panel must weigh and balance the evidence and legal arguments presented by both sides.[5] However, an exchange-related dispute may be initiated by the author of an exchange rate action (in response to the aggrieved Member's unilateral imposition of trade remedies), or by the Member claiming to be aggrieved. The choice of action therefore has a direct impact on the burden of proof in any potential dispute. Indeed, in the former scenario the initial burden of proof would be on the author of the exchange rate action challenging the trade remedy taken as a reaction to the exchange rate action; in the latter scenario, the initial burden of proof would be with the victim of the exchange rate actions challenging the author of the exchange rate action.

II. Three legal bases for claims: violation, non-violation and situation complaints

GATT Article XXIII illustrates three ways in which a member may seek redress that remain applicable, under DSU Article 3.1, to the WTO Agreement as a whole. These include, first, violation complaints under Article XXIII:1(a), whereby the member alleges 'the failure of another

rule on the matter. The AB has confirmed that the WTO dispute jurisdiction is compulsory. In *US – Shrimp*, it noted that, '. . . in the absence up to now of any agreed amendments or modifications to the substantive provisions of the GATT 1994 and the WTO Agreement generally, we must fulfill our responsibility in this specific case, which is to interpret the existing language of the chapeau of Article XX by examining its ordinary meaning, in light of its context and object and purpose in order to determine whether the United States measure at issue qualifies for justification under Article XX'. See WTO Appellate Body Report, *United States – Import Prohibition of Certain Shrimp and Shrimp Products* ('*US – Shrimp*'), WT/DS58/AB/R, adopted 6 November 1998, para. 155.

4 WTO Appellate Body Report, *United States – Measure Affecting Imports of Woven Wool Shirts and Blouses from India*, WT/DS33/AB/R, adopted 23 May 1997, para. 335.

5 WTO Appellate Body Report, *United States – Measures Affecting the Cross-Border Supply of Gambling and Betting Services*, WT/DS285/AB/R, adopted 20 April 2005, para. 140–141; WTO Panel Report, *US – Sections 301–310 of the Trade Act of 1974*, WT/DS152/R, adopted 27 January 2000, para. 7.14–7.16.

contracting party to carry out its obligations under this Agreement'. The AB has interpreted this provision to cover violations of the letter of another GATT provision.[6] Second, paragraph (b) covers 'the application by another contracting party of any measure, whether or not it conflicts with the provisions of this Agreement'. This is the basis for all 'non-violation' complaints. Finally, the so-called 'situation complaint' under paragraph (c) covers 'the existence of any other situation'. Paragraph (c) has never been interpreted or applied by a competent WTO body and we therefore do not consider it further.

This leaves Members with two options in case of a complaint regarding another Member's exchange rate or currency measures. First, Members may raise a violation complaint. The aggrieved Member may go directly to the DSB claiming a (*de jure* or *de facto*) violation of one of the provisions of the WTO Agreement. These claims could include, *inter alia*, GATT Article XV covering 'Exchange Arrangements', GATT Article II on Members' Schedules of Concessions and the SCM Agreement regarding subsidies.[7] Alternatively, should the aggrieved Member take various trade remedies, the Member targeted by the trade may bring a (*de jure* or *de facto*) violation complaint to the WTO asserting that these remedies violate the provisions governing how Members impose trade remedies. Such claims may include, *inter alia*, the SCM Agreement and GATT Article VI on countervailing duties, the Agreement on the Implementation of Article VI of the GATT 1994 (AD Agreement)[8] and GATT Article VI on anti-dumping duties, and higher import tariffs under Article II.

Second, Members may initiate a non-violation complaint under GATT Article XXIII:1(b) and DSU Article 26.1. The purpose of Article XXIII:1(b) is 'to protect the balance of concessions under GATT by providing a means to redress government actions, not otherwise regulated by GATT rules, but which nonetheless nullify or impair a Member's legitimate expectations of benefits from tariff negotiations'.[9] The complainant could claim, either on

[6] WTO Appellate Body Report, *European Communities – Measures Affecting Asbestos and Asbestos-Containing Products* ('*EC – Asbestos*'), WT/DS135/AB/R, adopted 5 April 2001, para. 185.

[7] Agreement on Subsidies and Countervailing Measures, 15 April 1994, Marrakesh Agreement Establishing the World Trade Organization, Annex 1A.

[8] Agreement on Implementation of Article VI of the General Agreement on Tariffs and Trade 1994, 15 April 1994, Marrakesh Agreement Establishing the World Trade Organization, Annex 1A.

[9] WTO Panel Report, *Japan – Measures Affecting Consumer Photographic Film and Paper* ('*Japan – Film*'), WT/DS44/R, adopted 22 April 1998, para. 10.50.

its own or together with a violation claim, that a Member's exchange rate or currency practices nullify or impair its benefits or the attainment of any other objective under the GATT. Both potential violation and non-violation claims involving exchange rates are addressed in Section C below.

III. Possibility of de jure *and* de facto *violations*

A further important distinction frames the analysis below. Under the DSU, complainants may bring claims of either *de jure* or *de facto* violation of WTO provisions. The AB in *EC – Bananas III* found that the 'treatment no less favourable' requirement under GATT Articles I and II (as well as under other provisions such as GATS Article II) includes not only violations in law (*de jure*), but violations in fact (*de facto*).[10] As such, even when a member's exchange or currency measures do not violate the letter of a WTO provision, their operation and application may nevertheless be found to violate those provisions in fact. Although controversial, it has been suggested that complainants in exchange rate and currency disputes could raise *de facto* violation complaints under, *inter alia*, the most-favoured nation (MFN), market access or national treatment obligations of GATT 1994 (Articles I, II and III).

IV. Presumption of nullification and impairment

The conclusion of a panel that a challenged measure violates any WTO provision carries a presumption of nullification or impairment of the complaining party's rights under GATT Article XXIII:1(a).[11] In practice, this means that complainants do not have to submit evidence on the trade effects of a challenged measure. The respondent could rebut that presumption by showing that no such nullification or impairment exists. This GATT presumption, codified in DSU Article 3.8, has never been successfully reversed.

[10] WTO Appellate Body Report, *European Communities – Regime for the Importation, Sale and Distribution of Bananas*, WT/DS27/AB/R, adopted 25 September 1997, para. 232.

[11] DSU Article 3.8.

C. Scenarios involving exchange rates in WTO dispute settlement

This section briefly summarises the types of exchange-related actions that could be brought to the DSB, including both violation and non-violation complaints. Because the WTO DSM is compulsory, the DSB would probably be obliged to establish a panel, if in either scenario a Member so requested. We therefore examine briefly the various components of these two alternative procedural courses.

I. Violation complaints before the DSB

Violation claims are the most common cause of action in the DSB. Members could take either 'offensive' or 'defensive' actions against another Member's exchange-related measures. For example, a Member could go on the offensive by taking a claim of violation or non-violation of a WTO provision by another Member directly to the DSB. A Member could also take defensive action by imposing unilateral trade remedies such as CVDs, AD duties or import tariffs to offset the alleged trade effects of another Member's exchange rate actions. The affected Member could then challenge these duties before the DSB.

1. Taking the 'offensive': claim that an exchange-related measure violates a WTO provision

The likely object of a Member 'taking the offensive' would be to challenge the WTO-consistency of a measure directly, with a view to obliging the implementing Member to bring the exchange rate measure into conformity with the relevant WTO provisions. As noted above, these claims may be either *de jure* or *de facto* and they are organised as such in our discussion below.

(a) *De jure* violations It has been suggested that Members could attempt to make *de jure* violation claims against another Member's exchange-related actions under GATT Article XV, GATT Article II or the SCM Agreement. GATT Article XV governs Members' 'Exchange Arrangements', GATT Article II binds a Member's tariffs according to its Schedule of Concessions and the SCM Agreement regulates Members' use of subsidies.

(i) *GATT Article XV – exchange arrangements* GATT Article XV is the central provision dealing with exchange rates under GATT 1994. It prohibits WTO Member governments from frustrating the intent of the GATT or the IMF Articles through exchange action.[12] Article XV:4 and accompanying Ad Note provide:

> Contracting parties shall not, by exchange action, frustrate* the intent of the provisions of this Agreement, nor, by trade action, the intent of the provisions of the Articles of Agreement of the International Monetary Fund.
>
> *Ad Article XV, paragraph 4
>
> The word 'frustrate' is intended to indicate, for example, that infringements of the letter of any Article of this Agreement by exchange action shall not be regarded as a violation of that Article if, in practice, there is no appreciable departure from the intent of the Article. Thus, a contracting party which, as part of its exchange control operated in accordance with the Articles of Agreement of the International Monetary Fund, requires payment to be received for its exports in its own currency or in the currency of one or more members of the International Monetary Fund will not thereby be deemed to contravene Article XI or Article XIII. Another example would be that of a contracting party which specifies on an import licence the country from which the goods may be imported, for the purpose not of introducing any additional element of discrimination in its import licensing system but of enforcing permissible exchange controls.

Article XV establishes the terms under which a GATT panel is authorised to adjudicate a dispute involving a Member's exchange rate policies.[13] To date, the provision has never been formally interpreted, nor has it been the subject of a dispute settlement claim or proceeding. There is thus no clear guidance from WTO panels or the AB on how to interpret and apply the provision. The panel in such a dispute would

[12] The legitimate reasons for which a Member may take exchange actions are not covered by the WTO Agreement. Rather, these are determined by an evaluation under Article IV of the IMF Articles of Agreement.

[13] Some have suggested that the WTO DSB could be requested under Article XV to establish a panel to adjudicate a dispute in which a WTO Member complains that another WTO Member's *trade actions* violate its rights under the IMF Articles of Agreement. Note that, pursuant to Article XV, a panel would be bound by the IMF's determinations of consistency with the Articles of Agreement. Difficulty in the legal situation could arise if the IMF did not or could not make such a determination of consistency. In such a case, it is debatable whether a WTO panel would consider that it had the competence or the expertise to interpret IMF provisions. In this chapter, we focus on the more likely scenario that a WTO Member could bring an action against another Member's trade-related exchange actions claimed to be inconsistent with the WTO Agreement.

first be tasked with interpreting the meaning of the provision's terms, including 'exchange action', 'trade action', 'frustrate' and 'intent'.

It has been suggested that a Member could argue, in light of the Ad Note, that Article XV prohibits exchange actions that frustrate the intent of another GATT provision. Thus, perhaps provisions including GATT Articles I, II and III could be brought within the realm of consideration. For example, it has been argued that an exchange action could frustrate the intent of GATT Article III if it were found to be a discriminatory regulation, affording detrimental treatment to a group of imported products *vis-à-vis* the group of like domestic products.[14]

Given that Article XV has never been tested in dispute settlement, it is unclear how one should demonstrate that an exchange action contravenes Article XV. As noted above, the complexity of establishing that a currency is 'misaligned' is well-known. The panel's assessment would be likely to be based on a complex expert analysis, including experts from the IMF, the parties and any other authorities the panel deemed appropriate. The experts would need to analyse the situation and then report and explain to the panellists technically complex issues. It would therefore be difficult for the panel to determine the conclusion of the dispute. A complainant would bear the burden of proof in making a factual demonstration establishing a *prima facie* case that a Member's exchange actions frustrated the intent of a GATT provision under Article XV.

There is an important limitation to the scope of GATT Article XV:4. Article XV:9 carves out from Article XV:4 any exchange actions that are consistent with the IMF Articles of Agreement.[15] Article XV:9(a) provides that:

Nothing in this Agreement shall preclude:

> (a) the use by a contracting party of exchange controls or exchange restrictions in accordance with the Articles of Agreement of the

[14] Alternatively, it has been suggested that a Member could argue that 'intent' covers the GATT as a whole, thereby preventing any exchange actions enacted in order to restrict trade. As the GATT preamble suggests, the Agreement was entered into because the contracting parties desired, *inter alia*, 'the substantial reduction of tariffs and other barriers to trade and . . . the elimination of discriminatory treatment in international commerce'.

[15] Articles of Agreement of the International Monetary Fund, adopted at the United Nations Monetary and Financial Conference, Bretton Woods, New Hampshire, 22 July 1944, entered into force 27 December 1945, as subsequently amended.

> International Monetary Fund or with that contracting party's special exchange agreement with the CONTRACTING PARTIES. . ..[16]

The exact meaning and scope of Article XV: 9 is not clear, particularly the scope of the terms included in the phrase 'the use . . . of exchange controls or exchange restrictions'. Does this mean that all exchange-related measures that are consistent with the IMF Agreement are presumed to be GATT-consistent? Or is a positive consistency conclusion by the IMF needed in order to benefit from the presumption of this provision? In other words, does a Member who initiates a claim of violation of Article XV have to demonstrate, first, that the challenged exchange measure is inconsistent with the IMF provisions? Or is it for the respondent to demonstrate that its exchange measure has been approved by the IMF? In light of the fact that the IMF has never reached a conclusion of a consistency, the role of GATT Article XV:9 could become crucial in a debate over exchange measures reviewed by the DSB.

Moreover, Article XV:2 obliges the WTO to consult with the IMF in exchange matters and to accept its determination of consistency or inconsistency with the IMF Articles of Agreement. The extent of this obligation to consult is discussed hereafter.

The Panel in *Dominican Republic – Import and Sale of Cigarettes* concluded that, because the Dominican Republic had argued that its exchange restriction was imposed in accordance with the IMF Articles of Agreement under GATT Article XV:9, the panel needed to consult the IMF under Article XV:2 for a determination of consistency.[17] The extent of this obligation to consult is discussed in further detail in Section IV below. What is clear is that the IMF determination is essential for deciding whether or not the Article XV:9 carve-out applies.

[16] A similar carve-out exists under GATS Article XI:2, which states:

> 'Nothing in this Agreement shall affect the rights and obligations of the members of the International Monetary Fund under the Articles of Agreement of the Fund, including the use of exchange actions which are in conformity with the Articles of Agreement, provided that a Member shall not impose restrictions on any capital transactions inconsistently with its specific commitments regarding such transactions, except under Article XII or at the request of the Fund.'

[17] WTO Panel Report, *Dominican Republic – Measures Affecting the Importation and Internal Sale of Cigarettes* ('*Dominican Republic – Import and Sale of Cigarettes*'), WT/DS302/R, adopted 19 May 2005, as modified by Appellate Body Report WT/DS302/AB/R, para. 7.139. For a more detailed description of the case, see R. Howse, 'Towards an Equitable Integration of Monetary and Financial Matters, Trade and Sustainable Development', Chapter 12, this volume.

Finally, should the panel or AB find that the respondent's exchange measure did indeed violate Article XV, the implementing Member would be obliged to alter its exchange measures to bring them into compliance with WTO rules although again no clear lines of action exist.

(ii) *GATT Article II – schedules of concessions* GATT Article II establishes a Member's obligation to apply its tariff rates at a level no less favourable than that agreed to in its Schedule of Concessions. It anticipates that a Member's 'method of converting currencies' could impair the value of its concessions, that is, its bound tariff rates. Article II:3 states:

> No contracting party shall alter its method of determining dutiable value or of converting currencies so as to impair the value of any of the concessions provided for in the appropriate Schedule annexed to this Agreement.

Thus, it has been suggested that a member could raise a *de jure* claim of violation of Article II:3 in response to an overvalued currency.[18] The method of currency conversion could impair the value of a concession by raising the applied tariff rate to a level above the tariff bindings in a Member's Schedule.[19] In the case of a general currency misalignment, the situation of an artificially overvalued currency is unlikely to be the focus of a

[18] See U. Thorstensen, E. Marçal and L. Ferraz, 'Exchange Rate Misalignments and International Trade Policy: Impacts on Tariffs', *Journal of World Trade* 46:3 (2012) and also G. Hudson, P. Bentode Faria and T. Peyerl, 'The Legality of Exchange Rate Undervaluation Under WTO Law', *CTEI Working Paper* (2011). It has also been suggested that this provision – together with Article II:6(a) mentioned below – could be cited in a complaint involving a member's undervalued currency, to the extent that a method of converting currencies could impair the value of concessions by reducing a member's market access. Note, however, that Article II deals with market access as a result of tariff concessions, rather than market access in an MFN or national treatment sense. Importantly, Article II grants both a right and an obligation to members: a *right* to impose tariffs up to the bound rates and an *obligation* not to impose tariffs above bound rates. Both are reflected in the paragraphs of Article II. We therefore consider an Article II claim for an undervalued currency as a *de facto* violation claim, below.

[19] E.g., assume two countries' currencies, Currency A and Currency B, are of equal value. Country A's Schedule of Concessions allows it to apply a ten unit duty on the import of a widget from Country B. This duty is initially equivalent to ten units of Country B's currency. Next, Country A applies a method of converting currencies that overvalues its currency by 100 per cent relative to Currency B. Although the duty remains ten units of Country A's currency, it now takes twice as many units of Country B's currency to pay the duty. Thus, Country A's widget industry effectively enjoys twice as much protection relative to its bound tariff rates when faced with competing imports from Country B. Article II:3 is designed to prevent such an event.

WTO dispute. The potentially higher tariff rates on a Member's exports due to an overvalued currency may be of small concern relative to the benefit of increased price competitiveness for its exports.

Some have noted that Article II could provide guidance for when a member's undervalued currency could be determined to impair concessions under Article II. In particular, Article II:6(a) considers that a member's 'specific' duties or charges on imports – as opposed to import duties or charges made on an *ad valorem* basis, which is the case for the majority of members' imports[20] – may be upwardly adjusted if its currency's '*par value* is reduced consistently with the Articles of Agreement of the International Monetary Fund by more than twenty *per centum*'.[21] In such a case, the Article envisions a process of renegotiation to restore the member's devalued concessions and assure it the level of protection to which it had agreed.

The *par value* system mentioned in Article II:6(a) for assessing specific duties and charges under Article II became defunct after the collapse of the Bretton Woods system in 1971. In 1978, the IMF passed the second amendment to the Articles of Agreement. Since then, market exchange rates have been used.[22] For example, when making a comparison of export prices to normal value to determine appropriate levels of anti-dumping duties, AD Agreement Article 2.4.1 requires conversions of currencies to be calculated from the date of sale (or possibly the forward exchange rate) and exchange rate fluctuations must be ignored.[23] The revised international monetary system has potentially important implications for the IMF, and for a WTO panel, seeking to ascertain the IMF- or WTO-consistency of a member's exchange measure.

(iii) *SCM Agreement – actionable and prohibited subsidies* Some have suggested that the complainant could also make a *de jure* violation complaint under the SCM Agreement, claiming that the member's

[20] Hudson *et al.*, 'The Legality of Exchange Rate Undervaluation', pp. 22–3.

[21] This provision does not apply as a trade remedy, however, and does not confer any right to upwardly adjust tariff rates (whether specific or *ad valorem*) in response to another member's currency movements.

[22] Note by the Secretariat, WTO Provisions Relevant to the Relationship Between Trade and Finance and Trade and Debt, WT/WGTDF/W/3, 21 June 2002.

[23] Similarly, the Customs Valuation (CV) Agreement removed the GATT Article VII:4 reliance on the old *par value* system for calculating rates of exchange. CV Agreement Article 9(a) requires rates of exchange to reflect 'as effectively as possible. . . the current value of such currency in commercial transactions', as duly published by the competent authorities of the importing country.

exchange rate policies are somehow actionable or prohibited subsidies.[24] In order to do so, it would need to satisfy the terms of SCM Agreement Articles 1.1 and 1.2 that spell out what constitutes a 'subsidy' under the Agreement. Subsidies may be 'actionable' under SCM Agreement Article 5 or 'prohibited' under SCM Agreement Article 3.

The finding of a 'subsidy' is a threshold issue for considering exchange rate policies under the SCM Agreement. If it is not a 'subsidy', the provisions of the SCM Agreement do not apply. To determine that the member's challenged exchange rate policy is a 'subsidy', the complainant must show four elements. First, the 'subsidy' must constitute a financial contribution or price support under SCM Agreement Article 1.1. Second, the financial contribution must be made by a public body, which the AB has interpreted to mean an entity 'that possesses, exercises or is vested with governmental authority'.[25] Panels will make this determination on a case-by-case basis. In this case, because central banks are responsible for making monetary policy, the panel would be tasked with weighing a central bank's autonomy with the character of its authority, that is, whether or not that authority is 'governmental'. Third, the financial contribution must confer a benefit. Fourth, the 'subsidy' must be 'specific' to certain enterprises under Article 2. Prohibited subsidies are automatically specific under Article 2.3.

After finding that a measure is a subsidy, a complainant must show that it is either actionable or prohibited. For an actionable subsidy to be a violation, it must produce 'adverse effects to the interests of other Members' under SCM Agreement Article 5. Adverse effects include injury to another member's domestic industry, nullification or impairment of benefits accruing directly or indirectly under GATT 1994, and serious prejudice to another member's interests as defined by SCM Agreement Article 6. A prohibited subsidy is a subsidy that, in the present case, is 'contingent... upon export performance' under SCM Agreement Article 3.1(a). In other words, an exchange-related subsidy

[24] E.g., see R. W. Staiger and A. O. Sykes, '"Currency Manipulation" and World Trade' *World Trade Review* 9:4 (2010). As provided in several SCM Agreement provisions (including Articles 1, 25 and 26), the SCM Agreement's obligations regarding subsidies operate in tandem with GATT Article XVI. The Agreement also covers countervailing duties in tandem with GATT Article VI, as discussed below. The SCM Agreement does not apply to agricultural subsidies, which are governed by the Agreement on Agriculture.

[25] WTO Appellate Body Report, *US – Definitive Anti-Dumping and Countervailing Duties on Certain Products from China*, WT/DS379/AB/R, adopted 11 March 2011, para. 317.

would need to be tied in law or in fact to export earnings to be considered a prohibited subsidy.[26]

If a panel or, in case of an appeal, the AB, finds that a Member's subsidy is prohibited, that member is required to withdraw the subsidy within a time period specified by the panel following the adoption of the panel or AB report. If actionable, the relevant member is required to withdraw the subsidy or remove its adverse effects within six months following adoption of the panel or AB report. If the subsidy is not withdrawn or the adverse effects not removed, the complainant may take appropriate countermeasures in line with SCM Agreement Articles 4.10 or 7.9, unless the DSB decides by consensus to reject the request.

(b) *De facto* violations It could also be argued that a WTO Member could attempt to raise a claim of *de facto* violation of certain WTO provisions, including GATT Articles I, II or III on members' most-favoured nation (MFN), tariff binding and national treatment obligations.[27] Rather than focusing on the wording of the challenged measure, as in the case of a *de jure* violation, a *de facto* violation implies that the actual effects of the measure, as applied, violate a WTO provision.

(i) *GATT Article I on MFN* GATT Article I provides that any advantage a member bestows on the trade of any product from any country be immediately and unconditionally granted to like products of all WTO Members. This provision assures that no member will privilege trade with one country over that with other WTO Members. Some suggest that a complainant could raise a *de facto* claim of violation under GATT Article I, arguing that the responding member's exchange actions *de facto* raise or lower levels of market access between countries. Because such variation might favour some members while providing less favourable treatment to others, the exchange or currency measures might be said to violate the MFN principle.

(ii) *GATT Article II on market access* As noted above, GATT Article II binds members' tariff rates according to each of their Schedules of

[26] This would include currency retention schemes or similar practices that involve a bonus on exports, according to SCM Annex I's 'Illustrative List of Export Subsidies'.

[27] In this light, GATT Articles I, II and III could also serve as the basis for claims that an exchange action under Article XV frustrates the intent of another GATT provision or for claims of nullification and impairment under GATT Article XXIII:1(b).

Concessions, thereby guaranteeing a predictable level of market access to each member's exports and imports. Arguably, a *de facto* violation claim could be made under Article II if it could be claimed that the exchange rate of the importing country reduces market access for imported goods. Article II:1(a) provides:

> Each contracting party shall accord to the commerce of the other contracting parties treatment no less favourable than that provided for in the appropriate Part of the appropriate Schedule annexed to this Agreement.

A member seeking to make a *de facto* violation claim under Article II:1 would bear the burden of proof, requiring a *prima facie* case that a member's allegedly misaligned exchange rate had resulted in a market access restriction. The complainant would thus need to show that the restriction amounted to less favourable treatment than that provided in the importing member's Schedule.

(iii) *GATT Article III on national treatment* GATT Article III requires that internal taxes, charges, laws and regulations not be applied on imports in order to protect domestic industry. As such, taxes on imports may not be applied in excess of those on like domestic products, nor may laws and regulations accord less favourable treatment to imports than to like domestic products. Could a complainant allege that a set of member's exchange actions constitute an import tax applied to imports in excess of that applied to domestic products because no such import barrier effect applied to domestic products? Similarly the complainant might claim that the member's exchange measures accorded less favourable treatment to imports by having a detrimental impact on their competitive opportunities in the domestic market. As such, the alleged exchange rate misalignment would be argued to *de facto* violate GATT Article III.

2. Raising the 'defensive': claim that a member's defensive duties in response to an alleged currency misalignment violate a WTO provision

Some interest groups are asking their governments to impose unilateral duties on imports to protect their industries from the trade effects of perceived currency misalignments that affect the value/price of exported products. Under this scenario, the affected exporting member may seek to bring a violation complaint to the DSB. In so doing, the affected exporting member would bear the initial burden of proving that the imposition of such duties is WTO-inconsistent.

Depending on the facts, a member is entitled to consider either *de jure* or *de facto* claims of violations of provisions of the SCM Agreement, AD Agreement or GATT.

(a) **Countervailing duties** Members may impose CVDs to offset the trade effects of a subsidy, as set out in the SCM Agreement. An (exporting) Member challenging the exchange-related CVD would need to demonstrate a *prima facie* case that the CVDs were *de jure* WTO-inconsistent by showing that they did not counteract an actionable or prohibited subsidy that causes or threatens to cause injury to the domestic industry. In situations other than *de jure* subsidies, that member would need to show that the challenged measures *de facto* violated an SCM Agreement provision in their manner of application.

In either case, the respondent would then have to rebut the complainant's *prima facie* case. In its rebuttal, as discussed above, the responding Member imposing the CVDs would be required to show that the alleged exchange action constituted a subsidy under the SCM Agreement. That is, it would need to show that the exchange action made a financial contribution or other price support from a public body that was 'specific' and conferred a benefit. If the exchange action were argued to be a prohibited subsidy, specificity would be assumed, but the additional requirement that the subsidy was 'contingent upon export performance' would need to be demonstrated. If the subsidy were claimed to be 'actionable', it would have to be shown to cause 'adverse effects', including injury to a domestic industry, nullification or impairment, or 'serious prejudice' to the interests of another member.

Additionally, if the CVDs met these criteria, the member imposing them could be required to show that they were appropriate countermeasures applied consistently with SCM Agreement Article 4.10 or 7.9 and Articles 19–21. As provided in SCM Agreement Article 10, CVDs must also be in accordance with GATT Article VI and the other clauses of the SCM Agreement.

Moreover, the Ad Note to GATT Article VI could, arguably, be relevant in this context. It provides that 'multiple currency practices' can 'in certain circumstances' be considered an export subsidy or a partial depreciation of a country's currency. It further provides that in such cases these multiple currency practices may be countered with CVDs or AD duties. Some suggest that this provision could offer guidance to a panel required to interpret both GATT Article VI and the SCM and AD Agreements in the context of an alleged currency misalignment.[28] Like GATT Article XV, the Ad Note to Article VI has never been tested or interpreted in dispute settlement proceedings.

(b) AD duties It has also been suggested that in some circumstances exchange rate measures may be equated to dumping and could be argued to allow for the imposition of AD duties under the AD Agreement. Normally, AD duties are applied to offset the unfair trade practices of private actors selling products at lower prices abroad than on the home market. In this case, the complainant would again bear the initial burden of proof of offering a *prima facie* case that the duties imposed could be inconsistent, either *de jure* or *de facto*, with the AD Agreement. In order to do so, the complainant would need to show that the duties had not been calculated based on the normal value of the products in question, either for market or for non-market economies, according to the terms of AD Agreement Article 2. Alternatively, it would need to show that there was no injury or causation arising from the alleged dumping. It would then be for the respondent to rebut the *prima facie* case.

Additionally, if the AD duties met these criteria, the member imposing them could be required to show that they did not exceed the margin of dumping, determined under AD Agreement Article 2, and that they had been applied consistently with AD Agreement Articles 9–11. As provided by AD Agreement Article 1, AD duties must also be in accordance with GATT Article VI and the other clauses of the AD Agreement. As noted above, some have suggested that the Ad Note to GATT Article VI could be relevant in a currency-related AD dispute.

(c) Collecting tariffs above the bindings of GATT Article II A member could argue that it is justified to raise its tariffs above bound levels in response to the trade effects caused by the alleged currency misalignment. As noted above, Article II:1 prohibits members from applying tariffs less favourable than the bound levels in their Schedules of Concessions. It could be argued that Article II:3 prohibits a member from altering its method

28 In respect of CVDs applied to offset the alleged export subsidy effect of 'multiple currency practices', the Ad Note to GATT Article XVI carves out 'multiple rates of exchange' that are in accordance with the IMF Articles of Agreement. These are not required to fulfil the obligations of Article XVI Section B, which includes the obligation to cease granting any export subsidy on non-primary products when it results in the sale of a product for a lower price than on the domestic market. The relevance of this Ad Note could be modified by the subsequent export subsidy provisions under the SCM and Agriculture Agreements.

of converting currencies in a manner that impairs the concessions made in its schedule under Article II. The initial burden of proof would be on the complainants to show that the tariffs collected were above bindings or otherwise contrary to Article II. It would then be for the respondent to justify why it believed that its import tariffs were consistent with Article II.

It should be noted that, as a general principle, DSU Article 23 requires members to seek redress of all claims through dispute settlement procedures and not to seek redress unilaterally. Thus, many believe that it would be difficult to demonstrate that above-binding, exchange-related tariffs could be consistent with Article II. Nevertheless, the duty-imposing member could seek to defend its increased import tariffs breaching Article II by invoking Article XV as a defensive justification (as we invoke Article XX in other circumstances). To support this argument, GATT Articles I–XI generally lay out Members' core substantive market access obligations under the GATT, while Articles XII–XXI generally allow flexibilities, justifications or exceptions to these rules. Article XV could be seen as a justification for defensive responses to another member's exchange actions, including higher import tariffs under Article II.[29] If this view is correct, in such a case, after the complainant had made a *prima facie* case that the import tariff hikes were inconsistent with Article II, the respondent would claim that the tariff hikes were justified under Article XV because the exchange actions in question allegedly frustrate the intent of another GATT provision. Although so far Article XV has been argued as a basis for claims, a panel could nonetheless consider whether Article XV can be interpreted as allowing for (conditional) justifications of violations of other GATT provisions.

In the event that Article XV could be used as a justification, the invoking Member would need to comply with related obligations such as consultation with the IMF and accepting certain IMF factual assessments would be likely to apply. Arguably paragraph 9 of Article XV could be invoked as a defence in response to claims of GATT violation and this seems to include all GATT provisions. It is not clear, however, whether and how GATT Article XV could justify non-GATT violations such as those resulting from SCM claims.

[29] G. Z. Marceau, 'L'OMC et la crise financière', in R. Chemain (ed.), *La Fécondation du Système Monétaire et Financier International. Actes du colloque du Cédin des 16 et 17 mars 2010* (Paris: Ed. A.Pedone, 2011), pp. 329, 336.

II. Non-violation complaints

In sum, several violation claims might involve exchange-related actions that would oblige a WTO panel to assess the WTO-consistency of an exchange-related measure. Members could also initiate a non-violation claim. The object of a non-violation complaint would be to claim that, although the challenged exchange rate or currency measure violates no WTO provision in particular, it does amount to nullification or impairment of some benefit to which the complaining member is entitled under the GATT. The non-violation claim could be raised by, together with or as an alternative, a claim to a violation. The burden of proof would be on the complaining member to present a *prima facie* case that the measure nullified or impaired its benefits. It would then be for the responding member to show that it did not.

The AB in *EC – Asbestos* ruled that GATT Article XXIII:1(b), the non-violation provision 'should be approached with caution and should remain an exceptional remedy'.[30] Article XXIII:1(b) covers the application of 'any measure, whether or not it conflicts with the provisions of this Agreement'. It is clear from the text of Article XXIII that it applies very broadly. Indeed, the AB has determined that 'measures of all types may give rise to such a cause of action [under Article XXIII:1(b)]'.[31]

The non-violation claim will require consideration of at least three conditions. First, the application of a measure by a member that is not WTO-inconsistent; second, the existence of a benefit or objective accruing under the applicable agreement; and third, the nullification or impairment of that benefit or the obstruction of any objective under GATT 1994 as a result of the application of the measure.[32] Moreover, it will require some consideration that the nullification or impairment was not reasonably anticipated at the time of the last tariff's negotiation.[33]

[30] WTO Appellate Body Report, *EC – Asbestos*, para. 186. As noted above, Article XXIII:1 paragraphs (a) and (c) also provide remedies for nullification or impairment due to a violation of a GATT provision or for 'any other situation' not covered by paragraphs (a) and (b).

[31] *Ibid.*, para. 187.

[32] WTO Panel Report, *Japan – Film*, para. 10.41; WTO Panel Report, *EC – Asbestos*, WT/DS135/R and Add.1, adopted 5 April 2001, as modified by Appellate Body Report WT/DS135/AB/R, para. 8.283.

[33] WTO Panel Report, *Japan – Film*, 10.82.

It has been suggested above that the responding member could attempt to invoke GATT Article XV as a defence to a non-violation claim under Article XXIII. As noted above, Article XV:9 carves out all exchange rate measures consistent with the IMF Agreement. In this light, a respondent to a non-violation claim could argue that its exchange actions are in conformity or are not inconsistent with the IMF provisions and therefore could not be the subject of any DSB recommendation. The exact scope and meaning of Article XV:9 are not clear.

DSU Article 26:1 sets out special rules for non-violation claims. It requires the complaining party to make a detailed justification in support of its complaint against a measure that does not violate a provision of the WTO Agreement. If a panel or the AB finds a challenged measure nullifies or impairs benefits without being a violation, there is no obligation for the imposing member to withdraw it. Instead, the respondent ought to provide a form of compensation. Would this imply no obligation for the Member concerned to modify the challenged exchange-related trade measure?

D. The role of the IMF, experts and other considerations

I. *Obligation to consult the IMF and related case law*

GATT Article XV establishes the terms under which a GATT panel is authorised to adjudicate a dispute involving a member's exchange measures. Among other obligations, it notes the dual responsibility of the WTO and the IMF and obliges the WTO to consult with the IMF on all exchange-related matters. As noted above, the Panel in *Dominican Republic – Import and Sale of Cigarettes* decided that, under GATT Article XV:2, a panel needed to consult the IMF in cases where the respondent claims that its exchange actions are consistent with the IMF Articles of Agreement.[34] This is especially important because members' exchange actions cannot violate Article XV if the IMF determines them to be consistent with the Articles of Agreement.

According to GATT Article XV:2:

> In all cases in which the CONTRACTING PARTIES are called upon to consider or deal with problems concerning monetary reserves, balances of payments or foreign exchange arrangements, *they shall consult fully with the International Monetary Fund. In such consultations, the*

[34] WTO Panel Report, *Dominican Republic – Import and Sale of Cigarettes*, para. 7.139.

> *CONTRACTING PARTIES shall accept all findings of statistical and other facts presented by the Fund relating to foreign exchange, monetary reserves and balances of payments, and shall accept the determination of the Fund as to whether action by a contracting party in exchange matters is in accordance with the Articles of Agreement of the International Monetary Fund*, or with the terms of a special exchange agreement between that contracting party and the CONTRACTING PARTIES. The CONTRACTING PARTIES in reaching their final decision in cases involving the criteria set forth in paragraph 2 (a) of Article XII or in paragraph 9 of Article XVIII, *shall accept the determination of the Fund as to what constitutes a serious decline in the contracting party's monetary reserves, a very low level of its monetary reserves or a reasonable rate of increase in its monetary reserves, and as to the financial aspects of other matters covered in consultation in such cases.* (emphasis added)

Thus, to the extent that they represent the contracting parties of the WTO in a dispute under Article XV, panels would be obliged to consult with the IMF 'on problems concerning monetary reserves, balances of payments or foreign exchange arrangements'. The meaning and scope of such terms, in particular 'exchange arrangements', and their relationship to a specific exchange-related trade dispute, are not clear. It should also be noted that DSU Article 13,[35] further discussed below, generally allows panels to consult with experts. The AB has not yet interpreted the relationship between the specific obligation to consult the IMF under GATT Article XV and the right of panels to consult experts under DSU Article 13.

Moreover, it is unclear to what extent the IMF consultation requirement holds in disputes that are not directly concerned with GATT Article XV, albeit involving exchange rate considerations. Does Article

[35] DSU Article 13, Right to Seek Information, states:

1. Each panel shall have the right to seek information and technical advice from any individual or body which it deems appropriate. However, before a panel seeks such information or advice from any individual or body within the jurisdiction of a Member it shall inform the authorities of that Member. A Member should respond promptly and fully to any request by a panel for such information as the panel considers necessary and appropriate. Confidential information which is provided shall not be revealed without formal authorization from the individual, body, or authorities of the Member providing the information.
2. Panels may seek information from any relevant source and may consult experts to obtain their opinion on certain aspects of the matter. With respect to a factual issue concerning a scientific or other technical matter raised by a party to a dispute, a panel may request an advisory report in writing from an expert review group. Rules for the establishment of such a group and its procedures are set forth in Appendix 4.

XV impose a general requirement to consult the IMF whenever an exchange action is involved? Or must that provision be cited by the parties? For example, a member could impose trade remedies against another member in response to an alleged currency misalignment. If the duties were challenged solely under the SCM or AD Agreements, and the parties invoked exchange rate arguments, would the panel be required to consult the IMF? The extent of the IMF consultation requirement under Article XV and its impact on the operation of other GATT or WTO provisions remains open to interpretation.[36]

There have been at least two cases in which the DSB has determined that panels should consult the IMF in matters subject to IMF jurisdiction. The AB found that, in the specific matter of *Argentina – Textiles and Apparel*, the Panel had discretion not to consult the IMF despite suggestions from both parties, Argentina and the US, that it should do so. This was because only Article XV *required* consultation and only under conditions not at issue in the dispute, namely, 'problems concerning monetary reserves, balances of payments or foreign exchange arrangements'.[37] Nevertheless, the AB found that consultations could have been useful and that other situations under Article XV could require consultation.[38] In *Dominican Republic – Import and Sale of Cigarettes*, the panel determined that a fee claimed to be an exchange restriction required consultation with the IMF for three reasons. First, the IMF's role in making determinations under GATT Article XV; second, paragraph 8 of the IMF/WTO Cooperation Agreement[39] (discussed below); and third, the AB decision in *Argentina – Textiles and Apparel*.[40] However, in *India – Quantitative Restrictions*, the Panel decided not to make a finding on whether or not the DSB was bound by certain determinations of the IMF in its consultations under Article

[36] The DSU may be instructive in this case. Article 7.2 requires panels to address 'the relevant provisions in any covered agreement or agreements *cited by the parties to the dispute*' (emphasis added).

[37] WTO Appellate Body Report, *Argentina – Measures Affecting Imports of Footwear, Textiles, Apparel and Other Items* ('*Argentina – Textiles and Apparel*'), WT/DS56/AB/R and Corr.1, adopted 22 April 1998, paras 84–6. For a more detailed description of the case, see R. Howse, 'Towards an Equitable Integration of Monetary and Financial Matters, Trade and Sustainable Development', Chapter 12, this volume.

[38] WTO Appellate Body Report, *Argentina – Textiles and Apparel*, para. 86.

[39] WT/L/195, Agreement Between the International Monetary Fund and the World Trade Organization, 9 December 1996.

[40] WTO Panel Report, *Dominican Republic – Import and Sale of Cigarettes*, paras. 7.132–7.142.

XV:2. The Panel also refused to determine whether it was bound to consult the IMF and instead consulted the IMF on the basis of Article 13 of the DSU.[41] Because the decision was not appealed, the AB had no opportunity to make a final determination on this issue.[42]

II. The role of the IMF/WTO Cooperation Agreement

The IMF/WTO Cooperation Agreement was adopted pursuant to Article V of the WTO Agreement. Even if the legal nature of the IMF/WTO Cooperation Agreement is not clear, it could be argued to provide important context for interpreting the consultation requirement. As noted by the AB in *Argentina – Textiles and Apparel*, the Agreement 'provides for consultations and the exchange of information between the WTO Secretariat and the staff of the IMF in certain specified circumstances, and grants to each organization observer status in certain of the other's meetings'.[43]

Recently, in *US – Tuna II* and *US – Clove Cigarettes*, the AB concluded that decisions from the Technical Barriers to Trade (TBT) Committee and the Doha Ministerial Decision of 14 November 2001 constituted a 'subsequent agreement between the parties' pursuant to Article 31.2(a) of the Vienna Convention.[44] If a panel were to reach a similar conclusion with respect to the IMF/WTO Cooperation Agreement, its provisions could be used to interpret GATT Article XV and other WTO provisions.

The IMF/WTO Cooperation Agreement was not, however, written in the context of dispute settlement.[45] In *Argentina – Textiles and Apparel*, the AB noted that it explicitly excludes cooperation in dispute settlement proceedings under paragraph 6, except where 'matters of jurisdictional

[41] WTO Panel Report, *India – Quantitative Restrictions on Imports of Agricultural, Textile and Industrial Products* ('*India – Quantitative Restrictions*'), WT/DS90/R, adopted 6 April 1999, paras 5.11–5.12.

[42] WTO Appellate Body Report, *India – Quantitative Restrictions*, WT/DS90/AB/R, adopted 22 September 1999, para. 152.

[43] WTO Appellate Body Report, *Argentina – Textiles and Apparel*, para. 71.

[44] WTO Appellate Body Report, *US – Measures Concerning the Importation, Marketing and Sale of Tuna and Tuna Products*, WT/DS381/AB/R, adopted 16 May 2012, para. 378; WTO Appellate Body Report, *US – Measures Affecting the Production and Sale of Clove Cigarettes*, WT/DS406/AB/R, adopted 4 April 2012, para. 268.

[45] D. E. Siegel, 'Legal Aspects of the IMF/WTO Relationship: The Fund's Articles of Agreement and the WTO Agreements', *American Journal of International Law* 96:3 (2002), 569–70.

relevance to the Fund are to be considered'.[46] Moreover, dealing with an Article II violation claim by the US, the AB noted that the Cooperation Agreement included no provisions 'that require a panel to consult with the IMF in a case such as this'.[47] Under paragraph 8, the IMF/WTO Cooperation Agreement requires the IMF to 'inform in writing the relevant WTO body (including dispute settlement panels) . . . whether such measures are consistent with the Articles of Agreement of the Fund'.[48] This provision requires the Fund to respond to a DSB request for a determination of consistency with the Articles of Agreement – probably with GATT Article XV in mind.[49] Paragraph 8 also provides that the IMF 'may communicate its views in writing on matters of mutual interest to the [WTO] or any of its organs or bodies (excluding the WTO's dispute settlement panels). . .'. The AB concluded that, '[e]vidently, the IMF has not been authorized to provide its views to a WTO dispute settlement panel on matters not relating to exchange measures within its jurisdiction, unless it is requested to do so by a panel under Article 13 of the DSU'.[50]

Two further declarations could also be relevant to the WTO/IMF relationship: the Declaration on the Contribution of the World Trade Organization to Achieving Greater Coherence in Global Economic Policymaking (the 'Declaration on Coherence') and the Declaration on the Relationship of the World Trade Organization with the International Monetary Fund (the 'WTO/IMF Declaration'). The Declaration on Coherence establishes principles of cooperation between the WTO and certain other international institutions in response to a 1994 Ministerial Decision. Paragraph 5 states that the WTO should 'pursue and develop cooperation with the international organizations responsible for monetary and financial matters, while respecting the mandate, the confidentiality requirements and the necessary autonomy in decision-making procedures of each institution. . .'. The WTO/IMF Declaration reiterates that the relationship of the WTO with the IMF 'will be based on the provisions that have governed the relationship of the contracting parties to the GATT 1947'. These provisions were also reviewed by the AB in *Argentina – Textiles and Apparel*.[51]

[46] WTO Appellate Body Report, *Argentina – Textiles and Apparel*, para. 71.
[47] *Ibid.*, para. 85.
[48] The same requirement was reviewed in the context of *Dominican Republic – Import and Sale of Cigarettes*. See WTO Panel Report, para. 7.140.
[49] Siegel, 'Legal Aspects of the IMF/WTO Relationship', 570.
[50] WTO Appellate Body Report, *Argentina – Textiles and Apparel*, para. 85.
[51] *Ibid.*, paras 67–74.

III. *The role of experts and IMF determinations in WTO disputes*

Panels are granted the right to consult Members, other international organisations, experts, expert review groups and any other relevant source under DSU Article 13.[52] The procedures for setting up expert review groups are provided in DSU Appendix 4. Other WTO agreements also refer to the use of individual experts. For example, SPS Agreement Article 11.2 requires consultation with experts for scientific or technical determinations, SCM Agreement Article 24.3 allows panels to refer to the 'Permanent Group of Experts' for determinations of a 'prohibited' subsidy, and the TBT Agreement refers to consultations with 'technical expert groups' (Articles 14:2 and 14:3). Typically, even in the case of the TBT Agreement, panels have preferred to consult with individual experts.[53] Any experts selected by the panel must be independent and impartial. Indeed, the AB in *US – Continued Suspension* found that the Panel had infringed the European Communities' due process rights by consulting with two experts considered to be partial.[54]

Panels have the right to seek or decline expert advice at their own discretion, even in cases when parties have requested it.[55] The AB noted in *Argentina – Textiles and Apparel* that 'a panel is not duty-bound to seek information in each and every case or to consult particular experts under this provision'. Pursuant to GATT Article XV:2, the WTO would be bound only by 'all findings of statistical and other facts presented by the Fund relating to foreign exchange, monetary reserves and balances of payments'.

Notwithstanding the requirement of IMF consultation, it would be for the WTO panel alone to critically assess all factual considerations, apply WTO law and make final determinations on whether or not a Member's exchange actions had violated a provision of the WTO Agreement.[56] The

[52] G. Z. Marceau and J. K. Hawkins, 'Experts in WTO Dispute Settlement', *Journal of International Dispute Settlement* 3:3 (2012), 503.

[53] *Ibid.*, 497.

[54] WTO Appellate Body Report, *US – Continued Suspension of Obligations in the EC – Hormones Dispute*, WT/DS320/AB/R, adopted 14 November 2008, para. 481.

[55] WTO Appellate Body Report, *Argentina – Textiles and Apparel*, para. 86.

[56] WTO Appellate Body Report, *US – Import Measures on Certain Products from the European Communities*, WT/DS165/AB/R, adopted 10 January 2001, para. 92. Similarly, DSU Article 3.7 states that 'the aim of the dispute settlement mechanism is to secure a positive solution to a dispute'. It is for the panel to resolve disputes and consultations are meant, under DSU Article 13, only to further that purpose.

IMF determinations would need to be examined next to and including additional considerations, such as the representations of the parties.[57] However, given the important place of the IMF in GATT Article XV, GATS Article XI, and potentially other WTO provisions relating to exchange actions, the IMF experts' testimony would carry heavy weight in a dispute settlement proceeding. This is all the more so given the subsequent agreements on the coherence of international organisations and the IMF/WTO Cooperation Agreement.

E. Conclusions

This chapter has reviewed the various types of OSU actions that have so far been argued to be relevant to potential exchange-related trade disputes. In such disputes, the jurisdiction of the DSB will be compulsory and the panel will have full discretion for assessing and making recommendations based on the parties' claims. Members may bring the disputes to the DSB in a number of ways, either by taking 'offensive' actions through positive claims of violation, non-violation or situation, or in reaction to 'defensive' imposition of unilateral trade remedies or import tariffs that cause the affected member to make a challenge. Violation claims could be made on a *de jure* or a *de facto* basis. The panel will have full discretion for seeking and assessing expert opinion, but may be obligated to consult the IMF under certain circumstances under GATT Article XV. It is unclear to what extent this obligation applies in exchange-related disputes other than under GATT Article XV, such as under the SCM or AD Agreements. Moreover, the scope of the general carve-out of GATT Article XV:9 is not clear as to whether or not, and to what extent, an exchange rate measure generally subject to IMF surveillance could nonetheless be considered GATT-inconsistent when it has not been declared IMF-consistent. In any case, it is anticipated that such disputes would be very complex and difficult to assess.

[57] WTO Appellate Body Report, *India – Quantitative Restrictions*, para. 150.

15

Monetary affairs in the WTO Trade Policy Review

MATHIAS KENDE

A. Introduction

The Trade Policy Review Mechanism (TPRM) as contained in Annex 3 of the Marrakesh Agreement establishing the World Trade Organization (WTO) provides a peer review mechanism for the appraisal of Members' trade policies and practices and their impact on the functioning of the multilateral trading system.[1] This chapter analyses whether and to what extent the TPRM can and has been able to review trade policies in a holistic way by taking into account monetary and financial policies. Trade policy – the core object of review under the TPRM – does not exist in clinical isolation. It is underpinned by wider monetary and financial fundamentals. This chapter examines the relationship between the TPRM and those underpinnings. The decrease in traditional trade barriers (e.g., tariffs) has led to the increased emergence of non-tariff barriers (NTBs) of a (i) social, (ii) environmental or (iii) economic and financial nature.[2] This last category of NTBs has not only gained in importance as a consequence of an increased number of (uncontrollable) financial crises[3] with negative trade repercussions but also as a result of their (controlled) misuse as a political or monetary instrument for national trade gains.

This chapter expresses the personal opinion of the author and does not necessarily represent the views of the Belgian Foreign Ministry or any of the institution's staff members. Various International Monetary Fund (IMF) and WTO staff members provided invaluable comments on earlier versions of this chapter. All possible remaining errors are the author's and the author's alone.

[1] Marrakesh Agreement Establishing The World Trade Organization, Marrakesh, 15 April 1994, in force 1 January 1995, *The Legal Texts – The Results of the Uruguay Round of Multilateral Trade Negotiations* (Cambridge University Press, 2003), pp. 380–2; A. C. Chayes and A. H. Chayes, *The New Sovereignty – Compliance with International Regulatory Agreements* (Cambridge, MA: Harvard University Press, 1995), pp. 244–6.

[2] *World Trade Report 2012 – Trade and Public Policies: A Closer Look at Non-Tariff Measures in the 21st Century* (Geneva: World Trade Organization, 2012), p. 252.

[3] T. Cottier, 'Challenges Ahead in International Economic Law', *Journal of International Economic Law*, 12:1 (2009), 7.

Two caveats apply. First, the TPRM's core object of review is concerned with national trade policies and practices and not by their monetary and financial underpinnings. This chapter aims to find out whether there is a link between these intrinsically separate topics. It therefore forms part of a wider reflection on trade and monetary affairs. Second, this chapter focuses on country-based TPRMs and not on the TPRB's monitoring of developments of the international trading system. The link between the latter and monetary affairs would merit a separate chapter.

B. Contextualising the TPRM

I. Foundations and development of the review mechanism

The history of the TPRM can mainly be traced back to six major events: (i) Article X of the General Agreement on Tariffs and Trade (GATT) (1947),[4] (ii) the Tokyo Round negotiations resulting in the Understanding Regarding Notification, Consultation, Dispute Settlement and Surveillance (1979),[5] (iii) the (so-called) wise men's report – Trade Policies for a Better Future: Proposals for Action (1985),[6] (iv) the Functioning of the GATT System (FOGS) negotiations (1986),[7] (v) the provisional adoption of the TPRM during the Montreal mid-term review of the Uruguay Round (1989)[8] and (vi) the final establishment of the TPRM in Annex 3 of the Marrakesh Agreement establishing the World Trade Organization (1995).[9]

[4] Article X GATT (1947). See *The Legal Texts*, p. 435.

[5] General Agreement on Tariffs and Trade, Understanding Regarding Notification, Consultation, Dispute Settlement and Surveillance, adopted on 28 November 1979, Basic Documents and Selected Documents (BISD), L/4907, 3 December 1979, p. 10 (DSU Agreement).

[6] Trade Policies for a Better Future, Proposals for Action (Geneva: GATT, 1985), p. 60; *Trade Policies for a Better Future: The Leutwiler Report, the GATT and the Uruguay Round* (Dordrecht: Martinus Nijhoff, 1987), 174. This report was also inspired by the 1982 Conference on Trade Policy organised by the Institute of International Economics in Washington, DC – see also C. F. Bergsten and W. R. Cline, *Trade Policy in the 1980s* (Washington, DC: The Institute for International Economics, 1982), p. 84.

[7] General Agreement on Tariffs and Trade, Draft Ministerial Declaration on the Uruguay Round; Punta del Este - Uruguay, adopted on 20 September 1986, Basic Documents and Selected Documents (BISD), Min (86)/W/19, p. 20 (Uruguay Declaration).

[8] Uruguay Round of Multilateral Trade Negotiations, Mid-term Review Agreements, NUR 027, 24 April 1989, MTN.TNC, 21 April 1989, 33–36; 'Forty Years on GATT', *The Economist*, 24 October 1987, 89.

[9] Trade Policy Review Mechanism – Arrangements for the Continued Operation of the Mechanism, Decision of 10 May 1994, L/7458; Annex 3 to the Marrakesh Agreement. See *The Legal Texts*, p. 380.

Article X of GATT (1947) may be considered as the earliest precursor to the TPRM. It provides the requirement for member states to notify their trade policies and practices in order to enhance their transparency. Nevertheless, the mechanism of Article X has always been found wanting in several regards: the notification requirements were seldom met; the analytical follow-up by the GATT Secretariat of the notified information was often lacking; and Article X of GATT (1947) did not contain a mechanism to nudge member states into greater adherence to the rules if the notified trade policies were perceived to be protectionist.

Further discussions therefore took place in the Tokyo Round Understanding Regarding Notification, Consultation, Dispute Settlement and Surveillance (1979). On the topic of surveillance, the Understanding requires that:

> The Contracting Parties agree to conduct a regular and systematic review of developments in the trading system. Particular attention would be paid to developments which affect rights and obligations under the GATT, to matters affecting the interests of less-developed contracting parties, to trade measures notified in accordance with this understanding and to measures which have been subject to consultation, conciliation or dispute settlement procedures laid down in this understanding.[10]

As a result of the Understanding, the Secretariat prepared twice-yearly reports on general developments in the world trading system. These reports were reviewed during the biannual special meetings of the GATT Council.

In the first half of the 1980s, the GATT Director-General Arthur Dunkel asked a group of seven experts 'to identify the fundamental causes of the problems afflicting the international trading system and to consider how these may be overcome during the remainder of the 1980's.' Within this framework, the report – drafted under the chairmanship of Swiss National Bank President Fritz Leutwiler – recognised the need for more comprehensive (individual) and regular (periodic) surveillance.[11] Proposal number eight of the report therefore stated that 'At the international level, trade policy and the functioning of the trading system should be made more open. Countries should be subject to regular oversight and surveillance of their policies and actions, about which the GATT Secretariat should collect and publish information'.

[10] DSU Agreement 10.

[11] *Trade Policies for a Better Future* p. 60; *Trade Policies for a Better Future: The Leutwiler Report, the GATT and the Uruguay Round*, p. 174.

The report furthermore proposed two alternative institutional options. Option one would consist of 'the establishment of a panel representing three to five governments that would review a GATT Secretariat report on the trade policies of the country in question and that would subject its representatives to questioning and make recommendations'. Option two would be the creation of 'an independent Trade Policy Committee, serviced by the GATT Secretariat, that would publish periodic reports on policy developments'. Moreover, the report attempted to reinforce the increased adherence to the rules function of this nascent surveillance mechanism by creating an almost prosecutorial role for the Secretariat while arguing that the Secretariat should 'act as a watchdog (though not judge) on behalf of the trading system as a whole' by analysing, publishing, discussing and questioning national trade policies.

In order to elaborate the concrete modalities hereto, the Punta Del Este Ministerial Declaration (1986) established the Functioning of the GATT System (FOGS) negotiating group.[12] Its modalities were, *inter alia*, 'to develop understanding and arrangements to enhance the surveillance in the GATT to enable regular monitoring of trade policies and practices of contracting parties and their impact on the functioning of the multilateral trading system'.[13] The FOGS thus engaged in a series of discussions with regard to surveillance during 1987 and 1988. Developed countries were mainly interested in improving the Secretariat's understanding and reporting on Member States' economic policy by placing greater emphasis on economic analysis and on the verification of increased adherence to contractual obligations. Developing countries focused more on the need for better trade surveillance capacity (especially of the major trading countries), on the improvement of their respective trade and investment policies and on being accorded international recognition thereof.[14]

Since almost all modalities of the TPRM had been elaborated at the end of 1988, the Montreal mid-term review of the Uruguay Round (1989) approved the temporary adoption of the TPRM. The first part, dedicated to objectives, mentioned the double objectives of the TPRM: transparency and increased adherence to the rules without enforcement.

[12] *Ibid.* [13] Uruguay Declaration, p. 20.

[14] S. Laird and R. Valdès, 'Trade Policy Review Mechanism', in A. Narlikar, M. Daunton and R.M. Stern (eds.), *The Oxford Handbook on The World Trade Organization*, (Oxford University Press, 2012), p. 465; A. Gosh, 'Information Gaps, Information Systems, and the WTO's Trade Policy Review Mechanism', *CEG Working Paper*, Vol. 40 (2008), p. 38.

These objectives were to be fostered by reviewing the contracting parties' national trade policies although such policies were to be placed in the wider context of (i) contracting parties' economic and developmental needs and policies, as well as (ii) their external environment.

The mid-term review moreover provided for a balanced periodicity of the reporting requirements: more important trading partners were to be reviewed on a more regular basis and TPRM reporting requirements were to be minimised in case of simultaneous consultation requirements under the GATT balance-of-payments provisions. The review furthermore set out the modalities for TPRM overview and revision. The GATT council – mandated with special prerogatives – would at periodic special meetings assemble as the Trade Policy Review Body (TPRB) before a final review of the TPRM, which would take place at the end of the Uruguay Round. The last section of the mid-term review provided – in addition to the (country-specific) TPRMs – for continued enhanced surveillance in the form of regular overviews of developments in the international trading environment that were having an impact on the multilateral trading environment.

A last (minor) review of the temporarily adopted TPRM followed in the spring of 1994. It essentially focused on the reporting requirements (form of the government reports and explicit recognition of the fact that 'trade policies must, to the extent necessary, be seen in the context of overall macro-economic and structural policies').[15] Some minor points were also made with regard to the periodicity of the reviews, the documentation requirements and TPRM organisational-specific requirements.

The entry into force of the Marrakesh Agreement coincided with the final adoption of the TPRM in its Annex 3.[16] Paragraph A(i) of Annex 3 states that:

> The purpose of the Trade Policy Review Mechanism ('TPRM') is to contribute to improved adherence by all Members to rules, disciplines and commitments made under the Multilateral Trade Agreements and, where applicable, the Plurilateral Trade Agreements, and hence to the smoother functioning of the multilateral trading system, by achieving greater transparency in, and understanding of, the trade policies and practices of Members.

[15] Trade Policy Review Mechanism – Arrangements for the Continued Operation of the Mechanism, Decision of 10 May 1994, L/7458.

[16] Annex 3 to the Marrakesh Agreement, see *The Legal Texts*, p. 380.

Paragraph A(ii) of Annex 3 furthermore clarifies that '. . . the function of the review mechanism is to examine the impact of Member's trade policies and practices on the multilateral trading system'.[17]

In conformity with paragraph F of Annex 3 to the Marrakesh Agreement,[18] four TPRM revisions followed in 1999,[19] 2005,[20] 2008[21] and 2011.[22] These appraisals – unequivocally and repeatedly – found that the TPRM functioned effectively. Although there is some academic debate with regard to the TPRM's main purpose (increased adherence without enforcement of the rules versus better understanding),[23] there is no historical or current doubt as to the TPRM's core object of review: paragraph A(ii) of Annex 3 to the Marrakesh Agreement explicitly states that '. . . the function of the review mechanism is to examine the impact of a Member's *trade policies and practices* on the multilateral trading system' (emphasis added).[24]

II. The scope of review

Trade policies cannot be assessed in isolation from broader macroeconomic policies and implications. Whether the TPRM is able to do so, raises the question of the legal and political limitations of its object of

[17] The peer review of national trade policies and practices within the framework of the TPRM has, since its establishment, also included the review of services and intellectual property.

[18] Paragrah F (Appraisal of the Mechanism) of Annex 3 to the Marrakesh Agreement. See *The Legal Texts*, p. 382.

[19] Appraisal of the Operation of the Trade Policy Review Mechanism – Draft Report to Ministers, WT/TPR/W/24, 30 September 1999, p. 4.

[20] Second Appraisal of the Operation of the Trade Policy Review Mechanism – Draft Report to Ministers, WT/TPR/W/33, 12 August 2005, p. 4.

[21] Draft – Third Appraisal of the Operation of the Trade Policy Review Mechanism, WT/TPR/W/38, 15 October 2008, p. 4; Third Appraisal of the Operation of the Trade Policy Review Mechanism, WT/TPR/229, 11 November 2008, p. 4.

[22] Fourth Appraisal of the Operation of the Trade Policy Review Mechanism, WT/TPR/W/44, 17 November 2011, p. 11.

[23] See, e.g., P. Mavroidis, 'Surveillance Schemes: The GATT's New Trade Policy Review Mechanism', *Michigan Journal of International Law* 13:2 (1992), 374–414 versus A. H. Qureshi, 'The New GATT Trade Policy Review Mechanism: An Exercise in Transparency or 'Enforcement?', *Journal of World Trade* 24:3 (1990), 142–60; A. H. Qureshi, 'Some Reflections on the GATT TPRM, in the Light of the Trade Policy Review of the European Communities – A Legal Perspective', *Journal of World Trade*, 26:6 (1992), 103–20 and A. H. Qureshi, 'Some Lessons from Developing Countries' Trade Policy Reviews in the GATT Framework: An Enforcement Perspective', *The World Economy* 18:3 (1995), 489–503.

[24] Chayes and Chayes, *The New Sovereignty*, pp. 244–6.

review. This section focuses on the TPRM's history and on its actual standard of review and reporting requirements.

The negotiating history of the TPRM demonstrated that the (nascent) TPRM's focus on policies affecting the international trading system went hand in hand with the member states' interest in examining the potentials and limits of further trade-related reporting that paid attention to the international trading system's wider monetary and financial context. The FOGS negotiations (1987–8) are replete with examples. Australia's first FOGS proposal regarding surveillance explicitly included the possibility of countries reporting on 'other economic ... (including external) factors affecting policy'.[25] Furthermore, some member states highlighted that:

> Closer cooperation in a wider range of areas between GATT and the international financial organizations would strengthen the coherence of international economic policies and ensure that trade policies were given their proper place in macro-economic policy as a whole: the expertise of GATT in trade policy questions could contribute to the operations of the IMF and the IBRD just as the expertise of these organizations in the areas of monetary and financial policies could contribute to the work of the Contracting Parties.[26]

This connection between GATT surveillance and coherence of policies was, *inter alia*, underlined by Jamaica while stating that

> the surveillance of macro-economic policies carried out by the IMF under its Article IV, while not involving any binding commitments, could provide a degree of moral suasion on all members; while by contrast, the surveillance carried out by the World Bank, limited to the policies of borrowing countries, did not cover the macro-economic policies or trade policies of developed economies. These would be covered by the proposed GATT review mechanism.[27]

[25] Multilateral Trade Negotiations, The Uruguay Round, Negotiating Group on Functioning of the GATT System, Communication from Australia, MTN.GNG/NG14/W/1, 3 April 1987, p. 5; Multilateral Trade Negotiations, The Uruguay Round, Negotiating Group on Functioning of the GATT System, Meeting of 7 April 1987, Note by the Secretariat, MTN.GNG/NG14/1, 10 April 1987, p. 2.

[26] Multilateral Trade Negotiations, The Uruguay Round, Negotiating Group on Functioning of the GATT System, Meeting of 28 September 1987, Note by the Secretariat, MTN.GNG/NG14/3, 8 October 1987, pp. 1–2.

[27] Multilateral Trade Negotiations, The Uruguay Round, Negotiating Group on Functioning of the GATT System Meeting of 26–30 September 1988, Note by the Secretariat, MTN.GNG/NG14/9, 18 October 1988, p. 8.

These delegations were therefore clearly of the view that 'reviews should be as broad as possible in scope; trade policy should be set in the context of overall macro-economic policy'.[28] Nevertheless, it was also highlighted that 'the review mechanism should confine itself to trade policies and could not be extended to general macro-economic policy'.[29] Moreover, some member states urged that 'Note should be taken . . . to avoid duplicating the work already undertaken by other international organizations (OECD, IMF)'[30] and stated that there was a need 'to keep a clear distinction between the surveillance functions exercised by the international financial organizations, particularly the IMF, and the development of monitoring of trade policies by GATT'.[31] A minority of members even explicitly cautioned against such 'background' considerations becoming themselves a subject for review. In this context, the suggestion was made that 'the country under review should decide on aspects of the "background" which should be considered relevant'.[32] Member states' *ad hoc* interests in, and approaches to, analysing trade policies and practices in their wider economic and financial contexts therefore gradually moved towards a more systematic quest for further horizontal policy analysis and coherence. TPRM activities would henceforth be fully aligned with the Marrakesh Declaration on the Contribution of the World Trade Organization to Achieving Greater Coherence in Global Economic Policy Making.[33] It is therefore not

[28] Multilateral Trade Negotiations, The Uruguay Round, Negotiating Group on Functioning of the GATT System Meeting of 3 and 4 November 1987, Note by the Secretariat, MTN.GNG/NG14/4, 30 November 1987, p. 3.

[29] Multilateral Trade Negotiations, The Uruguay Round, Negotiating Group on Functioning of the GATT System, Meeting of 21–23 March, Note by the Secretariat, MTN.GNG/NG14/6, 15 April 1988, p. 1; Multilateral Trade Negotiations, The Uruguay Round, Negotiating Group on Functioning of the GATT System Meeting of 6 and 9 November 1989, Note by the Secretariat, MTN.GNG/NG14/13, 12 December 1989, p. 27.

[30] Multilateral Trade Negotiations, The Uruguay Round, Negotiating Group on Functioning of the GATT System, Communication from Japan, MTN.GNG/NG14/W/8, 23 June 1987, p. 2.

[31] Multilateral Trade Negotiations, The Uruguay Round, Negotiating Group on Functioning of the GATT System, Meeting of 28 September 1987, Note by the Secretariat, MTN.GNG/NG14/3, 8 October 1987, p. 2.

[32] Multilateral Trade Negotiations, The Uruguay Round, Negotiating Group on Functioning of the GATT System, Meeting of 26–30 September 1988, MTN.GNG/NG14/9, 18 October 1988, p. 9.

[33] Marrakesh Agreement; WTO Agreements with the Fund and the Bank – Approved by the General Council at its Meeting on the 7, 8 and 13 November 1996, WT/L/195, 33; M. Auboin, 'Fulfilling the Marrakesh Mandate on Coherence: Ten Years of Cooperation between the WTO, IMF and World Bank', *WTO Discussion Papers*, No. 13, 2007, p. 33.

surprising that several elements of the TPRM's actual framework (including the TPRM's actual 'standard of review' and its reporting requirements) do not disbar the members from reporting on the economic and financial underpinnings of the trading system.

The TPRM's actual standard of review is very wide. Paragraph A(ii) of Annex 3 to the Marrakesh Agreement explicitly states that: 'The assessment carried out under the review mechanism takes place, to the extent relevant, against the background of the wider economic and developmental needs, policies and objectives of the Member concerned, as well as to its external environment'. Hence, paragraph A does not disbar member states from paying increased attention to the economic, monetary and financial underpinnings of the international trading system although the end of the same paragraph also states that '. . . the function of the review mechanism is to examine the impact of a Member's *trade* policies and practices on the multilateral trading system' (emphasis added).

The breadth of the TPRM's standard of review is moreover reflected in the flexible formal and content-based requirements for TPRM reporting. Annex 3 of the Marrakesh Agreement is quite succinct with regard to the formal requirements. Paragraph C (v) and (vi) of Annex 3 to the Marrakesh Agreement only provides a basic outline for TPRB reviews based on (i) the publication of a government report produced by the member under review, (ii) the publication of a report drafted by the WTO Secretariat and (iii) a compilation of the minutes of the TPRM meeting. Paragraph D of Annex 3 to the Marrakesh Agreement furthermore indicates that 'this format is to be decided upon by the Trade Policy Review Body' and that 'the initial format (subject to further potential review) was based on the Outline Format for Country Reports established by the Decision of 19 July 1989 (BISD/36/S/406–409)'. This formal reporting format has remained the general standard providing for flexible contours within which the TPRM department or the government under review can decide to pay more or less attention to any TPR chapter(s) or section(s). The succinct nature of the formal reporting requirements is matched by the relative absence of requirements as to the content of the various formal reports. The specific scope and depth of the Secretariat report is hence (again) very much left to the discretion of the members of the Trade Policies Review Division (TPRD). Practice has demonstrated that members under review can decide to engage in a narrow or a wide review of trade policies and practices.

A review of the evolution of successive TPR reports drafted by the Secretariat shows a broad and flexible understanding of reporting requirements. Two periods can be distinguished: the period before the start of 1996 and the period thereafter.[34] From 1991 until the first three reports in 1996, the Secretariat reports were structured into six chapters: (1) the economic environment, (2) trade policy regime: framework and objectives, (3) foreign exchange regime (in TPR reports from 1991 to 1993) or foreign direct investment and trade (in TPR reports from 1993 to 1996), (4) trade policies and practices by measure, (5) trade policies and practices by sector and (6) trade disputes and consultations. As from the 1996 TPR report on Switzerland,[35] the Secretariat reports have been structured into four main chapters: (1) the economic environment, (2) trade policy regime: framework and objectives, (3) trade policy and practice by measure and (4) trade policy and practices by sector. This revised format generally dispenses with the previously traditional third chapter on investment.[36] TPR reporting on investment is however channelled to the other chapters (mainly Chapter 2).

The Secretariat's TPR reporting on trade-related economic and financial factors determining the setting of the trade policy of the member under review therefore mainly occurs in the context of Chapter 1 (economic environment).[37] Chapter 1 generally covers the main macro-economic policy developments determining a country's trade performance including the framework of the country's fiscal policy, monetary policy and foreign exchange system, its exchange rate policy and its trade balance as well as trade-related structural reforms. In addition to Chapter 1, some reporting on trade-related economic and financial factors can be found in the pre-1996 Chapter 3 (although the reporting on a country's foreign exchange regime was moved to Chapter 1 after 1994) and in the post-1996 Chapter 3 (although economic and/or financial information is often spread around

[34] D. Keesing, *Improving Trade Policy Reviews in the World Trade Organization*, Policy Analyses in International Economics 52 (Washington, DC: Peterson Institute for International Economics, 1998), p. 17.

[35] Trade Policy Review Switzerland, Report by the Secretariat, WT/TPR/S/13, 26 April 1996, p. 124.

[36] It also generally dispenses with the (previously traditional) chapter on trade disputes. However, trade disputes are sometimes briefly discussed under the new Chapter 2 (trade policy regime: framework and objectives).

[37] Although chapter 1 of the Secretariat report on a member under review does *not* form the Secretariat's core object of reporting, this chapter only aims to assess the coverage of economic and financial elements that underpin international trade (the TPRM's core object); Keesing, *Improving Trade Policy Reviews*, pp. 17–21.

several subsections, for instance covering export finance, investment and regulation of prices).

The Secretariat's TPR coverage of trade-underpinning or trade-related factors has therefore varied considerably in depth and scope. Governmental TPR reporting is done at national discretion but with regard to the Secretariat's TPRM reporting, some academics mention the risk that there 'is insufficient restraint on the WTO Secretariat in the crafting of the report' with 'international civil servants getting embroiled in the domestic politics of the country under review'.[38] Nevertheless, this (isolated) argument seems to be erroneous and can easily be rebutted on the grounds that successive TPRM reviews have demonstrated that the WTO membership seems to rate highly the (objective and economic rather than legalistic) approach of the TPRM. Moreover, too flexible reporting by individual TPRM authors seems to be generally rectified in view of the fact that the drafting of the Secretariat's report for TPRs generally entails collaboration between several individual authors as well as a close coordination with other WTO divisions.

III. The review of monetary and financial affairs

The question remains whether the TPRM has properly employed its institutional flexibility and scope of review to report on the wider context in line with its double objectives – increased transparency and increased adherence to WTO rules. This section examines whether and to what extent these objectives have been achieved in the context of TPR reporting on monetary and financial elements.

Two cases are examined: (i) TPRM reporting with regard to the first financial crises during the history of the WTO (the Mexican crisis of 1995 and the Asian financial crisis of 1997–8) and (ii) TPRM naming-and-shaming with regard to the Chinese exchange-rate misalignment. These two cases can be distinguished by the fact that they are either more-or-less clearly delineated in time (i.e., the Mexican and the Asian financial crises) or by the fact that the TPR naming and shaming seems to have some increased relevance in this context – not only as a direct mechanism for peer pressure in the field of trade – but also as an indirect vehicle for peer pressure in the field of monetary and financial affairs (i.e., the Chinese TPRs). The ongoing European sovereign debt, banking

[38] A. H. Qureshi, *The World Trade Organization – Implementing International Trade Norms* (Manchester University Press, 1996), p. 114.

and growth crisis might offer another interesting case study. However, financial problems involving some of the European member states may (and will) probably result in further TPR coverage before the crisis is finally over. It should be noted that the 2009 and 2011 TPRs of the European Union have – so far – respectively argued (i) for a continued EU contribution towards making trade play a key role in reversing the (global) economic slowdown but also (ii) for a phasing out of (EU and national) financial support to several sectors including finance, automobiles, construction and tourism once the economic recovery has taken hold. Furthermore, the naming and shaming that originates in the successive Chinese TPRs seems to be mainly concentrated on the (single) problem of perceived exchange rate misalignment. This can be contrasted with the more heterogeneous naming and shaming that has resulted (so far) from the successive EU TPRs, a reminder that the ongoing EU crisis has a variety of causes (in the sovereign debt, banking and economic growth areas).

1. TPR reporting in the aftermath of the Mexican financial crisis (1995) and the Asian financial crisis (1997–8)

The Mexican financial crisis erupted in December 1994 when the Mexican government devalued and then floated the peso.[39] But, the so-called Tequila crisis was also based on a longer-standing explosive cocktail of dangerous factors. These included: (i) a strong monetary expansion in view of the 1994 presidential elections, (ii) lax regulation and supervision of the financial system, (iii) the overvaluation of the peso linked to the dollar, (iv) high capital inflows that were volatile as a result of the political instability in Mexico, (v) the issuance of dollar-denominated debt and (vi) the fatal rise of US interests.

The WTO did not formally respond to the Mexican financial crisis for several reasons. First, the WTO came into being through the Marrakesh Agreement that came into effect during the crisis on 1 January 1995. The WTO therefore did not start to function until a few months after the start of the Mexican Tequila crisis. Second, although the TPRM today provides for the possibility of TPRM monitoring of developments in the international trading environment (including monitoring of trade-related monetary affairs), the WTO Agreement (unlike the IMF) does

[39] P. Krugman and M. Obstfeld, *International Economics: Theory & Policy* (Boston, MA: Pearson International Edition, 2006), p. 618; J. A. Whitt, Jr., 'The Mexican Peso Crisis', *Economic Review, Federal Reserve Bank of America* (1996), 20.

not provide any instruments to formally deal with international financial crisis management. Finally, even (co-incidental) TPR reporting on the Mexican financial crisis was wanting in view (i) of the existing TPR periodicity and (ii) the fact that member states' economic and financial fundamentals do not form the core object of TPR reporting. Mexico's first (GATT) TPR took place in 1993.[40] At that time the Mexican TPR (or the preceding analysis by the IMF on which it was based) was not able to warn the international community about the looming signs of a financial crisis.[41] In accordance with the existing TPR cycle of reviews, Mexico's second TPR (1997) took place after the crisis but the WTO's main (and adequate) answer to financial crises was the creation of the monitoring exercise.

The Asian financial crisis came to the forefront in 1997–8 when one of Thailand's largest financial institutions, Finance One, defaulted and the Thai government unsuccessfully tried to resolve the situation.[42] Nevertheless, the Thai crisis was also based on longer-standing elements including (i) excessive investment especially in the real-estate sector, (ii) high borrowing (much of it in dollar-denominated debt) and (iii) a deteriorating balance-of-payments position. Furthermore, following the forced devaluation of the Thai baht, several speculation waves hit the respective currencies of Malaysia, Indonesia, Korea and Japan. The Asian crisis had a (marginally) greater impact on the WTO than its Mexican predecessor. It coincided quasi-simultaneously with several TPRs and the crisis indirectly fostered some other (non-TPRM-related) institutional WTO developments.

Almost all the Asian countries that were affected by the financial crisis went through a TPRM: either in the period preceding the crisis period (Korea in 1996), during the full-blown crisis period (Malaysia in 1997, Japan in 1998 and Indonesia in 1998) or in the period after the crisis (Thailand in 1999 and Korea underwent a second TPRM in 2000). Although TPRs were described as 'a constant learning process about

[40] Trade Policy Review of Mexico: 19–20 April 1993, GATT Council's Evaluation, Basic Documents and Selected Documents (BISD), GATT/1575, 22 April 1993, p. 7; Trade Policy Review of Mexico: Minutes of the Meeting, Basic Documents and Selected Documents (BISD), GATT, C/RM/M/35, 8 July 1993, p. 45.

[41] T. J. Kehoe, 'A Review of Mexico's Trade Policy from 1982 to 1994', *The World Economy: Global Trade Policy* (1995), 135–7.

[42] L. Cuyvers and B. Kerremans, *Internationale Economische Organisaties* (Antwerp: Garant; 2005), pp. 114–16; Krugman and Obstfeld, *International Economics*, pp. 622–4.

trade reforms and the linkages between trade and other policies',[43] the TPR's periodicity remains (as it should) firmly based on a members' share of world trade in a representative period of three years and not on its involvement in a financial crisis. The WTO membership did not see the need for a (gradual or rapid) alteration of the TPRM's periodicity because of the financial crises, nor did it perceive the need to alter the scope or depth of TPRM reporting with regard to the monetary or financial context.[44] Monetary and financial coverage within the framework of a TPR remains therefore very much confined to the utilisation of government sources unless there is a lack of such data, in which case IMF data are used.

Nevertheless, the Asian financial crises contributed indirectly to the creation of a Working Group on Trade, Debt and Finance (WGTDF). The establishment of this group was initially proposed at the WTO Ministerial Conference in Seattle (1999) as a response to developing countries' trade concerns stemming from a variety of international financial problems.[45]

Although this linkage (between the activities of the WGTDF and the TPRM) is quite weak, TPR analysis has been sporadically cited in WGTDF context.[46] Moreover, some (minimal) TPRM-specific reflection was undertaken in the context of the WGTDF. For instance, in the framework of the greater coherence debate between the WTO, the IMF and the World Bank, an analysis was carried out on possible synergies between the respective investment reviews by the United Nations Conference on Trade and Development (UNCTAD), the Organisation for Economic Co-operation and Development (OECD), the IMF, the World Bank and the TPRM.[47] Another example can be found in an

[43] S. Laird and R. Valdès, 'Trade Policy Review Mechanism', in A. Narlikar, M. Daunton and R. M. Stern (eds.), *The Oxford Handbook on The World Trade Organization* (Oxford University Press, 2012), p. 465.

[44] Interview with WTO officials of the TPRD; S. J. Evenett, *The Role of the WTO During Systemic Economic Crises* (Geneva: The Graduate Institute, 2009), pp. 7 and 10.

[45] The WGTDF was established at the 4th Ministerial Conference in Doha in November 2001. Ministerial Declaration, Doha – Qatar, adopted on 14 November 2001, WT/MIN (01)/DEC/1, 20 November 2001, para. 36.

[46] Working Group on Trade, Debt and Finance, The Relationship Between Trade And Finance, A Review Of Selected Literature Related to Financial Crises in the 1990s, WT/WGTDF/W/4, 26 May 2002, pp. 5–7; TPR analysis was also cited in the context of the WTO/Economic Research and Statistics Division. In this context see M. Daly, 'Evolution of Asia's Outward-looking Economic Policies: Some Lessons from Trade Policy Reviews', Geneva, WTO, *Staff Working Paper ERSD*, 2011, p. 59.

[47] Working Group on Trade, Debt and Finance, Towards Greater Coherence, Note by the Secretariat, WT/WGTDF/W/17, 13 November 2002, 11.

(unsuccessful) proposal by the African, Caribbean and Pacific Group of States (ACP) to establish a regular Committee on Trade, Debt and Finance whose tasks would include the review of the TPRM 'to have it cover developed countries' policies on the provision of development assistance, debt reduction and export credit, with the view of agreeing on commitments to ensure that such policies do not undermine the development objectives of developing and least-developed countries'.[48]

2. TPR and exchange rate alignments

The relationship between exchange-rate regimes and trade is complex. Coric and Pugh demonstrated that 'on average, exchange rate variability exerts a negative effect on international trade' but also that the result 'is highly conditional'.[49] Even on the stricter issue of exchange rate misalignments, the majority of theoretical and empirical studies have shown that 'the relationship between the level of a currency and trade is so multifaceted and complex that it is hard to take a firm line in any particular direction'.[50] At first sight, it would indeed seem obvious that – all else remaining equal – governmental intervention in exchange rate markets in order to lower the price of the national currency *vis-à-vis* other currencies leads to cheaper national exports and to more expensive foreign imports.[51] However, economists have been able to demonstrate that this assumption is fraught with complexities – both under a so-called flexible price scenario and in a fixed price context.[52] Under the former, the 'long-run neutrality' of money would equate a governmental devaluation simply with a change in the monetary unit of account, whereas the latter sticky-price context would completely ignore the effect of exchange rate movements on other prices in the global economy.

[48] Working Group on Trade, Debt and Finance, Communication From The ACP, WT/WGTDF/W/30, 15 April 2005, 3.

[49] The Relationship between Exchange Rates and International Trade: a Review of Economic Literature – Note by the Secretariat, WT/WGTDF/W/57, 27 September 2011, p. 31; B. Cavic and G. Pugh, 'The Effect of Exchange Rate Volatility on International Trade: A Meta-Regression Analysis', *Applied Economics*, 42 (2010), 2631–44.

[50] The Relationship between Exchange Rates and International Trade: A Review of Economic Literature – Note by the Secretariat, WT/WGTDF/W/57, 27 September 2011, p. 31. Also, for a discussion of the impact of exchange rate misalignment on trade imbalances, see J. Marchetti, M. Ruta and R. Teh, 'Trade Imbalances and Multilateral Trade Cooperation', Chapter 13, this volume.

[51] R. W. Staiger and A. O. Sykes, 'Currency Manipulation and World Trade', *NBER Working Paper*, No. 14600, 2008, p. 3.

[52] *Ibid.*, pp. 5–14, 15–25.

However, this complex economic relationship did not deter countries from developing several national and international trade-related instruments to deal with monetary misalignment.[53]

At the national level, Title III of the US Omnibus Trade and Competitiveness Act of 1988 (the Trade Act of 1988)[54] provides that 'The Secretary of the Treasury shall analyse on an annual basis the exchange rate policies of foreign countries, in consultation with the IMF, and consider whether countries manipulate the rate of exchange ... for purposes of preventing effective balance of payments adjustments or gaining unfair competitive advantage in international trade'. If the US Treasury Department is of the opinion that such a manipulation is occurring, it is supposed to resolve the issue by negotiations unless 'such negotiations would have a serious detrimental impact on vital national and economic and security interests'.

Under the Trade Act of 1988, the US Department of Treasury labelled Taiwan (1988 and 1992), Korea (1988) and China (1992) as currency manipulators. Each citation by the US Treasury Department lasted for at least two six-month periods, while China's lasted for five periods ending in 1994.[55] Subsequent Treasury negotiations generally led to reforms of the respective exchange rate regimes, to an appreciation of the currencies involved and to a decline of the respective trade balances.[56] While the Chinese exchange issues remained unresolved from a US perspective, no new instances of currency manipulation under the Trade Act of 1988 were raised after 1994 mainly because the strict conditions for a finding of currency manipulation – i.e., when an economy has a material global current account surplus and a significant bilateral trade surplus with the US – were not met.[57]

[53] A. Mattoo and A. Subramanian, 'Currency Undervaluation and Sovereign Wealth Funds: A New Role for the World Trade Organization', *World Bank Policy Research Working Paper*, No. 4668, 2008, p. 28; Staiger and Sykes, 'Currency Manipulation and World Trade', p. 42; J. E. Sanford, 'Currency Manipulation: The IMF and the WTO', *Congressional Research Service*, 2010, p. 6; C. D. Zimmerman, 'Exchange Rate Misalignment and International Law', *American Journal of International Law*, 105:3 (2011), 423–77.

[54] US Omnibus Trade and Competitiveness Act of 1988, §§3001–3006, Pub. L. No. 100–418, 102 Stat. 1107 (1988) (codified at 22 USC §§5304–5306), www.treasury.gov/press-center/press-releases/Documents/js1335attachmentjs1335.pdf.

[55] R. E. Scott, 'Currency Manipulation – History Shows That Sanctions Are Needed', Washington, Economic Policy Institute, *Policy Memorandum*, No. 164, 2010, p. 7.

[56] US Government Accountability Office (GAO), 'International Trade: Treasury Assessments Have Not Found Currency Manipulation, but Concerns About Exchange Rate Continue', Washington, *US Government Accountability Office (GAO-5-351)*, 2005, p. 85.

[57] *Ibid.*, 2.

A new Currency Exchange Rate Oversight Reform Act of 2010, aiming at China, was introduced by a bi-partisan group of Senators led by Charles Schumer, Debbie Stabenow and Lindsey Graham.[58] This Act requires twice-yearly reports by the US Treasury Department identifying fundamentally misaligned currencies and the designation of such currencies for priority action in certain circumstances. Upon designation, the US Treasury Department would have to consult bilaterally with the country that issues the currency in order to facilitate the adoption of appropriate policies to address the fundamental misalignment. The Act furthermore provides that 'failure' and 'persistent failure' to adopt appropriate policies can result in several steps of increasingly punitive action. A presidential waiver for potential punitive action is nevertheless foreseen, though limited by final Congressional authority.

The Schumer-Stabenow-Graham Act was described as 'legally flawed, economically dangerous and unnecessary'.[59] It is blinkered to the fact that legal experts disagree on the extent of a possible application of WTO rules to correct exchange rate misalignment[60] and to the eventuality that a WTO panel might reach a different decision on the topic from that reached by the IMF.[61] Furthermore, the Act risks sparking new trade wars – a rather unwelcome outcome in view of the still gloomy state of affairs of the Doha Development agenda negotiations.

At the international level, the main venues for action on exchange rate problems are situated within the framework of the IMF or within the realm of the WTO.

Article IV, Section 1 of the IMF Articles of Agreement requires each member of the Fund 'to collaborate with the Fund and other Members to assure orderly exchange arrangements and to promote a stable system of

[58] Currency Exchange Rate Oversight Reform Act of 2010, www.gpo.gov/fdsys/pkg/BILLS-112s1619es/pdf/BILLS-112s1619es.pdf.

[59] 'Trade with China, and Now Protectionism – America's Latest Anti-China Bill Tackles a Problem Already Solved', *The Economist*, 15 October 2011.

[60] T. Cottier and T. Payosova, 'Challenges in International Monetary Law', in I. Govaere, R. Quick and M. Bronckers (eds.), *Trade and Competition Law in the EU and Beyond* (Cheltenham: Edward Elgar, 2011), pp. 42–4 versus C. D. Zimmerman, 'Exchange Rate Misalignment and International Law', *American Journal of International Law*, 105:3 (2011), 423–77.

[61] Independent Evaluation Office of the International Monetary Fund, *IMF Involvement in International Trade Policy Issues* (Washington, DC: Independent Evaluation Office of the International Monetary Fund, 2009), pp. 78–9.

exchange rates'.[62] It further requires that the membership shall in particular 'avoid manipulating exchange rates or the international monetary system in order to prevent effective balance of payments adjustment or to gain unfair competitive advantage over other members'. The 2007 Decision on Bilateral Surveillance specifies that this could mean either 'to cause the exchange rate to move or to prevent such movement . . . for the purpose of securing fundamental exchange rate misalignment in the form of an undervalued exchange rate and for the purpose of securing such misalignment to increase net exports'.[63] The 2007 Decision moreover introduces a non-binding principle D with the recommendation to 'avoid exchange rate policies that result in external instability' (regardless of their purpose).[64] The IMF Articles of Agreement and its subsequent 2007 Decision are very difficult to enforce. Article IV, Section 1(iii) of the IMF Agreement is subject to (hard to provide) evidence of 'bad intent'. Moreover, an amendment of the IMF Articles of Agreement in order to establish a more robust enforcement mechanism would be hard to obtain. In practice, such an amendment would not only require an 85 per cent majority vote of the IMF membership but would also run counter to the interests of most of its members.

With regard to the WTO, academic writing has essentially focused on four possible venues: (i) a complaint based on Article XV of GATT (1947) (based on the assumption that exchange rate misalignment violates the WTO membership's obligation to cooperate with the IMF on questions relating to freedom or restrictions concerning exchange and trade),[65] (ii) a complaint based on Articles 1 to 3 of the WTO Agreement on Subsidies and Countervailing Measures (ASCM) (axed on the understanding that Chinese exchange rate practices amount to WTO-inconsistent export subsidies),[66] (iii) a complaint based on Article XXIII:1 of the GATT (1947) (based on the assumption that exchange rate misalignment would result in the nullification or impairment of

[62] The IMF Articles of Agreement are available at www.imf.org/external/pubs/ft/aa.index.htm.

[63] The IMF Bilateral Surveillance over Members' Policies – 2007 Decision is available at www.imf.org/external/np/sec/pn/2007/pn0769.htm.

[64] The 2007 Decision was replaced with the new Integrated Surveillance Decision in March 2012, www.imf.org/external/np/exr/facts/isd.htm.

[65] Article XV of GATT (1947), see *The Legal Texts*, pp. 443–4.

[66] Articles 1 to 3 of the Agreement on Subsidies and Countervailing Measures. See *The Legal Texts*, pp. 231–3.

a benefit or an impediment to the achievement of an objective)[67] and (iv) a (more general) amendment of the above-mentioned WTO rules. Nevertheless, each of these venues is fraught with difficulties.

Article XV of GATT (1947) provides for WTO–IMF cooperation in order to pursue a coordinated policy with regard to exchange questions. Within this framework, Article XV:4 of GATT (1947) explicitly stipulates that: 'Contracting parties shall not, by exchange action, frustrate the intent of the provisions of this Agreement, nor, by trade action, the intent of the provisions of the Articles of Agreement of the IMF'.[68] Article XV would however be difficult to enforce since the evidence of a 'wrongful' intent would be near impossible to provide.

Articles 1 to 3 of the WTO Agreement on Subsidies and Countervailing Measures (SCM Agreement) specify the conditions under which countries may and may not provide subsidies to help promote their national exports. However, legal experts either (at minimum) agree that SCM Agreement rules are currently not ideally equipped to deal with exchange rate misalignment[69] or (at maximum) completely disagree – in principle – on the possibility.[70]

Another venue for legal action could theoretically be provided by Article XXIII:1(b) of GATT (1947). A so-called non-violation complaint would result in legal adjudication based on the assumption that the exchange rate misalignment would have resulted in the nullification or impairment of a benefit or in an impediment to the achievement of an objective, irrespective of a violation of a legal norm. Currency misalignment has so far never been interpreted by GATT or WTO adjudication in light of Article XXIII:1(b) of GATT (1947). The conditions are difficult to meet. In the *Japan – Film* case, requirements for the fulfilment of a non-violation complaint stated: 'It must be demonstrated that the competitive position of the imported products subject to and benefiting

67 Article XXIII:1 of GATT (1947), *The Legal Texts*, p. 457; G. C. Hufbauer and Y. W. and K. Sheth, 'US-China Trade Disputes: Rising Tide, Rising Stakes', Washington, Institute for International Economics, *Policy Analyses in International Economics*, 78: 2 (2006), 122. For a study on the potential exchange rate disputes that may be brought before the DSB, see the contribution by G. Z. Marceau and J. J. Maughan, 'The WTO Dispute Settlement Mechanism in Matters Involving Exchange Rates and Trade', Chapter 14, this volume.

68 The Annex to GATT (1947) clarifies the word '*frustrate*' in Ad Article XV. See *The Legal Texts*, p. 483.

69 Mattoo and Subramanian, 'Currency Undervaluation and Sovereign Wealth Funds'.

70 T. Cottier and T. Payosova, 'Challenges in International Monetary Law', pp. 42–4 *versus* Zimmerman, 'Exchange Rate Misalignment and International Law', 423–77.

from a relevant market access (tariff) concession is being upset by the application of a measure not reasonably anticipated' would be difficult to prove.[71] Furthermore, none of the recent non-violation complaints have been successful. The Appellate Body in the *EC – Asbestos* and the *US – Offset Act* cases even underlined that 'the non-violation remedy . . . should be approached with caution and should remain an exceptional remedy'.[72] It would therefore be difficult to argue that the use of a non-violation complaint in order to redress a macro-economic malpractice would stand.

Finally, a legal amendment of any of the above-mentioned WTO rule(s) to enable them to deal appropriately with currency misalignment would be hard to obtain in view of the legal unanimity requirement. The political will for such an amendment seems to be lacking. A WTO seminar on exchange rates and trade in 2012 was marked by some words of caution from the then Director-General: 'Exchange rates are not a new issue for the WTO/GATT, trade policy alone cannot be the answer and the WTO system cannot solve it all'.[73]

In light of this unclear legal situation and the prudent approach that is generally taken, it is interesting to observe that views were expressed and efforts made within the TPRM on alleged currency misalignment. In comparison to national action and action undertaken in the context of the IMF or WTO, the TPRM's 'action' (at least with China) has had the effect of drawing attention to the problem in a trade-related setting. Unlike the venues for national action, the TPRM is not hindered by strict legal requirements (such as those emanating from the 1988 Trade Act) or based on an (incorrect) interpretation of the legal WTO possibilities (such as the Currency Exchange Rate Oversight Reform Act of 2010). Its international naming and shaming practice confers greater legitimacy than a purely national (or bilateral) approach.[74] Unlike the IMF venues for international action, the TPRM has the advantage of being able to

[71] WTO Panel Report, Japan – Measures Affecting Consumer Photographic Film and Paper, WT/DS44/4, adopted 22 April 1998, para. 10.82.

[72] WTO Appellate Body Report, EC – Measures Affecting the Asbestos and Asbestos Containing Products, WT/DS135/AB/R, adopted 5 April 2001, para. 7.125.

[73] Speech by Director-General Pascal Lamy on the occasion of a WTO seminar on Exchange Rates and Trade, 27 March 2012 www.wto.org/english/news_e/sppl_e/sppl222_e.htm.

[74] The Trade Act of 1988 has been described by the US President as 'Sons of Smoot-Hawley' and 'Rambo-esque' in D. E. Birenbaum, 'The Omnibus Trade Act of 1988: Trade Law Dialectics', *University of Pennsylvania Journal of International Business Law* 10:4 (1988), 654–61.

explicitly link international trade practices to underpinning monetary and financial factors. In contrast to the other non-TPRM WTO venues that were provided, the TPRM does not suffer from any legal handicaps when undertaking its operations within its broad mandate and objectives.

Since China's accession to the WTO on 11 December 2001, China has been subject to TPRs in 2006, 2008, 2010 and 2012. In each of these, IMF data and analysis have been used in order to name and shame China within the framework of the WTO and push it in the direction of an economically more appropriate exchange rate regime. In this regard, it is noteworthy that the TPRM's call for improved adherence to WTO rules has varied over time but was (and is) always intrinsically linked to IMF data and analysis. Initially, it grew louder. Later, the TPRM's call became more muted in response to China's positive role in the recovery of the (still) fragile international economic and financial environment.

The Secretariat's TPRM reports generally have been most prudent with regard to naming and shaming.[75] In 2006, the Secretariat noted that: 'The move to a more flexible exchange rate could enable China to operate a more independent monetary policy and allow the market to play a greater role in determining interest rates and therefore in allocating resources' and 'With a de facto fixed exchange rate in relation to the US dollar (until July 2005), the resulting accumulation of foreign reserves has caused rapid growth in the money supply and bank lending, which could lead to economic imbalances and contribute to increased inflation'.[76] In 2008 and notwithstanding the increased flexibility of the Chinese exchange rate regime, the IMF-backed WTO calls grew louder. The report underscores that:

> A more flexible exchange rate policy could enable China to operate a more independent monetary policy, which would be better suited to ensuring a low and stable rate of inflation, and therefore contribute to a macro-economic environment more conducive to sustained strong economic growth. A more flexible exchange rate and thus more independent monetary policy would complement structural reforms, especially those concerning the capital market, and obviate the need for price-controls and other non-market measures to contain inflation.

[75] The Secretariat's coverage of economic and financial underpinnings of member states' trade practices is entirely based on IMF data and analysis.

[76] Trade Policy Review People's Republic of China, Report by the Secretariat, WT/TPR/S/161, 28 February 2006, IX, pp. 8–9.

Explicit IMF analysis underscores the statement: 'According to the IMF, the observed path of the exchange rate was mainly determined by official action'.[77] The 2010 Secretariat report again was entirely based on the IMF assessment. It states that 'the IMF welcomed the important progress made in the past few years in increasing the market's role in determining the exchange rate, as well as the consequent substantial real appreciation that has been achieved since the exchange rate reform in 2005' but also that 'some IMF directors nevertheless supported the view that the Renminbi remains "substantially undervalued"'.[78] In 2012 – probably due to a smaller Chinese capital account and the role China played in the global economic recovery – the report became somewhat muted: 'Since July 2005 (when China's exchange rate reform started), the Renminbi has appreciated in nominal terms by about 31 % against the dollar' and 'this rate of appreciation has been somewhat slower in the last few years than at the beginning of the reform programme'. However, existing IMF criticism is again referred to. The report notes that 'IMF directors welcomed the authorities' commitment to move gradually to more price-based tools of monetary policy and continue to improve the monetary policy framework and the interest rate structure'. But the report also states that: 'They (the IMF directors) also saw room for a further tightening of monetary conditions through greater reliance on interest rates and nominal exchange rate appreciation, while taking care to safeguard financial system stability.'

In their quest for increased adherence to the rules, member states are generally quite vocal during TPRB meetings and in their written questions. Sometimes, an increased 'legalisation' of peer-pressure arguments can be noted. In 2006, member states either directly urged China to develop a more flexible exchange rate or (more indirectly) asked when and how this could or would be achieved (based on the Secretariat's TPRM reporting).[79] In 2008, (even) the discussant was rather critical, wondering 'what the inflation rate would be had the RMB not

[77] Trade Policy Review People's Republic of China, Report by the Secretariat, WT/TPR/S/199, 16 April 2008, XV-XVI, pp. 10–11 and 23.

[78] Trade Policy Review China, Report by the Secretariat, WT/TPR/S/230, 26 April 2010, VIII, pp. 4–5.

[79] Trade Policy Review People's Republic of China, Minutes of the Meeting, WT/TPR/M/161, pp. 13, 21 and 23 – Thailand however described the more flexible exchange rate regime reforms as 'an example of success'; Trade Policy Review People's Republic of China, Minutes of the Meeting, Addendum, WT/TPR/M/161/Add. 1, pp. 23, 29, 34, 98, 112 and 160.

appreciated, or by less'. He furthermore stated that 'if the focus of attention was on one side (too much money or too few goods) whereas the problem was more on the other, there was risk, for example, of causing the economy to slow down further without an abatement in the inflation statistics' and asked 'whether China would explore the possibility of reforming its exchange regime ... in order to allow for greater flexibility in its monetary policy'.[80] In 2010, the negative effects of the undervalued Chinese exchange rate were especially felt in South America. Ecuador, Columbia and the Dominican Republic were therefore very much at the forefront with arguments for the establishment of a better exchange rate regime.[81] Moreover, legal arguments were also introduced by India. It explicitly reminded the members that: 'The exchange rate of China under its fixed exchange rate policy is seen to be trade distorting and protectionist as it gives undue advantage to its exporters and inhibits imports into China. This regime may be in violation of Article XV(4) of GATT, 1994 and Article IV, Section 1 Articles of Agreement of the International Monetary Fund'.[82] In 2012, the comments of the WTO membership were primarily positive given the continued appreciation of Chinese currency and China's role in the recovery of the (still) fragile world economy.[83]

In view of the prudent nudging by the Secretariat and the more critical naming and shaming by the member states, China has been isolated and very much on the defensive in regard to its exchange rate regime. China's position in 2006, 2008, 2010 and 2012 consequently came down to a political and a legal argument. First, China liked to mention the ongoing reform process of its exchange rate policy, which in the long term should lead to full convertibility of the renminbi under both the current and the capital accounts. This process should take the domestic *and* the foreign context into account.[84] Second, China argued that

[80] Trade Policy Review China, Minutes of the Meeting, WT/TPR/M/199, 24 July 2008, pp. 9, 17, 27, 31 and 32; Trade Policy Review China, Minutes of the Meeting, WT/TPR/M/199/ Add. 1, pp. 38 and 150.

[81] Trade Policy Review China, Record of the Meeting, WT/TPR/M/230, 29 June 2010, pp. 24, 37, 40, 47.

[82] Trade Policy Review China, Record of the Meeting, Addendum, WT/TPR/M/230/ Add. 1, pp. 272–3, 474–5.

[83] Trade Policy Review China, Record of the Meeting, WT/TPR/M/264, pp. 17, 34, 40, 55, 56.

[84] Trade Policy Review, Report by the People's Republic of China, WT/TPR/G/161, p. 7; Trade Policy Review People's Republic of China, Minutes of the Meeting, Addendum, WT/TPR/M/161/Add. 1, p. 160 onwards; Trade Policy Review People's Republic of

neither the WTO nor the IMF have legal jurisdiction to adjudicate and enforce these issues.[85]

Given the frequent opposing remarks between the country under review and its peers, the concluding remarks of the Chairman are generally prudent. This has also been the case with regard to the Chinese exchange rate regime. In 2006, the Chairman (rather laconically) underlined that 'Regarding the exchange-rate regime, which some Members raised, China said it was taking steps to further develop its foreign exchange market'.[86] This declaration goes in the same direction as the Chairman's intervention in 2008 whereby attention is (succinctly) drawn to the fact that: 'Some Members called for a greater flexibility in China's monetary/exchange rate policy, which would be facilitated by a more smooth-functioning capital market'.[87] In 2010, the Chairman's statement was even congratulatory in view of China's positive role in the aftermath of the global financial crisis.[88] The same congratulatory tone can be observed in 2012. Here, the Chairman states that: 'Prompt actions by China through fiscal stimulus and prudential monetary policies were welcomed' and (diplomatically) that 'It was noted that this had resulted in ... some easing of macroeconomic imbalances that had been remarked on in previous reviews'.[89]

The broad standard of review, flexible reporting requirements and the TPRM's twofold objectives (increased transparency and increased adherence to the rules without enforcement) provide theoretical scope for increased reporting and naming and shaming with regard to the economic, monetary or financial elements that underpin international trade. Nevertheless, in practice, both have been inhibited by the periodicity of the TPRM and by the fact that the international trading system – and not its context – remains the core object of the TPRM review.

China, Minutes of the Meeting, Addendum, WT/TPR/M/161/Add. 3, p. 45; Trade Policy Review, Report by China, WT/TPR/G/199, p. 11; Trade Policy Review China, Minutes of the Meeting, WT/TPR/M/199, pp. 4, 6, 7; Trade Policy Review China, Minutes of the Meeting, Addendum, WT/TPR/M/199/Add. 1, p. 150 onwards; Trade Policy Review, Report by China, WT/TPR/G/230, 26 April 2010, p. 15; Trade Policy Review China, Record of the Meeting, Addendum, WT/TPR/M/230/Add. 1., 22 February 2011, pp. 474–5; Trade Policy Review, Report by China, WT/TPR/G/264, 8 May 2012, pp. 15–16; Trade Policy Review, Report of China, WT/TPR/M/264, pp. 5, 6, 56.

85 Trade Policy Review China, Record of the Meeting, Addendum, WT/TPR/M/230/Add. 1, 22 February 2011, pp. 272–3.

86 www.wto.org/english/tratop_e/tpr_e/tp262_crc_e.htm

87 www.wto.org/english/tratop_e/tpr_e/tp299_crc_e.htm.

88 www.wto.org/english/tratop_e/tpr_e/tp330_crc_e.htm.

89 www.wto.org/english/tratop_e/tpr_e/tp364_crc_e.htm.

IMF analysis and data therefore remains essential, especially – but not only – with regard to the TPRM's improved adherence objective.

C. Conclusion

This chapter shows that the TPRM is able to review the international trading system in a holistic way. TPRM is not only equipped to review member states' international trade policies and practices *strictu sensu* but is also institutionally not disbarred (and is even encouraged by the coherence mandate and the TPRM's flexible framework) to pay due attention to international trade's wider monetary and financial underpinnings within the overall context of trade policy and regulation.

In this context, the TPRM's twofold objectives – increased transparency and increased adherence to the WTO rules – also have their role to play. Reporting and naming and shaming with respect to the internal trading system's monetary and financial underpinnings, have enabled the TPRM to pursue its objectives in a flexible but generally appreciated way. The fact that dispute resolution is not readily available in the monetary field – either within or outside the WTO – renders the instrument of TPRM perhaps even more important in this area.

Nevertheless, the potential for increased TPRM reporting and naming and shaming with regard to the monetary or financial underpinnings of the international trading system, have been inhibited by the periodicity of the TPRM and by the fact that the international trading system – and not its context – remains the core object of the TPRM review.

Therefore, the TPRM cannot fully meet the need for more effective instruments addressing the monetary and trade linkages within the WTO and in particular within the IMF.

PART IV

The quest for law in monetary policy

16

The potential of law and legal methodology in monetary affairs

THOMAS COTTIER AND LUCÍA SATRAGNO

A. Introduction

The role of law in monetary affairs is an important one. Today, it focuses on the allocation of powers and competence in managing the public monopoly of money. It defines, based upon constitutional norms and acts of parliament, the provinces of central banks and currency boards, of government departments and agencies. If courts of law have been involved at all, this involvement has been in assessing these powers in the context of the constitutional prerogatives of these different authorities, in particular of parliament facing challenges to democratic legitimacy of monetary policies. A series of important decisions of the German Constitutional Court (Bundesverfassungsgericht) in 2011, 2012 and 2013 assessing the European Stability Mechanism (ESM) and financial commitments made by parliament in the light of budgetary powers are cases in point.[1]

In contrast to financial regulation of banks, intermediaries and insurance, and to international trade in general, the law governing monetary affairs does not generally extend to substantive rules and requirements. It may define broad goals of aspiration, such as combating inflation or securing full employment. Yet, beyond that, proper policy-making is exclusively a matter of developing and applying economics, based upon economic analysis and modelling. Monetary affairs are ruled by policies: interest rate policy, exchange rate policy and policies expanding or limiting the supply of money (M) are influenced by the regulatory framework relating to financial services, trade regulation and carve-outs, investment protection, fiscal law and policy and labour market regulation and cannot be separated from it.

The authors are most grateful to Rosa M. Lastra co-editor and Rekha Oleschak for their valuable comments.

[1] For the Decisions by the German Constitutional Court see, www.bverfg.de/en/decisions/rs20120912_2bvr139012en.html.

Yet, the law and its institutions have no place in defining monetary policies properly speaking, today. The law, at best, and beyond defining powers and separation of powers, is context.

This, of course, has not always been the case. The international monetary system based on the gold standard and fixed exchange rates, known as the Bretton Woods regime, was essentially rule-based, relying upon decisions made by governments and coordination within the legal framework of the International Monetary Fund (IMF). The same was true of the gold standard in Great Britain in the interwar period, and in the US until the abandonment of the system of fixed exchange rates (*de facto* in the early 1970s, *de jure* in 1978). The system was accompanied by administrated capital controls and export and import restrictions.[2] In Europe, rules remained operational, first until the abandonment of the par value regime and, then, from 1978–9 with the fixed but adjustable bands for the fluctuation of currencies (colloquially known as 'snake in the tunnel') that were established under the Exchange Rate Mechanism of the European Monetary System, which sowed the seeds that eventually led to the adoption of the euro. Within the monetary union, a single currency among its members is set by law without any flexibility.[3]

The move to floating exchange rates followed political expediency and monetarist theory essentially adopting free market paradigms.[4] It was argued that capital markets would essentially be able to define relations between currencies most efficiently and would produce better welfare effects than regulated currency regimes operating capital controls and exchange rate policies often influenced by prerogatives of trade and labour policies. The monetarist policy has been largely influenced by the theory of free markets, and a belief that matters are best left to the invisible hand of the market.

[2] For a history of the Bretton Woods regime, see, *inter alia*, R. M. Lastra, *Legal Foundations of International Monetary Stability* (Oxford University Press, 2006), pp. 356–64 and A. F. Lowenfeld, 'The International Monetary System: A Look Back Over Seven Decades', *Journal of International Economic Law*, 13:3 (2010), 575–95, also in T. Cottier, J. H. Jackson and R. M. Lastra (eds.), *International Law in Financial Regulation and Monetary Affairs* (Oxford University Press, 2012), pp. 52–71.

[3] See, for the history of European monetary integration, Lastra, *Legal Foundations*, pp. 173–206.

[4] M. Friedman, 'The Case for Flexible Exchange Rates', *Essays in Positive Economics* (New York: Fordham University Press, 1959).

We do not discuss the merits of different monetary policies in this chapter. The point we seek to make is that different policies seem to operate under the assumption that monetary policy is either rule-based or not; that it is either regulated or left to capital markets and policy intervention by central banks. From a legal point of view, the options seem to imply that they are either law-based or not. *Tertium non datur*, apart from institutional allocations of powers for the purpose of decision-making and responsibility. It would seem that monetary policy is either defined by law or by economics.

This finding is interesting, as it contrasts with almost all other policy fields, which are normally characterised by a combination of law and policy. For example, trade policy is strongly anchored in the multilateral trading system of the World Trade Organization (WTO), increasingly supplemented by preferential trade agreements. It is based upon domestic law often implementing these agreements. It is not limited to allocation of powers, and trade policy is still left to a considerable degree to policy-making influenced by economic analysis and economic interests. The rule-based system, in other words, combines law and policy. The same could be said of many other fields in international relations: investment, innovation and intellectual property, environmental policies and climate change, and market access in goods and services, among others. In all these areas we have seen an interaction of law and policy in defining outcomes, all operating under a different mix of law and policy. The same, finally, is true in operating state monopolies. Not only are they constituted by law, but they are also required to take into account obligations under non-discrimination and competition law which offers disciplines against their abuse.

We are thus interested in exploring whether a comparable relationship of law and policy could also exist in monetary affairs and hence in regulating and operating a public monopoly to supply money to society and to economies at large, or whether the matter is inherently unsuitable for a proper combination of legal principles, rules and economics. To this effect, we look into the relationship of law and policy within markets (Section B) and expound the foundations of legal approaches and methodology (Section C). We argue that taking into account the flexibility of legal methodology, there is an unexplored potential to combine legal and economic components in monetary affairs with a view to achieving stability and equity of the overall system (Section D). Finally, we explore other areas of law with a close interaction between law and economics (Section E).

B. Law and policy in markets

Leaving matters to the invisible hand[5] often implies that matters should be deregulated and it should be left to the laws of supply and demand to bring about efficient and welfare-enhancing results. The neoliberal schools, before the financial and debt crisis, argued, on these grounds, for deregulation of monetary affairs, in particular exchange rate formulation. This view, it would seem, implies that there is not room for law and regulation, accordingly. It implies, in other words, a specific perception of law which, in our view, was linked to perhaps excessive and inefficient control and command while ignoring the fundamental importance of law for the operation of markets.

Markets, we submit, are primarily constituted by law. Without legal assignment and protection of property rights, without contract law, without liability rules, markets cannot exist and operate. Institutional economics has long recognised the importance of these and other legal institutions.[6] Leaving matters to the invisible hand does not mean operating outside the bounds of law.[7] Indeed, Adam Smith, in his main work on morality, expounds and reiterates the importance of values and responsibility which are expressed in these fundamentals of the legal system. The debate on regulation, deregulation and reregulation does not affect these fundamentals of law, but essentially deals with additional legal goals and requirements in order to set and achieve public interest goals commensurate with justice and thus prevailing precepts of

[5] A. Smith, *The Theory of Moral Sentiments* (1759), Knud Haakonssen (ed.) (Cambridge University Press, 2009), p. 215.

[6] On the importance of law and institutions in the functioning of markets see, *inter alia*, R. H. Coase, *The Firm, the Market and the Law* (University of Chicago Press, 1988) and D. C. North, *Institutions, Institutional Change and Economic Performance* (Cambridge University Press, 1990).

[7] Adam Smith first referred to the invisible hand in describing the even distribution of surplus goods in *The Theory of Moral Sentiments* (1759), p. 215. The statement here, as well as a further reference in A. Smith, *The Wealth of Nations* (1776) depicting the pursuit of private interests 'to promote an end which was no part of his intention' (i.e. the public interest), Edwin Cannan (ed.) (New York: The Modern Library, 1994), p. 485, were not aimed at law and trade regulation, as opposed to unregulated commerce. Instead, the importance of order and good governance is particularly stressed: 'commerce and manufactures gradually introduced order and good government, and with them, liberty and security of individuals, among the inhabitants of the country, who had before lived almost in a continual state of war with their neighbours, and of servile dependency upon their superiors'; Smith, *The Wealth of Nations*, p. 440.

morality in a particular field.[8] They often take the form of government regulation with a view to monitoring the operation of markets, taking into account public interests and certain defined goals.

The debate is about government intervention beyond the fundamentals of the law. It is on this level that regulation is a matter of degree, and not of principle. A sector may be left to the fundamentals of market operation. It may be fully regulated leaving virtually no market to operate on the basis of supply, demand and price determination. The electricity sector is a case in point. The physical properties of electricity require a very high degree of regulation and intervention to bring about stability and a proper mix of different forms of electricity. Deregulation, in most cases, has not worked and has left the electricity industry short of appropriate investment.[9] Most areas are in between these extremes. It is a matter of politics to arbitrate the diverging interests involved and to define the degree of regulation and government intervention. In a particular sector, there is no single model of regulation, and regulations often vary from country to country in the same sector. This essentially flows from the notions of sovereignty and self-determination, and the role of government in a particular society.[10] Following the financial crisis of 2007–9, we witnessed a debate on proper governmental regulation and intervention in financial markets.[11] Overall, levels of regulation have

[8] Cf. R. Baldwin, M. Cave and M. Lodge, *The Oxford Handbook of Regulation* (Oxford University Press, 2010). The volume offers a comprehensive discussion of underlying theories of market regulation and the pursuit of public interests, in particular the contribution by M. Feintuck, 'Regulatory Rationales Beyond the Economic: In Search of Public Interest', p. 39; cf. also K. M. Meessen (ed.) *Economic Law as an Economic Good: Its Rule Function and its Tool Function in the Competition of Systems* (Münich: Sellier European Law, 2009).

[9] See Panel and Appellate Body Reports – Certain Measures affecting the Renewable Energy Generation Sector, WT/DS 412/R and Canada – Measures Relating to the Feed in Tariff Program, WT/DS426/R, adopted 19 December 2012, WT/DS412/A/B and WT/DS426/A/B, adopted 6 May 2013.

[10] As argued by Greene and Boehm, 'the value of sovereignty in global financial regulation is no longer absolute and must be weighted – on a strategic, tailored basis – against countervailing costs of unilateral action.' See E. F. Greene and J. L. Boehm, 'The Limits of "Name-And-Shame" in International Financial Regulation', *Cornell Law Review* 97 (2012), 1083–138.

[11] For an analysis of the debate on the role of regulation after the global financial crisis, see, *inter alia*, R. M. Lastra and G. Wood, 'The Crisis of 2007–09: Nature, Causes, and Reactions', *Journal of International Economic Law* 13:3 (2010), 531–50 and P. Delimatsis and N. Herger (eds.), *Financial Regulation at the Crossroads: Implications for Supervision, Institutional Design and Trade* (Alphen aan den Rijn: Kluwer Law International, 2011).

increased with the aim of bringing about financial stability.[12] It is no longer a matter of principle whether markets should be left to their own devices. It is a matter of defining the proper level and degree of regulation in a pluralist debate.

C. Law and policy in monetary markets

We have not seen a similar debate in the field of monetary law to the one that is going on in financial law. Discussions relate to the proper definition of powers of central banks in light of the expansion of policy activities beyond setting interest rates and influencing exchange rates, to intervening in markets and defining the amount of money available in the system.[13] Purchases of government bonds in support of banks and possibly government, and the power of lender of last resort are at the forefront. It is essentially about institutional powers. Whether or not the law may play a role in the setting of interest rates by central banks, defining parameters for intervening in currency markets, in combating inflation and unemployment does not seem to be on the table. The legal debate again relates to the context, in particular fiscal policies and tax law, levels of indebtedness and whether there should be a legal limit to public borrowing, but not to monetary policy as such.

There may be a number of reasons for this absence of legal discipline in monetary affairs.

First, some monetary affairs may not be considered to be a matter of markets, but rather of public monopoly. Central banks have exclusive powers to manage the supply of money in a particular monetary system. Yet, in international relations, we see different currencies stemming from monopolies and the power to print money, competing with each other.[14] In that sense, there is a market of currencies which currency traders operate and by which the ratio between different currencies is influenced. We may conceive the relations as competitive relations, and the law may play a role in bringing about fair competition, avoiding cartels and abuse not only by banks and traders, but also by central banks

[12] M. Giovanoli remarks that, '. . .the global financial crisis has been widely perceived as a failure of market mechanisms to maintain financial stability'. See 'The International Monetary and Financial Architecture – Some Institutional Aspects', Chapter 3, this volume.

[13] See, on the role of central banks in monetary affairs, R. M. Lastra, 'The Role of Central Banks in Monetary Affairs: A Comparative Perspective', Chapter 4, this volume.

[14] See F. Hayek, *The Denationalization of Money* (London: Institute of Economic Affairs, 1976).

or governments. Manipulations of exchange rates are manipulations in a market and may need legal disciplines of some sort. Monetary law at the international level, as a matter of international law, includes legal disciplines by defining competitive relations of currencies on a global market of currencies.[15]

Second, independence of central banks delinks rule-making for regular procedures in government, in parliament, in the executive branch and before courts of law. Independence of central banks forms a self-contained system, deliberately detached from government intervention.[16] As noted by Lastra in her contribution to this volume, the theory of independence is not only applied to central banking, but it is widely used in other areas of administrative law.[17] The main feature of this theory is the delegation of regulatory powers. Accordingly, Rosenfeld pointed out that the administrative regulation that emerges from this type of delegation facilitates the legal and institutional means for the state to deal with areas that require specialised expertise and also a distance from politically driven decisions.[18] Internationally, national systems co-exist, cooperate and coordinate within the IMF and the Bank for International Settlements (BIS) in a relationship of principals and agents. Accordingly, these processes are also formally delinked from normal intergovernmental processes, such as the G-20 or other international fora.[19] Importantly, central banks do not have the power to engage in treaty-making, which constitutionally is subject to the control of parliament and often requires consent before ratification.[20] They

[15] For a further discussion on the issues of monopoly and competition in the provision of currencies, see E. Baltensperger and T. Cottier, 'The Role of Law in Monetary Affairs', *Journal of International Economic Law* 13:3 (2010), 913–18, also in Cottier *et al.* (eds.), *International Law in Financial Regulation and Monetary Affairs*, pp. 357–81.

[16] For a study on central bank independence, see R. M. Lastra, *Central Banking and Banking Regulation* (London School of Economics, Financial Markets Group, 1996), pp. 10–44 and 'Central Bank Independence and Financial Stability', *Revista de Estabilidad Financiera*, 18 (2010), 49–66.

[17] See Lastra, Chapter 4, this volume.

[18] See M. Rosenfeld, 'Constitutional versus Administrative Ordering in an Era of Globalization and Privatization: Reflections on Sources of Legitimation in the Postwestphalian Polity', *Cardozo Law Review* 32 (2011), 2339.

[19] See, on international financial architecture, M. Giovanoli, 'The International Financial Architecture and its Reform After the Global Financial Crisis' in M. Giovanoli and D. Devos (eds.), *International Monetary and Financial Law: The Global Crisis* (Oxford University Press, 2010), pp. 3–39 and Giovanoli, Chapter 3, this volume.

[20] Arguably with the exception of the BIS, although the legal nature and treaty making power of this institution, originally founded between central banks and private operators and recognised by the Swiss Government as an international organisation remains unclear; cf. Convention respecting the Bank for International Settlements, 20 January

necessarily refer to soft law instruments. Recourse to soft law expressed in instruments such as the Basel III rules[21] is mainly taken for this reason, rather than the substance of the matter. The complex rules on minimal capital requirements of systematically relevant banking institutions could well be presented in the form of binding international agreements as a matter of substance. It is merely soft law due to allocation of regulatory powers, preserving independent powers of central banks. Despite the fact that lack of treaty-making power of central banks is viewed as a positive aspect of soft law by some scholars (e.g., the possibility to participate in the standard-setting process without the capacity to make treaties),[22] we consider that the situation should be revisited from the point of view of accountability.[23] Governments and parliaments, in implementing these soft law rules, are not in a position to formally influence the negotiations of such instruments. This conveys a perception that action and regulation is taking place outside the realm of the law properly speaking.[24] The same is true in matters directly addressing the relationship among central banks. Monetary policy is informally determined, and explicit agreements, such as the Plaza Agreement of 1985, are exceptional and retain a soft law character.[25] There have been calls to reconsider the soft law approach in favour of moving to a treaty-based system in international financial regulation, after the past global financial crisis demonstrated the inability of the informal procedures to maintain financial stability especially in times

1930; Constituent Charter of the Bank for International Settlements, 20 January 1930; Status of the Bank for International Settlements, 20 January 1930 as amended 27 June 2005 ('a company limited by shares'); Protocol Regarding the Immunities of the Bank for International Settlements, 30 July 1930. Also, see Lastra, *Legal Foundations*, pp. 451–3 and C. Brummer, *Soft Law and the Global Financial System – Rule Making in the 21st Century* (Cambridge University Press, 2011), pp. 89–90.

21 See, www.bis.org/bcbs/basel3.htm.

22 See E. Ferran and K. Alexander, 'Can Soft Law Bodies be Effective?, The Special Case of the European Systemic Risk Board', *European Law Review* 35:6 (2010), 751–76 and C. Brummer, 'Why Soft Law Dominates International Finance – and not Trade', *Journal of International Economic Law*, 13:3 (2010), 631, also in: T. Cottier *et al.* (eds.), *International Law in Financial Regulation and Monetary Affairs*, pp. 95–113.

23 For an analysis, on the issue of accountability in international financial regulation, see Brummer, '*Soft Law and the Global Financial System*', pp. 177–209.

24 On this point, Brummer stated that, 'international financial regulation is largely posited as the product of more rudimentary forces of political or economic (and for some, military) power. Simply put, in the absence of a forceful legal regime, it is "power", not law, which promotes the promulgation of international standards.' See, *ibid.* 22, 623–43; also in: T. Cottier *et al.* (eds.), *International Law in Financial Regulation and Monetary Affairs*, pp. 95–113.

25 G-8, 'Announcement the Ministers of Finance and Central Bank Governors of France, Germany, Japan, the United Kingdom, and the United States' (Plaza Accord), 22 September 1985, www.g8.utoronto.ca/finance/fm850922.htm.

of crisis.[26] Consequently, there is a need to engage monetary policy with law and that is why we argue that governments should contend the possibility to give limited and well-defined treaty-making powers to central banks.[27] Indeed, during the crisis the central banks considerably expanded their policy toolkits and, thus, now is the moment to consider such expansion in the central banks' mandates.[28] The limits to the treaty-making power can be set by the so-called 'goal constraint' to central banks' independence.[29] Once the present preoccupation with financial regulation and architecture is settled, legislators should turn to these issues.

Third, the absence of legal regulation may be due to a perception that the law simply is not suitable to address complex issues of monetary policy. We submit that perceptions are often informed by an understanding of law that it either regulates a matter or it does not. In other words, the matter is either subject to law – as was the gold standard – or it is left to the invisible hand and to economic policies of central banks in line with the insights and recommendations of monetary economists. Managing the monopoly, it would seem, is not suitable for law. The main objections to legal disciplines, therefore, are likely to relate to the equivalent of government intervention, i.e., the regulation of currency exchanges, such as capital controls, addressing exchange rate policies or conditions for lending by central banks.

However, defining the interaction of different currencies, and thus monopolies, as a competitive relationship implies that they operate on a global currency market. The fundamentals of markets thus equally apply, in particular property rights, securing entitlement to money, contracts and liability rules. Selling and buying by central banks and the BIS, as well as lending, are subject to these disciplines and could not take place without them. The same is true for more complex operations among central bank institutions. Moreover, the IMF is mandated to

[26] On this issue, Tietje contends that, 'a stable international monetary system cannot rely exclusively on soft law. In fact, one may argue that the entire phenomenon of soft law essentially rests on the existence of "hard" law. Soft law fills gaps and in this it depends on gaps, gaps in a legal system.' See C. Tietje, 'The Role of Law in Monetary Affairs: Taking Stock', Chapter 2, this volume.

[27] Monetary policy is usually conducted by an independent central bank. See C. Proctor, *Mann on the Legal Aspects of Money*, 7th edn (Oxford University Press, 2012), p. 42.

[28] For a detailed analysis of the objectives of central banks, see F. Gianviti, 'The Objectives of Central Banks' in M. Giovanoli and D. Devos (eds.), *International Monetary and Financial Law, The Global Crisis* (Oxford University Press, 2010), p. 449.

[29] On the limits to central bank independence, see Lastra, *Legal Foundations*, pp. 50–61.

review periodically the central bank policies of its member states, which is yet another layer in the complex relationship. Article IV assessments are also related to law, albeit international law, the Articles of Agreement of the IMF.[30]

For example, the central banks by exercising their regulatory powers may opt to conduct an expansionary monetary policy, by increasing the money supply and lowering the interest rates. As explained by Gianviti in his chapter in this volume, the benefits derived from the application of an expansionary monetary policy are obvious and manifold. However, he also remarked that there could be losses from the application of such policy (e.g., pensioners and savers may lose purchasing power if salaries and pensions are not promptly adjusted).[31] Indeed, these distributional effects of monetary policy measures (conventional and unconventional) are some of the reasons why the law is needed when it comes to the conduct of monetary affairs. Zimmermann, in his contribution, addresses the elusive role of law in setting global and reference interest rates, both by central banks and commercial banks.[32] Today, monetary policies are exclusively based on economic analysis and considerations. The role of law is limited to institutional issues and setting broad goals and targets. Yet, the recent London InterBank Offered Rate (Libor) scandal and the manipulation of interest rates among competitors equally show that the boundaries between law and economics are not as clear-cut as they might seem. Thus, the question we want to raise here is whether law and methodology should have a say in a case where the effects of monetary policies go beyond economics.

[30] The IMF oversees the international monetary system and monitors the economic and financial policies of its member states, in its function known as surveillance. In this process, the IMF highlights possible risks to stability and advises on the policy adjustments needed. This function was established by Article IV of the IMF's Articles of Agreement, and revised in the late 1970s. In 2010, the IMF undertook a review of its surveillance mandate. This resulted in measures to integrate all dimensions of IMF surveillance – multilateral, bilateral and financial – and make it more effective. See generally on surveillance, IMF, 'IMF Surveillance – FactSheet' (30 March 2013), www.imf.org/external/np/exr/facts/surv.htm. Lastra, *Legal Foundations*, pp. 399–406 and N. Rendak 'Monitoring and Surveillance of the International Monetary System – What Can Be Learnt from the Trade Field', Chapter 9, this volume.

[31] See F. Gianviti, 'Relationship between Monetary and Exchange Rate Policy', Chapter 17, this volume.

[32] See C. D. Zimmermann, 'Global Benchmark Interest Rates: Conflicting Objectives and Increasing Hybridisation', Chapter 7, this volume.

D. The essence of law and regulatory theory

We submit that an exclusive choice between law and economics may result from an understanding of law and regulation which is obsolete. Such a view does not sufficiently take into account the nature of law and the fact that legal methodology is able to include economic considerations, offering guidance without prejudging a clear-cut result. The perception of regulation versus policy and markets is perhaps informed by traditions of overly dense regulation of financial markets in the past and again in the present.[33] It may be informed by the perception that regulation simply implements certain economic policies and at the same time freezes them. All too often, regulation and law are simply perceived as tools to implement economic policies, without bringing content, objectives, values and norms of their own to the table. They may also be informed by perceptions which limit rules and regulation to the application of specific norms to specific facts, inevitably producing specific outcomes without flexibility. Such perceptions may be true for classical areas like criminal law, which depend upon a high degree of predictability and legal certainty. But they certainly do not fit with the nature of law and legal methodology in the field of economic law.

While law and its enforcement mechanisms are used to implement economic policy, often in the form of detailed regulations, there is more to law than this. The law is based upon a number of fundamental principles which, on their own, call for respect in shaping policies. It is important to distinguish different types of norms of law.[34] Dworkin distinguished principles and rules. While the latter can be directly applied to a set of facts and offer a predictable outcome, the former form the basis of a more complex assessment and operation. Principles inform decisions injecting direction and values, but essentially depend upon taking into account a broader set of considerations which themselves are not rooted in law, but in experience and life and often expressed by other fields: science and technology, economics,

[33] For a study on regulation and market economies, see T. Daintith, Chapter 10 ‘Regulation’ in R. Buxbaum and F. Màdl (eds.), *International Encyclopedia of Comparative Law*, Volume XVII (Tubingen, Mohr Siebeck, 1997).

[34] For further analysis on the principles of the law see, *inter alia*, R. Kolb, ‘Principles as Sources of International Law (With Special Reference to Good Faith)’, *Netherlands International Law Review* 53:1 (2006), 1–36 and J. Wouters, D. Coppens and D. Geraets, ‘The Influence of General Principles of Law’ in S. E. Gaines, B. E. Olsen and K. E. Sørensen (eds.), *Liberalising Trade in the EU and the WTO – A Legal Comparison* (Cambridge University Press, 2012), pp. 43–74.

psychology, history, theology, linguistics, and the arts.[35] They all inform the operation of principles.[36]

I. *Principles of law*

The principles are often constitutional in nature. They are sometimes enshrined in international agreements and form part of customary law.[37] Partly, they form general principles of domestic law which also apply in international relations.[38] These principles, for example, entail emanations of equality, in particular equality before the law, equal treatment, principles of non-discrimination both internationally and in human rights protection.[39] They include principles containing powers against abuse of rights, against arbitrary decisions and against excessive intervention, in particular the principle of proportionality. It entails principles of transparency, fairness or due process shaping decision-making. It contains principles translating fundamental beliefs into law, mainly by recourse to human rights which are bound to inform the life and operation of the law and activities of government. Overall, they form a

[35] The general principles of law are recognised as important sources of law. Article 38.1 of the Statute of the International Court of Justice establishes that:

> 'The Court, whose function is to decide in accordance with international law such disputes as are submitted to it, shall apply:
> a. international conventions, whether general or particular, establishing rules expressly recognized by the contesting states;
> b. international custom, as evidence of a general practice accepted as law;
> c. the general principles of law recognized by civilized nations;
> d. subject to the provisions of Article 59, judicial decisions and the teachings of the most highly qualified publicists of the various nations, as subsidiary means for the determination of rules of law.'

[36] R. M. Dworkin, 'The Model of Rules', *The University of Chicago Law Review* 35:1 (1967), 14–46.

[37] According to F. A. Mann: 'While normally the State is entitled at its discretion to regulate its monetary affairs, there comes a point when the exercise of such discretion so unreasonably or grossly offends against the alien's right to fair and equitable treatment or so clearly deviates from customary standards of behaviour that international law will intervene.' See F. A. Mann, *The Legal Aspect of Money*, 5th edn (Oxford: Clarendon Press, 1992), pp. 472–3.

[38] Procter, *Mann on the Legal Aspect of Money*.

[39] See, on the principle of equality, Baltensperger and Cottier, 'The Role of Law in Monetary Affairs', pp. 934–6; also in T. Cottier *et al.* (eds.), *International Law in Financial Regulation and Monetary Affairs*, pp. 357–81 and T. Cottier, 'From Progressive Liberalization to Progressive Regulation in WTO Law', *Journal of International Economic Law* 9:4 (2006), 795–7.

core of standards of justice, often with competing goals. They specify standards of justice in a particular context. Finally, the law is complemented by considerations of equity. While expressing a separate legal tradition in former periods of common law, equity today is part of the law and allows new challenges to be addressed. It allows the law to be interpreted, complemented, but also corrected if need be.[40]

II. Rules of law

Rules by nature are more precise than principles. Ideally, they respond to the syllogism, i.e., they can be applied to a set of facts and offer a response defined by legislation, implemented by government and reviewed by courts. However, it is important to note that rules show great variety in their density and determination. Rules can be drafted in an open-textured manner, delegating power to the authority making detailed determinations and often exercising ample discretion within the bounds of the rule.[41] As a corollary, these rules do not offer predictability and suffer from a lack of legal security. Open-textured norms are close to principles and depend upon authoritative interpretation and application. They are not inherently self-executing. The more detailed rules become, the more they correct the shortcomings of indeterminacy and lack of predictability and security. As a consequence, they lack flexibility and fail to adjust easily to altered conditions and often produce results which do not match the original intentions of the legislator. It is important to understand the concept of rules as a continuum, stretching from open textured norms to detailed regulation, all of which is linked to a continuum of allocations of powers in decision-making.

III. Regulatory theory

Regulatory theory brings together the different components of law, in particular the interaction of principles and rules. It is sophisticated and

[40] There is extensive literature on equity and international law. See, *inter alia*, M. N. Shaw, *International Law*, 6th edn (Cambridge University Press, 2008), pp. 105–9 and C. R. Rossi, *Equity and International Law: A Legal Realist Approach to International Decision-making* (Irvington, NY: New York, Transnational, 1993). See on equity and international finance and trade, R. Howse, 'Fragmentation and Utopia: Towards an Equitable Integration of Finance, Trade, and Sustainable Development' in A. Cassese (ed.), *Realizing Utopia: the Future of International Law* (Oxford University Press, 2012), pp. 427–41.

[41] See Dworkin, 'The Model of Rules'.

elaborates on the relationship of density of norms, separation of powers, checks and balances, and the role of parliament, government and the courts. It essentially asks which body, given its legitimacy, composition, working modes and procedures, is most suitable to take decisions based upon law. This may be parliament, it may be the executive branch, it may be agencies, or it may be the courts of law. The process of law is understood as a continuum, starting from broad principles and ending in detailed regulation, the latter often made in specific cases and thus case law. There is no separation of powers in the sense that legislation and the application of law can be strictly separated. Rather, it is a matter of allocating, by law, powers to the authority most suitable to take decisions in the field, given its legitimacy and mode of operation.[42] Structure and substance are paired, and need to be paired in a meaningful manner. This is the essence of what we call structural due process in law.[43] Naturally, decisions of a general nature will be taken by parliament and the legislator, while the executive branch and courts follow up by rendering these decisions more specific. Yet, it is important to note that not all of the important decisions are made by parliament. In some areas, they are taken by the executive branch, in particular in areas requiring swift action. In other areas, they are entrusted to courts, in particular when it is a matter of protecting human rights and due process, but also matters of market access rights. The theory of direct effect in European constitutional law and the concept of self-executing treaties and the doctrine of justiciability of norms amounts to the most elaborate discussion of separation of powers and checks and balances between different bodies involved in the legal process.[44] The privileges and independence of central banks is an excellent example of how not all important decisions are reserved to parliament and the executive branch. Independence of central banks is shaped in such a way as to allocate powers in matters of vital importance to the economy, deliberately

[42] The regulatory theory is based upon T. Cottier, *Die Verfassung und das Erfordernis der gesetzlichen Grundlage*, 2nd edn (Zurich: Verlag Rüeger, 1993). See, also, T. Cottier, 'Constitutional Trade Regulation in National and International Law: Structure-Substance Pairings in the EFTA Experience', in M. Hilf and E. Petersmann (eds.), *National Constitutions and International Economic Law* (The Hague: Kluwer Law International, 1993), pp. 409–42.

[43] L. Tribe, 'Structural Due Process', *Harvard Civil Rights – Civil Liberties Law Review* 10:2 (1975), 269.

[44] See, e.g., T. Cottier, 'International Trade Law: The Impact of Justiciability and Separations of Powers in EC Law', *European Constitutional Law Review* 5 (2009), 307–26.

removing such matters from interest-driven decision-making in parliament and the executive branch.[45]

Regulatory theory thus equally and fully applies to monetary affairs. The breadth of principles, the broad scope of rules, ranging from flexibility to detailed prescription, and the modes of allocating powers to different authorities are equally as relevant to this field as they are to any other field of public governance. The allocation of special powers to central banks does not establish an exception, but confirms the operation of regulatory theory in the field. Furthermore, it shows that it is not a matter of separating law and economics or policy, but rather of integrating them in a set of principles and rules suitable for bringing legal principles, values and economics to the table.

It is, therefore, a matter of assessing the potential applicability of principles and of the wide scope of diverging density of rules to monetary affairs. Which are the legal principles relevant to the field? How can one shape the density of norms in order to bring about proper allocations of power taking into account proper structure–substance pairings in the field? How can law and economics be linked? Monetary affairs may learn from other areas of economic law and regulation, both in domestic and in international law.

A second and more recent dimension of regulatory theory concerns the vertical interaction of different principles and rules. Based upon the tradition of federalism, scholars addressing multilevel governance expound upon the interaction of different regulatory levels and communities.[46] This doctrine essentially seeks to define optimal allocation of regulatory powers with a view to bringing about respective public goods. It also looks into the role of vertical checks and balances in bringing about principles and rules which vertically interact and assist in avoiding failures of a particular layer of government, be it local, national, regional or global. Many of the functions of current international and federal institutions can be understood and explained in such terms. This is

[45] Lastra, Chapter 4, this volume.

[46] See, on the topic of multilevel governance, E.U. Petersmann, 'Framework of Analysis: Multilevel Governance', Chapter 21, this volume; T. Cottier, 'Multilayered Governance, Pluralism and Moral Conflict', *Indiana Journal of Global Legal Studies* 16:2 (2009), 647; T. Cottier and M. Hertig, 'The Prospects of 21st Century Constitutionalism', *Max Planck Yearbook of United Nations Law* 7 (2003), 261–328; T. Cottier, 'Challenges Ahead in International Economic Law', *Journal of International Economic Law*, 12:1 (1999), 3–15, and T. Cottier, 'Towards a Five Storey House', in C. Joerges and E. U. Petersmann (eds.), *Constitutionalism, Multilevel Trade Governance and International Economic Law* (Oxford: Hart Publishing, 2011), pp. 495–532.

particularly prominent in the field of trade regulation. Both globally within the WTO, and regionally within the European Union, and to a lesser extent in other instruments of regional integration, the main purpose of these instruments is to prevent and remedy state failures producing rent/seeking protectionism, given domestic power structures and relations. The same is true, albeit in a less effective manner, for human rights protection in international law.

Regulatory theory therefore entails both horizontal and vertical allocations of powers in defining the interaction of different authorities, but also of facts and findings informing the complex operation of the law.

E. Lessons from other areas of law

I. International trade regulation

The regulatory framework of international trade regulation, built upon fundamental premises of comparative advantage and welfare enhancing liberalisation, is closely intertwined with economic factors and thresholds throughout the system. Law and economics interact and influence each other in a dialectical relationship.[47] The fundamental principles of non-discrimination, most-favoured nation treatment and national treatment, essentially rely upon an economic analysis of like and competitive products as a basis for assessing requirements to ensure treatment of imported products is no less favourable than that of domestic products, both in goods and services.[48]

The operation of the WTO is inherently intertwined with economic analysis. Fundamental concepts of non-discrimination are based upon concepts of likeness which in return are closely related to product substitution and the notion of relevant markets, both in goods and services.[49] The

[47] This relationship should be distinguished from the economic analysis of law which explores the operation and efficiency of law from an economic point of view; see R. A. Posner, *Economic Analysis of Law*, 8th edn (New York: Aspen Publishers, 2011).

[48] For an analysis on the role of the principle of non-discrimination in the field of international monetary law, see T. Cottier and M. Krajewski, 'What Role for Non-Discrimination and Prudential Standards in International Financial Law?', *Journal of International Economic Law* 13:3 (2010), 817–35 also in: T. Cottier *et al.* (eds.), *International Law in Financial Regulation and Monetary Affairs*, pp. 271–87.

[49] See, generally, P. van den Bossche, *The Law and Policy of the World Trade Organization*, 2nd edn (Cambridge University Press, 2008); T. Cottier and M. Oesch, *International Trade Regulation: Law and Policies of the WTO, the European Union and Switzerland*, (Bern and London: Cameron May and Staempfli, 2005); T. Cottier and P. Mavroidis (eds.), *Regulatory Barriers and the Principle of Non-Discrimination in World Trade Law*

law of trade remedies, in particular, essentially depends upon economic analysis of dumping margins and determination of injury. The law prescribes taking into account a number of factors.[50] The same holds true for assessing benefits essential to the notion of a subsidy under the Agreement on Subsidies and Countervailing Measures (SCM Agreement). Safeguard measures essentially depend upon assessing increase of imports. All instruments are subject to injury determination which relies upon assessing economic impact on the basis of data available. Although the WTO does not rely upon trade flows in its determination of nullification and impairment of benefits, economic data and impact assessment within the legal framework is of paramount importance. These rules cannot operate without recourse to economic data and analysis. In the field of dispute settlement, determination of the amount of concessions to be suspended in response to non-compliance is based upon the analysis of past trade flows as a basis for projection of future trade restrictions to be approved by WTO members and to be imposed by the member concerned. Again, the application of the rules is closely dependent upon economic data and analysis.[51]

Finally, special and differential treatment of developing countries partly relies upon economic thresholds in limiting export subsidies. Such thresholds form the basis of graduation, an emerging concept for replacing special and differential treatment. Inspired by models applied to debt relief, graduation seeks to differentiate the operation of rules on the basis of economic thresholds and indicators. Differentiation is according to the level of competitiveness which, in return, triggers the

(Ann Arbor, MI: Michigan University Press, 2000); N. F. Diebold, *Non-Discrimination in International Trade in Services* (Cambridge University Press, 2010).

50 Article 3.4 of the Agreement on Implementation of Article VI of the General Agreement on Tariffs and Trade 1994 (www.wto.org/english/docs_e/legal_e/legal_e.htm) explicitly provides for, and epitomises, a topical approach to legal methodology, taking recourse to enumerated economic factors:

> The examination of the impact of the dumped imports on the domestic industry concerned shall include an evaluation of all relevant economic factors and indices having a bearing on the state of the industry, including actual and potential decline in sales, profits, output, market share, productivity, return on investments, or utilization of capacity; factors affecting domestic prices; the magnitude of the margin of dumping; actual and potential negative effects on cash flow, inventories, employment, wages, growth, ability to raise capital or investments. This list is not exhaustive, nor can one or several of these factors necessarily give decisive guidance.

51 For a more detailed analysis of the existing regulations based upon economic factors in WTO Law, see T. Cottier, 'From Progressive Liberalization to Progressive Regulation in WTO Law', *Journal of International Economic Law* 9:4 (2006), 795–7.

application of specific rules within a given agreement. This approach is particularly useful with regard to standard-setting agreements, for example on intellectual property protection.[52]

Importantly, close dependence upon, and interaction with, economic analysis and data does not exclude a rule-based approach which is subject to binding dispute resolution in the WTO under the Dispute Settlement Understanding. Panels and the Appellate Body are competent to interface legal and economic analysis and apply this to areas often felt to be beyond the realm of law. It may even touch upon monetary law to the extent that exchange rate policies may be argued and challenged under the SCM Agreement.[53] The economic nature of a problem does not *per se* remove it from the rule of law.

II. Competition law and policy

The operation of competition law and policy in the field of anti-trust and abuse of dominant position is perhaps the most prominent field of interaction of law and economics in domestic and European law.[54] While based upon fundamental principles and rules, the assessment of cartels and dominant positions inherently depends upon economic data and analysis that goes beyond assessing corporate behaviour. The field also allows an examination of the tensions between law and economics, and tensions inherent to such interaction. While the law seeks predictability and legal security by emphasising the need for clear rules relating to hard cartels, economics takes what has been called 'the more economic approach'. It essentially focuses on detailed examination of a particular case, assessing the pros and cons of a constellation from the point of view of consumer welfare in a particular context. A rule-based approach, on the other hand, stresses the protection of competition as an institution and the importance of predictability and legal security. It would seem that a proper balance has not yet been found between law and economics in this field, which is subject

[52] *Ibid.*

[53] For a discussion of the problem and the relationship of WTO law and the IMF see T. Cottier and T. Payosova, 'Challenges in International Monetary Law' in: Inge Govaere, R. Quick and M. Bronckers (eds.), *Trade and Competition Law in the EU and Beyond* (Cheltenham: Edward Elgar, 2011), p. 35.

[54] See, generally, V. Rose and D. Bailey (eds.), *Bellamy and Child, European Union Law of Competition*, 7th edn (Oxford University Press, 2013) and for an economic analysis of anti-trust law, see R. A. Posner, *Economic Analysis of Law*, 8th edn (New York: Aspen Publishers, 2011), p. 29.

to fluctuations and fashions over time. But competition law and policy clearly shows the need to work within a given legal framework in which economics will apply. It is a matter of assessing the proper density of rules in determining the appropriate scope and function of economic analysis.[55] Accordingly, Baltensperger and Cottier – while exploring the applicability of the principles of graduation to currency competition in international monetary affairs – suggested that, 'Economic indicators to assess and define thresholds could be commonly developed and used in the field of trade and financial regulation as well as monetary affairs'.[56] Again, the Libor scandal of 2012 shows to what extent the setting of reference interest rates is subject to competition law in a manner that was unexpected prior to this event.[57]

III. Maritime boundary delimitation

The field of maritime boundary delimitation in the United Nations Convention on the Law of the Sea (UNCLOS)[58] is of importance as it relates to the relationship of law and economics in areas of distributive justice among states, even in a domain pertaining to classical areas of international coexistence. The allocation of marine spaces for the purpose of resource extraction (oil, gas, fish and other genetic resources, but also tidal and wind energy) essentially follows the natural contours of the coasts projected in a seaward direction. The coastal configuration provides the basis for claims under the doctrine of the territorial sea, continental shelf and the exclusive economic zone (EEZ). The problem of vastly overlapping claims has been addressed throughout the past fifty years by the International Court of Justice and courts of arbitration on the basis of the principle of equity and, later, in terms of the treaty-based goal of bringing about an equitable solution to the issue of maritime

[55] For a comprehensive analysis of the reliance of economic factors in competition law, see E. M. Graham and J. D. Richardson (eds.), *Global Competition Policy* (Washington, DC: Institute for International Economics, 1997).

[56] Baltensperger and Cottier, 'The Role of Law in Monetary Affairs', 913–18, also in: T. Cottier *et al.* (eds.), *International Law in Financial Regulation and Monetary Affairs*, pp. 357–81.

[57] See Zimmermann, 'Global Benchmark Interest Rates'. For an assessment of a traditionally minor role of competition policy in financial regulation and monetary affairs prior to the Libor scandal, *cf.*, P. Marston and I. Kokkoris, 'The Role of Competition and State Aid Policy in Financial and Monetary Law', *Journal of International Economic Law*, 13:3 (2010), 875–92, also in: T. Cottier *et al.* (eds.), *International Law in Financial Regulation and Monetary Affairs*, pp. 321–36.

[58] See the text at www.un.org/Depts/los/convention_agreements/texts/unclos/unclos_e.pdf.

boundary delimitation relating to the continental shelf and the EEZ.[59] Equity formed the foundation of a doctrine of equitable principles, based upon which a boundary is essentially composed. These principles were subsequently identified and developed in an extensive series of case law, in a process of trial and error, and squared with the tradition of regulation based upon strict rules. In doing so, negotiators and courts took into account a number of criteria and relevant circumstances and factors relating to these principles. These developments in case law entail the principle that the coast dominates the sea, the principles of non-encroachment and non-cutting-off, and the principle of equal division of marine space and of reasonable proportionality between coastal length and marine space allocated. These principles are further refined by relevant geographical circumstances and factors, in particular the location of resources, unity of deposits, existing concessions and ecological criteria. They further take into account circumstances and factors relating to human conduct, in particular historical conduct and fishing patterns, social and economic considerations, economic viability, national security and third-generation interests.[60] Principles, circumstances and relevant factors were all derived from the general principle of equity, thus from a void of law at the outset. The field therefore is of particular comparative interest in the present context, given the legal vacuum in monetary policy today. It is of particular importance from the point of view of methodology.

Competing with a strict rule-based system, relying upon the operation of an equidistance line subject to exceptions, the principle of equity forms the foundation of a methodology which computes boundaries on the basis of the principles, circumstances and factors indicated above. These principles, circumstances and factors often lead to conflicting perspectives and interests being brought to the table. Hence, they are considered within the operation of the overall set of equitable principles which gradually emerged based upon the broad principle of

[59] There is extensive literature exploring the relationship of economic factors and normative concepts of delimitation based on the fundamental concept of equitable principles. See, *inter alia*, N. M. Antunes, *Towards the Conceptualisation of Maritime Delimitation: Legal and Technical Aspects of a Political Process* (Leiden: Martinus Nijhoff, 2003); S. P. Jagota, *Maritime Boundary* (Dordrecht: Martinus Nijhoff, 1985); C. R. Rossi, *Equity and International Law: A Legal Realist Approach to International Decisionmaking* (Irvington, NY: Transnational, 1993).

[60] For a detailed account of equity and the methodology of equity, see T. Cottier, *Equitable Principles of Maritime Boundary Delimitation: Foundations and Legal Methodology* (forthcoming 2014).

equity. Based upon equitable principles, it is a matter of assessing all the relevant circumstances and factors which the law requires to be taken into account, assessing them in economic terms, and engaging in a careful process of balancing these interests with a view to achieving a reasoned, legitimate and thus acceptable result. It has been seen that a proper interaction of law and economics can also be built on the basis of broadly defined principles and subsequently developed by case law, which enhances guidance and predictability in the field for negotiators and courts alike. It shows that the law can be built gradually by trial and error. It leaves sufficient flexibility to combine normative, economic and behavioural circumstances and factors.

F. Conclusions for legal methodology in monetary law

A brief survey of other areas of international economic law and competition law shows a close interaction between law and economics. While the latter informs broad principles of trade regulation within the WTO, the growing network of preferential trade agreements, legal principles and rules define the framework within which economic analysis operates, providing the necessary data and impact assessments required for a legal determination. Broad principles may also offer a starting point for gradually encompassing and developing a field of law that would engage in considering and weighing different principles, circumstances and factors in a topical manner. The operation of economic law is thus much more complex than simply applying strict and detailed rules, or applying specific facts to norms which in return produce predetermined results. While such rules exist, complex areas of policy-making operate on the basis of broader principles and open textured rules, the operation of which depends upon economic data and impact assessment. The law offers criteria, direction and predictability, but depends upon economics for detailed determination within the legally defined framework. This approach is not limited to international economic law. Originally defined in civil law and turning away from strict syllogism, topical jurisprudence emerged as a factor- and fact-intensive manner of assessing constellations and bringing about fair and just results.[61] This

[61] See T. Viehweg, *Topics and Law: A Contribution to Basic Research in Law* (Frankfurt am Main: Peter Lang, 1993) and J. M. Balkin, 'A Night in the Topics: The Reason of Legal Rhetoric and the Rhetoric of Legal Reason' in P. Brooks and P. Gewirth (eds.), *Law's Stories: Narrative and Rhetoric in the Law* (New Haven, CT: Yale University Press, 1996), pp. 211–24.

model is predominant in constitutional law inherently dealing with open textured norms in a complex environment.

It is submitted, based upon methodological experience that the future relationship of law and economics in monetary affairs should build upon the lessons learned from fact-intensive topical jurisprudence. The law defines goals, principles and factors to be considered in a particular area. It offers a framework within which the operation of economic analysis should take place, and which it should consider and respect. Regulatory theory, with both its horizontal and vertical components, is able to serve as a basis for defining the future relationship of law and economics in monetary affairs. The task ahead is to define the legal framework and to identify the principles and factors which should guide and inform key features of monetary policy. Beyond defining goals of monetary stability and welfare, such as employment in the case of the US, monetary law will seek to define principles, factors and circumstances to be taken into account in defining interest rates[62] and in defining the amount of money available in a system, and related activities (such as quantitative easing and forward guidance). Beyond stimulation of growth, relevant principles and factors the framework also needs to take into account the interests of savers and segments of the population dependent on returns on capital. It will develop legal principles relevant to lending and conditionality, both for government and private banks, taking into account human rights.[63] It will develop legal principles applicable to exchange rate policy and determination beyond existing rules relating to subsidisation in WTO law.[64] It will identify principles defining the relationship of monetary policy, fiscal policy and sovereign debt[65] as well as for rating countries and financial institutions,[66] and the role of federal and international institutions in bringing about financial stability.[67]

[62] See C. D. Zimmermann, 'Global Benchmark Interest Rates: Conflicting Objectives and Increasing Hybridisation', Chapter 7, this volume.

[63] See M. Krajewski, 'Human Rights and Austerity Programmes', Chapter 19, this volume.

[64] See G. Z. Marceau and J. J. Maugham, 'The WTO Dispute Settlement Mechanism in Matters Involving Exchange Rates and Trade' Chapter 14, this volume and J. Marchetti, M. Rutta and R. Teh, 'Trade Imbalances and Multilateral Trade Cooperation', Chapter 13, this volume.

[65] See I. Feichtner, 'Taxation in Times of Austerity: A Question of Political Economy', Chapter 11, this volume and A. Viterbo, 'The Impact of Sovereign Debt on EU Monetary Affairs', Chapter 10, this volume.

[66] See I. MacNeil, 'Credit Rating Agencies: Regulation and Financial Stability', Chapter 8, this volume.

[67] See contribution by R. Lastra, Chapter 4, this volume.

The point we wish to make at this stage is that law and regulatory theory and past experience of interfacing law and economics does not exclude a more active role of legal principles and rules in the field, even within the current system of free-floating currencies. There is more to monetary law than defining very broad goals and allocating powers without offering further legal guidance as to what course of action central banks should take. There is a potential to be explored in law in defining principles, factors and circumstances which authorities should take into account in making reasoned decisions in monetary affairs in support of economic analysis. The law can potentially guide and assist in rendering these decisions fully accountable.

17

Framework of analysis: towards multilayered governance in monetary affairs

ERNST-ULRICH PETERSMANN

A. Introduction

The international monetary, financial, trading and related legal systems are governed by private and public regulations at the local, national and transnational levels. They interact both 'horizontally' and 'vertically' in order to produce and protect interdependent 'aggregate public goods', such as an efficient world trading system and price and financial stability, through mutually coherent rules and institutions. While the Agreement establishing the International Monetary Fund (IMF) and the General Agreement on Tariffs and Trade (GATT 1947) were designed as mutually complementary instruments for protecting an efficient world trading system based on stable exchange rates and freedom of payments, financial regulation continues to be essentially based on *national law* and '*soft rules*'. There is no adequate *international regulation* of financial cross-border problems, such as capital requirements, prudential standards, disclosure and transparency of systemically important financial institutions, their restrictive business practices and bankruptcy procedures for global banks. Transnational cooperation among central banks and banking regulators, sovereign wealth funds and sovereign debt crises likewise lacks adequate multilateral treaty regulation to avoid systemic risks.[1] The financial crises since 2008 not only revealed failures of financial markets (e.g., in terms of self-regulation of banks, proper evaluation of lending risks to eurozone member countries, such as Greece), but also failures in regulation and in supervision by national and international monetary, financial and related governance institutions.

This chapter clarifies interrelationships between 'governments' and 'multilevel governance' (Section B) and the need for justifying governance regimes (Section C) before explaining why political, economic and

[1] Cf. T. Cottier, J. H. Jackson, R. M. Lastra (eds), *International Law in Financial Regulation and Monetary Affairs* (Oxford University Press, 2012).

legal theories of multilevel governance remain contested and incoherent (Section D). In order to promote transnational rule of law for the benefit of citizens, multilevel governance needs to be constituted, limited and justified by coherent 'constitutional principles' (Section E). These findings apply to monetary and financial affairs no less than to the multilevel governance of the world trading system. The interrelated monetary, financial and trading systems require stronger 'multilevel regulation' of 'governance failures' and judicial protection of cosmopolitan rights and transnational rule of law in order to operate more efficiently and legitimately for the benefit of citizens (Section F).

B. Governments depend on 'multilevel governance'

The term '*governance*' (*gubernare*, meaning 'to steer' and 'to regulate') refers to the image of steering a ship (e.g., the 'state ship'). Governance differs from *government* in terms of its different performance of government functions without a unifying authority, as illustrated by decentralised performance of information provision, allocation, coordination and sanctioning functions through market competition, intergovernmental network cooperation in the common market of the European Union (EU), and the dynamic process of invoking, challenging and progressively developing constitutional, legislative, administrative and judicial rulemaking by civil society. Even inside states that have a *centralised government authority* controlling them, there are many diverse forms of decentralised governance (e.g., through market mechanisms), centralised governance (e.g., through regulatory agencies), multilevel governments (e.g., in federal states) and 'network governance' (e.g., among central banks). The rule-systems and institutions governing money markets, financial markets and goods markets differ in response to their diverse regulatory problems (e.g., of monetary exchange rates, banking regulation or import tariffs). National government systems for the supply of *national public goods* legitimately differ even among constitutional democracies. Similarly, international regulatory systems for multilevel governance of *international public goods* differ depending on the regulatory challenges they face, as illustrated by the 'veto powers' in the UN Security Council, the 'weighted voting' in the Bretton Woods institutions, the tripartite structure of the International Labour Organization (ILO), the 'supranational' structures of the EU and the more decentralised structures of the European Economic Area (EEA). The governance of the global financial system (e.g., by the G-7, G-8, G-20, IMF, Bank for International Settlements (BIS), national finance ministries or central banks) lacks a worldwide treaty and compulsory dispute settlement system similar to the law of the World Trade Organization (WTO). Unlike the hundreds of regional free trade area regimes, regional monetary and financial regulation remains underdeveloped outside the EU. The breakdown of national monetary systems (e.g., due to hyperinflation), the use of bimetallic monetary standards (gold and silver) in European countries before the victory of the gold standard in the 1870s, and the European Monetary Union (EMU) illustrate the often experimental nature of monetary governance (e.g., in the Latin Monetary Union and today in the eurozone). The *de facto* limitation of 'monetary sovereignty' by global financial markets is a reminder of the ancient Roman maxim of *pecunia regimen est rerum omnium* (money is the ruler of all things).

Multilevel governance refers to the increasing fragmentation of central government authority in nation states – notably in the field of economic policy – entailing ever more diverse public and non-governmental governance institutions, regulatory systems and 'private–public partnerships' at local, national, regional and worldwide levels for the collective supply of 'aggregate public goods'. The functional reallocation of regulatory powers – both upwards to *international* and downwards to *subnational* institutions – entails new overlapping jurisdictions (like the European Central Bank System) challenging traditional government functions, related legal hierarchies, concepts (e.g., of state sovereignty), democratic accountability and 'participatory democracy'.[2] The persistent violations by more than twenty of the twenty-eight EU member states of the agreed fiscal, debt and economic convergence disciplines of the Lisbon Treaty illustrate how multilevel governance risks undermining the rule of law. Multilevel governance arrangements aim at promoting synergies (e.g., in the cooperation between the IMF, the EU Commission and the ECB in determining the conditionality of the bailout agreements for Greece, Portugal, Ireland and Cyprus). Yet, diverse monetary and trade policies may also 'nullify or impair' each other as acknowledged in Articles XV and XXIII GATT 1994, just as inadequate fiscal and financial regulation in the eurozone has contributed to the private and 'sovereign debt' crises in some eurozone countries with harmful effects abroad (e.g., by imposing losses on foreign lenders).

The more globalisation and regionalisation transform *national* into *transnational public goods*, the more multilevel governance is necessary for limiting governance failures and for protecting 'aggregate public

[2] See, generally, C. Joerges and E. U. Petersmann (eds), *Constitutionalism, Multilevel Trade Governance and International Economic Law* (Oxford: Hart Publishing, 2011).

goods' (like liberal international monetary, financial and trading systems) for the benefit of citizens. The prevailing 'Westphalian model' of intergovernmental power politics among nations means that most existing multilevel governance mechanisms fail to protect international public goods efficiently and legitimately.[3] As the reallocation of central government powers inside regional monetary unions (like the EU) often does not follow traditional theories (e.g., 'fiscal federalism' based on centralised macroeconomic stabilisation and income redistribution), multilevel governance must engage in 'regulatory experimentation', for instance inside the EMU protecting comprehensive *national* fiscal, debt, economic and social policy powers, 'opt-outs' from monetary integration and 'bailout prohibitions' (cf. Articles 120–126 Treaty on the functioning of the European Union (TFEU)). Traditional policy assumptions (e.g., of 'competitive federalism' among governments maximising social welfare) may not hold in regional economic integration, for instance because some jurisdictions (like Greece) are dominated by rent-seeking interest groups distorting the national fiscal, economic, political and legal system in their pursuit of private self-interests.[4] The human rights 'to a social and international order in which the rights and freedoms set forth in this Declaration can be fully realized', as universally recognised in Article 28 of the 1948 Universal Declaration of Human Rights (UDHR) as well as in numerous UN resolutions on 'the right to development' as a human right of citizens and people, require 'constitutional reforms' aimed at improving the 'problem-solving capacity' and democratic legitimacy of multilevel governance. They also necessitate adequate regard – by all governments and multilevel governance institutions – is paid to human rights in the management of financial crises and their social impact within and beyond debtor states.

C. Public choices among alternative governance regimes require democratic justification

Law and governance need to be justified by 'principles of justice' in order to be recognised as legitimate by citizens and enforced by courts of

[3] *Cf.*, E. U. Petersmann, *International Economic Law in the 21st Century. Constitutional Pluralism and Multilevel Governance of Interdependent Public Goods* (Oxford: Hart Publishing, 2012).

[4] Transparency International's *Corruption Perception Index 2012* ranked Greece as the most corrupt EU Member State (Berlin: Transparency International, 2012).

justice. In view of the universal recognition by all UN member states of 'inalienable' and 'indivisible' human rights to be 'protected by the rule of law' (Preamble UDHR), UN law (e.g., Article 1 UN Charter) and the Vienna Convention on the Law of Treaties (VCLT) also emphasise the need for settlement of 'international disputes . . . by peaceful means . . . in conformity with the principles of justice and international law', including 'human rights and fundamental freedoms for all' (Preamble and Article 31 VCLT). As human rights also protect individual and democratic diversity, multilevel governance must respect legitimate 'constitutional pluralism' and legitimately diverse conceptions of social and political justice. UN human rights law (HRL) recognises not only equal freedoms as the 'first principle of justice', but also human rights to the justification of all government restrictions of equal freedoms, notwithstanding disagreement on the scope of 'access to justice' and judicial review of governmental restrictions.

These constitutional premises are equally valid in the field of monetary affairs. Yet, they are not effectively limiting political reality. The slow evolution, through trial and error, and the 'moral hazards' of European monetary regulation illustrate the importance of democratic and judicial control of multilevel economic governance in order to protect rule of law and limit 'rent-seeking' (e.g., by overindebted eurozone member states living at the expense of taxpayers in other eurozone member states financing bailouts of foreign debts). Respecting human rights requires ceasing to interpret national and international legal systems only from a formal perspective as a union of 'primary rules of conduct' and 'secondary rules' of recognition, change and adjudication[5] that dynamically interact with changing *legal practices* by private and public legal actors. The more human rights and 'general principles of law' are recognised as integral parts of national and international legal systems, the more it becomes necessary to acknowledge that the 'dual nature' of modern legal systems (as 'positive law' including 'principles of justice') requires constitutional restraints of 'intergovernmentalism' through stronger protection of the transnational 'rule of law', cosmopolitan rights and judicial remedies of citizens.

The competing approaches and diverse value systems of international governance continue to impede adequate international regulation of financial markets in view of the political insistence of governments and central banks on national monetary sovereignty and the insistence of

[5] *Cf.*, H. L. A. Hart, *The Concept of Law* (Oxford University Press, 1994), Chapter V.

banks on financial self-regulation. The legal design of multilevel governance arrangements depends on how, and at what level of regulation, the ubiquity of conflicts between rational private interests and reasonable public interests can be resolved. For instance:

- *producers of private goods and services* (e.g., financial services) pursue rational self-interests in maximising profits through private law (e.g., law merchant), restrictive business practices (e.g., manipulation of the London Interbank Offered Rate (Libor)), excessive financial bonuses for 'risk-taking') and 'private–public partnerships' (e.g., bank purchases of government bonds in exchange for governmental bailouts of banks that are 'too big to fail');
- *consumers and taxpayers* have different rational self-interests, for instance to insist on governmental correction of 'market failures' with harmful externalities (e.g., conditionality of financial bailouts, at the expense of taxpayers, of private and sovereign debtors in peripheral eurozone countries);
- *producers of national and international public goods* (e.g., governments) pursue different 'public interests' (e.g., in terms of rule of law, monetary stability and general consumer welfare); but their 'public choices' of alternative governance mechanisms risk being distorted by their private self-interests (e.g., in avoiding accountability, offering bailouts to national banks in exchange for their political support and purchase of government bonds);
- *reasonable citizens* have self-interests in 'institutionalizing public reason' through constitutional, legislative, administrative and judicial rules and institutions protecting 'principles of justice' (like 'monetary stability', human rights and accountability mechanisms) and limiting abuses of power and 'moral hazards' (e.g., through individual rights, judicial remedies, central bank independence, prohibitions of 'central bank financing' and 'bailouts' in Articles 123–125 TFEU).

Solutions to the ubiquity of conflicts of interests (e.g., between 'Wall Street' and 'main street') have to be sought through democratic discourse and legal regulation. Even if certain areas of monetary and economic policies claim to be based on purely economic considerations (such as 'quantitative monetary easing' by central banks), their micro and macroeconomic effects (e.g., on private and public access to financial markets or the 'spread' of interest rates for bonds by over-indebted eurozone member states) may give rise to legal challenges. One example of this is the purchases of government bonds by the European Central Bank

(ECB) in 'secondary markets' whose legal consistency with the prohibition of central-bank financing of public expenditures (*cf.*, Article 123 TFEU) and with national constitutional law is being challenged in the German Constitutional Court.[6] The successful judicial challenges (e.g., in the Constitutional Courts of Latvia and Spain) of the 'financial conditionality' imposed by international 'bailout agreements' also entail challenges to the 'executive dominance' in 'intergovernmental rulemaking' that entail the risk of 'discourse failures' and democratic disagreement on the extent to which 'intergovernmentalism' should be constitutionally restrained or left to government discretion and majority politics. Disagreements on how to protect constitutional, representative, participatory and deliberative democracy in transnational governance also arise because – even inside the EU with its European Parliament, federal co-legislation and 'EU citizenship' – the competing models of national democratic control, multinational 'EU democracy' and 'cosmopolitan democracy' based on cosmopolitan rights have all too often failed to protect the common interests of EU citizens against the political self-interests of politicians (e.g., in accommodating rent-seeking lobbies in exchange for political support). The under-regulation of international financial markets illustrates how 'political markets for regulation' are often shaped more by competition (e.g., among jurisdictions issuing international reserve currencies and controlling financial centres) and power politics (e.g., in financial markets imposing excessive rates of interest on over-indebted borrowing countries) than by 'principles of justice'. The new 'euro governance' in response to the financial, fiscal and sovereign debt crises since 2008 continues to transform the EU's '*ordo*-liberal common market constitution' – based on the Court of Justice's (CJEU's) interpretation of the 1957 Rome Treaty – as well as the 'Maastricht principles' of euro-governance (e.g., *national sovereignty* over fiscal and debt policies, bailout prohibitions) by *ad hoc* intergovernmental rescue packages, new EU financial stability mechanisms, EU 'conditionality' of financial assistance, EU surveillance

[6] *Cf.*, K. Tuori, 'The European Financial Crisis – Constitutional Aspects and Implications', *EUI Working Papers Law* 2012/28, 29 ff. The German Constitutional Court judgment of 12 September 2012 on the European Stability Mechanism mentioned – in an *obiter dictum* – that Article 123 TFEU prevents the ECB from using 'the funds at its disposal for *direct* financial stabilization of its members'; 'an acquisition of government bonds on the secondary market by the ECB aiming at financing the Members' budgets independently of the capital market is prohibited as well, as it would circumvent the prohibition of monetary financing' (2 BvR 1390/12, 2 BvR 1421/12, 2 BvR 1438/12, para. 246).

mechanisms and judicial remedies aimed at protecting rule of law and limiting 'systemic contagion' of national governance failures. From the perspective of 'principles of justice' (such as human rights, democratic rulemaking, efficiency and fairness of governance), many multilevel governance mechanisms (e.g., financial markets, credit-rating agencies and systemically important banks) remain insufficiently accountable due to 'regulatory capture' and rational pursuit of private self-interests.

D. Disagreement on political, economic and legal governance principles

Similar to the diverse *political theories* on governance inside states and on designing private governance organisations and 'private–public partnerships' (e.g., for supplying public goods such as financial stability), there is no agreed 'doctrine of multilevel governance' for transnational public goods. For instance:[7]

- *'Realist' theories* continue to perceive states as key actors in world affairs and focus on 'national interests' in terms of power, security and separation of national from international law. The more hegemonic 'intergovernmental power politics' fails to protect international public goods demanded by citizens (such as financial stability and protection of consumer welfare), the more reason citizens and democratic parliaments have to insist on multilevel, constitutional safeguards limiting abuses of public and private power in order to protect common, reasonable self-interests of citizens, also beyond states.
- *Liberal regime theories* explain why international rules, procedures and institutions can help overcome 'collective action problems' in international relations, for instance through (i) formation of clubs excluding 'free-riders'; (ii) monitoring of rule-compliance (e.g., as a disincentive for 'cheating'); (iii) institutionalised long-term cooperation promoting trust and predictability; (iv) rules-based reduction of transaction costs; and (v) sanctions imposed on countries violating their 'duties to protect' human rights and other public goods.
- *Functional integration theories* offer additional strategies for depoliticising and transforming 'high politics' into mutually beneficial 'low politics'

[7] For an application of the following international relations theories to the GATT/WTO system, see E. U. Petersmann, *The GATT/WTO Dispute Settlement System. International Law, International Organizations and Dispute Settlement* (London: Kluwer, 1997), pp. 10 ff.

(e.g., inside free trade areas, customs and monetary unions) based on rational self-interests of subnational and supranational actors, as illustrated by the multilevel 'common market freedoms' of EU citizens and their multilevel, legal protection by independent institutions (like national and EU competition, monetary and judicial authorities). Reliance on citizen-driven market integration has increased the need for standard-setting bodies (such as the Basel Committee for Banking Supervision and the International Standards Organization) aimed at promoting transparency and integrity of product and production standards, market transactions and related government regulations (e.g., of money laundering or consumer protection).

- *Public choice theories* explain the ubiquity of 'market failures' and 'governance failures' in terms of the rational egoism of 'rent-seeking' individuals, interest groups and periodically elected politicians. For instance, national trade policy discretion risks being distorted unless interest group politics is legally constrained by multilevel safeguards of common reasonable interests of citizens (e.g., GATT/WTO law protecting non-discriminatory market competition). Similarly, the abuses of national fiscal, debt and economic policies in over-indebted eurozone member countries (like Greece) required the EU to introduce ever more multilevel legal and institutional disciplines, surveillance mechanisms and financial assistance in order to contain the financial crises since 2010. In order to avoid systemic risks, multilevel governance must coordinate the 'horizontal' and 'vertical' interdependencies among international movements of goods, services, persons, capital, payments, related rules and institutions at the national and transnational levels (e.g., coordination by the G-20 and the IMF of the 'international financial architecture' based on 'transnational governmental networking').
- *Constitutional theories* emphasise that legitimate and effective governance of public goods depends on mutually coherent constitutional, legislative, administrative, judicial and international rules and institutions for the benefit of citizens and their constitutional rights as ultimate constitutional values and guarantees of 'deliberative' and 'participatory democracy'. *Multilevel constitutionalism* aims at integrating legitimately diverse regulatory approaches in order to promote coherent and legitimate, multilevel governance of 'aggregate public goods'.[8] Just as morality requires limiting rational egoism by

[8] *Cf.*, E. U. Petersmann (ed.), *Multilevel Governance of Interdependent Public Goods. Theories, Rules and Institutions for the Central Policy Challenge in the 21st Century*

reasonableness, *cosmopolitan constitutionalism* aims at institutionalising 'public reason' (e.g., in terms of human rights, independent central banks, and 'courts of justice' limiting majority politics) so as to protect constitutional rights of citizens and decentralised enforcement of rule of law by individuals as 'agents of justice' entitled to cosmopolitan rights (as 'intermediate public goods').

As discussed in Section E, human rights law (HRL) and the democratic demands for international public goods require multilevel 'constitutional limits' of 'realist power politics' with due regard for the insights of liberal institutionalism, functionalism and 'public choice' theories.

The intergovernmental domination of UN and WTO governance institutions prioritising rights and self-interests of governments (e.g., in limiting their legal and judicial accountability *vis-à-vis* citizens) over rights of citizens lacks legitimacy and efficiency; for instance, human rights and consumer rights are not mentioned anywhere in the Bretton Woods, GATT and WTO Agreements, and citizens are not legally protected against welfare-reducing violations of transnational rule of law (e.g., violations of WTO law). HRL and the disagreement on the design of multilevel governance (e.g., the bailout prohibition of EU law) call for 'subsidiarity' of public governance mechanisms[9] and for decentralising some global governance institutions dominated and distorted by 'intergovernmentalism', for example by decentralising 'the dispute settlement system of the WTO' for 'providing security and predictability to the multilateral trading system' (Article 3 WTO Dispute Settlement Understanding) by transforming intergovernmental WTO disputes and related 'trade wars' into domestic disputes based on cosmopolitan rights and judicial safeguards of transnational rule of law in domestic courts based on the 'consistent interpretation' and 'judicial comity' principles recognised in national and international legal systems (*cf.*, Article 31 VCLT).[10] Yet, there is also an urgent need for new multilevel

(RSCAS 2012/13, Global Governance Program Working Paper 2012). In contrast to national (big C) Constitutions, (small c) 'constitutionalism' refers to the basic rules and institutions of transnational communities and their legal orders (such as the EU and WTO constitutions).

[9] The 2009 Lisbon Treaty defines the 'subsidiarity principle' in terms of constitutional, representative, participatory and deliberative democracy so that 'decisions are taken as openly as possible and as closely as possible to the citizens' (cf. Preamble, Articles 5, 9–12 TEU).

[10] On the need for 'cosmopolitan international economic law' in order to protect public goods more effectively and more legitimately, see Petersmann, *International Economic Law*, Chapters II and III.

governance institutions (e.g., for international financial and environmental regulation).

Economic theories remain crucial to the efficient design of multilevel governance institutions. For instance:

- The economic theory of 'optimal intervention' explains how alternative policy instruments for correcting 'governance failures' as well as 'market failures' should be regulated and 'legally ranked' (e.g., trade policy instruments in GATT/WTO law) in order to achieve their policy goals most efficiently.
- The economic theory of 'separation of policy instruments' explains why UN law and international economic law (IEL) allocate the multilevel governance of diverse international public goods (e.g., monetary governance, trade governance, international protection of public health and of labour market regulation) to different international institutions. Also, central banks have been given legal independence in ever more countries in order to protect monetary and financial stability efficiently.
- Economic theories of 'public goods' explain why the 'supply strategies' for the different types of public goods – such as 'best shot', 'weakest link' and 'aggregate public goods' – vary depending on their particular characteristics and the preferences of the citizens and governments involved (e.g., for 'internalising external effects' by means of taxes, subsidies or a change in property rights).
- Welfare economics explains why market regulation (e.g., in order to protect financial stability) must also provide for independent supervision of micro- and macro-policies (e.g., IMF surveillance or EU surveillance pursuant to Article 121 TFEU) and for crisis management (e.g., national central banks as lenders of last resort for governments and banks, deposit insurance and bank resolution).

In multilevel governance and intergovernmental regulation, *political* and *legal* arguments and pressures (e.g., regarding US veto rights and European over-representation in IMF institutions, and 'conditionality' of international 'bailouts') are often more influential than *economic* efficiency considerations. As governance institutions operate through legal rules and decisions, the legal design of multilevel governance institutions and their regulatory instruments are often shaped by legal theories. Due to the frequent disagreements on the role of national and international law in supplying international public goods, the thousands of diverse public goods regimes and private law regimes interact in a global space of 'legal pluralism' that often eludes coherent 'governance' and efficient coordination. Integration of the diverse political, economic and legal governance theories is also impeded because – similar to the story of the blind men touching different parts of an elephant and describing the same animal in contradictory ways – private and public, national and international lawyers continue to perceive 'international economic law' from competing perspectives, for instance as (i) public international law (e.g., the Bretton Woods Agreements), (ii) 'global administrative law' (e.g., the legal practices of UN Specialized Agencies and the WTO), (iii) 'conflicts law' coordinating 'legal pluralism' (e.g., in international commercial law), (iv) multilevel constitutional regulation (e.g., in EU law), or (v) multilevel economic regulation of the economy (e.g., NAFTA law) within the limits of national, democratic constitutionalism.[11]

E. Transnational rule of law requires justification of multilevel governance by constitutional principles

As 'globalisation' and 'policy externalities' increasingly mean that policy problems can no longer be effectively governed at the national level, multilevel governance becomes indispensable for international 'aggregate public goods' that can only be supplied collectively through international cooperation based on international law and institutions. Intergovernmental 'Westphalian governance' lacks democratic legitimacy in view of its inadequate democratic control and 'systemic failure' to effectively protect human rights and other international public goods. The existing 'legal fragmentation' and frequent lack of transnational rule of law need to be reformed on the basis of the 'constitutional principles' recognised in UN law as common framework for diverse 'multilevel public goods' regimes.[12] Progress will remain incremental and depend on struggles for stronger protection of cosmopolitan rights and other 'principles of justice' in multilevel governance of public goods.

[11] For a discussion of these five competing conceptions of IEL, see Joerges and Petersmann, (note 2).

[12] *Cf.*, Petersmann, *International Economic Law* and *The GATT/WTO Dispute Settlement System*. On this aspect also see T. Cottier and L. Satragno, 'The Potential of Law and Legal Methodology in Monetary Affairs', Chapter 16, this volume.

I. Limitation of 'governance failures' by 'multilevel constitutionalism'

The 'Westphalian traditions' of governments to insist on foreign policy discretion to violate international law and prioritise rights of governments over rights of citizens are inconsistent with the legal obligations of all UN member states to protect human rights through the 'rule of law' within and beyond national jurisdictions. In order to remain coherent, multilevel governance of 'aggregate public goods' must remain 'constitutionally embedded' and protect also cosmopolitan freedoms of citizens to engage in mutually beneficial cooperation across frontiers, with due respect for the legitimate diversity of 'constitutional pluralism' among jurisdictions. As 'democratic principals' of all governance institutions, citizens must be recognised as legal subjects of multilevel governance and of 'access to justice' to contest (e.g., in 'courts of justice') intergovernmental neglect of rule of law and other public goods. The primary aim of multilevel economic regulation must be to empower and protect individuals (e.g., traders, investors and consumers), and their legitimate trust in compliance with international treaties ratified by national parliaments for the benefit of citizens.

Multilevel regulation of the global division of labour is ever more important for satisfying consumer demand for scarce goods and services and for protecting the transnational rule of law, open markets, financial stability and freedom of payments. The private and public debt crises since 2008 have confirmed the need for additional international regulation of market failures (such as inadequate capital of global banks and the defaults of systemically important financial institutions) and of governance failures (such as sovereign debt defaults). Yet, there is no international agreement on replacing the informal coordination among central banks, banking regulators and 'regulatory competition' among financial centres by international legal harmonisation (e.g., of bank deposit insurance, bank insolvency proceedings, public debt restructuring and conditionality of bail-out agreements) and stronger, institutionalised control of systemic risks. The constitutional obligations of governments to protect public goods require constitutional limitations of foreign policy discretion by cosmopolitan rights and judicial remedies for citizens. In view of the failure of most UN and WTO 'public goods regimes' to effectively protect international public goods demanded by citizens, IEL must be interpreted in conformity with human rights as protecting cosmopolitan rights to challenge governmental violations of the transnational rule of law.[13] The 'emancipatory function' of cosmopolitan rights requires civilising and 'constitutionalising' the 'Westphalian model' of UN law, IEL and intergovernmental claims

- to limit international law to rights and obligations of states without regard to the democratic legitimacy of governments in UN member states;
- to focus on 'national interests' as defined by national interest groups rather than on protection of human rights and general consumer welfare that are not mentioned in most worldwide economic and environmental agreements;
- to separate national and international legal systems by excluding legal and judicial remedies of citizens against welfare-reducing violations of treaty obligations; and
- to treat citizens as mere objects of international law – without democratic justification of the welfare-reducing under-supply of international public goods and the unnecessary poverty endured by more than 1 billion people living on US$ 1 or less per day.

II. Protection of cosmopolitan rights through 'cosmopolitan constitutionalism'

The more national constitutions become 'partial constitutions' that can achieve many constitutional objectives only in cooperation with international law and institutions, the stronger the need for interpreting law and multilevel governance of international public goods on the basis of 'cosmopolitan constitutionalism' in order to promote stronger legal, judicial and democratic accountability of intergovernmental rulemaking based on cosmopolitan rights limiting, justifying and empowering multilevel governance. Denial by governments of legal and judicial accountability *vis-à-vis* citizens for intergovernmental failures to protect international public goods does not serve the reasonable interests of citizens. Hence, the legitimacy of secretly negotiated, intergovernmental agreements is increasingly challenged (e.g., the 2011 Anti-Counterfeiting Agreement rejected by the European Parliament). UN law and the 1969

[13] On such 'constitutional interpretations' and 'constitutional functions' of international guarantees of freedom, equality, rule of law and sovereign duties to protect public goods and domestic constitutional principles across frontiers for the benefit of citizens, see the interdisciplinary, comparative studies in M. Hilf and E. U. Petersmann (eds.), *National Constitutions and International Economic Law* (Deventer: Kluwer Publishers, 1993).

VCLT recognise that human rights are 'the foundation of freedom, justice and peace in the world'; 'respect for the obligations arising from treaties and other sources of international law' requires settlement of international disputes 'in conformity with the principles of justice and international law', including human rights and universal fundamental freedoms (Article 1 UN Charter, Preamble VCLT). Yet, in contrast to the 'cosmopolitan interpretations' of European economic law by European courts (e.g., in the EU, EEA and ECHR), many governments resist references to human rights in international economic and environmental treaties and dispute settlements outside Europe. Similar to 'human rights revolutions' aimed at reforming national governance systems and at protecting cosmopolitan rights of the 500 million EU citizens and more than 800 million European citizens protected by the ECHR, reasonable citizens have good reasons for insisting on their legal empowerment as 'UN citizens' and 'WTO citizens' through cosmopolitan rights. In interpreting HRL, IEL and related responsibilities of governments, international economic and environmental dispute settlement bodies must protect human rights and other cosmopolitan rights[14] such as

- *private freedoms* of 'economic citizens' to mutually beneficial cooperation (e.g., private property rights protected in investment and human rights treaties);
- *legal freedoms* of 'state citizens' to equal treatment and participation in legal communities, including 'negative freedoms' from unjustified government restrictions and 'positive freedoms' of participation and development of one's human capacities (as protected in UN HRL);
- *democratic freedoms* of 'political citizens' (e.g., EU citizenship rights) to participate as co-authors of democratic legislation in multilevel governance; and
- *cosmopolitan freedoms* empowering 'world citizens' to exercise their collective responsibility for jointly supplying transnational public goods (e.g., labour rights and representation protected in ILO law).

III. *Transnational rule of law for the benefit of citizens*

HRL and democratic self-government require 'rule of law' as a constitutional restraint on 'rule by law', as recognised in numerous constitutional

[14] *Cf.*, E. U. Petersmann, 'The Judicial Task of Administering Justice in Trade and Investment Law and Adjudication', in *Journal of International Dispute Settlement* 4 (2013), 5–28.

and human rights instruments and in the 'consistent interpretation' requirements of national and international legal systems. The effectiveness and legitimacy of 'aggregate public goods' based on local, national, regional and worldwide 'composite public goods' (such as efficient monetary and trading systems based on price and financial stability) inevitably depend on the transnational rule of law guaranteeing legal security and systemic coherence. The refusal by European courts to implement the UN Security Council's 'smart sanctions' violating human rights illustrates how intergovernmental 'rule by law' risks undermining human and constitutional rights of citizens and other 'constitutional checks and balances'. Non-inclusive 'Westphalian agreements' prioritising rights of governments justify often only a presumption of 'rule by law' rather than 'rule of law', for instance in case of their inadequate control by parliaments, courts of justice, their frequent exclusion of rights of citizens and of individual 'access to justice'. The jurisprudence of the CJEU and of the EFTA Court confirms that multilevel economic governance in the multilevel constitutional context of EU law and EEA law has only rarely entailed violations of HRL to the detriment of citizens.[15] Yet, in their external relations law, EU institutions also insist on 'freedom of manoeuvre'[16] – in the sense of freedom to violate WTO law and other international legal obligations of the EU ratified by national parliaments – without legal and judicial accountability *vis-à-vis* EU citizens adversely affected by violations of the EU's constitutional commitment to 'strict observance of international law' (Article 3 TEU).[17] As democratic parliaments have not delegated powers to international organisations (including the EU) to violate human rights and rule of law to the detriment of citizens, legal and judicial protection of interdependent 'aggregate public goods' through multilevel governance requires stronger accountability mechanisms protecting 'rule of

[15] *Cf.*, Petersmann, *International Economic Law*, Chapters IV and VIII.

[16] This term continues to be used by both the political EU institutions and the EU Court of Justice (e.g., in Joined cases C-120 and C-121/06 *P*, *FIAMM* [2008] ECR I-6513, para. 119) as the main justification for their disregard of legally binding WTO rules and WTO dispute settlement rulings.

[17] For an overview of the case law of the EU Court of Justice denying EU citizens rights to invoke and enforce WTO obligations in national and European courts and request compensation for injury caused by persistent violations of the EU's WTO obligations, see E. U. Petersmann, 'Can the EU's Disregard for "Strict Observance of International Law" (Article 3 TEU) Be Constitutionally Justified?', in M. Bronckers, V. Hauspiel and R. Quick (eds), *Liber Amicorum for J. Bourgeois* (Cheltenham: Edward Elgar, 2011), pp. 214–225.

law' for the benefit of citizens and judicial remedies against arbitrary government violations of IEL.

IV. *'Subsidiarity' of multilevel economic regulation*

HRL and constitutional, participatory and deliberative democracy require governance decisions to be taken 'as openly as possible and as closely as possible to the citizens' (*cf.*, Articles 1, 9–12 TEU). This 'subsidiarity principle' entails that assigning responsibility to international levels needs justification, as acknowledged in the Lisbon Treaty (Article 5 TEU) and in various judgments of the German Constitutional Court insisting on the responsibility of the German Parliament to exercise its democratic and budgetary powers rather than assigning them to EU institutions. Global financial markets remain governed primarily by national regulations and institutions. EU monetary and financial law recognises sovereign rights to opt out from eurozone membership and from the EU's 'banking union', notwithstanding increasing recognition of the need for additional international rules on restructuring and liquidating international banks in case of debt defaults. HRL and subsidiarity challenge the 'Westphalian conceptions' of foreign policy discretion as a privilege of the Executive. Cosmopolitan constitutionalism recognises every person's equal status as ultimate source of values (normative individualism), notwithstanding constitutional and democratic freedoms to distinguish between national citizens and foreigners. HRL limits national foreign policy discretion by 'duties to protect' also transnational public goods like financial stability and freedom of payments. Hence, similar to the requirement of the Lisbon Treaty that 'the Union shall act only if and in so far as the objectives of the proposed action cannot be sufficiently achieved by the Member States, either at the central level or at the regional and local level, but can rather . . . be better achieved at Union level' (Article 5 TEU), delegation of limited governance powers to international organisations does not justify 'Westphalian restrictions' of democratic, legal and judicial accountability of worldwide governance institutions *vis-à-vis* citizens. Cosmopolitan normative individualism calls for interpreting economic and environmental treaties not only in terms of rights and obligations of governments, but primarily in favour of citizens as cosmopolitan subjects of IEL and 'democratic principals' that must control their 'political agents' and multilevel governance more effectively. Many governments refusing 'state consent' to resolving 'collective action problems' are undermining the human rights of their citizens.

V. Multilevel enforcement of HRL and IEL based on 'access to justice'

The effectiveness of international monetary, financial and trade regulations depends on their implementation in domestic legal systems in ways that reduce economic transaction costs and enhance legal security, human rights and the value of property rights (e.g., in terms of monetary, financial and price stability). The WTO Agreement requires each member to 'ensure the conformity of its laws, regulations and administrative procedures with its obligations as provided in the annexed Agreements' (Article XVI:4); the WTO guarantees of access to justice at the international and domestic levels also protect individual access to domestic judicial remedies.[18] International monetary and financial regulation, by contrast, is often governed more by 'soft rules' (e.g., by the BIS or the Financial Stability Board) than by hard law enforceable in domestic courts. As long as citizens' rights to directly enforce international monetary, financial and trade regulations remain exceptional in IEL,[19] the lack of effective remedies and judicial accountability of governments undermines the transnational rule of law. For instance, the under-regulation of financial markets and lack of supervision of debt and economic policies inside the eurozone have contributed to private and sovereign debt defaults (i.e., violations of contract law) since 2010, inflicting huge financial losses on private and public creditors and taxpayers without effective judicial remedies. The Treaty on Stability, Coordination and Governance in the Economic and Monetary Union of March 2012 ('Fiscal Compact') also does not provide for judicial remedies for citizens in the monitoring process; only contracting states may challenge rule-violations in the CJEU, and the parties to the procedure must comply with the judgment within a time limit set by the Court (Article 8). European HRL, competition and common market law illustrate, by contrast, how decentralised legal and judicial enforcement of international rules can limit 'market failures' and 'governance failures' more effectively than intergovernmental procedures; the decentralised enforcement of EU trade rules meant that the CJEU has had to render

[18] *Cf.*, Petersmann, *The GATT/WTO Dispute Settlement System*, 194 ff.

[19] Exceptions include Article VIII:2(b) IMF Agreement (non-enforceability of exchange contracts violating IMF rules) and Article XX Government Procurement Agreement (domestic legal remedies against breaches of GPA obligations). In most countries (e.g., in the EU and US), governments oppose domestic judicial application of WTO rules in order to limit their judicial accountability.

only three judgments in trade disputes among EU member states over the past sixty years. Judicial protection of cosmopolitan rights can also increase the accountability of governments in politically controversial policy areas, as illustrated by the '*Kadi* jurisprudence' of the CJEU refusing to apply UN Security Council sanctions violating HRL as well as by the German Constitutional Court judgment of 18 July 2012 recognising a fundamental right of asylum seekers and other foreign migrants in Germany to receive higher cash benefits for their 'dignified minimum existence' protected by their human right to dignity (Article 1 sec.1 of the German Basic Law) in conjunction with the constitutional guarantee of a social welfare state (Article 20 sec.1).[20] Guarantees of 'access to justice' in HRL[21] justify extending judicial remedies in multilevel economic governance so as to empower citizens to hold governments more accountable for their failures to protect transnational rule of law for the benefit of citizens, and other public goods.

VI. Multilevel regulation of 'collective action problems'

Public goods theories emphasise that – depending on their respective 'provision paths' – some public goods can be supplied unilaterally by 'single best efforts' (e.g., an invention); the supply of some other public goods depends on the 'weakest links' (e.g., dyke-building, global polio eradication, or nuclear non-proliferation); 'aggregate global public goods' (such as monetary and financial stability, or open markets) tend to be supplied through a 'summation process' of local, national and regional public goods. Global public goods 'differ from their national counterparts in terms of the complexity – the multi-actor, multi-sector, multi-level nature – of their provision path, as well as in terms of the policy-interdependence they entail'.[22] The interdependence of multilevel governance of international movements of goods, services, persons, capital and related payments requires closer coordination of international monetary, financial and trade regulation in order to ensure that,

[20] Judgment of 18 July 2012 (1 BvL 10/10, 1 BvL 2/11). On the '*Kadi* jurisprudence' of the CJEU, see Petersmann, *International Economic Law*, pp. 205 ff.

[21] *Cf.*, F. Francioni (ed), *Access to Justice as a Human Right* (Oxford University Press, 2007).

[22] *Cf.*, I. Kaul, 'Global Public Goods: Explaining their Underprovision', in E. U. Petersmann (ed.), *Multilevel Governance of Interdependent Public Goods. Theories, Rules and Institutions for the Central Policy Challenge in the 21st Century* (RSCAS 2012/13, Global Governance Program Working Paper 2012), 41–60.

e.g., currency manipulation and fiscal stimuli programmes (e.g., with 'buy American requirements') do not undermine world trade rules. As the publicness and privateness of goods are often social constructs rather than innate properties, regulatory choices may legitimately differ. International financial markets, for example, are regulated by national and international public law organisations, numerous informal groups (like the G-7, G-8, G-10 and G-20) and standard-setting bodies (like the Financial Stability Board) and private bodies like the European Financial Stability Facility (EFSF) established by eurozone member states in 2010 as a limited liability company under Luxembourg law. The private law forms of the global governance of the Internet by the Internet Corporation for Assigned Numbers and Names (ICANN), and the settlement of thousands of international 'domain name disputes' by means of arbitration procedures administered by the World Intellectual Property Organization and enforced by ICANN, illustrate the global importance of decentralised, rights-based regimes transforming global public goods into institutionalised 'club goods' so as to limit incentives for free-riding and create incentives for supporting club goods. Public goods theories identify 'collective action problems' and argue for changing policy incentives, e.g. by

- sanctions *vis-à-vis* gross human rights violations in free-riding countries that refuse to cooperate in joint protection of public goods;
- transformation of public goods into 'club goods' excluding free-riders (such as countries unwilling to accept WTO legal disciplines); and
- granting of public or private property rights (e.g., in 'common pool resources' like fishery resources) so as to prevent the 'tragedy of the commons'.

VII. Constitutional pluralism and the limits of 'regulatory competition'

Just as HRL protects legitimately diverse 'constitutional pluralism', democracy and economic freedoms promote regulatory competition among jurisdictions. The global competition among national currencies and financial centres may lead not only to a 'race to the bottom' (e.g., favouring 'tax havens') but also to better prudential standards attracting scarce investments. The 'Maastricht principles' for monetary governance of the EMU focused on *ordo*-liberal 'monetary principles' such as primacy of price and monetary stability over fiscal policy, prohibitions on bailouts and on 'central bank financing', competition rules and surveillance disciplines (e.g., in Articles 121–126 TFEU) on *national* fiscal, budget and debt sovereignty. The assumption was that private and public debtors would be left to default in case of persistent rule violations and over-indebtedness caused by irresponsible fiscal and debt management. Yet, the unforeseen private 'bank defaults' and 'sovereign debt defaults' of euro member states violating the agreed fiscal, debt and economic convergence disciplines entailed risks of 'systemic contagion' of euro-governance beyond national jurisdictions prompting ever more intergovernmental transformations of the EMU. The financial rescue packages for Greece, Ireland, Portugal, Spain and Cyprus, the successive creation – since 2010 – of the European Financial Stabilisation Mechanism (EFSM, €60 billion), the European Financial Stability Facility (EFSF, €780 billion) and of the European Stability Mechanism (ESM, €700 billion) and the credit facilities made available by the ECB limited the financial market disciplines (e.g., the 'spread' of interest rates for bonds by eurozone member states) as incentives for domestic governance reforms. The legal consistency of these changes of European monetary governance by intergovernmental agreements, amendments of Article 136 TFEU, and expansion of the powers of the ECB in order to respond to unforeseen 'systemic risks' continues to be contested.[23] The fiscal and balance of payments crises in the eurozone have entailed legal and institutional fragmentation of the EMU in favour of intergovernmental eurozone governance mechanisms and EU rules differentiating among the eighteen eurozone member states and ten other EMU member states. Democratic control by citizens, civil society, the European Parliament and national parliaments of this 'fragmented governance' is increasingly difficult.

Similar to national 'fiscal profligacy' at the expense of foreign creditors, the redistributive consequences of multilevel governance often induce rent-seeking aimed at redistributing income through changes of the law. HRL and multilevel legal restraints of regulatory discretion limit both legitimate 'regulatory competition' and rule violations. Some global public goods – e.g., global transportation and communication systems – are better provided for than others due to more effective legal restraints

[23] The CJEU judgment of 27 November 2012 (Case C-370/12, *Pringle*) confirmed the legal validity of the amendment of Article 136 TFEU and of the related treaty establishing the ESM. Also see, A. Viterbo, 'The Impact of Sovereign Debts on EU Monetary Affairs', Chapter 10, this volume.

on market failures and governance failures (e.g., limiting fairness deficits in intergovernmental negotiations, contested distributional implications). As suboptimal supply of many international public goods is related to the property regime, redesigning the property rights and differentiating between different types of ownership rights (e.g., in case of bank defaults, rights of access to, and extraction and management of common pool resources) may enable more effective provision of public goods (such as protection of financial responsibility, or of biodiversity). Treaty provisions on 'enhanced cooperation' among 'coalitions of willing countries' (e.g., pursuant to Article 20 TEU), on 'plurilateral agreements' among some of the WTO Members (e.g., the 2011 Government Procurement Agreement), and on regional trade agreements (e.g., pursuant to Articles XXIV GATT and V GATS) can offer incentives for 'competing regulation' and institutional experimentation. Reconciling national and transnational self-interests requires 'responsible sovereignty' based on the neglected insight that – as a result of the transformation of ever more national public goods into international ones – national constitutions have become 'partial constitutions' that can protect ever more 'aggregate public goods' only in conformity with international law and international institutions.

VIII. Comparative lessons from public goods regimes

National public goods (like national currencies protecting price and monetary stability) continue to be supplied by states with legislative, executive and judicial powers (e.g., to tax and coerce citizens) that rarely exist in international institutions. As there is no one size fits all strategy for multilevel governance of all the diverse public goods, the collective supply of transnational public goods remains characterised by multi-level, legal and institutional experimentation. Transnational public goods regimes may be based on diverse legal instruments such as international treaties and intergovernmental organisations, informal intergovernmental networks among domestic regulatory agencies (such as the Basel Committee of national bank regulators), national authorities implementing international economic rules and policies (e.g., transnational currency unions based on gold or silver standards during the nineteenth century), hybrid public–private 'regulatory partnerships' and private regulatory bodies such as the International Organization for Standardization for the international harmonisation of standards that may also be used as a legal basis for intergovernmental regulation (e.g., in the WTO Agreement on Technical Barriers to Trade). The 'horizontal' legal regulation of 'overlaps', cooperation and conflicts between interdependent public goods (e.g., the relationships of the WTO to monetary and financial regulation) tends to be incomplete and to evolve dynamically in response to newly emerging regulatory challenges. Similarly, the regulation of the 'vertical interactions' among international and domestic legal regimes may follow diverse legal approaches, as illustrated by the more limited remedies for reparation of injury caused by treaty violations in the WTO compared with the rules on state responsibility applied by the ICJ or the CJEU, or by the diversity of treaty provisions on multilevel cooperation among courts in order to protect transnational rule of law. Multilevel rulemaking and compliance with rules depend on procedural fairness and 'responsible sovereignty', which becomes increasingly 'disaggregated' in IEL (e.g., due to the reallocation of previously national monetary sovereignty to eurozone governance institutions).

While the multilateral and regional trading systems continue to be coordinated within the global framework of WTO rules and institutions, the financial system lacks an equivalent central institution exercising overall regulatory, supervisory and dispute settlement functions and having related responsibilities for containing the recurrent financial crises. It is only since the 2008–9 international financial crisis that the initiation of G-20 leaders summits and the establishment and enlargement of the Financial Stability Board (now including twenty-four jurisdictions and a number of international organisations) have strengthened systemic, intergovernmental coordinating functions for the 'international financial architecture'. Yet, international cooperation among financial institutions (e.g., in the Bank for International Settlements composed of the sixty most important central banks of the world, and the OECD composed of thirty-four developed countries) and incorporation of the financial standards recommended by the numerous financial standard-setting bodies into national 'hard law' remain deficient. However, as the G-20 members hold a majority in the IMF and other financial organisations and have requested the financial standard-setting bodies to engage in public consultations, the restricted membership of most international financial institutions may not prevent effective legal coordination, implementation inside the most important jurisdictions, and sanctions against non-cooperative jurisdictions, so as to ensure that 'all systematically important financial intermediaries, markets and products irrespective of type must be subject to appropriate regulation and supervision in all jurisdictions'.[24]

[24] G-20 London Summit, Leaders' Statement of 2 April 2009, Section 15.

Comparative analysis of the existing international 'legal and institutional pluralism' suggests that citizen-driven, rights-based legal regimes (like the ECHR, EU and EEA law, investment and commercial law and arbitration) have protected transnational public goods for the benefit of citizens more comprehensively and effectively than state-centred agreements without equivalent accountability mechanisms and judicial remedies against violations of *erga omnes* obligations (such as human rights and fundamental freedoms of EU and EEA law).[25] The common evolutionary patterns of many environmental agreements – e.g., their initial design as framework conventions without enforcement powers, whose rules were progressively supplemented by additional Protocols with more precise regulations – illustrates how international institutions can promote learning processes and incentives for progressive rule-clarification in cooperation with non-governmental interest groups. Economic public goods theory offers few criteria for determining when global public goods should be regulated issue-by-issue (e.g., pursuant to the economic theory of separation of policy instruments underlying the separate UN Specialized Agencies) or by means of package deals facilitating compromises over the distribution of costs and benefits (as in the 1994 WTO Agreement and the 2013 Draft Trade Facilitation Agreement). Paradoxically, the evolution from the comparatively weak GATT 1947 – in spite of its lack of legal ratification, inadequate institutions and 'grandfather clauses' exempting inconsistent national legislation – into the worldwide WTO legal and compulsory dispute settlement system was more successful than the evolution of the Bretton Woods Agreements that had been duly ratified by national parliaments. Yet, the ever increasing number of trade agreements concluded outside the WTO, the failure to conclude the Doha Round negotiations, and other 'governance gaps' confirm the 'legitimacy deficits' and 'constitutional limits' of intergovernmental power politics as a legitimate tool for protecting global public goods. Waiting for global consensus (e.g., among 159 WTO members) has proven to be an unreasonable negotiation strategy, just as the 'single undertaking' method and consensus-based amendment procedures of WTO law risk being impractical 'implementation strategies'.

[25] *Cf.*, Joerges and Petersmann *Constitutionalism, Multilevel Trade Governance and International Economic Law*, Chapters II and VIIII.

F. Conclusion: cosmopolitan constitutionalism requires 'struggles for rights'

Multilevel governance is a normative necessity for the collective supply of most international public goods. The inadequate regulation of international financial markets confirms that collective supply of most international 'aggregate public goods' – like the international monetary system aimed at protecting monetary stability, liberal trade and international freedom of payments – requires going beyond 'realist', 'liberal', 'functional' and 'public choice' strategies by 'embedding' multilevel governance into 'multilevel constitutionalism' protecting rights of citizens, general consumer welfare and transnational rule of law 'bottom up' and justifying international public goods regimes in terms of human rights and domestic constitutional law.[26] Transnational rule of law is essential for the democratic legitimacy, effectiveness and overall coherence of interdependent 'aggregate public goods'. The judicial challenges by EU citizens of euro-governance (e.g., in national constitutional courts), like the political challenges by British citizens of their EU membership, promote 'deliberative democracy', 'public reason' and justice in the sense of requiring multilevel governance institutions to publicly justify their governance measures *vis-à-vis* citizens in more persuasive ways.

The evolution of the EMU – such as the increasing reliance on independent central banks, judicial remedies, multilevel constitutional restraints of abuses of national fiscal, financial and economic regulatory powers through multilevel regulation of eurozone governance – illustrates that most international public goods regimes remain 'incomplete agreements'. For instance, as the Lisbon Treaty included no adequate rules for dealing with 'systemic private and public debt crises' caused by persistent violations of the agreed fiscal, debt and economic convergence disciplines of the Lisbon Treaty, EU member states had to adopt *ad hoc* crisis measures in terms of bailout agreements, financial stability mechanisms, stronger multilevel governance disciplines and new EU banking

[26] Such 'bottom up multilevel constitutionalism' justifying international guarantees of freedoms, non-discrimination and rule of law in terms of corresponding domestic constitutional guarantees and emphasising the 'functional unity' ('constitutional functions') of multilevel protection of constitutional principles and rules has already been advocated in: E. U. Petersmann, *Constitutional Functions and Constitutional Problems of International Economic Law* (Fribourg University Press, 1991).

union rules. The multilevel governance failures of the eurozone confirm the 'constitutional insight' that – in order to be effective – 'constitutional principles' (like rule of law and the bailout prohibitions of the Lisbon Treaty) must be implemented through legislative, administrative and judicial governance inside domestic legal systems (e.g., in over-indebted 'peripheral countries' like Cyprus, Greece, Portugal and Spain) in order to restrain private and public abuses of power and protect international public goods. Without the support of citizens based on more convincing 'democratic justification' and multilevel regulation of the distributional conflicts underlying the euro crisis (e.g., who pays for the private and public debt and structural adjustment problems of over-indebted eurozone countries?), the monetary union and common financial market risk disintegration (e.g., due to non-membership of ten EU countries in the eurozone in 2012). As cosmopolitan rights entail responsibilities not only of governments but also of citizens, the proposed EU banking rules on imposing losses on bank shareholders and certain categories of bondholders and savers in case of bankruptcies are justifiable.

Unlike the 'hegemonic' US postwar leadership for adopting the Bretton Woods Agreements, the UN Charter, GATT 1947 and the UDHR, negotiating multilevel public goods regimes in the twenty-first century must go beyond multilateral 'institution building' focusing on the interests of hegemonic countries. As citizens and governments tend to accept international 'duties of justice' only reciprocally,[27] leadership by democratic 'civilian powers' must be based on bilateral, regional, plurilateral and worldwide initiatives for multilevel 'cosmopolitan constitutionalism' protecting human, democratic and cosmopolitan rights of citizens and legal, democratic and judicial accountability of multilevel governance. Section E of this chapter proposed eight 'building blocks' for 'constructivist public goods strategies' limiting the abuses of the prevailing, power-oriented 'Westphalian conceptions' of 'international law among sovereign states' and justifying multilevel governance and transnational rule of law in terms of 'common constitutional principles' that are already part of UN law. Promoting multilevel enforcement of HRL and IEL based on 'access to justice' and judicial remedies not only of governments, but also of citizens requires stronger empowerment of citizens through cosmopolitan rights to hold governments accountable for their failure to fulfil their

[27] *Cf.*, J. Rawls, *A Theory of Justice* (Cambridge, MA: Harvard University Press, 1971), p. 336.

'duties to protect' agreed 'common concerns'. Just as the EU's policy of extending the EU common market law to more than twenty new EU member states and additional associated states (like the European Economic Area (EEA) states and Switzerland) offers one of the most successful examples for progressively extending and improving public goods regimes, reforming UN and WTO institutions through bilateral, regional and plurilateral agreements and multilevel 'constitutional strategies' is likely to be more successful than waiting for global consensus on UN and WTO reforms. Complementing national constitutions protecting national public goods by cosmopolitan constitutionalism protecting transnational 'aggregate public goods' will require citizens to 'struggle for their rights' and to assume more democratic responsibility for protecting the transnational rule of law for the benefit of citizens. Without legal incentives for stronger 'participatory' and 'deliberative democracy' helping citizens to understand, monitor, criticise or support the complexity of multilevel governance, the prevailing 'Westphalian paradigm' of government executives and interest groups dominating international governance risks undermining democracy also at the national level. As emphasised in the conclusions adopted by about 300 members of parliaments from around the world at the end of their Parliamentary Conference on WTO at the WTO headquarters on 15–16 November 2012, the transparency and democratic legitimacy of multilevel governance institutions like the WTO can be enhanced by closer cooperation with national parliaments responsible for domestic implementation and democratic control of international rules aimed at promoting national economic welfare and transnational rule of law for the benefit of citizens.[28] Ultimately, however, individual citizens have to decide – e.g., in financial markets, democratic elections and through 'deliberative' and 'participatory democracy' – on the optimal level of democratic protection of public goods (such as monetary stability and regulation of financial markets). Cosmopolitan constitutionalism suggests that it is no coincidence that democracies with strong constitutional rights and accountability mechanisms tend to have the strongest national currencies. In view of the 'rational

[28] The parliamentary Outcome Document adopted by consensus on 16 November 2012 is published on the WTO website. On seven different ways of promoting domestic legitimacy of governments by multilevel governance institutions see: A. Follesdal, Epilogue: 'Towards More Legitimate Multilevel Regulation', in A. Follesdal, R. A. Wessel and J. Wouters (eds.), *Multilevel Regulation and the EU. The Interplay between Global, European and National Normative Processes* (Leiden: Nijhoff, 2008), pp. 377–98, 384.

ignorance' of most citizens *vis-à-vis* the complexity and abuses of multilevel governance, open markets, competition among currencies and citizens' struggles for cosmopolitan rights and transnational rule of law may also be the most reasonable safeguards against private and public abuses of 'rule by law'.

18

Transparency and monetary affairs

CHRISTINE KAUFMANN AND ROLF H. WEBER

A. Introduction

Transparency has for decades been a hotly debated topic in financial markets. In the aftermath of the financial crisis the transparency debate became a priority for politicians and regulators around the world. A hundred years ago, Supreme Court Justice Louis Brandeis expressed his concern about the lack of transparency in financial markets, mainly in view of the necessity to protect investors better: 'Publicity is justly commended as a remedy for social and industrial diseases. Sunlight is said to be the best of disinfectants; electric light the most efficient policeman'.[1]

According to the Oxford English Dictionary, transparency means 'easily seen through, recognized, understood, or detected; manifest, evident, obvious, clear'.[2] Transparency in government is to be realised by dissemination of information, both as a human right (in the form of freedom of information) and by making information public through institutional channels.[3] From an economic perspective, the availability of adequate information is a prerequisite for efficient free markets.[4] Therefore, the transparency principle encompasses the element of visibility and clarity on the one hand and the element of empowerment and capability on the other, entailing the process of 'seeing through' as well as the 'object' that is being looked at.[5]

[1] L. D. Brandeis, 'What Publicity Can Do' in L. D. Brandeis (ed.), *Other People's Money: And How the Bankers Use It* (Mansfield Centre, CT: Martino Publishing, 2009, first published 1914 by McClure Publications), p. 92.

[2] Oxford English Dictionary, online edition, 2012, www.oed.com/view/Entry/204968?redirectedFrom=transparency#eid.

[3] R. H. Weber, *Datenschutz v. Öffentlichkeitsprinzip*, (Zurich: Schulthess, 2010), paras. 18 and 24.

[4] G. A. Akerlof, 'The Market for Lemons: Quality Uncertainty and the Market Mechanism', *Quarterly Journal of Economics* 84 (1970), 488.

[5] See C. Kaufmann and R. H. Weber, 'The Role of Transparency in Financial Regulation', *Journal of International Economic Law* 13:3 (2010), 779–97, 779–80 with further references.

We developed a comprehensive, rule-based rather than purely process-oriented approach by suggesting a three-dimensional concept of transparency in financial markets.[6] This three-dimensional concept, upon which we can build, is summarised as follows:

- The first pillar is designed by institutional aspects, i.e., procedures and decision-making; by providing legal certainty, transparency can serve as an anchor for financial regulation.
- The second pillar encompasses the substantive backbone of financial regulation addressing the values and goals of financial market policies.
- The third pillar looks at the accountability of actors as an essential element for rebuilding confidence in the financial market system.

Transparency takes different shapes for different actors and different segments in financial markets. While transparency for commercial transactions and private actors has received substantial attention in legal discussions, legal research on the role of transparency in monetary affairs is still in its infancy. For a long time, central banks, as the key actors in monetary affairs, worked secretly, and 'a change in bank rate was no more regarded as the business of the Treasury than the color which the Bank [of England] painted its front door'.[7] Even in 1989, a book on the Federal Reserve with the catchy title *Secrets of the Temple* seemed to realistically reflect central banks' policies.[8] Clearly, these days are over. Central banks are now supposed to be open about their objectives, outlooks, policy strategies and even their mistakes.[9] This is particularly relevant for transactions that require confidentiality in order to be effective, such as market interventions with a view to influencing exchange rates. However, such transactions are not completely exempt from transparency requirements, yet they need to be communicated *ex post* rather than in advance. Recent central bank regulations take these considerations into account by, e.g., publishing the minutes of monetary

[6] *Ibid.*, 783 ff.

[7] Otto Niemeyer, director of financial inquiries at HM Treasury commenting on British monetary policy in 1929, quoted in: D. E. Moggridge, *British Monetary Policy, 1924–1931* (Cambridge University Press, 1972), p. 160.

[8] W. Greider, *Secrets of the Temple: How the Federal Reserve Runs the Country* (New York: Touchstone, 1989).

[9] N. Dincer and B. Eichengreen, 'Central Bank Transparency: Causes, Consequences and Updates', *Theoretical Inquiries in Law* 11 (2010), 75–123, 76.

authorities' meetings with a certain time delay[10] or requiring a central bank's governors to explain their past monetary policy decisions before parliamentary commissions.[11] *Ex post* transparency may therefore partially compensate for the lack of government or parliament involvement when urgent market interventions require confidentiality.

This chapter applies the above mentioned three-dimensional concept of transparency to monetary affairs as a key segment of financial markets.

B. Monetary affairs: mapping existing actors and their activities

Transparency in general has been a priority on the agenda of governments for a long time. When President Obama announced his initiative for open government in 2009,[12] he was able to build on a commonly accepted but not very specific principle of a democratic government required to be transparent while leaving room for the protection of essential state and security interests. This kind of balance, so far, has not been applied to monetary affairs. In fact the question is twofold: to what extent is transparency functionally possible and when does its operation depend upon confidentiality *vis-à-vis* governments and financial markets?

Since monetary affairs are neither a homogeneous field nor are they conducted by a single actor, a brief mapping of existing actors and their activities in this area is necessary. Apart from governments, monetary authorities, i.e., central banks and currency boards, are the key actors.[13]

[10] E.g. for the US Federal Reserve, see Sec. 10.10 of the Federal Reserve Act (12 USC 226) and the Government in the Sunshine Act (5 USC section 552b) and the Federal Reserve Board's Rules Regarding Public Observation of Meetings (12 CFR part 261b). The Governing Board of the ECB is currently (2013) considering to publish the minutes of its meeting: joint interview with Benoît Cœuré and Jörg Asmussen, Members of the Executive Board of the ECB, conducted by Andrea Rexer and Jean-Pierre Robin on 23 July 2013 and published on 29 July 2013 in *Süddeutsche Zeitung* and *Le Figaro* (www.ecb.europa.eu/press/key/date/2013/html/sp130729.en.html).

[11] Article 7 para. 2 Federal Act of the Swiss National Bank (SR 951.11).

[12] *Transparency and Open Government*, Presidential Memorandum for the Heads of Executive Departments and Agencies, 74 FR 4685, 21 January 2009.

[13] C. E. Walsh, *Monetary Theory and Policy*, 3rd edn (Cambridge, MA: Massachusetts Institute of Technology Press, 2010), pp. 135–43.

I. *Governments*

Many governments issued 'sunshine laws'[14] with Sweden taking the lead as early as 1766,[15] followed, *inter alia*, by the US with the Freedom of Information Act of 1966.[16] The starting point for government transparency is the normative concept of a right to know as a key prerequisite for democracy and participation. This general concept has only recently been further refined to support specific public policies such as the protection of the environment,[17] or fiscal and budget policy.[18] Thus, the normative concept is increasingly being complemented by *substantive criteria* on how specific policy goals can be enhanced by transparency.[19] The way in which transparency mechanisms are structured shapes their impact on public policy – on effectiveness on equity and on democratic accountability.[20]

Clearly, governmental activities have an impact on monetary affairs. Of particular relevance are fiscal and monetary policy measures. Often, the administration will take the lead in fiscal policy with a monetary authority – a central bank or a currency board[21] – being the main responsible institution for the monetary policy. Ideally, fiscal policy and monetary policy are complementary. However, a fiscal policy which does not factor in existing budget constraints may destabilise long-term inflation expectations and thus lead to increased macroeconomic instability.[22] Transparency can play an important role in

[14] Thus taking up Justice Brandeis' metaphor, Brandeis, 'What Publicity Can Do'. See for example the Swiss Freedom of Information Act of 2004 (SR 152.3).

[15] His Majesty's Gracious Ordinance Relating to Freedom of Writing and of the Press, 2 December 1766, English version in: J. Mustonen (ed.), *The World's First Freedom of Information Act – Anders Chydenius' Legacy Today* (Kokkola: Anders Chydenius Foundation 2006), pp. 8–17. The current version is the Public Access to Information of 2009, as amended in 2013 (Offentlighets- och sekretessförordning, 2009:641).

[16] The Freedom of Information Act, 5 USC § 552, as amended by Public Law No. 104–231, 110 Stat. 3048.

[17] The most prominent example is the Aarhus Convention on Access to Information, Public participation in Decision-Making and Access to Justice in Environmental Matters of 25 June 1998 (UN Treaty Series vol. 2161, 447); A. P. J. Mol, 'The Future of Transparency: Power, Pitfalls and Promises', *Global Environmental Politics* 10:3 (2010), 132–43.

[18] D. Heald, 'Why is Transparency about Public Expenditure so Elusive?', *International Review of Administrative Sciences* 78:1 (2012), 30–49.

[19] Mol, 'The Future of Transparency', 132.

[20] Heald, 'Why is Transparency about Public Expenditure so Elusive?', 32.

[21] Discussed in Section B.II.2.

[22] S. Kirchner, 'Reforming Fiscal Responsibility Legislation', *Economic Papers* 30:1 (2011), 29–32, 29; P. de Renzo and H. Masud, 'Measuring and Promoting Budget Transparency:

reconciling different policies and fostering predictability and legal certainty. In addition, in the light of increasing international connectedness, transparency is seen as a prerequisite for a modern concept of fiscal sovereignty in a globalised environment.[23]

These normative elements are fairly straightforward. What needs to be further developed in a monetary context, however, are *specific* transparency mechanisms to foster policy coherence as well as fiscal sovereignty. In order to partially fill this gap, the International Monetary Fund (IMF) developed specific standards for fiscal transparency, as discussed in Section C.

II. Monetary institutions

One of the major challenges in designing monetary institutions is the uncertainty about future social decisions. This uncertainty is due to both the impossibility and the undesirability of committing future monetary policy-makers to a previously defined strategy. An ideal framework would implement what is currently believed to be the optimal strategy and only deviate from it if there is a collective change of view on this strategy.[24] As Mervyn King put it so aptly, 'our ignorance is too pervasive to allow the adoption of a rule of how learning should occur.'[25]

1. Central banks

From an institutional perspective, with a few exceptions, central banks are rather 'youthful'.[26] It is therefore not surprising that the debate on central bank governance, including transparency, is relatively recent. Accordingly, new studies show a clear trend towards greater central bank transparency.[27] Yet, a caveat applies: most of these studies are based on a selective set of indicators for transparency, such as the publication of inflation targets.[28] Apart from this lack of conceptual rigour, the economic context in which a central bank operates, whether it is situated in an emerging or a developed country, is not always taken

The Open Budget Index as a Research and Advocacy Tool', *Governance: An International Journal of Policy, Administration, and Institutions* 24:3 (2011), 607–16, 608.

[23] P. Dietsch, 'Rethinking Sovereignty in International Fiscal Policy', *Review of International Studies* 37 (2011), 2107–20, 2117–18.

[24] M. King, 'The Institutions of Monetary Policy', Richard T. Ely Lecture, *American Economic Association Proceedings* 94:2 (2004), 1–13, 1 and 5.

[25] *Ibid.*, 5. [26] *Ibid.*, 2.

[27] Dincer and Eichengreen, 'Central Bank Transparency', 91.

[28] For a critical and more comprehensive approach, *ibid.*, 88–9.

into account. This empirical finding has been interpreted in various ways. One view is that transparency enhances the *effectiveness of monetary policy* because it allows for better communication and clearer expectations among market participants. Central bank transparency thus relates to three aspects: its price stability commitment, policy intentions and effective communication of its economic assessment.[29] Managing expectations, especially concerning inflation, is an essential element in order for monetary policy to affect outcomes.[30] Based on this rationale, the Governing Council of the European Central Bank announced its committment to give forward guidance to market participants by communicating its specific expectations on market developments.[31]

Another view relates central bank transparency to *democratic accountability*. Transparency is therefore seen as a mechanism to balance central bank independence.[32] From an economic perspective, transparency ensures accountability of policy-makers in an environment where the traditional instruments of fixed or pegged exchange rates and close central bank supervision by the government are replaced by flexible exchange rates and independence of central banks.[33]

The democratic rationale for implementing transparency and accountability measures played a major role when European central banks became independent in the context of the Treaty of Maastricht in 1992, and the establishment of the European Monetary Union. While the design of the new European Central Bank, to a large extent, followed the model of the independent German Bundesbank, other central banks such as the Bank de France were still under close supervision of the government at the time. Studies on data from the 1980s suggested that independence of the central bank was one of the key elements for success in maintaining price stability.[34] Prime examples at the time were the

[29] M. K. Tang and X. Yu, 'Communication of Central Bank Thinking and Inflation Dynamics', *IMF Working Paper* WP/11/209 (2011), pp. 6–7.

[30] M. Ehrmann, S. Eijffinger and M. Fratzscher, 'The Role of Central Bank Transparency for Guiding Private Sector Forecasts', *European Central Bank, Working Paper Series* No. 1146 (January 2010).

[31] Press conference of the European Central Bank, Introductory statement by Mario Draghi, President of the ECB, Frankfurt am Main, 4 July 2013.

[32] Dincer and Eichengreen, 'Central Bank Transparency', 77.

[33] S. C. W. Eijffinger and P. M. Geraats, 'How Transparent are Central Banks?', *European Journal of Political Economy* 22 (2006), 1–21.

[34] A. Cukierman, S. Webb and B. Neyapti, 'Measuring the Independence of Central Banks and its Effect on Policy Outcomes', *The World Bank Economic Review* 6 (1992), 353–98;

German Bundesbank and the Federal Reserve. More recent studies confirmed that greater central bank independence is associated with lower inflation.[35] In addition, there is evidence that greater transparency is associated with more use of public information and, in particular, central banks' forecasts. In such a context, the private sector will make greater use of information provided by the central bank.[36] If the public is better informed about monetary policy, it can react more quickly to policy decisions and thereby prevent public authorities from manipulating inflation in pursuit of other interests.[37]

2. Currency boards

Unlike central banks, currency boards are bound by rules that generally do not allow for discretionary monetary policy decisions. Typically, they will apply a fixed exchange rate with a reserve currency. As a result, conflicts between exchange rate policies and monetary policies are unlikely. Since currency boards are increasingly seen as an instrument for overcoming central banks' inherent lack of transparency, a brief critical review seems appropriate.

Although currency boards performed well until the 1930s, they were to a large extent replaced by central banks after World War II. In the 1990s, currency boards became relevant again. The reason for this unexpected revival was the desire to install a monetary regime to which the fiscal regime would be subordinate. In other words, currency boards were seen as means to impose fiscal discipline.[38]

The most prominent current example of a currency board is the Hong Kong Monetary Authority (HKMA). Hong Kong applies a linked exchange rate, with the Hong Kong dollar being linked to the US dollar at an exchange rate of 7.8 Hong Kong dollars to one US dollar. Typically, for a currency board system, the monetary base is fully backed by foreign currency reserves at this fixed exchange rate. The Basic Law for Hong Kong explicitly requires that the issue of Hong Kong dollars is backed by

A. Cukierman, *Central Bank Strategy, Credibility and Independence – Theory and Evidence* (Cambridge, MA: The MIT Press, 1992); for an update A. Cukierman, 'Central Bank Independence and Monetary Policymaking Institutions – Past, Present and Future', *European Journal of Political Economy* 24 (2008), 722–36.

35 C. Crowe and E. E. Meade, 'Central Bank Independence and Transparency: Evolution and Effectiveness', *European Journal of Political Economy* 24 (2008), 763–77, 769–70.

36 *Ibid.*, 771–2. 37 Dincer and Eichengreen, 'Central Bank Transparency', 88.

38 S. H. Hanke, 'Currency Boards', *Annals, American Academy of Political and Social Science* 579 (2002), 87–105, 99.

a 100 per cent reserve fund.[39] However, the fact that the mandate of a currency board and the objectives of monetary policy are built on legally binding rules does not automatically provide transparency, as the development of the Hong Kong Exchange Fund illustrates: established by ordinance in 1935, the accounts of the Exchange Fund were kept confidential until 1992. Since then, transparency has been steadily increased; since 1999 the Special Data Dissemination Standard (SDDS) of the International Monetary Fund[40] has been applied. In 2000 a new template for international and foreign currency liquidity was implemented:

> The public disclosure of such information on a timely and accurate basis promotes informed decision making in the public and private sectors, thereby helping to improve the functioning of global financial markets.[41]

Currently, the templates are published monthly. In addition, the record of discussion of the Exchange Fund Advisory Committee (EFAC) Sub-Committee on Currency Board Operations is disclosed to the public.

On its website, the HKMA identifies five characteristics of a properly run currency board: transparency, simplicity, reliability, predictability and credibility.[42] These characteristics are however not currency-board specific but rather seem to reflect what is currently understood as effective public policy-making. Similarly, HKMA's published statement on transparency remains rather general:

> The HKMA seeks to follow international best practices in its transparency arrangements. The HKMA places great emphasis on promoting a wide understanding of its policies and work. This is done through extensive contacts with the media, a range of regular publications, a comprehensive website, a public enquiries service and an educational programme.[43]

[39] Article 111 of the Basic Law for the Hong Kong Special Administrative Region: 'The Hong Kong dollar, as the legal tender in the Hong Kong Special Administrative Region, shall continue to circulate. The authority to issue Hong Kong currency shall be vested in the Government of the Hong Kong Special Administrative Region. The issue of Hong Kong currency must be backed by a 100 per cent reserve fund. The system regarding the issue of Hong Kong currency and the reserve fund system shall be prescribed by law.'

[40] Discussed in Section C.II.2.

[41] www.hkma.gov.hk/eng/key-functions/exchange-fund/transparency.shtml.

[42] www.hkma.gov.hk/eng/classroom/page/work/work_02_01.htm.

[43] www.hkma.gov.hk/eng/classroom/page/work/work_06_01.htm.

In sum, the classic blueprint of a currency board[44] which would emphasise its transparency in contrast to traditional central banks' secrecy cannot be applied to the new generation of currency boards which was introduced in the 1990s. These days, currency boards are still based on the rather mechanical principle of conversion and issuing fully backed base money. Yet, guaranteeing convertibility throughout a highly complex international financial system has become challenging. Due to the backing requirement, a currency board has limited possibilities for providing additional liquidity in times of systemic constraints.[45] As a result, stable monetary policy may come at the price of increased systemic risks. For this reason, most modern currency boards have applied specific policies in this regard and for example also serve as lender of last resort.[46] Not surprisingly, these policies require a clear division of tasks between the different actors and therefore call for transparency.

C. Transparency and the financial crisis

I. Lack of transparency as an underlying reason for the financial crisis

1. Financial markets

While the reasons for the recent financial crisis are manifold, a lack of transparency played a major role in undermining predictability of and trust in the financial markets and in the resulting volatility and instability. Intransparency may occur in three dimensions: *product*, *governance* and *organisation* related.

Newly developed structured financial *products* such as collateralised debt obligations (CDOS) were highly complex by nature and inherently intransparent.[47] Tools and instruments designed to hedge risks were sometimes (mis)used for increased leverage and, in the words of

[44] C. Ho, 'A Survey of the Institutional and Operational Aspects of Modern-day Currency Boards', *Bank for International Settlements (BIS) Working Papers* No 110 (March 2002), pp. 3–5.

[45] *Ibid.*, p. 13.

[46] *Ibid.*, p. 15. Hanke, 'Currency Boards', seems to have overlooked this development, at 100.

[47] J. Crotty, 'Structural Causes of the Global Financial Crisis: A Critical Assessment of the 'New Financial Architecture'', *Cambridge Journal of Economics* 33 (2009) 563–80, at 566.

Warren Buffet, became 'a weapon of financial mass destruction'.[48] Moreover, many financial innovations created links between formerly unconnected players as illustrated, for instance, by the US subprime crisis.[49]

New synthetic products and the related increase in interconnectivity among financial markets call for a *governance* reaction in the form of effective risk management systems both within institutions and at the government level. Hence, in many financial institutions the real financial exposure was not detected due to the lack of an effective risk management system. The abuse of economic models to build up derivative positions in order to profit from high returns, as long as the correlating risks did not materialise, had not been anticipated and accordingly was not reflected in the risk management systems available. A similar phenomenon could be observed at the *state* level: supervisory authorities and regulators failed to react and instead continued to rely on mathematical rigour and numerical precision in risk management and asset pricing tools. In particular, the Basel II Framework with its highly sophisticated risk assessment model[50] contributed to a certain information overload, which instead of promoting transparency led to opacity,[51] and eventually a control illusion.[52]

The financial crisis showed that financial groups and financial *conglomerates* can threaten the stability of the financial system. One of the reasons why these risks had not been detected earlier was the mix of regulated and unregulated entities (such as special purpose entities and unregulated holding companies) across sectorial boundaries and the related challenges for sector-specific supervisory oversight. A prime example in this respect was American International Group Ltd (AIG), the world's largest insurance company. AIG's problems stemmed from two main sources: its securities lending programme and its investment in

48 Cited in D. Colander, M. Goldberg, A. Haas, K. Juselius, A. Kirman, T. Lux and B. Sloth, 'The Financial Crisis and the Systemic Failure of the Economics Profession', *Critical Review* 21:2–3 (2009), 249–67, 254.

49 *Ibid.*, 263.

50 Bank of International Settlements, *Basel II: International Convergence of Capital Measurement and Capital Standards: A Revised Framework – Comprehensive Version*, June 2006: www.bis.org/publ/bcbs128.htm.

51 C. M. Bradley, 'Transparency is the New Opacity: Constructing Financial Regulation after the Crisis', *American University Business Law Review* 1 (2011) 7–34, 32.

52 Colander *et al.*, 'The Financial Crisis', 254.

credit default swaps (CDSs).[53] Despite its systemic relevance, AIG was, at the time, under the supervision not of the Federal Reserve Bank but of the Office of Thrift Supervision (OTS). OTS was the consolidated supervisor of AIG because it was considered a thrift holding company by virtue of its ownership of the AIG Federal Savings Bank. Given AIG's involvement in both financial and non-financial entities, consolidated supervision was not possible and systemic risks remained unidentified until autumn 2008 when AIG was on the verge of collapsing and was eventually bailed out by the Federal Reserve. One of the key lessons learnt from the financial crisis was therefore that it was necessary to strengthen *consolidated supervision* particularly for systemically relevant institutions with cross-sectorial activities.[54]

Finally, another phenomenon which has so far not attracted much attention is closely linked to the above-mentioned organisational and governance-related risks. As just noted in the context of the AIG, actors in financial markets which are not licensed as banks or securities dealers have become increasingly important. Such 'shadow-banking'[55] activities may create opportunities but at the same time become a source of risks. Since they are not covered by the traditional financial governance mechanisms and may therefore lack adequate regulatory frameworks and monitoring, problems may amount to systemic risks, especially when such institutions are performing bank-like functions such as leverage and when they are strongly connected with the banking system. It is therefore necessary for monetary and supervisory authorities to first map existing actors and then to identify and assess potential risks.[56]

2. Intransparent financial markets and monetary affairs

With risks in financial markets accumulating into systemic risks, monetary authorities and political bodies became involved in crisis management. In addition to insufficient information about the risk exposure of individual financial institutions, uncertainty about how monetary

[53] United States Government Accountability Office (GAO), Report to Congressional Requesters: Review of Federal Reserve System Financial Assistance to American International Group, Inc, GAO-11-616, (September 2011), p. 5.

[54] Basel Committee on Banking Supervision, Joint Forum, *Principles for the Supervision of Financial Conglomerates* (Basel: Bank for International Settlements, September 2012).

[55] Defined by the Financial Stability Board as 'credit intermediation involving entities and activities outside the regular banking system', *Global Shadow Banking Monitoring Report 2012*, 18 November 2012, p. 3.

[56] *Ibid.*, p. 6.

authorities and political institutions intended to react exacerbated the crisis. Clearly, poorly understood and unknown risks can barely be addressed in monetary policy. Not surprisingly, transparency has become a regularly debated topic during the last four years. The following section outlines some of the relevant policy discussions.

II. Reactions in policy making

The most noteworthy efforts to improve transparency are mirrored in the G-20 declarations and statements, but other organisations have also addressed transparency issues.

1. G-20

While decision-making in the G-20 itself cannot be defined as transparent and the group is not inclusive with regard to its stakeholders,[57] the 'transparency discourse' has appeared at different levels of intensity at several of the seven G-20 summits held so far:

(i) Transparency was most prominently mentioned at the G-20 Summit in Washington (November 2008).[58] The first of the five common principles for reform of financial markets addressed the strengthening of transparency and accountability. Transparency is also mentioned in the third common principle on the promotion of integrity in financial markets as well as in the list of the tasks of ministers and experts, requesting them to make efforts to strengthen the resilience and transparency of credit derivatives markets.

In the Action Plan for the implementation of the principles for reform, the word 'transparency' is again mentioned three times, among others in the section on prudential oversight.

[57] R. H. Weber, 'The Legitimacy of the G20 as a Global Financial Regulator', *Banking & Finance Law Review* 28 (2013) 389–407. C. Kaufmann, 'International Law in Recession? The Role of International Law when Crisis Hits: Food, Finance, and Climate Change', in U. Fastenrath, R. Geiger, D.-E. Khan, A. Paulus, S. von Schorlemer and C. Vedder (eds.), *From Bilateralism to Community Interest, Essays in Honour of Bruno Simma* (Oxford University Press, 2011), pp. 1189–206, 1202–3. M. Giovanoli, 'The International Monetary and Financial Architecture: Some Institutional Aspects', Chapter 3, this volume.

[58] See Declaration G-20 Leaders Summit, Washington 2008: www.g20.utoronto.ca/2008/2008declaration 1115.html.

(ii) The G-20 Summit in London (April 2009)[59] addressed transparency in the context of the strengthening of financial supervision and regulation, since transparency contributes to the restoration of confidence and the rebuilding of trust in the financial system.

(iii) The Declaration of the G-20 of the Pittsburgh Summit (September 2009)[60] mentions the word 'transparency' thirteen times in manifold contexts. Without going into the details of the various regulatory topics, two aspects are noteworthy:
- The G-20 welcomes the expansion of the Global Forum on Transparency and Exchange Information, including the participation of developing countries, as well as the agreement to deliver an effective programme of peer review.[61]
- The G-20 supports the voluntary participation in the Extractive Industries Transparency Initiative, which calls for regular public disclosure of certain payments.[62]

(iv) In the Declaration of the Toronto Summit (June 2010),[63] the G-20 particularly addressed transparency in the context of financial sector reform including aspects of banks' balance sheets. Again the word 'transparency' is mentioned more than ten times. The following Seoul Summit of November 2010 did not specifically look into these issues.

(v) The Cannes Summit of the G-20 (November 2011)[64] partly changed the perspective of the political agenda; transparency in this declaration is related to agricultural markets, energy markets and trade relations.

(vi) The Declaration of the G-20 leaders of the Los Cabos Summit (June 2012)[65] shows a two-sided picture: transparency was looked at from the angle of financial sector reform on the one hand and from the perspective of markets for agricultural products and energy, among others, on the other hand. Apart from general elements of

[59] See Declaration G-20 Leaders Summit, London 2009: www.g20.utoronto.ca/2009/2009communique0402.html.

[60] See Declaration G-20 Leaders Summit, Pittsburgh 2009: www.g20.utoronto.ca/2009/2009communique0925.html.

[61] *Ibid.*, No. 15. [62] *Ibid.*, No. 42.

[63] See Declaration G-20 Leaders Summit, Toronto 2010: www.g20.utoronto.ca/2010/to-communique.html.

[64] See Declaration G-20 Leaders Summit, Cannes 2011: www.g20.utoronto.ca/2011/2011-cannes-communique-111104-en.html.

[65] See Declaration G-20 Leaders Summit, Los Cabos (Mexico) 2010: www.g20.utoronto.ca/2012/2012–0619-loscabos.html.

transparency and accountability leading to greater credibility and confidence, as well as to improved surveillance (including the strengthening of competition among credit rating agencies), transparency of the exchange rate policy as a part of monetary law is explicitly mentioned (related to the renminbi exchange rate regime).

2. International Monetary Fund

In relation to its monetary stability objectives, the International Monetary Fund (IMF), together with the Bank for International Settlements (BIS), published a 'Code of Good Practices in Transparency in Monetary and Financial Policies (MFP Transparency Code). As a general rule, the MFP Transparency Code calls on the central bank of each country as the 'institution responsible for conducting monetary policy'.[66] The MFP Transparency Code addresses the clarity of roles, responsibilities and objectives (Part I), the open process for monetary policy decisions (Part II), the public availability of information on monetary policy (Part III), and the accountability and assurance of integrity by the Central Bank (Part IV).[67] Each section contains additional rules and guidelines.[68] Based on the MFP Transparency Code, the IMF encourages the authorities of member states to participate in a detailed assessment of transparency of monetary and financial policies, mainly in the context of their participation in the Financial Sector Assessment Program (FSAP); an FSAP evaluation entails detailed principle-by-principle assessments which are condensed in the Reports on the Observance of Standards and Codes (ROSC).[69]

In relation to fiscal matters, the IMF developed a 'Code of Good Practices on Fiscal Transparency',[70] a 'Manual on Fiscal Transparency', and a 'Guide on Resource Revenue Transparency'. The Code is based on four general pillars, namely clarity of roles and responsibilities (Part I), open budget processes (Part II), public availability of information (Part III), and assurances of integrity (Part IV). The implementation of

[66] IMF, *Code of Good Practices in Transparency in Monetary and Financial Policies* (July 1999), p. 18.

[67] See also R. H. Weber, 'Financial Stability – Structural Framework and Development Issues', *International and Comparative Corporate Law Journal* 6 (2008), 1–19, 1 and 7.

[68] For further details, see D. W. Arner, *Financial Stability, Economic Growth, and the Role of Law* (Cambridge University Press, 2007), p. 131.

[69] R. H. Weber and D. W. Arner, 'Toward a New Design for International Financial Regulation', *University of Pennsylvania Journal of International Law* 29 (2007), 391–453, 417 ff.

[70] IMF, *Code of Good Practices on Financial Transparency of 1998*, updated 2007.

the Code should follow the 'Manual' and the 'Guide'; the assessment of compliance with the Code can also be done in the context of the establishment of ROSC.

Another important aspect is the transparency of macroeconomic data since its public availability and comparability is important in combating financial crises.[71] As an instrument designed to provide guidance, the IMF has published standards in relation to data dissemination and compilation, such as the Special Data Dissemination Standard (SDDS)[72] and the General Data Dissemination System (GDDS).[73] These two standards encourage member states to substantially improve data quality, statistics and data disclosure.[74]

The problem with the transparency objective consists less in the availability of adequate transparency guidelines than in the willingness to publish the IMF's conclusive reports. In the past, the IMF often did not disclose its findings due to concerns that publishing the data could jeopardise the interests of the country concerned.[75] Over the last few years, however, the situation has improved: according to the IMF, as of September 2011, eighty-eight countries had completed an assessment of transparency in either monetary policies, financial policies, or both, in the context of an FSAP; furthermore, fifty-seven countries' ROSCs have been published on the IMF website.[76]

Other elements could impede transparency, namely the not always acknowledged functional, operational and economic independence of the central bank as well as the vague limitations of regulatory powers.[77]

3. World Bank Group

Starting in the 1990s, the World Bank sponsored the establishment of a worldwide database containing regulatory provisions and practices

[71] See Weber, 'Financial Stability', p. 8.

[72] IMF, *Special Data Dissemination Standard* (March 1996).

[73] IMF, *General Data Dissemination System* (December 1997).

[74] For more details, see Arner, *Financial Stability, Economic Growth, and the Role of Law*, pp. 132–3.

[75] Weber, 'Financial Stability', p. 7 and Arner, *Financial Stability, Economic Growth and the Rule of Law*, at p. 131.

[76] IMF, *Factsheet: Transparency in Monetary and Financial Policies*, www.imf.org/external/np/exr/facts/mtransp.htm. On this issue, see also N. Rendak, 'Monitoring and Surveillance of the International Monetary System – What Can Be Learnt from the Trade Field?', Chapter 9, this volume.

[77] R. M. Lastra, *Legal Foundations of International Monetary Stability* (Oxford University Press, 2006), pp. 44–6.

relevant to banking activities. The survey is very thorough and encompasses the banking regulations of more than 150 countries. Important aspects are the accounting practice, the external auditing and the financial statement transparency as well as the external ratings and the creditors' monitoring. The details are expressed in the form of variables that measure the extent of effectiveness or strength of a given entity in the different practices and enable comparisons across the countries.[78]

The World Bank Group has also emphasised its concerns about transparency by publishing a set of decisions issued by the World Bank Group's Sanctions Board. The disclosed cases concern alleged fraud and corruption and mark a step towards more openness and accountability in the field of anti-corruption.[79]

Furthermore, the World Bank Group, in collaboration with the International Finance Cooperation (IFC), published a guide called 'Doing Business 2012: Doing Business in a More Transparent World'.[80] The Report benchmarks the regulations that enhance business activities and those that constrain them, providing quantitative indicators on business regulations; the general comments are illustrated with case studies.

4. European Central Bank

In the past, central banks were notorious for being inscrutable, as reflected in Alan Greenspan's famous quip that 'if you understood what I just said, you must not have heard me correctly'. More recently, the situation has changed and central banks are increasingly trying to improve clarity in explaining their objectives and decisions to the public.

The European Central Bank (ECB) periodically publishes its monetary policy strategy and communicates its regular assessment of economic developments in order to help the markets to understand the systematic response patterns of monetary policy; such transparency makes policy adjustments more predictable for the markets over the medium term.[81]

[78] R. H. Weber, *Shaping Internet Governance: Regulatory Challenges* (Zurich: Schulthess, 2009), p. 126.

[79] See World Bank Press Release No. 2012/481/EXT of 30 May 2012.

[80] See www.doingbusiness.org/reports/global-reports/doing-business-2012.

[81] European Central Bank, Eurosystem, www.ecb.int/ecb/orga/transparency/html/index.en.html.

The improvement of transparency of the ECB also is a political theme: the Directorate General for Internal Policies of the European Parliament, Section on Economic and Monetary Affairs, prepared a document entitled 'Improving ECB's Accountability and Transparency', requesting further-reaching transparency of the ECB in September 2009.[82] The objective of this initiative is to transform the present 'Monetary Dialogue' with the ECB President into a 'Monetary Hearing'. However, such an approach requires a careful assessment with a view to central bank independence. The debate has recently been taken up again by members of the ECB's Governing Council who are calling for the release of the Council's meeting records.[83]

5. Basel Committee on Banking Supervision and Financial Stability Board

The Basel Committee on Banking Supervision (BCBS) realised enhancements, including with regard to transparency issues, to the Basel II capital framework in the reform package Basel III which was formally accepted in September 2010.[84] The regulations and guidelines prepared by the BCBS, however, concern the financial markets in general, not monetary affairs in particular.

The Financial Stability Board (FSB) has put considerable emphasis on transparency objectives and has taken steps to encourage improved disclosures. In March 2011, the FSB presented a "Thematic Review on Risk Disclosure Practices' addressing general transparency standards and disclosure requirements under Basel III; the practices are analysed and initiatives that are needed to keep risk disclosures relevant and useful in the future are discussed in detail.[85] In March 2012, the FSB organised a Round Table on Risk Disclosure, which provided the possibility for a debate about the key themes of transparency; the respective disclosure requirements mainly concern financial regulation related to market participants and touch less upon monetary affairs.[86]

[82] See www.europarl.europa.eu/document/activities/cont/200909/20090923ATT61084/20090923ATT61084EN.pdf.

[83] See below note 124 and accompanying text.

[84] Bank for International Settlements, *Basel III: A Global Regulatory Framework for More Resilient Banks and Banking Systems*, revised version (June 2011).

[85] FSB, *Thematic Review on Risk Disclosure Practices, Peer Review Report* (18 March 2011) www.financialstabilityboard.org/publications/r_110318.pdf.

[86] FSB, Press Release, 20 March 2012, www.financialstabilityboard.org/press/pr_120320.pdf.

6. World Trade Organization

Transparency rules are well known in the World Trade Organization (WTO), notably in the General Agreement on Tariffs and Trade (GATT), the General Agreement on Trade in Services (GATS), which addresses financial services, the Agreement on Technical Barriers to Trade (TBT) and the Agreement on Trade-Related Aspects of Intellectual Property Rights (TRIPS Agreement).[87] Article X GATS, which is of specific relevance here, attempts to achieve two transparency objectives: on the one hand, transparency is seen as a tool to prevent unnecessary barriers to trade by letting market participants know in advance what requirements would apply in international services trade. In this respect, transparency contributes to a predictable trade environment. On the other hand, transparency contributes to clear decision-making processes and thereby to legitimacy in democratic societies.[88]

The purpose of the transparency provisions is to provide a greater degree of clarity, predictability and information about regulations; the transparency achieved should facilitate the entry of WTO members into the cross-border trade of goods and services based on predictable trade regulations.[89] Transparent regulation is a core requirement for attracting investment and promoting economic growth; the WTO experiences demonstrate that transparency helps to overcome uncertainties in business processes and to improve the general basis for cooperation.[90] While trade statistics published by the WTO contain important information for market and policy-makers, its regulatory focus is – in contrast to financial organisations – not on quantitative indicators, but on transparent procedures.

III. Preliminary assessment

The analysis of the transparency discussions in international fora during the last five years has shown that this issue has played a key role and that politicians, regulators and expert bodies, among others, were addressing

[87] T. Cottier and M. Oesch, *International Trade Regulation* (Berne: Cameron May/ Staempfli, 2005), pp. 542–51 discuss transparency in the WTO as an element of the rule of law.

[88] Kaufmann and Weber, 'The Role of Transparency in Financial Regulation', p. 795; M. Krajewski, 'Democratic Legitimacy and Constitutional Perspectives of WTO Law', *Journal of World Trade* 35 (2001), 167–86, 169–70.

[89] See Weber, *Shaping Internet Governance*, pp. 124–5.

[90] See *ibid.*, p. 125.

many facets of transparency. In particular, the G-20 assigned a high priority to looking at transparency from various angles.

However, apart from transparency regulations governing (private) banks and other financial institutions or intermediaries, the global community paid hardly any attention to transparency issues in the monetary framework. Under the auspices of the IMF and the World Bank Group, efforts have now been made to improve the level of transparency related to the monetary policies of the respective members, among others. Nevertheless, the main achievement consists in the collection of general data. However, as for the specific needs of transparency in monetary affairs, there are still substantial analytical gaps. The following section attempts to enrich the discussions in other areas for monetary affairs.

D. The three pillars of transparency in monetary affairs

I. *Overview: conceptual framework and indicators*

From a legal perspective, transparency can be analysed by applying a three-dimensional concept, as indicated above. The three pillars are (i) institutional procedures and decision-making, (ii) substantive foundation and (iii) accountability. Applying this concept to empirical studies requires a comprehensive set of indicators, which has been developed by Eijffinger and Geraats.[91] They advocate fifteen indicators for political, economic, procedural, policy and operational transparency: the focus of *political* transparency is on policy objectives; that of *economic* transparency is on economic information, such as data, models and forecasts, used for monetary policy; *procedural transparency* relates to the way decisions are taken; *policy transparency* means prompt disclosure of policy decisions, together with an explanation of the decision, and an explicit policy inclination or indication of likely future policy actions; *operational transparency* applies to the implementation of monetary policy. It requires a discussion of the factors, including disturbances, that affect the transmission of monetary policy.

In Table 18.1 we situate Eijffinger's and Geraats' economic indicators (1) to (15) in the legal framework by aligning each indicator with one of the three pillars. In fact, Eijffinger and Geraats define transparency of monetary policy as the extent to which central banks disclose information that is related to the policy-making process.[92] Consequently, most of

[91] Supra note 33. [92] Eijffinger and Geraats, 'How Transparent are Central Banks?', 3.

the indicators, namely (4)–(6) and (8)–(15), reflect the different stages of the decision-making process and only indicators (1)–(3) refer to the institutional environment. With this focus it is possible to apply quantitative indicators to measure some aspects of monetary transparency. Despite this limited focus, the most recent study by Dincer and Eichengreen shows a correlation between greater transparency of central bank operations with more stable political systems and a higher ranking with regard to the rule of law.[93] With these empirical findings in mind we will discuss the three-pillar framework in the context of monetary affairs.[94]

II. *The first pillar: institutional framework and decision-making*

1. Institutional framework

Legal certainty and predictability are essential for creating a stable environment and are thus a prerequisite for efficient monetary policies.[95] What has been framed as 'political transparency' by economists,[96] reflected in indicators (1)–(3) in Table 18.1, refers to key elements of the rule of law: the applicable rules must be published, communicated and made accessible to the addressees of the regulations.[97] As simple as this may sound in theory, in practice, its implementation can be challenging. Empirical studies show that institutional transparency ranks high among the various dimensions of central bank transparency.[98]

Indicators for measuring institutional transparency are formal statements of the objectives of monetary policy combined with a quantification of these objectives as well as explicit contracts or other institutional arrangements between monetary authorities and the government.[99]

The institutional arrangements required for efficient monetary policymaking show some similarities with the transparency requirements under WTO law with regard to publishing trade-related regulations and restrictions. From an economic perspective, the rationale is the same: enhancing efficiency and facilitating business activities. Market

[93] Dincer and Eichengreen, 'Central Bank Transparency', 85.

[94] For a recent general description of legal and economic elements of monetary affairs (without aspects of transparency), see P. Nobel and H. Zimmermann, 'Money, Legally and Economically Speaking', in P. Nobel and R. Benevenuto (eds.), *Law and Economics of Money and Currency* (Zurich: Schulthess, 2012), p. 1 ff.

[95] Kaufmann and Weber, 'The Role of Transparency in Financial Regulation', 784.

[96] Dincer and Eichengreen, 'Central Bank Transparency', 81–3.

[97] See also Kaufmann and Weber, 'The Role of Transparency in Financial Regulation', 784.

[98] Dincer and Eichengreen, 'Central Bank Transparency', 82. [99] *Ibid.*, 92; Table 18.1.

Table 18.1. *Monetary transparency: indicators and conceptual framework*

	Legal concept (Kaufmann and Weber 2010)		
Economic indicators (Eijffinger and Geraats 2006)	Institutional procedures and decision-making	Substantive foundation	Accountability
Political transparency	(3) Are there explicit contracts or other similar institutional arrangements between the monetary authorities and the government?	(1) Is there a formal statement of the objective(s) of monetary policy, with an explicit prioritisation in case of multiple objectives?	(2) Is there a quantification of the primary objective(s)?
Economic transparency			(4) Is the basic economic data relevant for the conduct of monetary policy publicly available? (5) Does the central bank disclose the formal macroeconomic model(s) it uses for policy analysis? (6) Does the central bank regularly publish its own macroeconomic forecasts?
Procedural transparency		(7) Does the central bank provide an explicit policy rule or strategy that describes its monetary policy framework?	(8) Does the central bank give a comprehensive account of policy deliberations (or explanations in case of a single central banker) within a reasonable amount of time? (9) Does the central bank disclose how each decision on the level of

	its main operating instrument or target was reached?
Policy transparency	(10) Are decisions about adjustments to the main operating instrument or target announced promptly?
	(11) Does the central bank provide an explanation when it announces policy decisions?
	(12) Does the central bank disclose an explicit policy inclination after every policy meeting, or an explicit indication of likely future policy actions (at least quarterly)?
Operational transparency	(13) Does the central bank regularly evaluate to what extent its main operating targets (if any) have been achieved?
	(14) Does the central bank regularly provide information on (unanticipated) macroeconomic disturbances that affect the policy transmission process?
	(15) Does the central bank regularly provide an evaluation of the policy outcome in light of its macroeconomic objectives?

participants need to know the applicable rules. From a legal perspective, transparency of the institutional framework follows from the rule of law.

A further important element related to the institutional pillar is the independence of monetary institutions from governmental influence.[100] This independence is closely related to the above-mentioned need to learn about the economic environment and the discretion to deviate from announced policies based on new knowledge, if necessary. Nevertheless, the delegation of policy decisions and reactions to a changing environment to independent central banks or to other monetary institutions, requires democratic safeguards. These institutions need to be vested with the necessary legitimacy both politically and democratically. In this regard, communicating experiences and knowledge, as well as lack of knowledge, to society and thus making policy changes and the underlying 'learning process' transparent, is essential.[101] Such transparency requirements do not preclude measures such as market interventions which cannot be communicated in advance if they are to remain effective. What transparency requires in such circumstances is a timely *ex post* communication about the assessment of the situation by the central bank that led to the measures being taken as well as an evaluation of (the 'lessons learnt' from) the achieved results.

2. Procedural transparency

Related to the institutional framework is procedural transparency in terms of a clear allocation of tasks and responsibilities to authorities and the market participants, respectively. Members of society must be able to establish who is doing what under which circumstances and who can be approached and reproached.[102] Uncertainty with respect to responsibilities and procedures should be avoided. This criterion is (partially) reflected in indicator (3) in Table 18.1.

An example of non-transparent policy goals and uncoordinated standards occurred in Switzerland in summer 2012: notwithstanding the fact that Credit Suisse is permanently supervised by FINMA, the

[100] K. Hielscher and G. Markwardt, 'The Role of Political Institutions for the Effectiveness of Central Bank Independence', *European Journal of Political Economy* 28 (2012), 286–301.

[101] King, 'The Institutions of Monetary Policy', 5–6 and 12: 'A central bank needs to explain to the population both what it knows and what it does not know.'

[102] See also the similar question raised by Kaufmann and Weber, 'The Role of Transparency in Financial Regulation', 785.

Swiss financial market supervisory authority, the Swiss National Bank (SNB), published a statement (without having properly pre-informed Credit Suisse) that in its view Credit Suisse was substantially undercapitalised. While it was undisputed that Credit Suisse, as well as other banks, needed to increase its capital base, FINMA as the competent supervisor had granted an implementation period until 2019.[103] Not surprisingly, the SNB's statement triggered market turbulence. Obviously, contradictory statements of FINMA and the SNB created uncertainties in the market and thereby jeopardised transparency of the current analysis of facts by different public agencies.

III. The second pillar: substantive foundation

The Atlantic Charter signed by Franklin D. Roosevelt and Winston Churchill in August 1941, and the subsequent negotiations at the Bretton Woods Conference in 1944, emphasised what is broadly accepted today: transparency is not a goal in itself but rather a means to an end. In fact, the negotiators at Bretton Woods agreed that stable monetary and financial systems were a key condition for a peaceful postwar order.[104] Transparency was seen as a catalyst for re-establishing trust in stable currencies after the turmoil of the 1930s.[105] The means of achieving the desired objectives was the establishment of the IMF and the World Bank and a fixed exchange rates regime tied to gold.

Still, the important criterion is not the quantity of information but its quality. As pointed out above in Section C, many institutions have become involved in standard-setting and regulation in the aftermath of the financial crisis. In increasingly interconnected financial markets, proposals for regulation and the responses by different stakeholders tend to multiply among the different fora and at the national and international level.[106]

It seems that in the global quest for transparency, the need for good quality information rather than information overload has been partially neglected, not only as far as the regulation of financial markets in general

[103] FINMA Newsletter 38 (2012), 20 July 2012, Eigenmittelnachweis – Basel III (German only), www.finma.ch/e/finma/publikationen/Pages/finmamitteilungen.aspx.

[104] See Weber and Arner, 'Toward a New Design', 393 ff.

[105] See Kaufmann and Weber, 'The Role of Transparency in Financial Regulation', 787.

[106] Bradley, 'Transparency is the New Opacity', 28.

is concerned,[107] but also in monetary affairs.[108] In fact, information overload may make it impossible to adequately process, digest and use the information[109] and can lead to the so-called 'Cassandra effect'[110] or to ignoring 'the prospect of future changes about the actual character of which we know nothing'.[111]

In essence, the impact of transparency measures on public policy depends on their structure and on the balance between the 'value of sunlight' and 'over-exposure'. The latter may result in information overload, excessive politicisation or dysfunctional surveillance.[112] In addition, consumers may be overwhelmed with information which may hamper their ability to make informed good decisions.[113] As Caroline Bradley noted, complex transactions lead to complex rules and standards and this complexity impedes transparency. At the same time, efforts to make transnational standard-setting processes more transparent risk making the information overload problem worse rather than better.[114]

Generally speaking, any policies for enhancing transparency require not only a solid conceptual basis but also a substantial relation to the purpose for which the information is sought, to the capacity of and the incentives for actors to provide the information.[115] If different organisations and supervisory bodies for financial markets succeed in clarifying the content of tasks as well as the regulatory responsibility and transparency, the confidence of market participants will increase.[116] Moreover, apart from their substantial value, clearly defined mandates

[107] The Sarbanes-Oxley Act of 30 July 2002, 116 Stat. 745, 15 USC § 7201 is a good example of an extremely detailed (and complicated) 'rule book' which, however, does not allow the addressees of the rules to gain easy 'access' to the basic underlying message of the detailed regulations.

[108] Bradley, 'Transparency is the New Opacity', 28–32.

[109] D. Heald, 'Varieties of Transparency', *Proceedings of the British Academy* 135 (2006), 25–43, 35.

[110] For further details, see R. H. Weber, 'Kassandra oder Wissensbroker – Dilemma im Global Village', in J. Becker, R. M. Hilty, J.-F. Stöckli and T. Würtenberger (eds.), *Recht im Wandel seines sozialen und technologischen Umfelds, Festschrift für Manfred Rehbinder* (Bern: Stämpfli, 2002), pp. 405–21, 407.

[111] J. M. Keynes, 'The General Theory of Employment', *Quarterly Journal of Economics* 51 (1937), 209–23, 214.

[112] Heald, 'Why is Transparency About Public Expenditure So Elusive?', 32.

[113] Bradley, 'Transparency is the New Opacity', 28. [114] *Ibid.*, 31.

[115] See Kaufmann and Weber, 'The Role of Transparency in Financial Regulation', 790; R. B. Mitchell, 'Sources of Transparency: Information Systems in International Regimes', *International Studies Quarterly* 42 (1998), 109–30, 109–10.

[116] See Kaufmann and Weber, 'The Role of Transparency in Financial Regulation', 790.

and tasks are important elements of accountability which, as indicated in Table 18.1,[117] is a key criterion in shaping efficient monetary policies.

IV. The third pillar: accountability

Accountability is a concept with many facets:[118] together with checks and balances it is a prerequisite for legitimacy and a key element of any governance discussion. Obviously, accountability depends on reliable information.[119]

Accountability must be assessed with regard to the manifold relationships in the financial sector, in particular between the state and the financial institutions, between supervisory authorities and market participants and between different (quasi-)governmental organisations.[120] These relationships should be based on a transparent data regime: *ex ante* mechanisms help to prevent the abuse of power, *ex post* accountability applies instruments such as a judicial review or non-traditional remedies to assess monetary activities.[121] Indicators (2)–(6) in Table 18.1 focus on measures to make information on the policy framework accessible and are therefore related to *ex ante* accountability, while indicators (8)–(15) focus on *ex post* assessments.

In addition, a distinction needs to be made between a *retrospective* reporting cycle and *real-time* surveillance. The key difference between the two lies in the length of the accountability window. In a *real-time* setting, the accountability window is always open and surveillance is an ongoing process. Examples of this type of system are macroeconomic forecasts, including changes. In a *retrospective* system, the accountability window will be interrupted by the reporting lag during which the institution is preparing the information for the public.[122] Retrospective transparency may prevent political pressure on central bank board members when it comes to disclosing the minutes of board meetings.

[117] Above Section D.I; Dincer and Eichengreen, 'Central Bank Transparency', 88.

[118] R. M. Lastra and H. Shams, 'Public Accountability in the Financial Sector' in E. Ferran and C. Goodhart (eds.), *Regulating Financial Services and Markets in the 21st Century* (Oxford University Press, 2001), pp. 165–88, 166–9; Weber, *Shaping Internet Governance*, p. 133.

[119] Kaufmann and Weber, 'The Role of Transparency in Financial Regulation', 791.

[120] See also *ibid.*, 791.

[121] R. W. Grant and R. O. Keohane, 'Accountability and Abuses of Power in World Politics', *American Political Science Review* 99 (2005), 29–43, 30–1; slightly different, Lastra and Shams, 'Public Accountability', p. 169.

[122] Heald, 'Why is Transparency About Public Expenditure So Elusive?', 32–4.

An example of a retrospective system is the proceedings of the Federal Open Markets Committee of the Federal Reserve, which are released with a delay of one month.[123] In contrast, the European Central Bank has, since its establishment, justified its refusal to publish the minutes and voting records of its council on the grounds that individual members would then be subject to pressure from special interest groups (national interests, in this context) that might compromise their independence and lead to inefficient policy decisions. Recently, this policy has become controversial with at least two members of the ECB's Governing Council advocating increased transparency, by, *inter alia*, releasing the minutes of the meetings.[124] A possible middle-way could be to publish voting *patterns* instead of individual council member statements, which may foster predictability while still protecting independence.[125]

Clearly, in a monetary context, reliable quantitative indicators for communicating and evaluating monetary objectives, such as inflation targets, are essential for establishing credible accountability mechanisms. Recent empirical studies suggest a positive correlation between transparent accountability mechanisms as captured by indicators (8)–(15) in Table 18.1 and lower inflation rates.[126]

E. Conclusions

This chapter shows that the present lack of a comprehensive analytical framework for transparency in monetary affairs can at least partially be compensated by adapting existing instruments available in other areas of law. We suggest complementing the general three-pillar framework – institutional and/or procedural elements, substantive foundation and accountability – with criteria that are empirically proven to enhance efficiency of monetary policy. Examples include the fifteen indicators developed by Eijffinger and Geraats[127] which are highly relevant for our framework as shown in Table 18.1.

[123] Federal Open Market Committee – Statements of Policy, Policy Regarding the Government in the Sunshine Act, 12 CFR 281; as amended effective 16 February 2005.

[124] 'Making the European Central Bank more Transparent', *Financial Times*, 19 September 2012; 'Wie viel Transparenz verträgt die EZB?', *Neue Zürcher Zeitung*, 20 September 2012, 25.

[125] P. M. Geraats, 'ECB Credibility and Transparency', *European Economy, Economic Papers* 3330 (European Commission, June 2008), p. 25.

[126] Dincer and Eichengreen, 'Central Bank Transparency', 90.

[127] Eijffinger and Geraats, 'How Transparent are Central Banks?'.

As for procedural transparency, lessons can be drawn from WTO law, in particular the GATS, with its strong emphasis on the rule of law. This approach is supported by empirical findings according to which a stronger adherence to the rule of law is correlated to higher transparency. Moreover, transparency is particularly relevant for the publication of monetary policy and related instruments as reflected in indicators (1), (3)–(6), (8)–(9) and (13)–(15) in Table 18.1.

Since transparency in monetary affairs requires quantitative, measurable criteria, transparency indicators, such as those established by the IMF, should be included and elaborated further to meet the specific needs of monetary policy.

Finally, we conclude that, in monetary affairs, striking a balance between transparency and other policy goals is necessary. Recent debates illustrate that enhanced transparency may lead to increased political pressure and thus jeopardise central bank independence. In our view, the parameters for such a balancing test should be defined in a democratically legitimised process.

19

Human rights and austerity programmes

MARKUS KRAJEWSKI

A. Introduction

In June 2011 the United Nations Independent Expert on foreign debt and human rights,[1] Cephas Lumina, issued a warning that the austerity measures and structural reforms proposed to solve Greece's debt crisis may result in violations of basic human rights. He warned that the austerity measures and structural reforms, including privatisation of state-owned enterprises and assets, were 'likely to have a serious impact on . . . the enjoyment of human rights by the Greek people, particularly the most vulnerable sectors of the population such as the poor, elderly, unemployed and persons with disabilities. The rights to food, water, adequate housing and work under fair and equitable conditions should not be compromised by the implementation of austerity measures.'[2]

The Independent Expert also urged the Greek government to strike a careful balance between austerity and the realisation of human rights and to maintain some fiscal leeway to meet its people's basic human rights, particularly economic, social and cultural rights. He also called on the International Monetary Fund (IMF), the European Union (EU) and

I would like to thank Thomas Cottier, Robert Howse, Ernst-Ulrich Petersmann and Sofia Massoud for helpful and clarifying comments as well as the participants of the World Trade Forum 2012 for a stimulating debate. All errors that remain are mine.

[1] The Independent Expert on the effects of foreign debt and other related international financial obligations of States on the full enjoyment of all human rights, particularly economic, social and cultural rights, carries out his mandate on the basis of Human Rights Council Resolution 7/4 of, 27 March 2008, A/HRC/RES/7/4, which requests him to pay particular attention, *inter alia*, to the effects of foreign debt and the policies adopted to address them on the full enjoyment of all human rights, and the impact of foreign debt and other related international financial obligations on the capacity of states to design and implement their policies and programmes, including national budgets that respond to vital requirements for the promotion of the realisation of social rights.

[2] Greek crisis: 'Keep in mind the people's basic human rights' – UN expert on rights and foreign debt, www.ohchr.org/en/NewsEvents/Pages/DisplayNews.aspx?NewsID=11195&LangID=E (last accessed 2 October 2012).

the European Central Bank (ECB) to remain aware of the human rights impact of the policies they design in the attempt to resolve the sovereign debt crises in Greece and other countries.[3]

Later, in July 2012, the Human Rights Council formally endorsed the Guiding Principles on foreign debt which were drafted by the Independent Expert earlier that year.[4] Principle 8 stipulates that foreign debt strategies 'must be designed not to hamper the improvement of conditions guaranteeing the enjoyment of human rights' while Principle 9 states that international financial organisations have an obligation to respect international human rights, which implies a duty to refrain from policies and programmes which directly or indirectly contravene the enjoyment of human rights.[5] Even though these principles were adopted by a sharply divided Human Rights Council – thirty-one developing countries voted in favour and eleven developed countries voted against the resolution, while five members of the Council abstained – their adoption and the statement of the Independent Expert on Greece indicate the recognition by international human rights bodies that foreign debt and associated austerity programmes may have detrimental effects on the realisation of human rights.

This observation is supported by the 2012 Concluding Observations on Spain of the Committee on Economic, Social and Cultural Rights (ECSR Committee).[6] The Committee which oversees the implementation of the International Covenant on Economic, Social and Cultural Rights (ICECSR) was concerned that the protection of human rights had been reduced as a result of the austerity measures adopted by Spain, 'which disproportionately curtail the enjoyment of their rights by disadvantaged and marginalized individuals and groups, especially the poor, women, children, persons with disabilities, unemployed adults and young persons, older persons, gypsies, migrants and asylum seekers

[3] *Ibid.*

[4] Human Rights Council, Resolution 20/10, The Effects of Foreign Debt and Other Related International Financial Obligations of States on the Full Enjoyment of All Human Rights, Particularly Economic, Social and Cultural Rights, 18 July 2012, A/HRC/RES/20/10, para. 2.

[5] Human Rights Council, Report of the Independent Expert on the Effects of Foreign Debt and Other Related International Financial Obligations of States on the Full Enjoyment of All Human Rights, Particularly Economic, Social and Cultural Rights, Cephas Lumina – Guiding Principles on Foreign Debt and Human Rights, 10 April 2012, A/HRC/20/23.

[6] Committee on Economic, Social and Cultural Rights, Concluding Observations of the Committee on Economic, Social and Cultural Rights – Spain, E/C.12/ESP/CO/5, 6 June 2012.

(art. 2, para. 1).' The Committee therefore recommended that Spain ensures 'that all the austerity measures adopted reflect the minimum core content of all the Covenant rights' and that it takes 'all appropriate measures to protect that core content under any circumstances, especially for disadvantaged and marginalized individuals and groups.'[7]

Neither the Guiding Principles on foreign debt and human rights as adopted by the Human Rights Council nor the Concluding Observations of the ESCR Committee on Spain are authoritative statements of international law. Yet, like the views of the Independent Expert on Greece, they offer an invitation to analyse the relationship between human rights and austerity programmes more closely. In particular, they raise the question whether international human rights could serve as legal guidance for the design and implementation of austerity programmes. Do international human rights obligations impose limitations on such programmes by requiring or prohibiting certain measures or by obliging states to implement austerity programmes in a certain manner?

This chapter develops the analysis of this question in five steps: it commences with conceptual clarifications by discussing the notion of 'austerity programmes' and by showing that economic, social and cultural rights will be at the centre of attention in this context (Section B). The next Section discusses which entities are bound by human rights (Section C). This concerns the issue whether and to what extent not only states, but also international organisations, such as the IMF or the EU, or hybrid transnational networks of states and international organisations, are obliged to respect human rights. The next aspect to be discussed is the jurisdictional scope of human rights (Section D). In particular, the question is raised whether human rights obligations extend beyond the territory of the state which is bound by them (extraterritorial obligations of human rights) which is one of the most controversial issues of the contemporary human rights discourse. The chapter then turns to the substance of the human rights in question (Section E). It establishes the three dimensions of human rights obligations and their relevance for austerity programmes. A crucial aspect of economic and social rights is the progressiveness of their realisation. Accordingly, upon entering a commitment, a state is not required to realise economic and social rights immediately, but is only obliged to fulfil its obligations 'to the maximum of its available resources' and 'with a view to achieving progressively' the full realisation of those rights. This raises the question whether the

[7] *Ibid.*, para. 7.

progressive realisation prohibits retrogressive measures which reduce the level of enjoyment of economic and social rights. In addition, this chapter analyses how limitations of economic and social rights can be justified on the basis of general public policy considerations. It will be argued that the application of these considerations triggers a debate about the economic and social effects of austerity programmes. This leads to the last Section of the chapter which will turn to the implications of human rights for public discourse (Section F). It will be argued that human rights can shape the process of economic policy-making by opening up a space for the debates on political alternatives. A summary of the main arguments and an outlook conclude (Section G).

B. Conceptual clarifications: what are we talking about?

I. Austerity

Austerity, as a principle shaping fiscal and economic policies, has regained particular prominence in recent years. The catalyst for the current focus on austerity policies and programmes was the Greek sovereign debt crisis.[8] Yet, austerity is not a new concept. In fact, the ideological history of the concept – although not the term – can be traced back to the writings of classical economists of the eighteenth and nineteenth centuries.[9] In contemporary political debates about the sovereign debt crisis in the eurozone, austerity refers to a policy of reducing public deficits by lowering expenses, in particular by wage reductions in the public sector, cutting social benefits such as pensions and decreasing expenditures on public services such as health and education. The latter is often achieved through the privatisation of government monopolies. Similar policies were required of many developing countries in the context of Structural Adjustment Programmes introduced by the IMF and the World Bank in the 1980s and 1990s. The current debate on the effects of the Greek austerity measures has therefore historical antecedents.[10]

[8] S. Konzelman, *The Economics of Austerity* (Cambridge, Centre for Business Research, University of Cambridge Working Paper No. 434, 2012), p. 1, ssrn.com/abstract=2127567. I. Feitchner, 'Taxation in Times of Austerity: A Question of Political Economy', Chapter 11, this volume.

[9] Konzelman, *The Economics of Austerity* (note 8), pp. 4 ff.

[10] T. Mahmud, 'Is it Greek or Déjà Vu All Over Again?: Neoliberalism and Winners and Losers of International Debt Crises', *Loyola University Chicago Law Journal* 42 (2011), 629 ff.

More recently, political sociologists suggested analysing the economic policy consensus which emerged in the 1980s and 1990s in many industrialised countries as an 'austerity regime'. For them, austerity is not limited to certain measures and programmes adopted by a state as a reaction to a particular crisis, but it is a political principle institutionalised and implemented for a longer period.[11] A key element of such a regime is a continuous reduction of the proportion of the national budget which can be spent based on political discretion, due to a combination of reductions in deficit-spending while rejecting an increase in taxation. An austerity regime does not necessarily entail cuts to public spending in absolute terms, but it reduces the availability of policy space for programmes which require additional funds. However, in relative terms, spending on social programmes and governmental services will be reduced in the long-term.

In addition, an austerity regime is characterised by a fiscalisation of politics which sees a focus of the public discourse on austerity as an objective of policy and not merely as a means to achieve macroeconomic stability.[12] Such a development may even lead to the adoption of constitutional limitations on public debts, so-called debt brakes or 'Schuldenbremsen'.[13] These debt brakes not only establish legal barriers to politics of deficit-spending, but they also have a profound impact on public discourse by branding proposals which would lead to an increase of government spending as potentially illegal from a constitutional perspective. As such, debt brakes more often than not narrow the policy options to reductions in government expenditure. Consequently, debt brakes severely reduce the space for a democratic decision-making process because constitutional rules are usually difficult to change once enacted.[14] This aspect will be of particular relevance when discussing the impact of human rights on debates about political alternatives.[15]

There is no need to develop a comprehensive understanding of the notion of austerity for the purposes of this chapter, in particular since there is no agreement on the exact meaning of the term austerity among economists either.[16] It is sufficient to recall that austerity measures and

[11] W. Streeck and D. Martens, *Politik im Defizit – Austerität als fiskalpolitisches Regime* (Cologne: MPIfG Discussion Papers 10/5, 2010), p. 10.

[12] Konzelman, *The Economics of Austerity*, p. 28.

[13] 'Germany's Debt Brake – Tie Your Hands, Please: Is Germany's Fiscal Straitjacket an Example for Others?', *The Economist* 10 December 2011, www.economist.com/node/21541459.

[14] Streeck and Martens, *Politik in Defizit*, p. 12.

[15] See Section F.

[16] Konzelman, *The Economics of Austerity*, p. 2.

austerity politics typically involve severe cuts in public spending which have negative effects on employment, social benefits and the provision of public services.[17] As a consequence private costs for health and education rise while private incomes decrease due to growing unemployment and reduced social benefits.

II. Relevant human rights

In light of the effects of austerity on the social and economic welfare of a society, economic, social and cultural human rights (ESC rights) are of particular relevance. These rights are sometimes dubbed as 'second generation' or 'second dimension' rights, because they were allegedly after the establishment of civil and political rights.[18] Labelling economic and social rights as 'second' generation or dimension obscures the fact that no such distinction exists in the international legal development of human rights.[19] In fact, the history of international human rights law is a history of a parallel development of civil and political rights on the one hand and economic, social and cultural rights on the other. The famous Four Freedoms declared as policy goals of the United States by President Franklin Roosevelt in his 1941 State of the Union Address included the freedom of speech, the freedom of religion, the freedom from fear and the freedom from want.[20]

The 1948 United Nations Universal Declaration of Human Rights, which is usually seen as the first codification of international human rights, though not formally binding, includes economic and social rights alongside political and civil rights,[21] in particular the right to social

[17] P. O'Connell, 'Let them Eat Cake: Socio-Economic Rights in An Age of Austerity', in A. Nolan, P. O'Connell and C. Harvey (eds.), *Human Rights and Public Finance* (Oxford University Press, 2013), ssrn.com/abstract=1915221.

[18] M. Ssenyonjo, *Economic, Social and Cultural Rights in International Law* (Oxford: Hart Publishing, 2009), p. 10.

[19] The development of human rights in national constitutions follows a different pattern. Here, civil and political rights did indeed precede social and economic rights. However, if one looks at the international level, there is no similar historical sequence.

[20] Congressional Record, 1941, Vol. 87, Pt. I. See also the Preamble of the Universal Declaration on Human Rights: 'the advent of a world in which human beings shall enjoy freedom of speech and belief and freedom from fear and want has been proclaimed as the highest aspiration of the common people.'

[21] P. O'Connell, *Vindicating Socio-Economic Rights: International Standards and Comparative Experiences* (London: Routledge, 2012), pp. 28–9.

security (Article 22), the right to work (Article 23), the right to an adequate standard of living and health (Article 25) and the right to education (Article 26). In 1966, political and civil rights as well as economic, social and cultural rights were enshrined in two international covenants which entered into force in 1976. More recent international human rights treaties also include both types of rights.

The 'Magna Carta' of international economic, social and cultural rights is the International Covenant on Economic, Social and Cultural Rights (ICESCR) of 16 December 1966.[22] It entered into force on 3 January 1976 and currently has 160 parties from all parts of the world. Despite its near universal scope there are a number of countries which have either signed but not ratified the Covenant (such as Cuba, South Africa and the US) or have not even signed the Covenant (such as Botswana, Mozambique, Myanmar and Saudi Arabia). Yet, for all parties of the Covenant, the human rights enshrined in it are legally binding international norms.

It should also be noted that special international human rights treaties such as the Convention on the Elimination of All Forms of Discrimination against Women of 1979[23] with 187 parties, the Convention on the Rights of the Child of 1989[24] with 193 parties and the Convention on the Rights of Persons with Disabilities (CRPD) of 2006[25] with 124 parties, also contain a number of economic, social and cultural rights designed specifically to address the special situation of women, children and persons with disabilities. It can therefore be concluded that economic, social and cultural human rights form an integral part of the legally binding international body of human rights. While their primary source is treaty law, it may even be possible that certain core obligations of economic and social rights are part of customary international law, in particular, since the rights have been recognised in all human rights codifications from the Universal Declaration to the most recent human rights conventions.[26]

Human rights enshrined in binding international agreements are subject to the general rules of international treaty law. In particular, a state may not invoke the provisions of its internal law as a justification for its failure to implement a treaty as stipulated in Article 27 of the Vienna Convention on the Law of Treaties. The irrelevance of domestic law for the application of a treaty extends to domestic constitutional law.

[22] UNTS Vol. 993, 3. [23] UNTS Vol. 1249, 13. [24] UNTS Vol. 1577, 3.
[25] UNTS Vol. 2515, 3. [26] See Section C.II.

Hence, debt brakes in domestic constitutions or other constitutional provisions limiting state spending cannot trump international legally binding human rights.

Economic, social and cultural rights differ from civil and political rights because they are usually not drafted in a way which requires states to grant these rights immediately and without any deference to the resources of the state. In particular, Article 2 ICESCR stipulates that the Covenant's parties undertake 'to take steps . . . to the maximum of [their] available resources, with a view to achieving progressively the full realization of the rights recognized in the present Covenant by all appropriate means, including particularly the adoption of legislative measures'. This recognises that the realisation of economic, social and cultural rights requires states to employ resources. Since countries at different levels of economic development may have different amounts of resources at their disposal the realisation of economic, social and cultural rights may differ between countries. This chapter will return to the issue of availability of resources and the legal consequences of a reduction of state resources due to financial or debt crises in Section E.II.

Recalling the working definition of austerity programmes developed in the previous Section, the following economic, social and cultural rights would seem to be most relevant when discussing the impact of human rights on austerity programmes: the right to work including just and favourable conditions of work (Articles 6 and 7 ICESCR), the right to social security, including social insurance (Article 9 ICESCR), the right to an adequate standard of living (Article 11 ICESCR), the right to the enjoyment of the highest attainable standard of health (Article 12 ICESCR) and the right to education (Article 13 ICESCR).

Apart from the substantive scope of these rights, the standard of non-discrimination is of particular relevance. According to Article 2(2) ICESCR the human rights guaranteed in the Covenant shall be exercised 'without discrimination of race, colour, sex, language, religion, political or other opinion, national or social origin, property, birth or other status'. The reference to 'other status' indicates that discrimination on the basis of disability, age or nationality is equally prohibited.[27] Austerity programmes which lead to cuts in public spending often have adverse effects on certain vulnerable groups such as children, the elderly, persons

[27] Committee on Economic, Social and Cultural Rights, General Comment No. 20: Non-discrimination in Economic, Social and Cultural Rights, E/C.12/GC/20, 2 July 2009, paras. 27 ff.

with disabilities, migrants or persons marginalised on ethnic grounds. Furthermore, the impact of such programmes is often more burdensome on women who traditionally bear more responsibilities regarding family support and care for relatives.

When applying and interpreting the relevant economic and social rights, due regard needs to be given to the work of the Committee on Economic, Social and Cultural Rights. The Committee was established as a body for overseeing the application of the Covenant. One of its instruments aimed at helping states to meet their human rights obligations through clarifications and guidance takes the form of the so-called General Comments (GC). The Committee issued GC on a number of general aspects and specific rights, including the right to social security (GC No. 19, 2008), the right to work (GC No. 18, 2005), the right to the highest attainable standard of health (GC No. 14, 2000) and the right to education (GC No. 13, 1999). Even though these comments are not legally binding or authoritative interpretations of the Covenant they can be used as interpretative tools. The Committee also issues Concluding Observations on the reports of the parties such as those on Spain mentioned in the introduction to this chapter. While these often contain reactions of the Committee to the specific situation of a particular country they may nevertheless include helpful clarifications of the scope of the obligations of the ICESCR.[28]

C. Obligated entities: who is bound by human rights?

Human rights are international legal obligations. They contain rights of individuals *vis-à-vis* other legal persons. Austerity programmes are usually implemented by states, but often in the context of policies and programmes involving other states and international organisations.

I. States

States bear the primary responsibility for the protection and promotion of human rights. As parties to a particular human rights treaty they are bound to respect the human rights laid down in the respective treaty. It is therefore not surprising that the Committee on Economic, Social and Cultural Rights reminded Spain of its obligations under the Covenant in light of the austerity measures Spain took to reduce its sovereign debt

[28] O'Connell, *Vindicating Socio-Economic Rights*, p. 41.

problem.[29] It is also worth recalling that the obligation of states to protect and promote human rights extends to all entities of the state, including regional units such as provinces as well as local governments. In addition, central banks are also bound by human rights, because they are entities of the state even if they are constituted as politically independent organs, sometimes even with a distinct legal personality. This is due to the design and to the fact that central banks exercise public functions, both managerial and regulatory.[30] These functions establish the attribution in international law of their activities to the state in question in accordance with Article 5 International Law Commission (ILC) Draft Articles on Responsibility of States for Internationally Wrongful Acts.[31]

An issue which may be of particular relevance in the context of this chapter is whether state enterprises which are owned and managed by the state are also subject to human rights obligations, in particular if these enterprises are organised as private law companies. This concerns in particular the supply of services of general interest such as water, energy, transportation, health and education.[32] Usually, these enterprises are not empowered to exercise public functions and therefore do not fall under Article 5 of the ILC Draft.[33] Generally, international law recognises that state companies are legal entities separate from the state except in cases of an abuse of rights.[34] *Prima facie*, states are not responsible for the conduct of entities which are legally distinct from

[29] See note 6.

[30] R. M. Lastra, 'The Evolution of the European Central Bank', *Fordham International Law Journal* 35 (Special Issue) (2012), 1260–81.

[31] 'The conduct of a person or entity which is not an organ of the State under Article 4 but which is empowered by the law of that State to exercise elements of the governmental authority shall be considered an act of the State under international law, provided the person or entity is acting in that capacity in the particular instance'. Draft Articles on Responsibility of States for Internationally Wrongful Acts, untreaty.un.org/ilc/texts/instruments/english/draftarticles/9_6_2001.pdf.

[32] See, e.g., B. Choudhury, *Public Services and International Trade Liberalization: Human Rights and Gender Implications* (Cambridge University Press, 2012), pp. 244 ff.

[33] International Law Commission, Draft Articles on Responsibility of States for Internationally Wrongful Acts, with commentaries, Report of the International Law Commission on the work of its fifty-third session, 2001, Article 5, para. 5, untreaty.un.org/ilc/texts/instruments/english/commentaries/9_6_2001.pdf: '[Entities] may include public corporations, semi-public entities, public agencies of various kinds and even, in special cases, private companies, provided that in each case the entity is empowered by the law of the State to exercise functions of a public character normally exercised by State organs, and the conduct of the entity relates to the exercise of the governmental authority concerned.'

[34] Draft Articles on Responsibility of States for Internationally Wrongful Acts, with commentaries, Article 8, para. 6.

them. Yet, if the company exercises elements of governmental authority or the state uses its ownership or control of the company to achieve a particular result, the conduct in question can be attributable to the state.[35]

States are obliged to protect human rights throughout their own territory. In its Advisory Opinion on the legality of the Israeli wall in the Palestinian Territory, the International Court of Justice held that states are also bound by economic, social and cultural rights on territory over which they have control as an occupying power.[36] Whether and to what extent states are also obliged to protect human rights in other extraterritorial circumstances, in particular if they participate in the development and implementation of the austerity programmes of other states, is less clear and subject to heated debates in the literature and in international practice. The chapter returns to this issue in depth in Section D.

II. International organisations

A more challenging question concerns international organisations which possess an international legal personality distinct from their member states.[37] Direct international law obligations can only arise if these organisations themselves are bound by the respective human rights. The fact that states which are members of an international organisation are also parties to international human rights treaties does not create such a direct obligation of the organisation to respect these treaties.[38] Typically, international organisations are not parties to international human rights treaties, because these treaties usually only provide for the membership of states.[39]

One pathway to establishing that the IMF and the World Bank are bound by human rights could be the fact that these organisations are specialised organs of the United Nations and that Article 103 of the UN Charter establishes primacy of the Charter over every other international agreement, including the founding treaties of the two Bretton Woods Institutions.[40]

35 *Ibid.*

36 ICJ, *Legal Consequences of the Construction of a Wall in the Occupied Palestinian Territory*, Advisory Opinion, ICJ Reports 2004, 186, para. 112.

37 A. McBeth, *International Economic Actors and Human Rights: Global Rules for Global Players* (London: Routledge, 2009), p. 65.

38 But see I. Saiz, 'Rights in Recession? Challenges for Economic and Social Rights Enforcement in Times of Crisis', *Journal of Human Rights Practice* 1 (2009), 277 289.

39 Ssenyonjo, *Economic, Social and Cultural Rights in International Law*, p. 131.

40 *Ibid.*, pp. 131–2.

However, since the UN Charter contains only general references to human rights and no specific link to human rights treaties, reliance on the Charter can only create a very general and broad obligation. It is also difficult to create a binding obligation of specialised UN organisations to respect specific human rights solely based on the UN Charter. Article 55(c) UN Charter establishes the principle of respect and observance of human rights as a binding rule only for the UN and its organs, but not for the IMF or the World Bank which are independent legal institutions.[41]

International organisations are, however, bound by customary international law including human rights of customary nature.[42] Economic, social and cultural rights, such as the right to work, the right to an adequate standard of living and health and the right to education, are enshrined in the Universal Declaration of Human Rights, which is generally considered to contain customary law obligations at its core. Furthermore, the large majority of states has signed and ratified international human rights treaties which contain these rights. It can therefore be concluded that the basic elements of these rights are of customary nature. The possibility that international organisations, such as the IMF, are bound by human rights insofar as they represent customary international law was also affirmed by the IMF's General Counsel François Gianviti in a paper presented in 2002.[43]

Even if one does not go as far as accepting positive obligations of international organisations under customary human rights law, it seems safe to assume that international organisations are obliged not to frustrate the attempts of states to honour their human rights obligations.[44] For example, if a state refuses to cut back on expenditures in the

[41] B. Simma, D. E. Khan, G. Nolte and A. Paulus (eds.), *The Charter of the United Nations*, 3rd edn (Oxford University Press, 2012), Article 55 (c), para. 15 (Riedel/Arend) and Article 57, para. 18 (Meng).

[42] M. Cogen, 'Human Rights, Prohibition of Political Activities and the Lending-Policies of Worldbank and International Monetary Fund', in S. R. Chowdhury, E. M. G. Denters and P. J. I. M. de Waart (eds.), *The Right to Development in International Law* (Dordrecht: Martinus Nijhoff, 1992), p. 387; A. Clapham, *Human Rights Obligations of Non-State Actors* (Oxford University Press, 2006), pp. 87, 148.

[43] F. Gianviti, 'Economic, Social and Cultural Rights and the International Monetary Fund', Paper presented at the Seminar 'Current Developments in Monetary and Financial Law', Washington, DC, 2002, para. 19, www.imf.org/external/np/leg/sem/2002/cdmfl/eng/gianv3.pdf. For analysis of this opinion see Clapham, *Human Rights Obligations of Non-State Actors*, pp. 145 ff.

[44] M. Ssenyonjo, 'The Applicability of International Human Rights Law to Non-State Actors: What Relevance to Economic, Social and Cultural Rights', *International Journal of Human Rights* (2008), 725–42; McBeth, *International Economic Actors and Human Rights*, p. 67.

health and social sector due to human rights considerations, an international organisation, such as the IMF, must refrain from putting any pressure on the government of that state to do otherwise.

In addition, the EU is bound by economic and social rights which are enshrined in the EU's own Charter of Fundamental Rights (Article 6(1) Treaty on European Union). The Charter of Fundamental Rights includes the right to education (Article 14), the right to fair and just working conditions (Article 31), entitlements to social security and social assistance (Article 34) and the right of access to health care and medical treatment (Article 35).[45] These rights are addressed to the institutions, bodies, offices and agencies of the EU without any reservation. They are hence also applicable in the relations of the EU with third states or in the context of austerity programmes associated with institutions of the EU, such as the ECB. However, the obligations of the Charter of Fundamental Rights do not have an *international* legal character. Instead they form part of internal EU constitutional law. They may therefore only serve as an indirect route to establish an obligation of the EU to respect international human rights.

A more direct approach could be based on Article 21 of the Treaty on European Union which stipulates that the EU's actions on the international scene shall be guided *inter alia* by the universality and indivisibility of human rights and fundamental freedoms. Arguably, this provision contains a unilateral declaration of the EU that it considers itself bound by existing international human rights.[46] In particular, this includes human rights laid down in the Universal Declaration and in the two international covenants of 1966. However, it should be noted that this provision only relates to external actions of the EU and may only offer indirect guidance regarding the EU's actions towards its member states.

III. Transnational networks of states and international organisations

Global governance is no longer restricted to activities of states and international organisations. Increasingly states form networks and institutionalised groups which have significant practical effects on international policies. Well-known examples include the G-8 or G-20. As these

[45] OJ, 14 December 2009, C 303/1.

[46] A similar constitutional unilateral promise can be found in Article 54 para. 2 of the Swiss Constitution. I would like to thank Thomas Cottier for pointing this out to me.

groups are not formal international organisations they cannot be considered separate legal personalities. Nevertheless, states acting jointly in such groups are bound by human rights obligations and cannot discharge themselves of these obligations in an informal network. Networks of international organisations can be seen in the same way.

The recent sovereign debt crisis in the eurozone triggered joint activities of the IMF, the European Commission (EC) and the ECB, often termed the 'Troika'.[47] These activities are not based on formal agreements between the participating organisations. The Troika is not an international organisation. It can best be described as an international network of three legally independent organisations based on expertise. Again from a public international law perspective, such networks do not constitute legal persons and therefore are not subject to obligations under international law. It may even be questionable whether their activities can be attributed to an entity which is legally distinct from the organisations forming them.

Since these networks do not constitute independent subjects of public international law, the international organisations which constitute them continue to bear their full responsibilities under international law. Like states, international organisations may not discharge their obligations by claiming that a certain decision or recommendation issued by the network was not supported by its representative. Instead, all activities of or within a hybrid transnational network can be attributed to all the international organisations which are part of the network. The situation is therefore rather different from a situation in which one international organisation places its organs at the disposal of another international organisation.[48]

D. Jurisdictional scope: how far do human rights reach?

The previous Section showed that states are bound by economic, social and cultural rights as they exercise territorial jurisdiction or control over a certain territory. In many cases, this observation may be sufficient in the context of the application of human rights to austerity

[47] IMF Factsheet, *The IMF and Europe*, 19 September 2012, www.imf.org/external/np/exr/facts/europe.htm.

[48] On such a situation, see Article 7 of the ILC Draft Articles on the Responsibility of International Organizations, 2011, untreaty.un.org/ilc/texts/instruments/english/draft%20articles/9_11_2011.pdf.

programmes, because these programmes are typically adopted and implemented by a state on its own territory.

The recent attempts to address the sovereign debt crisis in the eurozone show, however, that other states and international bodies may also be involved in the implementation of such programmes. This raises the controversial question whether and to what extent human rights obligations apply beyond the territorial jurisdiction of the state. UN human rights bodies increasingly apply such an extraterritorial dimension to international human rights law. The Committee on Social, Economic and Cultural Rights, for example, stated in its General Comment on the Right to Water that 'steps should be taken by states parties to prevent their own citizens and companies from violating the right to water of individuals and communities *in other countries*.'[49] The possibility of extraterritorial human rights obligations has also been addressed in the Maastricht Principles on Extraterritorial Obligations of States in the area of Economic, Social and Cultural Rights adopted in September 2011.[50] These principles were drafted by a group of internationally renowned experts on social and economic rights from academic institutions and other organisations all over the world including current and former members of international human rights treaty bodies, regional human rights bodies and Special Rapporteurs of the United Nations Human Rights Council. The Principles aim 'to clarify the content of extraterritorial State obligations to realize economic, social and cultural rights'.

The Maastricht Principles are not an act of an international law-making body, but they carry significant normative force.[51] Due to the qualification of the group's members and their goal of concretising the content of existing human rights obligations based on international practice rather than proposing new legal obligations, the principles have a similar authoritative value to that of the reports and statements of other international expert groups such as the International Law Association (ILA). They do not represent a formal source of public international law, but they can be

[49] Committee on Economic, Social and Cultural Rights, General Comment No. 15 (2002) The right to water (Articles 11 and 12), E/C.12/2002/11, 20 January 2003, para. 33, (emphasis added).

[50] Maastricht Principles on Extraterritorial Obligations of States in the area of Economic, Social and Cultural Rights, adopted on 28 September 2011, www.maastrichtuniversity.nl/web/Institutes/MaastrichtCentreForHumanRights.htm.

[51] M. E. Salomon and I. Seiderman, 'Human Rights Norms for a Globalized World: The Maastricht Principles on Extraterritorial Obligations of States in the Area of Economic, Social and Cultural Rights', *Global Policy* (2012), 458, 459.

seen as evidence of 'the teachings of the most highly qualified publicists of the various nations' in the meaning of Article 38(1)(d) of the ICJ Statute and therefore as subsidiary means for the determination of rules of international law.

According to Principle 8(a) of the Maastricht Principles, extraterritorial obligations encompass 'obligations relating to the acts and omissions of a State, within or beyond its territory, that have effects on the enjoyment of human rights outside of that State's territory'. One legal argument for such obligations can be found in Article 2 ICESCR. Unlike Article 2 of the International Covenant on Civil and Political Rights (ICCPR) which expressly limits the obligations of a state party to 'individuals within its territory and subject to its jurisdiction', Article 2 ICESCR contains no such language.[52] Some authors have concluded that this indicates that the ICESCR also contains extraterritorial obligations.[53]

An additional normative argument establishing a state's extraterritorial responsibility could be based on the principle of aid or assistance as established in the international law on state responsibility.[54] According to that principle, a state is internationally responsible for aiding and assisting in an internationally wrongful act of another state if the former state knew about the circumstances of the internationally wrongful act and if the act would be internationally wrongful if committed by that state.[55] The activities considered as aid and assistance must be a significant contribution to the act, but they do not have to be 'essential'.[56] It can be argued that a state supporting or even demanding the implementation of austerity measures of another state may constitute assistance to a human rights violation of the former state, i.e. the state implementing the austerity programme.

Accepting the general possibility of extraterritorial obligations requires the establishment of a standard of attribution, because extraterritoriality cannot be applied without limitations. Principle 9 of the Maastricht

[52] F. Coomans, 'The Extraterritorial Scope of the International Covenant on Economic, Social and Cultural Rights in the Work of the United Nations Committee on Economic, Social and Cultural Rights', *Human Rights Law Review* 11 (2011), 1, 7.

[53] S. I. Skogly and M. Gibney, 'Transnational Human Rights Obligations', *Human Rights Quarterly* 24 (2002), 781, 790–1.

[54] J. von Bernstorff, 'Extraterritoriale menschenrechtliche Staatenpflichten und Corporate Social Responsibility', *Archiv des Völkerrechts* 49 (2011), 34, 60–1.

[55] See Article 16 of the ILC Draft Articles on Responsibility of States for Internationally Wrongful Acts.

[56] ILC Draft Articles on Responsibility of States for Internationally Wrongful Acts, with Commentaries, p.66.

Guidelines contains useful guidance in this respect. It holds that a state has obligations to respect, protect and fulfil economic, social and cultural rights, *inter alia*, in situations 'over which it exercises authority or effective control' and 'over which State acts or omissions bring about foreseeable effects on the enjoyment of economic, social and cultural rights, whether within or outside its territory'.

Applying this definition to the involvement of states in the implementation of austerity programmes of other states, it seems clear that the first alternative is not relevant. States usually do not exercise authority or effective control over the situation in which the austerity programme of another state is implemented. Even the imposition of 'conditionality' by the Troika on Greece is not a formal exercise of authority or effective control in that sense. However, if it can be foreseen that specific austerity measures will have negative effects on the enjoyment of economic, social and cultural rights, the states participating in the implementation of such programmes may have a legal obligation to either actively oppose those measures or at least to refrain from any activity which would exacerbate such negative effects.[57]

E. Substance: do human rights limit or prescribe the contents of austerity programmes?

Having determined that states bear the primary responsibility to protect and promote human rights in their own territory while international organisations and other states are at least required not to interfere with measures taken (or not taken) to protect human rights in the context of austerity programmes, the analysis now turns to the substantive question: what obligations – if any – arise from international human rights concerning the development and implementation of austerity programmes? The answer to this question will be developed in three steps: first, the types of obligations states have will be briefly described in order to situate the duties of states in light of austerity programmes more precisely. Second, the content of the notion of progressive realisation of economic and social rights will be addressed. Third, an analysis will be made as to whether an infringement of economic and social rights can be justified on the basis of limitations or derogations of human rights.

[57] See also McBeth, *International Economic Actors and Human Rights*, p. 54.

I. State obligations to respect, to protect and to fulfil human rights

State duties under human rights law are usually classified on the basis of a triple typology of obligations, i.e. the obligation to respect, the obligation to protect and the obligation to fulfil.[58] The obligation to respect requires that states abstain from interfering directly or indirectly with the enjoyment of human rights. This includes refraining from policies which would directly or indirectly deny individuals access to food, water and shelter, for example.[59] States implementing austerity programmes usually do not pursue these kinds of actions. Cutting back public expenditure on social and health policies may result in a *de facto* deprivation of individuals of access to health care and social security, but this would not be regarded as an infringement of the obligation to respect, because it is not a direct interference in the health of individuals. However, states are prohibited from discriminating between different groups with respect to social and other benefits. This may be of greater relevance in the context of austerity programmes, in particular if states cut back benefits for immigrants or certain minority groups while maintaining the level of services or benefits for (the majority of) their citizens, as indicated in the Concluding Observations on Spain.[60]

The obligation to protect requires state parties to prevent third parties, including private corporations, from interfering with the enjoyment of human rights.[61] For example, states may be required to adopt and effectively implement measures which restrain third parties from denying individuals access to adequate water and from polluting or inequitably extracting from water resources.[62] This obligation is relevant in the context of privatisation policies which are often a key element of austerity programmes. The state may be required, through legislation and administrative measures, to prevent a privatised utilities company from deliberately cutting individuals off from the supply of water or energy.

[58] Ssenyonjo, *Economic Social and Cultural Rights in International Law*, pp.23 ff.

[59] See Committee on Economic, Social and Cultural Right, General Comment No. 12, The Right to Adequate Food (Article 11), E/C.12/1999/5, 12 May 1999, para. 15 and General Comment No. 15 (2002), The Right to Water (Articles 11 and 12), E/C.12/2002/11, 20 January 2003, para. 21.

[60] See note 5.

[61] O. de Schutter, *International Human Rights Law* (Cambridge University Press, 2010), p. 365.

[62] General Comment No. 15, para. 23.

Lastly, the obligation to fulfil requires states to take positive measures to assist individuals and communities to enjoy the relevant human right. Depending on the circumstances, states may also be obliged to provide goods and services (e.g., food and water) directly in circumstances where individuals or a group are unable, for reasons beyond their control, to gain access to these goods and services by the means at their disposal.[63] This obligation is of greatest relevance in the context of austerity programmes, because cutting back the expenditure on health, education and social services may result directly in a reduction of the possibility of individuals to enjoy their rights. As a consequence, the concept of a 'minimal state' which does not provide any public services or social benefits cannot be reconciled with the obligation to fulfil.[64]

Nevertheless, it is important to recall that economic, social and cultural rights in particular, do not require or prohibit a particular economic system. The Committee on Economic, Social and Cultural Rights underlined this in its General Comment No. 3 on the nature of states' obligations published in 1999.[65] The Committee noted that in terms of political and economic systems the ICESCR 'is neutral and its principles cannot accurately be described as being predicated exclusively upon the need for, or the desirability of a socialist or a capitalist system, or a mixed, centrally planned, or laissez-faire economy, or upon any other particular approach.' The Committee reaffirmed 'that the rights recognized in the Covenant are susceptible of realization within the context of a wide variety of economic and political systems, provided only that the interdependence and indivisibility of the two sets of human rights, as affirmed inter alia in the preamble to the Covenant, is recognized and reflected in the system in question.'[66]

II. Progressive realisation of economic, social and cultural human rights

As mentioned above, economic and social rights do not have to be implemented immediately to their full extent. In fact, since the realisation of these rights requires the employment of public resources and not

[63] *Ibid.*, para. 25. [64] Saiz, 'Rights in Recession?', 282.

[65] Committee on Economic, Social and Cultural Rights, General Comment No. 3 (1999), The Nature of States Parties Obligations (Article 2, para.1), E/1991/23, 14 December 1990, para. 8.

[66] *Ibid.*

'just' the adoption and implementation of laws and regulations,[67] the ICESCR allows states to realise economic and social rights in a progressive manner, paying due respect to the state's resources. Other international human rights treaties containing economic and social rights, such as the CRPD, also contain this principle (see Article 4(2) CRPD). The progressive realisation of economic and social rights offers states the necessary flexibility to fulfil their obligations, reflecting the difficulties involved for any country in ensuring the full realisation of those rights.[68]

The notion of progressive realisation of human rights should not be misunderstood as an excuse for states to take only minimal steps towards the realisation of economic and social rights, claiming a lack of resources. Furthermore, the requirement to progressively realise economic and social human rights should also not be misinterpreted to mean that none of these rights could be judicially enforceable or self-executing. In fact, the non-discrimination obligations which are inherent in every economic and social human right and which are explicitly mentioned in some provisions of the ICESCR can be directly applicable in judicial proceedings.

1. Core minimum standards

Despite the flexibility of the notion of progressive realisation, it is generally accepted in human rights law that economic and social rights contain minimum core obligations which every state must strive to fulfil.[69] The thinking behind this assumption is that the provisions of the ICESCR must have a minimum element of obligations without which they could not be considered 'law'. Those minimum standards are absolute and must be met by every country regardless of its level of development or available resources.[70] This also means that austerity programmes cannot lead to a situation which would fall below the threshold for fulfilling those core obligations. States should also ensure that their obligations arising from any debt repayment or restructuring agreement or arrangement do not hinder them from realising the minimum core standards.[71]

In its General Comments, the Committee on Economic, Social and Cultural Rights indicated which elements it considers to represent these

[67] O'Connell, *Vindicating Socio-Economic Rights*, p. 1.

[68] General Comment No. 3, para. 9. [69] *Ibid.*, paras. 10 and 11.

[70] Ssenyonjo, *Economic Social and Culutral Rights in International Law*, pp. 66–7.

[71] Guiding Principles on Foreign Debt and Human Rights, para. 16.

core obligations for the respective rights. Regarding the right to health the Committee considered the following to be core obligations: ensuring access to health facilities, goods and services on a non-discriminatory basis, especially for vulnerable or marginalised groups; ensuring access to the minimum essential food which is nutritionally adequate and safe, to ensure freedom from hunger to everyone; ensuring access to basic shelter, housing and sanitation, and an adequate supply of safe and potable water; provision of essential drugs; ensuring equitable distribution of all health facilities, goods and services; and the adoption and implementation of a national public health strategy and plan of action.[72] For the right to social security core obligations require a state party 'to ensure access to a social security scheme that provides a minimum essential level of benefits to all individuals and families that will enable them to acquire at least essential health care, basic shelter and housing, water and sanitation, foodstuffs, and the most basic forms of education.'[73]

These examples show that core obligations include non-discriminatory access to existing goods, services and facilities as well as providing a minimum set of these goods, services and facilities which are necessary for the physical and social survival of individuals and groups. States implementing austerity programmes cannot deviate from these minimum core obligations. From a practical point of view, the non-discriminatory part of the core obligations seems more relevant in this context, as shown by the comments of the Committee on Spain mentioned at the beginning of the chapter.[74]

2. Retrogressive measures

As mentioned above, an essential element of austerity programmes is the reduction of public spending on wages, benefits and services. In the context of the obligation to progressively realise economic and social rights this raises the question of whether this obligation prohibits specific retrogressive measures in social programmes. In other words, while

[72] General Comment No. 15, para. 43.

[73] Committee on Economic, Social and Cultural Rights, General Comment No. 19, The Right to Social Security (2008), E/C.12/GC/19, para. 59 (a). This core obligation is qualified by the following sentence: 'If a State party cannot provide this minimum level for all risks and contingencies within its maximum available resources, the Committee recommends that the State party, after a wide process of consultation, select a core group of social risks and contingencies.'

[74] See supra note 5.

it is accepted that progressive realisation refers to a gradual approach of moving forward step-by-step, it is less clear whether states are free to move backwards by reducing the resources they spend on the realisation of their obligation to fulfil. This question is not only relevant regarding austerity programmes, but also with regard to a general decrease of the state's available resources due to economic and financial crises.[75]

The Committee on Economic, Social and Cultural Rights takes a particularly sceptical view concerning the legality of retrogressive measures.[76] In General Comment No. 3 it takes the view that 'any deliberately retrogressive measures in that regard would require the most careful consideration and would need to be fully justified by reference to the totality of the rights provided for in the Covenant and in the context of the full use of the maximum available resources.'[77] In General Comment No. 15 on the right to water, the Committee declares that

> there is a strong presumption that retrogressive measures taken in relation to the right to water are prohibited under the Covenant. If any deliberately retrogressive measures are taken, the state party has the burden of proving that they have been introduced after the most careful consideration of all alternatives and that they are duly justified by reference to the totality of the rights provided for in the Covenant in the context of the full use of the State party's maximum available resources.[78]

General Comment No. 19 spells out the specific issues the Committee will look at when assessing retrogressive measures:

> The Committee will look carefully at whether: (a) there was reasonable justification for the action; (b) alternatives were comprehensively examined; (c) there was genuine participation of affected groups in examining the proposed measures and alternatives; (d) the measures were directly or indirectly discriminatory; (e) the measures will have a sustained impact on the realization of the right to social security, an unreasonable impact on acquired social security rights or whether an individual or group is deprived of access to the minimum essential level of social security; and (f) whether there was an independent review of the measures at the national level.[79]

The Guiding Principles on foreign debt and human rights adopt a similar approach. Paras. 19 and 20 of those principles stipulate that states have

[75] Saiz, 'Rights in Recession?', 283.

[76] Similar Ssenyonjo, *Economic, Social and Cultural Rights in International Law*, pp. 67–8.

[77] General Comment No. 3, para. 9. [78] General Comment No. 15, para. 19.

[79] General Comment No. 19, para. 41.

an obligation to avoid retrogressive measures, 'that is, any deliberate action which has the effect of impairing the advancement in economic, social and cultural rights and thus hindering the continuous realization of these rights' and that they 'should ensure that their rights and obligations arising from external debt, particularly the obligation to repay external debt, do not lead to the deliberate adoption of retrogressive measures'.[80]

From the outset, these quotations indicate that retrogressive measures are not completely prohibited, but that a strong presumption of incompatibility of retrogressive measures with the ICESCR exists. More importantly, the quotes suggest that any deliberate measure, i.e., a measure which cannot be justified, would violate the Covenant. The Committee on Economic, Social and Cultural Rights (ESC Committee) suggested that a state party has the burden of proof to demonstrate that any retrogressive measure was only adopted after considering all alternatives and that it was justified on the basis of all rights provided for in the Covenant taking the full use of the state party's maximum available resources into account.

Whether or not a state has violated the prohibition of deliberate and unjustifiable retrogressive measures can only be determined on a case-by-case basis. However, a few general observations are possible. First, if a measure was put in place without considering its impact on human rights at all, it would seem difficult to justify that measure. Second, if alternatives with a more limited impact on human rights are available and they achieve the same result, they must be chosen. Third, any measure with a discriminatory effect is presumed to be a violation of the Covenant unless that discrimination can be justified on the basis of the foregoing principles.

Moreover, austerity measures which only or predominantly affect human rights, because they focus on social and welfare programmes while leaving other sectors untouched, would be particularly problematic. For example, cuts in government spending on health and education, while not reducing expenditure on weapons for the armed forces is likely to violate the principle of non-retrogression.[81] It can thus be concluded that retrogressive measures are only reconcilable with the ICESCR if they can be justified on the basis of the standards developed by the Committee in its General Comments. This leads to the issue of

[80] Guiding Principles on Foreign Debt and Human Rights, paras. 19 and 20.

[81] R. Balakrishnan and D. Elson, 'Auditing Economic Policy in the Light of Obligations on Economic and Social Rights', 5 *Essex Human Rights Review* (2008), 6.

limitations of economic and social human rights and the conditions for invoking these limitations.

III. *Limitations of, and derogations from, economic and social human rights*

Human rights are generally not conceived as rights without any limitations.[82] International human rights treaties typically contain limitation clauses either in each article granting an individual right as in the ICCPR (e.g., Article 18(3) or 19(3) ICCPR) or in general limitation clauses such as Article 29(2) of the Universal Declaration of Human Rights. Such limitation provisions allow states to balance their obligations under specific human rights with other legitimate public policies. The ICESCR is no exception in this context. It contains a general limitation clause: according to its Article 4 the Covenant's Parties recognise that a state may subject the enjoyment of economic, social and cultural rights 'only to such limitations as are determined by law only in so far as this may be compatible with the nature of these rights and solely for the purpose of promoting the general welfare in a democratic society.'

While writings and case law – both by the Committee on Human Rights and by Regional Human Rights Courts – on such limitations for civil and political rights are abundant, Article 4 ICESCR has not yet received much attention in the academic literature and in the practice of the Committee on Economic, Social and Cultural Rights.[83] This can be partly explained by the understanding of the notion of progressive realisation in Article 2(1) ICESCR. The *traveaux préparatoires* of the ICESCR seem to suggest that the drafters of the Covenant did not want to apply Article 4 to retrogressive measures which a state takes because of resource constraints. Instead this was considered to be part of Article 2(1) ICESCR.[84] The Committee on Economic, Social and Cultural Rights seems to have adopted this understanding. Article 4 would then apply to any limitations necessary to pursue general

[82] F. Mégret, 'Nature of Obligations', in D. Moeckli, S. Shah and S. Sivakumaran (eds.), *International Human Rights Law* (Oxford University Press, 2010), pp. 140 ff.

[83] A. Müller, 'Limitations to and Derogations from Economic, Social and Cultural Rights', *Human Rights Law Review* (2009), 557, 566.

[84] P. Alston and G. Quinn, 'The Nature and Scope of States Parties' Obligations under the International Covenant on Economic, Social and Cultural Rights', *Human Rights Quarterly* 9 (1987), 156, 194.

welfare, but not to those measures taken (or not taken) due to the lack of resources.

This raises the question whether measures taken in the context of austerity programmes fall under the prohibition of deliberate retrogressive measures in accordance with Article 2(1) ICESCR or whether such measures should be considered as general limitations under Article 4 ICESCR. As indicated by the quotes from the Committee's General Comments and Concluding Remarks cited above, it can be assumed that the Committee treats retrogressive measures due to austerity programmes as an issue under Article 2(1) ICESCR. Yet, this is not the only possible perspective. It could also be argued that austerity measures are taken in order to reduce public debts and to regain fiscal independence, which could constitute elements of the general welfare within the meaning of Article 4 ICESCR.

However, the precise categorisation of austerity measures may be more of academic interest than of practical relevance. As shown by Müller, the requirements for limitations contained in Article 4 ICESCR ('determined by law', 'compatible with the nature of the rights', 'promoting the general welfare in a democratic society' and the principle of proportionality) may have similar effects to the requirements determined by the Committee on Economic, Social and Cultural Rights for the legality of retrogressive measures according to Article 2(1) ICESCR.[85] This leads Müller to conclude that the distinction between Article 2(1) and Article 4 ICESCR should be abandoned.

Even those who do not want to go that far will have to concede that regardless of which provision applies to austerity measures, a key requirement is the justification of the measure as proportionate or necessary. In addition, a deviation from the core minimum obligations may not be acceptable. It can therefore be concluded that economic and social human rights do not prohibit reductions in social spending or cuts in welfare programmes *per se*. Apart from a very basic standard, economic and social human rights do not establish an absolute level of social programmes which states must provide at all times. However, international human rights require that states can justify these measures as proportionate and necessary. The central aspect of this justification is the identification of alternatives and the proof that there is really no alternative to the measures taken in the context of austerity programmes.

[85] Müller, 'Limitations to and Derogations From Economic, Social and Cultural Rights', 590–1.

Identifying alternatives and proving that they were not suitable are elements of a political debate. Economic and social human rights may therefore be of greater relevance concerning the political decision-making process than its concrete outcomes.

Before developing the consequences of this perspective further and with a view to processes, a brief look at the question of derogations seems desirable. Civil and political human rights are often subject to derogation clauses which allow the parties to deviate from their human rights obligations in times of a public emergency which threatens the life of the nation, such as Article 4 ICCPR. However, parties may only derogate from their obligations to the extent strictly required by the emergency and provided that the derogations do not involve discrimination. Furthermore, human rights treaties usually contain a list of human rights from which no derogation is possible. The ICESCR contains no such derogation clause. In light of this, it seems safe to conclude that derogation from economic, social and cultural rights in times of public emergency is not permissible. This supposition is also supported by state practice and the practice of human rights organs.[86]

F. Discourse about alternatives: can human rights shape economic policy decision-making?

The above-mentioned considerations concerning limitations point to a function of human rights, in particular economic and social rights, which is increasingly discussed and recognised: economic and social human rights require political debates about the effects of economic and social policies and may therefore be powerful tools to reopen space for political debates about alternatives to dominant discourses.[87] At the outset it should be noted that human rights need to be considered at all stages of the development, design and implementation of any policy measure. This applies to monetary policies[88] as well as all forms of austerity programmes.

A debate about the necessity of austerity measures will inevitably include an assessment of the economic consequences of these measures. While there is no agreement in economic theory on the

86 *Ibid.* 592 ff. 87 O'Connell, *Vindicating Socio-Economic Rights*, p. 16.

88 T. Cottier and L. Satragno, 'The Potential of Law and Legal Methodology in Monetary Affairs', Chapter 16, this volume.

ultimate effects of such measures, many commentators have shown the devastating effects of such programmes on internal demand, which triggered severe economic recessions.[89] International human rights standards cannot determine the outcome of such debates, but they require that policy measures which limit the enjoyment of economic and social rights are assessed and evaluated in an open decision-making process. As clearly indicated in Article 4 ICESCR, but also by general human rights doctrine, limitations cannot be justified unless they are decided upon in a democratic manner and provided for by the law.

Discourses about the justification of any limitation of economic and social human rights will not only have to assess the economic and political consequences of austerity measures, but also need to consider possible alternatives. Among them are other potential means for reducing government spending, for example concerning military or security expenditures. More importantly, however, any debate about the proportionality or necessity of austerity measures also needs to consider ways of increasing state income through taxation. Human rights are therefore also relevant in the context of budgetary policy.[90] In the case of the eurozone members, another option which would need to be discussed is the withdrawal from the European Monetary Union and the re-establishment of national sovereignty over exchange rate policies.

For the sake of clarity and in order to avoid misunderstandings it should be reiterated that economic and social rights do not provide any substantial answers to these questions apart from the core minimum standards discussed above. As explained above, social and economic human rights do not require a particular economic system. Consequently, they cannot offer much guidance in terms of the outcome of an open debate. Yet, they require debates about distribution of income in resources within a particular country and on a global level.[91] In addition, they clearly question conventional wisdom and the often criticised economic and political

[89] E.g., P. Krugman, 'Legends of the Fail', *New York Times*, 10 November 2011. Generally, see M. Weisbrot, R. Ray, J. Johnston, J. A. Cardeso and J. A. Monteciso, 'IMF-Supported Macroeconomic Policies and the World Recession: A Look at Forty-One Borrowing Countries', Center for Economic and Policy Research, October 2009, www.cepr.net/documents/publications/imf-2009-10.pdf.

[90] O'Connell, *Vindicating Socio-Economic Rights*, p. 19.

[91] Saiz, 'Rights in Recession?', 287.

'*pensée unique*',[92] which does not seem to accept any alternative or heterodox visions or ideas.

The debates about alternatives to austerity measures need to take place at the domestic and at the international level. It is clear from Article 2 (1) ICESCR that states are obliged to realise economic and social rights through national measures and through international cooperation. On a more practical level this means that it is not sufficient for austerity measures to be formally legitimised by decisions of a national parliament. The events surrounding not only the Greek crisis, but also the crisis management in Italy, have clearly shown that formal parliamentary approval of austerity measures taken without a fully informed public debate about consequences and alternatives only reduces the legitimacy of the measures adopted and further erodes public trust in political institutions. If anything, adopting policy measures in a context which constitutes less than the shell of a democratic process violates economic and social human rights.

G. Conclusion and outlook

The arguments developed in this chapter do not claim to provide full and conclusive answers to the question raised in the introduction. However, they show that economic and social human rights are of the utmost relevance in the context of establishing and implementing austerity measures. Not only the states adopting such measures, but also international organisations and other states participating in such programmes are equally required to take human rights into consideration. Economic and social human rights do not prohibit austerity programmes or retrogressive measures taken in a particular context. However, they do establish a presumption of incompatibility which a state can rebut if the measures taken can be justified on the basis of a careful consideration of their effects and of any available alternative. In addition, no deviation from the core minimum obligations is possible.

The most important result of the foregoing analysis, however, is that human rights are significant in policy-making. Economic and social human rights do not predetermine the outcome of a political decision (except for the contents of core minimum obligations), but they may

92 I. Ramonet, 'La pensée unique', *Le Monde diplomatique*, January 1995, www.monde-diplomatique.fr/1995/01/RAMONET/1144.

shape the process of decision-making: they require an assessment of the consequences of a particular measure to determine its social and its economic effects as well as deliberation on possible alternatives and their effects. Most importantly, this assessment and deliberation must take place in an open and democratic decision-making process. Economic and social human rights therefore complement political human rights, which also require deliberation, openness and transparency.

20

International economic law and macro-prudential regulation

KERN ALEXANDER

A. Introduction

The origins of the financial crisis of 2007–9 have attracted a great deal of attention from academics and policy-makers, with most observers agreeing that the crisis was triggered by a liquidity crisis in the wholesale securities debt markets which later intensified with the collapse of Lehman Brothers and other banks, resulting in costly regulatory interventions and taxpayer bail-outs.[1] International regulatory reform efforts identified macro-prudential regulatory and supervisory weaknesses that allowed financial institutions to expand their balance sheets, along with their leverage, without regard to risks that were building up across the financial system.[2] Central bankers failed to understand the linkages between monetary policy and prudential financial regulation and, in particular, how accommodative interest rate policies can cause asset price bubbles and high levels of leverage in the financial system which can result in a severe economic downturn.[3] The prevailing approach

1 M. Brunnermeier, A. Crockett, C. Goodhart, A. Persaud and H. Shin, *The Fundamental Principles of Financial Regulation*, Geneva Reports on the World Economy 11 (Geneva: International Centre for Banking and Monetary Studies, 2009) p. 18. See K. Alexander, J. Eatwell, A. Persaud and R. Reoch, 'Financial Supervision and Crisis Management in the EU' (Brussels: European Parliament, 2007). See also *Financial Crisis Inquiry Commission Report* (Washington, DC: Government Printing Office, January 2011).

2 See, generally, T. Cottier, *International Law in Financial Regulation and Monetary Affairs* (Oxford University Press, 2012).

3 See Transcripts of the Meeting of the Federal Open Market Committee of the Board of Governors of the Federal Reserve System (7 August 2007). The minutes reveal that the members of the Open Market Committee did not understand the nature of the systemic risks that had built up in the financial system and the impact on the macroeconomy. E.g., Committee Vice Chairman, Donald Kohn, stated that '[m]y forecast for the most likely outcome for output over the next few years is . . . growth a little below potential for a few quarters, held down by the housing correction, and the unemployment rate rising a little further.' He added '[t]he most likely outcome (of the financial crisis) is that it will be limited in duration and effect.' *Ibid.*

to prudential regulation at the time of the crisis was essentially micro-prudential, that is, it was concerned mainly with the stability of individual financial institutions, and the management of risks on bank balance sheets, while ignoring structural risks across the financial system, such as asset price correlations, aggregate levels of leverage and counter-party credit and liquidity risks in wholesale securities and derivatives markets, and the role of interest rates and exchange rates in propagating these risks across markets and countries.[4] The main focus of macro-prudential regulation, in contrast, is to mitigate systemic risks across the financial system, which involves recognising the linkages between institutions and investors across markets and the risks embedded in complex financial instruments and the infrastructure of the financial system. Macro-prudential supervision could include, for example, monitoring cross-border capital movements and exchange rates, interest rates and the rate of growth of credit and the money supply relative to the rate of the growth in the broader economy.

The macro-prudential design of international financial regulation will have important implications for the international regime of rules and standards that govern financial regulation and related areas of international economic law. This chapter will address how international financial regulation is being redesigned to incorporate macro-prudential principles and rules. It does so by analysing how the international financial regulatory regime has evolved from what was essentially a micro-prudential framework to one that is primarily based on macro-prudential principles. The chapter then analyses how recent international regulatory initiatives by the Financial Stability Board in coordination with the IMF are attempting to redesign international financial regulation with a macro-prudential focus, and points out the weaknesses and gaps in this coordination. And, finally, it will offer some observations on the question of whether international trade law commitments undertaken in the World Trade Organization (WTO) General Agreement on Trade in Services (GATS) limit WTO members' policy autonomy to implement macro-prudential regulatory reforms. Before addressing these issues, the chapter will review the origins of the global financial crisis and how it has changed the philosophy of financial regulation.

B. The crisis and the need for macro-prudential regulation

The global credit and financial crisis, which began in 2007, intensified in 2008 with the collapse of Lehman Brothers, and became a sovereign debt

[4] Brunnermeier *et al.*, *The Fundamental Principles of Financial Regulation*, pp. 19–20.

crisis in 2010, has been the subject of much debate and analysis. The causes of the crisis have been attributed to over-expansive monetary policies in developed countries which led to a property and share price bubble in the US, the UK and many other developed countries. Other factors which induced the crisis include bank pay structures, which rewarded speculative trading, and the design of complex investment instruments which were based on high levels of leverage. Most large banks and financial institutions failed to measure and manage the risks to which their highly-leveraged balance sheets were exposed. Regulators and supervisors also played a role by failing to oblige banks to hold adequate levels of capital and also by failing to detect the serious liquidity exposures of financial institutions in the wholesale funding markets and the dramatic build-up of leverage in the financial system. Financial innovation took the form of securitisation, special purpose vehicles, structured investment vehicles and other financing conduits which were used to avoid regulatory requirements and to drive up leverage in the financial system. The limited liability ownership structure of banks and other financial companies created incentives for shareholders to demand higher risk-adjusted returns, which led to dangerously high levels of risk in the financial system. Also, credit rating agencies underestimated and under-priced the risks of structured finance products, and individuals were allowed by regulators and banks to take on excessive levels of indebtedness to purchase homes.

Few observers paid attention to the systemic risks which had arisen from global structural imbalances and short-term foreign exchange risks from the carry trade. A synchronised economic boom led to excessive liquidity. This was exacerbated by perverse regulatory incentives created by international soft law standards such as Basel I. Although Basel II enhanced regulatory capital requirements for certain financial instruments, it was pro-cyclical and its credit and market risk models failed to take adequate account of correlations between different asset classes and liquidity risks.[5] Interconnected financial agents and institutions in the

[5] The Basel II regulatory framework allowed banks to devise models that relied on their own internal default data and statistical value-at-risk models to determine regulatory capital. Banks were already using these models before Basel II was adopted to calculate their economic capital. The financial crisis demonstrates how these models failed to take account of the liquidity risks and counter-party credit risks in the wholesale debt markets while underestimating correlations across asset classes in the mortgage-backed securities market. These factors contributed significantly to an undercapitalisation of the banking system which weakened its ability to absorb losses when the crisis began. See K. Alexander, ‘Rebuilding International Financial Regulation’, *Journal of Banking Law* 23:5 (2011), 337–44.

capital markets trading in collateralised debt obligations and credit default swaps contributed significantly to systemic risk. Moreover, accounting standards impeded adequate provisions and valuation of assets when wholesale markets suddenly collapsed.

In addition, the crisis management measures of the G-10 regulators and central banks failed to cope with the fallout from the crisis. Central banks, including the Bank of England and the Board of Governors of the Federal Reserve, were slow to recognise the dangers from the collapse of confidence in interbank markets in late 2007.[6] Developed countries failed to learn from the 1990s Asian crisis and the Scandinavian and Japanese crises of the early 1990s that losses must be recognised early and bad assets on bank balance sheets must be separated from viable assets through the use of 'bad' banks.[7] Market panic and the collapse of confidence in counterparties should have triggered faster official guarantees.[8] US authorities failed to control the fallout from the Lehman Brothers collapse and most European states had inadequate resolution regimes and were unable to restructure the balance sheets of their largest and most systemically important banks. The fallout from the financial crisis has raised issues concerning the scope and role of international economic law in financial regulation.[9]

[6] In March 2007, at a time when US mortgage loan defaults were increasing sharply and mortgage lenders were going out of business, Federal Reserve Chairman Ben Bernanke testified before the US Congress that '[t]he impact on the broader economy and financial markets of the problems in the subprime market seems likely to be contained'. See also Federal Open Market Committee of the Board of Governors of the Federal Reserve System, Transcript of Minutes of Meeting of 7 August 2007, with Ben Bernanke stating after the crisis had begun '[m]y own feeling is that we should try to resist a rate cut until it is really very clear from economic data and other information that it is needed,' and he went on 'I'd really prefer to avoid giving any impression of a bailout or a put, if we can'. See also William Poole, President of the Federal Reserve Bank of St Louis, stating '[m]y own bet is the financial market upset is not going to change fundamentally what's going on in the real economy'. Based on these comments, it is apparent that US central bankers had no understanding of the risks faced by the financial system nor how to respond to the crisis once it began.

[7] See Mariko Fujii and Masahiro Kawai, 'Lessons from Japan's Banking Crisis – 1991–2005' in K. Alexander and R. Dhumale (eds.), *Research Handbook on International Financial Regulation* (Cheltenham: Edward Elgar, 2012), pp. 259–84.

[8] It was not until December 2007, after the crisis had intensified, that the US government established the Term Auction Loan Facility, the first in a series of government subsidised loans to the financial sector.

[9] See C. Tietje and M. Lehmann, 'The Role and Prospects of International Law in Financial Regulation and Supervision', *Journal of International Economic* Law 13:3 (2010), 663–82 and C. Tietje, 'The Role of Law in Monetary Affairs: Taking Stock', Chapter 2, this volume.

C. International economic law and financial regulation – general observations

Within the sphere of international economic affairs, sovereign authority ultimately resides in the member states which have decided to establish organisations like the IMF, the World Bank and the WTO to achieve specified economic objectives. In the case of the IMF, these objectives are to promote international monetary cooperation and exchange rate stability in order to facilitate balanced economic growth and increased international trade[10] – so member countries, their companies and private citizens can pursue their economic activities according to the rules of the game, subject to IMF treaty powers of surveillance and conditionality, if a country receives IMF financial assistance. The GATS provides a treaty regime governing members' negotiations of specific liberalisation commitments.[11] Regarding cross-border trade in financial services, WTO members must respect their GATS commitments and obligations but retain the discretion to take regulatory measures for 'prudential reasons' that may depart from the commitments and obligations so long as there is no avoidance thereof.[12]

In contrast, international financial regulation is primarily a system of 'international soft law' – meaning standards, guidelines, interpretations and other statements that are not legally binding or enforceable according to formal techniques of international law, but are nevertheless capable of exerting a powerful influence over the behaviour of countries, public entities and private parties.[13] Despite its legally non-binding nature, international financial 'soft law' has had an enormous impact

[10] See Articles of Agreement of the International Monetary Fund, Article 1.

[11] See World Trade Organization Agreements: Marrakesh Agreement Establishing the World Trade Organization and its Agreements (15 April 1994) reprinted in *The Legal Texts* (Cambridge University Press, 1999), *International Legal Materials* 33: 1143.

[12] The GATS Annex on Financial Services, para. 2(a) provides:

> Notwithstanding any other provision of the Agreement, a member shall not be prevented from taking measures for prudential reasons, including for the protection of investors, depositors, policy holders, or persons to whom a fiduciary duty is owed by a financial service supplier, or to ensure the integrity and stability of the financial system. Where such measures do not conform with the provisions of the Agreement, they shall not be used as a means of avoiding the Member's commitments or obligations under the Agreement.'

[13] See M. Giovanoli (ed.), *International Monetary Law: Issues for the New Millennium* (Oxford University Press, 2000), Chapter 1 and R. Lastra, *Legal Foundations of International Monetary Stability* (Oxford University Press, 2006), Chapter 14.

on state regulatory practices,[14] especially in the area of prudential bank regulation. The international body responsible for devising and overseeing the implementation of international banking regulation standards is the Basel Committee on Banking Supervision.[15] The Committee is responsible for the Basel Capital Accord and the Basel Concordat – probably the most important and influential international financial regulatory agreements – which establish respectively regulatory capital standards for banking institutions that operate on a cross-border basis and the principle of consolidated supervision that allocates jurisdictional authority over a bank's cross-border operations between home and host state supervisory authorities.[16] The Basel Committee's effectiveness was called into question during the crisis because of the failure of the Basel Capital Accord's (Basel II) risk-weighted measurement approach for calculating bank regulatory capital. The Committee has embarked on Basel III, which is designed to enhance and increase regulatory capital and to link its calculation to macro-prudential economic factors.[17]

International legal scholarship also recognises the concept of soft provisions within treaties or other binding legal instruments. See Sir Joseph Gold, *Interpretation: the International Monetary Fund and International Law* (London: Kluwer International Law, 1996) (discussing how soft law emerges in the gaps of the IMF Articles of Agreement). See also Christopher Brummer, *Soft Law in the Global Financial System* (Cambridge University Press, 2011), Chapter 3.

14 The international standards governing English cricket provide an analogy to the governance of international financial soft law. In cricket, the international equivalent to the Basel Committee or Financial Stability Board is the International Cricket Council, which promulgates the Code of Conduct and appoints umpires and referees for international matches; at the national or regional (i.e., EU) level are the umpires who specify the precise rules of play to ensure these rules are followed; and, finally, come the players (i.e., market participants) who wield bat and ball under the umpire's eagle eye!

15 Also, the Basel Committee has attempted to increase the accountability and legitimacy of its international standard-setting process by increasing its membership to twenty countries, with the addition of Australia, Brazil, China, India, South Korea, Mexico and Russia as full-voting members. In 2012, its full membership included: the central banks and national supervisory authorities of the following countries: Argentina, Australia, Brazil, Canada, China, France, Germany, Hong Kong SAR, India, Indonesia, Italy, Japan, South Korea, Mexico, the Netherlands, Russia, Saudi Arabia, Singapore, South Africa, Spain, Switzerland, Turkey, UK, US and non-state representatives including the European Central Bank, international financial institutions, international Standard-setting bodies and Committees of Central Bank Experts.

16 See K. Alexander, 'Global Financial Standard Setting, the G10 Committees, and International Economic Law', *Brooklyn Journal of International Law* 34 (2009), 861.

17 As discussed below, Basel III requires an increase in the level of tier one regulatory capital to 7.0 per cent (including a capital conservation buffer), a tighter definition of tier one capital to include only ordinary common shares and retained earnings, an additional 2.5 per cent countercyclical capital ratio (yet to be determined for

D. Micro-prudential supervision and international financial regulation

Before the crisis, micro-prudential regulation and supervision mainly focused on individual financial institutions and their investors and how they managed balance sheet risks in a liberalised financial system where capital movements, interest rates and exchange rates were (and remain) deregulated. Although micro-prudential regulation had been utilised by many national regulators prior to the 1970s, it became a primary focus of bank supervisors in the 1970s after countries began to dismantle the macro-prudential controls that had been used to maintain the Bretton Woods fixed exchange rate regime.[18] Micro-prudential regulation was premised on the notion that if bank supervisors could ensure that banks and other financial firms were managing their risks well on an individual basis they would not only be profitable and stable but the systemic risks across the financial system would be negligible.

During the Bretton Woods era, it was necessary for national authorities to maintain macroeconomic controls, such as limits on cross-border portfolio capital movements and on foreign exchange rate convertibility and operational restrictions on the banking business. These controls were deemed necessary to ensure that credit growth and other financial market activities did not undermine or put at risk the government's management of exchange rate and interest rate policies to serve broader economic growth. In contrast, the micro-prudential regulatory rules and supervisory practices that emerged after the Bretton Woods period focused on how individual firms managed their balance sheet risks, but failed to appreciate the effects of their risk-taking on the broader financial system and economy and how the structure of the financial

implementation); and liquidity requirements that include a ratio for stable wholesale funding, liquidity coverage ratios, and an overall leverage ratio. The Basel Committee also agreed on an additional capital charge of up to 2.5 per cent regulatory capital for large and interconnected systemically important financial institutions (SIFIs).

[18] The IMF had administered the exchange rates of the major reserve currencies by pegging their value to the US dollar and in turn pegging the US dollar's value to the price of an ounce of gold. During this period, the IMF also used its powers of surveillance to ensure that IMF member countries were complying with their obligations under the fixed exchange rate regime and used its power of conditionality to require (mainly) developed countries which were experiencing economic imbalances, and which sought short-term financial relief, to make adjustments to rebalance their economies, including in some cases to change the par value of their exchange rates. See K. Alexander, R. Dhumale and J. Eatwell, *Global Governance of Financial Systems* (Oxford University Press, 2005), pp. 41–2.

system – the interconnectedness of banks and other financial firms and correlations in asset prices and investor behaviour – could propagate systemic risks across the financial system.

The lifting of macro-prudential controls in the post-Bretton Woods system was a dramatic shift of financial policy and regulatory attitudes away from the notion that the financial system was to be tightly regulated and utilised as an auxiliary to serve broader economic policy objectives, towards a liberalised model of financial governance in which it was presumed that banks and their investors could do more to support economic growth by following their own self-interests in greater revenues and profits unrestrained by macro-prudential controls. Bankers and investors were presumed to understand the risks they were taking on through increased leverage and transferring risks away from regulated institutions to off-balance-sheet entities that were not subject to prudential controls and that the systemic risks of any miscalculation would be minimal.

Throughout the 1970s and 1980s the IMF and OECD pressured countries to lift macro-prudential controls by liberalising their capital accounts in order to attract increased foreign capital portfolio investment. The IMF used conditionality to pressure both developed[19] and developing countries to reduce inflation by limiting the money supply and increasing interest rates to control inflation and to reduce government budget deficits, even if it resulted in higher unemployment and lower economic growth. IMF conditionality substantially extended its scope and usage in the 1980s and 1990s as it became a major policy instrument to pressure countries into deregulating their financial systems and liberalising macro-prudential controls, such as capital account convertibility.[20] The increasing openness of global capital markets – especially debt markets – allowed large US, European and Japanese banks to grow dramatically in size and in the scope of their operations

[19] The IMF used the 1976 sterling crisis to pressure the UK to undertake internal economic adjustments that prioritised controlling inflation over economic growth policies, reducing government deficits and accepting higher unemployment and reducing corporate taxes. Kevin Hickson, *The IMF Crisis of 1976 and British Politics* (London: IB Taurus, 2005) pp. 132–6.

[20] See Randall Stone, 'The Scope of IMF Conditionality', *International Organizations* 62:4 (2008), 589–620. The IMF further used conditionality to pressure sovereign debtors in less developed countries to pay off arrears on their debts to private banks based mainly in the US and Europe. The IMF refused to provide more loans to countries which had not undertaken macro-prudential austerity measures (i.e., tax increases and government spending reductions).

and interconnectedness across financial markets. Moreover, the value of foreign financial assets as a percentage of GDP increased substantially for a large number of countries from 36 per cent in 1980 to over 110 per cent in 2004,[21] while the value of foreign exchange trading exceeded the value of foreign exchange reserves for all governments.[22] Finally, it should be noted that the post-Bretton Woods era has been accompanied by a large increase in the number of banking, currency and sovereign debt crises in comparison with the number of such crises that occurred during the Bretton Woods period.[23]

I. The changing philosophy of financial regulation: micro-prudential to macro-prudential

The micro-prudential approach to regulation and supervision has been predominantly concerned with the stability of individual financial institutions and their responses to exogenous risks.[24] However, by focusing on individual institutions, such forms of regulation tend to ignore the impact of financial institutions' risk-taking on the broader financial system. For example, the micro-prudential approach often failed to incorporate into regulatory assessments the impact of a bank's size, degree of leverage and interconnectedness with the rest of the financial system. Moreover, bank supervisors generally assumed that banks were primarily exposed to exogenous risks, that is, risks that are generated externally to the bank's operations, and that any change, for example, in their credit or market risk exposures would require them to make balance sheet adjustments (i.e., by buying or selling assets) in a more or less similar manner. Although each bank individually might be adjusting its balance sheet risk in a prudent manner, the cumulative effect of all banks acting in the same manner would be to increase system-wide risks across the financial sector. This could have the effect of exacerbating a market upturn or downturn. Indeed, the Turner

21 See Andrew Glynn, *Capitalism Unleashed* (Oxford University Press, 2008), p. 66.

22 See Mark Mazower, *Governing the World: the History of an Idea* (New York: Allen Lame, 2012), p. 350.

23 See Barry Eichengreen and Michael Bordo, 'Crises Now and Then: What Lessons from the Last Era of Financial Globalization NBER Working Paper No 8716, January 2002' asserting that between 1945 and 1971 there were just thirty-eight banking or currency crises in the world economy, whereas between 1971 and 1997 (post-Bretton Woods) there were 139 crises.

24 See Brunnermeier *et al.*, *The Fundamental Principles of Financial Regulation*, pp. 31–3.

Review (2009),[25] published in the aftermath of the crisis, argued that this sort of regulation mistakenly and fatally relied on an underlying philosophy and an ill-placed faith in market prices as accurate indicators of risk, while financial innovation was viewed to be wholly beneficial. In seeking to regulate at the level of the individual institution, regulators failed to take account of a number of internal amplifying processes which perpetuate the failure of one financial institution through affecting other institutions' balance sheets.

The financial crisis demonstrates the need to enhance the micro-prudential regulatory approach to include broader oversight of risks across the financial system and a concern for taking supervisory measures that support the stability of the financial system as a whole and take into account the interconnectivity of financial institutions and their effects on the global economy in times of crisis.[26] Macro-prudential regulation consists of three main areas: (i) adjusting the application of regulatory rules to institutions according to developments in the broader economy (i.e., countercyclical capital requirements);[27] (ii) imposing economy-wide controls on the financial sector to limit aggregate risk-taking (i.e., capital controls to limit foreign exchange risk or system-wide leverage limits); and (iii) prudential requirements for financial infrastructure or firms providing infrastructure services (i.e., capital requirements for derivative clearing houses). An extensive literature has analysed these different areas of macro-prudential regulation. However, the implications of macro-prudential regulation and supervision for international economic law and international financial regulation have not been analysed. What is clear in the macro-prudential regulatory literature thus far is the need to strike a balance between macro-prudential regulation and micro-prudential regulation: both are

[25] UK Financial Services Authority, *The Turner Review: A Regulatory Response to the Global Banking Crisis* (UK Financial Services Authority, March 2009), www.fsa.gov.uk/pubs/other/turner_review.pdf, accessed 7 August 2013.

[26] See 'Report of the High Level Group on Financial Supervision in the EU', chaired by Jacques De Larosiere (Brussels: EU Commission, 25 February 2009). See also UK Financial Services Authority, *The Turner Review* (March 2009).

[27] Under the Basel III 'Pillar 2' system, states have discretion to impose a range of measures, including additional capital requirements, on individual institutions or groups of institutions in order to address higher-than-normal risk. Therefore, theoretically, national supervisors should be able to impose higher requirements if they so wish. Experts have observed that countercyclical buffers could be difficult to implement. See Brunnermeier *et al.*, *The Fundamental Principles of Financial Regulation*, Chapter 4 (discussing design of countercyclical regulation).

necessary for maintaining financial stability and the conditions for sustainable economic growth.[28]

Despite the enthusiasm for macro-prudential regulation, it is certainly not a panacea, as it does not eliminate credit cycles in an economy. Nor does it address regulatory failure and government subsidies for banks and financial firms which create moral hazard and can induce unsustainable risk-taking. Moreover, there is an inadequate appreciation of how monetary policy and financial regulation should interact to prevent unsustainable credit cycles.

Ultimately, whereas the macro-prudential approach focuses on risks across the financial system as a whole, regulatory and policy measures must be introduced at the level of individual banks. The micro-prudential approach is focused on the individual bank and is largely rules-based and backward looking; it involves regulators asking themselves how best to handle a single bank if it falls into serious trouble.[29] In contrast, the macro-prudential approach is largely forward-looking and involves the regulator monitoring risks in the market and forecasting how they might evolve in the future; it requires discretionary authority to take measures that address risks that may not threaten the market today but which may lead to substantial risks in the future.[30] Despite these different approaches, micro-prudential regulation and supervision *and* macro-prudential regulation and supervision are not mutually exclusive.[31] Indeed, by recognising the links

[28] For instance, Stefan Ingves (2011) writes that they should reinforce, rather than conflict with, one another, and Brunnermeier *et al.* argue that the two areas of regulation should interact more. See Brunnermeier *et al.*, *The Fundamental Principles of Financial Regulation*, p. 33.

[29] Prudential Regulation Authority, *The Prudential Regulation Authority's Approach to Banking Supervision* (Prudential Regulation Authority, April 2013), p. 5, www.bankofengland.co.uk/publications/Documents/praapproach/bankingappr1304.pdf, accessed 7 August 2013. See also: Paul Tucker, 'Macro and Microprudential Supervision' (Speech at British Bankers' Association Annual International Banking Conference, London, 29 June 2011), pp. 4–5, www.bankofengland.co.uk/publications/Documents/speeches/2011/speech506.pdf, accessed 7 August 2013.

[30] As Goodhart has noted, it involves the regulators '[asking] themselves how to protect the system of banks, conditional on another bank, perhaps one of the biggest and most interconnected, having already failed.' See C. A. E. Goodhart, 'Bank Resolution in Comparative Perspective: What Lessons for Europe?', 2013, unpublished paper on file with the author, p. 10.

[31] Financial regulation is generally defined as the promulgation and development of rules, standards and guidelines that govern behaviour in financial markets (i.e., the adoption of bank capital rules), whereas financial supervision refers to the discretionary function of monitoring and assessing risks in financial markets, including whether to authorise or de-authorise firms or individuals, or to investigate breaches of regulation and if necessary to bring enforcement actions including imposing sanctions.

between micro-prudential and macro-prudential regulation, a more coherent and effective framework can be developed for mitigating excessive risk-taking in financial regulation.

II. Shadow banking

Macro-prudential regulation should also focus on the 'shadow banking' system where financial intermediation occurs outside the formal banking sector by non-bank financial firms which engage in maturity transformation and take on leverage by issuing debt-linked instruments to generate capital to invest in longer-term assets. Of particular concern are intermediaries involved in the money and credit creation process. Regulatory instruments should aim to affect the balance sheets of financial institutions by limiting the aggregate level of leverage and maturity mismatch in the financial system as a whole. These controls could be tightened during periods when there are asset price bubbles (when asset prices exceed trend economic growth) and relaxed when the economy or financial sector slumps.

The existence of other, non-bank financial institutions therefore imposes a constraint on the ability to place requirements on banks, as there is a danger of risky activities moving into non-regulated sectors. However, this also suggests that it may make sense to consider reforms across the sector as a whole, rather than focusing too much on particular types of institutions. Indeed, Goodhart takes the view that there should be a degree of harmonisation of 'margin controls' such as capital ratios, saying that:

> There is a 'level-playing-field' argument between institutional arrangements within countries, as well as between countries. The imposition of (asymmetric) penalties (taxes) on the most visible, largest and probably the most efficient intermediaries (i.e. the banks) may have an increasing effect in diverting such intermediation towards less visible, and possibly less efficient channels.[32]

E. International regulatory reforms and the Financial Stability Board

The financial crisis has triggered intensive efforts internationally, regionally and nationally, to enhance the monitoring of systemic stability and

[32] *Ibid.*

to strengthen the links between macro- and micro-prudential oversight, supervision and regulation.[33] The design and implementation of macro-prudential oversight and regulation at the international level raises practical policy and legal issues involving the operation of the recently created Financial Stability Board (FSB) and the need for it to adopt effective standards of macro-prudential regulation.[34] The FSB has not yet demonstrated itself to be a meaningful institution for enhancing the macro-prudential focus of international financial regulation. Although the FSB has been engaged with micro-prudential reform issues, its efforts so far do not inspire confidence that more effective macro-prudential measures are being adopted at the international level.

The FSB[35] is the international body that has been given the responsibility by the G-20 to develop international financial standards that control systemic risk and provide more effective oversight of the global financial system.[36] The FSB has adopted twelve key standards for sound financial systems, all of which are legally non-binding soft law but nevertheless are expected to be incorporated into the national regulatory regimes of all countries.[37] Since its establishment, the FSB has been addressing a diverse range of regulatory issues. For example, it has taken some of the work of the Financial Stability Forum forward by overseeing reviews of the system of supervisory colleges to monitor each of the largest international financial services firms.[38] It has developed guidance notes and draft bank recovery and resolution plans to assist

[33] Note, however, the de Larosière Report, para 230 suggesting that, over the medium term, thought should be given to establishing a full international standard-setting authority, established by treaty, with binding legal powers.

[34] The most recent embodiment of an international financial soft law institution is the Financial Stability Board (FSB). The FSB consists of twenty-six member countries, the European Central Bank and the IMF. The representatives of FSB member countries are the same as those of the Basel Committee, www.financialstabilityboard.org/about/overview.htm (last accessed 15 January 2012).

[35] The FSB is an institutional continuation of the Financial Stability Forum (FSF) and has continued more or less to follow similar financial policies and regulatory approaches that are market-based and sensitive to the needs of the major international banks.

[36] The FSB was formally created in April 2009 by the G-20 Heads of State, see G-20, 'London Statement' (2 April 2009) para. 15. The G-20 Washington Action Plan and the London & Pittsburgh Summit Statements on strengthening the financial system reaffirm the policy recommendations of the FSF's April 2008 and 2009 Reports that provided a roadmap on financial supervision and regulation, and set out the principles for a more robust supervisory and regulatory framework based on new rules, not only for financial institutions but also other actors, markets and supervisors.

[37] The list is published at www.financialstabilityboard.org/cos/key_standards.htm.

[38] See G-20/FSB protocol to establish colleges of supervisors for all major cross-border

with its advice to national authorities on implementing the FSB Principles for Cross-Border Cooperation on Crisis Management.[39] It has established Principles for Sound Compensation Practices,[40] and has collaborated with other international financial bodies such as the International Organization of Securities Commissions (IOSCO) to develop a consistent regulatory framework for the oversight of asset managers.[41] It is also overseeing the emergence of national and regional frameworks for the registration, regulation and oversight of credit rating agencies and encouraging countries to engage in bilateral dialogues to resolve home–host country issues, involving inconsistencies and disagreements that may arise because of different regulatory approaches.[42]

I. *Financial Stability Board and IMF coordination*

The FSB[43] is part of a new drive to devise more effective international regulatory frameworks that durably link micro-prudential supervision with broader macro-prudential systemic concerns.[44] As discussed above,

financial institutions; Reports of the Financial Stability Board to G-20 Finance Ministers and Governors, *Overview of Progress in Implementing the London Summit Recommendations for Strengthening Financial Stability* (FSB September Report 2009), pp. 2–3 and (FSB November Report 2009), p. 13. Other FSB initiatives include its principles for cross-border cooperation on crisis management (2009). The Basel Committee and FSB have also established a task force to review the practices of colleges.

39 FSB November, 2009 Report, p. 14.

40 FSB Principles for Sound Compensation Practices: Implementation Standards (September 2009).

41 FSB November 2009 Report, pp. 11–12.

42 For further details on this issue see I. MacNeil, 'Credit Rating Agencies: Regulation and Financial Stability', Chapter 8, this volume.

43 The FSB consists of representatives from the central banks and national supervisory authorities of the following countries: Argentina, Australia, Brazil, Canada, China, France, Germany, Hong Kong SAR, India, Indonesia, Italy, Japan, South Korea, Mexico, the Netherlands, Russia, Saudi Arabia, Singapore, South Africa, Spain, Switzerland, Turkey, UK, US, and non-state representatives including the European Central Bank, international financial institutions, international standard-setting bodies and Committees of Central Bank Experts. See Financial Stability Board, Press Release, Annex (9 January 2010).

44 As discussed above, micro-prudential supervision focuses mainly on the solvency and risk management practices of individual financial institutions, depositor protection and protecting bank investors. In contrast, macro-prudential supervision involves assessing the aggregate risks developing in the financial system, the financial system infrastructure and the linkages between financial institutions and markets and the risks of common shocks in the financial system. Jean C. Trichet, 'Macro-prudential supervision in Europe', Text of the 2nd City Lecture, 2009, www.ecb.int/press//key/date/2009/html/sp091211_2.en.html.

a major shift in regulatory focus is occurring from micro-prudential to macro-prudential regulation. The focus on macro-prudential regulation involves, among other things, devising regulatory standards to measure and limit leverage levels in the financial system as a whole, requiring financial institutions to have enhanced liquidity reserves against short-term wholesale funding exposures, and, more generally, counter-cyclical capital regulation whereby capital requirements are linked to points in the macro-economic and business cycle. This move to a more macro-prudential regulatory regime has led the FSB to work more closely with the IMF. The FSB–IMF have undertaken collaborative early warning exercises to strengthen assessments of systemic risks and to identify possible regulatory controls and supervisory practices as a response to the changing face of systemic risk in financial markets.[45] These exercises are aimed at providing policy-makers with policy options and, as such, they add to the data-gathering, analysis and evaluation work and information-sharing activity that the IMF already conducts with a view to preventing crises by identifying policies to control macro-economic and systemic risks.[46] It is argued that the combination of the IMF's macro-financial expertise with the FSB's regulatory perspective will provide an important link between the micro-prudential regulatory perspective and the macro-prudential supervisory perspective.[47] These exercises are expected to be incorporated into the IMF's surveillance activities and this could serve as a means by which findings and policy recommendations may achieve a more concrete effect.

The success of the FSB/IMF collaboration in macro-prudential regulation raises concerns about the effectiveness, accountability and legitimacy of its standards and recommendations.[48] For instance, Lord King of Lothbury, former Governor of the Bank of England, raised important questions regarding the accountability and legitimacy of FSB standards for countries not represented in the G-20. He observed that 'the legitimacy and leadership of the G20 would be enhanced if it were seen as

[45] *IMF-FSB Early Warning Exercise* (IMF Factsheet, 2009).

[46] The IMF's *Global Financial Stability Reports* and *World Economic Outlook Reports* are its 'flagship' global surveillance publications.

[47] IMF, *Initial Lessons of the Crisis for the Global Architecture and the IMF* (IMF Strategy, Policy and Review Dept, 2009), www.imf.org/external/np/pp/eng/2009/021809.pdf.

[48] Douglas W. Arner and Michael W. Taylor, 'The Global Financial Crisis and the Financial Stability Board: Hardening the Soft Law of International Financial Regulation?', Asian Institute of International Financial Law Working Paper No. 6 (2009), p. 6, www.law.hku.hk/aiifl/research/documents/AIIFLWorkingPaper6June2009.pdf, accessed 7 August 2013.

representing views of others countries too'.[49] Close collaboration between the FSB and the IMF is a step towards addressing this concern. However, the involvement of the IMF does not address fully the existing weaknesses in the international financial architecture because the IMF itself has been subject to extensive criticism on legitimacy grounds, most recently because of its allocation of Special Drawing Rights and the related allocation of weighted voting rights.[50] The IMF has also been criticised for its advice to member countries in the 1980s, 1990s and early 2000s to adopt *laissez-faire* models of financial regulation without effective macro-prudential controls.[51] The IMF's Executive Board should therefore develop a new multilateral mandate that recognises the importance of it adopting internal governance reforms to enhance its accountability and legitimacy and to re-orient its financial policy advice towards a more holistic approach to macro-prudential financial regulation that takes account of macro-prudential risks and the differential impact of regulatory structures on different financial systems and economies.

II. Reforming and restructuring financial supervision

The crisis has led to significant changes in regulatory standards, stricter supervisory practices and institutional restructuring of financial regulation. Nevertheless, weaknesses remain. Basel III continues to allow global banking groups to use risk-weighted internal models to calculate credit, market and liquidity risks that rely on historical data and risk parameters that are based on individual bank risk exposures and not to systemic risk across the financial system.[52] Although Basel III contains

[49] See Sir Mervyn King, Text of Speech at the University of Exeter (19 January 2010), p. 8.

[50] Also, the appointment of Christine Lagarde as Managing Director perpetuated the image that the IMF is governed by and for the interests of the advanced developed economies.

[51] Indeed, the International Monetary and Financial Committee (IMFC) of the IMF's Board of Governors proposed in 1997 that the IMF amend the Articles of Agreement so as to divest its members of jurisdiction over capital controls with the result that the IMF would have been able to regulate when a member country could impose controls on cross-border capital flows. See IMF, 'Statement on the Liberalization of Capital Movements under An Amendment of the Fund's Articles' (21 September 1997) (Washington, DC: IMF).

[52] Basel III requires an increased level of tier one regulatory capital to 7.0 per cent (including a capital conservation buffer), a tighter definition of tier one capital to include only ordinary common shares, an additional 2.5 per cent countercyclical capital ratio (yet to be determined for implementation); and liquidity requirements that include a

higher core tier one and tier one capital requirements, liquidity requirements and a leverage ratio, it remains essentially dependent on risk-weighted models that were proven to be unreliable prior to the crisis because of their disproportionate focus on risk management at the level of the individual firm. As discussed above, the G-20 and the FSB have adopted the overall objective of reconstructing financial regulation along macro-prudential lines. This requires not only stricter capital and liquidity requirements for individual institutions, but also monitoring risk exposures across the financial system, including the transfer of credit risk to off-balance-sheet entities and the general level of risk across the financial system. For example, the G-20–FSB objective of requiring systemically significant financial instruments (i.e., OTC derivatives) to be traded on exchanges and centrally cleared with central counterparties is an important regulatory innovation to control systemic risk in wholesale derivatives markets. Also, systemically important financial institutions will be subjected to more intensive prudential regulatory requirements, including higher capital requirements and more scrutiny of their cross-border operations.

In addition, the wide scope of macro-prudential regulation will require a broader definition of prudential supervision to include both *ex ante* supervisory powers, such as licensing, authorisation and compliance with regulatory standards, and *ex post* crisis management measures, such as recovery and resolution plans, deposit insurance and lender of last resort. Indeed, the objectives of macro-prudential regulation – to monitor and control systemic risks and related risks across the financial system – will require greater regulatory and supervisory intensity that will necessitate increased intervention in the operations of cross-border banking and financial groups and a wider assessment of the risks they pose. The broad area of recovery and resolution will necessarily involve authorities in restructuring and disposing of banking assets and using taxpayer funds to bail out and provide temporary support for ailing financial institutions. Indeed, the FSB has stated in its *Key Attributes of Effective Resolution Regimes* that:

> [t]o improve a firm's resolvability, supervisory authorities or resolution authorities should have powers to require, where necessary, the adoption of appropriate measures, such as changes to a firm's business practices,

ratio for stable wholesale funding, liquidity coverage ratios, and an overall leverage ratio. Recently, the Basel Committee has agreed on an additional capital charge of up to 2.5 per cent regulatory capital for large and inter-connected systemically important financial institutions (SIFIs).

> structure or organisation ... To enable the continued operations of systemically important functions, authorities should evaluate whether to require that these functions be segregated in legally and operationally independent entities that are shielded from group problems.[53]

The exercise of macro-supervision and regulation along with overseeing recovery and resolution programmes will require a greater role for host country authorities to ensure that the risk-taking of cross-border financial groups complies with the host country's macro-prudential objectives. Most host countries will be able to achieve macro-prudential objectives in part by utilising traditional tools of macro-economic policy – exchange rates, interest rates and fiscal policy – and by applying traditional tools of micro-prudential supervision. However, under the FSB–G-20 proposals, countries will be expected to intervene in a bank's or financial firm's business practices at an early stage to require prompt corrective action to comply with regulatory requirements and if necessary to alter the organisational structure of the institution by requiring, for instance, that the local operations of a cross-border bank be placed in a separately capitalised subsidiary or independent legal entity so that the local operations of a large systemically important institution could be compelled to undergo a restructuring and/or recapitalisation by local authorities. Indeed, a key element of any bank resolution regime is that the local authority can have tools at its disposal to intervene in bank management (i.e., restrict dividends), restructure creditor claims or use taxpayer funds to recapitalise a systemically important institution or facilitate the transfer of assets to a private purchaser when a bank becomes insolvent.

In addition, to enhance prudential oversight of cross-border financial groups, the Financial Stability Board has encouraged host state supervisors to participate in supervisory colleges to oversee the cross-border operations of financial groups. The main functions of colleges will be to exchange information between supervisors, coordinate communication between supervisors of the financial group, voluntary sharing and/or delegation of tasks and joint decisions on model validation (e.g., Basel II/III). The colleges will also be involved in joint risk assessment and joint decisions on the adequacy of risk-based capital requirements as well as in the planning and coordination of supervisory activities for the financial group and in preparation for and strategy for use during emergency situations (i.e., crisis management).

[53] FSB Key Attribute 10.5.

The use of supervisory colleges is expected to modify the existing principle of home country control with limited host country intervention in a bank's cross-border operations by recognising that host authorities should play a greater role in approving the risk models and engaging in other practices for supervision of cross-border banking groups. This is a departure from existing principles of home–host coordination under the Basel Concordat and the Basel Accord which places most of the responsibility for supervising the cross-border operations of a banking group with the group's home-country supervisory authority.[54] For example, the global banking group's risk models are ordinarily assessed and approved by the home country supervisory authority and applied on a global basis without much adjustment by host country authorities regarding cross-border risk exposures. By contrast, international regulatory regimes should encourage host country regulatory authorities to exercise greater powers to implement macro-prudential tools to control excessive risk-taking by global banking groups. For instance, national regulatory authorities should require cross-border banking groups to maintain subsidiaries in every jurisdiction where they have significant operations and to hold minimum capital in these subsidiaries. This would have the effect of subjecting the global bank's risk management practice to a local assessment by the host supervisor that would require the bank to show how its local operations are holding adequate capital and liquidity that are appropriate for the host country's macro-prudential objectives. This would result in global banking groups moving away from a centralised approach to risk management at the global level towards a decentralised approach for measuring and managing risks at the national or host state levels. This would have important implications for Basel III's present approach to cross-border supervision that encourages and rewards global banking groups with more favourable capital and liquidity requirements for centralising and consolidating

[54] Essentially, Basel II and Basel III are based on a home country regulatory control model that encourages cross-border banks to adopt centralised risk models based on data calculated and assessed by risk managers at the level of the banking group to be applied (without much adjustment) on a global basis for measuring and managing the banking group's risk-taking. Although not legally binding, these principles support limiting a host country supervisory authority's discretion to apply prudential regulatory controls to a foreign bank's operations in the host country. See discussion in K. Alexander, R. Dhumale and J. Eatwell, *Global Governance of Financial Systems: the International Regulation of Systemic Risk* (Oxford University Press, 2006), pp. 27–38.

risk management and measurement in the jurisdiction (or the jurisdictions) where the banking group is based.

Moreover, macro-prudential regulation will necessarily involve the application of regulatory requirements to fit the particular attributes of the local economy where the banking group operates. There is no one-size-fits-all macro-prudential regulatory approach. Moreover, macro-prudential regulation is not well defined in practice and there needs to be a period of experimentation by national authorities before tested approaches are adopted by international standard setters. Countries must be given discretion to experiment with different macro-prudential tools whose effectiveness will vary from country to country based on differences in economic and financial systems. Host country authorities will need a wider array of regulatory tools to address the particular risks that different banking groups and conglomerates pose to their financial system. Effective macro-prudential regulation therefore will require that host countries intervene and challenge risk management and measurement models that global banks use and which have been approved by their home regulatory authorities, but which may be inappropriate, in a macro-prudential regulatory sense, for some host countries.

All of the above developments in banking regulation and supervision will have important implications for the existing international banking regulation regime which has been based essentially on micro-prudential regulation and supervision. This in turn has important implications for international economic law, especially international trade law and the WTO agreements. Under the WTO General Agreement on Trade in Services (GATS) countries have made certain specific liberalisation commitments and are subject to general disciplines of transparency and the most-favoured nation principle in their treatment of other WTO members. It also raises important questions regarding the scope of regulatory discretion that members have to adopt and implement international macro-prudential regulatory reforms and their scope of authority to adopt macro-prudential controls that go beyond FSB–IMF recommendations. This is discussed in the next section.

F. The WTO GATS – prudential 'carve-out' and macro-prudential regulation

The scope and content of macro-prudential regulation raises important issues regarding the GATS rules on cross-border trade in financial services and the scope of the prudential carve-out. Indeed, interesting issues are raised regarding how far GATS market access and national treatment commitments go in accommodating macro-prudential regulatory measures and other reforms likely to constitute key elements of the new financial architecture. Interpretations of the 'prudential carve-out' in the GATS Annex on Financial Services will be crucial for determining the regulatory policy space of countries to adopt macro-prudential regulatory controls.[55] The negotiating history of the GATS Annex on Financial Services and the prudential carve-out suggests that member countries have broad discretion to impose regulatory measures that may depart from GATS commitments and obligations for a prudential reason, so long as they are not intended as protectionist measures. This section suggests some ideas to address the perceived limitations of the GATS rules to accommodate macro-prudential regulatory reforms.

A number of commentators have argued that the GATS rules do constitute an impediment to regulatory reforms and other policy measures under discussion or likely to be required as part of the response to the financial crisis. These include the Report of the Commission of Experts of the President of the United Nations General Assembly on Reforms of the International Monetary and Financial System – also known as the Stiglitz Commission – published in September 2009 (United Nations, 2009), the 2011 edition of UNCTAD's Trade and Development Report (UNCTAD, 2011), Barbados's communication to the WTO, and the position papers of some NGOs.[56] Alternatively, some policy-makers from developing countries have argued that the GATS provides broad enough domestic policy and regulatory autonomy for countries to develop strengthened prudential regulatory regimes, including macro-prudential regulatory controls.[57]

Thus far, the WTO Dispute Settlement Body (DSB) has not heard any cases that involve an interpretation of the meaning and scope of the prudential carve-out. The recent case of Chinese electronic payments

[55] WTO Committee on Trade in Financial Services, Communication from Barbados – Unintended Consequences of Remedial Measures Taken to Correct the Global Financial Crisis: Possible Implications for WTO Compliance, 16 February 2011, www.wtocenter.org.tw/SmartKMS/do/www/readDoc?document_id=112852, accessed 7 August 2013.

[56] See 'The New Financial Architecture and the GATS', *Public Citizen* (2011).

[57] See B. K. Zutshi, 'Regulatory Freedom under GATS: Financial Services Sector', *Economic and Political Weekly* 46:46 (2011) where B. K. Zutschi, former Indian Ambassador to GATT, argues that the GATS rules provide countries with broad policy and regulatory autonomy.

services brought by the US, the first case submitted to the DSB regarding the GATS rules on cross-border trade in banking services, nonetheless illustrates how some of these concepts involving GATS liberalisation commitments can be interpreted in the face of a state's national regulatory measures that appear to infringe a GATS liberalisation commitment.[58] Nevertheless, this case leaves many questions unanswered regarding the scope of WTO members' commitments in cross-border trade in financial services and the degree to which a member may depart from such commitments by taking regulatory measures for a prudential reason. The GATS, however, was never intended to be a regulatory code, it was designed to facilitate negotiations by members to make liberalisation commitments and not to use regulatory measures for protectionist purposes. Once members have made commitments to liberalise trade under any of the four modes of trade in services, they are precluded from taking regulatory measures that infringe those commitments without a valid non-protectionist regulatory objective.[59] This means that countries' policy autonomy with respect to implementing macroprudential regulation might be potentially restricted with respect to their control of cross-border capital flows and the structural regulation of financial firms if it cannot be shown that there is a valid prudential reason motivating the regulatory measure in question.

As commentators have discussed, the meaning of the 'prudential carve-out' has yet to be precisely determined, but has been given a broad scope by most observers.[60] By the time the GATS Annex on Financial Services and the prudential carve-out became effective in 1995, it was clear from the GATS negotiating history that members generally desired a broad definition of 'measures for prudential reasons', including a variety of regulatory practices.[61] Although varied, these

[58] WTO Panel Report, China – Certain Measures Affecting Electronic Payment Services, WT/DS413/R, adopted 31 August 2012 docs.wto.org/dol2fe/Pages/FE_Search/FE_S_S009-DP.aspx?language=E&CatalogueIdList=86862,101369&CurrentCatalogueIdIndex=0&FullTextSearch=, accessed 7 August 2013.

[59] Section 4 of the Annex on Financial Services provides that dispute settlement panels may be established to determine the validity of members' prudential measures with respect to the GATS ('[p]anels for disputes on prudential issues and other financial matters shall have the necessary expertise relevant to the specific financial services under dispute').

[60] See J. Marchetti, 'The GATS Prudential Carveout' in P. Delimatsis and N. Herger (eds.), *Financial Regulation at the Crossroads: Implications for Supervision, Institutional Design and Trade* (Alphen aan den Rijn: Kluwer Law, 2011), pp. 279–95.

[61] *Ibid.*, pp. 280–1.

regulatory practices had to be motivated by a 'prudential reason' or rationale. Since the 2007 financial crisis, however, the meaning 'prudential reason' in financial regulation has evolved further and arguably has taken on a broader scope to include macro-prudential regulatory and supervisory tools to control systemic risk.

To assess whether the 'prudential carve-out' includes macro-prudential measures, one must resort to accepted principles of treaty interpretation. Article 31(1) of the Vienna Convention on the Law of Treaties (VCLT) requires that treaty interpretation must take into account the 'ordinary meaning to be given to the terms of the treaty in their context and in the light of its object and purpose.'[62] This requires that the 'object and purpose' of the words given their 'ordinary meaning' and the circumstances under which the treaty text was adopted should be considered primary in interpreting the treaty. If the interpretation of the treaty according to Article 31 'leaves the meaning ambiguous or obscure' or 'leads to a result which is manifestly absurd or unreasonable' then recourse to supplementary means of interpretation, including the *travaux preparatoires* and the circumstances of the treaty's conclusion, may be resorted to.[63] The VCLT interpretive approach would support interpreting the prudential carve-out in a manner that reflects the 'ordinary meaning' of the text 'in the light of its object and purpose'. Because most commentators agree that the 'prudential carve-out' has a rather broad scope – any measure that is motivated by 'prudential reasons' can be valid under the GATS so long as the measure is not shown to be avoiding a GATS commitment or obligation. It can therefore be argued that this open-ended meaning of the text of the 'prudential carve-out', combined with the circumstances under which the negotiators agreed the text and their 'object and purpose' as set out in the negotiating history, would suggest that the 'prudential carve-out' provides WTO members with wide discretion to adopt any measures in the area of macro-prudential or micro-prudential regulation for a prudential reason that is not intended to avoid a GATS commitment or obligation.

It should be noted, however, that the wide scope of discretion members may have to adopt regulatory measures may not include certain macro-prudential controls if such controls were not considered within

[62] 1969 Vienna Convention on The Law of Treaties, UN Doc. A/Conf.39/27 / 1155 UNTS 331 / 8 ILM 679 (1969) / 63 AJIL 875 (1969), adopted on 23 May 1969, untreaty.un.org/ilc/texts/instruments/english/conventions/1_1_1969.pdf, accessed 7 August 2013.

[63] VCLT, Article 32 (a) & (b).

the ambit of possible regulatory measures that countries could adopt in the 1980s and 1990s when the GATS was being negotiated. This is based on the interpretive principle that when states use text in a treaty, the factual circumstances to which the text is applied cannot develop and change over the years. However, this view might militate against VCLT Article 31's requirement that the 'object and purpose', as set out in the negotiating history, should be taken into account in interpreting the text.

If one were to accept the general meaning of prudential regulation in the 1990s, it would be a definition that involved the supervision and regulation of individual firms and investors, policy-holders and bank depositors. The concept of macro-prudential regulation was not generally practised at the time. However, in light of the recent financial crisis, macro-prudential regulation has now become an internationally acceptable approach to prudential financial regulation. Does the treaty text of 'prudential reasons' include macro-prudential regulatory measures or supervisory decisions? It is submitted that, because the intentions of the negotiating parties at the time the GATS was negotiated in the late 1980s and early 1990s appeared to afford wide discretion to members to utilise a broad number of regulatory measures and practices, the 'object and purpose' of the prudential carve-out would indeed include regulatory principles and practices which were not clearly foreseen during the negotiations but would have been acceptable to the negotiators given the broad ambit of regulatory measures and objectives they intended to preserve for members at the time the treaty was agreed.

However, the question arises whether the carve-out should permit regulatory practices that are not recommended by international bodies, such as the FSB and the IMF in the macro-prudential realm? It is further submitted that because the future of effective macro-prudential regulation and supervision will depend on proactive host state authorities taking regulatory measures that may not be internationally mandated, but which may be viewed as necessary or appropriate for the effective regulation of the host state market or of foreign firms operating in the host market, that reliance on international standards should not be a factor in determining compliance with the prudential carve-out. This support of host country regulatory autonomy would be in accord with the views of most negotiators of the GATS and would most likely conform with the 'object and purpose' of the provision. This means that the GATS prudential carve-out should not cross-reference generally accepted international regulatory standards. Given the unknown terrain of macro-prudential regulation, the prudential carve-out should permit many different types of regulatory and supervisory rules and practices and encourage states to engage in regulatory experimentation. This would include innovative forms of macro-prudential regulation involving unorthodox forms of monetary policy and adjusting claims on private sector assets as well as foreign exchange controls and portfolio capital controls.[64]

Nevertheless, despite this argument for a broad interpretation of the carve-out, the reality of WTO GATS dispute settlement processes suggests that the particular facts, circumstances and regulatory and supervisory practices and policies of each case will be important for determining whether a member avoided a GATS commitment or obligation. The test will likely be an objective one – and not a subjective one – based on what an outside observer in the field would think of the measure in question.

G. Summing up and conclusion

To return to the aphorism that policy-makers should not let a good crisis go to waste, there might be a new paradigm in global regulation in theory, but how closely this is mirrored in policy is another matter as macro-prudential policy is undoubtedly still in its infancy. The financial crisis has triggered intensive regulatory reform efforts to enhance bank risk management and the use of micro-prudential and macro-prudential regulation to achieve financial stability objectives. The chapter suggests that international financial regulation and international economic law must be redesigned to take account of the need for national regulators to adopt and apply macro-prudential regulatory frameworks. This will have important implications for the fields of international monetary and trade law. For example, GATS commitments will need to be interpreted with a view to allowing members adequate regulatory discretion to adopt supervisory practices and regulatory structures that enable them to achieve macro-prudential objectives. It is now necessary to allow countries to build financial regulation taking a more holistic approach that involves linking micro-prudential supervision of individual banks with broader oversight of the financial system and to macroeconomic policy. Not only should regulation focus more on

[64] For a discussion of the utility of different macro-prudential measures, see C. A. E. Goodhart, '*The Macro-Prudential Authority: Powers, Scope and Accountability*' (London: Morgan Stanley, 2011) pp. 1–12.

macroeconomic factors, such as liquidity risks, but it should also develop capital adequacy standards that have linkages and reference points in the broader macro economy, such as countercyclical capital ratios. These regulatory reforms will have important implications regarding international trade law commitments, especially GATS national treatment and market access commitments and the scope of the prudential 'carve-out'. National authorities should be encouraged to experiment with different macro-prudential approaches that utilise different tools to control systemic risk.

It is clear that macro-prudential regulation will have important implications for economic policy. This is why democratic safeguards should accompany the decision to use macro-prudential controls. This has important consequences for the democratic accountability of bank supervisors and central banks involved in bank regulation and supervision. Moreover, macro-prudential regulation will have to be coordinated at the international level, but host country authorities should have the ultimate say in ensuring that these tools are applied effectively and adequately address the risks faced by that country's markets.

21

Relationship between monetary policy and exchange rate policy

FRANÇOIS GIANVITI

A. Overview

I. *Definitions*

Monetary policy is the course of action followed by the authority vested with the power to control the volume of the money supply[1] and the cost of credit within a particular (usually national) territory. The expansion or contraction of the money supply will affect prices.[2] The cost of credit, which affects the level of consumption and investment, varies with the volume of the money supply and with the cost of money available for loans.[3]

Exchange rate policy is the course of action followed by the authority vested with the power to control the buying and selling rates between a particular (usually national) currency and other currencies.[4] Not every foreign currency is traded in every country, but it is usually sufficient to control rates in terms of a major currency ('intervention currency'), which can be bought and sold in the exchange market and used, in two-step transactions, to make or receive payments in a third currency.

1 There are different definitions of the money supply (M0, M1, M2, M3), based on the liquidity of assets. 'Monetary base and bank deposits' (M2) is the most common definition. 'Monetary base' (M0) means currency (coins and notes that are legal tender) and commercial banks' reserves held with the central bank, which are book money equivalent to currency in interbank transactions. Because of the 'money multiplier' (currency makes deposits, deposits make loans and loans make deposits), the monetary base is 'high-powered money'.

2 In periods of recession, an increase in the money supply will have a limited effect on prices.

3 Lower interest rates generate growth, but if they fall too low the preference for liquidity will prevail: there will be fewer or no loans from the private sector. Conversely, the cost of private loans rises with growth. In an open economy, low interest rates may cause a capital outflow whereas high interest rates may cause a capital inflow.

4 What is called the exchange rate for one currency in terms of another is usually the mid-point between their buying and selling rates in spot transactions. In a generic sense, the exchange rate for a currency, when assessing its variations, is an average of its exchange rates, usually *vis-à-vis* major foreign currencies.

The authority in charge of monetary policy is generally the central bank. It can issue or retire money by expanding or contracting the monetary base, increase or decrease the cost of money issue ('*seigniorage*') and, within the scope of its powers, adjust the volume of the money supply in the banking system to meet its objectives.

The authority in charge of maintaining buying and selling rates in the exchange market is also generally the central bank, but the government will normally have the power to decide whether or not specified rates should be maintained.

Both monetary policy and exchange rate policy can be implemented through the use of contractual transactions[5] and the exercise of regulatory powers.[6]

II. Coordination of monetary and exchange rate policies

Although the conduct of a country's monetary policy is guided essentially by domestic objectives, such as price stability and/or economic growth and full employment, some decisions may be guided by exchange rate considerations. In order, for example, to prevent capital flight and an excessive depreciation of the exchange rate, the central bank may decide to raise the interest rates on its loans to commercial banks and to impose higher reserve requirements to restrict the extension of credit.

Conversely, in the conduct of a country's exchange rate policy, some decisions may be guided by monetary policy considerations. In the case, for example, of a country with a large balance of payments surplus, if the central bank were to buy all incoming foreign exchange to maintain the exchange rate, it would be creating domestic money, which would increase the monetary base. As an alternative, different types of actions may then be envisaged, such as the imposition of exchange controls to limit inflows, or the 'sterilisation' of these inflows to prevent their conversion.[7] One of the most effective measures, however, is to adjust

[5] These transactions are mainly loans (or other types of credit) to banks and open market sales and purchases of financial instruments (monetary policy), and sales or purchases of foreign exchange in the exchange market (exchange rate policy).

[6] Reserve requirements can be imposed on banks to limit the amount of deposits available for lending and thus the increase in the money supply. Specified exchange rates can be made mandatory.

[7] On the sterilisation of inflows, see Section C.II.

the exchange rate by revaluing the currency or letting it appreciate in the exchange market.[8]

When separate authorities are in charge of monetary policy and exchange rate policy, their actions have to be coordinated. If, for example, in a country facing a large outflow of currency, the central bank is in charge of monetary policy and the government determines the exchange rate, the central bank could try to defend the exchange rate by raising interest rates or the government could decide to devalue the currency. Or there could be a combination of both, with a smaller rise in interest rates and a smaller devaluation. Also, subject to the country's international commitments, these measures may be supplemented with the imposition of trade and exchange restrictions.

III. Other relevant policies

Both the money supply and the exchange rate can be affected by fiscal policy. An expansionary fiscal policy, which stimulates demand with budget deficits, has effects similar to those of an expansionary monetary policy. As large and sustained deficits conflict with an objective of price or exchange rate stability, an expansionary fiscal policy may have to be countered by a contractionary monetary policy.

Not only the volume of the budget deficit, but also its sources of financing may affect the money supply and the exchange rate. If, for instance, large amounts of government bonds are sold to foreign investors who buy them with foreign exchange converted into domestic currency, the increased demand for domestic currency could lead to an appreciation of the exchange rate. If, on the other hand, the central bank were to buy the foreign currency with newly created money in order to avoid an appreciation of the exchange rate, the monetary base would expand and the money supply could expand exponentially. If the budget deficit is financed with central bank loans,[9] the monetary base will also expand.

[8] Revaluation (or its opposite, devaluation) is a change in the official value of a currency. Depreciation (or its opposite, appreciation) is the result of market forces.

[9] As central bank credit to the government is an easy way to dispense with fiscal discipline, central banks in many countries are prohibited or refrain from extending credit directly to the government. In those countries, therefore, contrary to a common assumption, the central bank is not a lender of last resort to the government. Typically, however, the central bank may still buy and sell government securities in the secondary market; these open market transactions are supposed to be based on macroeconomic considerations, with a view to increasing (purchases) or decreasing (sales) the volume of liquidity in the economy. Government securities can also be accepted as collateral for central bank credit

A large expansion in demand or in the money supply leads to higher prices, making domestic goods and services less competitive. One likely consequence is a decline in exports, which means fewer jobs in export-oriented sectors, an increase in welfare costs and a loss of fiscal revenue. Another consequence to be expected is an increase in imports, both because their relative prices will have declined and because domestic production may not be able to adjust immediately to the additional demand for goods. The deterioration in the current account may cause a balance of payments deficit, which, if large or sustained, will lead to a devaluation or depreciation of the currency.

When the budget deficit is not financed with foreign money or with central bank money but rather with securities issued by the government to domestic lenders, these loans reduce the volume, and increase the cost, of liquidity available for private investment ('crowding out'[10]). If these securities are later mobilised by lenders in open market or credit transactions with the central bank, domestic money will be created, which will expand the monetary base, unless the purchase of these securities by the central bank can be 'sterilised', i.e., offset by an equal reduction in central bank credit to the private sector, leaving the total monetary base unchanged. A massive net transfer of resources from the private sector to the government has major economic and political implications.[11]

Another way of financing the budget is to levy more taxes. Higher taxes have a contractionary effect as they constrain demand. Also, the same amount of taxes, depending on how it is levied, will have a different impact on the country's economy and its balance of payments. One of the clearest examples is the difference between production taxes and consumption taxes. If a country levies taxes that increase production costs, it will be at a competitive disadvantage *vis-à-vis* another country that levies taxes on consumption. While the former will make its exports more expensive without raising the cost of

to commercial banks. Central bank purchases (or acceptance as collateral) of government securities help maintain their value and allow the government to issue more securities with low interest rates. The real motive guiding the central bank when making these transactions, however, is not always clear.

[10] In Keynesian economics, there is no crowding out in times of recession because investment opportunities are limited. The government should then step in and replace the failing private sector to sustain demand.

[11] Disciples of Hayek see this transfer as the 'road to serfdom'. For Keynes, the government would repay the loans with revenue generated by the return to growth at the end of the business cycle. On the debate between Keynes and Hayek, see N. Wapshott, *Keynes Hayek: The Clash That Defined Modern Economics* (New York: Norton, 2011).

imports, the latter will make foreign imports more expensive without raising the cost of its exports.[12]

Social policies that increase production costs have effects that are similar to those of production taxes and a similar impact on the country's international competitiveness.

B. Legal framework

In principle, a sovereign state may freely determine its monetary policy and its exchange rate policy as elements of its monetary sovereignty, but the exercise of monetary sovereignty is limited by the rules of the international monetary system.

I. Monetary sovereignty

The right to issue currency and regulate its value and use is an attribute of sovereignty. In the exercise of its monetary sovereignty,[13] a country may determine the organ allowed to issue the currency, the conditions under which the currency may be issued, the use of the currency (legal tender status and convertibility into other currencies) and its value, including its value in terms of foreign currencies (exchange rates and conversion rate).[14] A country may also regulate the use of foreign currencies in its territories.

In the exercise of its monetary sovereignty, a country has a number of options, with respect both to the issuance of a currency and the choice of an exchange rate policy.

Most countries have decided to have their own currencies.[15] With respect to the exchange rate, a few countries maintain a fixed exchange

[12] A value added tax is a consumption tax. Amounts paid during the production stages are refunded if the final product is exported, and imported goods are taxable. Its effects have been compared to those of an exchange tax.

[13] See F. A. Mann, *The Legal Aspect of Money*, 5th edn (Oxford University Press, 1992), p. 461; T. Treves, 'Monetary Sovereignty Today', in M. Giovanoli (ed.), *International Monetary Law, Issues for the New Millennium* (Oxford University Press, 2000), p. 111; F. Gianviti, 'Current Legal Aspects of Monetary Sovereignty', in *Current Developments in Monetary and Financial Law*, vol. 4 (Washington, DC: IMF, 2005), p. 3.

[14] The conversion rate used to determine the value of foreign currency holdings or earnings (e.g., for accounting or tax purposes) may differ somewhat from the rates used in exchange transactions.

[15] Some local governments are allowed to issue a separate currency and to conduct their own monetary and exchange rate policies. For example, the Special Administrative Region of Hong Kong in the People's Republic of China has its own currency.

rate for their currencies in terms of another currency ('pegging').[16] Other countries let the exchange rate fluctuate either under a managed float system or freely and independently in the exchange market.

In some of the countries that have their own currencies, a foreign currency is given legal tender status, or is *de facto* generally accepted as a means of payment within the country. When the national currency and the foreign currency circulate side by side with a fixed conversion ratio between them, the country can no longer determine its own exchange rate. The national currency is 'pegged' to the other currency.[17]

In a few countries, a foreign currency has fully replaced the national currency. The money supply is then limited to whatever amounts of that foreign currency are available (in foreign bank accounts or in cash) to the country's authorities, financial institutions and other residents.

The term dollarisation is often used as a generic term to describe situations where a foreign currency (usually the US dollar,[18] hence the term) is given legal tender status, or is *de facto* widely accepted in payments, within a country other than its country of issue, either as a substitute for, or as a supplement to, the national currency.[19]

In monetary unions, such as the European Economic and Monetary Union (EMU) or the West African Economic and Monetary Union (UEMOA), the exercise of monetary sovereignty, including the issuance of currency and the conduct of monetary and exchange rate policies, has been transferred by treaty from the national authorities of the member states to common supranational authorities,[20] including a common central bank (in UEMOA, the Central Bank of the West African States (BCEAO)) or system of central banks (in EMU, the European System of Central Banks (ESCB), which comprises the European Central Bank (ECB) and the national central banks[21]). In EMU, the Council could

[16] For instance, Bulgaria and Lithuania peg their currencies to the euro. Hong Kong pegs the HK dollar to the US dollar. See Section C. III.2.

[17] In the 1990s, Argentina used the US dollar in parallel with its own currency.

[18] 'Euroisation' is also sometimes used, though not as a generic term, but only in cases where the euro is the foreign currency circulating within a country.

[19] For instance, Liberia, Panama, Ecuador, El Salvador and Zimbabwe use the US dollar; Montenegro uses the euro.

[20] In EMU, the transfer has only taken place for countries of the euro area, i.e., those whose central banks have joined the 'eurosystem' of central banks (see next footnote).

[21] The ESCB includes the national central banks of all the member states of the European Union, including 'Member States with a derogation', such as the UK, which are outside the euro area. These central banks, however, are not part of the 'eurosystem' and do not participate in its decision-making process.

determine an exchange rate for the euro, but it has so far refrained from exercising that power.

II. *International monetary system*

Member countries of the International Monetary Fund (IMF) are subject to certain obligations, which limit the exercise of their monetary sovereignty with respect to both their monetary and exchange rate policies.[22]

These obligations underwent a major change, however, with the abandonment of the gold exchange standard, which occurred first *de facto* with the decision of the US on 15 August 1971 to suspend the international convertibility of the US dollar into gold and then *de jure* with the entry into force of the second amendment of the IMF's Articles of Agreement on 1 April 1978.

Under the gold exchange standard, IMF members had to maintain fixed exchange rates that were based on parity,[23] i.e., the ratio between the respective par values of their currencies in terms of gold.[24] A par value could only be changed 'to correct a fundamental disequilibrium' and with the approval of the IMF.

With the current system, IMF members are no longer under an obligation to maintain fixed exchange rates. Each member may freely determine its 'exchange arrangements'. For example, it can maintain the value of its currency in terms of another member's currency ('pegging'), or a basket of currencies, or the special drawing right, or any other denominator as long as this denominator is not gold. Several members may agree to maintain specified exchange rates between their currencies. Another possibility for a member is not to maintain any exchange rate but rather to let its currency fluctuate, either within certain limits *vis-à-vis* another currency, or freely and independently of any other currency.

[22] See R. M. Lastra, *Legal Foundations of International Monetary Stability* (Oxford University Press, 2006), Chapter 13, p. 371.

[23] Instead of maintaining exchange rates based on parity, a member could opt to exchange its currency for gold at a price based on the par value of its currency, for the settlement of international transactions. The US was the only country that availed itself of this option. The par value of its currency (the 1944 dollar, i.e., US$ 35 per ounce of fine gold), which remained in force until December 1971, was also the official price for international gold transactions between governments or the central banks of IMF members.

[24] The par value of each currency was defined in terms of either gold or the 1944 US dollar. The parity of each currency in terms of every other currency was calculated on that basis. Within a member's territories, exchange rates for spot exchange transactions could not be allowed to deviate from parity by more than 1 per cent on either side of parity, which meant that the maximum spread for spot transactions was 2 per cent.

If a member decides to let its currency fluctuate feely and independently, that is, without intervention, it will still be regarded as having an exchange arrangement. This exchange arrangement will have to be notified to the IMF under Article IV, Section 2(a), but the member will not be regarded as having an exchange rate policy.

Even after the second amendment, however, members remain obligated to avoid certain exchange practices, such as multiple or discriminatory currency practices[25] and restrictions on the making of payments and transfers for current international transactions.

In addition, and as a partial substitute for the former prohibition against unapproved changes in par value, a new obligation has been imposed on all members, which is to 'avoid manipulating exchange rates or the international monetary system in order to prevent effective balance of payments adjustment or to gain an unfair competitive advantage over other members' (Article IV, Section 1(iii)).[26]

Moreover, the amended Article IV, Section 1 has created a new obligation, which is for each member 'to collaborate with the Fund to assure orderly exchange arrangement and to promote a stable system of exchange rates'. Article IV, Section 3(b) requires the Fund to adopt specific principles for the guidance of members with respect to their exchange rate policies. Pursuant to these provisions, the IMF has adopted Principles for the Guidance of Members' Policies. Even if a member decides not to maintain exchange rates but rather lets its exchange rate fluctuate freely and independently, it will be expected to comply with Principle B: 'A member should intervene in the exchange market if necessary to counter disorderly conditions, which may be characterized *inter alia* by disruptive short-term movements in the exchange rate of its currency'.[27] Also, a member maintaining exchange rates will be expected to observe Principles C ('Members should take into account in their

[25] A spread of more than 2 per cent between buying and selling rates for spot exchange transactions, if it is due to official action, is a multiple currency practice; the spread may only be exceeded for transaction costs and exchange risks (IMF Decision No. 8648-(87/104) of 17 July 1987 in *Selected Decisions and Selected Documents of the International Monetary Fund*, 36th issue (Washington, DC: IMF, 2011), p. 604).

[26] See F. Gianviti, 'Stabilité et manipulation des taux de change', in *Le droit international économique à l'aube du XXIe siècle* (Paris: Pedone 2009), p. 113 and Annamaria Viterbo, *International Economic Law and Monetary Measures, Limitations to States' Sovereignty and Dispute Settlement* (Cheltenham and Northampton: Edward Elgar Publishing, 2012), Chapter 7, p. 289.

[27] Decision No. 13919-(07/51) of 15 June 2007, as amended, *Selected Decisions*, p. 39; these Principles have been incorporated into Decision No. 15203-(12/72) of 18 July 2012 on

intervention policies the interests of other members, including those of the countries in whose currencies they intervene') and D ('A member should seek to avoid exchange rate policies that result in balance of payments instability').[28]

Perhaps the most important development brought about by the second amendment, however, was the change in focus from a system based on specific obligations concerning exchange rates to a broader and much less precise set of obligations (often described as 'soft law') concerning domestic policies. The underlying postulate was that exchange rate stability, instead of being an objective *per se*, would be the result of appropriate domestic economic and financial policies, including fiscal and monetary policies, carried out by all member states under the Fund's surveillance (Article IV, Section 3(a)). The main obligations of each member in this regard are to '(i) endeavor to direct its economic and financial policies toward the objective of fostering orderly economic growth with reasonable price stability, with due regard to its circumstances' and '(ii) seek to promote stability by fostering orderly economic and financial conditions and a monetary system that does not tend to produce erratic disruptions' (Article IV, section 1).[29]

C. Interaction between exchange rate policy and monetary policy

Three configurations may be envisaged.

The first is where a country's economy has been fully dollarised. In that case, the country has no monetary or exchange rate policy.[30]

The second is where a country has its own currency. It will then have a monetary policy and an exchange rate for its currency, but, as noted

Bilateral and Multilateral Surveillance, which will become effective and replace Decision No. 13919 on 18 January 2013.

28 *Ibid.* According to paragraph 14 of Decision No. 13919 and paragraph 21 of Decision No. 15203, Principles B, C and D 'constitute recommendations rather than obligations of members'.

29 On members' obligations and IMF surveillance under Article IV, see J. Gold, *Exchange Rates in International Law and Organization* (American Bar Association, 1988) and F. Gianviti, 'Evolving Role and Challenges for the International Monetary Fund', *The International Lawyer* 35:4 (2001), 1371, 1378. In contrast with earlier decisions of the IMF on surveillance, Decision No. 15203 contains a recommendation on domestic policies (Principle E): 'A member should seek to avoid domestic economic and financial policies that give rise to domestic instability'.

30 See A. Berg and E. Borensztein, *Full Dollarization, The Pros and Cons*, Economic Issues 24 (Washington, DC: IMF 2003).

above, it will not necessarily have an exchange rate policy. If it has both an exchange rate policy and a monetary policy, they will have to be coordinated together and with other relevant (e.g., fiscal) policies. If it has no exchange rate policy, monetary and other relevant policies will drive the exchange rate.

The third is where a country has joined a currency union. The only difference from the second configuration is that it is then for the union rather than the individual members to conduct the monetary policy and to decide whether to have an exchange rate policy. As noted above, however, fiscal policies also have an impact on monetary policy and exchange rates. Unless the countries' fiscal policies are coordinated, there will be conflicts among union members over monetary policy and exchange rate issues.

In every case other than full dollarisation, several approaches can be identified. One is to give precedence to consumption- and/or investment-led growth and employment through an expansionary monetary policy, regardless of its effects on the exchange rate. Another takes the opposite view, which is to give precedence to export-led growth and employment through exchange rate competitiveness and to adjust the monetary policy accordingly. Yet a third is to adopt a common objective of monetary stability, which could cover both domestic prices and the exchange rate.

I. Expansionary monetary policy

Most central bankers would agree that preserving the value of money in terms of domestic prices is a desirable objective. They would also agree, however, that a zero price increase is not a desirable objective. The underlying assumption, based on Keynesian economics, is that inflation[31] and recession are mutually exclusive.[32] Therefore, a monetary policy achieving sustained price increases should avoid a recession.

The dominant view is that the best compromise between recession and excessive inflation is to have regular but low price increases. Over the medium term, annual increases of about 2 per cent in domestic consumer prices are deemed to meet the objective of price stability.[33] The

[31] Inflation has two meanings: increase in the money supply and price increase. It is used here in the latter sense.

[32] Keynesian economic theory does not explain stagflation.

[33] See F. Gianviti, 'The Objectives of Central Banks', in M. Giovanoli and D. Devos (eds.), *International Monetary and Financial Law, The Global Crisis* (Oxford University Press, 2010), p. 449.

rationale is that there has to be a safety margin against deflation. Smaller price increases could result in a 'liquidity trap', where interest rates are so low that savings are hoarded rather than lent[34] and, if the central bank's short-term interest rates are already close to zero, it may not be able to stimulate demand by lowering them. As growth remains sluggish or turns negative, unemployment rises. The authorities can try to boost demand with artificial injections of liquidity through fiscal measures (budget deficits resulting from increased spending and/or lower taxes), or a major expansion in the monetary base ('quantitative easing'), or a combination of both, but success is not guaranteed.[35]

Quantitative easing is a term commonly used to describe nonconventional expansionary monetary policy measures that have been used, in different forms and with different degrees of magnitude, by the Bank of Japan, since 2001 and, since 2007, by several other major central banks (e.g., US, UK, ECB, Switzerland). The basic tenet of quantitative easing is that, in a recessionary or quasi-recessionary economic environment with short-term interest rates already at zero or close to zero, a central bank should engage in a major expansion of its monetary base, largely beyond what is normally required for non-inflationary economic growth, by acquiring large amounts of diversified assets and, consequently, injecting an equivalent amount of liquidity into the economy. This will usually involve not only a substantial expansion in the central bank's balance sheet but also the purchase of financial instruments previously excluded from the central bank's open market transactions. Thus, while central bank financing is usually based on the provision of short-term liquidity to banks and the purchase or sale of short-term highly liquid assets, quantitative easing usually includes central bank

[34] Hoarding may also be preferred to spending because of a fear of recession and loss of employment.

[35] Japan's 'lost decade' of the 1990s, following the bursting of the real estate and stock market bubble of the 1980s, illustrates the ineffectiveness of conventional monetary policy, coupled with a weak fiscal stimulus (partly offset by tax increases), when trying to restart a stagnant economy where short-term interest rates have already been lowered to zero or close to zero. For Keynesian economists, this experience validates Keynes's views on the liquidity trap and his advocacy of increased public spending (financed with loans rather than taxes), as the most appropriate tool to combat deflation and avoid a recession when monetary policy has become ineffective. Keynes did not advocate the use of budget deficits, however, as an instrument of a continued expansionary fiscal policy to stimulate the economy, with ever increasing and costlier debt, but only as a countercyclical policy in times of recession and on the understanding that they would be reversed at the end of the cycle. On Japan's economic policies in the 1990s, see, for instance, T. Cullen and J. D. Ostry (eds.), *Japan's Lost Decade, Policies for Economic Revival* (Washington, DC: IMF, 2003).

purchases of medium- and even long-term assets.[36] Therefore, instead of focusing monetary policy on the cost of short-term debt, the central bank provides refinancing for large amounts of medium- or long-term debt, such as two to ten-year government bonds and mortgage-backed securities. The sellers may then reinvest the proceeds in more of the same securities, which can be sold again to the central bank. With more and more money being offered, interest rates on such securities may be expected to go down, thus lowering the cost of long-term borrowing for the government and private investors while providing them with substantially larger amounts of liquidity. For the same amount of interest payments, they can borrow more and spend more, which will normally stimulate demand and create jobs, unless the money is spent on speculative investments or on foreign imports of consumer goods. In a stagnant economy, quantitative easing has a limited effect on consumer prices, which may remain well below the 2 per cent limit, but it may lead to an asset price bubble, particularly in the stock market. It may also affect the exchange rate (unless other countries are taking similar actions). In any case, it is supposed to be phased out as the economy picks up, which will lead to a substantial but gradual reduction in the money supply, with a rise in interest rates and an increase in the cost of government and private sector borrowing.[37]

Although moderate price increases could be seen as the result of an expansionary monetary policy, this policy is still regarded as achieving monetary stability. Therefore, a truly expansionary policy would have to yield annual consumer price increases substantially higher than 2 per cent.

Such a policy, which would combine an increase in the money supply with low interest rates, would seem to have a number of benefits, at least in the short term.

- First, the additional amount of money injected into the economy would mean more money available for loans and, with lower interest rates, more consumption, more investment and higher economic growth, resulting in more and better-paid jobs.
- Second, as consumer prices would rise, so would many incomes and asset prices. Private and public debtors, including the state, would find

[36] It may also involve non-sterilised purchases of foreign exchange by the central bank.

[37] Only time will tell whether quantitative easing has created an addiction to cheap and plentiful long-term credit, which cannot be cured without first going through a long and painful withdrawal period.

it easier to repay their existing debt (unless it is inflation-adjusted) or to borrow by using their assets as collateral.

- Third, with higher incomes and asset prices, tax revenue too would rise, thus adding to the resources available for a fiscal stimulus, e.g., through public investments or an increase in welfare expenditure.
- Fourth, to the extent the addition to the money supply came from low-cost or interest-free central bank loans to the government ('monetisation of debt'), the savings would further alleviate the cost of the public debt for the budget, which would allow the government to expand the fiscal stimulus.

The expected benefits of an expansionary monetary policy are so obvious that it is no surprise it has its fervent supporters. Not everybody, however, would gain from this policy. While owners of real assets (equity or real property) would generally be well protected,[38] and independent professionals or contractors may raise their fees or prices, the main losers would be those who kept their savings in cash and the 'rentiers', who bought government or corporate bonds with their savings. Workers and pensioners may be better off if they are able to have their salaries or pensions adjusted to the cost of living, but not all pension schemes have a full cost of living adjustment clause, and in any case adjustments to salaries and pensions are usually delayed; in periods of high inflation, a delay means a substantial loss of purchasing power.

Moreover, every action triggers a reaction and, over time, the negative effects of continued inflation become stronger. As prices rise, borrowing from private lenders becomes more and more expensive, even for the government. With higher interest rates, the market value of existing bonds declines, the risk of default on new and existing bonds increases and so does the reluctance to lend. Private loans to the government may have to be replaced with central bank loans, thus expanding the monetary base.

As money loses its purchasing power, the expectation of ever-rising prices becomes a self-fulfilling prophecy: individuals and companies either spend their income as fast as they can for fear that their savings will soon be worthless, or invest them in real assets, which again drives consumer and asset prices even higher.

[38] When selling these assets, however, they may have to pay a capital gains tax levied on the increase in nominal value. They will also have to pay higher property and perhaps wealth taxes as long as they hold these assets.

Unless there is a reversal in monetary policy, inflation may accelerate, reaching three-, four- or five-digit annual levels and turning into hyperinflation.[39] In such a situation, new banknotes are printed with ever-increasing nominal values. Although these notes remain legal tender and penalties are inflicted for refusing to accept them in payment, they are increasingly replaced by barter of real assets or payments in foreign currencies. The budget becomes unmanageable as fiscal income is based on past prices while expenditure is based on current prices, which are substantially higher. Eventually, the country's monetary system collapses and either a new monetary policy can be put in place or the domestic currency is replaced by a foreign currency.[40]

Even if this point is never reached, a large expansion in the money supply will have had an impact on the country's balance of payments, foreign exchange reserves and exchange rate.

A loss of competitiveness of domestic products, combined with an increase in domestic demand, will have resulted in a deterioration of the current account in the balance of payments, with a loss of reserves, probably compounded by a large capital flight due first to low interest rates and later to the anticipation of a devaluation or depreciation of the currency.

Moreover, a high rate of inflation makes the country's currency unusable for external payments. Foreign creditors will not take a currency that is fast losing its purchasing power and may soon become inconvertible.

The country's options are then rather limited. It may impose trade and exchange restrictions, tax imports and subsidise exports, but at the risk of triggering protests, complaints that these measures are violations of the country's international commitments or even retaliatory measures from its trading partners.

[39] Hyperinflation occurred, for instance, during the French Revolution (with the massive issue of 'assignats', which eventually became worthless), in Germany under the Weimar Republic, and more recently in Brazil (1967–94), Argentina (1975–92), Zaire (1989–96) and Zimbabwe (2001–8). In Argentina, the 1992 peso was worth 100 billion 1983 pesos. Hyperinflation in Zimbabwe was even more spectacular. In 1980, when Zimbabwe became independent, the Zimbabwe dollar, which replaced the Rhodesian dollar, was worth more than the US dollar. In 2008, shortly before the Zimbabwe dollar (Z$) ceased to be used, it took 3 billion Z$ to buy 1 US$. In February 2009, new banknotes in a new Z$ were issued; the new Z$ was equal to 10 trillion trillion original Z$. In Zimbabwe, the double-digit inflation of 1981–2000 rose to triple digits in 2001– 5, four digits in 2006, five in 2007, and from nine to twelve digits in the course of 2008. In 2009, the authorities endorsed the *de facto* dollarisation of the economy, with the US dollar being the currency most widely used.

[40] See C. M. Reinhart and K. S. Rogoff, *This Time Is Different – Eight Centuries of Financial Folly* (Princeton University Press, 2011), particularly Chapter 12, 'Inflation and Modern Currency Crashes', p. 180.

Or it may try to finance the external deficit with borrowed foreign money, agree to pay whatever rate the market will charge and accept the terms imposed by foreign creditors. Gold clauses are no longer used,[41] but foreign creditors may insist on the inclusion in loan agreements of clauses stipulating repayment in a foreign currency, subjecting the contract to the law of a foreign country and giving jurisdiction to a foreign court in case of disputes between the parties.[42] Unless it agrees to such clauses, the government may not be able to borrow from foreign banks or to issue securities abroad.

Yet another option is to correct the deficit through a devaluation or depreciation of the currency. This third option may be the most attractive as it is initially the least painful, although it will inevitably raise the cost of non-substitutable imports, such as food, raw materials, energy (petroleum and natural gas) or even high-tech industrial products.

A comparison of the exchange rates between the French franc (FF) and the Deutsche mark (DM) in the period from 1960 to 1989[43] shows the contrast between a country (France) whose government was following expansionary monetary and fiscal policies, and a country (Germany) in which the conduct of monetary policy had been entrusted to an independent central bank with a mandate of price

[41] The last inclusion of a gold clause in government bonds seems to have been in 1973, when France issued Treasury bonds with a maturity of 15 years, a 7 per cent interest rate and a gold value clause. With the subsequent appreciation of gold, rising from US$ 97 per ounce in 1973 to US$ 437 in 1988, the repayment value of these bonds increased considerably: for 6.5 billion French francs (FF) borrowed in 1973, France paid a total of FF 92 billion (principal and interest) during the life of the bonds. After the 1981 presidential and parliamentary elections, the French Parliament considered amending their terms by removing the gold clause. The proposal was eventually dropped. At that time, France was issuing new bonds, with even higher interest rates. Amending the terms of earlier bonds would have cast a doubt on the future repayment of the new bonds.

[42] Foreign currency clauses protect creditors from a depreciation of the debtor's currency. Foreign law clauses protect creditors from legislation enacted by the debtor country to amend the terms of bank loans or bonds governed by its own law. Foreign court clauses protect creditors from legislation requiring courts in the debtor country to apply its own laws regardless of the law governing the contract. In addition, there may be a waiver of immunity from enforcement, but its effects on a sovereign debtor's assets are limited.

[43] A longer-term comparison would show the same trend until 1989. According to calculations published by the French Ministry for Economy, Finance and Industry, the depreciation of the FF in terms of the DM, over ten-year periods from 1949 to 2001, was as follows: 28.8 per cent in 1949–59, 25.7 per cent in 1959–69, 33.9 per cent in 1969–79, 30 per cent in 1979–89 and 0 per cent in 1989–2001 (J. C. Asselain, Le siècle des dévaluations, www.finances.gouv.fr/notes_bleues/nbb/nbb227/227_dev.htm).

stability as its primary objective.[44] In 1960, the DM/FF parity was 1 FF = 0.85 DM and 1 DM = 1.177 FF. At the end of 1989, the average exchange rates between the FF and the DM were 1 FF = 0.292632 DM and 1 DM = 3.41726 FF.[45]

The depreciation of the FF in terms of the DM was gradual, but it accelerated for a few years in the early 1980s with the adoption by France of fiscal and monetary policies designed to reduce unemployment[46] and pay for welfare programmes with substantially larger budget deficits[47] financed at market rates.[48] With a rapid deterioration of the balance of payments, there were soon four devaluations of the FF (1981, 1982, 1983 and 1986), followed by a shift in monetary policy with a view to maintaining a stable exchange rate between the FF and the DM.[49]

Countries joining a monetary union such as EMU are no longer able to resort to expansionary monetary policy. As the rules of EMU, however, did not restrict members' fiscal sovereignty, while giving them the benefit of low interest rates,[50] several EMU countries turned to expansionary fiscal policies. The result could have been expected: current account deficits coupled with crushing levels of public indebtedness.

Since these countries, as members of a monetary union, could not correct their external deficits through exchange rate depreciation, their

[44] For a description of the role played by the Bundesbank in the conduct of Germany's monetary policy, see Deutsche Bundesbank (ed.), *Fifty Years of the Deutsche Mark* (Oxford University Press, 1999).

[45] As the euro (introduced in 1999 as a unit of account replacing the European Currency Unit (ECU) at 1:1 and circulated as a currency in 2002) is equal to 6.55957 FF or 1.95583 DM, the implied conversion rate used for the euro was approximately 1 DM = 3.354 FF and 1 FF = 0.298 DM.

[46] The results were not as expected. From the end of 1980 to the end of 1985, average unemployment in France rose from 5.9 per cent to 9.3 per cent of the active population and, for young adults, from 13.9 per cent to 21.8 per cent.

[47] From 1981 to 1995, there was a sevenfold increase in public debt.

[48] Following a law passed in 1973, the Banque de France was no longer allowed to buy government securities directly from the government. It could still buy them, however, in the secondary market.

[49] Some believe that the adoption of a 'strong franc' policy in the mid-1980s, followed by France's membership in EMU, was a mistake and that a pursuit of 'Keynesian' policies would have avoided higher unemployment, probably with a continuation of the earlier policy of credit expansion and large budget deficits followed by periodic devaluations to restore competitiveness. It has also been argued that the financing of budget deficits should have been provided through interest-free central bank credit in unlimited amounts.

[50] This was made easier by the EU accounting rule assigning a zero-weight risk factor to banks' exposures to EU member states' governments and central banks if these exposures were denominated and funded in the borrowers' currencies.

only available remedy, in addition to fiscal reform (i.e., spending cuts and/or higher taxes, which usually hamper growth and are partly self-defeating in terms of fiscal revenue[51]), was structural reform with a view to restoring competitiveness and export-led growth. Major structural reform, however, is extremely difficult to achieve as it affects many parts of society and conflicts with powerful vested interests, which are often well organised and well represented in political bodies.

II. *Exchange rate competitiveness*

Under a mercantilist approach to international trade, a depreciation of the exchange rate is an instrument for achieving international competitiveness and boosting exports. Usually, when a country generates a trade surplus, the value of its currency rises, up to the point where the country loses its competitive advantage. The rise in value of the currency may be even stronger when there is an inflow of foreign capital either for investment or for speculative purposes. Moreover, if the foreign exchange is converted into domestic currency, it will add to the money supply, generating higher prices, which will accelerate the loss of competitiveness.

In order to maintain its competitive advantage, the country can take various measures. In particular, it may impose restrictions on transfers of capital from abroad.

Another possibility is to 'sterilise' the inflow of foreign exchange. For instance, in order to prevent an increase in the money supply, reserve requirements on increases in bank holdings of foreign exchange can be imposed. Or the central bank, instead of converting the foreign exchange into domestic currency, can exchange it for bonds. This amounts to borrowing foreign exchange and holding it without revenue, which can

[51] Spending cuts are a more reliable tool to balance the budget than tax increases, which are based on projections that may not materialise if growth is less than expected. There is also some empirical evidence that spending cuts impede growth less than higher taxes. Although spending cuts have a negative effect on growth at first, over time they are beneficial to growth as they release money for productive investment and reduce the cost of borrowing for the private sector. The expectation of these benefits may even accelerate investment decisions, thus shortening the time lag between the policy measure and its effects. In contrast, the prospect of higher taxes on income from investment may be a deterrent to investors, particularly foreign investors, as they may therefore opt to invest in another country. On this point also see I. Feitchner, 'Taxation in Times of Austerity: A Question of Political Economy', Chapter 11, this volume.

be costly for the central bank and is, therefore, an inadequate tool for stemming large or sustained inflows of foreign exchange.

A more effective measure, which prevents both an increase in the money supply and an appreciation of the exchange rate[52] while reducing the cost of sterilisation, is for the central bank first to borrow the foreign exchange, instead of buying it, from commercial banks or exporters, and then to invest it abroad.[53] For example, a surplus in China's trade with the US will generate US dollar balances, which can be invested in US government securities. These investments will produce income for China and help the US finance its budget deficit. Although US manufacturers may see this as exchange rate manipulation to their detriment, the US government, given its need for budget financing, will be reluctant to file a complaint with the World Trade Organization (WTO) or the IMF.

There is, of course, a risk that other countries will retaliate and engage in competitive exchange rate depreciation, thus sending their economies into a tailspin, to everybody's detriment. 'Beggar-thy-neighbour' policies, which were used in the 1930s as an instrument of economic policy, became so widely discredited because of their detrimental effects that one of the missions of the IMF, when it was established in 1944, was to prevent the recurrence of such practices.[54] Avoidance of exchange rate manipulation in order 'to gain an unfair competitive advantage over other members' is one of the obligations of members of the IMF under its Articles of Agreement (Article IV, Section 1(iii)).[55] The IMF has not, however, enforced this provision through official action, preferring instead to use peer pressure to dissuade countries from engaging in such practices.[56]

[52] Because of this dual effect, the country's authorities often claim that the purpose of sterilisation is not to manipulate the exchange rate but rather to avoid domestic inflation.

[53] When investing in foreign currencies, the central bank may not be able to cover the full cost of its borrowing. Also, it is exposed to the risk of an exchange loss, particularly if the currencies concerned are those of countries running large current account deficits.

[54] One of the purposes of the IMF was and still is to 'avoid competitive exchange depreciation' (Article I(iii)). On the shift from the pre-World War II practice of competitive depreciations to a post-war system of stable exchange rates enshrined in the original IMF Articles of Agreement, and the influence in particular of John Maynard Keynes and Harry Dexter White in the adoption of the gold exchange standard at the Bretton Woods Conference (1–22 July 1944), see Benn Steil, *The Battle of Bretton Woods* (Princeton and Oxford: Princeton University Press, 2013).

[55] See Gianviti, 'Stabilité et manipulation des taux de change', and Viterbo, *International Economic Law and Monetary Measures*, p. 289.

[56] Some clarification by the IMF of the meaning of Article IV, Section 1(iii) can be found in the Annex to Decision No. 13919 of 2007 (*Selected Decisions*, p. 42) and, in the same terms, in the Annex to Decision No. 15203 of 2012.

While exchange rate depreciation is usually envisaged as a questionable but effective instrument in export promotion, its negative side for consumers is that it raises the cost of imports. This will affect the cost of living, which may be an important consideration for a country that is largely dependent on imports for its food and energy. The greater the share of imports in a country's economy, the greater the effect of exchange rate depreciation on domestic prices. Moreover, higher import prices will raise production costs and higher domestic prices will trigger calls for higher salaries, which will raise the cost of exports. As the country loses its competitive edge, a further depreciation of the exchange rate will be needed.

In the EMU, no decision has been made on the determination of an exchange rate for the euro. It is clear, however, that the leaders of some countries (e.g., France and Italy) have expressed a strong preference for a weak euro, which would help their countries regain some of the competitiveness they have lost due to their countries' fiscal and social policies. The leaders of other countries (e.g., Germany) have not supported this view, because the painful reforms undertaken by their governments have helped sustain and even develop their exports.

In stark contrast with the mercantilist approach to international trade, an argument often made in favour of a strong exchange rate is not only that it helps contain price increases and achieve monetary stability, but also that it forces domestic manufacturers to develop better products, with high added value, rather than try to sell lower quality products simply by relying on periodic devaluations or gradual depreciation to lower their prices.

The counter-argument is that, instead of improving the quality of their products, domestic manufacturers may prefer to request the allocation of subsidies to make their products more competitive and/or the imposition of custom duties to make imports less competitive. A government anxious to preserve employment will find it difficult to deny these requests, particularly if they are not inconsistent with the country's international commitments.

III. Monetary stability

Monetary stability, or 'preserving the value of the currency', can be understood as a common objective of both monetary and exchange rate policies. Supporters of this view sometimes cite Article IV, Section 1 of the IMF's Articles of Agreement, where an explicit reference is made to the dual objective of 'financial and economic stability' and 'a stable system of exchange rates'.[57]

In most countries where an objective of monetary stability is assigned to the central bank, this objective is defined or understood either as stability of domestic prices or as stability of the exchange rate, but not both.[58]

The most common option is stability of domestic prices.[59] This is the case, for example, for the central banks of the US, the eurosystem, the UK, Japan, Sweden, New Zealand and Switzerland.

Some countries, however, have made the opposite choice and made exchange rate stability the objective assigned to the central bank.

Theoretically, a third option could be envisaged, which would be to define the objective of monetary stability in terms of both domestic prices and the exchange rate. Although a few countries have adopted this definition, the dual objective of price and exchange rate stability may actually reflect two somewhat different assumptions. The first is that, if a country refrains from engaging in inflationary or deflationary policies, its domestic prices will remain stable and, as a consequence, its exchange rate will remain stable. The second is that, if a country is able to maintain a stable exchange rate, it will be able to maintain stable domestic prices.

An examination of the first two options will show, however, that neither of the assumptions underlying the third option is fully correct.[60]

[57] It should be noted that it is the 'system of exchange rates', rather than the exchange rates themselves, that should be stable. The reason is that, with the second amendment, there was no longer an obligation to maintain fixed exchange rates. See Gold, *Exchange Rates*, p. 102.

[58] See Gianviti, 'The Objectives of Central Banks', pp. 465–73.

[59] Monetary stability is generally understood and often explicitly defined in central bank laws as stability of domestic prices (e.g., the ESCB's 'primary objective . . . shall be to maintain price stability'). A 2 per cent annual price increase in domestic consumer prices, as reflected in a country's consumer price index (CPI), is seen as consistent with that objective; asset prices (real property and equity) are not included in the CPI. Many central banks aim at 2 per cent annual price increases ('inflation targeting') to avoid the 'liquidity trap'. Price stability is not always, however, the sole main objective of a central bank. The most notable example is the US Federal Reserve System, with its 'dual mandate' of price stability and maximum employment. Moreover, financial stability is now often assigned as an additional core objective to central banks (e.g., the Bank of England), but it is usually not supposed to interfere with the objective of monetary stability. See Gianviti, 'The Objectives of Central Banks'.

[60] For instance, the Central Bank of Israel, whose mandate includes the dual objective of price and exchange rate stability, eventually concluded that they were not compatible and that price stability should be its primary objective. See Gianviti, 'The Objectives of Central Banks', p. 465.

1. First option: stability of domestic prices

While the stability of domestic prices in one country will avoid major exchange rate variations between that country's currency and those of countries following a similar policy, it is not a guarantee of exchange rate stability.

First, there is no such thing as a single exchange rate for a currency. There is an exchange rate for each currency in terms of every other currency. In practice, therefore, even if one assumes that there is always a direct and exact correlation between domestic prices and the exchange rate, exchange rate variations are still inevitable at least *vis-à-vis* some currencies.

Second, the inflation rate and the exchange rate are not exactly correlated because they reflect different variables. An exchange rate is simply the price of a currency in terms of other currencies, which may vary for reasons other than a variation in each country's consumer prices. The inflation rate is an average of consumer prices while the exchange rate reflects the relative capacity of a country to generate a balance of payments surplus through exports of goods and services and capital inflows. Two countries may have identical monetary policies and the same inflation rate, but if one of them runs a large current account surplus or attracts large foreign investments, this will cause an inflow of foreign exchange, resulting generally in an appreciation of its exchange rate *vis-à-vis* the other country's currency.[61] For instance, a country that is able to raise the added-value component of its export products through research and development is more likely to have a trade surplus than a country offering lower quality goods. Different social or fiscal policies (e.g., consumption taxes rather than production taxes) will also affect the balance of payments.

Third, given the consensus among central banks that some degree of expansionary monetary policy is the most appropriate course of action, a country adopting a zero or near-zero price increase policy would be most likely, *ceteris paribus*, to find that its exchange rate does not remain stable but rather appreciates *vis-à-vis* most other currencies.

2. Second option: stability of the exchange rate

As mentioned above, for each currency, there is an exchange rate in terms of every other currency. As many of these rates fluctuate in different directions, not only would it not make much sense for a country to

[61] Unless it is sterilised, a large inflow of foreign exchange will also have an inflationary effect.

try to maintain fixed rates *vis-à-vis* every other currency, but it would also result in broken cross rates, which would be a breach of the country's obligations under the IMF's Articles of Agreement.

More understandable would be the maintenance of an exchange rate in terms of a weighted average of a basket of currencies, which could be the currencies of the country's main trading partners. This would help maintain close economic ties with these countries but would not necessarily help the country achieve domestic price stability.

The most effective approach, therefore, is to select a single foreign currency, which should be the currency of a country that has a good record of sound monetary policy and stable prices and, preferably, is a major trading partner, with which it appears desirable to maintain a stable exchange rate.

This approach appeals to, and has been adopted by, countries facing high inflation levels, often after losing hope that their authorities will ever be able to achieve domestic price stability by themselves. The decision is then made to 'peg' the national currency to another country's currency (the 'anchor currency') by requiring the national authorities in charge of monetary policy to maintain a fixed exchange rate between the two currencies.

'Pegging' a currency to a foreign currency may take different forms. The most effective is the establishment of a currency board, which is required to hold international reserves, in the anchor currency and possibly other reserve assets, equal in value to the full amount of the monetary base.[62] There is no expansion or contraction of the monetary base without an equivalent increase or decrease in the reserve assets held by the currency board.[63] Any holder of domestic currency is thus confident that it can be converted into the anchor currency, at any time and at the official rate, for external payments or transfers.

A partial dollarisation, with the foreign currency and the domestic currency circulating side by side within the country at a fixed conversion rate, has the same effect.[64]

[62] Hong Kong and Bulgaria follow this model. There are also less stringent forms of similar arrangements. On currency board arrangements, see C. E. Enoch, 'Recent Financial Crises: Institutional Responses', in *Current Developments in Monetary and Financial Law*, Vol. 1 (Washington, DC: International Monetary Fund, 1999), p. 124, and Lastra, *Legal Foundations*, Chapter 2, pp. 73–82. Without full backing of the domestic currency, there is a risk of loss of confidence in its continued exchange value, causing a flight from the domestic currency into the anchor currency, leading to a collapse of the exchange rate.

[63] The profits generated by the reserve assets can be used for credit transactions.

[64] For a while, in the 1990s, Argentina used this system, but it ended in 2002 when the domestic currency was no longer sufficiently backed by holdings of US dollars. One of the most harmful measures was the issuance of large amounts of domestic currency,

A variation on this approach is to use monetary policy instruments, together with exchange market interventions, in order to maintain a floating exchange rate within narrow margins on either side of a mid-point rate.

The expected benefit of pegging is that, if the authorities in charge of the anchor currency are able to maintain stable domestic prices in their country, the same stability will prevail in the pegging country.

Linking a domestic currency to a foreign currency has two main consequences.

First, the exchange rate of the pegged currency will follow the fluctuations of the anchor currency against all other currencies. If the anchor currency appreciates, so will the pegged currency, which will make exports from that country less competitive in foreign markets.[65] If the anchor currency depreciates, so will the pegged currency, which will raise the cost of its imports and, to that extent, its domestic prices.

Second, in order to maintain a stable exchange rate, the authorities of the pegging country will not only have to refrain from following monetary, fiscal and other policies that could result in an appreciation or depreciation of the exchange rate in terms of the anchor currency, but must also engage in policies that will maintain this exchange rate when the anchor currency appreciates or depreciates in terms of other currencies. Under a pure currency board arrangement, the issue does not even arise because the pegging country has no monetary policy and the foreign exchange value of the domestic currency in terms of the anchor currency is fully covered by reserve assets. Under more flexible arrangements, however, the country does have a monetary policy, but it is no longer independent. It will be guided by decisions taken by the monetary authorities of the anchor currency. If, for example, these authorities adopt an expansionary monetary policy to reduce unemployment in their country, the pegging country will need to adopt a similar policy, even though it will probably result in domestic price increases.

There is no assurance, therefore, that the pegging of a currency to a foreign currency will achieve price stability. Nevertheless, although not an absolute guarantee of price stability, pegging a currency to the currency of a country that has a good record of price stability may be an improvement

which were not backed by actual dollar balances in the central bank's reserves, but only by dollar-denominated promissory notes issued by the government.

65 This was a problem faced in the early 1980s by countries that had either pegged their currencies to the US dollar or dollarised their economies. The strong appreciation of the US dollar due to US domestic anti-inflationary monetary policy (with very high interest rates) resulted in export shortfalls for these countries.

on a continuation of domestic policies that have proved unsuccessful at achieving price stability. But it should be borne in mind that, if pegging is easy, unpegging is economically and socially disruptive and costly.

D. Concluding remarks

Most countries officially recognise that preserving the value of money is a desirable objective, a 'public good', which has to be attained and preserved to achieve real growth. What this entails, however, is not uniformly understood. Between preserving the value of the currency in terms of one or more foreign currencies and preserving it in terms of domestic prices, a choice has to be made.

In the EMU, price stability has been assigned to the ESCB as its primary mandate, and the Maastricht Treaty on European Union of 1992 (Article 104(c)),[66] followed by the Stability and Growth Pact of 1997, enshrined the commitment of members of EMU to fiscal restraint in order to achieve monetary stability.[67] A few years later, however, it became clear that, for most of them, fiscal restraint was not one of their priorities. They enjoyed the benefits of monetary stability, and in particular the low interest rates that allowed them to borrow inexpensively, but they were not willing to meet their fiscal commitments.

Gradually, in several of these countries, a deterioration of the balance of payments led to questions about the 'excessive' appreciation of the euro, as if exchange rate competitiveness rather than price stability was the main objective of the ESCB. While consumers could reap the benefits of a strong

[66] This provision is now (with some changes) Article 126 of the Treaty on the Functioning of the European Union (TFEU). In addition, and given the particular importance of budgetary discipline for members of a monetary union, Article 136 of the TFEU contains provisions specific to EU member states whose currency is the euro, with a view to strengthening the coordination and surveillance of their budgetary discipline.

[67] The commitment was not to exceed 3 per cent of each country's gross domestic product (GDP) for the annual budget deficit (including the budgets of local governments) and 60 per cent of GDP for the national debt. These rules, which were seen as too rigid or even 'stupid', were slightly relaxed in 2005. After the debacle of the euro area, amended and partly tighter rules were incorporated into the European Fiscal Compact (Treaty on Stability, Coordination and Governance in the Economic and Monetary Union) that was signed on 2 March 2012 and entered into force on 1 January 2013. In principle, the annual 'structural deficit' of the budget (as contrasted with the 'cyclical deficit', which is no longer taken into account) may not exceed 0.5 per cent. The ceiling on national debt remains unchanged. These objectives will be reached gradually. Stronger enforcement procedures should make these commitments more effective. Also, adherence to the Compact is a condition for assistance under the European Stability Mechanism.

currency, exporters saw a strong euro as helping their foreign (i.e., non-euro-area) competitors. A competitive depreciation of the euro was advocated by several of the governments whose exporters were most affected.

An even more radical view is the assertion that the primary objective of a central bank should not be to maintain price stability, but rather to provide the government with the financial means to achieve its own objectives by acting as 'lender of last resort' to the government. After all, goes the argument, a central bank can never become insolvent as it can always issue more of its own currency, while a government may default on its debt if it runs out of money.[68] A government's default has unacceptable consequences for a country's social, economic and political stability. Therefore, a central bank should stand ready, or even be required, to 'bail out' the government, preferably with interest-free loans, in unlimited amounts, whenever there is a budget deficit.

As a central bank is not in a position to prevent the government from incurring additional debt, it would have to finance whatever budget shortfalls are generated by projects the government decides to embark on, and most governments tend to run out of money long before they run out of spending projects. In EMU, this means that the ESCB would have to create enough liquidity to finance not only existing sovereign debt but also future deficits incurred by governments pursuing an expansionary fiscal policy.[69] Unless this liquidity is offset by a contraction in credit to the private sector,[70] monetising all present government debt and future budget deficits will have solved the sovereign debt problem but also killed the currency.

[68] See, for instance, André Grjebine, 'La BCE doit devenir une banque centrale–Ses statuts actuels sont trop contraignants', *Le Monde*, 10 July 2012, 17.

[69] The official position of the ECB is that its purchases of government securities in the secondary market are not made to bail out heavily indebted governments, but rather to achieve monetary policy objectives, i.e., to stem excessive rises in interest rates that have an adverse effect on countries' economies.

[70] ECB Statement of 6 September 2012 on Outright Monetary Transactions (OMT) (purchases of government securities in unlimited amounts in the secondary market): 'The liquidity created through Outright Monetary Transactions will be fully sterilised'. For a more detailed explanation on the functioning of the OMT mechanism, see, A. Viterbo, 'The Impact of Sovereign Debts on EU Monetary Affairs', Chapter 10, this volume.

22

Monetary policy measures in investment law: the uneasy relationship between monetary stability and investment protection

FEDERICO LUPO-PASINI

A. Introduction

International investment law has become a fundamental feature of international economic policy-making. At present there are around 3,000 investment agreements in force, which require states to adopt a certain regulatory and policy regime with regard to the treatment of foreign investments in their territory.[1] The body of principles of international investment law has proved to be extremely useful in protecting the rights of foreign investors, and in guaranteeing them a level playing field against the arbitrariness of host states. However, the same principles have sometimes proved to be invasive of the policy space that countries normally enjoy in the regulation of their economy. Indeed, the particular formulation and the scope of protection of certain investment principles have sometimes constrained the ability of host states to adopt policies that, in spite of aiming at achieving legitimate policy goals, are nonetheless considered detrimental to the life of the investment.

Monetary policy, being one fundamental aspect of domestic economic policy, is not excluded from the regulatory oversight of investment law. Over the last ten years, international investment disputes have often dealt with host country monetary measures. Argentina alone has been involved in multiple disputes involving, directly or indirectly, regulatory

I would like to thank Professor Christian Tietje for his comments on the draft, as well as all participants at the World Trade Forum 2012 for their valuable inputs.

[1] According to The United Nations Conference on Trade and Development (UNCTAD), there are at present 3,164 international investment agreements (IIAs) in force, 'which include 2,833 bilateral investment treaties (BITs) and 331 "other IIAs", including, principally, free trade agreements (FTAs) with investment provisions, economic partnership agreements and regional agreements'. *World Investment Report 2012* (Geneva: United Nations Conference on Trade and Development, 2012), p. 18.

or administrative measures adopted within the framework of monetary or financial policy.[2] Setting aside the specific situation of Argentina, the number of disputes involving monetary policy measures can only be expected to increase in the near future. The expanded role and coverage of investment treaties as well as the increased proclivity of investors to resort to arbitration will bring under strict scrutiny the monetary and financial stability measures adopted in the context of the recent financial and economic crises in Europe and elsewhere.

This chapter will analyse the legal and policy regime that disciplines monetary stability in the context of international investment law, and it will highlight some of the most important (and provocative) arguments discussed by the legal and political economy literature on the relationship between monetary and investment law. The central argument of this chapter is that, from a theoretical perspective, monetary and investment law are two largely incompatible aspects of economic law. The invasiveness of investment principles in the formulation of domestic policy can hardly match with fundamental aspects of monetary sovereignty, such as central bank independence, and with the ultimate goal of monetary policy: the maintenance of monetary stability. The legal configuration of investment agreements often subordinates monetary sovereignty to the respect of investment principles. Consequently, the full protection of monetary stability is often dependent on the presence in investment agreements of 'economic stability' or 'emergency' clauses. Resolving the normative conflict between investment protection and monetary sovereignty is, however, fundamental to ensuring good governance in international monetary affairs. Investment law is a growing and increasingly sophisticated tool of international economic policy-making, and a new element that monetary authorities will need to take into account in the management of monetary policy. This chapter argues that the International Monetary Fund (IMF) should play a central role in the definition of monetary and financial stability in investment agreements and in monitoring abuses, similar to the role it is already playing within the framework of World Trade Organization (WTO) law with regard to balance of payments problems.

This chapter will be divided into two main sections. The first will introduce the basic features of investment law, and it will explain from a policy and a legal perspective how investment agreements constrain the

[2] See, for instance, J. E. Alvarez and K. Khamsi, 'The Argentine Crisis and Foreign Investors', in C. Sauvant (ed.), *Yearbook of International Investment Law & Policy* (New York: Oxford University Press, 2009).

policy space of monetary authorities in the management of monetary policy. The second section will constitute the central body of the research and it will present and analyse the theoretical foundation of the relationship, by discussing some of the main arguments proposed by the policy and legal literature.

B. The scope of investment protection and how it relates to monetary policy

The analysis of the interplay between monetary policy and international investment law must begin with an examination of the scope of investment treaties that delimits the boundaries of the interaction between these two spheres of economic law. At the outset it is important to clarify a particular aspect of investment agreements: unlike international trade treaties, most investment agreements do not have a market access function. They do not contain pre-establishment rights that allow investors to pull their capital into the host territory the same way the General Agreement on Trade in Services (GATS) does with regard to trade in services under mode 3.[3] On the contrary, the main goal of investment agreements (and, more generally, of investment law) is to ensure that, once already in the host state territory, the investment and the investors are granted legal protection against the arbitrariness of the host state. The main function of investment agreements, therefore, is providing a legal framework that prevents host states from adopting certain behaviours that are considered to impact negatively on the life of the investment. Consequently, the relationship between monetary policy and investment law will depend only on the impact that a domestic monetary policy measure will have on the foreign investments *already present* in the territory. This means that, in principle, host states are not constrained by investment agreements when managing monetary policy variables connected to investment inflows. For instance, monetary

[3] Investment agreements with pre-establishment rights are rare. Some BITs, and especially North American BITs such as the US BIT Model, the Canadian BIT, some free trade agreements, and the North American Free Trade Agreement (NAFTA) contain pre-entry obligations. Under these BITs foreign investors are allowed to be accorded treatment which is no less favourable than that enjoyed by domestic companies. Under these BITs a violation of tariff commitments or other violations that affect the right of the investor to establish its presence into the host country could amount to a violation of the principle of non-discrimination. For a good overview of the issue see G. Sacerdoti, 'The Admission and Treatment of Foreign Investments Under Recent Bilateral and Regional Treaties', *Journal of World Investment* 1:1 (2000), 105–26.

authorities are in principle free to impose controls on the inflow of capital (whether foreign direct investment (FDI) or portfolio flows) in order to curb the negative effects associated with excessive capital inflows, such as high inflation.

The scope of investment protection depends on the definition of 'investment'. The presence of an 'investment' in the host country defines the substantial scope and coverage of the investment agreement; only the kinds of investments covered by the treaty are given legal protection. The meaning of the term 'investment' in international law has undergone a substantial evolution over the years. From the early twentieth century until very recently, the protection of foreign investment was largely based on the assumption that only investment in physical assets deserved legal protection. Indeed, for most of the nineteenth century FDI was the most common form of foreign investment. Nonetheless, over the last thirty years the composition of international investment flows has diversified as a result of the progressive liberalisation of capital flows around the globe and now also includes intangible capital transfers, such as portfolio investment. Thus, the concept of investment, as defined in international treaties, has been modified in parallel with its economic evolution, in order to protect also those intangible assets that now constitute a large share of international capital transactions. At present it is impossible to provide a common definition of 'investment' applicable to all the 3,000 IIAs in force, as each of them contains its own classification.[4] However, most investment agreements contain a definition of investment that covers FDI and portfolio investment, as well as

[4] Most IIAs contain a similar description of investment, usually as 'every kind of asset' or 'every kind of investment in the territory', followed by a non-exhaustive list of the 'assets' that are considered as constituting an investment. Usually this list comprises five categories of assets:

1. Movable and immovable property and any other property-related rights, such as mortgages, liens and pledges.
2. Interests in companies, such as stocks, bonds, debentures and any other form of participation in a company. Usually the definition is broad enough to cover both direct and portfolio investment.
3. Claims to money and claims to performance under a contract having a financial value.
4. Intellectual property rights: this category includes trademarks, copyrights, trade secrets, 'technical processes' and know-how. One recent development has been to include in this category goodwill, which indicates the reputation of firms.
5. Rights conferred by law or by contract to undertake business activity in the territory of the host state. These business concessions usually grant the right to explore, to extract or to exploit natural resources.

those intangible assets that are collateral to the physical investment, but that at the same time cannot be separated and treated differently from it, such as contracts and intellectual property rights. Monetary policy does not have an equal and uniform impact on all types of investment, as certain investments will be more affected by monetary policy measures than others. In this chapter I will concentrate my analysis on three different forms of investment – portfolio investment, FDI and FDI in the banking sector – and I will briefly discuss their interplay with monetary policy.

Portfolio investment is probably the most important link between monetary policy and investment law. Portfolio investments now comprise almost one-third of the overall investment flows to developing countries and around two-thirds of the overall investment flows to developed economies.[5] Most investment agreements cover portfolio flows in the list of investment 'assets' protected by the treaty. An example in this regard is the Association of Southeast Asian Nations (ASEAN) Comprehensive Investment Agreement, which defines investment as 'every kind of asset, owned or controlled, by an investor, including but not limited to... shares, stocks, bonds and debentures and any other forms of participation in a juridical person and rights or interest derived therefrom.'[6] From a legal perspective, investment law might constrain the ability of monetary authorities to conduct monetary or financial policies affecting portfolio investment under various circumstances. The most cited example is the imposition of capital controls on the outflow of capital.[7] This measure is used in the context of a balance of payment or monetary crisis to prevent investors from moving their assets out of the country. Controls might be imposed on all sorts of capital account transactions, such as banking loans, securities trading, foreign exchange trading, or opening or closing of bank accounts. Portfolio investment could also be affected by new tighter or more burdensome regulations affecting securities trading. A hedge fund or a private investor, for instance, would be required to comply with new

[5] On the difference between portfolio investment and FDI, see K. Evans, *Foreign Portfolio and Direct Investment: Complementarities, Difference and Integration*, paper presented at the OECD Global Forum on International Investment (Shanghai, 5–6 December 2002). On portfolio investment in investment law, see M. Sornarajah, 'Portfolio Investment and the Definition of Investment', *ICSID Review: Foreign Investment Law Journal* 24:2 (2009).

[6] ASEAN Comprehensive Investment Agreement, Article 4(c).

[7] See, IMF, *Liberalizing Capital Flows and Managing Outflows*, International Monetary Fund, 2012, www.imf.org/external/np/pp/eng/2012/031312.pdf.

regulations that could impose an unexpected burden on its financial operations.[8] Lastly, investment agreements might reduce the policy space of host countries in the event of a sovereign default.[9] Sovereign defaults are relatively common, as was recently demonstrated in the case of Greece, and earlier in Argentina. In the event of a country being unable to pay its debts, investors might lose all or part of their original investment. However, since investment agreements expanded their coverage to portfolio flows (and sovereign bonds in particular) international investors can now rely also on investment treaties to protect their rights. One recent example in this regard is the investment dispute initiated by private bondholders over the restructuring of the Argentinian sovereign debt that is taking place in different legal fora. Based on the protection given by the Argentinian BITs, bond investors in Italy, Germany and the US have sued the Argentinian government in three different arbitration proceedings for the violation of investment law.[10]

FDI in the banking sector is another important linkage between monetary policy and investment law. Banks conduct operations in foreign countries by establishing branches or subsidiaries, which are then protected by investment treaties as a foreign investment. Monetary or financial authorities can affect the life of this investment in various ways. For instance, during a financial crisis monetary authorities could choose to privilege national banks over foreign ones, by refraining from providing emergency liquidity assistance or bailing out the foreign bank, or simply by favouring national creditors over foreign ones in the context of bankruptcy proceedings.[11] In the famous case *Saluka* v. *Czech Republic* that took place during the process

[8] On capital controls and investment treaties, see A. Kolo and T. Walde, 'Economic Crises, Capital Transfer Restrictions and Investor Protection Under Modern Investment Treaties', *Capital Markets Law Journal* 3:2 (2008); and K. P. Gallagher, 'Policy Space to Prevent and Mitigate Financial Crises in Trade and Investment Agreements', *UNCTAD G-24 Discussion Paper Series 58* (2010).

[9] M. Waibel, 'Opening Pandora's Box: Sovereign Bonds in International Arbitration', *American Journal of International Law* 101 (2007); see also K. P. Gallagher, 'The New Vulture Culture: Sovereign Debt Restructuring And Trade And Investment Treaties', *The IDEAs Working Paper Series* 02 (2011) and A. Viterbo, 'The Impact of Sovereign Debts on EU Monetary Affairs', Chapter 10, this volume.

[10] See *Abaclat and Others* v. *The Argentine Republic*, ICSID Case No Arb/07/5, Decision on Jurisdiction and Admissibility, 4 August 2011, 373–8. A quick analysis of the issues discussed in the case is provided in J. Beess und Chrostin, 'Sovereign Debt Restructuring and Mass Claims Arbitration before the ICSID, The *Abaclat* Case', *Harvard International Law Journal* 53:2 (2012).

[11] For a good overview of the legal problems affecting cross-border bank resolution, see R. M. Lastra (ed), *Cross Border Bank Insolvency* (Oxford University Press, 2011).

of privatisation of the Czech banking sector in the 1990s, Saluka – a foreign bank controlled by the Japanese bank Nomura – was not granted a fair bankruptcy procedure by local authorities.[12] The Czech government was found to be in violation of investment law and was condemned to pay US$ 236 million in damages to the investor. In particular circumstances, the refusal to grant a banking licence could also amount to a violation of investment law. Although there is no notable example with regard to the banking sector, various arbitral awards have dealt with licensing issues in other industrial sectors. Lastly, like the securities sector, the close scrutiny that investment law applies to domestic regulations in the light of the non-discrimination or fair and equitable treatment principles, might constrain a host state's regulatory policies in the banking sector. The close and ambiguous interaction between investment law and regulatory policy is well documented in the legal literature, and has given rise to various well-publicised disputes.[13]

Lastly, the management of *exchange rate policy might affect all forms of investment*, whether portfolio or FDIs. Exchange rate policy is one of the fundamental attributes of monetary sovereignty, and monetary authorities often rely on exchange rates to influence their trade, industrial and financial sectors. Investment agreements might sometimes constrain the ability of monetary authorities to manage their exchange rate, when a devalued currency has the adverse effect of reducing the profitability of foreign investment. Indeed, investors wishing to repatriate their investment and convert it into another currency, or investors that more simply rely on a stable currency to conduct their business, might suffer considerable losses in the event of devaluation. The most cited examples in this regard relate to the Argentinian monetary crisis of 2000 and the various disputes it originated.[14] Another policy measure related to exchange rate is the adoption of currency controls on the outflow. Unlike capital controls, currency controls target current international payments. The adoption of exchange controls has the effect of rendering difficult or

[12] *Saluka Investments BV* v. *The Czech Republic*, Permanent Court of Arbitration, Partial Award, 16 March 2006.

[13] See, for instance, C. Henckels, 'Indirect Expropriation And The Right To Regulate: Revisiting Proportionality Analysis And The Standard Of Review In Investor-State Arbitration', *Journal of International Economic Law* 15:1 (2012) 223–55; OECD, '"Indirect Expropriation" And The "Right To Regulate" In International Investment Law', *OECD Working Paper on International Investment* No 2004/4, OECD (2004).

[14] In *Continental Casualty* v. *Argentina* the decision of the Argentinian government to devalue the peso and set it to a new parity with the US dollar had the effect of reducing consistently the value of foreign investments.

impeding domestic investors from converting local into foreign currency, or from purchasing foreign currency.[15] However, the 'free transfer of funds' provisions contained in most investment treaties protect the right of investors to convert their investment into foreign currency, and they have the effect of rendering exchange controls illegitimate from an international investment law perspective.

C. Economic stability vs. investment protection: two incompatible objectives of economic governance?

Having briefly clarified how, from a technical perspective, monetary policy measures might be covered by the scope of investment law, the next issue is to assess how the relationship between these two areas of law is structured in international law. The relationship can be essentially described as a dichotomy between the need of host country monetary authorities to maintain monetary stability, through the adoption of particular monetary or financial measures, and the often competing right of investors to be protected in their legitimate expectations regarding the regulatory and policy framework affecting their investments. The two areas do not necessarily coincide. Indeed, for the most part, monetary policy decisions do not negatively impact the life of the investment. A sound monetary policy has the positive effect of maintaining a favourable economic environment where business can prosper. However, in certain circumstances, especially if the host country is experiencing economic turmoil, the administrative and policy mechanisms adopted by central banks to maintain monetary and financial stability might influence the productive function or the value of the investment.

At the outset of the Argentinian crisis of 2001 and the global financial crisis of 2007–8 various authors highlighted how the regulatory intensity of investment law, and the strict standards of treatment required for foreign investors might sometimes clash with the need of monetary authorities to maintain financial stability.[16] Recently, a growing body

[15] See A. Viterbo, *International Economic Law and Monetary Measures: Limitations to States' Sovereignty and Dispute Settlement* (The Hague: Elgar International, 2012), pp. 249–81.

[16] J. P. Commission, 'The Global Financial Crisis and International Investment Regimes', *American Society of International Law Proceedings* 104:443 (2010); A. Kolo and T. Walde, 'Economic Crises, Capital Transfer Restrictions and Investor Protection'; A. Van Aaken and J. Kurtz, 'Prudence or Discrimination? Emergency Measures, The Global Financial Crisis and International Economic Law', *Journal of International Economic Law* 12:4 (2009), 859–94.

of literature has been analysing possible areas of conflict between monetary and investment law.[17] It is not the goal of this chapter to provide a further analysis on the jurisprudence of investment law and how it relates to monetary policy. However, it is important to briefly analyse a few important points that are always emphasised and implicitly assumed in any analysis of monetary stability in investment law. This section will explain, in a provocative way, some of the main economic policy and legal arguments that usually lie at the foundation of any discussion on the role of monetary policy in investment law, and it will highlight the difficulty of reconciling monetary stability and investment protection.

I. The political economy of portfolio investment and the shifting of risks

The first set of arguments concerns the political economy of investment agreements and the role of portfolio investment in investment and monetary policy. The classical political economy argument that justifies the protection of investment is based on the positive externalities usually associated with FDI, and on the inherent asymmetry of powers between investors and host country typical of investment treaties.[18] The assumption is that the economic benefits associated with foreign investment justify a reduction of policy space available to the host country authorities. Indeed, foreign capital directed towards enterprises is usually associated with various economic benefits, such as technology and skills transfers, job creation, increased competition, increased external trade and, more generally, a positive contribution to the economic development of the host country.[19] The importance of this argument is such that

[17] The list of relevant publications is too vast to summarise in a few lines. However, in her book, Viterbo provides a good review of the literature on the main legal and jurisprudential developments. See A. Viterbo, *International Economic Law*.

[18] See, for instance, K. J. Vandevelde, 'The Economics of Bilateral Investment Treaties', *Harvard International Law Journal* 41:2 (2008).

[19] It is impossible to provide a comprehensive assessment of the economic effect of FDIs. The literature is vast and it is impossible to summarise in a few words. Nonetheless, for a general overview of the issue see: T. H. Moran, 'How Does FDI Affect Host Country Development? Using Industry Case Studies to Make Reliable Generalizations', in T. H. Moran, E. M. Graham and M. Bomstrom (eds.), *Does Foreign Direct Investment Promote Development?* (Washington: Institute for International Economics and Center for Global Development, 2005); OECD, *Foreign Direct Investment for Development: Maximizing Benefits, Minimizing Costs* (Paris: Organisation for Economic Co-operation and Development, 2002).

for a long time arbitral tribunals, when evaluating the presence of an investment that qualifies for protection under the International Centre for Settlement of Investment Disputes (ICSID) Convention, required the presence of certain characteristics, in the absence of which they would not consider that the investment merits legal protection. These characteristics concern the beneficial effects of the investment on the host country economy, and are commonly known as the *Salini* factors.[20] They comprise: (i) a substantial contribution of the investor, (ii) a certain duration, (iii) the existence of operational risk, (iv) a certain regularity of profit, and (v) a contribution to the economic development of the host state. The importance of the *Salini* test is now strongly disputed, especially since new forms of intangible investment now account for the majority of cross-border investment among developed economies. Indeed, as we will see later, in a recent ICSID award, the Tribunal concluded that the fulfilment of the *Salini* test is no longer necessary to trigger the jurisdiction of the Court.

However, it is undeniable that the political economy of financial flows is inherently different from that of FDI. First, portfolio flows are more volatile, as they seek short-term gains, rather than stable profits. This renders speculative capital a double-edged sword. On the one hand, the high sensitivity of portfolio investors to changes in the economic environment pushes host states to implement better economic governance. On the other hand, when the economic conditions deteriorate, the short-term vision of investors produces massive capital flights, which only magnify economic problems. Furthermore, as the majority of portfolio investments consist of the purchasing of pure financial products rather than the creation of industries or manufacturing plants, they do not produce the large beneficial spillovers on the host economy that are usually associated with FDIs, such as labour creation, or technology transfer.[21] Given the peculiarities and the different political economy

20 This definition was proposed in the case *Salini Construttori S.p.A. and Italstrade S.p.A. v. Kingdom of Morocco* (ICSID Case No. ARB/00/4), Decision on Jurisdiction of 23 July 2001.

21 Clearly if one presumes portfolio flows to share the same positive characteristics as FDI, this would be wrong. Nonetheless, even portfolio flows are beneficial to the economic development of a country. Imagine an economy without any banks or other sources of finance: it would be impossible for enterprises to obtain credit and to grow. Furthermore, financial flows promote market efficiency, better discipline and transparency, and efficient capital allocation in the domestic economy. Kimberly Evans, 'Foreign Portfolio And Direct Investment Complementarity, Differences, And Integration', Paper presented at OECD Global Forum on International Investment, 2002.

of portfolio investment, a question arises as to whether portfolio investments should deserve the same level of legal protection as is normally accorded to FDI. For instance, during the jurisdictional phase of the ICSID investment dispute brought by Italian bondholders against Argentina, the main argument of Argentina to deny the jurisdiction of the Court was that its sovereign bonds did not amount to international investment, as they did not meet the requirements set by the *Salini* test.[22] Their reasoning was based on the political economy argument that an investment that does not make a substantial and long-term contribution to the economic development of the host country shall not bind host authorities to a certain standard of treatment, as it would fall short of the basic economic trade-off at the core of investment law. The Tribunal, however, denied the exclusiveness of the *Salini* factors, arguing that, as long as an investment falls within the scope of the investment agreement – as sovereign bonds did with regard to the Italy–Argentina BIT – the jurisdiction of ICSID should not be denied.[23]

If one accepts the definition of investment proposed by the *Salini* test, it is difficult to fit portfolio flows into the political economy scheme of investment agreements. It is undeniable that while portfolio flows do indeed benefit the host economy in terms of better financing opportunities and diversification of risks, they might not produce the long-term, stable and more widespread economic benefits that are demanded by the *Salini* test, and that are implicit in the political economy bargain of international investment agreements.[24] The protection of portfolio investment under investment law creates a political economy and legal imbalance between investors and host countries. Host countries do not receive from portfolio investment the classical economic benefits associated with FDI, but they are nevertheless obliged by investment agreements to accord to portfolio flows the same right of protection accorded to FDI. This unbalanced trade-off benefits primarily foreign investors rather than host countries. More specifically, portfolio investment shifts the risk from the investor to the host country, thereby undermining the political economy trade-off between economic development and investment protection at the core of investment law.

Indeed, the making of an investment always implies a certain degree of risk. In the case of FDI the element of risk is usually on the investor's

[22] *Abaclat*, ICSID Case No. ARB/07/5, para. 341. [23] *Ibid.* paras 362–7.

[24] This argument was originally proposed by Sornarajah. See Sornarajah, 'Portfolio Investment and the Definition of Investment', 518.

side, which on top of the inherent business risk of the investment also bears the political and regulatory risk associated with having its assets located in another jurisdiction. By contrast, the host government is not subject to any specific risk.[25] The political economy of investment agreements consists of transferring the political risk from the investor to the host country. Indeed, the imbalance between the risk faced by the investor and the economic benefits the investment confers on the host country's economy are corrected through the obligation on the host country to ensure a certain legal standard to the investor and its assets. For this reason the 'fair and equitable treatment' and expropriation clauses usually contained in investment agreements are specifically designed to protect the investors from the arbitrariness of the host government, and to guarantee a level playing field between the investor and the host government anchored in certain international legal standards.

However, when a country receives portfolio investment or investment in the banking sector, the trade-off between the economic benefits of international investment and the reduction of regulatory autonomy, which are the basis of international investment law, are no longer present in their totality. The peculiar effects of portfolio investment on monetary and financial stability shift the risk from the investor to the host country economy. The economic literature and the experience gained demonstrate that financial flows need to be handled with care.[26] Without a sound financial infrastructure and a stable macroeconomic framework, both the inflow and outflow of financial assets could have a serious destabilising effect on the host country economy, and trigger a downward spiral of economic recession. Unlike FDI, portfolio investment

[25] But even in that case these risks are determined by the specificity of the investment and the regulatory framework in which the investment takes place, and not in its international character.

[26] The free flow of capital has profound effects on multiple aspects of a country's economy, influencing the country's ability to set an interest rate, to control the external value of the currency and, more generally, to conduct an independent monetary policy. If properly controlled, capital movements can influence the decisions of domestic and foreign investors. Furthermore, the strict linkages between capital movements and financial services make capital flows a fundamental element in the maintenance of financial stability; for countries with a fixed regime of exchange rates, these links are also an important element in managing the balance of payments. For an overview: Christopher J. Neely, 'An Introduction to Capital Controls', Federal Reserve Bank of St. Louis (1999); and IMF, 'The IMF's Approach to Capital Account Liberalization', International Monetary Fund (2005).

generates particular macroeconomic dynamics in the host country's economy that could render the opening of the capital account a particularly dangerous business.[27] In the event of an economic crisis the volatility of portfolio flows could create serious problems for the financial and macroeconomic position of the country, exacerbating existing weaknesses.

It is not the goal of this chapter to argue for the exclusion of portfolio flows from the benefits of investment protection. Investment law has the undoubted merit of ensuring a level playing field between foreign investors and host states and compelling host country authorities to respect fundamental principles of good governance. This is particularly important in monetary and financial affairs, where host authorities enjoy total discretion in the design and implementation of their policies. However, it is undeniable that according the same legal treatment and applying the same legal principles indiscriminately to both FDI and portfolio flows is in sharp contradiction with the different underlying economic dynamics of capital flows. As argued before, subjecting portfolio flows to the same legal treatment as is accorded to FDI would undermine the political economy bargain that is the foundation of investment agreements.

II. Portfolio investment and the entitlement to investment protection

Another line of argument, similarly focused on portfolio investment, disputes the entitlement of financial investors to be protected by investment treaties. Sornarajah, a prominent investment lawyer, argues that the particular way in which financial products are traded in the primary and secondary market undermines the right of the final buyer to benefit from investment protection. This argument is linked to the concept of '*privity of arbitration*' which in the case of investment law is structured on the promise of the host state to grant protection to the investors of another state with whom it has signed an investment agreement. The privity of arbitration would not be satisfied when the financial products offered in the host country are traded and sold in the secondary market to a third-party investor. In that case, Sornarajah argues, the last investor would not benefit from the protection of the treaty.[28] This argument

[27] It is important to note that the risk of instability associated with portfolio investment is typical only of foreign portfolio investment, and not of domestic investment.

[28] Sornarajah, 'Portfolio Investment and the Definition of Investment', 22.

hinges on the requirement of the territoriality of the investment that defines the scope of protection *rationae persone* of investment agreements. The concept of the territoriality of the investment requires the investment to be made in, and the capital to be transferred into, the host country territory. In the case of financial products this does not always happen. For instance, in some cases bonds or derivatives are sold to intermediary traders and sold in the offshore market.[29] Hence, one questions whether the investment is actually made in the host country territory. This argument, while applying to some financial transactions, does not hold for the large majority of them. Indeed, although financial products are traded through intermediaries, the investment is still made in the host country, and the capital is transferred to the host country economy.[30]

Most of the answers to these questions have been clarified in a recent ICSID case. In *Abaclat and Others* v. *The Argentine Republic* the tribunal was called upon to judge as to whether the purchase of Argentinian sovereign bonds by Italian investors would be considered as an investment, and whether this investment would satisfy the territoriality requirement. The tribunal put forward an interesting consideration on the specificity of financial products. The tribunal stated:

> With regard to an investment of a purely financial nature, the relevant criteria cannot be the same as those applying to an investment consisting of business operations and/or involving manpower and property. With regard to investments of a purely financial nature, the relevant criteria should be where and/or for the benefit of whom the funds are ultimately used, and not the place where the funds were paid out or transferred. Thus, the relevant question is: were the invested funds ultimately made available to the Host State and did they support the State economic development?[31]

The tribunal eventually concluded that although the Argentinian bonds were traded through third-country intermediaries, nonetheless the funds were ultimately transferred to the Argentinian government, thereby conferring an economic benefit to the host country economy.

29 *Ibid.*, 519; Waibel, 'Opening Pandora's Box'.

30 Indeed intermediaries do not sell their own products but only charge a commission for the intermediation.

31 *Abaclat and Others* v. *The Argentine Republic*, ICSID Case No Arb/07/5, Decision on Jurisdiction and Admissibility, 4 August 2011, 373–8.

III. *The problem of central bank independence*

One of the central problems of monetary policy in international law is how to maintain central bank independence in the context of the reduction of monetary sovereignty caused by trade and investment treaties. Although central bank independence does not have relevance in international customary or treaty law, in virtually any state with monetary sovereignty, central banks are endowed with a special status.[32] Indeed, in the conduct of monetary policy and in the achievement of any other objective that has been assigned them by the law, central banks cannot receive any order from the government and, more importantly, they do not need to respond to the government for their decisions. In the conduct of economic policy, this special status makes the central bank an independent organ of the state, which enjoys the highest discretion and autonomy in the pursuit of its objectives. The freedom that central banks enjoy in the management of monetary policy is an essential element in safeguarding monetary stability, as it ensures that the achievement of monetary stability cannot be undermined by short-term political goals. However, in the context of international law, central bank independence can sometimes be sacrificed to the rules of free trade or investment.

In order to understand the importance of central bank independence for the successful management of monetary policy and monetary stability it is necessary to briefly describe the functions of central banks. Modern central banks have two major objectives.[33] The first is the classical objective – to conduct monetary policy and ensure monetary stability. This is usually intended to cover domestic price stability (inflation) as well as external stability, which consists in managing the exchange rate. In so doing, central banks have the power to set the interest rate, conduct foreign exchange operations and to a certain extent, also to manipulate the exchange rate. All these tasks are conducted without any interference from other political organs, which need to rely on central banks' decisions even for the formulation of their

[32] R. M. Lastra, 'The Independence of the European System of Central Banks', *Harvard International Law Journal* 33:2 (1992); R. M. Lastra, *Central Banking and Banking Regulation* (London: Financial Markets Group, London School of Economics, 1996).

[33] See F. Gianviti, 'The Objectives of Central Banks', in M. Giovanoli and D. Devos (eds.), *Monetary and Financial Law: The Global Crisis* (Oxford University Press, 2010) and R. M. Lastra, 'The Role of Central Banks in Monetary Affairs: a Comparative Perspective', Chapter 4, this volume.

policies. The second objective, which is increasingly one of the major tasks of modern central banks, broadly consists of ensuring the stability of the domestic financial system. Defining a unique concept of financial stability is not easy, nor is distinguishing what is a central bank function from what is a competence of other organs of the state. In almost all jurisdictions, given the pivotal role of the central bank at the top of the pyramid of the banking and payment system, central banks are entrusted with lender of last resort functions, which entail injecting liquidity into a bank or into the banking system in order to prevent a lack of liquidity from triggering a systemic crisis.[34] In this endeavour, central banks decide on a case-by-case basis if and when to intervene in the market, based on the specific systemic risk. There is no specific legal and pre-determined framework that sets out precisely the conditions that should trigger the intervention or, in other cases, the decision not to intervene and to let a bank collapse. In other jurisdictions, central banks oversee the financial system, and are given a supervisory role over the banking system. While this is not the case for all central banks, in almost all cases the supervisory role does not extend to other financial intermediaries, such as insurance companies or securities firms.

Central bank independence is a function of monetary stability, and an aspect of domestic monetary policy. As such, central banks are protected as independent powers in the institutional architecture of the state, but the same is not necessarily true in the context of international law. Indeed, central banks' independence is not considered a customary norm of international law, and it is not protected in any international treaty. The question then is whether central banks shall enjoy in international law the same degree of independence that they enjoy in domestic law. For instance, a measure taken by the central bank on matters falling within its competence might be totally legitimate from a domestic law perspective, but at the same time it might amount to a violation of the investment agreement. The answer of international law in this respect is plain. Article 27 of the Vienna Convention on the Law of Treaties stipulates, 'A party may not invoke the provisions of its internal law as justification for its failure to perform the treaty'. Furthermore, Article 47 adds,

[34] One important note is that a central bank can inject liquidity, but not provide capital to private banks. Liquidity is a temporary shortage of funds, which is backed up by capital. On the other hand, a shortage of capital means that a bank is insolvent.

> A State may not invoke the fact that its consent to be bound by a treaty has been expressed in violation of a provision of its internal law regarding competence to conclude treaties as invalidating its consent unless that violation was manifest and concerned a rule of its internal law of fundamental importance.

It is indisputable that central bank independence is a matter of internal law. Indeed, a state decides autonomously whether to give this privilege to the central bank and which objectives would fall under its competence. Accordingly, although central bank independence is a fundamental principle of domestic law, it does not have any relevance at the international level.

In spite of the irrefutable logic of international law, however, it is doubtful whether it is acceptable from a monetary policy perspective that an international treaty can undermine the achievement of monetary stability. First of all, international investment treaties are rarely negotiated with the support of central banks or financial authorities (especially in the case of developing countries), but by officials of the ministry of foreign affairs or investment, who are unlikely to be aware of the implications of investment agreements for monetary policy. It is certainly puzzling that a country chooses to carve out its central bank from the influence of domestic politics, while at the same time it accepts to bind it with regard to foreign investors. If central banks are fully independent from the government in the conduct of monetary policy, they should be similarly independent of any other external influences.

IV. Investment protection and monetary stability

This last argument leads to what is probably the most important and hotly debated issue on the relationship between monetary policy and investment law: the constraints that investment law imposes on the ability of monetary authorities to intervene effectively to maintain monetary or financial stability. The overlap between the two regimes is particularly marked in the context of emergency measures adopted during an economic crisis. It is not easy to summarise emergency or stability policies. These generally take the form of interventions in the foreign exchange market, adoption of capital controls, lender of last resort or bail-outs, and prudential regulations. In the second section of this chapter, I introduced briefly some of the monetary policies that could be considered illegitimate under investment law. The common denominator of all these measures is that in the event of a conflict between a monetary policy measure and an investment right, host states have to choose between following their own domestic priorities and sacrificing them to protect the rights of a single investor. More bluntly, the question for the host state is to decide whether the rights of a single investor are more important than the economic and monetary sovereignty of an entire nation. There are two sets of considerations in this respect.

The first concerns the decision to give precedence to monetary stability over investment protection, or vice versa. There are different ways one can look at this problem. Historically, monetary policy, especially the aspect of monetary policy that promotes monetary stability, has been intentionally insulated from external influences. If one compares the international political economy of monetary policy to that of international trade or investment, it is clear that monetary policy does not require international cooperation to be implemented successfully. A central bank can easily implement monetary policies, such as inflation targeting, quantitative easing, or exchange rate determination without having to rely on the collaboration of external actors. This is because the scope of monetary policy is necessarily limited by domestic borders, and because the main goal of monetary authorities is not to increase exports, or encourage investment, but simply to protect the stability of the domestic economy through the adoption of monetary measures. Hence, the protection of economic stability is primarily a domestic policy matter, rather than an international one. This explains why monetary law is subject to limited internationally binding coordination compared to international trade or investment. Second, as already explained, the achievement of monetary stability necessarily depends also on the degree of independence that monetary authorities have when formulating their policies. The higher the level of interference of external factors, the more likely it is that monetary policy would be diverted from its main objective: economic stability. The need for independence and the national scope of monetary policies explains certain features of monetary law: central bank independence; lack of extensive multilateral regulations compared to international trade or investment law, and focus on national regulations; and soft law approaches to the few areas regulated at the international level.

Consequently, it is easy to see how the interference of external factors, such as the invasive principles of investment law, might constrain the policy space of monetary authorities for the management of monetary and financial stability and ultimately reduce central bank independence. One might nevertheless argue that monetary policy is also subject to various regulatory constraints in other areas of international law, such as WTO law. In the context of international trade agreements the maintenance of stability is subordinated to the respect of certain procedural and substantial conditions. For instance, the violation of Article XI or Article II of the GATT to maintain balance of payments equilibrium can be tolerated only in the presence of a balance of payments problem, as certified by the IMF.[35] However, even when monetary independence is sacrificed, the loss of monetary sovereignty is nevertheless offset by the benefits that the host country receives from free trade. More specifically, in the context of FTAs, the occasional loss of monetary sovereignty is nonetheless justified by the economic benefits that the host country receives in terms of market access concessions. In the event of a conflict between a monetary policy measure and investment law, however, the respect of international investment does not produce enough economic benefits to the host country that justify the reduction of policy space for the formulation of monetary policy. International investment agreements are one-sided in the protection of one particular interest, namely, the interests of the investors. Economic evidence is scarce and contradictory as to whether investment agreements produce economic benefits to the host country's economy. First, it is doubtful whether international investment agreements promote the inflow of capital.[36] Furthermore, unlike international trade agreements, investment agreements do not entail a reciprocal exchange of concessions by mutual market access benefits, or even by promoting a regulatory level playing field between the two states that are signatories of the investment agreement. The respect of investment law as opposed to respect for monetary stability is a net loss to the host country. Thus, from a policy point of view, monetary stability should always be prioritised over investment protection.

Having clarified that monetary stability is a compulsory choice, the next question is how to ensure that it prevails over investment

[35] See F. Roessler, 'Selective Balance-of-payments Adjustment Measures Affecting Trade: The Roles of the GATT and the IMF', *Journal of World Trade Law* 9 (1975); D. Siegel, 'Legal Aspects of the IMF/WTO Relationship: The Fund's Articles of Agreements and the WTO Agreements', *American Journal of International Law* 96 (2002).

[36] Hoeckman and Newfarmer do not find conclusive evidence on the role of BITs in attracting investment, see B. Hoeckman and R. Newfarmer, 'Preferential Trade Agreements, Investment Discipline and Investment Flows', *Journal of World Trade* 39 (2005), 949–73. On the contrary, Salacuse and Sullivan find a positive correlation. See J. W. Salacuse and N. P. Sullivan, 'Do BITs Really Work?: An Evaluation of Bilateral Investment Treaties and Their Grand Bargain', *Harvard International Law Journal* 46 (2005), 67.

protection. At the outset it should be noted that investment agreements do not provide institutional mechanisms to deal with the negative externalities of investment protection for the host country's economy. Investment agreements do not have an economic bargaining function based on mutual exchange of concessions, similar to that of FTAs. This means that the violation of an investment right cannot be compensated by the offer of new regulatory concession or further market access. Consequently, investment agreements do not normally provide a GATT-type safeguard clause (which is normally present in trade agreements) that would protect host countries from unforeseeable developments caused by the investment agreements themselves. In the presence of an unforeseeable development which forces a host country to violate the terms of the investment agreement, absent a necessity or essential security clause, the only option for the host country is to offer monetary compensation or to pay damages to the investor.

Therefore, in order to safeguard the policy space for monetary stability, the only option is to anchor monetary measures to the necessity or essential security exceptions, such as 'balance of payments' or financial stability clauses. Kurts and Van Aaken divide such clauses into three major types.[37] The first category is GATS-type prudential carve-outs for monetary or financial stability. They either offer exemption for prudential regulation or monetary policy, or they exclude the financial services industry from the scope of application of the national treatment provisions. Such provisions are a feature of the majority of FTAs with investment provisions, and of the model BITs negotiated by Canada, India and the US.[38] Second, certain BITs provide general essential security interest clauses, which comprise monetary and financial stability issues. Crucially, such clauses are self-judging. Thus, they leave the host state free to decide to which situations the clause applies. However, such clauses have only recently become a trend in investment law. Hence, not all investment agreements can benefit from the same level of legal sophistication, and often they do not contain any emergency or stability clauses.[39] In the event of a financial or monetary problem, which necessitates the adoption of exceptional measures, the problem for

[37] Van Aaken and Kurtz, 'Prudence or Discrimination?', at 891–2.

[38] See Viterbo, *International Economic Law*, pp. 249–73.

[39] An UNCTAD study found that BITs with emergency or stability exceptions are clearly in a minority, as only 12 per cent of BITs contains such exceptions. See UNCTAD, *The Protection of National Security in IIAs* (New York/Geneva: United Nations Conference on Trade and Development, 2009), p. 3.

host-country monetary authorities is to figure out a way to impose such measures without becoming liable for a violation of investment law. The first option is to link monetary policy decisions to the principle of necessity in international law. Certain BITs, for instance, included essential security interest or necessity clauses that leave it up to the tribunal to decide under what circumstances a certain measure will fall within the scope of the exemption.[40] Host states would be entitled therefore to derogate from investment law (for instance, by imposing capital controls), once they have demonstrated the necessity of such a policy to safeguard the essential security interests of the state. This approach has been widely analysed by the investment jurisprudence and literature. However, it has two main flaws. First, it excludes from the application of the exception all those monetary or financial policies that are not adopted in the context of an emergency situation, such as prudential regulations or monetary policies not necessarily linked to monetary stability. Second, it subjects monetary measures to the discretionary interpretation of 'necessity' by investment tribunals. The experience of Argentina shows how contradictory is the approach of arbitrators with regards to necessity clauses and state of necessity principle of international law.[41]

The next option would be to resolve the conflict of norms according to the classical criteria of *lex posterior derogat legi priori*, or *lex specialis derogat legi generali*. Unfortunately this approach has two main flaws. First, with the exceptions of the IMF rules on international payments, most of the norms disciplining financial and monetary law are of a non-binding nature, or are not even disciplined in international law. Monetary policy is largely unregulated even in domestic law, as monetary authorities need to maintain, at all times, full independence and freedom of thought. Furthermore, even for the few aspects of international finance and monetary policy that are disciplined, the regulation usually takes the form of soft laws. Voluntary

[40] Art XI of 1991 US–Argentine BIT.

[41] See M. Waibel, 'Two Worlds of Necessity in ICSID Arbitration: CMS and LG&E', *Leiden Journal of International Law* 20 (2007), 637–48; W. Burke-White, 'The Argentine Financial Crisis: State Liability Under BITs and the Legitimacy of the ICSID System', *Asian Journal of WTO & International Health Law and Policy* 199:3 (2008); W. Burke-White and A. Von Staden, 'Investment Protection in Extraordinary Times: The Interpretation and Application of Non-Precluded Measures Provisions in Bilateral Investment Treaties', *Virginia Journal of International Law* 48:2 (2008); A. Martin, 'Investment Disputes after Argentina's Economic Crisis: Interpreting BIT Non-precluded Measures and the Doctrine of Necessity under Customary International Law', *Journal of International Arbitration* 29:1 (2012), 49–70.

standards, codes of good practice and the recommendations of international institutions do not have any formal relevance in the classical definition of international norms.

The issue is therefore how to combine the respect of soft law standards or guidelines with the respect of the rules of international law. Various authors have suggested that monetary or financial stability clauses should make an explicit reference to IMF law, or to IMF decisions,[42] similar to Article XVIII of the GATT, or Article XII GATS in WTO law. This option has various merits. First of all, it would allow the respect of the principle of investment protection to be reconciled with the need to maintain the political and regulatory framework of monetary policy at the national level. Second, it would help in defining a division of labour between different international actors that would take into account and respect essential competences in different aspects of economic policies. One useful example in this regard is the adoption of capital controls, which, in the absence of specific stability clauses, is in principle a violation of investment law when it affects foreign investments. The current legal framework in investment law is unclear and contradictory on this point. Few investment agreements do not contain balance of payment or stability clauses that would allow monetary authorities to impose capital controls in the presence of stability or monetary policy concerns. Other agreements which contain such clauses leave it totally to the discretion of monetary authorities to decide whether capital controls are achieving a stability objective. The danger with this type of arrangement is that capital controls might be used to achieve policy goals other than monetary stability.[43] The adoption of balance of payments or economic stability clauses that would refer to the IMF for the assessment of the underlying problem and the proportionality of the stability measure would ensure a uniform interpretation of monetary stability problems in international law and prevent abuses. The IMF has recently argued for such an option in the context of its evolving role in the surveillance and soft regulation of capital flows and capital account measures.[44]

[42] See D. Kalderimis, 'IMF Conditionality as Investment Regulation: A Theoretical Analysis', *Social and Legal Studies* 104 (2004); see also Viterbo, *International Economic Law*.

[43] IMF, 'Multilateral Aspects of Managing the Capital Account', IMF Staff Discussion Note SDN/12/10, International Monetary Fund (2012).

[44] IMF, 'The Liberalization and Management of Capital Flows: An Institutional View', International Monetary Fund, 14 November 2012, pp. 33–4.

D. Conclusions

This chapter has discussed the main legal and political economy arguments regarding the relationship between monetary and investment law. The conclusions largely suggest an antinomy between the two. First, the peculiar feature of portfolio investment and the lack of tangible benefits to the host country economy do not justify the loss of policy space caused by investment treaties. Furthermore, the invasiveness of investment principles in the formulation of domestic policy poses a legal threat to fundamental aspects of monetary policy, such as central bank independence or the maintenance of monetary stability. The underdeveloped regulatory structure of investment agreements compared to that of international trade treaties, and the limited and ambiguous application of the customary principle of necessity in international law, make it difficult to resolve the normative conflict between investment protection and monetary sovereignty. A host country can enjoy full monetary sovereignty and independence only by explicitly carving out monetary and financial policy from the scope of investment agreements. Absent an explicit choice in this direction, investment agreements can probably be considered one of the most serious threats to monetary sovereignty today, and a new element that monetary authorities will need to take into account in the management of monetary policy.

INDEX